SEVENTH EDITION

The Complete Reporter

Fundamentals of News Gathering, Writing, and Editing

Kelly Leiter
The University of Tennessee

Julian Harriss

Stanley Johnson

Allyn and Bacon

Boston ■ London ■ Toronto ■ Sydney ■ Tokyo ■ Singapore

Vice President, Editor-in-Chief: *Paul A. Smith*
Series Editor: *Karon Bowers*
Series Editorial Assistant: *Jennifer Becker*
Marketing Manager: *Jackie Aaron*
Composition Buyer: *Linda Cox*
Manufacturing Buyer: *Julie McNeill*
Cover Administrator: *Jenny Hart*
Production Administrator: *Rosalie Briand*
Editorial-Production Service *Spectrum Publisher Services*

Library of Congress Cataloging-in-Publication Data

Leiter, Kelly.
    The complete reporter : fundamentals of news gathering, writing,
and editing / Kelly Leiter, Julian Harriss, Stanley Johnson.
        p.   cm.
    Rev. ed. of: The complete reporter / Julian Harriss, Kelly Leiter,
Stanley Johnson. 6th ed. 1991.
    Includes bibliographical references (p.   ) and index.
    ISBN 0-205-29586-X
    1. Reporters and reporting Handbooks, manuals, etc.
2. Journalism—Authorship Handbooks, manuals, etc.   3. Journalism—
Editing Handbooks, manuals, etc.   4. Report writing Handbooks,
manuals, etc.   I. Harriss, Julian.   II. Johnson, Stanley.
III. Title.
PN4781.L36   1999
070.4'3—dc21   99-39519
                                                                     CIP

Printed in the United States of America

10 9 8 7 6 5 4 3 2 1   02 01 00   99

Dedicated to
Julian Harriss
1914–1989

A quiet, gentle man whose intellect and immense writing talents
could never be hidden behind his shy demeanor.

CONTENTS

PREFACE

In his excellent book, *My Times: Adventures in the News Trade*, John Corry, who had a 31-year career at the *New York Times*, wrote:

> "Each story I wrote defined me. In a society where so many ache to be heard, a byline was better than money."

In this seventh edition of *The Complete Reporter*, the aim is to help students develop their skills as a reporter that will earn them by-lines as John Corry did during his distinguished career.

This new edition contains much that is new. Yet, it has retained the basic concept and organization that served students and teachers well in the first six editions.

All chapters have been rewritten in part to reflect changes in the newspaper profession, especially the increased use of computers as a research tool for reporters and the introduction of digital photography. New illustrations and photographs are included to help students visualize the principles discussed.

As in previous editions, the exercises are written in incomplete sentences to resemble a reporter's notes. They serve as an example of note taking which has proved useful to students using past editions. The exercises are designed to give students an opportunity to practice the principles discussed in each chapter and to challenge them to think carefully before writing. Some contain examples of libelous or unethical statements as well as trivia which will help the instructor make the point that careful reporters avoid using such material in their stories.

Incorporated in this edition are many of the suggestions offered by teachers who have used the textbook over the years. The features in previous editions that have been so effective as teaching tools have been retained.

The Complete Reporter is a practical, basic textbook designed to teach students how to gather, write and edit news stories. The techniques discussed in the book are the ones that are used daily at every newspaper. That makes it an excellent text for not only beginning but also advanced reporting classes as well.

Acknowledgments

I am indebted to the dozens of publishers, editors and reporters, many of whom are former students, for their ideas, suggestions and examples that have been used in this edition. I am also grateful to the teaching colleagues who have made valuable suggestions which also have been incorporated in the text, including Lois Bianchi, Queens College, City University of New York; and Jean Chance, Univer-

sity of Florida. I owe a debt of gratitude to everyone who has given me unstinting support and encouragement, especially to the late Bill Golliher and to Andrew
R. Pizarek. And Betty Bradley and Janine Jennings have my everlasting gratitude
for their hard work on my behalf. Thank you all.

PART ONE

Reporting Today

"The day of the printed word is far from ended."

That statement is as true today as it was when made by Erwin Canham, long-time editor of the *Christian Science Monitor*, several decades ago during a period when the demise of the American newspapers was being predicted by countless futurists then enamored with television.

In fact, there may be even more printed words around today than ever before. Many people just may be reading or seeing them in new and different sources such as Web pages on the Internet and electronic mail.

The explosion in the electronic delivery of news and information has brought dramatic changes to the newsroom just as it has to society, which in turn has presented journalists with a greater challenge than any they have faced in the past.

The long-held belief that newspaper editors and reporters were writing and editing for a "typical" reader is no longer valid. Today, they try to reach a vastly segmented and rapidly changing audience that has a wide choice of alternative sources of news, information and entertainment.

Among the many changes that challenge editors and reporters to produce newspapers that are relevant to the needs and demands of the readers are the continuing change in the role of women in the workforce and as a consumer group; the rise in the number of single-family households; the increase in the number of persons older than 65 in the general population; the mobility of the American family; and the public's general mistrust of the news media.

Those and many other changes in society mean that reporters today must have a far broader perspective than ever before. No longer can a reporter simply tell the reader, "Here's what happened." Readers want to know, "What does this mean to me?" and "What, if anything, can I do about it?" They want news they can use.

An excellent example of that kind of news is the "Ms. Cheap" column created by veteran reporter Mary Hance for the *Nashville Banner* and continued in the *Tennessean* in Nashville after the *Banner* ceased publication. Mary Hance set out to help readers find the best buys in town on literally anything the reader might want or need. She haunts store sales, swap meets, church auctions, secondhand shops and any other place there may be a bargain and she tells her readers about it. In turn, her readers share bargain spots they have found with her. The column was an instant hit and remains one of the most popular features in the newspaper.

In Indiana, several newspapers got together to do a collective statewide audit of how public officials and employees respond to the taxpayers and the press when they seek information under the state's open records law. They found widespread violations of the law by public officials as well as open hostility by state legislators and other public officials to the law and the people who sought to use it. The results of the audit, published in a series of shared stories, brought calls from the citizens to enforce penalties on officials who violate the law, a promise from the governor to review the open records law and a move by several state senators to rewrite the law to make public records more accessible.

Reporters need to know how to gather facts for a story as well as how to write in a clear and coherent style so that readers can immediately understand the story. That's not always easy because many stories are far more complex than who did what to whom, when, why and how.

News does not exist in a vacuum. The reporter shouldn't either. Every reporter should be a voracious reader, a collector of information about everything that is going on. A civil war in an African nation may have an immediate local impact, especially if the local National Guard or Army Reserve unit is activated and sent to the war zone. That makes it a local story.

In addition, it is important for reporters to know as much about the complete operation of the newspaper as possible—not only its editorial policies, but its business, technical and mechanical divisions as well. Newspapers are a team effort, and reporters should know and understand the important role of all the departments.

Beyond that, reporters must know the characteristics of journalism as it is practiced not only at his or her newspaper, but also in the profession in general. To be successful, reporters must keep up with current trends in the profession and be flexible enough to change as the profession and the society it covers changes.

A reporter needs to understand the unique role of a newspaper in society. It is basically a business, but it is a very special business. After all, the press is the only private business singled out in the Bill of Rights. The First Amendment to the Constitution thrusts a tremendous responsibility on journalists. The true professional will always be aware of that.

What Is News?

There are almost as many answers to that question as there are editors and reporters. In fact, no uniformly satisfactory definition has been found. The question will be thoroughly explored in Chapter 3. However, it is a given in most city rooms that news is what the editor says it is.

While there may be no definitive definition of news, there is a body of knowledge dealing with writing and presenting news that every reporter should master. To be effective, a reporter simply has to understand the theories and concepts of how news is gathered and written as well as the particular role a newspaper plays in a community.

Developing News Style

News writing follows all the accepted rules of English grammar, sentence structure, spelling and punctuation. Yet it differs in many ways from other forms of writing. It strives for certain qualities of style: simplicity, conciseness, vividness, directness, clarity, brevity and accuracy. News style is discussed in Chapter 4.

Responsibilities and Restrictions

A reporter's first obligation is to tell a story as accurately, clearly and fairly as possible. However, this task is not always as easy as it may sound. A variety of restrictions can make writing a news story difficult. Some may be the reporter's own, based on how thoroughly he or she has gathered the information needed to make the story complete. Some restrictions may result from a particular newspaper policy. And still others are imposed by the laws regarding libel and invasion of privacy. It should be noted that while legal restrictions are somewhat limited, violation of them could cost a reporter a fine or a term in prison.

Most restrictions, however, come under the voluntary classification, recognized in journalism as codes of ethics that are observed for the welfare of both the press and society (see Chapter 5).

1

Journalism as a Career

"Newspapers are a wonderful collection of people, people of all colors, both genders, all human experiences, people with a concern for justice and compassion for those who are without hope or voices to express their hopes," Gregory Favre told members of the American Society of Newspaper Editors when he was their president.

They are "people who love the language and try to use it with care and dignity, people who don't mind hard work and who are always ready to answer the alarm bells."

Favre, executive editor of the *Sacramento Bee* in California, was speaking from nearly 50 years of newspaper experience that began in his youth when he worked on his family's weekly in rural Mississippi.

A career in journalism continues to attract bright, talented and interesting young women and men to the nation's newsrooms because journalism gives them an opportunity to be creative and offers them a daily challenge.

"There is abundant evidence that today's newspaper employees are still not only hardworking but dedicated to the highest ideals of journalism," the authors of a report on "The Newspaper Journalist of the '90s" wrote.

The report, sponsored by the American Society of Newspaper Editors and published in 1997, shows that the vast majority of today's newspaper journalists are quite happy with their work. Seventy-six percent of those responding said they like their current job better than their most recent previous one. A similar percentage said their jobs either met or exceeded their expectations. And three-fourths said they would choose newspapering if they had it all to do again.

The ASNE report was based on 1,037 valid responses to 1,191 questionnaires sent to journalists at 61 newspapers randomly selected from circulation sizes ranging from more than 500,000 to 5,000 or less. The response rate was 87.1 percent, which is considered unusually high in survey research.

The responses to the survey came from journalists who, for the most part, will not become more famous than many of the men and women they cover, as a number of leading television news anchors have. Nor will they command million-dollar salaries as some "star" journalists do. Yet they play important roles in their communities and enjoy exciting and rewarding careers. They are the women and men Gregory Favre was talking about in his ASNE speech.

There is far more hard work than glamour and glory involved in being a journalist. Even those who gain some measure of fame and fortune do so because they are talented and work hard. There is no escaping it—the journalist's work often is so routine and exacting that it is boring. But it is this very routine, boring—and extremely vital—groundwork that often leads to interesting and exciting news breaks that can turn a journalist into a public personality.

In their daily work, most American journalists write more news stories about city council meetings than they do about the rich and famous. They spend more time reporting activities of the police and fire departments and local schools than they do writing about sensational scandals in high office. And if they do their work with care and accuracy, they perform a far more vital function daily for their readers and their communities than the reporter who does major investigations or who writes only about the stars of stage, screen and television.

In a democracy, information is vital, and in the information explosion that has marked the last half of the twentieth century, the role of the journalist is not only to report this information but also to analyze and interpret it for the public. Through the journalist and the mass media, most Americans gain most of the information that has an impact on their daily lives. That makes the journalist a vital cog in the democratic system.

A Writer on Current Events

Journalists are writers who deal chiefly in current events. As contrasted with some other types of writers who employ imagination in their quest for reader appeal, reporters must deal with facts. Their chief role is to record what has happened and sometimes to analyze or interpret what has happened or will happen. Occasionally reporters give their own opinions on events they have reported, but opinion traditionally is not included in news stories. Opinions are expressed on the editorial pages.

Vitality and drive are important assets for journalists, but even more important are the passions for facts and the ability to write well. The two distinctive functions of journalists are gathering facts—more information than can be used—and composing accurate and interesting stories with that information.

The term *journalist* as used above is interchangeable with "newspaper reporter," for reporting the news is fundamental to virtually all journalistic occupations. Although television has challenged newspapers as a principle channel through which news is widely disseminated (studies show that the public turns to it for national and international news), newspapers still are the major source of local news for most persons. With few exceptions, most television stations provide little more than a headline summary of local news. This is particularly true in the non-metropolitan areas. The typewritten script of most television news shows would fill less than three-fourths of a single page of standard-sized newspaper.

And, despite the rapidly increasing technology in the field of electronic communications, data banks and other information storage systems, newspapers remain the chief permanent record of current events. This does not imply, however, that careers in journalism are largely limited to reporting and editing. Many journalism school graduates find successful and fulfilling careers in newspaper design and production as well as various business functions in the advertising and circulation departments of newspapers. Other communications media offer as many or more journalistic opportunities. But, historically, newspaper reporting is the grandfather of all modern journalistic careers.

Reporting: Doorway to Many Vocations

Experience as a newspaper reporter often is the foundation for a variety of other careers. A hurried check of the backgrounds of public persons both living and dead will produce an impressive list of former newspaper reporters who became mayors, governors, representatives, senators, ambassadors, actors, corporation presidents, college professors and even a U.S. president and a president's wife.

The history of American literature, for example, is laced with names of authors who were former newspaper reporters—Walt Whitman and Ernest Hemingway among them. In its long and illustrious life, the *Chicago Daily News* was the training ground for poets, playwrights, humorists, biographers, novelists, screenwriters, critics and historians. The list of former Daily News reporters includes Carl Sandburg, poet and Lincoln's biographer; Ben Hecht, novelist, playwright and screenwriter; and Meyer Levin, novelist.

Some of the most widely read popular authors of the past several decades, such as Tom Wolfe, author of *The Right Stuff* and other books, began their careers as newspaper reporters. So did Patricia Cornwell, a former police reporter for the *Charlotte Observer,* who writes best-selling suspense novels featuring medical examiner Kay Scarpetta. A number of current journalists—Pete Hamill, a veteran New York newsman, and young Rick Bragg, a Pulitzer Prize–winning *New York Times* reporter—are authors of important fiction and nonfiction works.

Intangible Benefits

The common reward for all newspaper men and women is being where the action is. They have a front seat at most public events. They are ex officio members of public organizations and committees. Even beginning reporters carry with them the influence of the newspaper, and doors are opened that often remain closed to persons in other professions. Reporters observe events in the making, and in the words of Philip Graham, late editor of the *Washington Post,* they write "the first rough draft of history." Especially for a beginner, this can be a heady ego trip. In fact, some reporters never get over it.

But exposure to the reality of a reporter's life tends to bring the truly dedicated person back down to earth. Practical experience ripens a reporter's character as perhaps no other schooling can. Reporters soon learn that not everyone loves newspapers and that people—often those in high places—will try to use newspapers for their own gain. They also learn quickly that not everyone is cooperative, and some are hostile, if not violent, when reporters arrive. Nevertheless, the conscientious reporter never stops growing as a reporter, a writer and a judge of others. And through it all, the serious reporter will develop and maintain a sense of personal and professional integrity.

The movie and novel stereotype of the reporter who takes periodic breaks from the party circuit to turn the scoundrels out of office and to rescue and uplift the downtrodden is more fiction than fact. To be sure, some reporters lack manners, morals and integrity. Some, in fact, abuse their rights and privileges. Others succumb to the temptations thrown into their paths. But most reporters, like other professionals with jobs to do, develop a code of conduct and personal integrity in keeping with the responsible positions they hold in the community.

Opportunities on Newspapers

The future of most reporters is limited only by their talents and their ambition. A talented, self-disciplined ambitious reporter can become a "big name" news writer whose by-line is readily recognized and respected or a columnist or commentator who analyzes current events. News writing opportunities are available on thousands of daily and weekly newspapers or with the wire service, the Associated Press (AP), syndicated newspaper services, news magazines and a variety of other organizations dealing in news.

Another newspaper career open to the reporter is the field of editing. In general, editors supervise the news-gathering activities of reporters, review and copyread their stories, write headlines and plan the design of the pages using their stories and pictures. These responsibilities generally do not include gathering and writing news, but some persons carrying the title of editor may have fewer or more duties than those mentioned here.

The science editor, sports editor, education editor and other staff members with similar titles are generally by-lined reporters who specialize in one area of journalism, but some of these editors may also edit copy and write headlines. The editor of a small daily or weekly newspaper usually combines news writing and editing and sometimes is responsible for business management as well. The duties of the principal editor (editor in chief) of a metropolitan daily may be limited to writing editorials, supervising the entire staff and making policy decisions.

The editor is sometimes (but not necessarily) the owner or part owner of the newspaper, and as such he or she is the publisher—another newspaper opportunity open to reporters. The publisher is the chief officer of the newspaper, responsible for its entire operation—editorial, business and mechanical. To be successful as a publisher, one obviously needs management ability in addition to a knowledge of printing processes and a capital investment to purchase or lease either an existing newspaper or the plant and equipment needed to start one. The *Editor & Publisher Yearbook* lists more than 10,000 weekly, semiweekly, small- and medium-sized dailies and large metropolitan daily newspapers in the United States. Publications serving the newspaper industry, such as *Publisher's Auxiliary*, frequently have a number of smaller newspapers listed in the "For Sale" columns. Often they may be bought on the installment plan with a reasonable down payment and the balance in periodic payments.

Opportunities in Other Fields

Although the editorial departments of newspapers do not like to be considered as training grounds for other professions, the truth is that some reporters leave after several years of experience to take positions in a variety of other fields. Reporting is an invaluable introduction to life at many points. Because reporters go everywhere and meet hundreds of people, they can make excellent contacts and learn of other opportunities that might be available to them. Often the skills developed in gathering facts, interviewing people and writing news will increase a reporter's chances for success. The worlds of business and public service are well populated with men and women who got their start on newspapers.

But by far, most of the reporters leaving newspaper work find employment in related journalistic areas—press associations; general circulation magazines; trade journals and industrial publications; radio and television stations; publicity and public relations agencies; and publications of business firms, industries, institutions and associations. Advertising is another large field that frequently absorbs individuals with newspaper experience, for journalistic techniques are applied in its various communications efforts.

Finally, the newspaper is a splendid training ground for creative writers. Many successful authors and playwrights of yesterday and today acquired their basic training as newspaper writers. The list is long, but a few excellent examples are Ernest Hemingway and Charles MacArthur, as well as Bruce Catton, Tom Wicker, David Halberstam and Gay Talese. The varied experience and constant practice in the careful and precise use of the English language provide an excellent basis for literary achievement.

Qualifications of a Reporter

What makes a good reporter? There probably are as many answers to that question as there are reporters, for few agree completely on what makes a good reporter. However, most do acknowledge that, although some persons are better fitted than others to become reporters, it is not true that reporters are born and not made. Given reasonable intelligence, most of the attributes of a successful reporter are acquired, not inherited. Perhaps the best qualifications for a reporter—aside from desire and ability to write for print—are insatiable curiosity (which surely will express itself in part through a strong habit of reading), a flexible and social personality, a nature that relishes a variety of experiences, a temperament to work under the pressure of deadlines and a tolerance permitting objective observations of people and events. A successful reporter also needs ambition, drive, determination, and, most certainly, self-discipline.

Richard J. Cattani, editor of the *Christian Science Monitor*, listed the attributes needed by professional journalists as self-operating, productive, caring, exemplary, versatile, authoritative, expansive, supportive, visionary, sensitive, considerate, confident, distinctive, intuitive, teachable, selfless, responsible, active, paced and, finally, impelled: "If you don't wake up writing, try a different trade," he advised.

Attributes Needed for Success in Reporting

A broad knowledge of the English language and the ability to use words with style and grace are the essential tools of a good reporter. Journalism is not a logical career choice for anyone who does not enjoy writing.

In a career guide published by The Newspaper Fund, Paul McKalip, editor of the *Tucson Citizen*, said the following is what he looks for in an applicant for a reporting position: "Intelligence, wide range of interests, ambition to advance, skills, thoroughness, accuracy, ability to meet deadlines, excellence in spelling and grammar."

Other editors added such attributes as "insatiably curious," "patient but persistent" and "the ability to write a clear, carefully constructed sentence." These attributes may seem unrealistic in a profession not known for its unusually high salaries. Nevertheless, they are the qualities and abilities that editors of good newspapers expect. Without them, the staff would produce a dull, routine, lackluster newspaper.

Anyone seeking a career in journalism should be aware that although much of a reporter's work is routine, it is essential never to fall into the trap of treating a story routinely. Each story, whether it is about a local rose festival or an interview with the president, should be the best possible story the reporter can write at that time. There really are no dull stories, only unimaginative, lazy reporters.

Most of the routine a reporter faces is part of a daily kaleidoscope of events. Assignments may change rapidly from the commonplace to the exciting. A reporter must be alert and think fast to move smoothly from one assignment to another when stories vary greatly in news value.

Reporters work under a great deal of pressure much of the time. They constantly race against the clock to meet deadlines, so another important attribute is the ability to work calmly under pressure.

Perhaps the most difficult challenge facing every reporter is the ability to separate personal beliefs and biases from what is being written. A good reporter simply must take a position as an unbiased witness in reporting the news and accurately interpreting the facts.

Educational Needs of a Reporter

Although educational training for journalists dates back to the turn of the early 1990s, college-educated journalists were not common on most newspapers until well into the 1930s. Today, it is often difficult to obtain a position on a newspaper without a college degree and, in many cases, a degree in journalism. The 1997 American Society of Newspaper Editors' report showed that 89 percent of the journalists have college degrees compared to 86 percent eight years earlier. In 1982–1983, that figure was 70 percent. And 10 years before that, it was only 58 percent. Accredited colleges and schools of journalism require students to get a broad liberal arts education with a concentration of journalism courses. Because of the vast amount of knowledge needed by a journalist, students in accredited journalism programs take only one-fourth of their work in specific journalism courses; the other three-fourths of their college work is in the arts, sciences and humanities. Those students who hope to specialize in a particular area—politics, science, foreign relations, home economics, agriculture and other fields—are encouraged to bolster their education with additional courses in these specialized areas.

Journalism students generally are required to take courses in English composition and literature, history, political science, economics, psychology, one or more of the natural sciences and one or more foreign languages. A foreign language—Spanish, for example—would be a tremendous asset to a reporter working in an area where there is a large Latin American population, such as southern Florida, the southwestern states or southern California. A course in public speaking often is required. It can prove helpful when covering a speech or when asked to give one, as many reporters and editors are asked to do.

The ability to type with speed and accuracy is absolutely essential. Even the smallest newspapers have converted their newsrooms to electronic, computerized operations. Reporters compose their stories on the keyboard of a computer. In fact, technology is advancing so rapidly that many newspapers regularly upgrade to more highly developed computer systems that require even greater typing skills.

Education is tremendously important for a reporter. However, some persons without a college education have become successful as reporters. Many newspapers in the past have employed high school graduates and "brought them up" in the editorial department. A few still do. But most employers are aware that, in comparison with high school graduates, college-trained reporters generally have a greater capacity for success and thus are worth considerably more to the newspaper.

A college-trained reporter brings to the job not only knowledge of history, psychology, political science and the like, but also the ability to use that knowledge to help interpret the events of the day, to put them in their proper perspective so the reader can understand them. Journalism courses are designed to show how to use the knowledge obtained in other courses for the benefit of the readers.

Advantages of a Journalism Degree

Journalism education in college was ridiculed by some newspaper editors (and still is by a few), but today it is widely recognized as valuable for the beginning reporter. Some editors, because they were not college graduates, argued that the best education for a reporter was practical experience in the newsroom.

In more recent years the same editors admitted, somewhat reluctantly, that although the newsroom is good experience, it is also limiting. They discovered that college training in journalism not only affords a shortcut to learning the basic journalistic techniques and skills, but also gives the beginning reporter a broader understanding of his or her work. In short, city editors and other staff supervisors have not been as successful in teaching journalistic fundamentals with the trial-and-error method as have instructors using formal classroom procedures. Hour for hour, the student in the classroom learns those fundamentals in less than one-third the time spent by the beginning reporter taught by the trial-and-error process.

A Craft or a Profession?

Never before has so much information been available in so short a time. And never has so much attention been focused on the men and women who deliver that information.

Many journalists have become glamor figures or immediate public personalities, especially those reporting from Washington, D.C. In fact, in the view of several social critics, journalists have become part of a new society dubbed "mediacracy," described as a public aristocracy of people important in the media and people who gain power through the media.

Enrollments in journalism schools continue to rise. Some say it is because of the glamor surrounding the profession as a result of the Watergate scandals in the administration of President Richard M. Nixon. Others insist the increase is caused by the lure of fame and fortune offered by journalism, especially to those who become network television anchors. Still others say young men and women, aware of the declining popularity of the traditional liberal arts degree, are simply seeking an education that will make them more hirable.

But as Watergate faded into the past, enrollments continued to increase. Enrollments are near the 70,000 mark (this includes all programs—journalism, broadcasting, advertising and public relations). Now some journalists and educators are suggesting that enrollments be limited and that more rigid entrance requirements be established.

All this debate has done little to settle the long-standing dispute: Is journalism a craft or a profession? Despite the advancements in education and training and the sophistication in reporting and writing techniques, some insist that news writers and commentators have no right to place themselves among the professionals with such time-honored groups as lawyers, physicians, teachers, ministers and engineers.

The Press and Society

The press, both print and electronic, is an important institution in modern society. It is recognized as the principal medium of mass communication and has become increasingly important because scientific and technological advancements make it more essential than ever to keep people informed of day-to-day developments. The task of sorting this information and presenting it to the public in a clear, coherent manner has placed an increased burden on the press. Most news professionals realize this, just as they are aware that without an independent and often aggressive press, a democracy such as ours might not survive.

Particularly in a democracy, the role of the press is of vital importance, as the events surrounding Watergate and the Clinton administration scandals attest. The success of a democratic government depends on the wise decisions of an informed citizenry, for a democracy is ruled by people at the polls. Therefore, the press must be utilized to give the people the information they should have in casting votes on candidates and issues. In this respect, the press is a great educational institution. Its responsibilities in informing the public fairly, accurately and objectively in all matters of public concern are paramount. A responsible newspaper must remove itself from partisan politics in its news columns.

The press as an institution serving the people of a democracy was identified when journalists were designated as the "Fourth Estate." This unofficial title was given to members of the press near the turn of the nineteenth century by the British Parliament in recognition of the fact that the press represents the people and has strong influence on public opinion. The other three recognized "estates" or classes representing the British people were the clergy, the nobility and the commons. The "Fourth Estate" title is just as applicable today as it was then, for as government grows larger and more complex by the day, it is not humanly possible for a single individual to understand even a small amount of what it does without the aid of the mass media as sources of information and interpretation.

Just as it is used to enlighten the people, the press, under the thumb of dictatorial control, can be used to enslave a nation. The mediums of mass communications can be employed to disseminate either truths or falsehoods. Hitler, like other dictators before and after him, gave the world a tragic lesson on a controlled press. The efforts of several presidential administrations since the late 1950s to control or intimidate the American press (such as the Nixon administration's effort to prevent the publication of the Pentagon Papers, the Reagan administration's ban on journalists going ashore with the troops during the invasion of Grenada and the Clinton administration's stonewalling during the special prosecutor's investigations) demonstrate just how fragile the constitutional guarantee of freedom of the press really is. Fortunately, the press has successfully resisted most overt attempts at control with the aid of some enlightened public officials. Yet this is a battle the press must continue to fight.

Equally important for the press in a free society is its relationship with the people, because they keep the press in business. Readers and subscribers are the life blood of the press. As a member of a free enterprise system open to anyone who cares to venture into competition, a newspaper must maintain the confidence and respect of its readers or its competitors will take over.

The press can be described as a quasi-public agency. It has the responsibility of keeping the public informed, and it is given freedom to do so by the U.S. Constitution. But because the press operates under the private enterprise system, it is divorced from governmental control and its economic fate is placed directly into the hands of the people.

Journalism and the Professions

Although the press is accorded a special place in a democratic society, whether this warrants professional status for journalists can still be debated. Many of the attributes of journalists give them strong claim to this distinction. Compared to members of the accepted professions, journalists also have great responsibilities of public service that demand respect. Journalists are, to a large degree, educators. They influence public opinion, which, in turn, can influence the enactment or repeal of laws. They serve as guardians of the public by constantly monitoring and reporting on the actions of public officials and bodies. They have the power to bring credit or discredit to the names and reputations of everyone they write about. What other occupation provides so many important public services and carries so many responsibilities?

Yet journalism is unlike other professions in that it is not—and should never be—a licensed profession. Physicians, lawyers, teachers and others must be licensed (or certified) to practice, and to obtain a license they must complete specific educational programs and, in some cases, must pass examinations. Further, some of these professional people can lose their licenses if they are found guilty of unethical practices. Such requirements are designed to help maintain standards and to protect the public from damage that could be done by unqualified persons in the professions. (In reality, the licensing and examination system is far from perfect, and the enforcement of standards is highly erratic, resulting often in totally irresponsible delays in the revocation of licenses.)

Licensing journalists, however, would be a form of governmental control of the press. Through license laws, a dictatorial or spiteful government, by hand-picking those who issue the licenses or those who are licensed to write for newspapers and other mediums, could nullify the constitutional guarantee of a free press. (Some members of the broadcasting industry charge that licensing radio and television stations, which has led to efforts to control content, is indeed a violation of the U.S. Constitution.)

Professional status for journalism cannot be attained by imposing high standards through license laws, but it can be achieved through voluntary efforts of journalists. Although no law should require beginning journalists to have a college education, this is a prerequisite that more and more employers are finding much to their advantage. Although no law can require that journalists abide by a professional code of ethics, journalists themselves, through organizations such as the Society of Professional Journalists (formerly Sigma Delta Chi) and the American Society of Newspaper Editors (ASNE), have established voluntary codes. Although journalists with a genuine respect for their responsibilities generally accept those voluntary standards, there are and will continue to be men and women in journalism who violate them for personal gain, without any feeling of guilt or fear of prosecution.

As a result of criticism leveled at the press from both inside and out, during the period of the war in Vietnam in particular, a number of watchdog publications came into being. They repeatedly called into question the actions and policies of individual newspapers, publishers, and the entire mass communications industry. Among the more notable of these were the *Columbia Journalism Review*, the *Chicago Journalism Review, More* and the *St. Louis Journalism Review*. There have been several other journalism reviews as well, and occasionally a new one will appear. However, most of them have ceased publication. The *American Journalism Review* and the *Columbia Journalism Review* continue as the chief and most vigorous sources of criticism of the media. Several national publications—the *Atlantic, Harper's* and the *Wall Street Journal*—report regularly and often critically on the media. *Brill's Content* added its critical voice in the late 1990s. And there is an increasing number of books critical of the media published each year by journalists as well as others.

It was during this period of turmoil, also, that a number of press councils were established in several cities and states, and the National Press Council was created by the Twentieth Century Fund in the early 1970s. The councils generally investigate complaints against the media but at the same time work to defend freedom of the press. The councils did not have the overwhelming support of some of the nation's newspapers or the broadcasting industry, and most of them have ceased to function. The National Press Council ceased operation in 1984.

Several so-called independent organizations were founded to serve as watchdogs for the media. The most active has been Accuracy in Media (AIM). Other organizations such as the Pew Research Center for the People & the Press have brought a more scholarly and less strident voice to the study of the press than most of the self-appointed watchdogs. In addition, some newspapers have named ombudsmen—in-house critics—to review and critique the performance of the newspaper staff. The *Louisville Courier–Journal* and the *Washington Post* have used this technique for a number of years. In addition to reporting, as it were, their views to the senior editors, they often write a column critical of the way in which a particular story or issue was handled. This in-house critic idea has been praised by many outside the profession, but is generally not popular among newspaper staffs. A number of newspapers, among them the *Washington Post* and the *Los Angeles Times*, also have media critics who evaluate the performance of the press on a regular basis.

Even with these watchdogs, the press has its unethical journalists just as medicine still has its quacks, law its shysters and education its tenure-protected and inept teachers. Those who faithfully serve the profession of journalism, like those serving other professions, can only hope that the unethical encroachment on their privileged profession can be kept at a minimum and prosecuted as far as possible through regular legal channels.

EXERCISES

1. Using out-of-town newspapers available in your university library or the local public library, compare the front pages of three dailies from major cities for the

same day. Prepare a report on their similarities and differences, especially in the selection of the major story of the day, the story length, its placement on the page, and the size of the headline.

2. Using the *Editor & Publisher Yearbook*, look up the web site address of those same papers. Visit the web sites and compare what the major stories used on the web site that day with those used in the newspaper. Prepare a report on the similarities and differences you find.

3. With a copy of the local daily or a major newspaper such as the *New York Times* in hand, watch both the major local and national evening newscast of a local television station. Compare the difference in stories used on the front page of the newspaper and those used on the local and national newscasts. Write a report on your findings.

4. Invite the editor of the local newspaper and the news directors of the leading television and radio stations in your area to class for a panel discussion on journalism careers. Prepare a list of at least 10 questions to ask the panel members, such as, "What attributes do you look for when interviewing an applicant for a position as a reporter?" Write a report on what members of the panel say.

5. Ask a local by-lined reporter or newspaper columnist or a television anchorperson to class to be interviewed about her or his career as a journalist. Prepare a list of questions to ask that person. Write a brief report on the discussion.

6. Interview at least 10 persons in your community (but not your fellow students) and ask them their views of the quality of the press (newspapers and television and radio stations) in your community. Write a brief paper on the results of your interviews.

7. Contact the executive director of the state press association and interview him or her about the health of the newspaper industry in your state. Find out if the industry is thriving or declining. Include statistics on the number of daily and weekly newspapers currently published. Ask for statistics on the number of new newspapers that have started publishing in the last five years and the number that have ceased operation. Ask about the number of chain-owned newspapers compared to those independently owned. Write a report based on the information you collect.

8. The press is the subject of constant review and criticism in a variety of national magazines and specialized publications such as the *Columbia Journalism Review* as well as a number of books. Study at least four issues of those specialized publications as well as the press sections in the national news weeklies as well as magazines such as the *Atlantic, Brill's Content* and *Harper's*. Make notes on the types of criticisms leveled at the press and write a report on your findings.

9. Using a copy of a daily newspaper that circulates in your city, select 10 stories that interest you the most. Then ask at least five individuals who are not students who read that same issue of the paper to tell you what stories interest them the most. Write a report on the results.

10. Press freedom on campus is an ongoing issue. Interview the editors of your campus newspaper, yearbook and literary magazine about the restrictions, if any, that have been placed on them by university officials. Using those interviews and material collected from articles in journalism reviews such as the *Student Law Center Report* and *Quill*, the national publication of the Society of Professional Journalists, write a report comparing press freedom on your campus to national trends in student press freedom.

CHAPTER

2

The Reporter in the News Organization

H. L. Mencken had this to say about reporters: "His overpowering impulse is to gyrate before his fellow man, flapping his wings and emitting defiant yells. This being forbidden by the police of all civilized countries, he takes it out by putting his yells on paper."

Mencken was speaking from experience because he was one of the most celebrated writers, editors and social critics of his time, and he certainly emitted defiant yells in print often.

Was he being unkind? Was he being funny? Yes, unless you are a humorless reporter. Was he accurate? In many cases, yes.

It has been said that a reporter's ego is like an unskulled brain, a quivering mass of vulnerability. But no matter how big an ego a reporter may have, the simple fact of newspapering is that no story, no matter how well written, would be printed and seen by readers without the important work of dozens—often hundreds—of men and women in all departments of the newspaper, starting in the newsroom.

Most of the public's attention is focused on reporters chiefly because they are the "point" men and women of the news business. More people know reporters by name or reputation than they do press operators. Yet both are essential to a newspaper.

A newspaper's reputation often is based on the public's perception of its reporters. They usually are blamed by the public for all the perceived sins of the press simply because they are the most visible members of the staff.

Despite the prominent role of the reporter, increasing attention has been given in recent years to the dramatic advances in the technology of printing and the speed with which news can be delivered to the public. At times, in the trade press in particular, it has appeared that the technology of the industry was more important than the human beings involved in the news process.

Like printing technology, however, the American reporter is better than ever. At the same time, reporters cannot afford to be arrogant about their importance, because without the important work performed by all the others in the organization, business and technical as well as editorial personnel, their work would be useless. Each of the three major departments of a typical newspaper plays a significant role in the delivery of news to readers.

Editorial Department.   The function of the newspaper's editorial department is to gather news from various sources and to write it into readable, interesting stories, edit them and plan how they will be displayed on the printed pages. Other functions of the editorial department are to instruct or influence the public through editorials, commentary and analysis, as well as to entertain the public through its by-lined columns, comics and other features. All the editorial content of the newspaper is processed by the editorial department.

Many newspapers have established their own web pages on the Internet and the editorial department is responsible for preparing stories for that page (Fig. 2.1). If a newspaper has a web site, it will be listed in the *Editor & Publisher Yearbook.* Newspaper web addresses also can be found through the use of Internet search engines.

Mechanical Department.   The complicated and highly technical process of transforming the reporter's stories into type and reproducing them on thousands of pages of newsprint is done by the mechanical department, which includes the composing room and the pressroom. The printing process has become highly computerized.

Business Department.   To finance the two other departments, advertising space must be sold, subscriptions must be solicited and the finished product must be delivered to the readers. To handle these important duties, most newspapers have separate advertising and circulation departments under the business department.

A third division handles problems of management, personnel and business administration at many newspapers. Advertising, circulation and management may be combined into one unit at small newspapers. But at larger ones, they generally operate as separate units and report to a business or general manager.

Details of Organization

The organization of a newspaper will vary considerably, depending on its size. Metropolitan newspapers frequently have highly developed organization charts similar to that in Fig. 2.2. At smaller newspapers, some of the duties of various departments may overlap. And in rare cases, there may be no formal organization chart at all; everyone does what has to be done to get the paper out.

All papers have a publisher. The title often is assumed by the owner or the majority stockholder in the corporation or it can be given to someone hired to serve in that position. The latter is particularly true at newspapers owned by both large and small chains. The men and women hired as publishers may have no direct ownership in the publication, although some companies do offer opportunities to buy stock in the firm.

The degree of involvement by the publisher in the daily operation of the newspaper varies greatly. On smaller newspapers a publisher may also be the ed-

FIGURE 2.1A   The *Knoxville News–Sentinel* established its own web page early. Here is an example of the front page of the *News–Sentinel* reporting President Clinton's acquittal by the Senate.

FIGURE 2.1B The same story reported on its web page.
(Reprinted by permission of the *Knoxville News–Sentinel*.)

itor and general manager. On larger newspapers he or she may serve as the chief executive officer of the company and delegate authority for daily operation to a general manager.

Although a publisher technically has the power to dictate all policies, editorial as well as business, it usually does not work that way. Policies are generally worked out among the publisher—or owners, if the publisher is hired—the editors and often members of the business staff. The publisher is ultimately, and legally, responsible for everything that appears in the newspaper.

On smaller dailies and weeklies, the publisher may be the owner, editor and even one of the reporters. The late Nancy Petrey, copublisher of the *Newport Plain Talk* (Newport, Tn), the largest nondaily in the state, sold advertisements, took photographs, wrote stories, sold subscriptions and delivered her prize-winning newspaper. She was also known to put on a pair of coveralls and crawl up on the press when a mechanical problem developed.

The business manager generally has authority over advertising, circulation and the office manager, if the newspaper is large enough to need an office manager. In many instances the business manager also fills that position. In that type of organization, the advertising and circulation managers report to the business manager, who then reports to the general manager or publisher. On smaller newspapers it is not uncommon for the publisher also to act as the business manager and an advertising sales representative.

Since the late 1970s, the process of getting a story into print has changed dramatically. The Age of the Computer is in full flower at newspapers all over the nation. Reporters write their stories on a computer terminal. Copy editors use computers to edit stories and write headlines. Graphic artists use personal computers for designs, charts, graphs, maps and many papers to design the pages as well.

The designed pages are sent by the newsroom computers to the computer in the printing department, where the stories, photographs, charts and advertisements are assembled into a finished page by the image-setter (photocomposition machine). The image-setter produces a negative of the page, which is burned onto thin, sensitized plates that are attached to the press. The image is produced on newsprint by the offset method. In that process, the ink adheres only to the image that has been burned onto the plate; it is then imposed on a rubber roller on the press that transfers the image to the newsprint. The result is generally a much sharper, cleaner-appearing newspaper. Most modern newspaper presses are computer driven.

Major benefits of computerization have been increased speed and the reduction of personnel, particularly in the composition and printing operations. However, there is still considerable debate in newsrooms over whether the product is as good. Some worry that the editing is not as carefully done, although a number of studies show that there is little or no difference in the quality of editing whether it is done on a computer or by hand. Some reporters complain that the computer turns them into typesetters and proofreaders. And other studies have been conducted on the possible health hazards that could be caused by working on computers for extended periods. San Francisco was the first city to establish safety guidelines for persons who use computers in their daily work.

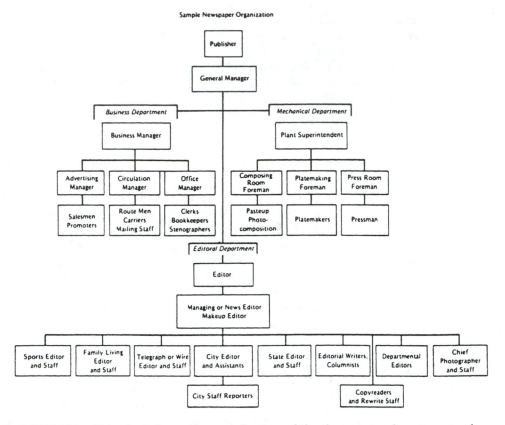

FIGURE 2.2   This chart shows the organization of the three major departments of a typical daily newspaper.

Although the editor of a newspaper works in concert with the publisher and often the business manager, he or she is primarily responsible for the editorial content. At larger papers, the editor generally delegates the responsibility for running the daily operation to a managing editor, who in turn directs the activities of the city editor and the various department editors.

All local news stories are written by staff reporters who work under the city editor. Stories received from the national wire services are handled by the wire editor. Correspondents (out-of-town reporters) work through the state editor. Editors in charge of lifestyles, sports, entertainment, business and other editorial departments handle all the stories for their pages. However, they work closely with the managing editor, the city editor and the graphics editor in an effort to coordinate their efforts.

Editorials are written by editors and editorial writers. Usually, if an editor has administrative duties, he or she may write few editorials. Newspapers that are owned by chains may receive some of their editorials from the home office. In addition, the public relations offices of a number of the state and national business and professional organizations and other special-interest groups send materials for editorials to newspapers. Some newspapers use them, but others consider their use unethical and will not print them.

Stories written on computers by staff reporters are carefully read on computers by copy editors not only for errors in spelling, grammar and punctuation, but also for errors in facts and style. Staff members also serve on the rewrite desk. They may take stories by phone from out-of-the-office reporters working their beats or covering a breaking news event, or they may be given press releases to rewrite.

On larger newspapers most headlines are written by the copy editors. On smaller ones much of the copyreading and headline writing may be done by the city, wire and state editors. And on very small publications, a reporter may write the headline on the story he or she has just composed.

Photographers may serve under a chief photographer, but their assignments generally come from a photo editor or one of the departmental editors. They may accompany a reporter on an assignment, or they may cover an event alone. On smaller newspapers, reporters often serve as their own photographers.

Department editors are in charge of special sections devoted to such topics as business, sports and entertainment, including radio, television, motion pictures, the arts, music, and books. Department editors also are responsible for the special Sunday sections of most newspapers. However, on smaller newspapers, coverage of those areas may be assigned to various staff reporters in addition to their regular duties. The book page editor may be an editorial writer, for example. Or a beat reporter may also do movie reviews.

The availability of personal computers and the growing use of computers to collect data and sort vast collections of government records introduced a new term to the journalism lexicon at the start of the 1990s: *computer-assisted reporting*. Reporters quickly learned to make good use of Nexis, Lexis, Vu/Tex, and other commercial databases, and many have moved on to using computer software programs to analyze government databases.

The *Atlanta Journal–Constitution* analyzed bank records with a common Lotus software program for its Pulitzer Prize–winning series on racial bias in bank lending practices, for example. Two reporters for the Washington bureau of Cox Newspapers used government records to develop a database on the ownership of assault weapons. Then they analyzed it to see if assault rifles really were serious problems in American society. Their analysis allowed them to determine how often assault guns, as opposed to more conventional firearms, were used in crimes. They also were able to determine the preferred gun of drug traffickers and terrorists and compare the numbers of foreign and domestically manufactured assault weapons that had been traced to crimes.

Investigative reporters say computer analysis of databases can cut months or years of legwork. To promote the use of personal computers as reporting tools, the National Institute for Computer-Assisted Reporting was established at the University of Missouri.

The Library/Morgue

An important tool for all reporters and editors is the newspaper's reference file, traditionally called the "morgue" but more often the "library." Most libraries keep rather complete clippings of all previously reported major news stories and photographs that have been printed. In many cases, they also keep extensive background material gathered by reporters on various subjects and persons as well as clippings from competing newspapers and other sources. Pictures, both used and unused, generally are kept in the library also. In addition, most libraries keep a wide variety of reference books, from world almanacs to the various *Who's Who* publications, along with social, political and economic data on the city and state.

A complete library also has on hand biographies of prominent persons—city, state, national, and international—ready for instant use. In fact, many newspapers have these biographies written as news stories and stored in their computer memory bank. They are updated regularly. A newspaper the size of the *Chicago Tribune* or the *Los Angeles Times* will have hundreds of them already prepared, and when a famous person is thrust into the news, the staff has only to write a brief new lead on the story and it is ready for instant printing.

Depending on the size of the newspaper, the library may range from a few files to a large reference collection. Some newspapers keep their files on microfilm, but more and more are computerizing their libraries.

The *Knoxville News–Sentinel* (Knoxville, Tn), for example, has computerized everything that has appeared in the newspaper since 1990, and reporters can call up previous stories on their computers without going to the library. It also has retained all clippings before 1990. Large newspapers such as the *New York Times*, and the *Wall Street Journal*, have established databanks for the complete storage of all information that has been printed in the publications. Some of them sell the information to other newspapers. In fact, today's newspapers have a choice among a number of databanks and information retrieval services that can be used by reporters conducting research for stories.

News Channels

The editorial department of a newspaper receives news through a variety of sources and channels.

1. From local sources through the newspapers' own reporters, who gather news from regular beats, flesh it out with background from the newspaper's library, and do most of the writing in the newspaper office under the direction of the city editor or one of the departmental editors.

2. From national and foreign sources through the wire services and syndicates such as *AP, Reuters,* the *New York Times*, the *Los Angeles Times* and the *Washington Post* news services. In addition, commercial syndicates provide many of the features and columns. Some of this material is received by wire and, except for copyreading, is ready for publication. Some feature services send material to their client newspapers by mail if it does not fit into the immediate-news category. The wire editor or a department editor is responsible for handling this material, although the task may be assigned to a copy editor. Credit is given by use of the name or initials of the press service that provided the material on each story used. The press service or syndicate may be credited in a by-line, or the initials may be included in the dateline, which is the line at the beginning of a story giving its place of origin: WASHINGTON (AP). A local story needs no dateline, although some papers—the *New York Times,* for example—use them. Some papers reserve the right to combine stories from various press services to which they subscribe. In those cases the story usually carries a by-line saying "Compiled from press services."

3. From state and regional sources through correspondents. Much of this material is written and ready for publication, although many state editors either rewrite the stories or heavily edit them. Occasionally, a correspondent simply dictates his notes to a state desk reporter, who will write the story. Such stories often have "Special to the [name of newspaper]" preceding or in the dateline. In addition, some state editors gather stories by telephone from news sources such as police and city officials in communities in the newspaper's circulation area.

4. From various individuals and organizations, such as chambers of commerce; public information offices of various social, fraternal and educational organizations; public relations agencies through the mail, by telephone, by e-mail or during personal visits. Most of this material is rewritten by the city staff under the direction of the city editor.

Sources and Beats

At most newspapers, as much as 90 percent of all local news comes from regular beats and sources. Beats are the same at almost every newspaper. Reporters are assigned to them by the city editor to cover daily. They are:

1. The city police station, county jail, sheriff's office, state police, fire department and local hospitals.
2. The city hall, which houses the offices of the mayor and the city manager, most of the city department offices and the meeting room for the city council or aldermen.
3. The county courthouse, which houses the offices of the county's chief executive officer, the county departmental office, meeting room for the county commissioners and the county courts.
4. The state capitol or state offices, which house the governor, members of the governor's cabinet and various state departmental offices. State government departments usually maintain satellite offices in many cities and towns.

5. The federal building or offices, which house the post office, federal law enforcement agencies, and other federal operations such as the Internal Revenue Service and the Immigration and Naturalization Service. The federal courts also are housed in the federal building. However, some agencies maintain offices outside the federal building.

6. City, county and private schools, colleges, universities, trade schools and associated organizations.

7. Chambers of commerce, business firms, industries and labor organizations.

8. Civic, fraternal and professional organizations such as the local medical society.

9. Churches and associated organizations.

10. Organizations and welfare agencies associated with the local Community Chest or United Fund, as well as health organizations in such fields as medicine, mental health and alcohol and drug counseling, which might be financed independently or through public fund drives.

11. Motion picture theaters, radio and television stations and all organizations offering theatrical or musical productions, such as the local symphony orchestra, amateur and professional theater groups, athletic events, or performances by nationally and internationally known music groups and individual performers.

12. Funeral homes.

13. Convention centers, hotels, airlines and other firms engaging in tourism or accommodating meetings and visitors, such as the local tourist bureau.

14. Businesses and industries important to the local community, such as shipping and mining.

Many newspapers also have specialized beats dealing with the environment, agriculture, science and medicine and other areas of public interest. One of the newest beats at newspapers of all sizes deals with technology in general and specifically with the impact of computers on our lives and the changes brought about by the growing popularity of the Internet for news, information, entertainment and shopping. The *San Jose Mercury News* in the heart of California's Silicon Valley has been a leader in reporting on the computer industry and the computer's impact on daily life. Other papers such as the *New York Times* and *USA TODAY* have regular "technology" sections. And as more and more Americans begin to use the Internet—by the late 1990s, 70 million of the 202 million U.S. adults (34.9 percent) use the Internet—it is almost certain that most newspapers, even the small ones, will be covering technology in depth.

A number of newspapers have experimented with doing away with beats altogether. Others have rearranged and consolidated them. In an effort to cover the "texture and fabric" of the Silicon Valley, Jerry Ceppos, executive editor of the *San Jose Mercury News*, reallocated resources and set up a five-person team to concentrate on the "Valley" and the people who live and work there. "It's just good local reporting," Ceppos says. The *Mercury News* was a pioneer in newspapering online with its Mercury Center. A number of other newspapers have reconfigured their newsroom staffs, creating teams to cover topics in areas like health coverage rather than letting it be the exclusive prerogative of a single reporter or wire editor.

It should be apparent from this list of beats that most news is gathered in a regular, formalized, systematic way. A reporter does not stroll about the streets looking for news to happen. Every day, the beat reporter is responsible for covering the special offices and organizations in which most news originates. Even news of murders, fires, accidents and disasters generally comes from regular sources—police and fire departments, hospitals and the local weather service.

The number of beats often is determined by the organization of the newsroom. For example, some newspapers in larger cities have a metropolitan editor who attempts to coordinate all the news in the city and the area immediately surrounding the city. In others, everything beyond the immediate city limits may be the responsibility of the state editor or zone section editors. The physical location and other conditions may cause a reporter to cover parts of several beats.

In addition to beat reporters, every newspaper has general assignment reporters who cover a wide range of stories, depending on the particular need on any given day.

The Story Process

Although the process varies from paper to paper, generally speaking, a story follows this path from the event itself, into print and then into the hands of the reader.

1. A reporter is sent to cover a newsworthy event. He or she gathers the facts by interviewing the participants and others and makes careful notes for the story. A beat reporter may interview an official, cover a meeting or search public records to gather information for a story.

2. Most reporters return to the office to write the story. In some cases, because of deadlines a reporter may write the story on the spot and dictate it over the phone to another staff member in the office. Or the reporter may use a computer modem to send the story back to the office. At some newspapers, the reporter may give only the basic facts of the story over the phone to a staff member in the office who will write the complete story. Some metropolitan dailies have installed computers in the pressrooms at city hall and the courthouse; the reporter writes the story on the computer and feeds it directly into the computer at the newspaper by telephone.

3. After a reporter writes the story and files it in the computer, the city editor (or department editor) calls up the story on another computer screen and reads it. Changes may be made at that point by the editor, or the story may be sent back to the reporter for rewriting. Once the story meets the city editor's approval, it is filed in the computer again until called up by a copy editor, who completes the editing process and writes the headline. When ready for publication, the story can be sent directly to the photocomposition machine, which sets it in type, or it can be stored for later use.

4. During a news meeting involving the managing editors and all department editors (or during the editing process), where the story will appear in the newspaper is decided. The person responsible for designing the pages works closely with the editors. At some newspapers all the page layouts are done by the same designers. But at larger papers, one group of designers handles the news sections while others do the layouts for the special sections such as business and sports.

5. Wire copy generally is fed directly into a newspaper's computer and called up on the computer screen by the wire editor or a copy editor for editing and headline writing.

6. Once the stories have been set in type in the composing room, they are pasted on a page-form by staff members who use the page dummy drawn by the designer as a guide. The completed pages are generally checked by someone from the newsroom before they are released. Many papers do the page layouts on a computer screen.

7. From the page-forms a photographic negative is made. The image from the negative is burned onto a thin, sensitized plate, which is then fitted on the presses in the pressroom where the newspaper is printed, cut and folded in one operation.

8. The printed newspapers are delivered to the circulation department for home delivery, street sales and mailing.

Although there are a number of complaints about the impact of computerization on the quality of newspapers and the health of the staff, it is apparent that advancing computer technology will continue to have a significant influence on the gathering of news and the printing of newspapers.

EXERCISES

1. Tour a daily and a weekly newspaper in your city or a nearby community. Take extensive notes how the newsrooms of each operate. Write a report comparing the organization, chain of command and staff size, among other factors.

2. Interview the heads of the advertising, circulation and mechanical departments of a local newspaper. Write a report on how each of those departments relates to the news department.

3. Interview a reporter and a copy editor at a local newspaper. Write a report on how their roles at the newspaper are related.

4. Tour the news department of a local television station. Write a report comparing its operation to the news department of the newspaper you toured.

5. After visiting the local newspaper, draw up a plan of news coverage of a new newspaper that you would establish in the community. Describe what your newspaper would offer the readers and advertisers that the established one does not provide. Include the type of news, information and entertainment you would feature and describe the appearance of your newspaper.

6. Using a recent copy of the newspaper in your community or a nearby city, examine the front page carefully and make a list of the beat each story came from and the source or sources.

7. Ask the city editor of your local newspaper to let you spend a day with a reporter on a beat. Write a report on your day "in the field."

8. Arrange to spend a day observing the staff of one of the non-news departments at your local newspaper, such as advertising or circulation.

9. Most newspapers contribute much more to their communities than simply covering the news. Interview the editor or public service director of a local newspaper about the various public events and social service projects the newspaper supports. Write a report on your findings.

CHAPTER

3

What Is News?

"News is anything that will make people talk."

That is how Charles A. Dana, editor from 1868 to 1897 of the legendary "newspaperman's newspaper," the *New York Sun*, defined news.

More than a century later, it is still a good definition. Listen to conversations any day and compare them to the front page of your local newspaper. There's a good chance there will be a striking similarity.

Of course, Dana hasn't been the only person to define news over the years. In fact, there are almost as many definitions as there are editors and reporters. Most readers have their own ideas of what news is as well. And they often let editors know in strong words.

In truth, there is no single all-encompassing definition of news because the elements that constitute it are constantly changing, and so are the women and men who select it for print, broadcast and other sources such as the Internet.

The dramatic social, economic, political and technological changes sweeping the world continue to have a profound impact on what is considered news today, just as they have had on the readers and the way readers get the news.

What may be important news in one city may not be in another. A newspaper in Oregon, for example, may focus special attention on the battle between environmentalists and the timber industry, while one in Kentucky or North Carolina may devote a lot of the front page space to the fortunes of the tobacco industry.

Reader interests varies greatly. That's why an event that may rate the front page in a community of 10,000 may not make the calendar of events in a newspaper in a city of 500,000. Although there are some events such as major airline disasters or violent weather patterns that leave a path of destruction and death across vast sections of the country uniformly make the front pages of both large and small newspapers.

Despite the fact that some of the new mediums are attempting to recast the definition of news, there is general agreement in most of the nation's newsrooms about the kinds of events and individuals that are newsworthy.

News Values

The qualifications or characteristics of news generally recognized by editors and reporters are known as *news values*. They include:

Conflict

Most conflicts are newsworthy to some degree because they disrupt the status quo. Physical conflict is considered newsworthy because it may lead to injury and damage. Violence arouses emotions, not only in the participants, but also in the spectators, and can be of enormous and immediate importance.

War is a classic example of conflict. It will dominate the news. However, a fistfight between two partisans at a championship football game may rate no more than a single line of type, if that, in a game story. But let the partisan fans riot after the game, damaging cars, blocking traffic, breaking windows in stores and looting, and the story probably will be spread all over the front page because of the magnitude of the "conflict."

Wars, murders and violent strikes—conflicts of a more disruptive nature—always receive space on the front page, which leads critics to complain that newspapers devote too much space to violence. Until recently, other conflicts—political, economic, social, scientific—did not always receive similar attention. However, that has changed, and today the often impassioned debates over the safety of nuclear energy, global warming, protection of the environment and other less violent clashes often are played out on the front pages of newspapers, too. Here's an example from the Associated Press (AP):

> BOMBAY, India (AP)—Members of Hinduism's lowest cast burned buses, hurled stones at police and blocked trains in Southern India in widespread rioting Saturday to protest police killings and the desecration of a monument.

This story from the *San Francisco Examiner* focuses on a conflict of a more personal nature:

> SACRAMENTO—A Carmel woman, who, along with her late husband, donated nearly a quarter of a million dollars to the Placer County Society for the Prevention of Cruelty to Animals, has withdrawn further financial support for the agency in a dispute over its euthanasia policies.

Progress and Disaster

In conflict, one side usually wins and the other loses. From the routine struggles of life, not generally newsworthy in themselves, shining successes frequently emerge. For example, from quiet laboratories come new inventions, new advances in science and medicine and new devices to improve the quality of life that genuinely represent progress.

Sometimes progress can lead to disaster. Such was the case with DDT, hailed as a major breakthrough in the control of crop-destroying insects. But after 20 years it became the subject of major news stories when the federal government finally banned its use after it was linked to cancer in humans. Saccharin was for years a seemingly harmless substitute for sugar welcomed by diabetics and persons with weight problems. But it, too, became the subject of major news stories when it was linked, in some scientific studies, to cancer. Congress even debated banning it. The great promise of nuclear power after the splitting of the atom lost some of its luster more than 30 years later due to the accident at the Three Mile Island nuclear plant in Pennsylvania.

Tornadoes and earthquakes strike suddenly. Lives are lost and millions of dollars' worth of property is damaged. Hundreds, sometimes thousands, of persons are displaced. Businesses are closed. The recovery from such a disaster often becomes a story of progress. The *Atlanta Journal–Constitution* led its front page with this local air disaster:

> Four prominent Atlanta lawyers and a pilot flying alone were killed Saturday when a private jet and a single engine plane collided in midair over East Cobb County.

The *Seattle Times* displayed this agriculture story on the front page of its business section to show economic progress in eastern Washington:

> MOSES LAKE, Grant County—After a 20-year hiatus, sugar beets are back. The crop, a mainstay in the Columbia River Basin until the late 1970s, is being grown again in the rich, irrigated land around this eastern Washington city. It's providing a stable crop for growers and a boost to the local economy.

Consequence

Any event that causes or is capable of causing a sequence of activities that affect many persons is newsworthy. Obviously, certain events are of more consequence than others, and they will receive more space and larger headlines. For example, the newspapers in Knoxville, Tn., gave extensive coverage to consequences of a U.S. Department of Education order to desegregate the local public school system. The desegregation plan called for the closing of a number of elementary and high schools: Parents who did not want their children to attend schools outside their neighborhoods bitterly opposed the plan.

It should be noted that all newsworthy events, for whatever other reason they are newsworthy, have some consequence. Conflicts have consequence. For example, one consequence of the war in the Persian Gulf was the problem of caring for the thousands of Kurdish people who were fleeing Iraq to avoid further repression by the Iraqi army.

Disaster and progress also have consequences, as noted earlier in this chapter.

FIGURE 3.1 When the worst terrorist attack in American history—the bombing of the federal office building in Oklahoma City—took place, the *Tulsa World* devoted its entire front page to the story that would dominate the news for months. This front page is an excellent example of how newspapers cover major disasters. (Reprinted with permission of the *Tulsa World*.)

The *San Jose Mercury News* prominently displayed this story about the fight between rural residents and environmentalists over the newest national monument, the Grand Staircase Escalate National Monument:

> ESCALATE, Utah—The red rock canyons surrounding this rugged town were the last place in the continental United States to be mapped. Dotted with juniper and sage under sweeping blue skies, southern Utah's most remote landscape has remained largely undiscovered since the Mormon pioneers of the 1880s first rolled up in their wagons. But now people are paying attention. Passionate attention.

A storm that dumped 17 inches of snow in Lexington, Ky., and 22 inches across the state resulted in serious consequences for residents of that city and state as reported by the *Lexington Herald–Leader*:

> WHITLEY CITY—Thousands of Kentuckians continue to live in crisis today as crews work to clear snow and tree-covered roads and restore power to nearly 20,600 homes.

Prominence

It is a given in the news business that names make news and big names make bigger news. The "name" must do something or have something done to her or him to be newsworthy. A prominent person may do no more than stop over in the city en route to a national conference to rate a story in the local paper, for example.

What a prominent person says or does often makes news because of its consequences. A nationally known economist's predictions could influence the stock market. A national political leader might enhance a local political candidate's chances for election by joining the local campaign for a dinner or speech. State-level politicians have been known to fly great distances at enormous costs and considerable inconvenience just to be seen and photographed with a president or a leading candidate for the presidency. They know it is almost certain to rate space in the state's newspapers or on local television. Prominent individuals are newsworthy for the same reason a political conference or a summit meeting of world leaders is newsworthy. The potential is there for significant change that makes news. The decision of a U.S. Supreme Court justice to step down, for example, could lead to a shift in the balance between conservatives and liberals on the court and influence the court's rulings on such issues as abortion for decades.

The National Aeronautics and Space Administration's decision to allow Sen. John Glenn, the first astronaut to orbit the earth on Feb. 20, 1962, to return to space at the age of 72, touched a frenzy of media attention, the likes of which he hasn't enjoyed during a 24-year career as a Democratic senator from Ohio. Here's how the *San Francisco Examiner* handled the story after that announcement:

> COCOA BEACH, Fla.—It's T-minus two months to liftoff for the second flight of America's most famous astronaut, and the countdown is underway for what one local tourism official terms "a John Glenn frenzy." Not in three decades has a flight generated as much hoopla as was ignited by NASA's announcement in January that the 77-year-old senior senator from Ohio would be returning to space.

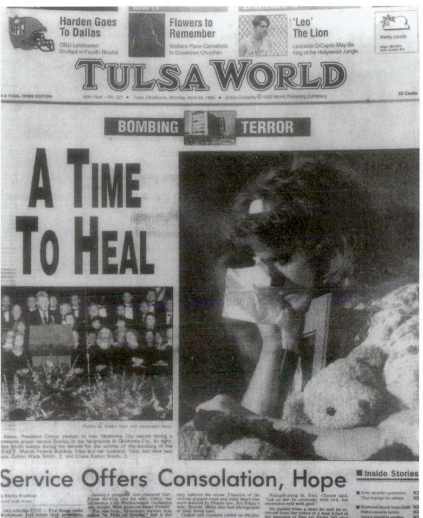

FIGURE 3.2 Four days after the bombing of the federal building in Oklahoma City, the tragedy still dominated the front page of newspapers. This front page from the *Tulsa World* reports on the services, led by President Clinton, honoring the victims of the domestic terrorists attack that killed more than 160 men, women and children. (Reprinted with permission of the *Tulsa World*.)

"Lordy, we haven't seen anything like this since the moon missions—or maybe all the way back to the Project Mercury, say," Cocoa Beach Mayor Joe Morgan said.

Timeliness and Proximity

Two other news values commonly recognized are timeliness and proximity. Both are important measures of news. Although they alone do not make an event or individual automatically newsworthy, in combination with events that have other news values they can help determine newsworthiness. An accident today that tied up local rush-hour traffic for two hours is more timely than one that happened even 24 hours before and will rate more attention in a newspaper. That same accident is more newsworthy because it happened locally than a similar one that tied up rush-hour traffic in the state capital 200 miles away.

The violent fluctuation of the stock markets around the world during the financial crisis of 1998 dominated the news for days. Here's how the *New York Times* reported the story on the morning after the U.S. stock market suffered its biggest drop in eight years:

> Waves of selling by investors large and small engulfed the stock market yesterday.
>
> The selloff erased the last of the market's gains this year and sent stock prices down more than 19 percent from their peak set just six weeks ago, the sharpest decline in eight years.

Novelty

Readers and editors alike are attracted by novelties in the news. They are a staple in all newspapers: the two-headed calf, the 350-pound pumpkin, the cat that walks 200 miles to find its owner who moved to another city, the whale that keeps getting stranded in San Francisco Bay. Novel ways of making a living, unusual habits and hobbies, superstitions—anything different—all have strong reader appeal. The common element is simply that the event or the individual is unusual.

The *Washington Post* displayed this novelty story prominently:

> NEW YORK—St. Clement's Episcopal Church serves a small, poor parish in Hell's Kitchen, just west of Broadway's bright lights. The congregation is a diverse one that includes indigents, immigrants and a lot of struggling performers. On this particular Sunday morning, the attendance totals 39: 35 humans and four dogs.
>
> When it is time for communion, the humans gather in a circle around the altar and join hands. The dogs come forward too. The Rev. Barbara C. Crafton, who has headed up the church for two years now, makes her way from person to person, offering bread and wine. Each dog gets a blessing.

Human Interest

Many stories that appear in newspapers at first glance do not seem to be news because they do not meet the tests of conflict, consequence, progress and disaster, or any other specific news value. Generally they are called "human-interest" or "feature" stories. Although they may border on being novelties, they frequently have considerably more substance. They may be about the desperate efforts of a lifeguard to save the life of a stranded dolphin, a famous author's battle with depression, or a 78-year-old man who returns to high school to work for his diploma. There are hundreds of such stories in newspapers every day. They have broad reader appeal.

Some events and individuals lend themselves more readily than others to human-interest treatment. They may lack the basic values that would make them a news story, yet they have special qualities that have reader appeal.

Often major news events spawn a variety of human-interest stories. One such story grew out of the crash of a Northwest Airlines jet at Detroit's Metropolitan Airport in which 158 people were killed. Four-year-old Cecilia Cichan was the only survivor. The child's recovery from injuries she suffered in the crash and her adjustment to the death of her parents and brother captured the attention of millions of readers who flooded her hospital room with gifts.

The *Orlando Sentinel* reported this human interest story on a whistling prodigy:

> WINTER PARK—It all started with a canary. At 3, Michael Barimo was fascinated by the whistling of his new pet.
> Nine years later, Michael walked away with four top prizes at the international competition for whistlers in Louisberg, NC.
> The 12-year-old Winter Park boy, who also sings opera, is undoubtedly a whistling prodigy. When he started whistling at age 3, his preschool teachers were amazed. Few children that age can even pucker up enough to make a sound.

Sex

Most editors consider sex a news value. This is especially true when it is coupled with prominence. The marital problems of millionaire–developer Donald Trump rated almost as much space in the press as his financial wheeling and dealing. The multiple marriages of movie star Elizabeth Taylor have been reported in detail and read avidly. Each new alliance between actress–singer Cher and a younger man grabs an inordinate amount of space. The on-again-off-again romances, marriages and casual housekeeping arrangements of many major rock stars have lasting reading appeal, especially when they contain such other elements as conflict or, perhaps, disaster.

Although presidential sex scandals dominated the news in the late 1990s, youthful sexual activities got the press' attention as this AP story from England shows:

> A highly precocious lad named Sean Stewart—who is all of 11—is on biological course to become Britain's youngest dad when next-door neighbor Emma Webster, 15, gives birth to their child in January.
> Webster admits making a mistake. She thought her man was 15.
> "I think he will be a good father," said Webster. "He may be only 11, but he is quite mature and responsible for his age."

Miscellaneous Values

Stories of animals often are well read, even by people who do not like animals. Write a story critical of cats and hundreds, perhaps even thousands, of cat owners will respond with vehemence, if not violence. Tell the story of a singing dog and you'll be swamped with requests to do stories about other clever canines. Some editors believe the only story better than an animal story is one that involves an animal and a baby, especially if the animal rescues the baby.

Many other types of stories used in newspapers are not news from the standpoint of such news values as conflict, progress and timeliness. But they are used because they inform or entertain the reader. Stories about current fashions, trends in leisure time activities and unconventional health care fit this category.

This *Wall Street Journal* story is an example of the miscellaneous category:

> The doctor is in . . . right over there by the canned gravy.
> At the Pick 'n Save Mega Food Center in Milwaukee, near the donuts and decorated cakes, is a health clinic with five examining rooms and a full-service laboratory. Two doctors and four nurse practitioners treat everything from allergies to bladder infections.
> In Syracuse, NY, Wegman's houses diabetes disease-management centers in two of its supermarkets . . .

Summary: Nature of News and News Values

Newspapers deal in a commodity—news. It can be defined this way:

1. News is an account of man's changing relationships.
2. News is an account of events that disrupt the status quo or have the potential to cause disruption.
3. News is an event of community consequence.

Items of news have intrinsic characteristics known as news values. The presence or absence of these values determines the newsworthiness and reader appeal that in turn establish an event's worth to the newspaper. The intrinsic characteristics of news values are

1. Conflict (tension, surprise)
2. Progress (triumph, achievement)
3. Disaster (defeat, destruction)
4. Consequence (effect on individuals or community)
5. Prominence (the well-known or famous)
6. Novelty (the unusual, even the bizarre)
7. Human interest (unusual or emotional)

Desirable Qualifications
8. Timeliness (freshness and newness)
9. Proximity (local appeal)

General Interest
10. Sex
11. Animals

Measuring the Importance of News

Reporters quickly learn, by intuition or applying news values, to recognize news. They also quickly become aware that not everything that happens in a city in a day can be printed, even if it meets all the standard categories of news. From the mass of material gathered daily, only the most important, significant and interesting is offered to the reader.

To know what is the most important, significant and interesting, reporters must know their community and the readers of the newspaper. One of the greatest handicaps a reporter can have is to not know his community and the people who live in it.

News always must be measured for its comparative importance to the reader. Stories must be compared to determine their relative reader appeal, which will influence not only their length, but also where and how they are displayed in the paper. The following factors are generally considered by editors in measuring the relative importance of stories.

1. The extent of disruption of the status quo
2. The number of persons affected by the event
3. The nearness of the event
4. The timeliness of the event
5. The extent of the results of the event—its consequence or significance
6. The variety of news values in the event

Story Types

Generally, reporters and editors do not discuss news values or the relative importance of most stories, although in some cases they may. They merely apply these values instinctively in writing and editing the news. They do, however, recognize and discuss stories in other terms. They talk of "fire stories" or "accident stories" perhaps, or a "meeting," a "speech" or a "murder" story and, always the "weather" story.

Most newspaper stories fall into well-defined types. Here are the types of stories newspapers generally recognize:

General Types
1. Personals and briefs
2. Speeches, publications, interviews
3. Meetings and events

Stories that are classified by a "package" in which they are "wrapped" rather than the content or subject matter

Simple Types

4. Illnesses, deaths, funerals	Stories that generally require little
5. Fires and accidents	interpretive writing by the reporter
6. Seasons and weather	
7. Crime	

Complex Types

8. Courts, trials, lawsuits	Stories that generally require
9. Government and politics	interpretation from the reporter's
10. Business, industry, agriculture,	background of specialized information
labor	
11. Eduction, research, science	
12. Religion, philanthropy, promotion	

Special Types

13. Lifestyles (including social events)	Stories and articles that encompass a
and consumer news	variety of subjects often requiring a
14. Sports	high degree of specialized knowledge
15. Entertainment (films, television,	on the part of the writer
popular music, art, theater, criticism)	
16. Editorials and editorial columns	
17. Interpretative and investigative	

Some story types are more clearly defined than others. Many of the classifications overlap. For example, accidents frequently figure into weather stories, or a trial may also be a political story; a major sporting event could be an economics story. Because the lines of distinction between types of stories are not always clear, the reporter who masters each type will have no trouble writing a story in which several types merge.

News Sources

Newspaper stories obviously come from many sources. The main beats covered regularly by reporters were noted in Chapter 2. They include all available offices of the state, county, city and federal government; the headquarters of all civic and professional organizations; churches, schools and charities; and many individuals, public and private, who occupy key positions in business, industry, transportation, utilities and other major fields. A number of "events" are purposely staged for the news media by public relations people to promote an opening or gain space in a newspaper about a new product, for example. Editors and reporters should be skeptical of being "used" by the sponsor of such pseudo-news events. However, they should also remember that public relations people can be important sources of legitimate news.

Many stories come from a single source. The public relations chairman of a national convention, for example, may provide all the necessary information for a story on the event in a press kit. On the other hand, information will have to be pieced together from several sources to ensure a balanced final story.

A careful reporter will always double-check the facts with at least a second source. In the case of the national convention, it might be the manager of the hotel where the convention is headquartered. Many reporters have been told by public relations representatives that 1,000 persons were expected, when only a couple of hundred actually registered.

Many stories will have to be pieced together from a half-dozen or more sources. To write a complete story about a major labor strike, a reporter should talk to the strikers; their labor union representatives; the employers; the police; the mayor; the governor; hospitals, if there is violence; charities, if it is a protracted strike; and others, including the president, if the strike is of nationwide significance.

Because all details in a news story are facts gathered by the reporter, the information in every story should be traceable to its source. The source should be named, and statements should be attributed to the person who made them. Here is an analysis of news story showing how the facts in the story were drawn from various sources:

Source of News	*News Type: Crime*	*News Content*
Police	An Eastside man knocked down two police officers with his car during a dramatic chase after they tried to arrest him on drug charges Thursday.	What took place
Police	Lamont Jones, 32, of 1009 Granada Ct., was jailed under $250,000 bond. He was charged with two counts of aggravated assault on a police officer, one count of evading arrest and one count of soliciting to purchase drugs.	Identification of man arrested and charges
Police	Metro Police had raided a known drug house at 504 Vernon Ave. and arrested four other people on drug charges when the incident occurred about 8 p.m.	Specific details
Police	Jones allegedly purchased what he believed to be cocaine from undercover officers, then ran to his Buick when they attempted	More details

	to arrest him, Homicide Detective E.J. Bernard said.	
Police	Officer Jim K. Reed opened the passenger door just as Jones slammed the car into reverse. He was dragged 10 to 15 feet before he fell to the ground.	More details
Police	The car struck Officer Ron D. Riddle, who was behind the vehicle, "a glancing blow and knocked him down." Bernard said.	More details
Police	Jones wrecked his car about a half-block away, then tried to escape on foot before he was caught by police.	More details
Hospital officials and police	Reed and Riddle of the West Central Sector crime suppression units were treated at Metro General Hospital and released.	Details of injuries
Corrections Department	State Corrections Department officials said Lamont C. Jones was sentenced to a maximum of eight years in prison in Hamilton County in 1987 for receiving and concealing stolen property, and simple robbery.	Background details
Corrections Department	He was paroled last July.	More details
Police	Others who were arrested and charged with soliciting to purchase a controlled substance were: —Timothy E. Pratt, 21, 2926 Old Buena Vista Rd. —Robert Lee McCormack, 40, 1100 Hemlock Ave. —Kevin Wilson, 23, 1515 Seymore Ave. —Gwenevere A. Gross, 31, 1100 Hemlock Ave.	Other police action

The outstanding news value of this story is conflict—a police raid, an attempted escape, two police officers injured. It also is timely because it happened the day of publication. It was given more length and displayed prominently because of the unusual aspect of the man's attempting to flee and the injury to the police officers. In addition, the ongoing "war on drugs" by police had strong reader appeal.

EXERCISES

1. Using the most recent edition of your local daily newspaper, read and then classify each story on the front page, first by story type and then by its news value. Identify the new source or sources in each story.

2. Although most daily newspapers cover local, state, national and international events, many smaller dailies tend to emphasize local news. With that background, read the following items and determine which are worth publishing in a nonmetropolitan daily. List the five most important ones that you would consider for the front page along with any significant state, national or international stories that may be selected. List each story's primary news value as well as the source(s) from which you would seek more details to develop a complete story:

   a. Three traffic accidents happen in a 20-minute period on the interstate that runs through the middle of the city. Three persons are seriously injured. No fatalities. Traffic tied up nearly two hours.

   b. Out-of-state company buys the largest food processing plant in the city which is also the city's largest employer.

   c. City council votes to raise pay for the mayor and council members, but refuses to increase property taxes.

   d. Sales taxes account for nearly half the city's $4.7 million budget.

   e. City police confiscate 300 sticks of dynamite from the owner of the Red Dog Tavern.

   f. First City Bank contributes $100,000 to the Campbell County Community College scholarship fund.

   g. Bulldozer driver clearing highway across Smoky Mountains killed by tons of ice and snow from an avalanche.

   h. An initiative to allow the sale of horsemeat for human consumption has gotten enough signatures to qualify for a place on the Nov. 3 general election ballot.

   i. Officials break ground for a new 150-bed regional health center.

   j. School board delays vote on pay raise for teachers despite threat of a strike.

   k. Local man on probation after killing his first cousin shoots and kills his brother.

   l. Credit card firm to bring $8 million payroll to the city.

   m. Two county jail escapees give up after four-hour standoff.

   n. Four Centennial High School students win $3,000 grant to start a peer tutoring program in their school.

   o. Local woman charged with starving and freezing her two daughters in a tool shed behind her home.

   p. Sheriff proposes making all inmates in his county jail pay for keeping them there.

   q. Outbreak of swine disease cancels greased pig contest at the county fair.

   r. New principal appointed for Eastside High School over objections of some parents.

s.   Father arrested after leaving 2-year old in car in 101 degree heat.

t.   Mother, father and six children die of carbon monoxide poison in their rural home.

u.   Police chief shoots self in foot while cleaning his service revolver.

v.   Search continues for 72-year-old man missing for three days from a local nursing home.

w.   County unemployment rate dips to 6.2 percent.

x.   County agent warns that retail tomato prices will increase if rain and cold weather continues.

y.   One of five teenage boys hospitalized after overdosing on PCP says he didn't know he was taking the powerful drug.

z.   A former courthouse clerk has been charged with running a call-girl racket out of the county courthouse.

3.   Invite the city or managing editor of a daily newspaper in your area and the editor of a weekly newspaper to your class to discuss news values. Bring a copy of each editor's newspaper to class and ask her or him to discuss why each story on the front page was selected. Look through the papers carefully and select stories that are not on the front page but have a strong appeal to you. Ask the editors why those particular stories were not used on the front page.

4.   If your local daily has a web site, invite the editor in charge of selecting the stories for the page to class to discuss what influences her or his choices of the stories that are used.

5.   These story leads were taken from small daily and weekly newspapers. Classify each by one or more of the story types discussed in this chapter. List the news value of each story and the source(s) you would turn to for additional information:

a.   Police say it began as a drug deal, turned into a rip-off, and then ended in gunfire that left Melvin Christo, 17, 1220 Laurent St., dead and another teenager charged with homicide.

b.   A berserk 900-pound bull ran over an animal control officer, smashed a police cruiser and chased a young boy up a tree in Lebanon before it was finally killed Friday.

c.   A Henry County High School student is due in juvenile court tomorrow to face charges of spiking her teacher's coffee with a prescription drug.

d.   Only residents living within the city limits would be required to clean up their dog's mess under an ordinance that will come before the city council Wednesday.

e.   Detective Justine Crabb, 39, a 17-year veteran of the city police force, was arrested Sunday on charges of stealing cocaine that had been seized as evidence, Prosecuting Attorney Carlos Santiago said.

f.   More than 100 homes, businesses, schools and utilities were damaged or destroyed at sunset Friday as a freak storm sent tornadoes ripping across Rutherford County.

g.   The federal government is seeking $2.2 million in a settlement from three local hospitals it says it overpaid in Medicare bills.

h.   One man was killed and another critically injured when they were thrown from a speeding car about 3:45 a.m., Saturday on Interstate 5 near the Ferndale exit.

4 News Style

"A perfect writer would make words sing, dance, kiss, do the male and female act, bear children, weep, bleed, rage, stab, steal, fire cannon, steer ships, sack cities, charge with the calvary or infantry, or do anything that man or woman or the natural powers can do," poet and one-time newspaper man Walt Whitman wrote in his day book.

That is a tall order for any writer and especially for a newspaper writer faced with his fifth two-car accident story of the day. Yet the history of 20th Century American journalism is laced with the names of writers who made their words do all that Whitman called for and more.

Among them are Ernie Pyle, the celebrated World War II correspondent; Don Whitehead and Hal Boyle of the Associated Press; Walter W. (Red) Smith, a sportswriter with the soul of a poet; Edna Buchanan of the *Miami Herald*; Russell L. Baker, John Nobel Wilford and Anna Quindlen of the *New York Times;* and Mike Royko, the redoubtable Chicago columnist.

Each has her or his own special writing style, yet all conformed to basic news writing style: short words, short sentences, short paragraphs and active verbs. Not every news story lends itself to artistry but the well-written ones are clear, precise, succinct and accurate. This lead by Patricia Lynch Kimbo in the *Nashville Banner* is a good example of news style:

> Nasir Phillips Lual and his family came to America from Sudan, searching for the American dream.
>
> What they found was a nightmare.
>
> Lual, 29, became Metro's first homicide victim of this record-breaking year. He was gunned down on his front steps Jan. 2 as he brought groceries home to his wife and two children.

Here is another lead from a story by Chris Poore in the *Lexington Herald Leader* in Kentucky:

> Kentucky doctors own enough tobacco to produce 63 million packs of cigarettes a year.
>
> But they say they don't want you to smoke them.

At a time when volumes of research blame smoking for a growing number of deadly illnesses, more than 300 of Kentucky's doctors own the right to grow and sell tobacco.

Both leads give readers of the newspaper what they want—news written in a way that will not confuse them, bore them or waste their time. The remainder of both stories packed in enough details to give readers a clear picture of the tragedy that overtook an immigrant family and the paradox of doctors growing a product that has been linked with deadly illnesses.

Readers also want writing that illuminates people, places and things with the subtle light of well-used language, as James P. Gannon wrote in a special report on better writing for the *Bulletin* of the American Society of Newspaper Editors. Here is an example of writing that illuminates: Ira Berkow's story on Cus D'Amato's Gym, written for the *New York Times*:

> Nighttime, and the walk up the poorly lit, steep, narrow wooden staircase to the shadowed area on the third floor seemed long. The street noises grew muffled and the creak of the stairs became louder.
>
> The climb Tuesday night in this old building at 116 East 14th Street to the Gramercy Gymnasium at the top of the stairs—quiet now, because it is just past closing time, 8 o'clock, and the punching, skipping, snorting fighters have gone home—brought to mind the words of Cus D'Amato.
>
> "Any kid coming here for the first time who thinks he wants to be a fighter, and who makes the climb up those dark stairs." said Cus, "has it 50 percent licked, because he's licking fear."
>
> Cus D'Amato, the sometimes strange, usually sweet, often suspicious, invariably generous teacher and philosopher and boxing manager and trainer, owned this gym for some 30 years. . . .

The best thing a newspaper has to offer the reader is good stories, well told. That is why good newspapers put so much emphasis on good writing, which begins with a mastery of the language. It is difficult to write with clarity, precision and accuracy if you do not know the accepted rules of punctuation and grammar and the principles of rhetoric.

No newspaper intentionally permits its writers to misuse the English language. Most spend countless hours and amounts of money attempting to make certain that the language is used properly, but errors still slip through the editorial safety net.

Newspapers follow accepted rules of English grammar and sentence structure. But they also strive for certain qualities of style: simplicity, clarity, brevity, accuracy, precision and originality. These qualities cannot be sharply defined. However, they can be developed by every writer who cares about using the right words in the right order.

Most newspapers have their own style book or use the *Associated Press Stylebook* as a basic guide for reporters when they write their stories. Style books not only deal with such fundamentals as grammar, punctuation and spelling, they also set the standards for the use of titles, addresses and numbers in an effort to bring a uniformity to those aspects of writing that are common to all stories. Many of them also offer suggestions and examples of clear, precise, succinct and expressive writing of stories and headlines.

Here are some general principles of news style. Most of them conform to the *AP Stylebook.*

Newspaper English

Eliminate Unnecessary Words

a. Unnecessary articles
   Weak: The club members attended the meeting.
  Strong: Club members attended the meeting.
   Weak: He returned a part of the money.
  Strong: He returned part of the money.
(However, only unnecessary articles should be eliminated. For example, the article in "Club members attended the meeting" cannot be eliminated. The same applies to "a" and "an.").

b. Circuitous verb forms
   Weak: The group will hold a meeting.
  Strong: The group will meet.
   Weak: The judge arrived at a decision.
  Strong: The judge decided.

c. Adjectives, adverbs, prepositions
   Weak: Both cars were completely destroyed.
  Strong: Both cars were destroyed.
   Weak: A tall 18-story building
  Strong: An 18-story building
   Weak: He stepped off of the train.
  Strong: He stepped off the train.
   Weak: The club will meet on Friday.
  Strong: The club will meet Friday.

d. Connectives
   Weak: He said that he would go.
  Strong: He said he would go.
(However, when two or more "that" clauses follow a verb, the conjunction should be used with all clauses for purposes of clarity.)

e. Well-known place names
   Weak: He came from Chicago, Ill.
  Strong: He came from Chicago.

f. Phrases
   Weak: The accident occurred at the corner of Vine and Maple streets.
  Strong: The accident occurred at Vine and Maple.

Weak: The debate lasted for a period of two hours.
Strong: The debate lasted two hours.

g. Clauses

Weak: All who are interested can vote.
Strong: All can vote.
Weak: The drought that occurred last summer.
Strong: Last summer's drought.

h. Redundancies

Weak: Past experience had taught him the way.
Strong: Experience had taught him the way.

Use Simple, Accurate, and Vivid Words

a. Short words are usually best. The newspaper is written to be read hurriedly by persons of all levels of intellect.

Use	*Rather than*
fire	holocaust, conflagration
died	passed away, deceased
man	gentleman
woman	lady
left	departed
body	remains
buried	interred
cancer	carcinoma

b. Superlatives are usually inaccurate. There are few "catastrophes," "panics" and "fiascos."

More Accurate	*Less Accurate*
a beautiful woman	the most beautiful woman
an exciting game	the most exciting game
seldom	never
frequently	always
probably true	absolutely true
escape	miraculous escape

Improper: The decision was unjust.
Proper: The attorney general said the decision was unjust.
Improper: The prisoner lost his temper.
Proper: The prisoner kicked the chair over.
Improper: The witness lied.
Proper: The prosecuting attorney said the witness lied.
Improper: He committed suicide by jumping from the window.
Proper: He was killed in a fall from the window, and the coroner ruled it a suicide.

Improper: Little Johnny Black, 6-year-old darling son of Mr. and Mrs. W.R. Black, died today.
Proper: Johnny Black, 6, died today. He was the son of Mr. and Mrs. W.R. Black.
Improper: The young lady will win the hearts of all visitors when she begins serving as hostess at the chamber of commerce next week.
Proper: The young woman will begin serving as hostess at the chamber of commerce next week. ("Attractive young woman" is permissible in some newspapers if she is attractive and young, but many newspapers consider such phrases puff.)
Improper: The judge told me (told this reporter) the case was dismissed.
Proper: The judge said the case was dismissed.

Sentences and Paragraphs Should Be Short

The news paragraph rarely should exceed 50 words and should be broken up into two or more sentences, if possible. Thirty to 40 words often makes a well-proportioned paragraph, although at some newspapers paragraphs often are considerably longer.

The object of the paragraph is not only to provide facts and information for the reader, but also to present it in an easy, readable fashion. Although newspaper paragraphs should be short, they should not sacrifice standard qualities such as unity and coherence.

News style calls for short sentences. They are easier to read than long, involved ones. But the writers should avoid overusing short sentences exclusively. A blend of short and slightly longer sentences generally makes a news story read more smoothly.

Here is an example of a long, one-sentence paragraph that tries to tell too much at once:

> One man died and another was critically injured about 6 p.m. Tuesday when their Mercury Cougar crossed the median on Interstate 24, just past the Old Hickory Boulevard exit, and struck a Cadillac headed in the opposite direction, then was "totally destroyed" by a tractor-trailer rig loaded with steel bars, State Highway Patrolman Frank Biggs said.

That lead is more than 50 words. It is just too long and too involved. This rewritten version shortens it considerably. The details omitted from the first lead can be used later in the story:

> One man died and another was critically injured Tuesday when their car crossed the median on Interstate 24, struck another car and ran under a tractor-trailer rig.
>
> State Highway Patrolman Frank Biggs said the Mercury Cougar, driven by Michael Pritzl, 27, Gallatin, was dragged nearly 150 feet by the semi. Pritzl is in critical condition at Vanderbilt Hospital.

His passenger, Edwin L. Roberts, 27, also of Gallatin, died of massive internal injuries at 8:30 p.m. Tuesday at HCA Southern Hills Hospital.

The remainder of the story gave the time of the accident, the exact location on the interstate, the names of the drivers of the other two vehicles involved and other pertinent facts about the accident.

Identify Persons in News Stories

When using the name of a public official, it is sufficient simply to use a title. For example: Mayor Paula Casey or Senator Frank Gibson. However, if a person named in a story is not well known, the reporter should find another way to identify him or her.

Numerous types of descriptive facts are used to identify persons named in news stories. The most common include age, home address and occupation. But reporters also can use well-known nicknames as well as affiliations with social or religious organizations if the person holds or has held a prominent post in them. For example: former president of the chamber of commerce or former director of the YMCA. It is also possible to use the relationship of a person to local or prominent individuals such as "nephew of Congressman Tom Jones." Or a person's achievements ("city golf champion") or infamy ("ex-convict") may be used. The most commonly used identification for anyone who is not well known is the home address. Some newspapers use both age and home address as a general rule. But the reporter should use other identification if it leads to a clearer understanding of who the person is. For example, in a story about the manager of a local motel being robbed, more persons would know the person by his occupation than by his street address. In that case the identification should be "Richard Bodkin, manager of the Downtown Holiday Inn, was robbed" rather than "Richard Bodkin, 52, 1109 Bennet St., was robbed." More people will know Bodkin by his occupation than by his residence.

Sources Should Be Named in News Source

"Attribution" means naming the source of the facts used in the story. Unless a reporter is an eyewitness to an event, the facts will have to come from another source. And that source should be identified. The facts in a news story should be attributed to a person, group, document or report.

The reporter usually has three options in attributing facts:

a. To state the source explicitly

Senator Mark Pizarek said the United States will have to impose a tax increase to pay for a long-term Middle East presence if we don't get more financial help from our allies.

> The California Independent told the Exchange Club . . .

or

> The state Supreme Court today ordered a new trial for convicted drug dealer Paul Pullen.
> Pullen, serving two life sentences for the murder of his partner in a 10-state drug distribution ring, did not get a fair trial, the Supreme Court ruled.

b. To leave the source implied

> Five more Mid-state National Guard units have been put on alert for possible deployment to the Middle East as part of Operation Desert Shield.
> They are: . . .

The implied source in the lead is the National Guard itself. Later in the story a direct quote from the commander makes that plain.

c. To conceal the source purposely to protect some individual or to maintain a news advantage

> Gov. Betty Bradley is expected to seek a 5-cent hike in gasoline taxes this year, a high-ranking member of central administration said today.
> The official, who asked that his name not be used, said the money would be used to support the governor's educational reform package.

These are common options reporters face daily. The use of unnamed sources continues to be debated, sometimes hotly, by reporters, editors and publishers. Some studies show the readers are skeptical when a source is not named in a story. Critics, and some reporters and editors, agree that not using a name gives the source an unfair advantage. Sources cannot be held responsible for what they say because their names are not made public. But others argue that without the guarantee of anonymity, some sources will not speak and reporters will miss excellent stories. In one of the more celebrated legal cases involving the press, a source who had been assured anonymity sued a major daily after his name was printed as the source of a derogatory story about a political candidate and won on the trial-court level.

Except in unusual cases, editors always insist that the reporter give the source of all opinionated statements:

> Community activist Nancy DeCosta today accused the Solid Waste Authority of "playing politics" with the lives of Eastside residents.
> "None of you want a rat-filled cesspool of garbage in your section of the city," DeCosta told the stony-faced members of the board, "but you are willing to ruin property values and threaten the lives of the poor people who live on the Eastside because they are poor."

It is essential to be fair. Every derogatory statement or accusation in a news story should be attributed to a source. The reporter must make an exceptional effort to seek out the person or persons subjected to the attack or allegation and allow him or her a chance to reply in the same news story.

The best way to attribute facts in a story is to state the source explicitly. However, to avoid the monotony of repeating "DeCosta said" throughout the story, a reporter should use direct and indirect quotations and other devices.

In news stories, the authoritative expression commonly is placed at the end of the sentence. The word "said" may be replaced with other words such as "declared," "insisted," "stated," "pointed out" and others, if they are applicable. But remember: "Said" is still the strongest choice.

Variety can also be achieved by presenting the authoritative phrase within the sentence rather than at the end.

"I can't recall, "Tucker told the Council, "when I have seen a worse proposal."

instead of

"I can't recall when I have seen a worse proposal," Tucker said.

Words used to replace "said" should be chosen with care. Reporters often use words like "asserted," "stated" and "declared" to avoid repeating "said." But they really aren't the same. In fact, they are stronger and more formal words. "Pointed out" implies an indisputable fact. "Admitted" implies guilt. "Claim" casts doubt on the statement. Descriptive words such as "whispered," "screamed," "thundered," "declared," "insisted" and others should be used for the sake of accuracy only, not for the sake of variety.

The Story Should Be Well Organized

The incidents of a story may actually occur in great chaos and confusion. The written story must analyze and relate these incidents one to another and to the central story theme. A speaker may actually ramble in this fashion:

> Gentlemen, this is a bad bill and ought not to pass. I was talking to Senator Williams last night, and he said the state can't afford all these welfare payments. I'm just as anxious to help the unfortunate as the next man, but I know down in my section we've got more people on welfare than we have people working. Some of them make more money off welfare than they did when they were working. That's why we shouldn't increase payments. This state's practically bankrupt. This bill might just push it over the edge. All we're doing if we pass this bill is paying people to rip off the taxpayer some more. You know it's true.

But the news story would probably read:

> Senator Jones opposed the bill. He argued that the state is nearly broke and cannot afford to increase welfare payments. He warned that this bill might push the state over the edge into bankruptcy.

The Stylebook

Before attempting to write news stories, the reporter should study thoroughly the stylebook of the publication for which he or she works. This guide, which usually is handed to a news reporter on the first day, explains the newspaper's style in preparing copy, spelling, punctuating, capitalizing, abbreviating and other such details. The common style is observed by all staff members.

The stylebook does not pretend to be an English grammarbook or a guide to composition and rhetoric. A reporter is expected to know common grammatical rules before beginning a newspaper career. Also, the careful reporter should make constant use of a standard handbook of English composition. The stylebook is designed to clarify certain disputed or difficult points and explain certain accepted usages. One newspaper capitalizes "street" and "avenue" when they are used in place names ("Fourth Street"), which is called the "up style." Another newspaper uses a lowercase letter (Fourth street), the "down style." Some newspapers use a short form for a word such as "through," making it "thru." Obviously, not all stylebooks are alike, but the following style specifications can be studied as typical.

Spelling

Any standard dictionary is the reference for spelling. Also, a city directory, telephone directory, almanac and Bible are useful in checking on the spelling of proper names. The *Associated Press Stylebook* and others also have sections on spelling. Do not rely solely on Spellcheck on your computer.

Punctuating

Use of the Period

1. Omit the periods in abbreviations of well-known governmental and other agencies.

   FBI   ROTC   AAA   FCC   ICC   PTA   USDA

2. Use three periods (. . .) to indicate quoted matter that has been omitted (four periods if at the end of sentence and another sentence follows).
3. Use a period to indicate cents only when the figure is more than one dollar and when the dollar mark is used. Otherwise, write the word "cents."

   $1.01   43 cents   nine cents

4. Omit periods in headlines, subheadings, captions and with Roman numerals and letters used in formulas.

Use of the Comma

1. Avoid superfluous use of commas, but do not violate accepted rules as set out in a standard handbook of English composition.
2. Use commas to set off the identification of a person, unless the identification is preceded by "of."

John Smith, 1012 Towne St.
John Smith of 1012 Towne St.

3. Use commas in listing a series (see Semicolon, 1).
4. Do not use a comma between a man's name and "Jr.," "Sr." or "II."

John Jones Sr.   James Smith Jr.   George VI

Use of the Colon

1. Use a colon to introduce a formal series of names or statements.

The following officers were elected: John Smith, president . . . (but "Officers elected are John Smith, president . . .").

2. Use a colon before minutes in writing the time of day, as in "3:30 p.m." (but "3 p.m.")
3. Use a colon between chapter and verse in referring to the Bible.

Luke 1:3–5

Use of the Semicolon

1. Semicolons should be used to separate a series of names and addresses or similar series containing commas.

Those attending were John Jones, 405 Trace St.; James Smith, 910 Drew Ave.; . . .

2. Semicolons should be used instead of periods in headlines.
Six Convicts Escape; Prison Guard Wounded

Use of the Dash

1. Use dashes to indicate unfinished sentences or broken sentence structure.
2. Use dashes to set off highly parenthetical elements and to enclose appositives containing commas.

A crowd assembled in front of the building, but the sheriff—the man for whom they called—was not to be found.
The six students selected—three seniors, two juniors and one sophomore—will receive . . .

3. Use dashes to indicate omitted letters.
4. Use a dash to separate a dateline from the first word of the lead.
5. Form the dash with two hyphens -- on the keyboard.

Use of the Hyphen

1. Use the hyphen in compound adjectives.

   coal-brick chimney   well-known man
   old-fashioned dress   so-called enemy
   10-year-old girl   10-yard gain

2. Use a hyphen with prefixes to proper names.

   un-American   pre-Christian   anti-Wing

3. Use a hyphen in writing figures or fractions.

   sixty-five   two-thirds

4. Use a hyphen between two figures to indicate the inclusion of all intervening figures, as "May 1-5."
5. Use a hyphen instead of "to" in giving scores, as "13-6."

Use of Parentheses

1. Use parentheses to insert a word within a title.
   The Bridgetown (Conn.) Fire Department
2. Use parentheses in a direct quotation to insert words that are not the speaker's.

   "They (the strikebreakers) shall not pass," said the foreman.

3. Use parentheses to enclose figures or letters that indicate subject divisions within a sentence.

   The committee decided (1) to refuse permission. . . .
   The board voted (a) to build a new athletic field. . . .

4. Parentheses are no longer used to indicate the political party or state, or both, of a government official, in abbreviated form. Current style is "Sen. John Smith, D–R.I."

Use of Quotation Marks

1. Use quotations marks to set off direct quotations.
   Special Note: While most sentences can be written as either direct or indirect quotations, the use of direct quotations in newspaper stories is reserved largely for statements that are best displayed within quotation marks. Examples are highly controversial statements, ironic expressions,

facts made inaccurate by rewording, ideas made ineffective by para-phrasing and unusual combinations of words.

2. Use quotation marks to set off titles of speeches, articles, books, poems, plays, operas, paintings and television programs.

"Pride and Prejudice"   "Hamlet"   "Mona Lisa"   "Aida"

(Note: Newspapers generally do not use italic body type, and quotation marks are employed as a substitute. However, quotation marks are not used in naming newspapers and magazines.)

3. Use quotation marks to set off coined words, slang and unusual words, or expressions the first time such words are used in a story. Do not use quotation marks if the same words are used again.

4. Use quotation marks to set off nicknames when the full name is used but not when the nickname is used instead of the full name.

John "Bud" Smith   Bud Smith

5. In a series of quoted paragraphs, use quotation marks at the beginning of each of these paragraphs and at the end of the last paragraph only.

6. Use single marks for a quotation within a quotation.

7. In headlines use the single quotation mark.

8. Quotation marks should always follow adjoining periods and commas.

"Here," she said.
His style recalled "Leaves of Grass."

If the punctuation belongs to the quotation, the question mark, the exclamation point, the colon, the semicolon and the dash also are followed by quotation marks.

"What do you want?" she asked.

Otherwise, quotation marks precede these punctuation marks.

Have you seen the new motion picture "May Queen"?

9. Do not use quotation marks with Q-and-A quotations.

Q: How old are you? A: Fifty-four.

Use of the Apostrophe

1. Use the apostrophe to form the plural of letters but not the plural of figures, as "A's," "70s."

2. Use the apostrophe to indicate the possessive case.

New Year's Day   master's degree   children's home

3. Omit the apostrophe in such names as Bank County Farmers League and City Lawyers Association.

Capitalizing

Capitalize

1. Religious denominations and orders:

    Protestant   Baptist   Jesuit   Franciscan
2. Nationalities, races:

    Germans   Afro-American   Chinese
3. Names of animals, as Fido or Rover (no quotation marks).
4. Names of political organizations:

    Democrat   Republican   Communist Party
5. National, state and local subdivisions:

    North   South   West Montana   East Blankville
6. Political divisions:

    First District   Fifth Ward
7. Words used with numerals to form a proper name:

    Operator 7   Room 32   Lot 21   Journalism 301
8. Titles preceding proper names but not "former" or "ex" preceding such titles:

    President K.L. Burns   Prof. T.M. Smith   former President K.L. Burns
9. Nicknames, including those of states, cities and schools.
10. Complete titles of all public or private organizations.:

General Assembly	City High School
City School Board	First Baptist Church
City Council	City Department Store
First National Bank	Jones and Company
Southmoor Hotel	Center Country Club
11. Place names:

Lake Michigan	Ohio River	Vatican City
First Creek	Atlantic Ocean	Great Smoky Mountains National Park
12. The first and all principal words in titles of speeches, plays, books and poems:

    "An Answer to Questions on War"   "The Way of the World"
13. Complete titles of streets, avenues, boulevards and roads:

    King Street   Elm Lane   Queen's Way

14. Holidays:

Fourth of July   Labor Day   Lincoln's Birthday

15. The "Union," in referring to the United States.
16. Abbreviations of college degrees, as "B.A."
17. Abbreviations of "junior" and "senior" to "Jr." and "Sr."
18. Names of legislative acts or sections of documents, as Smith Law, Title D. (A final reminder: If in doubt about capitalizing a word, make it lowercase.)

Do not capitalize

1. Seasons of the year, as "spring" or "summer."
2. Points of the compass, as "northeast."
3. The abbreviations "a.m." and "p.m."
4. Titles that follow proper names, as "K.L. Burns, president."
5. Names of studies, except languages, as "mathematics," "French" and "literature."
6. Scientific names of plants and animals, except names derived from proper nouns ("Hereford cattle").
7. "National," "government," "state" and "federal," except in titles.
8. "Association," "club" and "society," except in titles.
9. "Alma mater."

Abbreviating

Abbreviate

1. Months of the year of more than five letters when the day of the month is given:

Nov. 24   the last week in January   March 21

2. Times of the day, as "6 p.m."
3. Familiar college degrees, as B.A., Ph.D., M.D.
4. Names of states only when they follow names of cities or countries:

Blankville, Ark.   a town in Arkansas

5. "Mr.," "Mrs.," "Dr.," "the Rev.," "Prof.," "Gov.," "Gen." and so on when they precede the name of a person.
6. "Saint" and "mount" only when preceding names:

St. Louis   Mt. Mc Kinley   "Sermon on the Mount"

7. "Sr.," "Jr.," "III" following proper names.
8. Titles of public and private organizations that are well-known by the readers after such titles have been used once in spelled-out form:

FBI   SEC   CIO   YMCA   UCLA

Do not abbreviate

1. "Christmas."
2. "Percent" as "%," except in tabulation.
3. Names of persons.
4. Points of the compass.
5. Names of cities or countries.
6. Days of the week.
7. "Street," "avenue," "boulevard" and so on when not preceded by both the house number and the name.
8. "Company," except when a part of the official name.
9. "Association," "fraternity" and "university."
10. "Department" or "building."
11. "And" as "&," unless it is part of a formal name of a firm.
12. Weights or measures, as "pound" and "foot."

Titles

1. Always give a person's first name or initials with the surname the first time any name is used. Use the first name of unmarried women, not their initials, unless they are known by those initials. For example: M.F.K. Fisher, the California writer of a series of classic books with food as their central theme, was known to her legions of fans, editors and readers as M.F.K. Fisher. No one called her "Mary," her first name.
2. On second reference and thereafter, most newspapers use just the last name. However, some still use so-called courtesy titles such as:

Ms. Fisher   Miss Fisher   Mrs. Fisher
Or in the case of a man:

Mr. Smith   Dr. Smith   Prof. Smith

3. For most religious denominations, it is correct to refer to a minister first as "the Rev. John Smith," and thereafter in the story as "Mr. Smith." "Dr. Smith" should be used only if the minister holds a doctor of philosophy degree. There are exceptions: For Roman Catholic clergy, "the Rev. Patrick O'Malley" becomes "Father O'Malley" or whatever his rank in the priesthood may be. Jewish clergy should always be referred to as "Rabbi," "Rabbi Samuel Brown" on first reference and "Rabbi Brown" in the rest of the story. Latter Day Saints (Mormons) refer to their leader as "President John Smith," following which it should be "Mr. Smith." Christian Scientists have official titles such as "Practitioner," "Lecturer" and "Reader" instead of "the Reverend."
4. Do not use long and cumbersome titles before a name. Instead of "Director of Public Parks John Smith," make it "John Smith, director of public parks."

5. Do not refer to a woman as "Mrs. Dr. John Smith" or "Mrs. Prof. John Smith." A wife has no claim to her husband's title, and a husband has no claim to his wife's title.
6. Instead of "Mesdames" or "Messrs.," use titles singly.
7. Write "Mr. and Mrs. John Smith" instead of "John Smith and wife."
8. Do not use "honorable" in a title unless quoting someone else.
9. Do not use double titles such as "President Dr. John Smith." Choose the higher title or the one of greater relevance to the story.
10. Give exact titles of faculty members, public officials, business executives. "Professor" and "Instructor," for example, are not synonymous.

Figures

1. Spell out numbers from one through nine and use digits for all numbers above nine, except for the following:
   a. Spell out any number that begins a sentence.
   b. Spell out numbers referring to centuries, such as "tenth century."
   c. Spell out ordinal street names, such as "Fourth Street," up to "twenty-first."
   d. Instead of "thirty-fifth" and "fiftieth," use "35th" and "50th," except in referring to centuries.
   e. Spell out numbers in such phrases, such as "one in a hundred."
   f. Use figures for all sums of money: "$5," "$6.01," "$23."
   g. Use figures for the time of day, such as "3 p.m.," "8 o'clock."
   h. Use figures in tabulations.
   i. Use figures for any whole and fractional number, such as "91½" and "4.1."
2. Spell out fractions, except after whole numbers, such as "one-third."
3. Do not use "st," "nd," "rd," or "the" after dates. Write "Aug. 10, 1984."

Miscellaneous Rules

Use the following style:

all right	cheerleader	homecoming	re-elect
all-state	cooperate	Joneses (plural)	somebody
anti-Catholic	everybody	line up	someone
anybody	everyone	newspaper	statewide
anyone	ex officio	nobody	text book
attorney general	governor-elect	no one	two-thirds
baseball	half-dollar	Old Glory	upstate
basketball	half-dozen	Post Office	

Preparing Copy

For the convenience of those who may not yet write their stories on a computer terminal, instructions for preparing copy on a typewriter and correcting copy with a pencil are included in Appendix A.

E X E R C I S E S

1. The following sentences have errors in style, language use and spelling. Retype them on your computer, correct them and then make a copy to turn in. Or retype them on a separate sheet if you use a typewriter, correct them, and turn in the corrected copy. There is at least one error in each sentence.
   a. Ms. Martinez told polcie she found the money bag with $4,000 in it lying in the gutter about a half a block from the bank entrance.
   b. "Oh! Calcutta," the 1960s Broadway musical that shocked audiences with its nudity but seems tame and oddly old-fashioned today, will open at 8 p.m. Tonight in the restored Olympia Theater.
   c. "Gollihowski certainly has a flare about him," Coach Frank Biggs said about his 7-foot freshman center.
   d. Several Democratic members of the House of Representatives were pushing for censor not impeachment.
   e. University officials said that about two thousand students were involved in the demonstration outside the President's office about 4 o'clock yesterday afternoon.
   f. Police said the ransom note was written on fine bond stationary with the name and address cut off.
   g. Dale Gollamore, chief inspector for the 10th region of the U.S.D.A., says the fire ant infestation ahs reached a critical stage at the state's commercial nurseries.
   h. Autumn colors in the Green Moutnains have reached their peak, State Forester Joseph Bundy said.
   i. Soochan Shin, a prominent businessman and community leader, has been chairman of the Mayor's committee on racial tolerance.
   j. Jessica Javelina, of 1621 San Carolos Boulevard, told police whe she work up she saw a man wearing a ski mask standing next to her bed.

2. Each of the following sentences is packed with more words than a sentence can comfortably hold or a reader can wade through. They also contains misplaced elements. Rewrite each sentence to conform to news style.
   a. A gunman was wrestled down by police and 26 children and a teacher who were held hostage at a private school were released Thursday night, ending a day-long siege by a man who said he wanted to help the homeless in America.
   b. Rep. Bo Lolly, D–Camden, explained his proposed bill that would restrict abortions in the state to members of the state House of Representatives.
   c. Multnomah County Sheriff's Department duputies, working until 2 a.m. today, have arrested 10 more persons, bringing the total to 11, among the 16 indictments on drug charges handed down by the county grand jury last week.

d. Carrie "Big Tussie" Jackson attacked photographers Leon Chin and Sonny Boy Vaughn of the *Daily News* when they took her picture as she was about to enter criminal court Thursday to stand trial on charges of forging a $337 check which she used to pay on a rental car at the Volunteer Rent-A-Car on Chapman Highway 10 days ago.

e. Ten people on crowed Main Street were injured today when a 65-year-old woman lost control of her car, jumped the curb and ran 10 feet among pedesterians on the sidewalk in front of the Bon Marche Department Store during the lunch hour, police said today.

3. Analyze the following sentences and select the correct work of the choices given in parentheses:

   a. The defendant (secures, hires) a lawyer if he can afford one, or is appointed one by the court.

   b. County Medical Director Dr. Mary Reed said the birthrate here has declined because many women have chosen to (prolong, postpone) both marriage and childbearing.

   c. The two-month draught will have an (adverse, averse) (affect, effect) on the color of fall leaves in the Great Smokey Mountains, chief Forester Alice Land predicted.

   d. "There will be (fewer, less) peaches on the market this year (because of, due to) the late killing frost last month," County Agent Elbert Hooker said.

   e. Football Coach Paul "Bubba" Ashdown said his team is (anxious, eager) to challenge the Coalfield Miners for the Division 5 championship this Saturday.

4. Clutter is a common problem in many news stories. In these examples, delete the unneeded words, substitute shorter ones or rewrite the sentences to shorten them.

   a. The Pametto County Coroner, Dr. Max Kappelhoff, said this was the 10th drowning death in the first month of the summer swimming season which still has four months to go until Labor Day.

   b. The Securities and Exchange Commission is loath to embark on new and stricter regulations of the bond market due to the unstable nature of the financial condition of the stock markets in Asia and the European countries that are important to the health of the American financial community.

   c. Although public service workers in many areas of the state will lose their jobs March 31 due to the cutbacks in federal funds, David O. Bowman, county executive, said that because Alpine County has a population of less than 50,000 it may not be affected as quickly as some others.

   d. Bradly County School Board's negotiating team agreed to take under advisement a request by Bradly County Education Association negotiators to change the date of payment from the second day of the month to the 20th of the month during Wednesday's session of contract talks for next year.

   e. Polk County resident Doyle Smith was listed in stable condition Saturday at St. Mary's Memorial Hospital in Dayton after a shooting incident early Friday morning in which the bullet entered his chest, exited through his back and entered a china cabinet in the dining room of his double-wide home on Yellowood Road about five miles south of Dixie Lee Junction.

5. Select five news stories with opening sentences (leads) that are more then 40 words long from any newspaper available to you. Rewrite them using no more than 25 words.

6. Select five news stories from any daily or weekly newspaper. Read them carefully and mark each place in them where you think attribution should have been used but was not.

7. If your local newspaper has a web site, compare the length of the opening sentences (leads) of five stories used on it to the opening sentences used in the printed edition of the newspaper that same day.

5   Ethics and Libel

"I think every reporter or editor responsible for coverage ought to be covered himself or herself. It's a wonderful object lesson."

If that suggestion by David Lawrence, former editor of the *Miami Herald*, were to come true, there might not be so much public animosity toward the news media today. And there might not be as many libel suits.

"I think you truly do treat people in the fashion you would want to be treated—you don't pull your punches, you're tough in your reporting, but you don't see compassion as a weakness, thoughtfulness as a weakness," Lawrence said in an interview for a special report on media fairness in the *Media Studies Journal* published by the Media Study Center of the Freedom Forum.

The fact that readers see bias in the way newspapers, television and radio continually report what they perceive as negative stories contributes to the low credibility the press has with the general public.

In a survey by the Pew Research Center in 1998, some 63 percent of the respondents said they believe news stories are often inaccurate, up from 56 percent the previous year. Sixty-five percent said the press gets in the way of society solving its problems.

The reputation of the news media isn't helped when an important opinion magazine like the *New Republic* fires a star writer for making up several dozen stories that it ran, apparently without much fact checking. This was followed by the *Cincinnati Enquirer* publicly disavowing a major investigative report that was highly critical of Chiquita Brands International, Inc., a company controlled by the city's most powerful corporate figure. Then it took the usual step of printing a public retraction and apology on its front page three days in a row and paying Chiquita $10 million.

The public retraction by CNN and *Time* magazine of a story charging American forces used nerve gas on our own troops in Vietnam and a very public firing of two *Boston Globe* columnists for making up people and events in their columns did little for the image of the press.

But few stories have contributed more to the declining respect for the press than the scandal involving President Clinton and a White House intern, Monica Lewinsky, and the protracted investigation of it by Special Prosecutor Kenneth Starr. The media feeding frenzy about illicit sex in the Oval Office turned off more than half the public. There was widespread perception that the media wanted to "bring down" the president. Polls showed that 60 percent of the public was prepared to let the president get on with his job while editorial writers and columnists were calling for his ouster—either by impeachment or resignation.

Many reporters and editors have a conflicting view about the media's performance during the Clinton sex scandal. In a survey for *Columbia Journalism Review*, 89 percent of senior journalists said they would not change the way they cover the private lives of political officials and candidates. And 56 percent said that journalist's personal lives, including their sexual behavior, should not have been held to as high a moral standard as the personal lives of political officials.

A number of newspaper editors, however, have expressed their concern that the presidential sex-scandal coverage has been harmful to the credibility of the press. And credibility was on the minds of most editors who attended the 1998 American Society of Newspaper Editors convention.

During a panel discussion, Rich Oppel, editor of the *Austin American–Statesman*, said credibility can be restored by being accurate and fair, and admitting it publicly when you are wrong.

Karla Garret Harshaw, editor of the *Springfield News Sun*, said credibility is not only accuracy and getting names, dates and places right, but also the way a newspaper covers its community. "We should be able to reflect the range and dimension of views, perspectives and the fabric of life in the community. And sometimes I think that's where we fall short, and that's where credibility comes into question."

Sissela Bok, a distinguished fellow at the Harvard Center for Population and Development Studies, said that in the public's view, credibility has to do with believability. "That's very easy when you have an immediate way of checking what you hear. But, of course, the reading public or the public that looks at television has no way of checking. So they have to say, 'How believable is this person who is speaking?' 'How believable is this newspaper?' That's where the trouble comes in for the public."

A number of editors at the meeting said the speed with which news is distributed today causes mistakes. But others said that was a "cop out."

Jack Tinsley, vice president/community affairs for the *Fort Worth Star Telegram*, offered editors these credibility messages:

— The first priority in news coverage is accuracy. Don't sacrifice accuracy and fairness to be first, although it is desirable to be right and first.
— Display corrections prominently.
— Avoid bias. Strive for fairness and balance.
— Try to avoid anonymous sources.

Credibility will remain a problem for the press, especially for those diehards in the news business who hold to the cherished hope that the First Amendment literally means that a newspaper has the right to print anything it wants to print.

Most responsible editors and reporters know better. A newspaper simply cannot, and in a number of cases should not, print anything it wants to, even if the courts have permitted. There are numerous reasons—social, ethical, legal and economic—that the First Amendment cannot be applied in its broadest, most literal sense to every story.

The ethics and credibility of newspapers have been questioned over such stories as:

— The late tennis star, Arthur Ashe, being forced to announce publicly that he had AIDS because a newspaper was about to reveal it.
— The *Dallas Morning News* reporting first on its web site and then on its front page the next day that Timothy McVey admitted to his lawyers that he had bombed the Oklahoma City federal building.
— The saturation and often excessive coverage of the O.J. Simpson murder trial.
— The repeated use of Richard Jewell's name as a prime suspect in the Atlanta Olympics bombing before any charges were filed. None were.

And, of course,

— The obsessive coverage of the sex scandal involving President Clinton.

The coverage of most of those stories was dominated by rumor and innuendo, especially the presidential sex scandal. From newspapers to magazines and television newscasts, there was a journalistic standards meltdown, Sherry Ricchiardi wrote in the *American Journalism Review.* She cited the most common lapses in standards as:

— A knee-jerk impulse to be first at the expense of being right.
— Unrestrained speculation portrayed as news.
— A rush to judgment.
— An overwhelming use of thinly sourced stories.
— Reporting unconfirmed information as fact.

Debate over ethical issues goes on daily in every newspaper. Usually it does not involve individuals as prominent as the president, but the debate is just as intense.

The erosion of the public's faith and trust in newspapers led the American Society of Newspaper Editors (ASNE) in 1997 to embark on a three-year, million-dollar initiative to identify and address the root causes of journalism's dwindling credibility.

"The Journalism Credibility Project is among the most ambiguous initiatives ASNE has ever undertaken," said ASNE President Sandy Rowe. "It is an extraordinary opportunity. Never have I seen journalists more determined to understand and reverse the damaging erosion of our credibility with the public."

Public interest frequently collides with special private interests in the news. And where these two are clearly conceived, the newspaper's policy (discussed in Chapter 14) may influence its decision and dictate its course of action. Normally, however, newspaper editors deal with each story of this nature on an individual basis.

Where certain larger issues of ethics and policy are concerned, newspapers frequently are influenced by what they consider to be acceptable community standards and by public opinion. For example, how graphic and detailed should a newspaper's description of a murder–rape case be? Should a newspaper publish more, or less, crime news? Under what condition, if any, should a newspaper report the name of a rape victim? Should the names of juveniles be printed if not forbidden by state law? Most newspapers attempt to be responsible to the opinions of their readers in these areas, although no newspaper can please every reader every day. Even the most well-meaning, carefully reasoned decision dealing with a moral or ethical issue may bring howls of protest, angry letters to the editor and, on occasion, a canceled subscription.

Members of a news staff can and sometimes do influence a newspaper's ethical or moral standards. In one instance, protests by the reporters forced an editor to reverse a decision to print the name of every woman who brought rape charges against a man. Every reporter wants to be proud of the newspaper's general moral or ethical standards. However, the reporter's principal concern should be for his or her own professional code of ethics.

Relations to the Public

Reporters cannot ignore the fact that the public welfare may be involved in much that they write. Newspapers are addressed to the general public. In many cases, what appears in a newspaper is the only, or chief, source that the public (individually or collectively) has for information. This responsibility makes careless, slipshod, inaccurate or biased reporting inexcusable.

One of the major criticisms of the press—one that creates a credibility problem—is "the press is biased." Often what is mistaken by the reader as bias is careless, inaccurate reporting by the writer of the story and the headline.

Ideally, a reporter would not make mistakes in judgment, but such mistakes are sometimes made. All reporters face situations in which they have to make decisions on what, how, when and how much information should be revealed in a story. Most reporters are guided by their conscience in these cases. A carefully trained, educated and enlightened reporter ordinarily should be able to make sound and unbiased judgments.

Relations to the Newspaper

Most newspapers are genuinely concerned about their reputation for fairness and accuracy. Editors want the respect of their readers and insist that reporters be fair and accurate. However, some publishers, in pursuit of a particular policy that may be social and economic as well as political, may expect much more or much less than the plain, unvarnished truth as the reporter sees it. In some instances, a change in ownership may cause a newspaper to reverse a policy, political or otherwise.

A reporter faces a difficult choice if instructed by the editor or publisher to twist the truth in a story. Three possible courses seem to be open: Refuse to alter the story and resign; write a fair and accurate story and insist that it not carry a byline if the editor inserts material that would make it misleading; and, finally, attempt to work out with the editor a change of assignments to avoid such conflicts in the future. There can be no doubt that the first and third of these choices are strictly ethical and should be satisfying in the long run, in terms of self-respect if not money.

The problem of ethics was one of the motivating forces behind the establishment of a number of journalism reviews. Perhaps the best known are the *Columbia Journalism Review*, published at Columbia University in New York City, and the *American Journalism Review*, established as an independent magazine and later given to the College of Journalism at the University of Maryland. Both evaluate the performance not only of newspapers but also of all the mass media.

The *Chicago Journalism Review* was among the first of the reviews established by staff members of local newspapers. Although it ceased publication after several years, it was a lively and often provocative publication that pointed out what its editors considered to be the shortcomings of the local media. Others were established in a number of cities, but most have disappeared.

Industry trade publications such as *Presstime,* published by the American Newspaper Publishers Association, and *Editor & Publisher,* the industry's oldest publication, do from time to time include press criticism. But generally they report current events and trends in the industry and are not known for biting critical analysis of the performance of newspapers.

In addition, several national organizations have been established by individuals or groups to monitor the performance of the mass media. The most prominent of these is AIM—Accuracy in Media—which represents a conservative point of view in its approach to the news.

Relations to News Sources

The reporter's access to news sources is a major professional asset. Sources must be carefully cultivated, honorably maintained and respected. On the other hand, reporters must not become the "captive" of their sources and work as their personal "press agents." Sources often attempt to use their close relationship with reporters to control the news in some fashion.

Good reporters know much more than they can get into print. And they do not divulge secrets or betray confidences. Of course, if ordered to do so by a judge, the reporter faces a dilemma: to reveal the source or go to jail. The U.S. Supreme Court has ruled that the First Amendment does not guarantee the right to protect the confidentiality of news sources. A number of states, however, do grant that right in cases tried in state courts. Sometimes it is wise for a reporter not to accept some so-called confidences, for the same information may be obtainable from other sources. Reporters who are intelligent and who work hard developing a network of sources should have little difficulty managing the ethics of this type of situation.

Reporters should have a clear understanding with every person they deal with. They should explain the role of the reporter as well as that of the editor so the source will know what to expect. They need to make it clear that reporters gather facts and write stories, whereas editors decide how much of a story goes into the paper and on which page. Reporters should be careful about making promises to sources and should not agree to let a source read a story in advance of publication. And they should be constantly aware that many sources, particularly in the area of politics, attempt to use reporters to personal advantage in an effort to color the news. On the other hand, they should respect confidences and release dates.

Increasing numbers of persons in public life are resorting to backgrounding sessions or informal conferences during which they will speak to reporters "off the record." Often they use these sessions to get information out to the public without being identified as the source. A number of reporters willingly cooperate, but the practice is criticized soundly by others. And some newspapers have a policy of not permitting their reporters to remain at such sessions if the source insists on not being identified in the news story that may grow out of the meeting.

Accuracy as a Protection

The best protection against bias in reporting is the indefatigable pursuit of facts and the careful checking of all facts. It has often been said that the three cardinal rules of journalism are accuracy, accuracy, accuracy. As long as reporters present the news as it actually occurs, without any ideological shading or emotional coloring, they are performing their duty professionally.

Of course, this will not make them or their newspapers immune to resentment or attack. A large proportion of the news will be injurious to someone or some cause or will be thought so by the individuals involved. The more important the revelation, the more resistance there is, usually, to the reporting of it. (Certain technical problems of privileged and non-privileged documents will be examined later on.) Every reporter should remember that in many cases, especially in the area of public affairs, even the most recalcitrant news source often is dependent on the media for his or her public image. But a reporter should never use that as a lever with a news source. In general, a reporter's reputation for accurate, professional reporting will often overcome resistance, solve problems and open many doors to the sources of news.

Importance of Authoritative News Sources

The careful use of authority in the news is an important means of solving certain ethical problems for reporters. The facts in every news story should be attributed to a reliable source. Reporters should know their sources well enough to know if they are trustworthy as well as authoritative. Even then, the careful reporter will seek verification of material with another source. Verification is especially critical if the reporter is dealing with an unfamiliar source. Despite precautions taken to cite authority and to confirm or verify information with additional sources, the reporter must occasionally face the fact that sources will lie, which is why some newspapers require two or more sources for controversial stories.

Codes of Ethics

Although there are no concrete "rules of honor" that apply uniformly for newspapers and their staffs, an increasing number of publications are developing written codes in response to growing criticism by readers. There always is a danger in trying to put together an all-inclusive list of what the newspaper will and will not permit its staff to do because such restrictions can "handcuff" the staff, and there always will be someone who will find a way to circumvent the standard. Nevertheless, a written code does indicate what the newspaper considers ethical and can serve to raise the consciousness of the staff.

Whether they have a written code or not, most newspapers today attempt to follow a set of principles or a code of ethics established by such professional groups as the ASNE and the Society of Professional Journalists (SPJ). Here is a Statement of Principles adopted by the ASNE in 1975, which supplanted the organization's Code of Ethics, originally written in 1922:

Preamble

The First Amendment, protecting freedom of expression from abridgement by any law, guarantees to the people through their press a constitutional right, and thereby places on newspaper people a particular responsibility.

Thus journalism demands of its practitioners not only industry and knowledge but also the pursuit of a standard of integrity proportionate to the journalist's singular obligation.

To this end the American Society of Newspaper Editors sets forth this Statement of Principles as a standard encouraging the highest ethical and professional performance.

Article I—Responsibility

The primary purpose of gathering and distributing news and opinion is to serve the general welfare by informing the people and enabling them to make judgments on the issues of the time. Newspapermen and women who abuse the power of their professional role for selfish motives or unworthy purposes are faithless to that public trust.

The American press was made free not just to inform or just to serve as a forum for debate but also to bring an independent scrutiny to bear on the forces of power in the society, including the conduct of official power at all levels of government.

Article II—Freedom of the Press

Freedom of the press belongs to the people. It must be defended against encroachment or assault from any quarter, public or private.

Journalists must be constantly alert to see that the public's business is conducted in public. They must be vigilant against all who would exploit the press for selfish purposes.

Article III—Independence

Journalists must avoid impropriety and the appearance of impropriety, as well as any conflict of interest or the appearance of conflict. They should neither accept anything nor pursue any activity that might compromise or seem to compromise their integrity.

Article IV—Truth and Accuracy

Good faith with the reader is the foundation of good journalism. Every effort must be made to assure that the news content is accurate, free from bias and in context, and that all sides are presented fairly. Editorials, analytical articles and commentary should be held to the same standards of accuracy with respect to facts as news reports.

Significant errors of fact, as well as errors of omission, should be corrected promptly and prominently.

Article V—Impartiality

To be impartial does not require the press to be unquestioning or to refrain from editorial expression. Sound practice, however, demands a clear distinction for the reader between news reports and opinion. Articles that contain opinion or personal interpretation should be clearly identified.

Article VI—Fair Play

Journalists should respect the rights of people involved in the news, observe the common standards of decency and stand accountable to the public for the fairness and accuracy of their news reports.

Persons publicly accused should be given the earliest opportunity to respond.

Pledges of confidentiality to news sources must be honored at all costs, and therefore should not be given lightly. Unless there is clear and pressing need to maintain confidences, sources of information should be identified.

These principles are intended to preserve, protect and strengthen the bond of trust and respect between American journalists and the American people, a bond that is essential to sustain the grant of freedom entrusted to both by the nation's founders.

The Pitfalls of Libel

Every reporter works with the specter of a libel suit nearby because there simply is no sure-fire method of preventing libelous material from getting into a newspaper story. In writing news it is not always easy to determine the exact point at which the public's right to know is greater than the individual's right to his or her good name. A reporter must never forget that every person is protected by law from the publication of libelous or slanderous statements. A person's name—reputation—is of tangible value. And if a reporter damages it, even unintentionally, he or she could do irreparable harm to a person's position in society or that person's means of earning a living.

Damage to a person's reputation, if it is beyond the bounds of what a newspaper is legally entitled to print, is called "defamation." As a general rule, defamation is divided into two categories—libel and slander. In the view of the courts, libel is written defamation; slander is spoken. Over the years, the courts have expanded the definition of libel, making it include all defamation that offers a greater possibility of harm than does slander because it is written (and is therefore more permanent than slander). Written materials, signs, cartoons, television and even radio broadcasts that have been taped or presented from written scripts have been held by the courts to be libelous.

Libel Defined

Libel laws vary in each state. As a result, definitions of libel may be slightly different from state to state. However, they are all essentially the same. Libel can be defined as:

> A false statement printed or broadcast about a person that exposes that person to public hatred, ridicule, or contempt, lowers him in the esteem of the community, causes him to be shunned, or injures him in his business or profession.

It is important to remember that a person may libel another either by outright expressions or by insinuation or innuendo. A person also may be libeled even though he or she may not actually be named.

Elements of Libel

Anyone filing a libel suit, regardless of status, has to establish these elements:

— *Publication*—that the statement was published (communicated) in some form. In the case of the news media, the most common way is either a newspaper article or a radio or television broadcast.

— *Identification*—that the statement was generally understood to refer to the person suing by persons who knew him or her or members of the general public. The person suing does not have to be specifically named. And members of a group, such as a school board, can be libeled even though they are not individually named.

— *Injury*—that the statements caused actual damage in some tangible manner. This could mean actual loss of money as a result of a lost job or a business contract, for example, or damage to the person's reputation, humiliation, or mental anguish and suffering.

— *Fault*—the status of the person suing determines what must be proved. If the person suing is a public official or public figure and the alleged libelous statement concerns his or her public role, he or she must prove that the statement was made by the newspaper or broadcast station even though it was known in advance to be false or that there was serious doubt as to its truth. But if the person suing is a private individual, or a public official or figure suing about a statement concerning a purely private matter not affecting his or her public role, then all that has to be proved is that the publisher or broadcaster was negligent in failing to determine that the statement was false and that it defamed the person suing.

Who Can Be Defamed?

Any living person can be defamed. A dead person cannot be defamed; however, if the words reflect upon any living survivor of that person, he or she can bring an action. A corporation or a partnership can be defamed by language that casts aspersions on its honesty, credit, efficiency and other business character. Individual professionals such as doctors and lawyers can be defamed if the language casts aspersions on their honesty or ability to practice their professions. For example, to call a doctor a quack or a lawyer a shyster could be libelous.

Every person instrumental in the publication of a libelous statement is responsible. This usually includes the person making the statement, the reporter, the editor and the newspaper itself, but the newspaper alone is made the defendant in many suits. Most newspapers carry libel insurance.

Interpretation of Defamatory Words

In all actions for libel and slander, the words alleged to be defamatory must be interpreted as such; they must be understood in the defamatory sense whether or not they are believed by the listeners or readers. It is not necessary that the defamatory meaning be apparent on the face of the communication; a communication may be defamatory as a result of circumstances known to the reader. For example, a false report that a woman had given birth to twins was held to be defamatory when the woman was able to prove that readers knew she had been married for only one month. A subject may be defamed even though the communication does not refer to that subject by name if the subject can show that the defamatory meaning referred to him or her. Such statements as "it is alleged," "it was reported," or "according to police" do not protect a reporter who writes a libelous statement.

Proof Needed

Formerly, all libel was actionable without proof of some injury or harm to persons or property. Today, however, many jurisdictions treat libel like slander in that they require proof of damages incurred, except in the following cases:

1. The imputation of a serious crime involving moral turpitude
2. The imputation that the party is infected with a contagious disease
3. The imputation affecting the plaintiff in his or her business, trade, profession or office
4. The imputation reflecting upon the chastity of a woman

However, all jurisdictions hold that words that are libelous per se are actionable without damage having to be shown. In most libel cases, however, an effort is made to show damage in order to increase the amount of the judgment.

Intent to Libel

The U.S. Supreme Court, under the late Chief Justice Earl Warren, changed the direction of libel law to favor the news media. In its landmark decision in 1964—*New York Times* vs. Sullivan—the Court ruled that the constitutional guarantees of a free press prohibit a public official from recovering damages for a libelous, false statement relating to official conduct unless the official could prove that the statement was made with actual malice. To prove actual malice, the court said, the public official must prove that the statement was made with deliberate knowledge that it was false or that it was made with reckless disregard of whether it was false. The burden of proof was on the public official.

The so-called *New York Times* rule was expanded in the Butts vs. Curtis Publishing Co. case in 1967 to apply not only to public officials but also to public figures. In 1971, it was expanded again in the Rosenbloom vs. Metromedia, Inc. case to include private individuals involved in matters of general and public interest.

The problem of determining who qualified as a public official frequently plagued the press after the *Times* ruling. Generally, the press gave the *Times* rule a broad interpretation. However, in 1974, the Court, under a new chief justice—Warren Burger—took another look at who was public and who was private and came up with a new interpretation in the case of Gertz vs. Robert Welch, Inc.

Gertz, a Chicago lawyer known for his trial work on behalf of civil rights and other causes and the author of several books, charged that he was libeled by the John Birch Society magazine *American Opinion*. Among other things, the magazine called him a Leninist and a communist fronter. The magazine article appeared while Gertz was representing a family who had sued the Chicago police department over the death of their son, who had been shot and killed by a policeman.

The magazine alleged that the suit was part of a plot to destroy the Chicago police department. Throughout the trial against the police department, Gertz kept a low profile, refusing to be interviewed and rejecting efforts of the media to get him to discuss the case publicly.

When he sued the magazine for libel, Gertz was able to find twelve jurors who claimed they had never heard of him despite his local fame. It was a major factor in helping him prove that he was not as well known as the magazine would claim in defending the suit. A jury found that Gertz had been libeled and awarded him $50,000 in damages. In the legal maneuvering that followed, the trial judge threw out the jury's award and said that Gertz was a public figure under the *Times* rule. Gertz appealed and the District Appeals Court upheld the trial judge, ruling that, because the story concerned matters of public interest, Gertz should have to show actual malice on the magazine's part, even though he might be a private citizen. He had failed to do this, the Appeals Court ruled.

Gertz appealed to the Supreme Court, which reversed the Appeals Court. The Supreme Court ruled that Gertz was not a public figure in this case and did not have to prove actual malice. In this decision, the Court established that there are two kinds of public figures. One kind is the individual who achieves such pervasive fame or notoriety that he or she becomes a public figure for all purposes and all contexts or the individual who voluntarily injects himself or herself or is drawn into a particular public controversy and thereby becomes a public figure. Gertz did neither, the Court ruled. The second kind is the limited public figure. Under this concept, the Court said, the nature and extent of an individual's participation in a particular controversy giving rise to the defamation must be considered. In short, the Court was saying that an individual must play a prominent role in a particular controversy before being considered a full public figure. Both types of public figures have to prove actual malice to collect punitive damages.

In 1976, the Court further narrowed the definition of public figure in Time, Inc. vs. Firestone. That case involved a divorce suit and resulted from a blurb in *Time* magazine that said Russell Firestone had been granted a divorce from his wife, Mary Alice, on the grounds of adultery. In fact, he had not. The wife sued *Time,* claiming she had been called an adulteress. *Time* claimed she was a prominent socialite and a public figure. It said the 17-month divorce case was well publicized and that she had held several press conferences during the trial. But the Court said a divorce suit was not the kind of public controversy referred to in the Gertz decision. It noted that while there was public interest in the case, it was not an important public question.

Under the *Times* rule, a public official seeking to prove actual malice was barred from inquiring into the state of mind of the reporter and editors when the alleged libelous story was being prepared for publication. Over the years, the Supreme Court has chipped away at that concept. Finally, in 1979, in the Herbert vs. Lando decision, the Court reversed the *Times* ruling on that point. In that case, Col. Anthony Herbert, an army officer who gained national recognition for his charges that he reported misconduct of troops and officers in Vietnam but was ignored by his superiors, sued Barry Lando, a television producer for the Columbia Broadcasting System. Herbert charged he had been libeled in a CBS program produced by Lando that discredited him and his charges against the army. In preparing for the case, Herbert's lawyers sought to ask questions about Lando's state of mind when preparing the telecast. Lando refused to answer their questions. When the case reached the Supreme Court, it ruled that a libel plaintiff, obliged to prove actual malice because he is a public figure, has the right to inquire into a reporter's state of mind. The decision brought a warning from the Reporters Committee for Freedom of the Press that it "will encourage harassing libel suits and will discourage news about public events."

Late in 1979, the Court acted again to put additional restraints on who might be considered a public person. One case involved U.S. Senator William Proxmire and a scientist. The other involved a former State Department interpreter and *Reader's Digest*.

Proxmire, in a press release, had ridiculed the scientist, Ronald Hutchinson. He awarded Hutchinson his monthly "Golden Fleece" award for wasting taxpayer's dollars with his publicly funded research. Hutchinson had received more than $500,000 to study aggression in monkeys to help the Navy and the National Aeronautics and Space Administration better select crews for submarines and spaceflights. In his press release, Proxmire called the research "monkey business." Hutchinson sued for $8 million.

The other case involved Ilya Wolston, a former State Department interpreter, cited for contempt by a federal grand jury when he refused to appear during an investigation of Russian spying in the United States. Wolston later cooperated with federal officials and was never indicted for espionage. However, in 1974 he was listed as "among Soviet agents identified in the U.S." in a book called *KGB: The Secret Work of Soviet Agents.* He sued the author, John Barron, and the publisher, Reader's Digest Association, Inc.

At the lower court trials, both Hutchinson and Wolston were ruled to be public figures and their libel suits dismissed. When the cases finally came before the U.S. Supreme Court, it reversed those decisions. In its decisions, the Court said that neither Hutchinson nor Wolston had "thrust" himself into a public controversy in order to affect its outcome. Mere involvement in a newsworthy event, the Court ruled, did not automatically make a person a public figure. (This is a reversal of the Rosenbloom decision and several others of the 1960s.) The Court also rejected Proxmire's defense that he was immune from libel suits by the Constitution, which states that "for any speech or debate in either House," members of Congress "shall not be questioned in any other place." Proxmire argued that congressmen cannot be held liable for what they say on the floor of Congress. The Court pointed out that what the senator had said was not said on the floor of Congress but in a press release. It ruled that congressional press releases and newsletters were not immune from libel suits.

The U.S. Supreme Court continued to consider libel cases during the 1980s and early 1990s. Several cases dealing specifically with the First Amendment protection of "opinion" led to what libel lawyer E. Eddie Wayland termed "a revolutionary turnabout in the judicial interpretation of the First Amendment."

In their libel manual, *The Media and the First Amendment in Tennessee,* Wayland and his colleagues at King & Ballow, a Nashville law firm that has gained a reputation as one of the leading media law groups in the nation, say that was particularly true in Milkovich vs. Lorain Journal Co. In that case, the Supreme Court concluded that a sports column implying that a high school wrestling coach had committed perjury during a court proceeding investigating a fight between two rival wrestling teams did not rate separate privilege in addition to existing First Amendment protection.

The coach had lost his original lawsuit largely because the Ohio court held that the article expressed the columnist's "opinion," which under the law at that time was fully protected by the First Amendment. But after 15 years of litigation in the Ohio courts, the U.S. Supreme Court decided that a separate privilege for opinion was unnecessary.

Wayland and his colleagues explained that before the Supreme Court's Milkovich decision in 1990, the lower courts had classified statements three ways: (1) pure fact, (2) pure opinion, and (3) mixed fact and opinion. Reporters used those classifications as guidelines. False statements of facts were actionable. Statements of opinion were not actionable. However, courts required that the facts underlying the opinion be presented. And if they were false and defamatory, the writer and the publication could be sued.

The mixed opinion category required that a court determine whether the opinion was based on undisclosed facts that could be considered defamatory. If the plaintiff could prove that the mixed opinion was reasonably understood as relying on defamatory, undisclosed facts, then the mixed opinion was actionable.

The significance of the Supreme Court decision in this case, Wayland said, is its rejection of the proposition that the First Amendment requires a separate privilege for opinion. He pointed out that the Court reiterated its earlier Philadelphia Newspapers vs. Hepps ruling that "a statement of opinion relating to matters of public concern which does not contain a provable false factual connotation will receive full constitutional protection." This means that a writer or speaker must fully disclose the injurious facts underlying the opinion or rely on nondefamatory undisclosed facts in order for the opinion to be protected.

The Philadelphia Newspapers vs. Hepps case, decided in 1986, is considered an important victory for the media. It deals with libel suits brought by private individuals against the media. The Court held that private figures must prove the falsity of the defamatory statements in order to recover damages if the article or broadcast covered is a "matter of public concern." The decision brought private figures under the same constraint as public officials and public figures who have been required to prove falsity in order to recover damages.

Television and Radio—Libel or Slander?

Defamation via television is generally considered libel because it is the type of defamation that can be detected by the sense of sight. The vast audience and the ensuing increase in the likelihood of harm are additional reasons given for this interpretation. Radio presents a different problem. Most courts have held that defamation through the medium of radio is slander unless the broadcast is made from a prepared script or from a tape or other recording.

Defenses of Libelous Statements

There are five basic defenses in a libel suit:

> The statement is the truth.
>
> The newspaper is "privileged" to print the statement.
>
> The statement is fair comment or criticism.
>
> The statement was made with the consent of the person who claims he or she was libeled.
>
> The newspaper offered the persons the right of reply to the alleged libelous statement.

In general, the first three are the most significant defenses. However, the last two could prove to be of extreme importance to the newspaper's defense in a libel suit. In defending itself against a libel suit, the newspaper has the responsibility to prove that one or more of the defenses existed when the story was published.

Truth as a Defense

A newspaper's strongest defense against libel is to be able to prove what it prints is true. A reporter must not rely on hearsay, opinions or rumors if a statement in any way borders on libel. A report that "Detective Smith said Tom Johns robbed the store" is libelous unless the reporter can prove Johns actually robbed the store (or unless the report is privileged, as explained in the following paragraphs). Calling a building an "alleged house of ill repute" libels every person living in that house unless the statement can be proved. Fortunately, it is not necessary to prove that a story is meticulously true. Slight inaccuracies of expression are immaterial provided the defamatory charge is true in substance.

If a statement is true, a libel suit probably will not arise, for truth is generally accepted as a "complete defense." In some states, however, the newspaper must show a good motive for publishing the statement, even if it is true.

A common misconception is that a newspaper or a radio or television station is safe as long as it merely repeats or attributes the false and libelous statement to a particular person. This simply is not true. And a newspaper cannot base its defense on the fact that the person it has libeled is guilty of even worse conduct than that implied in the libelous statement. If a newspaper falsely publishes that a person is guilty of robbery, it is no defense to be able to prove that he or she committed a murder. Likewise, a newspaper cannot imply that a person is guilty of repeated misconduct and then offer as its defense that the person was guilty of such conduct at least one time.

Privilege as a Defense

The reporter is privileged to report derogatory statements that are taken from legislative, judicial or other public and official proceedings and records without fear of successful libel or slander action. Because the meetings and records of such groups as city councils and state legislatures are generally open to the public, the newspaper has a right to step in and represent the public. If a person is defamed in those proceedings, he or she cannot recover damages. The public's interest in such cases outweighs the individual's right to reputation, even though he or she may suffer real harm. The immunity for the participant in official proceedings is called "absolute" privilege. As long as what is said is relevant to the business of the proceedings, it is privileged and therefore not actionable. Anyone reporting such proceedings is also given an immunity from successful suit for defamation.

The protection granted the reporter, however, is somewhat more limited in that in most states it does not protect malice in reports. As a result, it is known as "qualified" privilege. There are other considerations that must be met by the reporter to enjoy this qualified privilege. The story must be a fair and accurate account of the proceedings. Great caution is necessary in quoting from official proceedings, public records, police reports and other public sources of information. Some states have laws that spell out in considerable detail the kinds of proceedings and records protected as privileged communications. The Proxmire case, cited earlier, is an example of how the concept of privileged material has been narrowed down by court decisions.

Fair Comment

Newspapers and other mass media have the right to comment on and criticize the acts of public persons who offer themselves or their particular talent for public approval. But the comment must be:

> Fair
> Made without malice
> Not unjustifiably extended to the private life of the person involved.

Actors, artists, authors, composers, speakers and others who offer themselves or their works for public acceptance are subject to comment or criticism by the press. The press also has the right to criticize the public performance of public officials. However, the defense of fair comment is lost in most cases when a newspaper invades the private lives of such persons. To say that an author is a poor writer because he or she knows nothing about plotting a novel could be fair comment. To say that the author is a poor writer because of his or her sexual proclivities could bring a libel suit. Writers should be careful to criticize only the substance of an author's book, the caliber of an artist's painting or the quality of an actress's performance.

A classic example on how far a publication can go in commenting on a matter submitted for public acceptance was illustrated by the Cherry Sisters case (114

Iowa 298). The defendants had published an article in which a reviewer gave the following graphic description of a public performance by three sisters who danced and sang:

> Effie is an old jade of 50 summers, Jessie is a frisky filly of 40, and Addie (the plaintiff in the case), the flower of the family, a capering monstrosity of 35. Their long skinny arms, equipped with talons at the extremities, swung mechanically, and anon waved frantically at the suffering audience. The mouths of their rancid features opened like caverns and sounds like the wailing of damned souls issued therefrom. They pranced around the stage with a motion that suggested a cross between the danse du ventre and fox trot—strange creatures with painted faces and hideous mien.

That style of criticism is still practiced by some critics today. John Simon, theater critic for *New York* magazine, gained considerable reputation for his biting, sometimes even savage, attacks on performers. In a review of a musical starring actress-singer-dancer Liza Minnelli, he wrote:

> I always thought Miss Minnelli's face deserving—of first prize in the beagle category. Less aphoristically speaking it is a face going off in three directions simultaneously: the nose always enroute to becoming a trunk, blubber lips unable to resist the pull of gravity, and a chin trying its damnedest to withdraw into the neck, apparently to avoid responsibility for what goes on above it. It is, like any face, one that could be redeemed by genuine talent, but Miss Minnelli has only brashness, pathos and energy.

Miss Minnelli did not sue despite the fact that Simon's attack was not directly related to her performance in this particular musical. He made no attempt to relate her physical appearance to the role she was playing or the plot of the musical, but the implication was clear.

In writing about public officials, a newspaper reporter has the right to comment on or criticize that official's performance on the job. The courts have even given the press more latitude in commenting on public officials than they have allowed in criticizing the work of creative artists. Some comment on the private life and personal conduct of the public official is allowed if the official's private conduct has an influence on the way he or she conducts the public's business. For example, the late Drew Pearson and Jack Anderson, syndicated columnists, were not sued for libel when they reported in a series of columns that a very influential senior member of the House of Representatives was an alcoholic. He was subject to fair comment, no matter how damaging it might have been, because he was unable to separate his alcoholism from the conduct of his public office.

However, every reporter should be aware that the Supreme Court has continued to narrow the definition of who is a public person or public official. Its recent decisions indicate a growing concern for the privacy of even the most public persons.

Consent

It is not uncommon for a person to give consent to the publication of material and then change his or her mind after it is in print. On occasion the person may even sue because the material is libelous. In most cases, the newspaper is privileged to publish libelous matter if the libeled person has consented to it. A person does have a right, however, to place restrictions on consent. The person may, for example, want to limit publication to a particular time or for a particular purpose. The publication loses the defense of consent if it breaks the agreement. Consent is not needed for news stories, however.

A person may consent to publication of material by either oral or written authorization, or consent may be implied from the person's words or other conduct. Implied consent may be obtained by requesting and receiving a voluntary acknowledgment and confirmation of the libelous material. But the mere denial of, or refusal to answer questions concerning, the libelous material does not qualify as consent. A publication is on much safer ground if it has written consent when potentially libelous statements are involved.

The Right of Reply

Right of reply is a much stronger defense than consent. "Right of reply" simply means that a newspaper gives the person who has been libeled an opportunity to answer the charges or attack. Generally newspapers, simply as a matter of good faith, will not print a libelous attack, even if privileged to do so, without giving the attacked person a right to reply in the same article. It is important to note that the reply cannot exceed the scope of the original attack. The reply must be limited to answering the original attack only. It cannot be expanded to include any other area of concern or to introduce any new material. The chief purpose the right of reply serves is to demonstrate that the newspaper is acting in good faith and is not simply being a party to the original libelous attack. It helps the newspaper prove that it was not acting maliciously.

Statute of Limitations

Most state libel laws set a specific time limit on the filing of libel suits. Generally this ranges from one to three years after the first publication of the libelous material. A newspaper that circulates in several states should take the precaution of learning about the statute of limitations in each of those states.

Criminal Libel

Most libel cases go to civil courts, with the plaintiff suing for damages. Some libel cases can be tried in criminal courts and may be punishable by fine and imprisonment. A number of states have laws under which criminal prosecution is possible if the statements tend to provoke the wrath of the person about whom they are printed; to expose that person to public hatred, contempt or ridicule; or to deprive him or her of the benefits of public confidence and social intercourse. However, the Garrison vs. Louisiana case has done away with this area as a serious threat to journalists.

Two other special circumstances can be involved. One is libel of the dead, which is presumed to provoke relatives and friends of the deceased to violence; the other is libel of groups when the libel provokes violence. Both are quite rare. Because criminal statutes vary on these points, it is advisable for the reporter to consult state laws for the exact rules to follow.

Retractions of Libelous Statements

Newspapers attempt to avoid libel suits by publishing retractions of statements that are unquestionably libelous. The retraction should point out and correct the newspaper's errors, and the newspaper should apologize to the person or persons concerned. The retraction notice, in order to be effective, must generally be given space or time that is equivalent to that of the defamatory matter. For instance, if the defamatory material was printed on the first page of a newspaper, the retraction notice should be published on the first page. (In several states, all retraction notices are required by law to be published on the front page no matter where the original story appeared in the paper.) The retraction does not nullify the claim for damages against the newspaper, although it satisfies many libeled persons and causes them to decide against filing suit. If a libel suit is filed, the retraction may help reduce the damages awarded by indicating lack of actual malice.

Invasion of the Right to Privacy

Although laws of libel date back almost to the dawn of civilization, the right of privacy—the right to be let alone—is relatively new. The concept was first introduced formally in the 1890s. Originally it related to the use of a person's consent. However, privacy law has been expanded over the years and has been recognized as a constitutional right by the U.S. Supreme Court. Simply stated, the right of privacy is the right of a person to be let alone. It guarantees all citizens that they can, under most circumstances, expect to be free from unwarranted publicity and to enjoy life without fear of waking up and finding their names, photographs or personal activities in print. Of course, they can waive that right. The right of privacy is personal, protecting the feelings and sensibilities of living persons only. A corporation or public institution such as a university has no right of privacy, unless granted by special law. A person's right to privacy ends at death and is generally not transferable to relatives.

A person's privacy can be invaded by newspapers, radio stations, television stations, photographers, motion pictures, books, advertisements and dozens of electronic means ranging from wiretapping to supersensitive microphones that can pick up conversations at great distances. However, the extent to which anyone is protected generally depends on his or her status as a public or private figure. Public officials and public figures are more legitimately open to public comment, criticism and scrutiny than are ordinary citizens. However, there are limits on the press even in the case of public officials and public persons.

A person's privacy can be invaded in four ways:

Wrongful Intrusion.   Wrongful intrusion generally involves the invasion of a person's solitude or private affairs without his or her knowledge or consent. It often involves the use of spying devices such as hidden microphones, wiretaps, hidden tape recorders and high-powered cameras or illegal obtainment of a person's private documents. A reporter who gains access to a place or a person by misrepresentation, especially on private property, could be subject to an invasion of privacy suit.

Publishing Private Matters.   A newspaper may be guilty of invading privacy when it publishes facts about the private life of a person that would offend ordinary sensibilities and that may cause that person mental suffering or embarrassment. Publishing sensational private matters about a person's economic, social or sexual activities, for example, could lead to an invasion of privacy suit.

Placing a Person in a False Light.   Placing a person in a false light may be said to occur when a news story or photograph, for example, implies something other than the facts. The nature of the published material must not lead the public to assume or believe something that is not specifically mentioned or portrayed by the material. This commonly occurs when a writer embellishes facts for dramatic effect.

Appropriation.   A publication is guilty of invading a person's privacy if it uses that person's name, likeness or personality for advertising or other commercial use. This does not apply to news coverage. For example, a newspaper could photograph Dolly Parton arriving at the local airport to begin filming a movie. That's news. That same publication could not reproduce Dolly's photograph on a poster and sell it to make money without her permission.

Most states have laws that grant the mass media the right to use the name or a picture of a person without previous consent in connection with a current or even previous news event as long as there is genuine public interest. The Supreme Court has upheld that right in several important cases. On the other hand, the courts have granted entertainers, sports figures and other public persons the "right to publicity." That means they have a right to protect themselves for commercial exploitation. They can "sell" their names and likenesses and profit from so doing. The press cannot use a name except in connection with a legitimate news story.

Defenses

Truth is normally not a defense in invasion of privacy suits. However, there are three standard defenses:

1. *Newsworthiness.* The newsworthiness defense requires the publication to establish that the information revealed about the person who is suing was newsworthy or in the public interest.

   a. *Public figures.* A publication can use the name or photograph or information about a public official; candidate for public office; or public figure such as a writer, actor or musician without prior consent as long as it is reporting matters of legitimate public concern about that person's life. Even such a person's private life can be made public without consent as long as the information relates legitimately to his or her role as a public official or person. The case involving Drew Pearson and Jack Anderson cited earlier is a good example. In addition, the courts have ruled that the public has a continuing interest in public figures even after they retire from public life.

   b. *Private individuals.* Private persons generally cannot sue successfully for invasion of privacy if they become part of a public event, even unwillingly. A person who happens to be in a crowd watching while police raid a local pornographic bookstore has no legitimate cause for a suit if his or her picture appears in a newspaper report of that raid. Any private citizen may become the object of legitimate news interest to the public either as an individual or as part of a group event, even though the involvement was unexpected or involuntary.

2. *Consent.* A consent defense requires that the publication show it had the prior consent of the person who is suing. Consent is not needed for legitimate news events. However, an invasion of privacy suit might grow out of such an event if the reporter obtained information illegally or wrongfully intruded on the private property of a person in order to collect information for a news story. Consent, as noted under the section on libel, is not a strong defense.

3. *Constitutional Privilege.* The constitutional privilege provides that persons involved in matters of public concern cannot recover damages for a story that may place them in a "false light" unless they can prove the newspaper printed the material knowing it was false or had serious doubts about its truth.

Courts have held that public officials and public figures have virtually no right of privacy insofar as the facts relate, even remotely, to their public lives. And almost any logical connection between a private person and an event of public interest places them in the same category as a public official or figure. Disclosures of arrests, births, deaths, marriages, divorces, personal tragedies, civil suits and interesting accomplishments generally have been found to be protected.

In almost all cases, disclosed material that is a part of a public record has been held to be nonactionable. A publication generally cannot be held accountable for public disclosure of private facts when it simply further publicizes matters that are already public or that the plaintiff has left open to public scrutiny.

Wayland and his colleagues cite these examples of unsuccessful claims of invasion of privacy: the publication of a plaintiff's jail term and a discussion of his six marriages (information gathered from public records open to public scrutiny); a magazine article's estimation of an attorney's wealth (newsworthy); property ownership and business ventures (public records); a newspaper's publication of confidential child abuse information that had been included in the prosecution's case file and lawfully obtained by the reporter (public records); a newspaper's publication of events surrounding a suicide attempt by a jail inmate who tested positive for AIDS (newsworthy); the unauthorized disclosure of a confidential report that a plaintiff had been found unqualified for judicial appointment (newsworthy and public figure); and publication of a plaintiff's homosexuality in a story dealing with his efforts to avert the attempted assassination of a U.S. president (newsworthy and already open to public scrutiny).

It should be noted that many persons—scholars, writers, lawyers, journalists and lawmakers—believe that the right of privacy is in great peril as a result of sophisticated electronic equipment that permits almost undetectable spying on individuals. There also is a great concern about the invasion of privacy as a result of law enforcement agencies, credit bureaus, insurance firms, governmental agencies and a host of others who are collecting dossiers on private citizens for a variety of reasons and storing them in computer data banks.

Major scandals have developed out of the practice of certain government agencies of spying on private citizens, and both the federal government and many state governments have passed laws seeking to control the collection of information about private citizens. Despite these efforts, collection of data continues and more and more computer data banks come on line each year containing all types of information, both true and false, and posing a threat to the right of privacy of millions of Americans.

Nontraditional Claims Against the Media

Since the early 1980s there has been an increase in the number of nontraditional claims against the media. Among them have been charges that the media inflicted emotional distress and that a newspaper violated a contract by disclosing the name of a source of derogatory remarks about a political candidate.

Most individuals who have sued over emotional stress have not been successful. To prove an emotional distress claim, the person suing has to prove that the publication or broadcast station's actions (1) were intentional or reckless, (2) offended generally accepted standards of decency or morality, (3) was causally connected with the plaintiff's emotional distress, and (4) caused severe emotional distress.

Here are several examples of emotional distress suits in which the newspapers were found not guilty of inflicting emotional distress: (1) a story that a family of the plaintiff in a highly publicized lawsuit had been in 13 lawsuits in 10 years; (2) a feature story about the murder of the plaintiff's daughter that quoted from the deceased's diary, obtained from the police department; and (3) a newspaper story based on trial testimony that identified the plaintiff as a victim of sexual assault.

The breach of contract suit was brought by Dan Cohen, who provided information to the *Minneapolis Star Tribune* and the *St. Paul Pioneer Press Dispatch*. Cohen, who was working for a candidate for governor, provided damaging information about the criminal record of another politician. He had been promised he would not be identified in the story as the source. However, the newspapers used his name in the story and he was fired.

Cohen sued the newspapers for breach of contract because they did not give him the confidentiality they promised. Two courts in Minnesota agreed that the newspapers had violated their "contract" and awarded him $700,000. The U.S. Supreme Court agreed to hear the newspapers' appeal of the case and ruled in Cohen's favor.

The Supreme Court also agreed to review the $10 million libel suit in which the psychoanalyst, Dr. Jeffrey M. Masson, sued magazine writer Janet Malcolm. He charged that she fabricated quotations that he claims made him look ridiculous. Eventually, she won the case.

Other Legal Aspects of Journalism

In addition to the laws of libel and invasion of privacy, which are the most important legal provisions that limit a reporter's freedom, there are other legal aspects of journalism that can restrain both the reporter and the newspaper.

Censorship

The Constitution of the United States guarantees freedom of the press as a fundamental right in a democracy, but the extraordinary power of the federal government during times of national stress (insurrections, wars, threats of war) has resulted in a body of law that encroaches upon this freedom. Throughout our history there have been repeated efforts to censor the press under a variety of disguises. Chief among them have been the various sedition acts that have been passed, restricting publication of information that would "aid and comfort an enemy." The nation does not have an official secrets act; however, official secrets are protected under a variety of other acts, especially since the onset of the atomic age in the mid-1940s. In addition, repeated attempts to revise the U.S. Criminal Code, to include provisions that would essentially be a secrets act, have been made. Official secrets also are protected by the classification system for documents established by presidential executive order. Since government officials and newspaper people have not always agreed on what should be censored, the press continues to fight a battle to protect its right to print.

The press's constitutional rights were upheld in the famous Pentagon Papers case. The "papers" were classified Department of Defense documents detailing the historical development of the war in Vietnam. They were given to the *New York Times* by Daniel Ellsberg, a former Pentagon official who was working for the RAND Corporation, a firm that did consulting work for the Department of Defense. The *Times* began printing excerpts from the papers on June 13, 1971, and four days later Attorney General John Mitchell asked the *Times* to print no more of the documents "because they would do irreparable injury to the defense interests" of the nation. The newspaper refused, and the Department of Justice asked U.S. District Court Judge Murray I. Gurfein to halt publication of the stories. Judge Gurfein, serving his first day as a federal judge, issued a temporary injunction of June 15 preventing the *Times* from continuing the publication. The *Washington Post* and other publications began printing parts of the papers. The Justice Department also obtained a temporary injunction against the *Post*.

The case was rushed to the Supreme Court, and after two weeks the Court, in a 6–3 decision, ruled that the government had not shown sufficient justification for imposing prior restraint. Although the press won eventually, many journalists were gravely concerned that a precedent may have been set in which, for perhaps the first time in American history, federal court injunctions imposed prior restraint upon American newspapers.

The media are not free to print everything, of course. The U.S. Criminal Code and the statutes of all states carry numerous penalties for the publication of pornography and obscenity. Although those laws may not directly affect a newspaper of general circulation, many reporters have a genuine concern about them because there is no clearly accepted definition of obscenity and pornography. As a result, the laws are subject to broad interpretation and certainty might cause difficulty for a newspaper, especially one that tends to print the more explicit types of material.

Reporters should also be aware of additional Supreme Court decisions that have a direct influence on their work. In 1972, the Court ruled in Brandzburg vs. Hayes that a reporter has no right to withhold information about his or her sources from a grand jury in criminal investigations. Because that case involved the federal courts, a number of states quickly passed laws to permit reporters to keep the names of their news sources confidential in state criminal cases. However, several later Supreme Court decisions have cast a cloud over the validity of the state confidential sources laws.

As a result of the Zurcher vs. Stanford Daily case in 1978, police, with a warrant, were permitted to make a surprise raid on a newsroom to search for evidence of crimes committed by others. In short, police could go into a newsroom and search through the newspaper's files. However, the power of police to conduct searches of newsroom files was curtailed when President Carter signed a federal law that limited such searches except where they would prevent a death or injury. In 1979, the Court refused to review an appeals court ruling that allowed government investigators access to the telephone company's records of phone numbers called by journalists.

In a series of three cases between 1974 and 1978, the Court ruled each time that the press has no more right of access to public institutions than does the general public. These rulings can successfully block reporters from investigating conditions in jails, prisons and mental hospitals, for example.

The Court handed the press another setback in 1979, when it refused to hear the appeal of *New York Times* reporter Myron Farber, who spent 40 days in jail for contempt for refusing to turn over to the defendants his notes at a murder trial. He had claimed protection under a New Jersey law protecting confidential sources.

A decision that created great concern about court control of the press came in the Gannett Co. vs. DePasquale case in 1979. The case dated back to 1976, when Judge Daniel DePasquale, at the request of defense lawyers in a murder case, barred the press and the public from a pretrial hearing. The lawyers argued that the adverse publicity would jeopardize their clients' chances for a fair trial. The prosecutor did not object. However, reporters for Gannett's *Rochester Democrat & Chronicle* and *Times Union* challenged the judge's ruling on the basis of the Sixth Amendment's guarantee of a public trial. Judge DePasquale refused to open the pretrial hearing. His decision was first overturned on appeal and then upheld before it finally reached the Supreme Court in 1979.

In a 5–4 decision, the Supreme Court upheld Judge DePasquale. In the majority opinion, Justice Potter Stewart wrote that the Sixth Amendment's public-trial guarantee belongs only to the criminally accused, not to the public itself. He refused to concede that the press or the public possesses a constitutional right under the First Amendment to attend criminal trials. In a separate opinion, Chief Justice Burger stressed that the ruling applies only to pretrial hearings, not to trials themselves. Justice William Rehnquist, who concurred, wrote that defendants, prosecutors and judges should be free to bar press and public from any trial for any reason they choose. He wrote that the public had absolutely no right to attend any criminal proceedings. He said that the First Amendment was not some kind of "constitutional sunshine law."

The decision resulted in so much judicial confusion that Justice Burger and Justice Powell broke a long-standing court tradition and began discussing the case in public. Both of them gave a number of public speeches defending and explaining the decision. They insisted that the Court meant only pretrial hearings could be closed. But in the first five weeks after the decision, judges across the nation had closed their courts to the public and the press more than 30 times, and at least eight of them involved full trials. Several news organizations—Gannett among them—issued cards to reporters on which was printed a formal protest. The reporters were instructed to read the statement aloud in court if a judge decided to close the court to the public or the press.

The following year, the Supreme Court handed down a decision that cleared up much of the confusion created by the Gannett case. In the case Richmond Newspapers Inc. vs. Commonwealth of Virginia, the Court ruled that both the public and the press have a constitutional right to attend trials. The case grew out of the murder of a Virginia motel manager in 1975. Three men were charged with the murder and were granted separate trials. One of the defendants was tried three times in secret before charges against him were finally dismissed. The Commonwealth attorney did not object when the judge closed the court to the public and the press. However, the *Richmond Times–Dispatch* and the *Richmond News–Leader* did object because their reporters were barred from covering the trials. Their appeal to the Virginia Supreme Court was turned down. That court said the judge had acted with legal authority when he ordered the secret trials. The newspapers pushed the case all the way to the U.S. Supreme Court. In its 7–1 decision, the Court said, "We hold that the right to attend criminal trial is implicit in the guarantees of the First Amendment: without freedom to attend such trials, which people have exercised for centuries, an important aspect of freedom of speech and of the press could be eviscerated." The decision was hailed as a victory for the public and the press by news executives and First Amendment attorneys.

The Court also recognized that the right of access is not absolute and that closing a trial may be justified under certain circumstances. Two years after the Richmond case, in the Globe Newspapers case, the Court reaffirmed the right of access and said that the press and the public can be barred from a criminal trial only in very limited circumstances where the justification for exclusion is substantial. Before closing a criminal trial, or a portion of a trial, the judge must have a hearing and must make findings supporting the closure.

In a later decision (*Press-Enterprise* I), the U.S. Supreme Court ruled that courts could not be closed during jury selection except in extreme circumstances. And in *Press-Enterprise* II, the Court ruled that preliminary hearings before a magistrate are presumptively open to the public and cannot be closed unless specific, on-the-record findings are made that "closure is essential to preserve higher values and is narrowly tailored to serve that interest."

In addition to censorship, there are other legal aspects of journalism that restrain the newspaper and reporter alike.

Copyrights

The U.S. Constitution provides for copyrights just as it does for freedom of the press, and newspapers must observe the copyright holdings of others. By the same laws, the newspaper can prevent unauthorized use of original material it publishes by obtaining copyright privileges.

Obtaining a copyright is a relatively simple procedure. Application forms are available from the Register of Copyrights, Library of Congress, Washington, D.C. An author or publisher may obtain a copyright by submitting a completed application, a small fee and the required number of copies of the material, and by carrying a notice of copyright on all published copies.

Written materials may be protected by copyright in the form in which they appear. However, the news facts or the ideas stated in the materials cannot be copyrighted. Copyright protects the way the story is organized and treated. In other words, newspaper cannot obtain exclusive use of the facts pertaining to a murder story, for example, by copyrighting the initial news break on that story, but it may obtain a copyright to the story as it is organized and presented.

Even though a newspaper cannot claim exclusive rights to the facts in a news story through the copyright procedure, it can employ other legal methods to protect itself from the wholesale use of its stories by competing news media. Several state courts have ruled that such unauthorized use of news items, taken from a newspaper and not independently gathered, is unfair competition and "violation of property right."

Reporters may quote copyrighted material verbatim without permission provided such quotations do not exceed a reasonable length and provided the quoted material is properly acknowledged. The privilege protects newspapers' use of quotations in book reviews and other types of stories. However, as a common practice, most newspapers do seek permission before printing copyrighted material other than news stories. In using copyrighted material from another newspaper, most papers give the other paper credit almost immediately in the story in this fashion: "The *Miami Herald*, in a copyrighted story today, said that . . ."

For a fuller understanding of copyrights and especially the fair use standards, reporters should read the current copyright law passed by Congress in 1976.

Internet Law

In reality, there are no specific Internet or cyberspace laws. There have been some cases of libel, invasion of privacy and copyright infringement on the Internet, but they were tried under the same laws that apply to the print and electronic media.

As the 20th century draws to a close, there is no special protection for reporting information obtained on-line. Reporters simply must verify information gathered from on-line sources the same as they must when gathering information from other sources.

Proper verification can avoid libel and invasion of privacy suits growing out of information gathered from on-line sources. It is important to remember that on-line sources often are anonymous, so information provided by an on-line source must be verified. The source may not be who he or she says he or she is. Simply reporting that the Internet is abuzz with allegations of wrongdoing by an individual will not protect the reporter from liability if the allegations are false.

When it comes to libel, privacy and copyright law, there are no special protections or exceptions for information obtained on-line.

EXERCISES

1. Using the codes of ethics in this chapter as your guide, select four major crime stories from a local or regional newspaper, read them carefully to determine if any part of them violates any part of those codes of ethics. Write a brief report on your findings.

2. Look up your state's libel law in a copy of the annotated state code in your college library. Write a brief report on the major provisions of the law, such as the definition of libel, the defenses permitted and the state's statute of limitations for filing a libel suit.

3. If your state has a privacy law, look it up in a copy of the annotated state code in your college library. Write a brief report of the law's major provisions, such as the definition of invasion of privacy and the defenses permitted.

4. Most states have open meetings and open records laws. And some states have laws that give reporters the right to protect the names of their confidential sources. Look up those laws for your state in the annotated state code in your college library or obtain a copy of them from your state press association. Write a brief report on the major provisions of the laws.

5. Invite a newspaper, radio or television reporter who covers the courts in your city to speak to your class about how she or he covers that beat and any problems they may encounter in obtaining records related to trials. Write a story on that class discussion.

6. Contact the editor of the local newspaper and ask him or her to visit the class to discuss the safeguards used by his newspaper to avoid libeling individuals.

7. Using any newspaper available to you, look for examples of stories or photographs you consider to be of questionable taste. Clip them and paste them on blank sheets of paper. In the margins, explain why you think the material is objectionable and why it should not have been used.

8. Using a standard journal publication, such as *Media Law Reporter, Quill, The American Editor, American Journalism Review* or *The Student Press Law Center Report,* available in your college library, look up a recent libel suit and a recent invasion of privacy suit. Write a brief report on each. Most trade publications such as *Editor & Publisher* also carry reports of significant legal cases.

9. Using any newspaper available to you, clip five stories that contain several types of derogatory statements about individuals that you think may be libelous. Paste them on a blank piece of paper and explain in the margins why you believe them to be libelous.

10. In some, but not all, of these paragraphs, some statements are libelous, some invade the privacy of a person, and others are of questionable taste. Rewrite those paragraphs you believe contain libelous statements, invade the subject's privacy, or are of questionable taste. Note that some of these paragraphs are from news stories and others from editorials or by-lined reviews.
    a. In a law suit filed in Circuit Court today, Nesty Morrow charged that real estate promoter Tom Barry made "unfair and illegal profits" in the sale of 350 acres of her Whitower Road estate and broke an agreement he signed not to sell the land for a mobile home park development.
    b. Mary Edith Pullen, a former nurse at Dr. Simon Wellstone's heath clinic, told the *Daily News* today that the doctor often conducted illegal abortions at night after regular office hours for wealthy clients willing to pay $5,000. She said he fired her when she complained that he was violating state and federal laws.

c. Going to a home game of the Dixon Devils is a fate worse than death. The fans are a stupid, boorish, drunken lot about six rungs lower on the food chain than British soccer fans.

d. CourtWatch, an unofficial organization of local citizens, today announced that it was going to seek the removal of Criminal Court Judge Albert "Take No Prisoners" Sidney Johnson for his "outrageous personal conduct in the courtroom, his verbal abuse of witnesses and attorneys, his total lack of knowledge of the law and blatant sexual harassment of female lawyers and witnesses."

e. Police today arrested two 13-year-old boys and an 11-year-old girl in connection with the vandalism of Cedar Creek Elementary School that did an estimated $43,000 in damage to the building and equipment. The juveniles were identified by police as Floyd Giger, James (Bubba) Lolly, and Precious Van-Horn. All were students at the school.

f. Now, here's one for the books—maybe even the police blotter. The newest business to open in the city is the "Gotcha Burglar Alarm Service," and the three owners have got to be experts. One is an ex-cop who served 20 years on the burglary detail and the other two are convicted ex-burglars.

g. Does Bumpkin County need a prosecuting attorney who is soft on drunk drivers because he's been arrested for drunk driving himself? Do we need a prosecuting attorney who refused to pay child support until threatened by the court system? Do we need a prosecuting attorney who violates the state's Open Record law by refusing to allow the press and the public access to public records? Prosecuting Attorney Harold Biggs has done all of that and more. That's why the *Daily News* recommends you vote for his opponent, Judson Cartwright, in the upcoming election for prosecuting attorney.

h. A headline in the local daily said: "Safety Director Orders Baby to Jail." The story that followed explained that a policeman had stopped a woman for speeding with a 10-month-old infant in her car. He contacted police headquarters for instructions. The safety director who was in the radio room ordered the policeman to bring both the mother and child to city jail, which he did. The newspaper, which monitors the police radio, had a tape of the safety director's conversation with the policeman.

11. Interview a local judge about the possible influence of pretrial publicity on major criminal cases. Then ask the editor of your local paper to respond. Write a news story presenting both views.

PART TWO

Writing the News Lead

"Words are sacred. They deserve respect. If you get the right ones, in the right order, you can nudge the world a little," Tom Stoppard wrote in *The Real Thing*.

Anyone who has ever written a news story, or read one, will tell you that the most sacred words in any story are the first ones. The opening sentence—the lead—is what lures the reader into the story. It is what gives the reader a reason for going on with the story.

"If it doesn't induce the reader to proceed to the second sentence, your article is dead," William Zinsser says in his excellent book, *On Writing Well*.

A good lead reaches out and grabs the reader. It charms. It teases. It piques the reader's curiosity. If forces him or her to want to know what happens next.

Here is a classic news lead from the Associated Press (AP):

> If oil was liquor, the United States government would know where to find every drop of it.

The story, written during an energy crisis when motorists were waiting in long lines to buy gasoline when it was available, went on to compare how much more money the federal government had spent on tracking down bootleggers than it had on oil exploration.

And here's a clever weather story lead by Steve Carney of the *Lakeland Ledger* in Florida:

> If March goes out like a lamb, the lamb was sweating Tuesday.

The story was written on March 31, when the temperature hit 90 degrees.

Good leads look deceptively simple because they flow effortlessly; they don't strain. Good leads have a strong sense of rhythm, unity and pace. They don't overwhelm the reader. They reach out and touch the reader with excitement or drama or humor and make her or him face a critical decision: Should I go on?

The lead may be a compelling subject. A triple murder, perhaps. Or it may be a descriptive passage that sets the stage for a mini-drama. It may be an amusing turn of a phrase or play on words. Whatever the technique used, most good leads are marked by tight, dynamic and energetic writing.

Lead writing may appear to be simple. It isn't. While some reporters may be able to dash off a lead in a hurry, most cannot. Often writing the lead is the most difficult part of writing a complete news story for many reporters.

Some basic forms and principles of writing the news lead are discussed next. However, every reporter should remember that although forms and principles are extremely helpful, they are not substitutes for the clarity and precision in writing needed to grab the attention of readers and compel them to read on.

6 The Simple News Lead

"For a journalist, it is imperative to get the audience's—and the editor's—attention with the lead . . . regardless of what kind of writing is involved, the principle is the same. The first words, the first phrases, the first paragraph are critical," says author and freelance writer Robert M. Knight.

In news writing, unlike narrative writing, the opening sentences should emphasize what is the most important, the most newsworthy. The narrative prose writer does the opposite. The emphasis is on the end of the story.

The two writing styles also differ in other ways. News writing style calls for short words, short sentences, short paragraphs and a generous use of quotes. Sentences and paragraphs in narrative writing tend to be longer, and the choice of words often is more expansive. Both, however, follow all standard rules of grammar, punctuation and sentence structure.

This example illustrates the difference in the two writing styles:

Ordinary Narrative Style

Andrew R. Pizarek, one of the city's leading philanthropists and founder of the high-tech accounting firm, CyberAudit, left his office in the Galleria Tower in Plaza Park about 3:30 p.m. yesterday. He drove to Guadalupe Municipal Park in North Santa Clara County to meet members of his seniors' soccer team for a match with a team made up of local lawyers. When he arrived at the park, he was joined in his 1999 BMW roadster by a teammate, Harold Graham, a retired Navy officer. All others were late. As the two sat talking in Pizarek's convertible, two men pulled up in a van, got out and approached Pizarek's car. Both men pulled guns and demanded money, jewelry and a cellular phone. When Pizarek and Graham refused, the two gunmen threatened them. Pizarek forcefully shoved open the driver's-side door, trying to knock the robber nearest him off balance. He managed to get out of his car and struggle with the robber. In the fight, the robber fired several shots that struck Pizarek in the stomach, chest and back. Graham fled from the passenger side of the car and shielded himself from a spray of bullets being fired by the second robber by hiding behind a nearby tree. When Pizarek collapsed to the ground, the robbers took off in their teal-colored Chrysler minivan without the money, jewelry and cellular phone they had demanded. Graham used the cellular phone to call 911 and tried to help Pizarek until police arrived. Pizarek was flown by Medivac helicopter to St. Cecilia's Hospital where he underwent two hours of surgery to remove the bullets and to repair damage to his chest, back and stomach. He is listed in serious but stable condition by hospital officials. Graham was treated for scrapes and bruises. He told Police Sgt. Joseph Walsh that he wasn't wearing a watch and had less than $10 in his wallet. He said Pizarek, who had given millions to churches and local charities, was wearing a diamond-encrusted wristwatch, but had less then $25 on him. Sgt. Walsh said a search is underway for the van and the two robbers.

The News Story

A prominent Santa Clara businessman and philanthropist was shot three times yesterday by gunmen who attempted to rob him and a friend as they waited for teammates to arrive for a city-league soccer game at Guadalupe Park.

Andrew R. Pizarek, founder of CyberAudit, a high-tech accounting firm, was wounded when he struggled with one of the gunmen in the parking lot at the municipal park.

He is in serious but stable condition at St. Cecilia's Hospital, where he underwent two hours of surgery to remove three bullets and repair the damage to his stomach, chest and back, hospital officials said.

Harold Graham, a retired Navy officer and accountant, was with Pizarek and was treated for scrapes and bruises.

Police are searching for a teal-colored Chrysler minivan the gunmen fled in.

Graham told Police Sgt. Joseph Walsh that he and Pizarek were sitting in Pizarek's 1999 BMW convertible in the parking lot of Guadalupe Park, waiting for other members of their seniors' soccer team to arrive. They were late. So were members of the opposing team, which is made up of doctors.

He said two men drove up in the van, got out and approached Pizarek's car. Each pulled a handgun and demanded money and jewelry and Pizarek's cellular phone. When they refused, the gunmen threatened to shoot them.

Pizarek shoved open the driver's-side door, trying to knock the gunman nearest him off balance. He managed to get out of the car and struggled with the robber. During the struggle, the gunman shot Pizarek three times. Graham said he struggled with the other gunman briefly and he took refuge behind a nearby tree while the gunmen fired shots at him repeatedly.

When Pizarek fell to the ground bleeding, the gunmen ran to their van and fled, Graham said. He used Pizarek's cellular phone to call 911 and tried to help Pizarek until police and an ambulance arrived.

Sgt. Walsh said Graham told him he had left his jewelry and all but about $10 at home before he drove to the park to meet Pizarek and their teammates for the soccer game.

Pizarek was wearing a diamond-encrusted wristwatch but had less than $25 on him, Sgt. Walsh said.

Since founding his high-tech accounting firm that serves major corporations in the computer software and chip industry, Pizarek has opened CyberAudit offices in 16 cities statewide. He has contributed millions to churches and charitable groups over the past 25 years.

Pizarek has served on the boards of nearly a dozen civil and charitable organizations. And last year he was recognized as the Chamber of Commerce's Businessman of the Year.

There is considerable difference in the telling of these two stories. The events in the prose story are recounted in chronological order. In the news story, they are arranged, from beginning to end, in order of their newsworthiness. The shooting of Pizarek during the attempted robbery of him and Graham and the escape of the gunmen are the most newsworthy events of the story. They are the first things told. In the narrative version, they are presented well into the story.

In ordinary narrative, the entire story becomes clear gradually. In the news story the most newsworthy fact is flashed before the reader in the opening sentence—the lead. The object of the lead is to tell the reader as quickly as possible what the story is about. This generally is done in a single sentence or two that form a single paragraph.

The narrative story will include all the minute details. The news story generally omits details or includes them in a final paragraph. This style of writing is usually called the "inverted pyramid" because the "bottom," or end or climax, of a story told in chronological order is inverted and placed at the top of the news story.

The style is an outgrowth of the Civil War, when correspondents were restricted from sending long stories by telegraph. To make certain all the essential information was sent, writers gave the most important facts first. Although the style has been refined considerably since then, most basic news stories still follow that pattern.

All good news writing is based on careful and accurate reporting. And to do that well, the reporter has to "think." In fact, the late Saul Pett, a Pulitzer Prize–winning writer for AP, said, "Writing begins and ends with thinking: Ideally, a reporter should think about the story, about what he or she wants to know, what readers will want to know, before asking the first question or putting the first word on paper."

Thinking helps the reporter probe deeper, ask more penetrating questions, and seek out the small and unusual details so that when she or he is ready to write there will be much more information about an event than is needed to write a clear, accurate, fair and compelling story.

Remember, no amount of flashy writing will cover up the fact that the reporter did not follow Pett's advice to "think" about the story beforehand. Good writers listen, watch and absorb first; then they write.

The Five W's

Every news story should answer the questions: Who? What? When? Where? Why? and, for good measure, How? They should be answered as quickly as possible for the reader. Some writers still attempt to cram answers to all those questions into the opening sentence, which frequently results in 60 to 70 words of almost incomprehensible prose. For example, a lead containing answers to all those questions might come out like this:

Andrew R. Pizarek, a prominent Santa Clara businessman and philanthropist, is in stable condition at St. Cecilia's Hospital today, recovering from three
gunshot wounds to his stomach, chest and back that he suffered while struggling
with a gunman who attempted to rob him and another accountant while they were
waiting for their teammates to begin a seniors' soccer game about 3:45 p.m. yesterday in the parking lot at Guadalupe Municipal Park.

That certainly answered all the questions:

Who? Andrew R. Pizarek, a Santa Clara businessman and philanthropist
What? Was shot in the stomach, chest and back
When? About 3:45 p.m. yesterday
Where? In the parking lot at Guadalupe Municipal Park
Why? Two men were trying to rob him and a teammate and he resisted
How? With a handgun

But it also is 71 words and is ponderous. It would have been even longer if
the fact that the assailants arrived in and fled in a teal-colored Chrysler minivan
and the source—in this case, the police—had been included.

Readership studies continue to show that shorter words, shorter sentences
and shorter paragraphs are more understandable and easier to read. As a result,
most news writers now do not attempt to cram all of the traditional five W's into
the lead sentence or even the first paragraph of a story. Generally, newspapers
strive to keep the lead sentence to 30 or so words, depending, of course, on the
story. Some even try for shorter leads. But others continue to burden the reader
with 50, 60 or even 70 word leads.

Playing Up a W

Simpler, shorter leads can be written that feature the single W that is more important than the others. Occasionally, it may be difficult to select a single W as the
most important, especially if a news event is complex. However, here are some examples of how one news element can be featured effectively:

The "Who" Lead.   If the "Who" is a prominent person or place or thing, it is usually the feature of the lead. The name alone attracts the reader's attention. Unless
one of the other elements is particularly outstanding, the "big name" comes first,
as in these examples:

Publicly, Vice President Al Gore refuses to acknowledge the obvious: that he
is running for president.

Actor Michael J. Fox, who revealed that he has Parkinson's disease, is one of
only a small number of people under 50 diagnosed with a disease much more commonly considered a scourge of the elderly.

Joe DiMaggio now has more room to recover from lung cancer surgery. The New York Yankees legend remains in intensive care in a Hollywood, Florida, hospital Thursday, but he was moved to a larger room to accommodate family and friends.

The Hall of Fame center fielder was buoyed by a visit from his granddaughters, Valerie, 9, and Vanessa, 11, who marked his 84th birthday Wednesday by singing "Happy Birthday."

A "Who" lead frequently is used even when a person is not widely known. In such cases, it is usually the person's occupation, sex, age or other distinguishing characteristics that are featured.

MINDEN, La. (AP)—A 70-year old man walking across his yard to pick up his morning newspaper was charged by a male deer that gored him with its antlers.

A woman, her mother and a cousin died in a two-alarm fire that destroyed a two-story house in Camden early yesterday, officials said.

MODESTO—A man rented a revolver and bought ammunition, then shot himself to death at a gun range here, police said.

Walter Henry Vaccaro, 59, a Modesto resident, apparently had been depressed, Detective Sgt. Mike Harden said.

He was the second suicide at the Gun County range in recent years. In 1995, a Ceres man rented a gun and purchased ammunition, then killed himself.

The "What" Lead. If an event or action is more important than the persons involved, that element should be featured.

Fire destroyed one of Miami Beach's oldest grocery stores early Thursday.

Firefighters were called to the 1051 Supermarket, 1051 Washington Ave., shortly before 1 a.m., and found smoke rising from the second floor and roof, Miami Beach Fire Chief Luis Garcia said.

OVIEDO (AP)—A cross-burning in the front yard of a well-known wild animal trainer who has a racially mixed son is being investigated by sheriff's deputies.

A proposal to open a "boot camp" for unruly Knox County schoolchildren has been put on hold by the county school board to allow more time to explore alternative ways of dealing with "kids who don't want to go to school so bad that they would commit a zero-tolerance offense."

Although the following example starts with a "Who," the "What" circumstances probably would be considerably more significant than the persons involved.

A 75-year-old Smithville man, who told police he "accidentally took a wrong turn," almost crashed into a twin-engine plane that was landing at Downtown Island Airport Monday.

The "Where" Lead.   On occasion, the "Where" is significant enough to overshadow the other W's. Often it is used by writers trying to establish a mood or recreate a scene. Here are several examples:

> MARINELAND—This little town sleeps with the fishes. Whether it will wake up with them remains to be seen.
> Marineland, population 12, home of the world's first oceanarium and perhaps the smallest town in Florida, is going through a patch of rough water right now. The number of visitors is down, the 60-year-old tanks are rusting in patches, and the investors who bought the land have filed for bankruptcy, cutting the tourist attraction adrift to fend for itself, $9.7 million in debt.

Francis X. Clines of the *New York Times* filed this report on one of the more colorful pages of life in early Fort Smith, Ark.:

> FORT SMITH, Ark.—In 1904, an enterprising prostitute named Laura Ziegler dropped into a local bank, negotiated a $3,000 loan and opened an enduring house of ill repute here in this wicked depot of American frontier history.
> Miss Laura's Social Club, as the handsome apple-green, mansard-roofed establishment was known, became the most seductive brothel in a city steamy with bawdy houses. They were arrayed along Bordello Row, an old riverfront strip that glittered with red lights and a supermart of pleasure.

Susan Cocking, *Miami Herald's* outdoors writer, found mystery almost in her back yard:

> Alligators blink at you lazily as you pass. You come face to face with otters and raccoons. The rapid hammer of a palliated woodpecker echoes in the distance. Cypress trees, port apple and leather ferns are in your face. You could almost touch the tarpon rolling right in front of you.
> Guess what? You are within spitting distance west of where I-95 and the Florida turnpike run parallel. You are on the Loxahatchee River.

The "When" Lead.   "When" is automatically included in most leads, but it is not often the most important feature. There are some instances when the writer elects to emphasize "When" in the lead.

This "When" lead by Carole Tarrant, on a cosmetic expert who rails against exaggerated claims by the beauty industry, was cited in the "Write Stuff" column in the American Society of Newspaper Editors' publication, *The American Editor:*

> It's 8 a.m. in Seattle, the city of Starbucks, but Paula Begoun doesn't need caffeine to jump-start her long-distance rant.

Scott Bowes of *USA TODAY* used "When" effectively in his story on the slay-ings of three students at Heath High School by a fellow student in Paducah, Ky.:

> PADUCAH, Ky.—It began Friday morning with a gentle but firm warning from Michael Carneal as he sidled up to his friend, Ben Strong, between classes at Heath High School.
> "Stay away from Bible Study," Strong recalls the freshman whispering. "Something big is going to happen."

Bowes went on to describe how the following Monday, 14-year-old Carneal calmly put in ear plugs, pulled out a .22-caliber handgun and opened fire on 35 students participating in a weekly prayer circle in the front lobby of the school just before classes began. Three students were fatally wounded, and five others lay bleeding on the floor.

The "When" element can be used effectively in feature stories. Here's an ex-ample of a feature lead by Greg Melikov of the *Miami Herald*:

> ST. AUGUSTINE—In 1882, a New York businessman toured tiny St. Augus-tine in a horse-drawn carriage.
> The businessman, a partner in Standard Oil Co., was so impressed he de-cided to turn the city into a winter playground for the wealthy.
> His name? Henry Morrison Flager.
> His legacy? The Hotel Alcazar, now a museum, and the Ponce de Leon Ho-tel, now a college. And churches. And a hospital. And City Hall. And the jail. And the train depot for his railroad.

The "Why" Lead. The motive or cause of an event sometimes can be the most important element of a story to feature in the lead. Writers may avoid it because it could make for a long lead. Here are a couple of examples of strong, direct "Why" leads:

> Failure to stem the growth in medical costs over the past several years means many working Americans will pay 8 to 20 percent more for health insurance pre-miums next year.
> That's the sharpest price increase since the early 1990s. Insurance executives blame the hike on the large price increases for prescription drugs, advanced surgi-cal devices and techniques, and services to patients outside hospitals.

> Four months of extremely dry weather has brought the water level in the state's main water supply to dangerously low levels, which could lead to water ra-tioning, state officials warned today.
> They urged residents to reduce water use by installing faucets and shower heads that conserve water and to limit watering lawns and shrubs.

HAVANA (Agence France-Presse)—Because they "pose a threat to our ideology and our culture," foreign magazines will no longer be sold to the Cuban public, Alejandro Gonzales, a Foreign Ministry spokesman, said today.

However, the sale of these publications to foreigners—residents, diplomats, and tourists—can continue in hotels and at tourist sites, he said.

The "How" Lead.   Although it can be an effective device, the "How" lead is not used as often as the others. Some reporters shy away from it because it can become too wordy. Here are several examples:

FRESNO—A beagle is the first line of defense against unwanted agricultural pests that may have stowed away on planes landing at Los Angeles International Airport.

The U.S. Department of Agriculture has developed a "Beagle Brigade" of about 60 small hunting dogs who have been trained to sniff out infested fruits, vegetables, flowers and meat that come into the country in the cargo holds of planes on international flights.

The dogs are stationed at 21 airports across the nation, where they sniff the baggage on incoming planes.

An anonymous letter to a Madison biotechnology company saying one of its scientists stole equipment has led to the arrest of three men.

Detective Ray Rice said the three scientists stole pumps, supplies and other lab equipment to outfit their own start-up labs to produce proteins and other products used by biotech companies. All three hold doctorates.

Crowding the Lead

The lead of a simple news story should not say too much or too little. In this type of story the best leads generally are those that emphasize a single W. If other W's deserve attention, they can be emphasized in the second paragraph.

The shorter the lead, the better, as long as it tells the reader the most important details. Newsworthy details not included in the lead will fall properly into the body of the story. If no single element in the story seems to stand out above the others, reporters generally write a "Who" lead:

A 67-year-old real estate agent was convicted of trying to hire a hit man to kill his partner so he could be the sole owner of a painting some think is the work of Vincent Van Gogh.

Frank Ravenall will be sentenced April 2 for soliciting the murder of Albert Papandelli.

A Davidson County sheriff's deputy went boating early Saturday—in his patrol car.

The deputy, Charles Pullen, was chasing a burglary suspect about 4 a.m. when his patrol car hit a patch of black ice, skidded off the highway and flopped into the Uvas Reservoir, near the Davidson and Coffee county lines.

A sheriff's department spokesperson said Pullen got out a window of his patrol car and swam to shore. He called the dispatcher from a pay phone at a boatdock.

Although the "Who" lead certainly is adequate, it also tends to be dull. Reporters should always examine the facts of a story carefully before writing to find an angle that will make the story more interesting.

Often reporters are faced with determining who is the "Who" in a story, especially when two or more individuals or groups are involved. For example, if the police chief and a city council member have a heated verbal exchange during the council's budget hearings, the reporter has to determine which of the two is to be the "Who" in the lead. In this case, of course, the reporter might evade the issue and use both by writing: "Two public officials clashed today . . ." However, the reporter could have focused on the person who apparently provoked the argument.

Complete Reporting

Reporters should remember to answer every question the reader might have about a story. The reader should not have to make a phone call after reading a story about an upcoming event to find out what it will cost, if the event is open to the public, if it will be telecast and when and over what channel. The complete story should give all those details. It is not enough to identify a person by his or her address if other forms of identification are available. They all should be worked into the story at some point. It is not enough to say "Fire destroyed the Marvel Manufacturing Company" without telling what the firm manufactured and how many persons worked for it. Incomplete reporting can produce lackluster leads such as:

The state's citrus producers today asked the Environmental Protection Agency to lift its ban on the pesticides Aldren and Dieldrin to help fight an invasion of the Apopka bug.

Although that lead is adequate, it really doesn't give the reader any indication of the seriousness of the problem and what it could mean to the state's economy. The following is another version that provides the reader with a clear picture of the impact the bug could have on the citrus crop:

Florida's billion-dollar citrus crop will be destroyed if the Environmental Protection Agency doesn't lift its ban on two pesticides that control the Apopka bug, citrus producers predicted today.

The beetlelike insect has already infested 30,000 acres of fruit trees, causing an estimated loss of $100 million to producers.

"The bug is eating its way across the groves of Central Florida leaving behind a trail of bankrupt grove owners," Thomas Ballard told EPA officials.

The second lead gives the reader a more dramatic picture of what the insect is doing to an important industry in the state. The first gives the reader only a minimum amount of information.

Obviously, there are limits to how much material can be crowded into a lead. But there should be no limit on the quality of the material. In his excellent book on writing, *The Word*, Rene (Jack) Cappon said writers should think of leads "as though they cost you 10 bucks per word, each word to be engraved on stainless steel while you're sitting on a hot stove." That is good advice.

Testing the Lead

There is no single formula for writing leads. Every reporter has to develop his or her own way to measure how adequate the lead is after it is written. No matter what device is used, reporters must never forget that a good lead makes a direct statement of the essential facts of the story. In addition, it must say something to readers in such a way that a reader is hooked on that story and will continue to read beyond the opening sentence.

This lead by John Noble Wilford, Pulitzer Prize–winning science writer for the *New York Times*, is a classic example of one that hooks the reader:

Move over, Chuck Yeager, and give way to supersonic dinosaurs. At least 150 million years before Mr. Yeager in 1947 became the first human to break the sound barrier in a rocket plane, the largest dinosaurs, a group known as sauropods, could have mustered the right stuff to send sonic booms resounding over the Mesozoic landscape.

No, the 100-ton creatures never got off the ground. All they would have had to do was flick their long tails like a bullwhip.

Once Wilford had the reader hooked, he went on to explain a researcher using computer models proposed that the Apatosaurus used its tapered tail like a bullwhip, making noise to attract a mate or establish dominance. And the energy waves would have picked up speed as they rippled along the tail from the wide base to the narrow tip. The end of the tail could have moved faster than sound, creating a loud sonic "crack."

Note: Few reporters write complete sentences while gathering information for a story. In keeping with that practice, some of the notes and exercises in this

ONCE IN A LIFETIME: A construction engineer and photography enthusiast took this shot from the 27th floor of a condominium project on Brickell Avenue. Details, 8A.

AT THE FINISH: Dr. Michael Stein helps Susie Maroney ashore at Key West after her 112-mile swim from Havana.

FIGURE 6.1 Reporters at the *Miami Herald* told the readers in a very direct fashion what happened when a hit-and-run tornado ripped its way through the middle of the city shortly after lunch one day in May.

(Reprinted with permission of the *Miami Herald*)

chapter and the following chapters are deliberately written in incomplete sentences.

At the end of each set of notes the source of the information is given in parentheses unless the source is otherwise included or obvious. Remember, in many stories it is absolutely essential to credit the source of information in a very specific way, often in the lead. However, if the source is obvious, it is not necessary to attribute the information.

This is an example of a story in which the source should be credited specifically:

> Seven members of an elite Lincoln County Sheriff's Department narcotics unit have been charged with stealing $1.4 million in cash seized during drug raids, District Attorney Donald Scroggins said today.

A reporter would have no way of knowing that the police officers had been charged with the crime unless the district attorney announced it. In the following example, however, the source is obvious:

> NORTH POLE, Alaska—Santa Claus is getting a gift from the U.S. Postal Service: a bar code to help sort the tens of thousands of letters sent to him at the North Pole.

In that story, it is apparent that the announcement came from the Postal Service. It is not absolutely essential to say "Postal Service officials said" in the lead.

Students should use good judgment in the use of direct quotations in completing these assignments. The notes within quotation marks indicate direct quotations. If they are used, additional words may have to be added to make them complete sentences. But only obvious additions should be made.

Because these are reporter's notes, they should be viewed as accurate statements from the sources of information. If the instructor permits, the students may convert an unquoted note into a direct quotation. For example: A note reading "Thomas refused to comment on the council's action" may be written " 'I have no comment to make,'" Mayor Thomas said. However, in converting an indirect quotation into a direct quotation, the student should not embellish it with imaginary facts.

Students also should be aware that the exercises may contain some material that, if used as given and sometimes if used at all, will constitute errors. These notes contain trivia, editorialized matter, statements violating newspaper ethics, libelous statements and misspelled words.

Some instructors may require students to hand in all completed and corrected assignments at the end of each quarter or semester. Students should keep a folder of all their work as a means of tracking their progress in the writing assignments.

EXERCISES

1. Using any newspaper available to you, or the web page of any newspaper, on a given day, identify the W's in the lead on each of the stories on the front page.

2. If your city has both a morning and afternoon newspaper, compare the leads on the main story of the day. If there is not a morning and afternoon newspaper in your city, compare the lead on the main national or international story used in your city's paper to the lead on that same story in a paper from a neighboring city.

3. Identify the five W's in each of the follow set of notes for story leads and then write a lead on each one:

   a. Jack Fuller, 2, 6519 Pine St.
      Riding a sled down an icy hill
      With his grandfather, John Fuller, 52
      In front of the Fuller home
      Hit a tree when grandfather
      Lost control of sled
      Jack was pinned between
      Between tree and the sled
      Suffered fatal injuries
      Grandfather in serious condition
      At St. Mary's Hospital

      (Sources: Policeman David Gorcyca, hospital spokesperson)

   b. Angel Valencia, 28, 105 Earle St.
      Driving on Highway 242
      Car went off an embankment
      Flipped over landed
      On street below at
      Intersection of Concord
      And Commerce streets
      Highway Patrolman Gus Blockman said
      She is in critical condition
      At John Muir Medical Center
      Her Rottweiler was riding
      In the car with her
      It was injured and is being
      Treated at an emergency
      Veterinary clinic in Concord

      (Sources: Blockman, hospital spokesperson)

   c. Fire Chief Leonard Basler
      Said five-story commercial building
      At Duboce Avenue and Wallace Lane
      Extensively damaged by fire that
      Started around 8:50 this morning

Roofers putting a new roof on the building
Apparently started the blaze with
With a propane torch, Basler said
"The torch got out of control
And ignited things."
No one was injured in the two-alarm fire
But there was extensive
Smoke and water damage
Tenants will have to move
Until building is repaired.

(Source: Chief Basler)

d. Samantha Grabstein, 2,
1821 Whitewater Lane
In critical condition
At Metro Medical Center
Bitten dozens of times
By father's pet ferret
John B. Grabstein, 22, father
Olga Torres, 21, mother
Held in city jail
Charged with child endangerment
Child bitten 50 times
On face and chest
She required 100 stitches
Parents were asleep during
The attack, social workers said
Police Sgt. Mark Hastings said
Parents had been drinking beer
And fell asleep
Four other children, under 7,
Placed with relatives

(Source: Sgt. Hastings)

e. Federal Courthouse in downtown
Evacuated for 30 minutes today
After a fake bomb was found
In shrubs beside the courthouse
At 301 N. Dade Ave.
By a gardener trimming shrubs
Police blocked off a two-block
Area around the courthouse
Bomb squad detonated device
Police spokeswoman Dorrine Moss
Said it was a cluster of
Wires and a timing device
"The maker went to great lengths
To make it look like a real
Bomb," Moss said.
The building reopened in about 1 hour.

(Source: Moss)

4. In the following notes for story leads, identify the fact or facts (Who, What, When, etc.) you think deserve the most conspicuous play in each lead. Then write the lead.

    a. A 15-year-old high school student
        Charged with spiking
        Her teacher's coffee
        With prescription drugs
        At Giles County High School
        Police declined to name
        The student or the teacher
        Teenager claims it was accident
        Police Investigator Joe Dill
        Says the drug was an antidepressant
        Could prove fatal if taken
        By someone already taking
        Certain other prescription drugs
        Teacher took a sip of coffee
        Realized it had been altered
        Reported incident to principal
        Who questioned students in class
        Then called police
        Teenager admitted putting
        The drug in the coffee

        (Source: Joe Dill)

    b. Timon Cobb, 66, 728 Lomax St.
        Working on his Lincoln Mark IV
        In garage at his home
        Used bumper jack to lift car
        Off the ground
        Jack apparently dislodged
        Car fell on him, crushing him
        Family members found him
        When they arrived to
        Take him to church about 7 p.m.
        Police, fire department
        Emergency medical service
        Personnel arrived and
        Removed the vehicle off
        Cobb who was pronounced
        Dead at the scene

        (Source: City police report)

    c. Mike Dunleavy, 43
        Central High football coach
        Will resign at end of season
        Claims school officials and fans
        Have lost faith in him
        His team has a 2–16 record

During his 3 years as coach
"I'm sorry I didn't accomplish
What I wanted to," he said
Praised his players for their
"Great team spirit despite
Our disappointing record."
School officials said
They'd start a search
For a new coach immediately.

(Sources: Dunleavy, School Principal Clarence Schmartz)

d. School Superintendent Margaret Perez
Says last three days of term
Will be shortened this week
High schools close at noon
Instead of 3:30 p.m.
Middle schools close at 2:30 p.m.
Instead of 3:40 p.m.
All elementary schools to close
At 1 p.m. instead of 2
Early dismissal allows
Teachers time to grade papers
And turn in final grades
Perez said slow driving zone hours
In front of schools
Will start earlier than usual
Working parents reminded
To make certain children
Are picked up at the
New dismissal hours.

(Source: Perez)

e. Van hauling 14 farmworkers
Blew a tire and rolled over
On Highway 99 about 7 o'clock
Thursday morning
Highway Patrolman Rusty Biggs
Said four men were killed
Five others injured
All treated at Valley Hospital
Santiago Jacobo, 23, and
Celestino Gusman, 31
Died at the scene
Hilario Solis, 38, and
Rolando Calvario, 19
Died at the hospital
Van was enroute to
Napa Valley for
Grape harvest season

(Source: Biggs)

7

The Complex Lead

"Writing is the art of the second thought. What first springs to mind is seldom good enough; the skill lies not in a ready gush of words, but in sifting them."

Those words by Rene (Jack) Cappon, for many years the Associated Press (AP) newsfeatures editor and writing coach, are especially true when writing a complex news lead.

Many stories are far more complex than the single-incident story. A reporter may be faced with having to sift many facts and juggle two or more important news elements in a lead. The complex type story can't be written in a gush of words. It must be planned and carefully organized to make certain that the separate parts come together clearly and coherently for the reader.

Suppose, for example, the following happened in your community late one afternoon:

1. Two persons were killed and 12 injured when tornadoes damaged their homes and businesses
2. The Weather Service said three back-to-back tornadoes ripped through the area in a matter of minutes
3. About 100 homes and businesses and dozens of vehicles were damaged or destroyed
4. Torrential rain and large hail and thunderstorms had pounded the area all day
5. Emergency shelters were opened in schools
6. 4,000 homes without electric power and telephone
7. The governor activated National Guard units
8. The county executive ordered a round-the-clock curfew for damaged areas

The general rule in writing a story about a news event is to place the most noteworthy item first. This rule presents no serious problem as long as the story has only a single incident to be the focus of the lead. However, when the story has more than one significant incident, as in the above event, the reporter's job becomes more complicated. One of two basic methods generally is used in handling a more complex story:

1. Summarize all features—in order of importance—in the lead sentence or paragraph.
2. Emphasize the most important or significant of the features and then quickly summarize all the other important ones in logical order in succeeding paragraphs.

In either approach, all of the features should be clearly established in the reader's mind as quickly as possible before the reporter proceeds very far into developing any open feature.

Here is an example of how the details might have been summarized in a lead:

> Two persons were killed and 12 injured, more than 100 homes and businesses and dozens of vehicles destroyed or damaged and 4,000 customers left without power or telephones when three back-to-back tornadoes cut a wide swath of destruction across Cumberland County at sunset Thursday.

Like most summary leads, this one is too long. Most editors do not like summary leads with too much information crowded into a single sentence.

Here is how that summary lead might have developed. At the left are numbers that correspond to the numbers on the separate features listed on page 111.

Feature Number	*The Written Story*
1, 2, 3, 6	Two persons were killed and 12 injured when three back-to-back tornadoes cut a wide path across Cumberland County just before sunset Thursday, destroying or damaging 100 homes and businesses and dozens of vehicles and leaving 4,000 customers without electric power and telephones.
1	The names of the persons killed have not been released, pending notification of next of kin. Harry Hicks, director of Emergency Planning for Cumberland County, said one victim was a 57-year-old farmer who was killed when he was caught in the middle of a field on his tractor. The wind, clocked at more than 120 miles an hour, blew the tractor over, trapping him under it. The other was an elderly woman who apparently was outside trying to find her cat when a tree, uprooted by the wind, fell on her.

2

The injured were being treated at area hospitals for injuries they suffered when struck by broken glass and debris when the tornadoes struck their homes and businesses.

4

Torrential rain, hail, and thunderstorms lashed the area most of the day, sending water in creeks and ditches over their banks, making it difficult for rescue workers to reach remote parts of the county that were in the path of the tornadoes, Hicks said.

5, 7

Four emergency shelters were opened in schools, and were manned by the Salvation Army and volunteers. The governor activated several National Guard units to help search for victims and patrol the devastated areas to prevent looting.

9

And County Executive Thomas J. Calhoun declared a 24-hour curfew for the hardest hit areas.

Other Paragraphs Develop
Additional Details

The tornados touched down within minutes of each other, Hicks said. Most of the destruction . . .

Emphasizing an Outstanding Feature

Feature Numbers

The Written Story

1, 2

Two persons were killed and 12 injured when three back-to-back tornadoes swept across Cumberland County just before sunset Thursday.

3, 6

At least 100 homes and businesses and dozens of vehicles were destroyed or damaged and 4,000 customers were left without electric power and telephones, Harry Hicks, director of Emergency Planning for the county, said.

The names of the persons killed have not been released, pending notification of next of kin. One was a 57-year-old farmer who was killed when he was caught in the middle of a field on his tractor. The wind, clocked at 120 miles an hour, toppled over his tractor. He was pinned under it. The other victim was an elderly woman who apparently was caught outside while trying to find her cat. A tree, uprooted by the wind, fell on her.

1

Additional Details Supporting 1	The injured were being treated at area hospitals for broken arms and legs and cuts and bruises suffered when they were struck by broken glass and debris in their homes and businesses. (Further details of all the features would be developed in the rest of the story.)

In that example, all the emphasis is placed on the dead and injured. However, because of the unusual concentration of tornadoes, an editor may want emphasize the number of tornadoes in the lead. In that case, here is how the story might be written:

Feature Number	*The Written Story*
1	Three tornadoes ripped across Cumberland County within minutes of each other Thursday, killing two persons and injuring 12 others.
3, 6	At least 100 homes and businesses and dozens of vehicles were destroyed or damaged and 4,000 homes were left without electric power and telephones, Harry Hicks, director of Emergency Planning for the county, said.
	"In three areas there's hardly a house left standing," Hicks said. "But we are lucky that more people weren't killed or injured."
1	Names of the two victims have not been released, pending notification of kin. One was a farmer who was caught in the middle of a field on a tractor. The wind, clocked at 120 miles an hour, toppled the tractor, pinning him beneath it. The other was an elderly woman apparently outside looking for her cat. A tree, uprooted by the wind, fell on her.
	The tornadoes were located in the Barfield community, the Hickory Groves area, and the Southridge subdivision, all south of Clarksville. Some homes were reduced to rubble while others were blown off their foundations.
3	The roof of a strip mall on old Jefferson Pike collapsed, damaging 12 stores, scattering their contents for miles.
	"It sounded like a herd of 18-wheelers coming down the highway and all of a sudden everything seemed to explode," said Mary Rose Hooker, whose dress shop was destroyed.
	(Further details on all the features would be developed in the rest of the story, which would include quotes from persons whose property was damaged or destroyed.)

Here is a more complicated story. A reporter covering a meeting of a county commission has the following facts, each worth considering for the lead, to work with:

1. County Commissioner Roy McKenzie introduced a list of major cuts totaling nearly $60 million in the proposed $968 million budget for next year.

2. McKenzie accused County Manager Charles Whitehead of "dragging his feet" in making cuts in the budget.

3. Whitehead accused McKenzie of a "personal vendetta" against him and resigned immediately.

4. A majority of the commission agreed that Whitehead's original budget was too high and approved McKenzie's cuts.

5. Approximately 250 persons will be cut from the Sheriff's Department, the staff of the County Hospital and the County Highway Department.

6. Whitehead said McKenzie's cuts were not made in the interest of efficient government or for financial reasons but "just as a means of getting rid of me." McKenzie and several other commissioners have tried to force Whitehead's resignation on three other occasions.

Each of these is worth considering as a separate lead. However, all are related, so the reporter has to weave most, if not all, of them into one lead. Here is an example of how the story might be written:

The Diagram	*The Written Story*
	The County Commission today slashed nearly $60 million from the $968 million budget for next year and cut 250 County Hospital, Sheriff's and Highway Department jobs.
1, 4, 5	
3	The action brought the immediate resignation of County Manager Charles Whitehead.
	Here's what happened at the Commission meeting today:
1	—County Commissioner Roy McKenzie introduced a list of major budget cuts totaling nearly $60 million.
2	—McKenzie told his fellow commissioners he made the cuts because County Manager Whitehead had been "dragging his feet" about trimming the budget.
4	—The commissioners, by a 5-4 vote, approved McKenzie's cuts.
3	—Whitehead accused McKenzie of carrying on a "personal vendetta" against him and resigned immediately after the Commission approved the cuts.

6   —Whitehead said McKenzie's cuts weren't made in the interest of "efficient government" or for "financial reasons" but as a "means of getting me."

5   —The cuts will cost 250 persons in the County Hospital and Sheriff's and Highway Departments their jobs.

(Details of the cuts and Whitehead's resignation as well as other features would be presented in the body of the story.)

Other Leads

The Combination or Scrambled Lead

There are no hard and fast rules for writing the several-feature lead. The leads illustrated here show two basic methods of "placing first things first." Both of them have variations. The choice of the exact variety usually will be determined by the facts and incidents of the story. Some of the features, for example, may be summarized, but not all. Or an outstanding incident may be singled out. It might also be combined with related incidents. And in some cases the reporter may want to take advantage of the drama of an event to depart completely from the hard news lead. Here are several examples:

The city school board took the following actions at its meeting:

1. Rejected a plea from several hundred parents to ban a controversial reading book for sixth-grade students.

2. Voted not to appeal a federal court order prohibiting Bible classes as part of the public school curriculum.

3. Hired The Survey Group, Inc., an engineering firm, for $9,900 to survey all school buildings in the system for asbestos-containing material.

4. Approved a plan, ordered by the State Fire Marshal, to correct "life-threatening" fire hazards in 14 schools.

Feature Numbers

1, 2

The Written Story

The city school board last night rejected a plea from parents to ban a controversial sixth-grade reading book and voted not to appeal a court order prohibiting Bible classes in the schools.

3, 4

In other action, the board hired an engineering firm to survey all school buildings for asbestos-containing material and approved a plan to correct fire hazards in 14 schools.

(Details of each piece of action would be developed in logical order in the paragraphs that follow.)

In this version of the story, the first two paragraphs summarize two of the features because they deal with academic issues in the system. The second paragraph adds other features that are related because they deal with the condition of school buildings, a concern of parents. These features are equally important but are not as emotionally charged as the issues reported in the lead paragraph. This method can be called the "scramble" lead, but a name is unnecessary. If a reporter organizes and relates several features properly and places the most significant items first, a proper lead will result, whatever its name.

Tabulations

Many newspapers use tabulations either above or within the story as a way of summarizing for the reader the action reported in the body of the story. It is a way of letting the reader know a lot of information quickly. It permits the reporter to focus on a single fact. Some papers use numerals with tabulated items; others use dashes or dots. Here is an example:

A One-Column Box or a Boldfaced List Preceding the Story

Highlights of Yesterday's Election

—Governor: William Branson
—Lt. Governor: Gwen Stocks
—State Income Tax Referendum: Defeated 4–1
—State Lottery Referendum: Defeated 2–1

The preceding tabulation made this simplified lead possible.

For the first time in the state's history, Independent Party candidates won the two top offices in state government.

William Branson, a former corporate executive who was running for public office for the first time, was elected governor by a three-to-one margin over both the Democratic and Republican candidates.

Gwen Stocks, who joined him on the Independent Party ticket after Chester Gould withdrew because of failing health, won the lieutenant governor's post. For many years she headed "Save Our Seashore," a group opposed to commercial development along the coast.

Governor-elect Branson credited the crossover vote for his stunning defeat of the major party candidates. "I believe the voters have grown tired of the same old promises made by Republicans and Democrats," Branson told supporters at his victory rally. "Now it is up to me to keep my promises. And I pledge to do that with all the energy I can muster."

Another type lead is a variation of the summary. Instead of a single sentence including all the important features, this style briefly itemizes each feature, as in this example.

Dr. Alexander Schultz, the new executive director of the state's Higher Education Commission, today introduced his "Twenty-First Century Education Agenda," which calls for:

— Higher admission standards at all state-supported universities
— Abolishing the tenure system for faculty members
— Term limits for all university administrators
— Increased financial support for academic programs
— Increased emphasis on technology
— Decreased emphasis on college sports

"We simply have to set our admission standards higher," Dr. Schultz said. "We can no longer accept the ill-prepared students coming to us from the state's high schools."

He said the universities must "weed out the dead wood on the faculty and administration."

His proposal drew immediate criticism from all quarters, but especially from supporters of the athletic programs at the universities. But he defended his proposal, saying, "There is something drastically wrong with our priorities when a head football coach can make $500,000 while the instructor teaching students basic English skills is paid almost minimum wage."

(Details of each of the items in the list would be developed fully in the body of the story.)

The Interpretive Lead

Rather than using one of the news leads already discussed, a reporter may elect to write an interpretive lead. In this type of lead, the reporter attempts to tell readers what the facts mean. Interpretation should always be fair and objective. It should be based on the facts and the background knowledge of the event or situation, and it should be an accurate analysis of the facts. If the interpretation is simply the reporter's subjective view, then it becomes editorial opinion.

The standard straight news lead simply reports on an event, but the interpretive lead attempts to put the event into perspective for the reader. This type of lead is often used on a second-day story or by a newspaper whose competition got the story first. However, it is not uncommon for papers to use an interpretive lead when telling the story for the first time.

For example, if the executive director of the state's Higher Education Commission asked the state legislature to call for a constitutional convention to establish a state income tax to finance his "Twenty-First Century Education Agenda," a standard story might begin:

Dr. Alexander Schultz, executive director of the state's Higher Education Commission, urged the state legislature to call for a constitutional convention to establish a state income tax to finance higher education.

In the rest of the story, the reporter would give the details of the proposal, citing overall cost of financing higher education and the limited revenues generated by the sales tax, which is the state's main source of income.

A reporter interpreting Dr. Schultz's request for the reader might have written:

> Ignoring fierce opposition from university faculty members and administrators, business and consumer groups and college sports fans, Dr. Alexander Schultz, Executive Director of the state's Higher Education Commission, called for a state income tax.
>
> He said there "simply isn't enough money generated by the current state sales tax" to support his "Twenty-First Century Education Agenda."
>
> "Our state universities face a decline into second-rate status if they are not overhauled and receive increased funding," he added.
>
> Faculty members and administrators bitterly oppose . . .

If this type lead is used, it is important to include as quickly as possible the highlights of the education agenda. Some editors try to get those details into the second or third paragraph. Others include them in the third or fourth, depending on the circumstances of the story. In no case should they be placed much farther down in the story than the fourth or fifth paragraphs. The reader needs those facts to understand why Schultz has proposed a state income tax and why various groups oppose it.

Some editors would put the highlights of Schultz's proposal in a bold faced box and place the story around it. Or they might use it as a boldfaced precede to the story.

Considerable debate about interpretive reporting continues among journalists, and many newspapers still approach it with extreme caution. But it is being used increasingly in reporting government and politics, and it frequently brings cries from the persons whose action is being interpreted that the reporter is "biased" or, worse, "simply dead wrong." Nevertheless, the increasing complexity of modern society—not just government and politics—tends to require that newspapers explain facts as well as report them. Newspapers have a responsibility to make certain that the reporter who does the interpretation is careful and thorough and has the necessary background and maturity to present an accurate and fair analysis of the facts.

Separate Stories

Elections, storms, strikes, wars and frequently large fires and other major events may demand more than one story. For example, a story about persons killed and injured in the chain-reaction crashes would require a main story about the crashes plus stories on the rescue efforts; stories on the survivors; interviews with officials about the causes; a story on similar crashes, especially if others occurred in the same area; and a story on what might be done to prevent similar crashes. In each one of these "sidebar" stories, the original event would need to be recapped in a brief paragraph early in the story.

Many of these stories lend themselves to strong dramatic feature leads. Often these stories are grouped in one section of the newspaper to make it easier for the reader to have immediate access to everything that is written about the event. It is not uncommon for a newspaper to collect all of its coverage of a major event such as an earthquake or major air crash in which lives are lost into a special section that is issued a week or so after the event.

Identifying the Features

It is difficult if not impossible to write a clear, coherent news story without identifying the features in the mass of story details the reporter has collected. Simply defined features are the highlights—the outstanding, most interesting and most significant items in any news event. The reporter has to determine which of these features are the most interesting and newsworthy.

For example, a reporter assigned to cover a speech should always look for the main arguments or contentions of the speaker to emphasize in the lead. However, the speaker's ad-libbing that the president should be impeached, a fist fight's starting in the audience, or hecklers' being ejected would be "features" that might rate even more attention than the highlights of the formal speech.

Perhaps the best guide in recognizing the worthwhile features is to look for these elements first: "Who" was involved; "What" happened; "When" it happened; "Where" it happened; "Why" it happened; and "How" it happened. Obviously the news values discussed earlier in this chapter will influence the process. Reporters should always remember that the purpose of the lead is to give the reader an accurate and complete picture of what is to come later in the story.

Summarizing the Features

Once the features have been recognized, the reporter's job is to decide whether to try to summarize them or select one to emphasize in the lead. Here are several examples of leads in which the efforts to summarize all of the features produced leads that really are too vague:

> Four points in favor of consolidating city and county schools were given today by Mrs. Cyndi Tipton, president of Save Our Schools, Inc., in a speech to the . . .

> Problems of taxation and public health were debated today by the State House of Representatives.

> Four important pieces of consumer legislation were passed by Congress today.

Each of these leads recognizes the existence of several features, but the attempt to summarize them results in vague, dull and uninteresting leads. "Four points in favor" has little reader appeal and actually does not summarize those points. A brief summary of the points would make the lead more specific and catch the reader's attention.

Mrs. Cyndi Tipton, president of Save Our Schools, Inc., told the Downtown Kiwanis Club that the consolidation of city and county schools would:

— Sharply reduce the cost of public schools
— Bring uniform educational standards to all students
— Reduce teacher-pupil ratios
— Reduce the number of students who would be bused

Another approach would be to emphasize one feature in the lead sentence and summarize the others in the next one, as in the following example:

The cost of public schools would be reduced sharply by consolidating the city and county school systems, Mrs. Cyndi Tipton, president of Save Our Schools, Inc., told the Downtown Kiwanis Club.

Consolidation would also bring about more uniform educational standards, reduce teacher-pupil ratios in the classrooms and greatly reduce the number of students who would have to be bused.

Combining Stories

Separate stories about a single event naturally will differ in content, although there will be some overlapping of facts in each one. As a result, some newspapers will combine the stories into one. But combined stories have a tendency to be long, and some editors prefer to group individual stories about the event on the same page with separate headlines or group them under a single major headline. To avoid long stories, some reporters will write a lead story on the major action taken and separate shorter stories on secondary actions.

EXERCISES

1. Using any newspaper available to you, clip stories that illustrate three leads that illustrate the different methods of writing a several-incident story lead. Bring them to class and be prepared to discuss their strengths and weaknesses.

2. Here are rough notes for several-incident stories. Use them to (1) list the various factors in order of their newsworthiness; (2) write a summary lead, a second lead emphasizing an outstanding feature and a third lead in one of the forms discussed in this chapter.

   a. The State Senate yesterday voted to:

      i. Raise the speed limit on all state roads and highways to 75 miles an hour
      ii. Increase the state sales tax on cigarettes by 35 cents a pack, making that tax now $1 a pack
      iii. Increase the tax paid by wholesalers on beer from the present $3.90 for a 31-gallon barrel to $5 a barrel
      iv. Increase the price of hunting and fishing licenses from $25 to $50

v. Charge a $5 entrance fee for individuals at all state parks and recreation areas

b. Anthony Chavez was fishing on Lake George about 7:30 yesterday morning. He found the body of a woman floating near the shore about a half mile from the Twin Cove Marina. He called 911 on his cellular phone. Police and Rescue Squad members pulled the body from the lake. Medical examiner said body had been in the lake 24 to 36 hours. Victim was identified as Caroll Jefferson, 42, 139 Pine Tree Drive, who had been reported missing 48 hours earlier by her husband, Jacob, 49. He told police his wife went out to "get some cigarettes" and never came home. Medical examiner said woman's skull had been crushed with a blunt object like a hammer. Police got search warrant for the Jefferson home. They confiscated a number of tools, including several hammers, 12 marijuana plants growing in pots in the basement, 100 bags of a white powdered substance police believe to be crack cocaine and drug paraphernalia, including needles and syringes. Neighbors told police they suspected Jefferson "was up to something because there were more cars in and out of his driveway than at a McDonald's drive through." They also told police the Jeffersons have violent quarrels. Police arrested Jefferson on charges of possession of illegal drugs. He is being held in County Jail under $50,000 bond. Police Chief Sonny Tuffs said he will wait until the medical examiner determines the cause of death before bringing other charges. "Mrs. Jefferson's death sure looks suspect to me," he added.

(Sources: Police Chief Tuffs, Anthony Chavez, Medical Examiner Dr. Horace Wells.)

c. Killer heat wave continues for the 16th day across the state. Five more heat-related deaths were confirmed, bringing the state's death toll to 26 since the current heat wave began, Governor Paula Casey said. National Weather Service says 100-degree days are likely to continue for another week. Since the heat wave began four weeks ago, the temperature has never been lower than 98 and for the last 16 days has gone above 100, including a 105, 108, 110 and two 115-degree days, Weather Service spokesperson Amy Lin says. Power distributors report that they are buying electric power from producers in six nearby states to meet the increased demand. They warned of possible "brown outs" if the heat wave continues for another week. They urged homeowners to turn off air conditioners when they are away from home during the day and to turn off their hot water heaters except when absolutely needed. The state's farmers report their corn and soybean crops are dying in the fields. Jesse Ricks, the state Agriculture Commissioner, estimated that the crop loss will be nearly $30 million. Hospitals and clinics across the state report the number of individuals treated for heat exhaustion and other heat-related illnesses has tripled.

(Sources: Governor Casey, Amy Lin, Emergency Planning Services, Commissioner Ricks, Hospitals)

d. Three teenagers under arrest for vandalizing lights, Sheriff's Department helicopters, and six private planes. Because they sprayed the cockpits of the planes with fire extinguisher, they're facing federal charges, Dancie Taylor, chief sheriff's deputy said. Chemicals in the extinguisher are corrosive and can cause the instruments to malfunction and the planes to crash. Damages could exceed

$250,000. One 19-year-old and two 17-year-olds are being charged. Taylor said they broke 20 runway lights, broke out the windows in one of the helicopters parked outside the hanger. Broke into the locked hanger and spray painted another sheriff's department helicopter and poured oil all over the cockpit, ripped the doors off and set two fire extinguishers off in it. They spray painted six private planes, poured oil in all the cockpits, broke out windows and set off fire extinguisher in them. When investigators arrived at the airport, one of them found a class ring with the owner's initials etched inside. They went to the high school and checked the list of enrolled students until they found the ring's owner. He led them to the others. Names withheld.

(Source: Deputy Taylor)

e. John Forsythe, 67, retired railroad engineer, worked as the engineer of the miniature train at the City's Oak Park Zoo. Was hauling 10 passengers Sunday over the one-mile scenic route through the zoo when the train went out of control and jumped the track. Forsythe was thrown from the train, died at the scene. The engine overturned and its cars left the track. Witnesses said they heard him yelling that he could not stop the train. Ten passengers were injured, none seriously. They were given first aid at the scene by zoo paramedics. Witnesses said some passengers jumped off when the train was about to crash. The red miniature train, with partly open sides, bench seats, and five cars normally travels 3 to 5 miles an hour. Forsythe had worked for the zoo for two years. He had been a locomotive engineer for the Southern Pacific Railroad for 41 years. Zoo Director Lucy Driscoll said the miniature railroad would be shut down until the staff completes an investigation of the accident and all the tracks and rolling stock have been carefully examined.

(Sources: Lucy Driscoll, Witnesses to the accident)

CHAPTER

8 Polishing the Lead

"You want a lead that makes your reader exclaim, 'Gee whiz!'—a lead that makes his eyes pop, that so captures his attention that he can't wait to gobble up the rest of your story."

James Reynolds, then a member of the editorial staff of the *National Graphic,* offered that sage advice a long time ago in an article he wrote for the *Quill.*

But he acknowledge that it isn't always easy to write a lead that rivets the attention of readers. Part of the problem is that news is repetitive. And part of the problem is that some reporters do not use their skills or imagination when faced with writing essentially the same story over and over again. That's why so many leads begin this way:

The President signed into law today . . .
The House of Representatives passed a law today requiring . . .
The County Commission voted unanimously last night to . . .
The City Council voted 16—4 last night to . . .

Or they become "said" leads such as these:

The President said yesterday . . .
The Governor said yesterday . . .
Vols coach Phil Fulmer said yesterday . . .
Actor Michael J. Fox said yesterday . . .

In many of these leads such words as "announced," "revealed," and "admitted" replace said. But the effect is still the same: a dull, unimaginative lead.

A person who writes that type lead is tempting fate because there is little in it to make the reader want to go on reading the rest of the story. And that's the purpose of a lead.

Reporters generally agree that the lead is the hardest part of a newspaper story to write. Some call it sheer agony, and that is often obvious in what they finally produce.

Frequently a lead will follow all the rules and principles discussed so far but still not be interesting enough to grab the reader's attention. It may contain all 5

W's, the proper identification and attribution, and it may emphasize a significant feature. In short, it may be adequate, but it may also be dull and uninteresting. It may lack originality, vividness, style, class, distinction and imagination.

A good lead is more than just adequate. It is clear, crisp and inviting. The Associated Press' Rene Jack Cappon says in his excellent book *The Word* that "A good lead makes a clear statement of the essential news point and when possible includes a detail that distinguishes the story from others of its kind."

Here is an outstanding lead written by Camilla Warrick for the *Cincinnati Enquirer*:

> On one side is a church with a mission.
> On the other side is a city with a need.
> In the middle is an aging, former elementary school.
> These are the ingredients of a church–state confrontation that is pitting Northside Baptist Church against the North College Hill City Council.
> It is a familiar story about one party coveting what the other has. In this case, it is the city hankering after what the church bought from under its nose.

Good leads, compelling leads, take time and effort and thought. Often the best leads form in the writer's mind before a single word is written on the computer screen or that blank sheet of paper.

Here's a lead that shows the writer thought before writing it:

> You can run, but you can't hide—from technology, that is.
> If you try, someone might hunt you down by tucking a portable global positioning system (GPS) device in your pocket.

The remainder of the story detailed all the devices and software programs that are allegedly designed to make our lives simpler.

And here is a clever lead by Charlie Appleton of the *Nashville Banner:*

> You've taken cats home from the mall but you've probably never heard of one going back.
> One fortunate feline is counting how many lives he has left after surviving a 25-mile trip to Hickory Hollow Mall in the engine compartment of a car.
> "We think he's from Murfreesboro, and once he climbed under the hood, just wouldn't get out until he got here," says George Earls, operations manager for Dillard's Department Store, where the cat now stays in a storage room.

Rhetoric

Good writing demands the use of clear, crisp, colorful, precise language. When such language is combined with short sentences and short paragraphs, you have the essence of good news writing. But a reporter must always use variety in sentence and paragraph length as well as in sentence structure.

The most common sentence form is subject–predicate:

> More than half of the people killed or maimed worldwide by terrorists are Americans, a U.S. diplomat said Friday.

It is favored by many reporters and editors, especially when dealing with straight news. But if all leads were written that way, they would fail in their basic goal to grab the reader's attention. While this type of lead sentence often is adequate, it just as often is dull. Focusing on one of the various W's gives variety to the lead.

Reporters often turn to other sentence forms to avoid writing all leads in the subject–predicate form. Here are some examples:

Phrases

Infinitive: To halt the flow of illegal drugs into South Florida, the U.S. Coast Guard today launched a . . .

Participial: Trying to shore up his crumbling political machine, Gov. Elbert Hooker called a secret meeting of . . .

Prepositional: In a slashing attack on the administration's treatment of the homeless, Senator Elise McMillan accused . . .

Gerund: Naming another so-called blue-ribbon panel of all-white males to investigate sexual and racial bias in hiring police and fire personnel is a joke, Councilwoman Marian Martin said . . . .

Clauses

Substantive: That Congress will vote to support the President's plan to use force in the Middle East is a forgone conclusion in the minds of political observers.

Adverbial: If the public does not take a strong stand against drug dealers, pushers and users, the police won't push the "War on Drugs," Jeanne Barry, president of Mothers on the March . . .

Although there is nothing wrong with these leads, many writers avoid them and many editors rewrite them simply because they have a tendency to be clumsy. They can, if not written with great care, sound stilted and often are quite long.

Emphasizing News Values

It is important for the reporter to study all the features carefully to avoid over-looking a newsworthy feature or angle that might make the difference between a routine lead and a bright, imaginative one. While it is important not to bury the news, the reporter should always seek out that special angle that might make the lead reach out to the reader. There are a number of approaches, based on the traditional news values, available to a reporter. Here are several examples:

Timeliness

The words "today" and "tomorrow" characterize most newsworthy leads on straight news stories. Occasionally, however, a story concerns events that happened "last night," "last week" or even "last month" that result in a current story. In such cases the reporter should look for a "today" angle. It isn't always easy. Here are two versions of a "today" story that illustrate the point:

> *First Version*
> Despite threats of a revenue shortfall and budget increases, state employees will get a pay raise.
> "That's good news," Linda McGill, executive director of the State Employees Association, said today at a press conference on the state capitol steps.

> *Second Version, Today Angle Emphasized*
> The state's 65,000 employees got good news today—they are getting a pay raise for the first time in four years.
> Linda McGill, executive director of the State Employees Association, said hard work by the state legislature as well as healthy state pension plan earnings means state employees will receive increases from 4 to 6 percent, depending upon their length of service and . . .

> *Other Today Angle Leads*
> Today marks the 25th anniversary of Skylab, the nation's first space station.
> The National Aeronautics and Space Administration launched the first Skylab from Cape Kennedy with a three-man crew on . . .

> When Harry Cohen, 73, married Lucille LaTour, a widow from his retirement community, today, the groom's cousin said in his toast the bride had landed the most eligible bachelor in the state.
> "Besides being a great guy," Marcus Cohen said, "Harry drives at night . . . "

The story went on to detail the problem older Americans encounter when their eyesight and health forces them to give up driving.

Proximity

Reporters should always look for a "local" angle to a story in addition to emphasizing "today."

A General Lead

Members of the U.S. Conference of Mayors today praised the Clinton administration for its "support of urban America." "The Administration's record shows it has made a commitment to urban America," Mayor Betty Bradley, the Conference president, said.

A Localized Lead

Knoxville Mayor Victor Ashe today was named to the board of directors of the U.S. Conference of Mayors.

He is one of three mayors who joined the group's board at its national convention, which ended today in San Francisco.

National and international stories often have a local angle. Certainly a major story such as a war involving American forces will produce hundreds of stories with a local angle. So do stories of major natural disasters in which Americans respond as volunteers or as a part of the armed services. Here's an example:

A Terrytown nuclear scientist is serving as an adviser to the United Nations weapons inspectors searching for weapons of mass destruction in Iraq.

Dr. James Zuchar, distinguished professor of nuclear physics at Middleboro University, has been in Iraq since June and will remain with the weapons teams until the end of August.

Prominence

It may be considered a cliche by some in the news business, but names really do make news, especially prominent names. Here are several examples:

A General Story

WASHINGTON, D.C.—Americans gave $100 billion to charity last year—10 times the amount given by all the foundations in the United States.

"Put simply, some people engage in philanthropic activity because it makes them feel good," said . . .

Prominent Name Emphasized

Bill Gates, the beleaguered billionaire founder of Microsoft, and his wife, Melinda, said Tuesday they will donate an unprecedented $100 million to get the latest vaccine to the world's poorest children.

The Gates are the wealthiest Americans to contribute to charity recently. But they are not alone. Americans from every economic category gave $100 billion to charity last year.

When you think Debbie Reynolds, you can't help but think wholesome.

"I wish people would stop thinking I'm this wholesome, sappy woman," the 66-year-old actress said.

Susan Wioszczyna of *USA TODAY* wrote this lead on a famous personality about to be receive one of the Kennedy Center Honors, the nation's tribute to artists, writers, actors, musicians and dancers who have had distinguished careers:

> Oh, my goodness! Mrs. Black is going back to Washington.
> This time, though, it's as Shirley Temple.
> The ex-actress, 70, who worked for the United Nations and the State Department under four presidents, last visited the capital in 1992, when she wrapped up a stint as U.S. ambassador to Czechoslovakia.
> But it's Black's Hollywood incarnation—the most successful child star ever to sparkle on the silver screen, the No. 1 box office attraction for four years running in the '30s—who takes a bow this weekend.

Novelty Leads

Reporters today have considerable freedom in writing leads, although there are some editors who still prefer that every story have a straight news lead. "Novelty," as used here, simply means using any one of a number of devices from questions to quotations to attract the reader's attention.

There are as many approaches as there are imaginative writers and editors. Usually, the facts of the story will dictate the type of lead, and the reporter should not strain to write a novelty lead on a story that does not justify such treatment. Here are a few of the more common forms of novelty leads:

The Question Lead

A question lead works best when a problem with reader appeal or public interest is the central point of the story. Unfortunately, the question lead is used far too often as a crutch by a reporter who does not take the time to work on another more effective approach. Some editors put a limit on the number of question leads that can be used. Nevertheless, there have been some classic question leads, such as:

> O, say can you sing "The Star Spangled Banner" without mumbling the words and petering out on the high notes?

Here's a clever question lead from Leon Alligood of the *Nashville Banner*:

> David and Dorothy Counts want to know: RV having fun, yet?
> Spot them at their campsite and they don't look any different from any other couple in the campground. They appear to be typical owners of a recreational vehicle: retired, in good health and they love to travel.

> But this Canadian couple are not so much sojourners as they are re-
> searchers . . .

The rest of the story details how the retired anthropologists travel thousands of miles each year to study some of the estimated 2 million adventurous souls who are full-time RVers.

> "When does a pint of Haagen-Dazs become a guilt-free indulgence?

Jan Hollingsworth of the *Tampa Tribune* in Florida, who wrote that excellent question lead, answered it for her readers by explaining that a new recycling firm in town was offering to pay for the containers.

The Punch, Capsule, or Cartridge Lead

Short, punchy statements used to attract the reader's attention are not always easy to write. Here's a good example of one by Gina Stafford of the *Knoxville News–Sentinel* in Tennessee:

> MORRISTOWN—Hang out with him. Drink with him. Spit on his floor. But don't throw his cat around. For Timothy Paul Winegar Jr., the latter is a killing offense.
> James William Lane's 22 years of life ended with that fatal lesson in October, and on Monday, Winegar was sentenced for his former friend's murder.

The story went on to report how after drinking all day, the two men argued when Lane spat on his floor, but when Lane threw Winegar's cat against a wall several times, Winegar used a .22-caliber rifle to repeatedly shoot and kill Lane.

Betty Barnacle of the *San Jose Mercury News,* used a question to open her story on a not-too-bright bank robber:

> How should one flee after sticking up a bank?
> Obviously, not the way tried by a suspected bank robber Tuesday in Cupertino.
> For his getaway, the gun-wielding robber selected a Santa Clara County transit bus. But he evidently did not check the schedule.

Her story went on to detail how, after robbing the bank, the holdup man walked across the street and stood at a bus stop waiting for the next bus. When police arrived at the bank, one of the tellers pointed out the robber standing at the bus stop. He was arrested and rode off in a police car before a bus ever arrived.

The Direct-Quotation Lead

A direct quote can be an extremely effective lead—if the quote is a good one and if it is not too long. Quote leads should be avoided if it takes several follow up paragraphs to explain them to the reader. Here's an effective direct-quote lead by Octavia Roca, staff critic of the *San Francisco Chronicle*, on an interview:

> NEW YORK—"A good song is a good song, no matter how it's presented. But a great song is more than a song—it's a whole play in a few moments of music," says Liza Minnelli, who should know.

Michael Kernan of the *Washington Post* used a direct quote effectively in this story of a survivor of the Holocaust:

> "I saw him at the railway station watching us leave on the train. He got smaller and smaller, and he just stood there looking rather nostalgic, as if he was sorry to see us go, sorry that the job was done now . . ."

The statement sounds unexceptional, until one learns that the train was full of Hungarian Jews headed for Auschwitz. And that the man at the station was Adolph Eichmann.

The boy on the train, now remembering as a man, was Elie Wiesel, a survivor of the Holocaust, who has become a legend through the novels in which he tries to distill the experience, tell the untellable and pass it on.

The Contrast Lead

A contrast lead reaches for the reader's attention by comparing extremes—the big with the little, comedy with tragedy, age with youth, the past with the present.

Lance Cowan of the *Nashville Banner* used the contrast between a school with money troubles and one that had an excess:

> FRANKLIN—A local high school had a problem other schools would like to have—too much money.
>
> The Williamson County School board has agreed that Franklin High School's general fund balance of $180,000 is too high and the money should be spent to keep the balance more in line with other county schools.

The rest of the story explained how the money was raised for the fund and how a committee had been appointed to review ways to spend the money.

In this AP lead, the contrast between birth and death during the poison gas disaster in Bhopal, India, adds a dramatic touch to the story updating the tragic event:

> BHOPAL, India—Six years ago, as Rani drew her first breath, hundreds of others nearby took their last. She was born as clouds of poison gas spewed from a Union Carbide plant and billowed deep into the city of 1 million people.
>
> The Bhopal accident was the world's deadliest industrial disaster, and its medical, legal and economic cost is still being reckoned. More than 3,800 people

have died because they inhaled the gas that leaked from the plant at midnight on Dec. 2, 1984.

And there certainly is implied contrast in this unusual rape story by Edna Buchanan of the *Miami Herald:*

> A 39-year-old man, jogging in a Southwest Dade residential neighborhood, told police he was abducted by a gang of women and raped, Metro-Dade police said Thursday.
> "He's very hysterical, very traumatized," Rape Squad Lt. Linda Blue said.
> The victim, whose name is being withheld, is a professional man, with children, police said.

The Direct-Address Lead

Writers frequently speak directly to the reader in a lead, often when the story may have broad interest or appeal. Consider this story written by Gene S. Sloan for *USA TODAY:*

> If you were thinking of getting away to Canada, now might be the time to do it.
> The U.S. dollar has soared to record levels against the Canadian dollar in recent weeks, making everything from Rocky Mountain resorts to Montreal bistros much less expensive for U.S. vacationers.

Direct-address leads can be effectively used on weather stories. Here's an example:

> You knew it all along, didn't you?
> It always rains more on the weekends when you are off, spoiling your plans, right?
> Well, now you can say, "I told you so" because a new study shows that Saturdays receive an average of 22 percent more precipitation than Mondays.
> Climatologists at Arizona State University reported in the current issue of *Nature* magazine that . . .

The Descriptive Lead

In a descriptive lead, the reporter tries to paint a word picture of an interesting person, place or event. A descriptive lead also helps create the mood for the story and for that reason should match the subject carefully. In the next example, John M. Crewdson of the *New York Times* describes the scene as illegal aliens cross the border from Mexico into the United States:

> WHY, Ariz.—It was the sweetest and gentlest of desert evenings, pitch-black except for a sliver of new moon and the light from a hundred thousand stars.

Nearby, a coyote scampered among the stately organ pipe cactuses, its occasional mournful howl slicing the night like a jagged knife.

Presently the stillness was broken by a softer sound, a brief two-toned whistle. For half a minute there was nothing, then an identical whistle was heard from beyond the rise, followed by a flash of light and an answering flash, the signal that the way was clear. Within seconds, shadowy figures emerged from the desert. Smiling and talking softly, they gathered in a circle near the little-used highway.

This story by Mike Sager for the *Washington Post* describes the change of season in the Virginia countryside:

CULPEPER, Va.—The dawn is chilly inside the barn, and Greg Smith's breath hangs in the air like puffs from a hand-rolled smoke. A Holstein stands motionless before him, and he strokes the cow's black and white face with a rough, stained hand. A few steps away, the sun outlines the open barn door on the earth, and there summer lingers, warm to the skin.

It is autumn, harvest time at Ashland Farm. And while Smith still rises, with the certainty of the chime, at 5:30 sharp, the sun dawdles 60 seconds more each morning and moves imperceptibly to the south. Smith pulls a handful of brown corn silage from the trough, stirring the kernels and the chopped pieces of cob, stalk, and shuck with a finger. He closes his hand tightly. When it opens again, the coarse, fluffy matter springs back to size. Perfect. The right amount of moisture to last the winter.

It has been a good year at Smith's 1,112-acre dairy farm, so bountiful.

The *Christian Science Monitor* used a descriptive lead in recounting the story of the first woman to drive a car across the United States:

It was pouring rain that gloomy June morning as a crowd gathered under umbrellas at curbside on a New York City street. The Maxwell, a forest green touring car with a leather-like pantasote top, was parked by the curb exactly at the place where Lincoln Center now stands. The year was 1909, the same year that Robert E. Peary set foot on the North Pole.

Next to the car stood a dimpled and impatient Alice Huyler Ramsey. She wore a bulky, ankle-length black poncho and rubber helmet with detachable goggles. Someone had given her a bouquet of carnations. Undaunted by rain or tradition she smiled for the photographers, as did the three women next to her.

But the dimples and smile were mere camouflage. This 21-year-old Alice H. Ramsey was half steel, half lightning rod in an era when nearly all women washed, ironed, changed diapers and cleaned their houses instead of even thinking of driving a 2,100-pound car 4,000 miles from New York to San Francisco. Ramsey didn't toy with the idea; she was doing it.

The Parody Lead

Writers frequently use widely known proverbs, quotations, song titles, currently popular sayings, book titles and often holiday or seasonal references to help establish an immediate identification for the reader and bring a little pizzazz to what otherwise might have been a routine story. Here are several examples:

> TALLAHASSEE—Lawmakers stuffed the coming year's budget with a record number of "turkeys."
>
> Just in time for the Thanksgiving season, legislators added 380 pet projects, costing taxpayers $266.4 million, to the budget. They include $100,000 to help farm cannonball jellyfish; $100,000 to buy a trailer to haul catfish; and $750,000 to add a high-speed training track at the Gainesville Raceway, where the National Hot Rod Association operates a quarter-mile drag strip.
>
> Love may be forever, but support is a different matter.

The Historical or Literary-Allusion Lead

Using a familiar character or event from history or literature is a good way to attract and hold a reader's attention, as long as the reference isn't too obscure. Doreen Carvajal used a play on the title of Marcel Proust's famous novel for this lead:

> The remembrance of things past is too fresh to imagine Random House without its showy impresario of a publisher and president, Harold Evans.
> But with the resignation of Mr. Evans, 69, last week, . . .

Geoffrey Tomb of the *Miami Herald* used this Biblical allusion in a lead on a story about the demolition of the newspaper's old printing plant in which the ashes of its first editor had been scattered secretly when it was built:

> Ashes to ashes, literally. The onetime office building and printing plant of the *Herald* is being torn down, and with it go the ashes of its first editor, Frank Stoneman.

The story details how the editor's colleagues secretly scattered his ashes into the wet cement of a support column during the construction of the building.

Jay Boyar of the *Orlando Sentinel* used a play on words in this short but effective movie review:

> Don't expect greatness from Great Expectations.
> An updating of Charles Dicken's 1861 literary classic, the new film takes some of the characters, themes and plot devices from the novel and attempts to give them a modern spin.

The Staccato Lead

A staccato lead consists of short, clipped words, phrases and sentences, sometimes separated by dashes or dots or simply made into a list, to help create a certain mood for the story. Often this type of lead is descriptive in nature. Although it is not used as often as other types of leads, it can be effective, as in the following examples:

> DICKSON CITY, Pa. (AP)—A dress factory was damaged. A lumberyard and department store were burned. Vacant houses were torched.
> And authorities say the men who set some of the fires went back to fight the flames. Eight volunteer fire fighters were arrested . . . .

> The noise begins high. Up in the rafters. It gathers strength. Spills down the aisles. Building relentlessly. It cascades over the railing. It engulfs the expensive box seats. And spills out into the playing field. A raging torrent of sound. The eardrums vibrate painfully. The heart flutters.
> Pele, the world's greatest soccer player, has just received another message of love from his adoring fans.

Leon Alligood, senior staff writer at the *Nashville Banner*, used the technique effectively in this prize-winning feature about students with learning disabilities:

> TRACY CITY—Sam Baker has a learning disability.
> Lena Cox has a severe speech impediment.
> Frankie King is autistic.
> They live in Grundy County, one of the poorest in Tennessee, where the number of students who quit high school almost equals the number who graduate.
> But the county school system's special education students, like Sam, Lena, and Frankie, defy those numbers. Their dropout rate is far below the rate for the entire school system.
> On Thursday, 29 special education students, those with the steepest path to academic success, will don cap and gown to receive their diplomas. . . .

Miscellaneous Leads

Occasionally, a reporter will attempt to give a story special treatment in the way it's written or displayed to catch the reader's attention. But that method can fall flat if not done with care. One of the more popular ways is to open with a quote, usually set off in italics, such as this one by Catherine Keefe O'Hare in the *Beverly Citizen* in Massachusetts:

> *There was an old woman who lived in a shoe. She had so many children*
> *she didn't know what to do. (Mother Goose)*
> Mary Driscoll loves so many children, and she knows just what to do—call Mom, or Dad, or Auntie, or one of the other 35 people on her list of friends or relatives all lined up to help.

Mary and David Driscoll are the parents of the almost-1-year-old quadruplets born last July 17 within three minutes of each other. And Mary sings in praise not just for these little "miracles," but for all her helpers.

Writers frequently take a quote from a novel or a famous speech or use a definition from a dictionary to start a story. Some editors like them; most don't—especially the definition from a dictionary, which tends to be overused. Computer graphics today makes it possible for newspapers to combine a reporter's story with charts, graphs, sketches, and headline type to create a novelty and eye-catching presentation. More and more newspapers are using colorful graphics, especially on their feature pages and the front pages of sports, living and business sections.

Complete Reporting

Good writers use words that tell the reader what he or she needs to know in as few words as possible. They use short words, strong words, colorful words and specific words. And they select details a reader can see. Good writers think about what they are going to write before they ever put a word on paper. Good writers have something to say and say it with style, grace and impact.

Most leads can be improved if the reporter stretches his or her imagination, knows what makes this particular story different and stresses that angle in clear and concise words. Here is an excellent example of a story by a writer who obviously thought about her lead before writing it. It was written by Lucette Lagnado of the *Village Voice* in New York City:

She was born in the maternity ward of Columbia-Presbyterian Hospital and that is also where she died.

Sharon Michelle Davis married her first love, flipped hamburgers at McDonald's, worked at a supermarket checkout counter. She was a working-class girl who saved her middle-class dreams for her unborn baby.

But early in the morning hours of Halloween, at perhaps the most prestigious medical center in the country, she suffered the most macabre trick of all. After enduring induced labor and surviving a difficult cesarean section, Sharon Michelle Davis, age 20, died in a maternity ward run by one of the nation's leading obstetrician-gynecologists. She died without being seen by any doctor—not even her attending physician—until it was too late.

Lucette Lagnado let the drama of the story speak for itself. She did not try to overdramatize the tragic situation. Her choice of words set just the right tone for the story.

In a lighter vein but equally effective is this story written by Jim Laise for the *Nashville Banner*. When the University of Alabama's football team, traditionally a national powerhouse, ran out of steam, so to speak, Laise went south to talk to the Crimson Tide's loyal fans and filed this story:

TUSCALOOSA, Ala.—Good gawd ya'll, they've done raised the white flag in the Heart of Dixie.

That's right. Alabama football fans, faced with their team's worst start in 26 years, have just about conceded. Already.

"People are always saying, 'Wait till next week,'" said Bill Hogue, a Dothan resident dining Tuesday in Bessemer's Bright Star Restaurant. "Now, we might as well say, 'Wait till next year.'"

The reason is simple. The Tide is 1-2. That's right. The same Tide that some fortune-teller from one of them girlie magazines picked to finish No. 2 in the whole darn shootin' match can't even beat Georgia Tech, for Pete's sake.

Although Alabama fans may take the team's poor showing seriously, Laise used the right light-hearted tone in his story.

Tone has to ring true to the subject of the story. If it does not, the reader will know it immediately—and you will lose her or him. Both reporters struck the right tone in their stories.

EXERCISES

1. Using any newspaper available to you, select five stories with leads that are 40 to 50 words long. Rewrite them using no more than 25 words. Turn them in at class.

2. The following leads are long; rewrite them to make them shorter and more direct.
   a. SEATTLE—Boeing, the world's largest aerospace company with workers in 27 states, announced Tuesday that it will cut 48,000 jobs by 2001, 20,000 more jobs than it announced two months ago that would be eliminated because the economic slowdown in Asia has caused several countries to cancel orders for Boeing's passenger jets.
   b. Three people were reported killed yesterday by a tornado in Wayne County where areas of the southern part of the county were so hard-hit that rescue personnel had to use a three-wheeler instead of an ambulance to rescue a critically wounded person who later died.
   c. In the first Federal Appeals court ruling on affirmative action in public school admissions, a three-judge panel in Boston yesterday struck down racial preferences at Boston Latin School, the city's most prestigious public high school that has been charged with turning down highly qualified white students in favor of less qualified minority students.
   d. WASHINGTON—Twelve consumer, environmental and religious organizations asked the Consumer Product Safety Commission today to ban vinyl toys for small children, four days after Canadian officials advised parents of small children to throw away vinyl teethers and rattles because of possible kidney and liver damage.

3. Reporters often have to update stories that took place after the previous daily or weekly edition was published. What information would you seek, and from what sources, to make the following leads more "timely"?

a. A Jefferson County woman was arrested for allegedly stealing checks from schools in seven north Alabama counties.

b. A military helicopter on a search and rescue training mission crashed today in the Great Smoky Mountains, killing four people. The fifth person aboard was still missing.

c. A 43-year-old rental car clerk was gunned down by two men while working at the Drive-In-Style car rental counter in the lobby of the Clewiston Inn last night.

4. Explain in detail how you would "localize" the following stories:
   a. WASHINGTON—Yielding to a stream of complaints from patients who say they were illegally denied emergency care, the Clinton administration told hospitals today that they must examine and stabilize patients without any delays to ask about insurance coverage.
   b. NEWPORT, R.I.—A new set of drinking water standards to control previously unregulated microbes as well as compounds found to cause cancer in laboratory animals that can result from chemicals used as water disinfectants have been established by the Clinton administration.
   c. WINCHESTER, VA.—Thousands of prospective gun buyers who should be disqualified may be able to buy a weapon anyway as a new nationwide system of instant background check goes into effect today.

5. Rewrite the following leads to focus on the prominent person.
   a. In what may be the largest private gift ever made to an American college or university, Vanderbilt University announced yesterday that it had received stock currently valued at more than $300 million. The gift was made by Martha R. Ingram, chairwoman of Ingram Industries Inc., a privately held wholesale distribution company based in Nashville.
   b. For decades, environmentalists watched the state's park endure quiet neglect while money went to myriad other state agencies and programs. Now, they say, it's time for the 51 parks to get some attention, says Walter Gilbert, president of Save Our State Parks, a conservation group that has lobbied the state legislature and Environment and Conversation Commissioner Jenny Yin for more money for maintenance.

6. Using the following situation, write a question lead based on the notes and another one on one of the other lead styles discussed in this chapter.
   a. Bay Institute for Health
      Care Communications conducting a study
      On training doctors
      To listen more carefully
      To their patients
      Doctors in Internal
      Medicine residency program
      At Irvine Medical Center
      Are taking classes
      In communicating carefully
      Their patient sessions are
      Videotaped and replayed
      Instructors critique tapes

Suggest way to communicate
More clearly, sympathetically
Earlier studies show
Doctors interrupted patients
After 18 seconds on average

b. Honor student Chris Grabenstein
Showed up at Clear Creek High School
Wearing a Santa Claus suit
Which had been made
By his mother and sister
After third class period
Vice Principal Victor Chavez
Removed Grabenstein from class
Sent him to school's
Intervention Center
As a form of discipline
Chavez said Santa suit
Was distracting to
Teachers and students
Costumes are not allowed
Principal Latasha Chappelle said
Fellow students started
"Free Santa" petition
Got 200 signatures
Grabenstein spent half day
In detention doing nothing
Called his punishment "dumb"
His first experience with
School discipline

7. Attend a campus event such as a homecoming parade, an art exhibit, a dance recital, a major athletic event or a concert by a popular music group and write a descriptive lead on that event.

8. Find what you consider the most scenic place on or off campus and write a descriptive lead for a story about that spot.

9. Write a parody or literary-allusion lead based on the following notes:
   a. Beatrice Pratt, 48
   Account clerk in city's
   Cashier's department where
   Residents pay water bills
   Arrested for allegedly taking
   More than $112,000 in city money
   Charged with grand theft
   Released on $10,000 bail
   Police recovered $79,000 in checks
   At her home
   Still looking for $32,700 cash
   She didn't explain why

She took the money
Police said she made $27,000
But drove a Jaguar sedan
And lived in a $250,000 home
She is not married

b. Redlands Commercial Bird Farm
Reported theft of $90,000
Worth of exotic birds
Owner Alta Rajput said
He found cage doors open
And 46 rare birds missing
When he went to feed them
About 7:30 this morning
Neighbors who lived next door
Found a pair of birds
In a pillow case
In their yard where
Thieves accidentally dropped them
Police said about
20 exotic bird thefts
Reported in area
In the last year
Stolen birds were mostly
African grays and Amazons
They were used for
Breeding purposes
And were not taught
To talk, Rajput said

PART THREE

Writing the Complete Story

"Some (reporters) turn in pieces that start out well, develop a few paragraphs, then trickle off into unrelated paragraphs, then unrelated sentences and sometimes sheer gibberish, with no ending," Don Frye, an independent writing coach, said in a column for the *American Editor*.

His comments are seconded by many editors who remind reporters that a news story needs more than just a good lead.

It is true that the lead is what attracts a reader's attention in the first place, but it is the body of the story that holds it.

A news story comes together in the body and delivers to the reader what the lead has promised. If the body does not support the lead in a careful and lucid fashion, if it isn't as interesting as the lead, the reader may feel cheated. What is worse, the reader might not finish the story.

Organizing and developing the body of a news story is tremendously important. Often it can present even greater problems than writing the lead. Just as there are a number of styles or approaches to handling leads, the body of a news story can be developed in a variety of ways.

Part Three presents organizational patterns for both straight news and feature stories. It also deals with four other areas that may present problems for which there are specific techniques to use in writing a complete story. These include the organization of (1) stories on events about which previous stories have been published; (2) cutlines to go with pictures, which are often important supplements to stories but which sometimes stand alone in the coverage of an event; (3) news stories for radio and television; and (4) stories requiring special treatment if a newspaper's policy is involved.

The chapters in this section form a basis for writing all of the types of newspaper stories considered throughout the book.

CHAPTER

9

The Body of the Story

"Some writers have the philosophy that when the lead is written, the rest of the story will simply flow. The result is often a rambling repetitive story."

DeAnn Evans of the *Desert News* in Salt Lake City made that point at a seminar conducted by the American Press Institute, the leading continuing education organization for journalists in the United States.

To be effective, a news story has to be more than just a loosely assembled collection of facts. First, the story must have something to say. Then it must have an interesting lead to grab the reader's attention. And the lead should be followed by the main body of the story, which expands and elaborates—documents—the lead. The story should come to a logical end.

Each part should be carefully tied to the other so the story progresses in an interesting, informative and logical manner. Often a single fact seems to have great possibilities as a lead, but there is nothing to support it. That is why the reporter has to carefully sort and organize the facts, first in her or his mind and then on the computer screen.

Like the lead, the body of the story should be clear and concise. It should take the reader through the details of the story in logical progression, emphasizing the facts in order of descending importance. Here is a long and convoluted lead that almost defies understanding:

> The Public Housing Authority, meeting in regular session Wednesday night, expressed optimism that City Council will vote Monday night to approve the Authority's selected site for the proposed 120-unit public housing project for low-income families here and decided to proceed with further arrangements for building the project.

The rest of the story was equally muddy and difficult to wade through. The basic problem is that the lead is too vague, too general, too wordy. It isn't specific. Obviously the writer did not organize the material carefully before writing it. And the copy editor apparently made no effort to rewrite it into a clear, crisp report. The writer might have tried a more direct lead such as this:

> The Public Housing Authority is going ahead with plans to build a 120-unit public-housing project for low-income families even though the City Council hasn't approve the site.
> "We are optimistic that the City Council will approve the site at the intersection of Timber and Hardwood," said Bernie Goldstein, PHA chairman. "So we decided to go head with . . ."

Here is a short lead playing off the lyric to a Christmas carol that gets right to the point and is quickly supported by the body of the story:

> "Tis the season for fraud and robberies." That's what police are singing in these days before Christmas as the number of reported thefts, robberies and check cashing scams increase almost daily in the city.
> "It's driving us crazy," Metro Robbery Sgt. Ron Parrish said. "Everything gets pretty wild this time of year . . . we need some relief."

The rest of the story gave the statistics showing the increase in crime and tied them to the fact that the period between Thanksgiving and Christmas is the prime shopping period of the year, and shoppers often have more money with them than they have at other times of the year.

The following is an example in which the lead and the first paragraph in the story are somewhat at odds, which damages the effectiveness of the lead:

> MONTEREY, Calif.—Adorable quotient aside, sea lions these days are more a rank and nasty nuisance to Monterey city officials than the cuddly creatures gliding through the water that tourists love.
> It's not cute, they say, when a dozen of the 800-pound mammals climb aboard a tugboat and sink it with their combined weight. It's not sweet when they take over entire boat slips, preventing even the proudest yacht owners from stepping out of their crafts.

The problem with this lead is that the writer calls an 800-pound sea lion cuddly and adorable. There are few things that weigh 800 pounds that are cuddly or adorable. Sea lions are very large and very ugly and often ill-tempered. It could be the writer has mistaken the sea lion for the sea otter. At any rate, the lead is certainly out of sync with the second paragraph of the story.

The reporter should use good judgment in writing the lead and in developing the body of the story. The object is to attract the reader's attention with the lead and then hold it by arranging all the significant facts and incidents of a story in their logical order of importance or newsworthiness. In telling the story in logical order—arranging facts in order of descending newsworthiness—the reporter should lead the reader carefully from one paragraph to the next. One weak paragraph preceding several interesting ones might mean that the latter paragraphs are not read.

Although editing techniques and the ability to match stories to available space are now more sophisticated than they were when the inverted pyramid style became common more than 60 years ago, the logical order is still an important aid to the mechanical process of the newspaper. If the copy editors or makeup editor must reduce the length of a story, he or she cuts paragraphs from the end of the story. The copy editor takes for granted that the final paragraphs contain the least important facts. The following rule is an excellent one to use when writing a standard news story: Write your story so that if it is terminated at any point, nothing below that point will be as newsworthy as anything above it, so that at the terminating point the story will be complete, intelligible and effective.

The body of the story serves one or both of two purposes: (1) it explains and elaborates the feature or features in the lead or lead block; (2) it adds and elaborates on minor features not summarized in the lead.

Developing the Single-Feature Lead

If a story contains only one feature, the lead is built around it. The body of the story will elaborate and document the lead by adding the pertinent facts. In this case the task is to judge the newsworthiness of all facts so that they may be presented in logical order. Here's an example of this type of story.

The Diagram	The Written Story
Single feature	Creation of a non-political Civilian Review Board to investigate all cases of alleged police brutality was recommended in a report sent to Mayor Elizabeth Ragsdale today.
	The report, from a special commission named three months ago by the mayor to study the Police Department, said:
	"A Civilian Review Board is needed because the Police Department is hopelessly politicized and incapable of fairly and impartially investigating itself.
Additional details	The report noted that the Police Department's internal security division had not taken disciplinary action against a single police officer although more than 30 persons have charged that they were beaten or manhandled by policemen during questioning and arrest in the past 18 months.
Further details	"In two cases where policemen were found guilty in court of assault and battery, the Police Department still failed to take any disciplinary action," the report said.
	The proposed Civilian Review Board would be appointed by the mayor and confirmed by City Council. One member would be selected to repre-

sent each of the council districts. They would serve three-year terms.

Mayor Ragsdale named the special commission to study the Police Department in response to dozens of complaints about police brutality.

(Additional paragraphs would give more details and background.)

Developing the Several-Feature Lead

The several-feature story often presents problems for the reporter. Chief among them is the organization of the body of the story.

Since the body of the story should explain and elaborate on all the features presented in the lead or lead block, the reporter is faced with the problem of giving each of the features the proper amount of attention without burying important facts deep within the story.

Too often reporters get carried away and load the body of the story with insignificant facts about one or more of the features, delaying the explanation of the other features. If a feature has enough reader appeal to deserve a place in the lead or lead block, it deserves to be supported high in the body of the story.

Reporters also frequently have problems with minor features not summarized in the lead. Minor features should not be introduced into the body of the story until all the features in the lead have been explained fully. When they are introduced, they should be summarized before their details are presented.

Summary Development

If more than one feature is summarized in the lead, often resulting in a long lead, each feature should be elaborated in the order it was presented (logical order) as in this example:

The Diagram
Lead: Summary
of all features

The Written Story
Creation of a non-political civilian board to investigate cases of alleged police brutality, special human relations training for all police officers and reorganization of the Police Department's Internal Security Bureau were recommended in a report sent to Mayor Elizabeth Ragsdale.

Details common
to all features

The report was prepared by the special commission named by the mayor three months ago to study the city's trouble-plagued Police Department.

Details of first
feature

The proposed review board would investigate all cases of alleged police brutality because the Police Department is "hopelessly politicized and incapable of fairly and impartially investigating itself," the report said.

Details of second feature	Asserting that most instances of alleged man-handling of citizens are unnecessary, members of the commission urged that all police officers be required to take special training in human relations.
	"Police are given no courses in human relations during their training period, and they obviously do not get any training in it after they are placed on active duty," the report said.
Details of third feature	Public dissatisfaction with the department stems chiefly from the work of the Internal Security Bureau, which is responsible for investigating civilian complaints against police officers.
	"The Internal Security Bureau has not recommended disciplinary action against a single police officer, although more than 30 persons in the last 18 months have charged that they were beaten or man-handled by police officers during questioning or while being arrested.
	"In two cases where police officers were found guilty in court of assault and battery, the Police Department did not take any disciplinary action," the report said.
More details on first feature	In recommending a Civilian Review Board, the report suggested that members be named by the mayor and confirmed by the City Council. Each member would represent one of the city's council districts and would serve for three years.
	(Additional paragraphs would give further details and background.)

Outstanding Feature Development

One feature may be so significant that the reporter may elect to emphasize it in the first paragraph and then summarize all the other features in the second paragraph. The third paragraph then should elaborate and explain the feature emphasized in the lead. The remainder of the body of the story should consider each of the features given in the second paragraph in their logical order, as in this version of the story:

The Diagram	*The Written Story*
Lead: Outstanding feature	Creation of a non-political Civilian Review Board to investigate all cases of alleged police brutality was recommended in a report sent to Mayor Elizabeth Ragsdale today.
Summary of other features	The report also urged that all police officers be given intensive training in human relations, and that the Police Department's Internal Security Bureau be reorganized. The report requested a special allocation of $150,000 to begin the training within 30 days.

Details common to all features	The mayor received the report from the special commission she appointed three months ago to study the Police Department. She took the action after a rash of reports of alleged police brutality over the past 18 months.
Details of outstanding feature	The Civilian Review Board is needed, the report said, because the Police Department is "hopelessly politicized and incapable of fairly and impartially investigating itself."
Details of first minor feature	Asserting that most instances of alleged manhandling of citizens are unnecessary, the report urged that all police officers be required to take intensive training in human relations.
	"Police are given no courses in human relations during their training period, and they obviously do not get any training in it after they are placed on active duty," the report said.
Details of second minor feature	Much of the public's dissatisfaction with the Police Department stems from the work of the Internal Security Bureau, which is responsible for investigating civilian complaints against individual officers, the report said.
	"The Internal Security Bureau has not recommended disciplinary action against a single police officer, although more than 30 persons in the last 18 months have charged that they were beaten or manhandled by police officers during questioning or while being arrested.
	"In two cases where policemen were found guilty in court of assault and battery, the Police Department still failed to take any disciplinary action," the report said.
More details of outstanding feature	In recommending a Civilian Review Board, the report suggested that members be named by the mayor and confirmed by City Council. One member would represent each of the city's council districts and would serve for three years.
	(Additional paragraphs would give further details and background.)

If the minor or secondary features are not as important as some of the details of the outstanding feature, they need not be introduced until the details of the outstanding feature have been spelled out. This organization still observes the logical order of presenting the information.

The Diagram	The Written Story
Lead: outstanding feature	Creation of a non-political Civilian Review Board to investigate all cases of alleged police brutality was recommended in a report sent to Mayor Elizabeth Ragsdale today. The report, made by a special commission appointed by the mayor three months ago to study the trouble-plagued Police Department, said: "A Civilian Review Board is needed because the Police Department is hopelessly politicized and incapable of fairly and impartially investigating itself." It pointed out the failure of the Department to take any steps to prevent "the kind of action on the part of police officers that has led to 30 citizens charging that they had been manhandled or beaten." "An apparent lack of concern for the public welfare pervades the entire Department," the report said.
Additional details	A Civilian Review Board would ensure the citizens that all complaints against police officers would be fairly and objectively investigated because the board would be non-political and not affiliated with the Department in any way, it added. Members of the board would be appointed by the mayor and confirmed by City Council. One member would be selected to represent each of the council districts in the city. They would serve three-year terms.
Summary of other secondary features associated with outstanding feature	The report also recommended that a special staff be hired for the review board, and it asked for an emergency appropriation of $150,000 to begin the board's operation as soon as possible.
More details	"A separate staff of investigators and special assistants is absolutely essential to the operation of the proposed board," the report said. "Without its own staff the board will have to rely on the Police Department for its investigative work. This obviously would create a serious problem for the board."
More details	The need for an independent office staff and team of investigators makes it essential that approximately $150,000 be appropriated on an emergency basis to get the board into operation, the report said.

It points out that a regular budget for the board would have to be included in the city's annual budget in future years, if the board is to operate as an effective independent, non-political agent.

Summary of
other features

The report also urged that all police officers be given intensive training in human relations and that the Police Department's Internal Security Board be reorganized.

(Additional paragraphs would elaborate and explain these two other recommendations of the special committee named by the mayor.)

It should be noted that some editors would consider this too far down into the story to introduce the recommendations for human relations training and the re-organization of the Internal Security Bureau. Some editors would have the reporter write separate stories to avoid making the lead story long. Some studies have shown that unless a story is compelling, readers begin to lose interest if it runs more than 15 inches.

The Combination Development

The Diagram
Lead: summary
of two-lead
features

The Written Story
    Creation of a non-political Civilian Review Board to consider cases of alleged police brutality and special training in human relations for all police officers were recommended in a report sent to Mayor Elizabeth Ragsdale today.

Summary of
other features

    The report also recommended that the Police Department's Internal Security Bureau be reorganized. And it requested an emergency allocation of $150,000 to begin the human relations training within 30 days.

Details common
to all features

    The report was made by a special commission appointed by Mayor Ragsdale three months ago to study the Police Department. The mayor took the action after a rash of reports of alleged police brutality over the past 18 months.

Details of first
lead feature

    In recommending a Civilian Review Board, the report said it is needed because the Police Department is "hopelessly politicized and incapable of fairly and impartially investigating itself."
    Board members would be appointed by the mayor and confirmed by the City Council. One would be selected from each of the city's council districts. They would serve three-year terms.

Details of second lead feature	Asserting that most instances of alleged police manhandling of citizens are unnecessary, the report urged that all police officers be required to take intensive training in human relations.
	"Police are given no courses in human relations during their training, and they obviously do not get any training in it after they are placed on active duty," the report said.
Details of first minor feature	Calling the Internal Security Bureau "ineffective" in its present form, the report said the bureau took months to conduct the most routine investigation. And then it rarely came up with any recommendations that "would help relieve some of the intolerable conduct on the part of some police officers."
	It noted that the bureau had not recommended disciplinary action against a single police officer, although more than 30 persons in the past 18 months had charged that they were beaten and manhandled by police during questioning and arrest.
Details of second minor feature	The $150,000 emergency allocation would allow the department to begin an intensive course in human relations on a crash basis within 30 days, the report said. Additional money would have to be allocated in the department's budget to include this kind of training for all new officers in the future and provide periodic review courses for veterans of the force.
	In advocating the Civilian Review Board, the report suggested . . .
	(Other details in logical order)

A combination development with some features buried deep in the story (note the following example) is a common form. This is much like the out-standing-feature form illustrated previously in this chapter. In long stories, minor features may be introduced in summary paragraphs at several points in the body of the story.

The Diagram	*The Written Story*
Lead: summary of two main features	Creation of a non-political Civilian Review Board and special training in human relations for all police officers were recommended in a report sent to Mayor Elizabeth Ragsdale today.
	The mayor received the report from the special commission she appointed three months ago to study the Police Department. She took the action

after a rash of reports of alleged police brutality over the past 18 months.

Details of first
lead feature

The Civilian Review Board is needed to investigate all cases of alleged police brutality because the Police Department is "hopelessly politicized and incapable of fairly and impartially investigating itself," the report said.

Details of second
lead feature

Asserting that most instances of alleged manhandling of citizens are unnecessary, the report urged that all police officers be required to take intensive training in human relations immediately.

Summary of
other features

The report also recommended that the Police Department's Internal Security Bureau be reorganized. And it requested an emergency allocation of $150,000 to begin the human relations training within 30 days.

Details of first
lead feature

"The Civilian Review Board would reassure the citizens that all complaints against police officers would be fairly and objectively investigated because it would be non-political," the report said. Members would be appointed by the mayor and confirmed by City Council. One would represent each of the city's council districts. They would serve three-year terms.

Details of second
lead feature

The report noted that "Police are given no courses in human relations during their training period, and they obviously do not get any training in it after they are placed on active duty."

"It is obvious that some police officers prefer to restrain rather than reason with persons they are questioning or arresting," it added.

Details of first
minor feature

The report stated that much of the public dissatisfaction with the Police Department stems from the work of the Internal Security Bureau, which is responsible for investigating civilian complaints against police officers.

It pointed out that the Internal Security Bureau "has not recommended disciplinary action against a single police officer, although more than 30 persons in the last 18 months have charged that they were beaten or manhandled by police officers during questioning while being arrested."

(Other details in logical order)

As noted earlier, some newspapers attempt to keep stories reasonably short and, when confronted with handling a report such as the one cited in these examples, elect to make it into a series of stories. The major story might be a general review of the report, emphasizing the major point and highlighting the minor ones. The secondary stories would be devoted to each of the other recommendations made in the report. Often, in a story of this importance to a community, the main story would be used on page one and perhaps continue to an inside page where the secondary stories would be displayed. A number of newspapers use the same technique when handling city council and school board stories in which a lot of action takes place. This is a graphic device used to attract readers who would read the shorter stories but would be unwilling to wade through one very long story.

Multiple-Casualty Story Development

Many newspapers have a standard form for stories involving several casualties. Here is an example of how an accident resulting in several deaths might be handled:

The Diagram	*The Written Story*
Summary lead	Three members of a Southside family were burned to death early today in a fire that destroyed their two-story home at 1165 Roswell Blvd.
	Two others were hospitalized in critical condition. They suffered burns over most of their bodies, fire officials said.
The dead	Jose Chavez, 31, his wife, Rosa, 29, and their six-month-old son, Luis, were trapped in an upstairs bedroom and unable to escape.
The injured	Two other sons, Jamie, 3, and Roberto, 6, who were sleeping downstairs, were rescued by firemen. They are in critical condition at St. Mary's Medical Center.
Summary of other features or details on lead	Fire Chief Leonard Basler said the fire apparently started about 5 a.m., and spread quickly to the upper floor. . . .
	(Details of the fire would follow in chronological order.)

Newspapers generally group the names of casualties into a single paragraph when they are related. However, if the casualties are not related and the list is long, the names are given on separate lines immediately following the leads, as in this example:

The Diagram	*The Written Story*
Summary lead	Five officials of the Rainbow Manufacturing Co. were killed today when the company's jet crashed on takeoff from McGee Tyson Airport.

	They are:
The dead	Michael Connely, company president
	Thomas Lewis, vice president for sales
	Gregory Thompson, vice president for manufacturing
	George Ramos, treasurer
	Darlene Yhieme, personnel manager
The injured	The pilot, Brian Prentice, and copilot, Gail Palmer, were critically injured in the crash.
Summary of details of other features	Airport officials said the plane . . .
	(Details of the accident would follow in chronological order.)

The object in using a list here is to make it easy for the reader to see the names of the dead quickly. Some newspapers even set the names of the victims in boldface type.

Chronological Order

Stories with strong narrative elements may sometimes best be told in chronological order, rather than logical order, in the body of the story. After the lead has summarized the outstanding feature or features, the body of the story may be developed as a narrative. In most cases, however, the narrative paragraphs are interrupted by paragraphs adding additional facts, as in the following example:

The Diagram	*The Written Story*
Lead: Summary	A gunman demanding $1 million and a plane to fly him to Mexico held two employees of the First National Bank hostage for three hours yesterday before surrendering to FBI agents and city police. The hostages were not injured.
	FBI Agent Joseph Westfall identified the gunman as Bobby Mack Cable, 41, a former mental patient.
Non-narrative details	Becky Barnette, secretary, and Jackson McDonald, vice president and comptroller of the bank, said Cable walked into her second-floor office in the bank building about 12:45 p.m.
Narrative	"When I asked him if I could help him, he pulled a gun out of his windbreaker pocket," Mrs. Barnette said. "I guess I screamed because Mr. McDonald came running out of his office. We were the only two there. All the others were out to lunch."

McDonald said Cable told them: "OK! Keep calm. Just do what I tell you and nothing will happen to you."

Cable ordered McDonald to lock the door from the inside and made the banker push a desk and file cabinet against it as a barricade.

Narrative details

"Now, get on that phone and call the president of this bank and tell him I want $1 million in small bills and an airplane to fly me to Mexico," Cable said. "If I don't get them and get them soon he'll be shopping for two new employees tomorrow."

McDonald said he called Harry Jameson, bank president, whose office is on the fourth floor. "He wasn't sure that I wasn't just kidding at first, but Cable yanked the phone out of my hand and repeated the demand. He also warned Mr. Jameson not to call the police. He wanted Mr. Jameson to drive us to the airport in his personal car and then, he said, he would release us just before boarding the plane."

Jameson said he talked to the bank security chief and they decided to call the FBI and the police.

Within 15 minutes, more than 50 city policemen and FBI agents had surrounded the bank. They cleared patrons from the first floor of the building and the parking lot. Police rerouted traffic in the downtown area so no cars passed the bank building at 911 Jefferson St.

Mrs. Barnette said Cable seemed calm and sure of himself. "He talked about the weather and how nice it is in Mexico at this time of the year for about 20 minutes. Then he forced Mr. McDonald to call Mr. Jameson again."

Cable grabbed the phone from McDonald and told Jameson: "Listen, turkey, I know you called the cops. You just bought yourself two dead ones," Mrs. Barnette said.

"He was very nervous then and when I started to cry, he told me to 'shut up, them tears ain't gonna do you any good where you're going.'"

Non-narrative details

Westfall said he called McDonald's office in an effort to speak to Cable. At first Cable refused to talk to the FBI agent, but then he repeated his demands. He agreed to give Westfall three hours to arrange for the money, the safe trip to the airport and the plane to Mexico.

Narrative	"That was the longest three hours of my life," McDonald said. "We sat there not knowing what was going to happen next."
Non-narrative details	Westfall, Jameson and Dr. Robert Marcetti, a psychiatrist, each talked to Cable on the phone during the three hours he held the two hostages.
Narrative	"When he would talk to Mr. Westfall or Mr. Jameson, he would get angry and scream his demands at them repeatedly," Mrs. Barnette said. "But when he talked to Dr. Marcetti he was just like a little boy who was ashamed of himself." McDonald said Cable kept repeating, "Yeah, I know, Doc. They ain't harmed me. Yeah, I know, Doc. But I gotta do it." "I think my hopes finally began to rise when I heard him talking to the doctor," McDonald said. "Before that I was just plain scared I'd never see sundown."
Non-narrative details	Dr. Marcetti said he talked to Cable four times, for a total of 45 minutes, before Cable agreed to release the hostages and give himself up.
Narrative	Westfall said Cable "agreed to send Mrs. Barnette and McDonald out with his gun, if we would agree to take him out the back way and not parade him in front of spectators who had gathered in the area."
Non-narrative details	Mrs. Barnette and McDonald were released about 3:45 p.m. McDonald handed Cable's gun to Westfall. Cable waited inside the office for Westfall and Dr. Marcetti. He was led down a flight of stairs and out a rear door to a waiting FBI car. Cable will be arraigned before U.S. Magistrate Carlos Wilson today. (Personal details about Cable follow.)

The chronological order in the body of the story is a popular form for many types of stories—accidents, fires, crimes, debates, trials, sports, even weddings. Most of these stories have strong narrative elements such as fast-moving action that lend themselves to being told in chronological order after the lead has summarized the major news elements.

Use of the chronological order does not relieve the reporter of the responsibility for adequate summarizations in the lead and throughout the story when they are appropriate. Care must be taken to avoid jumping into telling the story chronologically too quickly. Sometimes only one paragraph of summary is needed, sometimes more than one. A story written in chronological order may be either a single-feature or a several-feature story.

FIGURE 9.1   The death of England's Princess Diana in an automobile accident and her state funeral challenged writers to use their best descriptive powers. This front page from the *Sunday Sun–Sentinel* in Ft. Lauderdale, Fla., demonstrates how effectively a newspaper can handle the death of two major world figures at the same time.

(Reprinted with permission of *Sunday Sun–Sentinel*, Ft. Lauderdale, Fla.)

Direct Quotations

To overcome the problem of monotony in the body of the story, the reporter should use well-attributed indirect and direct quotations. The story should not be simply a series of direct quotations, just as it should not be wholly indirect quotations or summary statements. A "happy medium" is most effective.

Direct quotations aid a story if they are used carefully. Woven in between indirect quotations and summary statements, they breathe life into a story while helping to emphasize certain points. They also add authority to the story. Readers believe direct quotes. They often are skeptical of material summarized by the reporter. Direct quotations also help make the story look more attractive because they break up long blocks of type.

Some editors frown on a lead that begins with a direct quotation. This is largely a matter of personal choice. Direct quote leads work best if the quote is short and interesting. Unfortunately, too many reporters start stories with very long and very dull quotes. In most cases, a weak summary lead is better than a poor direct-quotation lead.

Most editors prefer that the reporter keep the quote to a single paragraph. However, an exceptional quote may be worthy of several consecutive paragraphs.

Transitional Devices

A news story must have unity, and to achieve it the reporter has to weave together the various parts of the story by using connective words and phrases. Unless the sentences within a paragraph or the paragraphs within a story are obviously related, the reporter must indicate their relationship. Sometimes such common connectives or transitions as "also," "on the other hand" or "meanwhile" may be sufficient. But in many cases the transition must be clarified by reference to the material that preceded it. In the previous example of combined development (page 150) the reporter needed to connect the material in the first three paragraphs with what was to follow, so this line was used:

In recommending a civilian board, the report said it is needed . . .

The transition refers to "Creation of a nonpolitical Civilian Review Board . . ." It is essential to clarify the relationship of the two parts of the story.

In making a transition, the reporter should avoid the verbatim repetition of previous wording in the story. The transition should be as short as possible.

Transitional words or phrases provide a minor problem for copy editors who may want to change the order of paragraphs in a story during the editing process. A paragraph cannot be shifted without editing if a transitional phrase directly connects it with a paragraph that precedes or follows it. That is why reporters should keep the transitional words and phrases as short as possible.

Clutter

Every reporter is faced with the question: How much detail should be included in a story? Some reporters never like to waste a fact. If it is in the notes, it will be in the story whether it adds anything or not. Others seem to horde the facts and don't include enough of them to make a complete story. They leave the reader wondering. The problem of how much detail to include is a real one because newspaper style calls for generally shorter stories, and news space in any edition is limited. There is no general rule to guide a reporter on what to put in and what to leave out. But once a story is completed, the reporter should read it over carefully and ask: "What have I left out that needs to be in here?" and "What have I included that really doesn't serve any useful purpose, no matter how interesting it may be?"

Complete Reporting

Quantity is not the object in a news story. Quality is. The effectiveness of the body of the story doesn't depend on how much is included but on what is included. Details alone do not make for good reading. Every reporter should be something of a human vacuum cleaner, sucking up every tidbit of information available about a news event or individual. But he or she doesn't have to dump all of that into the story as if emptying the dust bag. Reporters have to be selective. They have to use only those facts that are needed to make the story complete and understandable.

Complete reporting requires that a reporter develop the skills of a researcher. Reporters have to know how to gather facts. The best writers on a newspaper cannot produce a clear, crisp, informative news story if there are no facts to work with.

EXERCISES

1. Using a recent edition of the annual anthology, *Best Newspaper Writing for* [year], published by the Poynter Institute of Media Studies, St. Petersburg, Fla., analyze the organization of one of the stories reprinted in that collection. Be prepared to discuss the story in class.

2. Invite a by-lined reporter from your local newspaper to class to discuss reporting and writing techniques. Ask him or her to bring several examples of stories that required a great deal of fact gathering and analyze them for the class.

3. Using the following notes, write a story illustrating the single-feature story form:
   Christians Against Smut
   On the Internet
   Meeting in Fellowship Hall
   Of Bellbuckle Interfaith Church

Passed a Resolution
Demanding computers in
The Sunbright City Library
Be restricted to adults only
And that librarians monitor
What adults are viewing
"I don't want my tax money
Going for providing pornography,"
Said Mrs. Mary Edith Ricks
One of the founders of
The group which claims
It has 1,000 members
"If they want to poison their
Minds with filth let them
Buy their own computers,"
she told the audience and
Received a sustained cheer
When one person in the audience
Raised the question of
First Amendment rights
He was shouted down
Mrs. Ricks was asked
To deliver copies
Of the resolution to
All members of the City Council
All members of the Library Board
And the head librarian
She urged members of the group
"To show up at City Council and
Library board meetings to show
We mean business"

4. Add the following notes to those in Exercise 3 and write a story illustrating the several-feature summary story form:

At Mrs. Rick's recommendation
The group agreed to hire
"A Constitutional lawyer
To combat any legal efforts
Those fuzzy-headed liberals
Will try in an effort to
Thwart our will to protect
Our children from filth and
To stop wasting taxpayers'
Money on pornography."
Group agreed to seek donations
From other concerned citizens
To help pay legal fees
And it deputized Mrs. Ricks
To seek help from national

Christian Right organizations
"In our battle for the very
Soul of our community,"
Mrs. Ricks said.

5. Adding the following notes to those in Exercises 3 and 4, write a story illustrating
   the first outstanding-feature story form:
   Group also agreed to
   Organize library patrols
   To make daily checks
   Of computers at the
   Main library and all branches
   To determine how often
   They are being used
   To view pornographic material
   "We have to prove that libraries
   Are becoming cesspools of filth
   And degradation and that
   We are paying for it," Mrs. Ricks said
   More than 100 members
   Of the audience signed up
   To be library watchdogs
   "You can't trust librarians,"
   Mrs. Ricks said
   "They believe you have a right
   To see anything you want
   No matter how deviant
   Or how disgusting it is
   They really are into this
   Freedom of Speech thing
   Not that I'm against it
   You understand."

6. Adding the next set of notes to those in Exercises 3 and 5, write a story illustrating
   the second-feature story form:
   Group also agreed
   To organize a committee
   To lobby the state's
   Congressional delegation
   To support federal legislation
   Outlawing pornography
   On the Internet
   When one person in the audience
   Pointed out that the
   U.S. Supreme Court had
   Already declared a
   Similar law unconstitutional
   Mrs. Ricks replied
   "Well, we will just have to

Force Congress to keep trying
Until it passes
A law that is"
She recommended that the group
Enlist the aid of
Dr. Jack Haskins
Professor of Sociology at
State University to provide
Evidence on the effects of
Pornography on the Internet
On Adolescents and Young Adults
He is a specialist in deviant behavior

7. Using notes in Exercises 3, 4 and 6, write a story illustrating the combined from described earlier in this chapter.

8. The multiple-casualty story is commonplace in most newspapers. Using that form described earlier in this chapter, write a story from the following notes:

Three members of a family
Killed in crash on Interstate 75
City fireman critically injured
Dead are Robert C. West, 35
His wife, Betty Lou, 32
Their son, Craig, 5
Injured fireman is
Philip Wilson, 38, from
Engine House 98
State Trooper Javonna Blake
Said West's 1996 Dodge pickup
Slammed into the rear of
A City Fire Department van
Driven by Wilson who had stopped
To help a woman fix a flat tire
Family members killed instantly
Wilson flown by helicopter
To University Medical Center
He is listed in critical condition
With head injures and
A broken collarbone
The wreck occurred about 4 p.m.
In westbound lane of I-75
Between Fessler Land and
The Hermitage Avenue exit
Traffic blocked more than
And hour and a half
Rescue workers had to
Use axes to cut open the
Pickup's roof and removed
The bodies of the family

State police said a
Woman pulled her Cadillac
Next to the concrete median
When her right front tire blew out
Wilson stopped the
Fire Department van to help
Blocked off traffic on
The inside lane and switched on
Blue Lights to alert drivers
He had been there about
Five minutes when West's
Pickup slammed into the
Back of the van
The impact knocked
Wilson about 50 feet
Slamming him against
The concrete medium
State troopers said
Other drivers have
Driven around the van
They have no explanation
Why West's truck
Hit the van
West owned a dairy farm
About 10 miles out of Madison

(Source: State Trooper Blake)

9. Write a story using the chronological order from the following notes:
Woman called 911 about 11:20 a.m.

Requested help for daughter
Said she couldn't breathe
Paramedics and fire rescue team
Responded to the call
Woman lived in upstairs
Apartment at 900 N.E. 170th St.
First team of paramedics
Realized they couldn't move her
She weighed between
650 and 800 pounds
They called for help
Eventually 20 rescue workers
Were on the scene
They had to remove
Apartment window
Three sheets of plywood
Strapped to bucket of
Fire department ladder truck
Firemen slid woman on mattress

Through window and on to
The wooden platform
It was lowered to waiting
Flatbed tow truck
Loaned by Midtown Towing
Police stopped traffic on
167th Street while makeshift
Ambulance transported her
To Northside Hospital
Emergency room staff treated
Her for one hour
In the parking lot
Before a stretcher
Strong enough to support her
Arrived from Memorial Hospital
During that time
Her breathing stopped
But was restored in minutes
Oxygen tanks and other
Emergency equipment
Moved to parking lot
To treat her while
Waiting for the stretcher
Moved inside and was
Receiving additional treatment
Doctors would not say
What caused her breathing problem
The hospital and police
Refused to identify her

(Sources: Police Sgt. Venetta Coffey, Fire Lt. Roman Begatta)

10. Write a story based on each of the following sets of notes. In each case, explain at the end of your story your choice of lead and story form:

a. Sunnyland Police Chief
   Arthur Schwartz and
   His wife, Jennie,
   Arrived at home
   About 11 p.m. from
   A City Symphony concert
   He noticed neighbor's garage
   Was standing open
   When he went to investigate
   Three masked gunmen
   Stepped from shadows
   Pointed a gun at his head
   Demanded his money
   He handed wallet and
   His cellular phone
   Ordered to lie on ground

He refused when one gunman
Started to approach his wife
He started to reach for
His gun in his pocket
And the gunman fled
Next day three men arrested
During invasion at
A nearby home
One still had Schwartz wallet
Michael Henderson, 19,
Doug Crowell, 21, and
Sam Lakeland, 20, charged
With armed robbery

(Sources: Schwartz, Det. John Bailey)

b. State Representative Vic Vance
Introduced bill calling for
Higher pay for jurors
"I don't think $10
A day is enough," he said.
He pointed out it was a
"Civic duty" but also
"A tremendous burden"
He said many self-employed
Individuals are called
To jury duty and lose
"That day's salary"
Jurors in state court
Get $10 a day and $1
For parking although
Parking costs at least
$4 a day near the courthouse
Vance noted that jurors in
Federal court receive
$40 a day, parking, and mileage
"It's disheartening to people
To think their services are worth
Only $10 a day," Vance said

c. Maria Montez, 32, filed suit
In Superior Court
Challenging the will
Of Sidney Quevedo
Her companion of 10 years
He made millions
Manufacturing bathroom fixtures
When he died at age 60
He left his home and
Most of his $5 million estate

To his beloved dog
Samantha, a cocker spaniel
He left Ms. Montez
$60,000 a year as long as
She took care of the dog
When the dog dies
The house and money
Go to charity
She is seeking $2.7 million
Of the $5 million estate
"I gave him the best
Years of my life," she said.

CHAPTER

10 Features and Human-Interest Stories

"Journalists have forgotten why people read, and I think people read because they want to feel something," Thomas Hallman Jr. of the Portland *Oregonian* said after winning the American Society of Newspaper Editors Distinguished Writing Award for non-deadline writing.

"I am an emotional writer, and I want to make my readers feel the same emotions I feel," he said.

Dozens of readership studies show that Hallman is right on target. Readers say they want to know how it feels to be held captive by a gunman for six hours. They wonder what goes on in the mind of a mother who has just lost a son to AIDS. They are eager to share the rush of excitement with the housewife who has just won $50 million in a state lottery.

Details, numbers, statistics are important. But more than that, the reader wants to be right there—to feel, to share the whole mosaic of human emotions. The reader wants the drama and excitement, the joy and despair. Those emotions are the real story to the reader.

Carefully reported and well-written feature and human-interest stories will provide those emotions for the reader. Good feature writing is simply good storytelling. And good storytelling, says Rene (Jack) Cappon, a long-time editor and writing coach for the Associated Press (AP), "thrives on color, nuance, wit, fancy, emotive words, dialogue and character."

A good feature engages the reader emotionally. Here is the lead from an award-winning feature about the return to society of a five-year-old girl who had been burned beyond recognition. The emotionally charged story was written by Julie Klein of the *Albuquerque Tribune:*

> Denise Volkman cradled a daughter she didn't recognize and carried her through a house she didn't know.
>
> She wrapped the tiny naked frame in a towel, and the two of them sat in front of a full-length mirror. It would be the first time her daughter would see herself since the fire.
>
> The mirror reflected an incomplete face. "You're looking great, Sage," Denise told her 5-year-old daughter. "When I first saw you, you looked like a pumpkin." She hesitated. "You know, you don't have a nose."

"Yeah, I guess you're right. I don't have a nose," said Sage, studying her face in the mirror. "I don't have an ear either. Oh well."

Denise opened the towel. Sage's missing body parts could have composed a shopping list. A nose, a left ear, both eyelids, all her fingers. The fire that exploded the family camper also melted the skin on her face, chest, arms and legs.

While the word "feature" has many meanings in the lexicon of reporters, in this chapter it is applied to a story that is based wholly on human interest—the story that does not quite conform to the rigid standards of hard news.

At the heart of a feature or human-interest story are facts representing solid reporting techniques, just as in a straight news story. But the stories differ in style. The news story is timely and written in a straightforward, concise, unemotional style. The feature, on the other hand, may not be particularly timely (though it could be), and it is marked by a blending of imaginative and creative use of the language that can touch readers' curiosity, amaze them, arouse their skepticism, or make them laugh or cry. To complicate matters, in the relationship between features and straight news is the fact that it is a rare reporter who can handle human-interest or feature stories well until he or she knows how to write a compact, coherent, straight news story that is packed with names, facts and details.

Here's an example of a hard news event given feature treatment. It was written by Toni Lepeska of the *Commercial Appeal*, Memphis:

> She wasn't about to leave her 1-year-old son at the mercy of a man with a gun.
>
> Elena Jenkins, 27, refused to relinquish the keys to her moss-green 1995 Jeep Cherokee until she could unstrap her son from a child's seat in back.
>
> "I guess my attitude was, `You're going to have to kill me if you're going to take the car with my baby inside,' " she said Monday.
>
> She had just backed into a parking spot Sunday afternoon in front of the Wal-Mart in the 6900 block of East Shelby in the country.
>
> "I just opened the door and he was right on top of me," she said. "He put the gun to my stomach—and I'm five months pregnant."
>
> The man had the gun hidden under his clothing, but Jenkins saw the barrel sticking out at her.
>
> She told him he wasn't getting the keys or car until she got the baby out.
>
> The Jeep was still missing Monday.

Not all feature stories have to be long to grab the readers attention as this one shows.

Human-Interest Stories

One writer summed it up accurately when he said that there is no sharp line of division that runs between straight news and human-interest stories any more than there is an abrupt line between the colors of the rainbow. One hue may shade into the total rainbow and be lost to view, just as certain elements of a story that might make it a feature (or straight news) can be lost from the view of a not-too-perceptive writer. Frequently the straight news account contains strong feature elements, whereas the human-interest story may owe its very existence to a news event and in such cases has to be printed along with the news story or lose its impact. But it should be obvious that as the human-interest values are increased—as the dramatic, emotional and human background materials of the story are played up—they will become, at some point, more important than the news incident itself. When this point is reached, the story becomes primarily a human-interest (feature) story rather than a straight news story.

Consider the lead in this dramatic story by Charles Bowden of the *Tucson Citizen* about the plight of illegal aliens from Mexico and Central America trying to cross the western Arizona desert to seek entry into the United States:

> TACNA—They play a game but there are no spectators.
> The players are called wets by those who hunt them. They cross one of the hottest, most deadly deserts in North America with a gallon of water. They are looking for work. The walk is 30, 40, 50, 60 miles.
> Here are the rules:
> Get caught and you go back to Mexico.
> Make it and you get a job in the fields or the backroom.
> Don't make it and you die.
> Each month during the summer, about 250 people try the game in this section of western Arizona, a 3,600-square-mile stretch that lies roughly between Yuma and the Maricopa County line.
> Half get caught—mainly because the heat and thirst and miles grind them down. . . .
> Some die.
> Nobody pays much attention to this summer sport.

The remainder of the story details the writer's own trek across the relentless desert describing just how it feels to walk some 30 miles in the searing heat with little water.

The writer used his powers of observation and his command of the language to describe just what the illegal aliens experienced in their desperate effort to slip into the United States. Hundreds of stories have been written about the plight of illegal aliens, so the news value of the story was not great. What made it so special was that the writer, through his own experience, was able to take the readers right into the desert and let them share the painful journey with the aliens.

Any given incident or situation can be handled within the following degrees of human-interest appeal:

1. As straight news with little or no human interest
2. As straight news plus some or much human-interest treatment
3. As human interest with little or no hard-news value

Although there is a tendency now, probably as a result of competition from television, to give hard-news stories the feature treatment, the incident itself, if properly evaluated, will usually determine what treatment it deserves. In general, human-interest treatment of the kind listed as item 3 is selected for those incidents that have slight or nonexistent news value or values but that suggest a rich background of human interest. The human-interest treatment is applied to numerous stories every day that might not otherwise be reported. They have become an important part of what every newspaper offers its subscribers daily because of the broad appeal that human-interest stories have for readers. In this sense the human-interest story is considered as a separate story type, and it is one form of the more general feature stories.

In this example, Leon Alligood of the *Nashville Banner* examines the life of a young quadriplegic who was paralyzed by a stranger's gunfire four years earlier. It was the first in a series on the young man's efforts to forge a new life:

> Outside his window, the seasons were on the cusp of change. Winter's gray bleakness was yielding to spring's riot of colors, and Michael Dixon was ever so thankful.
>
> Soon he would go outside, Michael thought to himself. Just do nothing but sit in the sun and feel its warmth envelop him like a mother's hug.
>
> He would ask Shirley, his sister, to take him to the grassy area behind his apartment complex and just let him sit there, mild breezes washing across his face.
>
> For now, until the new season firmly established itself, his view remained limited to the small, one-windowed room of his townhouse apartment. It was a view he knew all too well, because it was the only view he had.

The remainder of the story described the small apartment and detailed how the three hollow-point bullets from the deranged stranger's 9-mm Lugar splintered Michael's spinal cord, leaving him a quadriplegic unable to shave himself, brush his teeth, scratch his nose, or even breathe without help. Subsequent stories describe how he has adjusted to his new life and the impact it has had on his family.

In the typical newspaper office both the human-interest story and the feature article are loosely termed "features" or "feature stories." (Some other newspaper features include columns, cartoons, comic strips and virtually all materials other than advertisements and editorials.) The story could also be a news feature, sometimes called a "sidebar," that depends on a timely news event for its peg. For example, the reaction of the survivors of an airplane crash might be printed beside the main story about the accident. Other examples include color story, such as a description of the crowd the night before the Kentucky Derby or Indianapolis 500; an interpretative piece on the impact of the new tax hike passed by Congress; or an informational piece on the new industries in the city.

Whatever the terminology, the human-interest story and the feature article are usually distinct and distinguishable in form, content and purpose. The former is usually a dramatic story proposing to touch the readers' emotions in some way.

The latter is usually an expository article, such as the kind used by magazines, and its major purpose is to inform.

Sources of Features

Today's straight news stories on the appointment of a new cabinet officer, the fire-bombing of a public building or the signing of a contract for construction of a new library could be tomorrow's feature presenting a personality sketch of the new official; the history of revolutionary activity in the nation; or the growth in book publishing, the use of libraries or the entire library system of a city. Much feature material is related to the news, as pointed out earlier, and many newspapers, as a result of television and radio's ability to "get there first," are turning more and more to feature treatment of the news. But giving news the feature treatment takes time and an inclination to do the necessary research.

Of the regular sources, the police beat yields a wealth of tragedy, humor and pathos from which many features may be developed. The most important news stories—murders, airplane crashes, spectacular fires, space shots and hundreds of others—can be highlighted and sidelighted by features: the murderer's life story or the impact of a murder on the victim's family; an eyewitness account of the crash; heroic rescues by firemen; life aboard a spacecraft.

Much of the content of material in magazines or documentaries on television is feature material suggested by the news. In most cases the reporter has to do little research beyond going to regular news sources to develop features. A reporter must be willing to take the time to dig deeper and to be curious enough to ask questions that go far beyond the obvious.

Many features are developed independently of the news, however. The following general classifications of situations and incidents suggest the varied fields in which features may be found:

1. *The unusual.* Oddities, freaks, coincidences, unusual personalities.

2. *The usual.* Familiar persons, places, things, landmarks. For example, the handicapped young man who sells newspapers outside city hall, the street-corner minister. The feature writer evokes the reader's "I've always wanted to know about that" response.

3. *Dramatic situations.* Sudden riches, the prize winner, the abandoned baby, the heroic rescue or nerve-shattering peril, hard luck, animal heroes, the underdog.

4. *Guidance.* Advice to the troubled, recipes, health, etiquette, stamp collecting, flower arranging, woodcraft, advice on how to vote and a host of others.

5. *Information.* Statistics, studies, records, historical sketches, analogies, comparisons and contrasts of then and now, biographies.

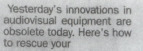

FIGURE 10.1 To help its readers deal with the advances in technology and how it influences their lives, the San Louis Obispo County *Tribune* began devoting a full page of news and feature stories and columns to the subject under the title *Personal Tech*. (Reprinted with permission of the *Tribune*, San Louis Obispo, California.)

Writing Feature Articles

No standard form or style is used for feature articles. They follow no set rules for leads or for the body or end of the story as news stories generally do. Some conform to the straight-news style with a five W's summary lead, but use of the novelty lead (see Chapter 8) is more common. Feature articles may be narrative, descriptive or expository. They tell stories, paint pictures, explain conditions—but are fact, not fiction. Features may differ radically from news stories in style of writing and arrangement of material, but the incidents, facts and persons involved are real, not created. The feature article is generally designed to convey information and not, as in the case of the human-interest story, to dramatize events for the sake of an emotional impact on the reader.

Because the feature article cannot rely on news values for reader appeal, it must deal with otherwise interesting and vital subject matter. The feature story must be written with a flair for words that will turn a somewhat pedestrian topic into an interesting story with high reader appeal. In brief, the chief rule in writing features is "make them interesting from beginning to end."

Features can be used to provide the reader with a variety of information. Laura Bly of *USA TODAY* brought readers up-to-date on the outlet shopping mall craze that has changed retailing in the United States with this feature that focused on the granddaddy of all outlet-catalog stores—L.L. Bean:

> FREEPORT, Maine—In the beginning, there was Bean's—a folksy backwoods emporium devoted to hunters, anglers and flannel-swathed New England college students.
>
> But 81 years after Leon Leonwood Bean opened his doors, this village that surrounds his flagship has embraced L.L.'s entrepreneurial mission with a vengeance.
>
> Today, some 140 outlet stores and specialty shops lure 4 million visitors a year, outstripping Acadia National Park as the state's top attraction and transforming manicured flower-strewn Freeport (pop. 7,000) into a Visa-toting browser's version of *The Truman Show*.
>
> Freeport isn't the only destination that has discovered discounts can be a major tourist draw. According to a Travel Industry Association of America poll, nearly 40 percent of business and vacation travelers journeyed more than 100 miles from home to visit one of the country's 300-plus outlet malls last year.

The story goes on to list some of the super outlet malls and interviews with shoppers who describe their savings made by purchasing at an outlet mall. It also included two sidebar stories, quoting *Consumer Reports* magazine's tip for smart shopping as well as a comparison chart showing savings on eight items from shirts to speaker systems when they were purchased at an outlet mall.

Writers often use a descriptive lead. In the following story, AP reporter Jay Reeves leads the reader into his story by describing the scene at an unusual mission in Alabama:

> STERRETT, Ala.—A bell tolls across a serene alley and dozens of people emerge from the shade of the woods, all walking across a pasture graced with wildflowers.

Rosaries in hand, they kneel before a concrete statue of the Virgin Mary. Everyone, young and old, seems oblivious to the blazing summer sun. Their words flow like water from a spring.

"Hail Mary, full of grace," the group prays as one, "the Lord is with thee . . ."

Thousands have been drawn to this field since 1988, when a Yugoslavian visionary came to Alabama and said she saw Jesus' mother there, near a towering pine tree.

Out of that event bloomed Caritas of Birmingham, a multimillion–dollar Roman Catholic mission, where families live apart from the world. Caritas is also a religious publisher and has a travel arm, arranging charter trips to the site of a vision in Bosnia.

Under the direction of founder Terry Colafrancesco, Caritas has quietly become one of the nations's largest organizations promoting devotion to Mary. Its name means "love" or "charity" in Latin.

There are no televisions at the mission, no newspapers. The day begins at 5 a.m. And the 60 or so residents pray as a group five times a day.

Children ride bicycles and play on the 150-acre compound, the oldest ones watching the younger ones while their parents work. The youngsters attend a one-room school on the grounds, about 20 miles southeast of Birmingham.

The remainder of the story describes life at the compound through interviews with the women and men who have given up their worldly life to become a part of this unusual mission.

Here is an example of how Wells Twombly used description to set the scene for his personality piece on baseball's great Cookie Lavagetto:

The autumn days slip past in silent splendor with no tongues of their own to tell you the story of old men who once were young heroes so very long ago.

Hairlines retreat and then surrender. Stomachs push forward and collapse entirely. All that remains are misty memories and newspaper clippings turned to soft powder in crypt-cold library files.

Some athletes litter the record book with their accomplishments. They own a hundred-agate line of dry statistics. A few explode for one glorious moment and then disappear into oblivion.

Harry (Cookie) Lavagetto, whose father was a trash collector, whose mother immigrated from Genoa, is the sole owner of one precious moment in history. Always it will belong to him. It cannot be bartered, sold or bequeathed.

It is Oct. 4, 1947 and the New York Yankees are playing the Brooklyn Dodgers in the fourth game of the World Series. . .

The similarity of feature articles and magazine articles has been pointed out, as has the writer's freedom in selecting the form used in composing the story. Although the reporter may abandon the regular news story organization and apply a narrative or expository form in feature articles, he or she is bound by other general rules of news writing: using short paragraphs, observing the newspaper's style, avoiding monotony in the use of direct quotations and unquoted summary, using transitional phrases to bridge paragraphs and achieve smooth reading, and so on.

The logical order is used to the extent that the reporter attempts to hold the reader by introducing new features and details in the order of interest or by an interesting narrative. But the general rule of logical order, which permits cutting a story from the end, may be ignored, as it is in the surprise-climax story form (illustrated later in this chapter). Many if not most feature articles end with a summary or conclusion, a characteristic of expository writing. This style of writing makes editing a feature story to cut its length a painstaking task.

Writing Human-Interest Stories

Because most human-interest stories are designed to evoke a certain response in the reader, they must rely heavily on the human background of the event, not just the plain, unvarnished facts. Even where a newsworthy event is lacking, there exist here and there predicaments and entanglements of human beings—stresses and strains and dramatic situations with which the human-interest story weaves its patterns. The thoughts, emotions, ambitions—the varied psychological and social data of humanity—are all part of the human background so essential to this type of story. They help dramatize the person, place or thing and create an emotional response in the reader.

Saul Pett, one of the AP's top feature writers for many years, put it this way:

We can no longer give the reader the fast brush. We can no longer whiz through the files for 20 minutes, grab a cab, spend 30 minutes interviewing our subject, come back to the office, concoct a clever lead that goes nowhere, drag in 15 or 20 more paragraphs like tired sausage, sprinkle them with four quotes, pepper them with 14 scintillating adjectives, all synonyms, and then draw back and call that an incisive portrait of a human being.

Today the reader wants more . . . he wants to be drawn by substance. He wants meat on his bones and leaves on his trees. He wants dimension and depth and perspective and completeness and insight and, of course, honesty.

After 500 or 1,500 or 2,500 words, the reader wants to know more about a man's personality than that he is "mild-mannered" or "quiet" or "unassuming" . . . Willie Sutton, the bank robber, was mild-mannered, quiet, unassuming. So was Dr. Albert Schweitzer.

How can you write about a man without knowing what others have written about him? How can you write about a man without knowing what others think and know of him? How can you write about a man without interviewing him at great length and in great detail and in such a way that he begins to reveal something of himself? How can you interview him that way without planning a good part of your questioning beforehand?

How, when you've collected all you're going to collect, how can you write about a man without thinking long and hard about what you're learned? How can you write about a man without writing about the man, not merely grabbing one thin angle simply because it makes a socko anecdotal lead and leaves the essence a vague blur?

How can you write about a man simply by telling me what he says without telling me how he says it? How can you write about a man simply by telling me what he is without telling me what he is like or what he'd like to be? How can you write about a man without telling me what he is afraid of, what he wishes he could do over again, what pleases him most, what pleases him least, what illusions were broken, what vague yearning remains? How can you write about a successful man without telling me his failures or about any man without somehow indicating his own view of himself?

Give me the extraordinary and give me the ordinary. Does the richest man in the world have everything he wants? Does he bother to look at the prices on a menu at all? That strange, remote, isolated little village way up in the Canadian bush. Don't just tell me about the polar bear and the deer. Tell me, buster, how do they get a suit cleaned there?

Tell me the large by telling me the small. Tell me the small by telling me the large. Identify with me, plug into my circuit, come in loud and clear . . . don't give me high-sounding abstractions. . . .

Don't tease me unless you can deliver, baby. Don't tell me the situation was dramatic and expect me to take your word for it. Show me how it was dramatic and I'll supply the adjectives. You say this character is unpredictable? When, where, how? Give me the evidence, not just the chapter headings.

Pett's comments help point out an important difference between the art of human-interest writing and the art of writing a play, novel or short story, although the purpose and materials of the reporter are much the same as those of other writers. The reporter must present life as it is; the dramatist may present it as it ought to be. In the similarity and difference between the two forms of writing, a few principles guiding the reporter may be found.

The temptation of the reporter is to improve on reality in order to make a better story. Pett's warning that the reader wants honesty should be ingrained in every human-interest writer's mind. Of course, the writer has some leeway, but it is not easy to define. He or she is justified in some rearrangement of events as long as the essential truth of the story is presented. But a writer certainly should not distort for dramatic effect. He or she should not force a quote on his or her subject any more than make up a quote out of whole cloth and put it in the subject's mouth. A writer who repeatedly asks a striking miner, "You suffered greatly after the mines closed down, did you not?" to get the striker to repeat the phrase in those words is presenting a false picture.

The reporter also may be tempted to adopt emotionalized language to achieve an emotional impact. To do so, however, is to defeat the purpose. The drama and its impact must be inherent in the facts of the story. Simple language is the best medium for transmitting those facts to the reader. Ernie Pyle's famous story on Captain Waskow, which was reprinted in a collection of his war dispatches under the title of *Brave Men*, is an excellent example of how a writer can achieve dramatic impact through the use of simple language.

The human-interest story takes no standard form. Almost any of the rhetorical devices and suspended-interest forms may be appropriate. A novelty lead with the body in logical order is a popular form. The summary lead with the body in chronological order is often used. Animal stories are extremely popular features. Here are two examples:

DUNSMUIR, Cal. (AP)—They call him Rudy the bungling Beagle. In his five years, he's been to the veterinarian 12 times. His master, Francis Lamere Jr., says Rudy is a good hunting dog but:

Once he leaped high as ducks flew over and caught part of the blast from Lamere's shot gun.

Another time, while tethered to a pickup truck on a hunting trip, Rudy jumped or fell off and ran the pads off his feet trying to keep up.

He has broken his tail twice, once falling off an ironing board on which he was sleeping.

He's been shot twice and caught once in a trap. He had eye surgery after one fight. Another fight cost him 28 stitches in one leg. He's had an emergency tonsillectomy and intravenous feeding for distemper.

Rudy now is recovering from an abdominal operation. He ate too much of a too-long-dead squirrel.

"We keep him for two reasons," says Mrs. Lamere.

"We love him—and he represents quite an investment."

DAWN, Va.—Snorts, grunts and squeals from the hog pen: How sweet it is to a Virginia Commonwealth University professor who electronically transforms hog small talk into music.

"I think it is important that we humans try to go to the stars, but I think it is important, too, that we try to know more about the other species with which we share this planet," says Loran Carrier.

He says he sees his work as aiding the understanding of communications between species.

The essence of the oinks he's recording from up to 40 hogs is going into a musical collection called "Swine Lake." Already on tape, scrambled, dissected and elongated, are "High on the Hog," "Thou Swill," "Road-hog," "Swine Song," "Scaredly Pig," "Overalls" and "Porkchop Sticks."

"I hope to make an LP someday," says Carrier, who holds a doctorate in music and is on sabbatical from VCU while he studies Greek and Latin at Hampden-Sydney College.

"This hog study," as he calls it, began last spring when he started taking a tape recorder into the hog pen at his six-acre Caroline County farm. But its roots lie in his childhood more than 40 years ago on a farm in northern Montana.

The remainder of the story tells how he grew up on a farm and went to a prep school in the East and taught at VCU for 14 years. It also explains how he transformed the hog sounds into music and tells of his remorse when the hogs he has recorded are shipped to market.

Surprise Climax Form

Still another form often used for human-interest stories is called the surprise climax, or "O. Henry ending." This example was written by Eldon Barrett of United Press International (UPI):

The Diagram	*The Written Story*
Narrative of details	SEATTLE, Wash.—Based on a premise expounded by a psychiatrist, Seattle has just gone through one of the glummest summers on record. It hardly rained at all.

The Written Story

SEATTLE, Wash.—Based on a premise expounded by a psychiatrist, Seattle has just gone through one of the glummest summers on record. It hardly rained at all.

Dr. S. Harvard Kaufman, a resident for 28 years, is convinced that nice weather in Seattle makes most of its residents gloomy.

Why?

"Because they figure it's going to get worse," said Kaufman. "People carry around a lot of guilt. When they are happy, they wonder when the knife is going to fall.

"Good weather in Seattle activates a deep-seated sense of guilt in most of the residents.

"From birth they are taught that the weather here is rainy," he said. "They also are taught that because of this the air is clear and the grass is green."

The fact is, there is less annual rainfall in Seattle than in New York, Philadelphia, Washington, Trenton, N.J., and Atlanta, Ga.

But the myth persists that Seattle is the sponge of the United States and Seattleites visiting elsewhere have found it usually expedient to let the legend linger on.

"We are not exactly promoting rain," said Bill Sears, publicist for the Seattle-King County Convention and Visitors Bureau. "But we are promoting its by-products—fresh air, cleanliness and greenery!

"If we can't scrub out the legend that Seattle is in a constant deluge, we might as well put the myth to work," Sears said.

As he spoke, the first downpour of fall was bathing the region, where the worst drought in 33 years had turned the evergreen state into a dusty brown.

And peering out from under umbrellas and foul weather hats were the smiling faces of passersby, obviously delighted that the ordeal of the long, pleasant summer was over.

Surprise Climax

The object of the surprise climax technique is to hold the reader's attention for an O. Henry type of story ending—a climax with a twist. No rules regarding the logical order or the five W's lead apply here; on the contrary, the story builds up as it continues. But the beginning must have an element of suspended interest to attract readers, and its narrative qualities must be strong enough to hold readers to the end.

Many newspapers use the feature story to tell the readers of very dramatic human events. One of the truly outstanding uses of this approach was made by Steve Sternberg to tell about the life and death of a young man from Atlanta who suffered from AIDS. The *Atlanta Journal and Constitution* devoted a 16-page special section to Sternberg's stories and the photographs taken by Michael A. Schwarz. Here is the beginning of Sternberg's story:

Tom Fox sat up as best he could and put his arms up for his mother's kiss. They kissed and hugged until he was exhausted and fell back weakly into the hospital bed.

"Are you afraid?" Mrs. Fox asked.

Tom shook his head. No.

"This is horrible," Mrs. Fox said outside her son's hospital room. "This is so horrible I can't believe it's happening." Inside, a chaplain was exhorting Tom to "go towards the light."

On this morning in July, family members were gathered in an intensive care hospital room in Eugene, Ore., to help Tom die. He had made the decision to go off the ventilator that forced pure oxygen into his AIDS-ravaged lungs. He knew he would never recover enough to go home to Atlanta, that even force-fed oxygen could not sustain him much longer.

"He's ready to see us all now," Robert Fox Sr. said to his two other sons, Bob Jr. and John.

It was 8:30 a.m. Tom was lying on his bed, wearing his glasses, his clipboard on his chest. With the oxygen tube threaded through his vocal cords, writing was the only way he could communicate. His skin was sallow.

The nurse was ready to start the morphine that would deaden the pain, minimize the struggle.

"It's going to be all right when they take the tube out of you," Doris Fox said to her son. "I'm going to give you the biggest hug you've had since you've been here. We're all going to give you hugs.

"I love you all very much, each one of you. You're all my favorite sons," she said to Bob Jr. "I love you," she said, hugging her husband. "We've done very well, haven't we?"

"Three wonderful sons," Bob Sr. said to his wife. He was crying openly, unashamedly, as the nurse busied herself with disconnecting Tom's heart monitor.

Tom appeared unruffled by the activity, and the unbridled grief. He asked for a cup of ice and, with difficulty, spooned some beneath the hose of the ventilator into his mouth.

Bob Jr. stood by the bed, stroking his brother's hair without looking at him. Eyes rimmed with red, he looked out the window at Spencer's Butte and the forest of fir trees outside the city.

"Do you need some relief, Bob?" Bob Sr. asked his son.

At 8:45, the doctor entered. He looked perfectly composed, powder-blue jacket, dark-blue tie, dark slacks. He unknotted the ribbon of tape holding the ventilator tube securely in Tom's nostril.

"Here we go, Tom," the doctor said.

He smoothly withdrew the corrugated ventilator tube.

For an instant, it appeared to be a relief. "He may be feeling fine for a while and can even talk to you," Dr. Matthew Purvis said.

"Handerkerchief," Tom said. He noisily blew his nose.

Doris, who was tearfully watching her son, broke her silence and laughed sympathetically for an instant. Over the past week Tom had asked repeatedly whether he could blow his nose.

"It must be a relief to blow your nose," his mother said.

"Beats that long catheter," the respiratory therapist said.

"It's a big 'un," Tom said. Then, "I can't breathe."

His chest heaved again and again, but weakly. He had no strength. "I can't breathe," he said again. It was as he had predicted all along: a fish out of water, no fight left in him.

"He's asleep," Doris Fox said, leaning over and stroking his forehead. "He's asleep now. I love you. I love you so much, son."

"Just relax and let it go. Slip on out, Tom, slip on out. We're all with you."

"He's letting go," his father said through his tears.

Tom gasped for breath. His eyes were open, but he could not speak.

"Good night, Tom," Bob Jr. said, his head thrown back, his mouth open, his voice a tortured sob.

"It's almost over," Dr. Purvis said.

"Almost there, Tom," Doris said.

The figure on the bed was motionless.

"It's over," she said.

It was 8:55. The dying had taken barely 10 minutes.

One by one, everyone passed by the head of the bed, kissing Tom on the forehead.

"I could never be so brave," John said.

"It's hard to leave him," Doris said. "I want to look at his lesions. He wouldn't let us look near the end."

She uncovered his legs. "They're like leather."

"So hard," his father said. "There'll be a cure someday."

"Not soon enough," Doris said.

The section included three other major stories by Sternberg about various aspects of Tom Fox's life and AIDS, along with nearly three dozen photographs by Schwarz. The section was the result of more than 1,000 hours the reporter and photographer spent with Fox during a 16-month period to chronicle the life of a person with AIDS.

The dramatic stories in that special section followed this advice offered at an American Press Institute seminar by Edith Hills Cooper of the *Atlanta Journal*:

For feature writing, there's only one rule: Be seductive.

EXERCISES

1. Select a prominent political leader, entertainer, artist, musician, or sports figure who currently is in the news. Using publications available to you, compare the profiles or personality pieces written about him or her in two daily newspapers and one major magazine. Write a brief report on which story you thought was the best written and tell why.

2. Using any newspaper available to you, select two hard-news stories you think would make good feature stories and tell why.

3. Select two major news stories from any newspaper available to you and rewrite them as feature stories.

4. Arrange to spend a night in a local hospital emergency room and write a feature story about it.

5. Volunteer to work for a day at the local animal shelter and write a feature story about it.

6. Select the most historic building in your city and write a feature story about it. Use reference material from the local libraries as well as the local historical society. Interview current occupants of the building who have been tenants the longest.

7. Interview the head of residence halls on your campus and write a feature story on what kind of "tenants" students are.

8. Arrange an interview with a prominent campus visitor—a nationally known concert performer, popular music performer or distinguished visiting speaker—and write a human-interest story based on the interview.

9. Interview the director of the local 911 emergency service and write a feature story based on the interview.

10. Interview 8 to 10 students about their use of the Internet and write a feature story on those interviews.

11. Alumni often leave their alma mater rare or unusual gifts. Interview the head of your college or university's alumni affairs office about the unusual gifts that have been received. Write a feature story based on that interview.

12. Select a little-known historical site in the city where your college or university is located and write a descriptive feature story about it. Use reference material, such as local histories and tourists guidebooks, to help you find such a site.

13. Write a story based on the following information collected from Jeremy Bangs, director of Leiden's American Pilgrim Museum. The museum is in New York City.

    What most Americans know is the Pilgrims, fleeing religious persecution in England, sailed off on the *Mayflower* and founded a colony at Plymouth, Mass., in 1620, Bangs said.

    But what they don't know is that the pilgrims actually spent 11 years laying over in the Dutch town of Leiden in Holland before arriving in America.

Actually, they had planned to stay in Holland, where the 100 Pilgrims were welcomed. But they became disillusioned and annoyed with the relaxed attitude of the Dutch about observing the Sabbath.

They wanted toleration for themselves. They weren't too happy with the results when this was also extended to other people, Bangs said.

So they got on board the *Mayflower* and headed west to the New World, where they could establish the religious society they dreamed about.

But they didn't leave Holland totally behind. In fact, they brought with them a lot of local customs and know-how from the Dutch.

For example, our federal system of government was greatly influenced by Holland, which was set up as a nation of semi-independent provinces, somewhat like our states.

The *Mayflower Compact*, drawn up as a blueprint for society on board one of the ships that took the Pilgrims to America, was modeled on Leiden's neighborhood organizations where local officers were voted into power.

The Pilgrims also brought the Dutch custom of civil marriages, the ladder-back chair and an early type of hockey stick from Leiden.

But what may surprise most Americans is that the tradition of the Thanksgiving feast actually was Dutch in origin. Usually, it is portrayed as a Native American custom to celebrate the end of the harvest season by giving thanks for another bountiful year of crops. However, Bangs said it probably was based on the annual feast in Leiden to celebrate a 1574 victory over the Spanish.

Bangs is a leading Pilgrim scholar and former chief curator at Plymouth Plantation in Massachusetts. He said the Leiden's American Pilgrim Museum is a celebration of the nearly forgotten decade the Pilgrims spent in Holland before sailing to America.

14. Write a short three- or four-paragraph feature story from these notes:
   a. 911 dispatcher Thomas Chang
   Took a call from a child
   Who said there was a fire
   At his home
   Firemen were dispatched
   The boy was 4-years-old
   The emergency was
   Gingerbread burning
   In the oven
   Firemen explained to boy
   Gingerbread men don't breathe
   And don't bleed so there
   Was no need to call 911
   The burned gingerbread man
   And five other cookies
   Were taken to the 911 center
   "We just want to keep them
   For sentimental value,"
   Chang said.

   (Sources: Chang, Fire Chief Robert Kenyon)

b. Study commissioned by
America OnLine
Shows Internet is
Cutting into time
People watch television
5000 Nielsen families
Were part of study
TV use was 19% lower
4:30–6 p.m., Monday–Friday
In homes with on-line access
Compared to nonwired homes
From 8–11 p.m. TV usage
Was 6% lower
"The networks can deny it
All they want. The world
Is changing," said
Nick Donatiello of Odyssey,
A San Francisco market
Research firm
More than 28 million
Households now on line
Advertisers spent $45 billion
On TV last year
Compared to $1 billion
In cyberspace advertising
Nielsen's Jack Loftus
Said study doesn't show
Whether higher family income
Could mean lower TV use

CHAPTER

11 Rewrites and Follow-Ups

"Rewriting is the essence of writing," William Zinsser says at the outset of his excellent book, *On Writing Well*. ". . . professional writers rewrite their sentences repeatedly and then rewrite what they have written."

His words are echoed daily by writers and editors who are aware that only a handful of reporters can pass along their copy as first written. The rest have to rewrite their stories—often several times.

Kevin McGrath, writing coach for the *Times* of Munster, Ind., put it this way in a column in the *American Editor:*

> The worst writers deny the awful truth that nobody produced perfection on the first try; the best writers embrace it. The best writers revise, then revise some more, then revise again.

Rewrites

In most newsrooms, the word "rewrite" has a variety of applications. It is commonly used by reporters who are trying to write clear, crisp, interesting stories. Some rewrite more often than others. Some do not rewrite often enough, leaving the job of smoothing out the rough spots, untangling words, answering unanswered questions to the copy editor.

Here's McGrath, again, on rewriting: "The essence of revision is to realize that it isn't an extra piece of work tacked onto the end of your day; it's where the payoff for your hard work comes, where you make it sing."

Beyond the act of the reporter rewriting her or his own story sometimes six or seven times before being satisfied with it, "rewrite" means other things. For example, on metropolitan dailies it usually refers to a group of writers whose chief role is to take information over the phone from reporters on regular beats and then write a news story, often with the reporter's by-line on it.

These same writers work with one or more reporters who may be covering the scene of a major fire, bridge collapse or other disaster. The reporters on the scene phone the information into the rewrite desk, where the facts are woven into an accurate and interesting story. Papers in smaller cities use this system of rewrite only occasionally, usually for last-minute stories gathered right on deadline.

"Rewriting" can also mean producing a new story from a clipping taken from another publication or a press release. It can also mean rewriting a story because the editor did not like the way it was written originally. Most editors will give the story back to the reporter who wrote it for rewriting. However, if the reporter is not available, a rewrite person may handle it.

Often the persons assigned to rewrite on larger newspapers are among the best writers and most capable members of the staff. They usually work with reporters on the beats. The job of rewriting less significant stories from clippings and press releases frequently goes to the newest reporter on the staff.

In rewriting a story from another newspaper or other source, the reporter must first verify the facts in the clipping and then attempt to get additional facts to use in the rewrite. The object is to have the story appear to be a new one, not simply a repeat of the original story. To accomplish this, a reporter may start the rewrite by (1) playing up an additional newsworthy fact or facts, or (2) reorganizing the story if no new facts are available. In the second case, the story often is shortened unless it is about a very important news event. Obviously, the first method is preferred, but sometimes there simply are no new facts to add to a story. In any event, the rewritten story, especially the lead, should be as different as possible from the original one.

Here are two leads for the same story. The first one appeared in an afternoon newspaper:

> CAPE CANAVERAL—Still a hero and still making history, John Glenn roared back into space today, retracing the trail he blazed for American's astronauts 38 years ago.

Because there were no new facts to add, the morning newspaper used a slightly different approach to the story:

> CAPE CANAVERAL—Discovery roared into orbit Thursday with six astronauts and a deliriously happy John Glenn, the aging hero who finally got his reunion with space.

These two wire service leads vary only slightly but they allow newspapers printed and delivered at different times of the day to not sound exactly alike:

> HOUSTON—In a positive report on the seven surviving octuplets, doctors said today that tests had shown no signs of a condition that could lead to developmental problems.

> HOUSTON—Ultrasound tests on the seven surviving octuplets found no bleeding on their brains, lessening chances of developmental problems such as cerebral palsy, physicians in Houston said today.

Meetings of city councils and county commissions frequently overlap a newspaper's deadline. In such a case, a reporter will have to base his or her lead on action taken early in the meeting, whereas a competitor from another paper can focus on action taken much later in the meeting. The following is an example of a lead on a story about a county commission meeting written for an afternoon newspaper. It was written to meet a deadline that came more than an hour before the morning meeting was over:

> County Commissioner James V. H. Brewer today accused the county school system of mismanagement and misstatement concerning budgetary matters.
>
> Brewer distributed his charges in a printed report at the regular meeting of the County Commission. Chairman Vernon Bradshaw said he will ask for a written response from County School Superintendent Mary Cimino and report back to the commission.

The rest of the story detailed Brewer's charges against the school system.

The morning newspaper's reporter was not on deadline, so he was able to stay through the entire meeting. His lead focused on other action taken by the commission:

> Members of the County Commission failed yesterday to override County Executive John Ragsdale's veto of an extra allotment of $46,450 for the sheriff to continue a drunken driving educational program to the end of the year. The vote was 9 to override and 10 against.

The story gave additional details on the veto action as well as other action taken by the commission. The morning newspaper also carried a much shorter, separate story on the commissioner's charges and focused on the response of the school board:

> County School Board Chairman Joyce Marshall labeled charges of mismanagement against the board by County Commissioner James V. H. Brewer "a self-serving, one-sided, perverse view of the county school system."
>
> She called the charges made yesterday at the commission meeting a mixture of "half-truths and innuendoes."

The rest of the story briefly summarized the charges and reported that the commission chairman had asked for a written reply from the school board.

Often the angle featured in the rewritten lead is taken from the body of the original story, as the next examples show. The morning newspaper used this lead on its city council story:

> A request to rezone 9.6 acres of land south of Northshore Drive and east of Willman Lane to permit construction of a $3.5 million apartment complex was delayed by the City Council last night.
>
> Councilwoman Brenda Frazier asked for the delay to give the developer and residents of the area, who oppose the development, an "opportunity to work out a compromise."

Earlier the Metropolitan Planning Commission ignored the opposition from the homeowners and recommended rezoning the property from single-family to multi-family to permit construction of the apartments.

If the Council gives final approval Tuesday, residents of the area say they will file a suit in Circuit Court to block the rezoning.

The story went on to give details of the apartment complex and the dispute between the homeowners and the developer, as well as other action taken by the council at the meeting. The afternoon newspaper's coverage of the same meeting used the following lead:

If you park illegally and your car is towed in, you'll have to pay $40 instead of $20 to get it out.

The City Council voted last night to double the towing and impoundment fee after police said the problem with illegally parked cars has become "epidemic."

The afternoon newspaper's story did not get to the rezoning until about the eighth paragraph. The morning newspaper's story did not introduce the hike in towing fees until the sixth paragraph.

Facts omitted purposely or otherwise by the reporter of the original story are often featured in the rewrite because they give the story a fresh aspect. In striving for a fresh angle, however, a reporter must guard against distorting the essential facts and significance of the story. Sometimes new events occur and give the rewrite person a feature that was not available to the reporter of the original story. In that case, the story is a combination rewrite and follow-up.

Press Releases

Hundreds of press releases are received each week by most newspapers. They come from private industry, civic groups, religious organizations, educational institutions and just about anyone else who has some information they want to get before the public. Many of them are extremely well written by very talented public relations writers. Others are, quite frankly, badly written. In many cases, the press release contains no news or information that is of any value to the newspaper's readers. The careful editor has them checked by a staff member and then rewritten for publication. However, at some newspapers, both large and small, press releases often find their way into print as originally written.

Often the task of rewriting a press release can be easy because the real news may be buried down in the third or fourth paragraph after the public relations writer has plugged his or her client shamelessly in the lead. However, a number of press releases are very well written, and the task of rewriting them can be tough. A person on rewrite handling a well-written press release needs all the skills and imagination at his or her command to improve what is basically a good story to start with.

PAGE ONE
NEWS Inside...

4 LUB nominations fail
before council agrees... 2A

Commission to fund Jellico
Rescue Squad building... 2A

Hill pays tribute to Seibers'
bravery at press conference... 5A

PRESS
LaFollette

Thursday, June 12, 1997   50 Cents

Local officials amazed, pleased at response to emergency

By MIKE McDONOUGH
LaFollette Press Reporter

Local officials are amazed at the way agencies and individuals responded to the recent fireworks disaster.

'What I feel is nothing at all to what the four families feel'

Pyro Shows to continue – for now

Memorial service set for Sunday

By CHARLES WINFREY
LaFollette Press News Editor

Hill, employees will decide company fate after July 4th

By LARRY SMITH
LaFollette Press Publisher

In remembrance
LaFollette's Centennial Committee placed this wreath in the James P. Freeman Memorial Park in downtown LaFollette Friday in memory of the victims of the Pyro blast.

LANSDEN HILL

Funerals for 4 victims held Sunday

Three of the dead lived in Caryville

By MIKE McDONOUGH
And CHARLES WINFREY
LaFollette Press News Editor

Stream of friends share family's grief

By LARRY SMITH
LaFollette Press Publisher

FIGURE 11.1 The aftermath of an explosion at a fireworks factory became a continuing story for the *LaFollette Press*. This front page was devoted to following up the impact of the tragedy, which killed four persons and damaged dozens of homes and businesses.

(Reprinted with permission of the *LaFollette, Tenn., Press*.)

Here is an example of how a press release was rewritten to emphasize the most important news element. The original lead on the press release read:

> WASHINGTON, D.C.—By a 2–1 decision, the U.S. Court of Appeals reversed a lower court decision in The Bubble Room, Inc. v. The United States and ruled the Internal Revenue Service (IRS) has the authority to assess restaurant employers FICA taxes on unreported tips without first determining which individual employees actually underreported their tips.

That lead is 55 words and bogs the reader down in details that can be used later in the story. Here's how it was rewritten to get right to the point:

> WASHINGTON, D.C.—The Internal Revenue Service has the authority to tax restaurant owners on tips their employees don't report on their income tax, the U.S. Court of Appeals ruled today.
> And the IRS doesn't even have to figure out which employees actually underreported their tips, the court said.

The rest of the story points out that the ruling reversed a lower court decision in the Bubble Room case and gives the details of that case. It would also include reaction from the National Restaurant Association, including any plans to appeal the decision.

In the following example, an awkward direct quote lead was rewritten to take the emphasis off the president of the company and focus on the news element. The original lead on the press release was:

> "For the first time in 19 months, the company's earnings have risen above the annual dividend rate of $1.54 a share," Alvin W. Vogel Jr., president of The Southern Company, announced today.

The rewritten lead put the company's name at the start of the sentence rather than at the end and told what the actual earnings were for an average share of common stock:

> The Southern Company today reported that the average earnings of its common stock rose to $1.54 a share for the 12 months ending January 31—an increase of 17 cents a share over last year.
> Consolidated net income for the electric utility totaled $231 million for the period—up nearly $33 million, Alvin W. Vogel Jr., company president, said.

Although many reporters object strongly to being assigned rewrites, it can provide excellent experience in handling a wide variety of news as well as human-interest and feature stories.

Follow-Ups

A follow-up is usually an updating of an earlier news story in which the latest developments are reported. A follow-up story naturally features the new developments, but the reporter must summarize enough of the background of the original story for the benefit of readers who did not see it and to refresh the memories of those who did. Because this summary refers to an earlier story, it is called a "tie-back."

The tie-back of one or two short paragraphs follows the lead or second paragraph, but no set rules govern its length or position in the story. One sentence or phrase within a paragraph or within the lead itself may be sufficient to make new developments clear. If the story remains prominent for several days, the tie-back becomes shorter and shorter because chances decrease daily that a reader has missed all the earlier stories. However, in some stories, several paragraphs may be necessary, particularly when the follow-up is published some time after the original story appeared.

The follow-up is handled in the same manner as the rewrite; the reporter uses the facts already in hand and diligently seeks new developments. Except for the tie-backs, follow-ups are written in the same form as a news story.

Most rewrites are brief and about rather insignificant items, as a general rule. The pressure to conserve space is so heavy that information previously seen by a large number of readers must be condensed as much as possible. However, if a big story—a natural disaster such as a flood or earthquake, for example—breaks on the competitor's time, the story is not rewritten, in the usual sense of the term. In fact, reporters are sent to cover the story just like the competition, only they have longer to write it. Subsequent stories will be follow-ups, just as they are when the newspaper's own first account deserves later development. Most stories of importance are pursued through later developments for days or weeks and, on rare occasions, even years. Reporting of the Watergate scandals in the federal government covered more than two years. A fire or a storm is followed by accounts of relief and reconstruction. Crime is followed through the trial and sentencing. Gradually, the force of the first explosive event plays out, and the follow-ups dwindle away.

Sometimes the follow-up can develop into a much larger story than the original one. A short story may be followed by a longer, more detailed account over several days or weeks until a major story develops. Bank failures, embezzlements of public funds or congressional investigations may be the bases for stories that will build slowly. That is what happened in the Federal Bureau of Investigation's Abscam investigation, in which congressmen and one senator were eventually convicted of accepting bribes from a phony oil sheik.

Here is an example of a follow-up story three days after the original story when there had been no major new developments. The tie-back comes in the fifth paragraph:

AMHERST, N.Y.—Police in upstate New York and Canada searched early Sunday for the sniper who killed a prominent abortion practitioner, making him the first fatality in a series of sniper attacks on doctors in the area since 1994.

President Clinton, Attorney General Janet Reno, New York Gov. George Pataki, and abortion rights activists and foes alike condemned the murder of Dr. Barnett Slepian, an obstetrician and gynecologist.

"It's beyond a tragedy," said Pataki, who said the killer should face the death penalty. "It's really an act of terrorism and, in my mind, a cold-blooded assassination."

Reno vowed to do "whatever it takes to track down and prosecute" the killer.

Slepian, 51, a target of anti-abortion protesters since the 1980s, was gunned down in his kitchen Friday night. The killing came . . .

This example by John Tierney of the *New York Times* is a follow-up of a different sort. It reaches back in time to bring the readers up to date of an event that made news 11 years before:

He had to wait 11 years after his first attempt, but yesterday Rocco Morabito finally drove his sister all the way to the beach. He was safe at last from the police, thanks to the learner's permit he got on his 16th birthday, and he handled the car even better than he had the first time.

"It's easier when you can see over the top of the steering wheel," he explained as he pulled out of the garage at his family's home in Port Chester, N.Y., navigating the same narrow driveway where his famous ride began the morning of Dec. 4, 1987.

At the time, Rocco was five-years old and three feet tall. His two-year-old sister, Brandi, wanted to go to the beach, and Rocco got halfway there, cruising at 20 miles an hour along a main thoroughfare in Westchester County. Then a police officer in Rye, Robert P. Vogel, spotted their car, which appeared to be driverless. Rocco responded to the flashing lights and siren.

"He pulled over perfectly," Officer Vogel reported. "He didn't even hit the curb. It was a beautiful job."

The two children, who were wearing pajamas, started crying for their mother, but Rocco regained his composure when Officer Vogel said she would be summoned to pick them up.

"My mommy can't come here because I have the only car," Rocco told the officer. "I can drive. I'll go get her."

The remainder of the story recounts Rocco's famous ride, the reaction in the press, and what his life has been like since then.

The Developing Story

Although it is not as common as it once was when many daily newspapers had as many as six or seven editions, reporters still may handle a developing story of several editions in a single day. If a major court trial is in progress, the newspaper may want an up-to-the-deadline report of the trial in every edition. A newspaper with three editions, each with a different deadline, may have one story (or parts of it) rewritten to include the latest newsworthy development for each edition.

A new lead, including the latest developments or revelation, may be all that is needed. Although some editors may want inserts, or "adds," for the original story to fill in details. However, as much of the original story as possible is left undisturbed.

Major events, such as a presidential sex scandal and subsequent impeachment, can be classified a developing story but they stretch over days, weeks, and months as new details are revealed. Natural disaster stories—floods, hurricanes, earthquakes—might be classified as developing stories because of the destruction that can affect the lives of thousands over weeks and months. But each of these stories is tied-back to the original event in about the third or fourth paragraph of the new story.

Here is an example of how a daily with several editions might handle a story of a fire that was reported at the city jail just before deadline. The first edition story might say:

> A fire swept through the jail on the second floor of City Hall shortly before 9 a.m. today, and at least three inmates are known to be dead.
>
> "It could be a lot worse," Police Chief Bill Joe Biggs said. "I just can't tell you anything for sure until the fire is out and we can get in there."
>
> He said he did not know how many prisoners were in the jail, because he had not received the daily head count before the fire started.
>
> "Things have been quiet this week. I think maybe we had 12 or 15 locked up. But I can't really be sure," Biggs said.
>
> He added that he did not have time to identify the dead men.
>
> Heavy black smoke billowed through the 156-year-old building and inmates could be heard screaming for help as fireman pumped thousands of gallons of water through the second-floor windows.
>
> Dozens of policemen joined firemen in trying to reach the prisoners. But most rescue efforts failed because of the intense heat and the heavy black smoke.
>
> "You can't get anywhere near the cell block," Patrolman Ira Bevins said. "If the flames and heat don't stop you, the smoke will."

To round out the story for the first edition, the writer should include information about evacuating city employees from other offices in the building. The story may include some information about the building and the jail, especially if a check of the clipping file at the newspaper shows there have been previous reports about safety conditions at the jail.

Examples of how the story might be changed to include up-to-deadline developments in later editions follow:

> *New Lead*
>
> At least eight prisoners were killed today when fire swept through the jail on the second floor of City Hall.
>
> The dead were trapped in a large holding cell in the jail. Other prisoners may have died in their locked cells at the rear of the second floor.

Insert After Fifth Paragraph of the Original Story

Two officers and a trustee who were downstairs smelled smoke and ran to the second floor. They opened one of two doors to the large holding cell, but were unable to open the other door, which may have been blocked by the body of an unconscious inmate, Biggs said.

Add to End of Story

Three firemen were hospitalized from smoke inhalation.

Biggs said it was too early to determine how the fire started. He added, however, that it was not uncommon for prisoners to start fires in their cells.

"They set fire to a half-dozen mattresses a month," he said.

Of course, if a final death toll is available by the final edition of the day, a new lead should be written. Additional details of the fire may be inserted or added at the end of the story. Because "patching" a story together in this fashion can result in mistakes, many papers will have the story for the final edition completely rewritten.

If time does not permit the revision of a story in an earlier edition, a short (usually one-paragraph) "bulletin" is written to precede the lead of the earlier story. However, this is usually done for the lead story on the front page and only in the event the latest developments are significant enough to warrant this special treatment.

EXERCISES

1. Rewrite this story, which appeared in the morning newspaper, for the competing afternoon daily using only the facts given here:

   A San Pedro man who abducted a county social worker and her teenage ward was sentenced Monday to 121 years to life in prison.

   Los Angeles Superior Court Judge William Garner sentenced Troy Lee Mendenhall, 34, two months after his conviction on two counts of kidnapping and one count of kidnapping for carjacking, robbery and assault with a deadly weapon.

   Mendenhill was arrested in January after a high-speed chase with police on the Harbor Freeway shortly after he had kidnapped social worker Lucie Whitcomb, 43, and a 14-year-old girl. The victims had been carjacked by Mendenhall as they drove away from the girl's foster home in Long Beach.

   Whitcomb was stabbed, tied, gagged and dropped off in Wilmington before Mendenhall continued with the girl, said prosecutor Vivian Davidson. Despite her ordeal, Whitcomb did not suffer any major injuries, Davidson said. The girl was not injured.

2. Rewrite the following story, which appeared in the afternoon newspaper, for the competing morning daily:

   A runaway horse took its carriage for a wild ride along Central Park South this morning, running over a tourist.

Julieta Partida was knocked to the ground and dragged for a few feet after the horse bounded onto the sidewalk and plowed into her, witnesses told police.

"She couldn't have done anything," said Mohammed Gulgar, a T-shirt vendor who watched the bizarre episode unfold about 10 a.m.

Partida, 26, of Pasadena, Calif., suffered minor injuries and was taken to Roosevelt Hospital, said Detective Joseph Pantangelo, a police spokesman. Partida was expected to be released tonight, the hospital said.

The horse, witnesses told police, began its rampage near Columbus Circle. Its first victim was a 1987 Ford parked along Central Park South, which it sideswiped.

"I was like `Oh . . . ,'" said Adam Castillo, 37, owner of the gray sedan.

Shortly after Partida was struck, the driver of the carriage arrived and allegedly took off—with the horse.

Police tracked him down, and the driver, whose identity was not immediately available, was issued a summons for leaving the scene of an accident, Pantangelo said.

3. Using the following information, do a follow-up story to the one in Exercise 2.

Police identified the driver of the horse and carriage as Ike Taskopoulas, 34, an illegal alien from the island of Crete. They said he apparently had been in the country for about a year, entering from Canada. He did not have an alien work permit (Green Card). When they searched him, they found about a dozen plastic bags of a white powder, which was sent to the crime laboratory for analysis. Other carriage drivers, whose identity police would not divulge, reportedly told police Taskopoulas was well known among regular visitors to the park for selling "high-quality" drugs to passengers in his carriage. The Immigration and Naturalization Service is working with police on the case but refused to comment on it.

4. Here is a press release that was distributed from a Congressman's office. It is reproduced here as it actually appeared. Nothing has been changed. Read it carefully and evaluate its news potential. If it has news value, rewrite it to give the news a stronger lead.

News Release

from Congressman
JOHN J. DUNCAN, Jr.
2nd DISTRICT, TENNESSEE
115 CANNON HOUSE OFFICE BUILDING
WASHINGTON, D.C. 20515
(202) 275-5435

PROVISIONS FROM DUNCAN'S DIPLOMAT BILL PASSED
BY THE HOUSE TODAY

FOR IMMEDIATE RELEASE   CONTACT: David Balloff
Wednesday, October 14, 1998

WASHINGTON, D.C. -- The House passed legislation today which included provisions from a bill that Congressman John J. Duncan, Jr. (R-TN) introduced with Congressman David Dreier (R-CA) last year, along with Senator Paul Coverdell (R-GA) in the Senate.

This bill unanimously passed the House and will now go to the White House.

The legislation directs the State Department to pursue waivers of diplomatic immunity when foreign diplomats commit serious crimes in the United States. And, if a foreign government of a diplomat who commits a crime will not agree to waive immunity, then that government will be encouraged to prosecute the criminal for the same offense in their own courts.

Duncan stated, "Foreign diplomats who commit felony offenses on U.S. soil should be prosecuted for those crimes."

According to Congressman Duncan, "This bill will encourage the State Department to hold diplomats accountable for crimes committed in the United States."

"It has been reported that there has been, on average, one death a year over the last ten years in which a diplomat has been involved and the perpetrator was not charged," Duncan said.

Duncan introduced this legislation following the tragic death of a 16-year-old girl in the Washington, D.C. area. The girl was killed in a collision with car driven by a diplomat from the Republic of Georgia. The diplomat was reportedly drunk and driving 80 mph in downtown Washington, D.C. when the accident occurred.

Initially, the driver was not going to be prosecuted because of his status as a diplomat. Under international law, foreign diplomats are immune from prosecution by the courts in the country where they are working.

The Republic of Georgia later waived immunity for the diplomat in question.

Duncan stated, "I welcome people of all nationalities into this Country, but at the same time, I do not think diplomats have the right to come here and maim or kill without expecting punishment."

12 Pictures

"Photographs are lucky! We get to share some of the biggest moments in people's lives. Every story we cover and every photo we shoot is important to someone," Linda Asberry-Angelle, vice president of the National Press Photographers Association, said in "The Best of Photojournalism" for 1997.

Those moments captured by newspaper photographers are a vital part of every modern newspaper. They not only document the news, but they also serve as a permanent visual record of history, for the newspaper and for the individuals in the pictures.

"As photographers, we may be assigned to our 100th high school football game, but for those kids, it is probably the first time they have been in the paper . . . the pictures we take will be cut out and framed . . . put in scrapbooks and taped to refrigerators. We have captured a moment in someone's life," Ms. Asberry-Angelle said.

Despite the dramatic changes in photography since the introduction of the digital still camera and the computerization of the photographic process at most newspapers, the basic role of the photographer remains the same—to capture a given moment in the life of someone, someplace, to take people places they would never go and show them people they would never meet.

A good news picture can speak quickly, vividly and simply, and it can give a newspaper a more colorful and readable appearance. Pictures are a major element of design.

A reporter does not have to be able to take pictures, but the ability to do so is an extremely useful talent, especially on smaller newspapers, where reporters often double as photographers. The late Nancy Petrey, copublisher of the *Newport Plain Talk*, Newport, Tenn., handed every new reporter a camera along with a stack of reporter's notebooks and pencils. If the new staff member didn't know how to use the camera, she gave him or her a short course right there on the spot. "In a paper our size, everyone has to be able to take pictures as well as report, write and edit," she said.

In general, pictures are used in connection with news and feature stories, usually on the same page with the story. Sometimes a picture may be used on page 1, for example, and the story will appear on an inside page. A number of editors, however, will not separate the picture from the story.

Frequently, a picture may tell its own story and stand alone, supported merely by cutlines. This type of picture usually features some vivid action that may not require a story. Often newspapers will use feature pictures of interesting faces or scenery with only a caption.

Newspapers generally prefer pictures that show action. Unfortunately, this often results in contrived and posed bits of action such as someone pointing at something or two persons shaking hands or one person handing a check to another. A formal head-and-shoulders photograph of an individual taken by a staff photographer or retrieved from the newspaper's files may be just as effective as the obviously posed action shot. More and more newspapers are using such photographs when action shots are not available. Today's flexible production methods have resulted in a number of newspapers combining head-and-shoulder photos with maps, charts and sketches to create a large visual to accompany a story whenever an action photograph is not available.

A creative photographer can make even the oldest situation seem new, just as an outstanding reporter can make the most routine story interesting. It is a matter of thinking innovatively, caring about the quality of the photograph and taking pride in one's work. Except for head-and-shoulder photographs (called "mug shots"), the gifted photographer avoids the stiff "facing the camera" pose and will have the subjects looking toward a focal point for the picture rather than "mugging" or looking straight into the camera.

A good photographer will avoid cliches—the handshakes, the ribbon cutters, the pointers, the check passers—whenever possible. If such assignments can't be avoided—many cannot—a good photographer will at least shoot them from a different angle.

Here are some general guidelines issued for photographers by Landmark Community Newspapers, Inc.:

— Avoid more than five people in a photo (except for crowd shots); ideally, three is enough.
— Insist that posing be tight. Space between heads is almost always wasted.
— Crop ruthlessly. Slash; don't slice.
— Full-length figures of adults should normally be cropped at the bottom of the rib cage.
— Enlarge generously. A good picture should always be one column wider than you first think it should be.
— Heads of people in photos should be at least the size of a dime.

Ideally, the photographer should always seek drama, human interest, conflict and other news values when taking a picture. All of this is important to a reporter who has to double as the photographer. In fact, to see creatively is just as essential for a reporter as it is for a photographer.

Picture Process

A reporter should be familiar with the picture process. Here is how photographs are generally processed at those newspapers that still have not yet installed digital photography systems:

1. The city editor, or photo editor if the newspaper has one, makes the assignment, which should be as specific as possible. The photographer should be given some idea of the type of picture the editor wants.

2. The picture is taken by a photographer; the film is developed and printed. (Some smaller newspapers use Polaroid cameras to eliminate the developing and printing process.) The glossy print is handed to the proper editor, usually the city editor for local pictures. The city editor as well as the Sunday, entertainment, sports or women's news editor will receive many pictures along with the press releases provided by other sources such as public relations persons.

3. The editor determines the news value of the picture, marks the picture where it should be cropped and indicates the size of the cut (or negative, in offset printing) that should be made of it. If the picture has flaws that can be corrected, the editor may give it to a staff artist, who may "retouch" it to strengthen weak lines or "paint out" objectionable features. The artist may also make a layout showing the arrangement of pictures to be used in a picture story.

4. The retouched print goes to the backshop. If the paper is printed by the offset method, a screened negative is made with the offset camera. If the newspaper is still printed by hot metal, an engraver makes a metal "cut" of it.

5. A proof (copy) of the cut is returned to the editor, who may mark it for a special place in the paper.

6. The editor gives the original print or proof to a reporter or copy editor for writing of cutlines. Often, however, the cutlines are written before the picture is sent to the backshop.

7. The print and its cutlines (checked by the editor or a copy editor) are returned to the composing room, where the cutlines are set and assembled with the negative or cut into the page where they will appear.

The introduction of highly sophisticated, computerized equipment in the late 1980s that permits a photo editor to rearrange the composition of a photograph has touched off a debate within the profession over the ethics of so-called doctored pictures. Several major magazines were criticized because they moved major elements in a picture to create a better visual impact shortly after the equipment became available. Critics of the new equipment argue that no longer will the public be able to "trust" photographs as an accurate historical record. As more and more newspapers and magazines begin to use the equipment, the debate is certain to continue.

Digital Process

The introduction of digital photography has changed the picture process dramatically. Traditional photo laboratories have been all but eliminated at many newspapers. The photograph goes right from the camera to the computer. Here are the basic steps in the process:

1. After a photographer takes the picture on a digital camera, the image is fed into the computer through a cable or a smart card.

2. Using a Photoshop program, the editor brings the photographic image up on the computer screen, where the color can be adjusted, the dot pattern increased and the picture cropped and reduced or enlarged to the exact size of the image that will appear in the paper. That image is then stored in a Pagemaker program file from which the entire page is composed.

3. All digital pictures are in color, but it is possible to remove all the color while manipulating the image on the computer screen and produce a black and white photograph at that point, if desired.

4. Some newspapers continue to produce a black and white image that is integrated with the negative of the entire page and burned onto a thin metal printing plate, which is attached to the press. Color photographs are fed into an image setter, which produces the color negatives that are integrated on the negative of the entire page and burned onto a thin metal printing plate, which is attached to the printing press.

Larry Smith, editor and publisher of the *LaFollette Press*, an award-winning Tennessee weekly newspaper that converted to digital photography in the late 1990s, said it has "saved us a lot of time and money and produced higher quality color photographs." He noted that there are some limitations on the less expensive digital cameras and that it is necessary to increase the dots per inch in the image that originally appears on the computer screen to get high-quality photographic reproduction in the newspaper.

Color Pictures

Today, color photography is standard for almost all daily newspapers and many weeklies. Black and white photographs have not been eliminated, but color photographs tend to dominate the front pages and the front pages of the sections such as sports, business and lifestyle.

Even the great gray *New York Times*, which had used color photographs on its feature sections front pages, gave in during the mid-1900s and began using them on its front page. The first color news photo on the front page of the *Times* caused a minor sensation among some of its readers and was the talk of the newspaper industry briefly. The only major newspaper that was still a holdout as the twentieth century ended was the *Wall Street Journal*. Its front page steadfastly remained vertical in design and colorless.

Photographic and printing technology is so advanced now, using color does not present the headaches it once did. And it adds a tremendous excitement to the front page of an otherwise gray publication.

Richard Curtis, managing editor for graphics and photography for *USA TODAY* and cofounder of The Society of Newspaper Designers, pointed out the importance of good photographs and art work. "You must design a page that effectively displays the right photographs/artwork because they carry a tremendous burden," he said. "Photographs and their captions and artwork are almost always 'read' before the text."

He recommends that they be treated "as news." And he urged editors and graphic designers to resist the urge to use "a beautiful photograph of a pelican backlit by a beautiful sunset, a photograph with absolutely no news value." He says to use them is a waste of a newspaper's time and resources and a lot of the reader's time, too.

Writing Cutlines

Writing cutlines (captions) is one of the most difficult assignments at a newspaper. It takes practice, patience and a command of the language. Not everyone writes cutlines well. In fact, they often are the most poorly written parts of a newspaper. Many cutlines lack grace and style.

In a study of cutlines used with Associated Press Laserphotos during a single month, 60 percent had punctuation, spelling, sentence construction and word-use errors. In addition, writing errors such as cliches, pejorative adjectives, incorrect verb tenses, incorrect noun–pronoun or subject–verb agreement and sentence fragments were found. One of the most common errors in captions is the use of "shown above" and "pictured here." They are unnecessary and are an insult to the reader. It is obvious that the subject is in the picture and that the picture is above the cutline.

Cutline styles vary greatly in newspapers. Most cutlines are placed underneath pictures. Some newspapers, however, place them at the side. This is commonly called "magazine style." Some newspapers make use of overlines placed above the picture. However, tests show that readers tend to miss or ignore them. Here are examples of various commonly used cutline styles:

An Iraqi boy learns how to hold an AK-47 during military training in Baghdad today.

MISPLACED: Tree directly in front of Colmon Chan's store door violates basic tenet of feng shui.

Motorcycle officers head east on Interstate 580 as part of John Monego's funeral procession on Friday.

Construction worker *Chanda Crockett hasn't been paying much attention to the mayoral campaign, but "I'll go over the voter's pamphlet with my mom."*

A day for remembering

Patricia Jones, left, and Madlyn Hightower, both of The United Daughters of the Confederacy, Captain James Monroe Briggs Chapter 2582, place a Confederate flag at one of 134 Confederate graves Saturday in Sunset Hill Cemetery. Saturday was Confederate Memorial Day.—Times photo by Mike Tanner

JIANG: Chinese president answers a question at news conference in Beijing yesterday.

ABANDONED BUILDING: Ruben Avila Jr., head of Miami's unsafe structures division, tells people found living in a condemned building at 224 NW 12th St. to vacate the premises.

"The Republican conference needs to be unified, and it is time for me to move forward."
House Speaker Newt Gingrich, announcing he would step down.

The most effective cutlines are brief and clear. They should tell what the picture is about and identify the people in it. An Associated Press Managing Editors Continuing Study Committee put together "Ten Tests of a Good Cutline." They are:

1. Is it complete?
2. Does it identify, fully and clearly?
3. Does it tell when?
4. Does it tell where?
5. Does it tell what's in the picture?
6. Does it have the names spelled correctly, with the proper name on the right person?
7. Is it specific?
8. Is it ready to read?
9. Have as many adjectives as possible been removed?
10. Does it suggest another picture?

The committee added what is called the Cardinal Rule, which should never, never be violated: Never write a cutline without seeing the picture.

Although cutlines are much like a story lead because they should include the five W's of the picture, they should not repeat the lead of an accompanying story word for word. In the case of a straight news picture, a cutline should emphasize the most important fact first. Cutlines similar to feature leads are appropriate with pictures that are not straight news.

When writing a cutline, the reporter should study the picture carefully first and know what is in it. Obvious features should not be described; after all, the reader will know if the person is laughing or crying. Everything a reader might misinterpret at first glance should be explained. Cutlines should be written in the present tense when describing the action taking place in the picture, but past tense should be used when giving additional details. Reporters should not mix tenses in the same sentence in a cutline any more than they would in a news story. And the cutline writer should never speculate on what the persons in the picture are thinking.

Remember that cutlines should not be loaded with excessive details. When a picture accompanies a story, many newspapers use the briefest possible cutline because the details are adequately covered in the lead or are high in the story. Under a photograph of voters in Haiti participating in that country's first democratic national elections, one newspaper used this brief cutline on a picture accompanying a detailed story on the elections:

Haitians lining up in Port-au-Prince to vote yesterday

Under a picture of a shelter for the homeless that was burning, one newspaper used this short cutline because the picture accompanied a lengthy story on the fire:

Fire engulfs a vacant homeless shelter in Elkins

Here are other examples of the use of pictures:

Story Lead, Figure 12-1
A steam roller owned by the Tennessee Asphalt Company lost its brakes, rolled down a steep hill, crossed South Main Street and came to a stop inside the home of Vicki and Mike Sanders.

No one was hurt, but the Sanders' home certainly was. Damages are estimated at $10,000.

Ms. Sanders, Campbell County School Food Supervisor, was at home with a "bug" Monday when the unmanned steam roller crashed into her home. Steve Spicer, who was operating the machine on a steep hill across from the Sanders' home, said when the brakes failed he jumped off and the machine kept right on rolling.

Caption, Figure 12-1
Vicki Sanders was home with a "bug" Monday when a steam roller's brakes failed and it rolled down a steep hill, crossed South Main Street and smashed into her home. No one was hurt in the accident.

Story Lead, Figure 12-2
The first snow storm of the season caught everyone by surprise yesterday. Snow wasn't even in the forecast but we got five inches of it, snarling traffic, closing schools and businesses and making almost everyone but the city zoo's polar bears unhappy.

FIGURE 12.1   Vicki Sanders was home with a "bug" Monday when a steam roller's brakes failed and it rolled down a steep hill, crossed South Main Street and smashed into her home. No one was hurt in the accident.
(Photo by Charles Winfrey, News Editor, *LaFollette Press*. Reprinted with permission of the *LaFollette Press*.)

"We goofed on this one," Dean Hitt, spokesman for the local National Weather Service office, said.

Caption, Figure 12-2
A surprise 5-inch snow storm dressed the countryside in white yesterday but many people were too busy digging out to enjoy its touches of beauty.

Story Lead, Figure 12-3
Sacred Heart rolled to an easy victory over Faith Christian Middle School in the first round of the Highland Hill Invitational Basketball tournament in Chattanooga yesterday.
Thomas Kollar lead Sacred Heart with a season and team high of 18 points.

Caption, Figure 12-3
Sacred Heart's Thomas Kollar takes aim at the basket on his way to scoring 18 points for a season and team high against Faith Christian.

FIGURE 12.2   A surprise 5-inch snow storm dressed the countryside in white yesterday, but many people were too busy digging out to enjoy its touches of beauty.
(Reprinted with permission of Gary Heatherly, Gary Heatherly Photography.)

EXERCISES

1. Using the *Photography Annual*, published by the editors of *Popular Photography* magazine, look at the photographs and evaluate their effectiveness. Then turn to the back of the publication and read what the photographers say about their photographs.

2. Review a recent edition of "The Best of Photojournalism," published by the National Press Photographers Association, and make note of the wide range of subjects covered by photographers for newspapers and magazines.

3. Ask the chief photographer and photo or graphics editor of your local newspaper to come to class to talk about their work. If possible, accompany one of the newspaper's photographers on assignment to observe her or him at work.

4. Using any newspaper available to you, clip three local news stories that might have had greater impact if they had been accompanied by pictures. Write a brief explanation of the type pictures you would have used with each.

5. Rewrite the cutlines for any five pictures in a newspaper available to you, using the cutline styles illustrated in this chapter. Use a different style for each cutline. Turn in the original cutlines with your written versions.

6. Make a walking tour of your campus and then suggest ideas for five picture stories involving people, events or places on your campus or the nearby area. Avoid the obvious such as athletic teams and static classroom scenes. Write a brief explanation of why you think each would make an interesting photo story. Suggest the various pictures you would use in the story.

FIGURE 12.3   Sacred Heart's Thomas Kollar takes aim at the basket on his way to scoring 19 points for a season and team high against Faith Christian.
(Reprinted with permission of Robert E. Kollar.)

7. Using the 10 tests of a good caption listed in this chapter, analyze the cutline style in one issue of any three newspapers available to you. Write a brief report on how those captions compare to the 10 tests.

8. Using these brief notes, write cutlines in any style of your choice for pictures that will not accompany a story. Explain specifically what kind of picture you would suggest be taken.

   a. Green Street Baptist Church
      Holds annual School of Religion
      Offering Christian education classes
      Program lasts for five days
      More than 200 persons enrolled
      Participants encouraged to tell
      How religion plays
      A role in their lives
      At the end of each day
      In the main sanctuary
      Of the church which
      Celebrates its 100th
      Anniversary in June
   b. Elana Peters reunited
      With her sister
      Wanda Bednarski
      At Midway Airport today
      Hadn't seen each other
      In 35 years
      Sisters were given up
      For adoption after
      Their mother died
      When Elena was 5 and
      Wanda was 4
      Elena grew up here
      Wanda in California
      Elena hired search firm
      That advertised on TV
      To help her find Wanda
      Sisters talked on phone
      A half dozen times
      Then decided to reunite
   c. Kablooie, 5-year-old
      Sea otter at city zoo
      Cools off in his tank
      As temperature soars
      High today will be
      At least 100
      For 10th straight day
      Weather forecasters say
      No relief in sight
      For at least 3 more days

CHAPTER

13 News for Radio and Television

"When we think of writing, we think first of print, but writing is just as critical to the spoken words on television and radio," Paula LaRocque, writing coach and assistant managing editor of the *Dallas Morning News*, said in her column in *Quill*.

She listed some of the misuse of words by radio and television reporters and commentators, such as the one who, in describing an automobile accident, said: "The car vareened around the curve and went off the road." She added that "vareened" probably was a hybrid of careened and veered.

In that column, Ms. LaRocque was critical of the graceless use of words both on the air and in print. "Every time a journalist fails to use words gracefully, the audience's esteem drops a bit."

Immediacy is the chief difference between print and broadcast journalism. Both deal in the same product—news. What makes an event news for a print journalist generally makes it news for television and radio journalists. Both use the same language, often carelessly, illogically and imprecisely. "Readers and listeners alike hope for better from professional writers and editors," Ms. LaRocque said.

The basic role of every reporter, no matter what the medium, is to tell the news. How it is told is largely a matter of style, dictated in large measure by technology. Writing is designed for readers who expect greater detail along with explanations and analysis. Radio and television newscasts are generally aimed at listeners and viewers who are seeking information rather than a detailed explanation. That is why broadcast news stories are condensed into a few sentences similar to the lead paragraph of a newspaper story.

News is a basic commodity. For the most part, no real differences exist in the elements that make something news for print or news for broadcast. All the news values used in selecting stories for newspapers apply to selecting stories for broadcast. Where the mediums differ is in the way those stories are told, and that often is affected by the audience.

Newspaper and broadcast audiences differ considerably in age and education. Newspaper readers tend to be older and have more education. Broadcast audiences tend to be younger—a lot of children—and generally are not as well educated. In fact, broadcast audiences include many persons who do not read because of lack of education or inclination.

In addition, technology for delivering news for broadcast in many ways confines the writer of a newscast. Because air time devoted to news is so limited, many stories have to be told in 30 to 45 seconds. Two minutes devoted to a single news item on a newscast is considered a long story.

Stories in newspapers often run 15 or more inches long. A 15-inch story would amount to about 600 words. By contrast, one minute of news read aloud amounts to about 150 words. A typical 30-minute newscast on television actually amounts to about 22 minutes after time for commercials and opening and closing credits is subtracted. The total number of words used in those 22 minutes would amount to little more than half of the words printed on the front page of a standard-size American newspaper.

So the newscast writer has to make every single word count. He or she has to emphasize the who, what, when and where first and then if there is time include the why or how. But much of the time, the why and how are left out of most broadcast news stories.

There are other differences in writing news for print and broadcast caused by time constraints and technology. The writer of a television newscast, for example, must coordinate the words with film, still photos, graphics and other available visuals. Some stories, in fact, are selected for television because there are dramatic pictures to illustrate them.

Newspaper reporters pay particular attention to the accurate spelling of names of persons, places and things. The newscast writer, however, is more concerned with the proper pronunciation of names. In broadcast news copy, correct pronunciation often is inserted in parentheses immediately following unusual names, in this manner: Buehler (BEE-ler), Spivey (SPY-vee), Iglehart (EYE-gull-hart) and Smythe (SMEYE-th).

News for broadcast is written in a conversational style because it is heard, not read. Simple, short sentences are used. Adjectives and adverbs are kept to a minimum. Strong, active verbs are used rather than passive ones. Broadcast news writers know that listeners cannot "rehear" a word, phrase, or sentence they do not fully understand, so every word has to count. On the other hand, a newspaper reader can go over a sentence as many times as desired, although the ideal newspaper sentence is as easy to comprehend as a well-written broadcast news sentence.

Writing Newscasts

Two important writing techniques mark the differences between news for radio and television and news for newspapers. One is the construction of sentences; the other is the casual, informal language. These and other differences are discussed in the sections that follow:

Sentence Structure

1. The inverted sentence structure used in newspaper writing generally is not used in newscasts. Often newspaper stories give the source at the end of the lead sentence unless the source is a major public figure such as the president or governor. Newscast writers generally start with the source or some other introductory phrase and place the important facts later in the lead sentence. For example, a newspaper reporter might write:

> An 86-year-old Clinton woman was struck and killed by a coal truck while trying to cross East Central Avenue on Thursday, Police Chief Gilbert Chavez said.

The broadcast writer might use this approach:

> Police Chief Gilbert Chavez said 86-year-old Matty Marlow died attempting to cross East Central Avenue Thursday. She was struck by a coal truck as she was crossing East Central Avenue at the Cumberland Avenue intersection.

2. Sentences are shorter than those generally used in newspaper stories, but variety in sentence length is still preferred. For example, a newspaper reporter might write:

> State legislators, who now are paid $16,000 a year plus other benefits, will get almost double that under a proposal by a special commission on salaries of elected officials appointed by Speaker of the House William Britt.

The broadcast news writer might use this approach:

> House Speaker William Britt is talking about giving state lawmakers a pay raise. They currently make 16 and a half thousand dollars a year, plus other benefits. Britt would like to see it go up to between 25 and 30 thousand, he told a special commission he named to study salaries of elected officials.

3. Only one principal thought is used in each newscast sentence. If longer sentences are used, they tend to be compound rather than complex sentences. (One newspaper sentence will sometimes be divided into two newscast sentences, as in item 2.)

4. Verbs and their subjects are kept reasonably close together. This rules out the use of long "interrupters" between the verb and subject. Broadcast writers generally avoid introducing a second proper name between the subject and the verb. For example: "Mary Ross, secretary of Mayor Jackson Turner, died this morning." A listener may not hear the opening words and might believe that the mayor died.

5. Identification of the person quoted is shortened as much as possible and placed before instead of after the names. Sometimes the identification only is used in one sentence and the name in another to break up extraordinarily long combinations of the two.

6. Incompleted sentences, if used only from time to time, are generally permissible in newscasts.

7. Although broadcast news is written in a conversational style, it still follows all the standard rules of English grammar.

Language

   1. The question of tense is often debated by radio and television news writers. Many stations insist that, to give news a sense of immediacy, the present tense rather than the past should be used at all times. Others consistently use the past tense. Some have adopted a practice of dealing with each story separately, using the most logical tense for that story. However, the present tense is most commonly used.

   2. To prevent awkward pronunciations by the announcer, such combinations as alliteration in the sequence of words should be avoided (example: "The professor protested provisions . . ."). Also, too many words starting with "s" will result in noticeable hissing (example: "Sister should send some . . .").

   3. The overworked "quote" and "unquote" are not used by most newscast writers today. They frequently break down long direct quotes into a combination of direct and indirect quotes. They use such phrases as "He said—and we quote him . . ."). If a long quote is used, newscast writers frequently insert a qualifier to let the listener know it is a direct quote. They use such terms as "he continued," "he went on to say" and "he concluded."

   4. If possible, numbers should be rounded off, especially large and detailed numbers. The city budget may be $20,568,987, but the broadcast news writer will make it "20 million 569 thousand dollars." However, if the number must be specific, for example, "a new tax rate of 3 dollars and 24 cents," it is not rounded off. Newscasters generally try to use figures sparingly and avoid lists of numbers altogether. They never start a sentence with a figure if they can avoid it.

   5. Contractions are acceptable in newscasts but should not be used to extremes. Contractions should not be used if they sound awkward on the air. The use of slang should be avoided unless it is in a direct quote or is germane to the story.

   6. Newscasters use adjectives sparingly. Nouns are much stronger words. In newscasts that are going to be augmented by film or still photos, adjectives should be avoided if they are relative words. The pretty blonde to the news writer may not be pretty to many of the viewers, for example, and the use of such a description may be considered sexist by others.

   Here is an example of the newspaper version and the broadcast version of the same story:

Newspaper Version

   WASHINGTON—It has been nearly three decades since Dr. Dennis P. Burkitt, a British missionary surgeon who studied the differences in disease of poor Africans and affluent Westerners, postulated that

Broadcast Version

   A study out today of nearly 90,000 women disputes the popular belief that a high-fiber diet protects against colon cancer.

   Fiber intake has no effect on the risk, according to research for the Nurses Health Study in The New England Journal of Medicine.

the Africans' high-fiber diet protected them against colon cancer. He
spread his thesis as dietary gospel,
prompting millions to change their
diets.

Now, the largest study ever to
examine Dr. Burkitt's theory has
found that, at least when it comes to
preventing colon cancer, all those
fruits, vegetables and cereals do not
do any good.

The research, by a team from
Harvard University and Brigham
and Women's Hospital in Boston,
tracked . . .

Researchers asked the women
about their diet in 1980, then followed
them for 16 years to see who got colon
cancer.

But don't replace bran cereal and
fruit with bacon yet, says Harvard
Medical School's Charles Fuch, lead
study author. A high-fiber diet clearly
cuts heart disease risk, he says. . . .

The newspaper story went on for another 20 inches, giving details of the
study and including quotes from its authors as well as statements from other researchers, nutritionists, and the National Cancer Institute.

Special Devices in Newscasts

Because a newscast is made up of a number of short stories, the newscast writer
often has to provide a "bridge" between them, particularly when the two have
something in common. A variety of transitional phrases is used. Some examples
are "Meanwhile, at City Hall, Mayor Jack Corn took action to . . ." (used between
two stories dealing with city government in some way) and "Today's hazardous
weather conditions did not keep Mayor Jack Corn from showing up at . . ." (used
as a bridge from a weather story to a story on the Mayor).

The best rule for the use of transitions is: Use them when they seem helpful
or logical; do not use them if they seem forced. Newscast writers should avoid using such editorialized transitions as "Here's an interesting item" or "You will like
this story." Datelines, however, which are often used to identify where an item
originates, can serve as good transitions from one story to another, as in the example: "And from Washington comes a report that . . ."

As a teaser to attract listeners, a newscast often begins with a series of three
or four rapid-fire, headline-style phrases from the leading stories of the day. Frequently they are flashed on the television screen at the same time the anchor is
reading them. The "headlines" generally are followed by a commercial break, and
then the regular newscast begins. Here are several examples of a television newscast headline:

COMING UP NEXT ON NEWS AT NOON . . .

FIRE DESTROYS RESORT HOTEL
IN THE SMOKY MOUNTAINS . . . WE'LL

HAVE AN EYE-WITNESS REPORT FROM
COSBY.

SEARCHERS FIND BODY OF MISSING
WOMAN FLOATING IN NORRIS LAKE . . .

AND AN OUTBREAK OF FLU HAS
CLOSED THE CHRISTIAN ACADEMY FOR
THE REST OF THE WEEK . . .

THOSE STORIES PLUS—
HOW TO BEAT THE WINTER BLAHS . . .
NEXT—ON NEWS AT NOON!

Stories told in chronological order are used from time to time on newscasts just as they are in newspapers. However, on newscasts they are generally extremely short, and they end with a surprise or a punch line.

The Extra Job of Television Writers

The television newscast writer has to make certain that the words selected for the anchors to read blend smoothly with the action films, videotape, still photographs, electronic graphics or other visual material selected to illustrate the story. The words and pictures have to complement each other. That's why it is important that a writer never attempt to prepare a script for a piece in which videotape or film is to be used without having seen the visuals. If the mood of the words does not match the action on the film, the viewer will notice it quickly.

Planning and selecting the visuals may be part of the responsibilities of the newscast writer. At some small-market stations, the writer may even do the filming. However, at most television stations there is a news director and an assignment editor who assigns reporters and camera operators to specific stories.

News operations at television stations are similar in a number of ways to the city room of a newspaper. The news director and assignment editor keep abreast of news developments in the city and schedule reporters and camera crews to regular events such as meetings of governmental bodies. Many stations have reporters regularly assigned to major beats just as newspapers do. Coverage of fires, accidents and natural disasters often becomes a team effort with all available hands contributing.

The overriding concern is to get excellent visuals to help tell the story. What the visuals don't tell, the writer should. At a fire, the film may show flames and smoke engulfing a building, but there may be no immediate identification of the building. That means the writer has to tell the viewer what is burning and where it is. For example, say a fire destroys the main building at a knitting mill where workers have been on strike for two months. The film will show the burning building, but the writer has to tell the reader that:

A four-alarm fire destroyed the main building at the strike-bound Riverside Knitting Mill in suburban Rockwood today.

When the scene switches, the writer has to reestablish the scene for the viewer. If the film shows the fire chief talking to company executives, the writer has to explain for the viewer:

Meanwhile, Company President George Everett urged Fire Chief Leonard Basler to begin an immediate arson investigation.

The viewer would then see and hear Everett making his request and explaining why he suspects arson. The writer follows this up with other details of the fire and gives some background on the labor troubles at the knitting mill while additional footage of the fire is being shown.

Broadcast Copy

Although each news operation will have its own particular format for preparing the news copy that is read on the air, generally radio newscasters prefer triple-spaced copy with each line of type averaging fewer than 10 words. Newscasters usually speak about 125 to 150 words a minute, so 12 to 15 lines will take about one minute of air time. At some stations, each story is prepared on a separate sheet of paper to allow for last-minute changes in the order the stories are presented. At others, the script simply runs from one page to the next. Some stations prepare their scripts in all capital letters. However, both capital and lowercase letters are easier to read than all uppercase and are more universally used in broadcast writing.

Television newscasts are generally written on the right half of the page with each line averaging five or six words. The left side of the page of a television script is used for the audio and video information so the anchors will know what pictures and audio material is being used. Of course, this material, usually in all caps, is not read aloud. Most stations use teleprompters so the anchors can look directly at the camera and not down at the script.

Here is part of what a typical script for a local 6 o'clock television newscast might look like:

OPENING CREDITS
Aerial view of Riverbend state prison
Voiceover
    The machines worked but the people didn't!
    State prison officials say human error is to blame for two high-profile
    prison breaks.
    Hello! I'm Rick Kaplan
    And I'm Kim Clark, and this is the 6 o'clock news.
    (Rick) It was a difficult day for state prison officials. They were called to
    Capitol Hill to explain two embarrassing escapes. The most recent involved
    six maximum security inmates who broke out of Riverbend two days after
    Christmas. All have been recaptured. In an earlier prison escape, four

inmates broke out of a Communications Corporation of America prison in
Wayne County in October.

David Wickert was on Legislative Plaza today when state officials
came clean.

ANCHOR QUESTION

(Kim) David, did prison officials explain what happened?

(David Full) Officials told the legislators that there were
procedural violations on the 3rd shift, the night shift where these maximum
inmates were brought out of their cells to work in violation of policy.

(Rick) Did they say why inmates would be out of their cells at 1 a.m?

(David Full) I have Rep. Tom Jester with me, Rick. Did prison officials
explain how this last escape happened?

(Rep. Jester Full) "We all know and you know and the commissioner
knows somebody screwed up. Just plain and simple. And I acknowledge that,
sir."

(Kim) Are lawmakers completely satisfied with the answers from prison officials?

(David Full) No. Senator Edna Mae Pullen said she wasn't sure she could believe the information prison officials gave. She called their explanation vague
and evasive.

(Rick) What did the Corrections Department's internal investigation show?

(David Full) "State officials say at least 6 months went into planning the
escape at Riverbend. But prisoners would never have made it over
the last chain link fence if at least 6 different employees would have done
their jobs.

(Rick) David, the tension at today's meeting was obvious. Are lawmakers calling for the commissioner's job?

(David Full) Not at this point. But they're not happy and neither is the governor.

(Kim) Thanks, David. When we come back, a gas leak in Springfield forces the
evacuation of three businesses.

There is a commercial break and the script continues with the gas leak story, the
kidnapping of a disabled teenager, a drug sting, a feature on personalized license
plates and a dozen other stories, including weather and sports. Fourteen visuals
were used to illustrate the stories.

EXERCISES

1. Arrange a tour of the news operation of a local or nearby television station. Interview the news director and write a story for a newspaper on that interview.

2. Using a copy of the daily morning newspaper that circulates in your city, watch a
   local television newscast that same evening. Compare the stories on the front page
   of the newspaper with the stories used on the television news program. Write a
   brief report comparing the two.

3. If the leading radio station in your city broadcasts a news program late in the day or early evening, make a similar comparison between the newspaper's front page and the stories used on the radio news broadcast. Write a brief report comparing the two.

4. Write a newscast version of each of the following opening paragraphs of these news stories and indicate what visuals you would use to illustrate the story:

a. A Long Island teenager was killed Wednesday night at the front door of his Bay Shore home after he was confronted by a young man who asked for him by name, then shot him once in the face, police said.

As the victim, Tim Halbritter, 15, fell to the floor, the unidentified gunman, who appeared to be no more than 20, fled on foot, Detective John Gorkas said.

b. Thirty-eight vehicles, including at least eight tractor-trailers, piled up in a fiery chain-reaction wreck on foggy Interstate 75 Friday, killing a woman and injuring 10 others.

The accident occurred shortly after 8 a.m. in the southbound lanes about 10 miles north of Athens. Smashed cars, motor homes, light trucks, big rigs and even snowmobiles were scattered over a tenth of a mile, State Trooper Ed Prieto said.

c. Friends of the Elderly is seeking volunteers to bring meals and gifts to isolated Cedar Rapids senior citizens on weekends.

The group needs 100 volunteers to commit themselves to about three hours a week, David Medved, the organization's spokesman, said.

Volunteers will be asked to deliver a hot meal on Saturday and Sunday to two or three elderly residents who are living alone.

d. The state's highest court yesterday made it easier for computer users suffering from repetitive stress injuries to take a byte out of keyboard manufacturers.

A unanimous state Court of Appeals yesterday extended the vote that potential plaintiffs have to sue, ruling that RSI Injuries are unique and must be treated specially under the law.

People who contend that their fingers, wrist, arm, neck and back problems were caused by computer keyboards now have three years to sue from the time RSI symptoms appeared or from the last time they used the crippling keyboard, whichever is earlier.

5. Write television newscast headlines on the following stories:

a. Police Chief Francisco Martinez has banned use of pepper spray by city police officers, citing the deaths of 60 people nationwide that have been blamed on the chemical.

b. The State Supreme Court today rejected the death penalty appeal of Edward Zakweski, 33, on grounds he was morally justified in hacking his family to death because he wanted to spare them the embarrassment of an impending divorce.

c. A suspect in a series of bank robberies in East Tennessee has been arrested and another man is being sought in connection with at least four area bank holdups, the FBI said today.

Michael Lovell, 29, of Greeneville, was arrested yesterday after FBI agents searched his apartment. He allegedly robbed the First American Bank of Rogersville on October 15.

d. Search and rescue crews located a small airplane that crashed in the eastern edge of Kings Canyon National Park a week ago, killing the pilot and her two passengers.

The single-engine Cherokee Piper 28 was found yesterday 75 to 100 feet below the summit of the 13,568-foot Mount Goddard.

6. Using the following stories, write a three-minute newscast (roughly 450 words) organized according to local, national and international news.

a. After more than 11 hours of deliberation Thursday, a jury found Fortunato Camberto guilty of manslaughter in the January 14 shooting death of his 69-year-old cousin.

Camberto, 75, had been facing a first-degree murder charge when the trial started 7 days ago. But the 12-member jury came back into the courtroom late Thursday with the guilty finding on the lesser criminal charge.

b. Tax bills for nearly 295,000 properties in Volusia County and about 60,000 in Flagler County for the coming year will soon be on the way to property owners.

Volusia County's property tax bills are scheduled to be mailed today and Flagler County's tax bills, will be mailed "first thing Monday morning," said Tina Smith, spokesperson for the Flagler Tax Collector's office.

c. A former legal secretary of a prominent local law firm was sentenced to 16 months in prison for embezzling $515,000 by Criminal Court Judge John Chang. With good behavior and credit for 90 days already spent behind bars, Angel Stephenson is likely to be freed in little more than five months.

d. Union officials said Thursday that a five-week strike at Valley Recycling Company has been settled after City Council members put pressure on the company.

Antonio Stallone, who heads the International Longshore and Warehouse Union, said that Valley Recycling had settled the labor dispute shortly after the City Council threatened to revoke the company's lucrative $14 million contract with the city.

Several council members said they were concerned that the materials that had been accumulating at the company's recycling plant were creating a public health hazard.

The 56 workers went on strike five weeks ago over overtime pay and health benefits. Stallone said the terms of the settlement were favorable to the workers.

e. FAIRFIELD—A teenager has admitted to fatally shooting his mother in front of her husband and five other children, Fairfield police said today.

Darrieus Hemphill, 18, shot Leonteen Jackson, 39, during an argument over money Wednesday, police said. He was arrested when the woman's husband called 911 and police responded.

"He wasn't calm, but he wasn't freaked out either. He admitted to shooting her," said Detective Georgia Sweeten.

f. STOCKTON—Mental health workers say they did everything right in restraining an out-of-control patient who died after he was wrestled to the ground and bound in leather restraints, Stockton Police Chief Joseph Dickerson said.

Rick Griffin, 36, died Wednesday at San Thomas Mental Health Institute where he had been for 30 days. His family was disturbed that he died in the care of people they thought would help him.

They believe hospital staff members used unnecessary forces because they were intimidated by Griffin's 340-pound, six-foot three-inch frame.

g. DENVER—The first blizzard of the season shut down much of the western Plains Wednesday, with up to three feet of wind-driven snow closing hundreds of miles of highways and leaving travelers snowbound in bus depots, airports and truck stops.

Even people trained for severe conditions couldn't reach their destinations. Search and rescue specialist Micki Marti tried to get from Denver to her home in Las Chance, but never made it beyond Byers, 25 miles east of Denver on Interstate 70.

"I even tried the back roads, but they were all closed," said Marti in a telephone interview from a Salvation Army shelter at the Byers American Legion Hall, where she was one of about 25 stranded travelers.

Interstates and other highways were closed across a large part of eastern Colorado and southeastern Wyoming, along with adjoining sections of Nebraska, Kansas and New Mexico.

h. CHICAGO—Moments after confessing to the shooting deaths of a young couple at the Oak Street beach, a former Marine shot himself in the head.

DeWayne Gesellschaft, 20, of Evanston, died yesterday morning at Micheal Reese Hospital, several hours after he admitted to police in a phone call that he had killed the couple.

He had reported finding the bodies of Cynthia Gormey, 19, and Estevan Jimenez, 24, while jogging on the beach. Later he was tied to the slayings by witnesses who saw him approaching the couple on the beach.

i. BETHLEHEM, West Bank—Israeli soldiers fired tear gas and rubber bullets yesterday at stone-throwing Palestinians who were marching for the release of Palestinian prisoners held in Israel's jails.

One of the 400 protestors was taken to the hospital after being hit in the leg with a rubber bullet. Ten others were treated for the effects of tear gas.

The protestors say the Palestinian Authority has neglected the issue of Palestinian prisoners in Israeli jails. But Hisham Abdel Razig, a Palestinian National Assembly member who deals with the matter, blamed the Israeli officials for stalling on the prisoner release agreement.

j. MANILA—The Philippines vowed to strengthen its armed forces, one of Asia's weakest, to defend its territorial claims in the South China Sea against alleged Chinese intrusions. But it made it clear it wanted no war with China over the potentially oil-rich cluster of islands, reefs and rocky outcrops, called the Spratlys, which are claimed wholly or in part by six Asian nations.

k. BERLIN—Chancellor Gerhard Schroder's chief of staff, Bodo Hombach, will visit the United States and Israel this month to discuss compensating the Nazi's slave laborers, a spokeswoman said.

Before taking office in October, Mr. Schroder's government decided to establish a fund to settle wage claims and suits for the thousands of Jews who were forced to work in Nazi factories producing guns, tanks and ammunition for the German army during World War II. They lived and worked in subhuman conditions, survivors claim.

1. CAIRO—Iraq has executed 18 political detainees, including army officers accused in a plot to kill Saddam Hussein, an Iraqui opposition group said today.

The executions took place in a prison near Baghdad in mid-December, the Center for Human Rights said. It provided a list of names of the prisoners it said were killed. Fifteen bodies were returned to their families with a warning not to conduct any public mourning, a Center spokesman said.

7. List the visuals you would suggest for the stories in Exercise 6.

CHAPTER

14 Policy in the News

"America's press failed the basic test of ethical journalism," said Steve Geimann, a past president of the Society of Professional Journalists and chair of its Ethics Committee.

The coverage "has put another dent in our credibility," said Diane McFarland, executive editor of the *Sarasota Herald–Tribune* in Florida and vice chair of the ethics and values committee of the American Society of Newspaper Editors.

"Competitive juices overtook common sense" James E. Shelledy, editor of the *Salt Lake Tribune* said.

"There was a real frenzy because of the ingredients: sex and a well-known figure," added Ben Bagdikian, journalism professor emeritus at the University of California and author of *The Media Monopoly*.

They all were talking about the press coverage of the White House sex scandal, which dominated the news for more than a year in the late 1990s.

Probably no story in the last decade of the 20th century generated as much criticism of the press, not only from media critics and the general public, but from members of the press itself.

"The 'feeding frenzy' by the news media in the White House sex scandal was quickly followed—and thereafter continuously accompanied—by a media frenzy of self-recrimination," Fred Brown, political editor of the *Denver Post* and president of the Society of Professional Journalists (SPJ), wrote in *Quill*, the SPJ magazine.

Yet a goodly number of journalists said they felt the press had done its job well in covering the story. In a survey conducted by the *Columbia Journalism Review*, 6 percent gave press coverage of the White House sex scandal an A; 55 percent gave it a B; 23 percent, a C; 14 percent, a D; and only 1 percent gave it an F. Another 2 percent weren't sure how to grade the media.

Other surveys indicated that the public had conflicting views of the performance of the press. In one, only one in 10 respondents gave the media "excellent" marks for its coverage. And in another, taken at approximately the same time, 64 percent said the quality of coverage by the news media was excellent or good.

The No. 1 complaint of those who participated in the surveys was the media's failure to verify the facts and its airing of unsubstantiated rumors and accusations. Others said they believed the press went overboard in its coverage, devoting too much time to the story and sensationalizing it. Many criticized the press for biased reporting and intrusiveness.

Complaints about the press being biased are not new. They have been around a long time. Usually they also include that the press is unfair, insensitive, inaccurate and unethical, among a host of other sins, both real and imaginary.

In addition, the consolidation of media ownership—85 percent of the daily papers in America are chain owned, for example and there is a growing concentration of ownership of the electronic media—has led to large numbers of individuals expressing concern about undue influence on the coverage of the news by owners of newspapers and broadcast stations.

While it is true that owners can and do influence the contents of their newspapers directly and indirectly from time to time, the same can be said for hired publishers, editors, managing editors or any person in authority at a newspaper. So it is essential that a reporter realize at the outset that most newspaper writers do not have total freedom to "do their own thing."

Every newspaper has specific policies that guide what news is reported and how it is presented to the public. Sometimes those policies are very specific and are included in the newspaper's stylebook. Some newspapers even carry the policy in their mastheads. The *St. Petersburg Times*, for example, states its ethical policies simply and directly: "The policy of our paper is very simple—merely to tell the truth."

Most often, however, a newspaper's policies are unwritten, and the reporter learns them through conversations with fellow reporters and editors, usually after he or she has violated one of them. Sometimes those policies are vague and may change with the circumstances of a story; other times they are blatantly obvious. For example, one newspaper may have a policy never to report divorce cases. Another may list divorces in its public record log. A third may even write news stories about divorces, especially those of prominent local persons. One newspaper may automatically support all candidates of a particular political party; another may mix its endorsements.

If a newspaper doesn't have a written policy guide for its staff, an astute reporter will learn the "policies" as quickly as possible. That does not mean a reporter should not work to change a policy, especially if it may be detrimental to the credibility of the newspaper. At one southern newspaper, for example, reporters worked for months to convince the editor to stop using the names of rape victims in news stories because they were aware the practice was resented by many readers.

But reporters should remember a newspaper is a business enterprise and can be operated as the owners see fit, no matter what the purpose, including personal, financial, political or social gain. A newspaper can promote political or other fortunes of the individual owner; the newspaper chain, if it is a part of one; or any special interests. Unfortunately, some newspapers do just that. However, responsible owners and editors will avoid any blatant misuse of the newspaper for personal reasons.

The newspaper is also—whether it wishes to be or not—a social instrument. It enters thousands of homes and is read by, or indirectly influences, every member of the family. It offers not merely news but information and entertainment. It promotes—whether it intends to or not—social, economic and political philosophies. The newspaper creates the atmosphere in which its character is nourished. Powerful and influential, it colors and infuses the character, ideals and institutions of the individual, the family and the community.

Because of its power and influence, the first duty of a newspaper is to keep its readers fully, accurately and truthfully informed. As long as it does this, a newspaper can promote its own policies without being accused of perverting the news.

In cities and towns served by only one newspaper, editors have a special responsibility to make certain they publish a wide range of opinion, not just their own. Unfortunately, it does not always work that way. Some editors take advantage of their position to force only their views on the public and exclude all others—especially opposing views. In other cases, editors are reluctant to adopt an outspoken editorial policy on controversial issues or political candidates. An editor may not want to face up to the pressure from various individuals and groups in the community, including some big advertisers. It may be that an editor sincerely believes the publication should be non-partisan and independent because it is the city's only newspaper. Rather than taking a stand, the editor may try to remain neutral by printing all the facts on all sides of public issues or campaigns for public office. However, this general policy should not prevent the editor from making certain exceptions.

When the public welfare of the community is at stake, every editor has an obligation to present and comment on the pros and cons of an issue. In such cases, the columns of the newspaper should be open to those who disagree with the newspaper's views. Even newspapers with admittedly strong partisan or other non-neutral general policies should be willing to print news and public statements that disagree with their policies. To do less would destroy the credibility of the paper.

Devices to Promote Policies

Editorials

The editorial section is generally recognized and accepted as the editor's (owner's) platform or soapbox. The editor has the same liberty to voice an opinion as the reader has to reject it.

Whether a newspaper should adopt strong policies or pursue a middle-of-the-road course—whether to attempt to shape public opinion or merely to reflect it—is an open question. Some newspapers take pride in their fighting qualities, but others boast of detached judgment. The answer is largely to be found in the personality of the editor (or owner if he or she is active as editor or publisher) and in the newspaper's circulation and advertising accounts. Some editors revel in a good fight. It wins them friends as well as enemies and perhaps a number of journalism awards for courage. Some even crusade at the risk of physical and financial danger. But, for the most part, a newspaper's editorial policy usually is determined on the basis of profitable reader appeal.

On smaller newspapers, most policy decisions are made by the owner, publisher or editor, who may be the same person. Larger newspapers may have an editorial board made up of the publisher, the editor, all the editorial writers and selected departmental editors. Some newspapers even have an advisory board of influential community leaders who regularly discuss the publication's policies with the editorial staff. Occasionally, they are called on to write columns for the editorial page as well.

On occasion, the publisher and the editorial board may disagree. That happened at the *Charlotte Observer* in North Carolina during a senatorial election campaign. The publisher wanted his newspaper to endorse the Republican incumbent. His two top editors and all the editorial writers preferred to endorse the Democratic candidate and eventual winner. They had prepared an editorial endorsing the Democratic candidate and were set to run it. But the publisher canceled it just before the election.

It was the newspaper's first non-endorsement in a Senate race in 20 years and it touched off heated internal discussions among the staff. They agreed that it was the publisher's prerogative to overrule an editorial board but they expressed their concern that the decision might have implications for the journalistic integrity of the newspaper. One editor charged that the paper, which should love the community, abdicated its role by failing to take a stand one way or the other.

Some larger newspapers also have an ombudsman, an in-house critic, who responds to letters of criticism from readers by investigating the complaints to determine their validity. Often, the ombudsman writes a column on the editorial page discussing a particular complaint. Sometimes ombudsmen are not popular with the editorial staff, especially when they are critical of how a particular story was handled by the reporter and editors. Staff members see this public discussion of their work as just another way of undermining their credibility.

One of the most difficult concepts for the public to accept is that a newspaper has the legal right to pursue any policy it pleases as long as it does not violate libel and other laws. In expressing editorial opinions, responsible newspapers will label them as such and confine them to the editorial page. In addition, they will publish opposing opinion.

Although some newspapers still present only their own views and opinions, many seek to balance their editorial pages by selecting columns that reflect a broad range of views. Several newspapers have selected local leaders or experts in a particular field and have asked them to express their views, which may or may not agree with the editor's stand on an issue.

On major local issues, the *St. Petersburg Times*, for example, often publishes its own editorial and in the next column an opposing point of view on an issue. The *New York Times* actively solicits diverse points of view for its "Op-Ed" page. Frequently its editors will take a particular stand on an issue in an editorial and print, on the opposite page, an article by someone diametrically opposed to the editor's view. Many other newspapers across the nation follow a similar policy.

Several newspapers have invited readers to participate in an exercise in editorial decision making by presenting a set of hypothetical situations involving the possible publication of private matters about the subject of a story. In most cases the readers tended to opt for privacy and compassion more often than the professionals. But they also tended to agree that it is difficult to produce simple, consistent, clear-cut resolutions of the ethical questions of journalism.

Other newspapers seek to accomplish the same goals through regular focus group sessions with readers. The focus groups usually are made up of a wide range of readers of the newspaper who meet regularly with an outside moderator to discuss the content of the newspaper. The moderator then reports the comments and opinions of the focus group members to the editorial staff.

The Front-Page Editorial

Occasionally, to reinforce the importance of an issue, a newspaper will print an editorial on the front page. The practice is generally accepted despite the criticism that it may be a confession of editorial-page weakness. The editorial should always be labeled as an editorial to let the reader know that he is reading an opinion, not news.

Other Policy Devices

A newspaper's policy is frequently reflected in cartoons as well as editorials. These "visual editorials" play an important part in political campaigns in particular, but they also are used most effectively to support other editorial points of view. A cartoon makes no pretense of being unbiased, as a general rule. It is frequently a frank and open criticism of an antagonist and in support of a definite policy. Patrick Oliphant, the Pulitzer Prize–winning cartoonist, told an interviewer that for him there "are no sacred cows . . . no forbidden areas. . . . If you are going to be in favor of something, you might as well not be a cartoonist."

Of course, not all editorial cartoons automatically support a particular point of view of the newspaper. Jim Borgman, editorial cartoonist for the *Cincinnati Enquirer*, wrote in the *Bulletin* of the American Society of Newspaper Editors that "at the *Enquirer*, to the everlasting credit of my publisher and editors, my cartoon has been allowed to roam, chancing upon the Official Editorial Stance only by coincidence. We get almost no letters that suggest readers are confused about the paper's position on issues by a contrary cartoon here and there. The signed cartoon is recognized as its own voice. What my editor may lose in control over the space, he gains in freshness, vigor and spontaneity, the stuff of debate."

Political cartoons were introduced in the American press by Thomas Nast in the mid-1800s and have since developed into a fine-art form. Many newspapers that cannot afford their own cartoonists regularly buy the work of major cartoonists, such as Oliphant, from feature syndicates. Lack of a cartoonist to support editorials of a purely local nature can sometimes handicap an editorial campaign. However, many editors employ photographs to help support editorials dealing with numerous local problems ranging from hazardous traffic conditions to slum housing.

In addition, columnists and other by-line writers may freely express opinions, and local citizens may be invited to contribute letters or articles to strengthen a campaign or crusade. Sometimes a newspaper adopts a slogan that promotes a policy.

The Newspaper Platform

Some of a newspaper's policies may be long-range programs. Others have immediate objectives. The policies of a Democratic, Republican or labor newspaper at election time may be predictable, but its responses to other issues will not be. In fact, newspapers that oppose each other politically often may support the same local programs on new schools, more city recreation areas, improved street lights, higher salaries for city policemen and a host of other issues dealing with civic improvement. Many newspapers begin each year with a list of civic goals at the top of the editorial page and then campaign all year long to bring them about. All of its policies taken together, including its more permanent attitudes toward such issues as politics, constitute the newspaper's platform. It has a right to work to achieve that platform. As long as it is a constructive platform, the newspaper's policy is a powerful influence for the common good. In promoting such policy, the editorial, the cartoon, the signed article and the slogan are legitimate devices beyond question. However, a newspaper that permits its policies to influence the writing and display of the news fails in its responsibility to its community and to the journalism profession as a whole.

Slanting the Policy Story

The temptation is always present for a newspaper engaged in vigorous promotion of a policy to utilize other resources at its command. Its most potent other resource, of course, is the news column. Several methods have been used to promote a policy through the news:

1. Featuring (and somewhat overplaying) an event in line with the newspaper's policy. This may be done with a large headline, a prominent position in the newspaper and a detailed account of the event. For example, a newspaper campaigning for safe driving may put every accident—major or minor—on the front page with large headlines, saying in substance, "I told you so."

FIGURE 14.1 Charles Daniel, editorial cartoonist for the *Knoxville News–Sentinel*, gave a local twist to a national story in this clever cartoon about the state's standing in a national survey.

(Reprinted with permission of Charles Daniel, *The Knoxville News–Sentinel*, Knoxville, Tenn.)

2. Ignoring or "playing down" events opposed to the newspaper's objectives. If mentioned at all, such events may be hidden under small headlines on an inside page or buried at the end of a story. If a newspaper opposes a candidate for sheriff, for example, it may give comparatively little space in which to present his or her side of the issues. If the candidate is an incumbent, the newspaper may suddenly discover, about two weeks before election time, that the county is riddled with vice and corruption. Apparently it does not expect its readers to ask why the vice and corruption had not been exposed months or even years earlier. Such transparent attempts to support a candidate by misleading readers can badly damage a newspaper's credibility.

3. Deliberately writing the news to emphasize certain points in a story while omitting others, thus interpreting an event so that it will best suit the newspaper's policy. Sometimes, unfortunately, facts themselves may be distorted or falsified. For example, suppose a speaker should say: "The working man does not deserve unemployment insurance. He deserves employment insurance, and it is the duty of the employer to see that he gets it." If, to make the speaker look bad, a reporter should play up the first sentence and purposely ignore the second, one would conclude that the speaker is against labor. Good reporting and honest newspaper policy would condemn such a purposely colored account.

4. Editorializing in the news. For example, if a newspaper favors a reduction in the tax rate, it may always refer to the existing *high* tax rate, taking for granted that everyone agrees the rate is high. The newspaper's opinions may be injected throughout the story in this manner. A review of some of the newspaper stories written about the increases in second-class postal rates would serve to illustrate this point extremely well.

5. Writing special stories deliberately designed to support the newspaper's policy. For example, the newspaper can always find prominent local persons or special-interest groups who agree with a given policy. These persons are interviewed, and their statements are prominently displayed in the newspapers. Persons against the policy are not usually interviewed, or their opposition is played down. Another example: If a newspaper wants to force an investigation of conditions at the jail, a local mental hospital or a nursing home, it might arrange to have a reporter locked up in the jail, committed to the hospital or hired at the nursing home to expose the "disgraceful" conditions that exist. Many editors consider such devices unethical.

Reporters should remember that under the law people who gather news have no more rights than ordinary citizens. They cannot break a law in pursuit of a story even if the person or institution they are investigating may be breaking the law.

Justification of Policies in News Stories

What are the justifications, if any, for promoting a policy by means of the news? Are all of the devices mentioned in the preceding section to be condemned? Obviously so, if their intent is to deceive. Obviously so, if their use prevents the complete, accurate and truthful presentation of the news. Under certain circumstances, however, there is some excuse—if not justification—for the influence of policy on the news.

Subjectivity

Few readers, but all editors, know that the process of gathering and writing news is subjective, despite all efforts to make it objective. The selection of assignments, the reporters picked to cover them and their approaches to handling stories are based on a series of value judgments. It is a cliche in the news business that seven reporters sent to cover the same speech probably will produce seven entirely different interpretations of that speech.

Although this may be an overstatement, it is based on sound observation. Theoretically, a speech has but one interpretation and that is the meaning that the speaker intends to convey. Actually, each person in the audience, including the re-porter, may get a different impression of a speaker's message. A careful reporter will focus on the most significant point or points the speaker makes, using quota-tions from the speaker to support the reporter's interpretation. Despite vast expe-rience in covering speeches, a reporter may give a speech story a slant quite different from what the speaker had intended. Yet the reporter is reporting the facts as seen and heard.

The complete objectivity necessary to perfect reporting has yet to be achieved by any reporter. All facts reported to newspaper readers must pass through the mind of the reporter. Every reporter observes events and understands facts against the screen of experience and through the film of human emotions. This human frailty plagues every reporter and all newspapers, but a reporter must not use this as an excuse for faulty or dishonest work.

Self-Censorship

Most newspapers practice self-censorship. Often this is dictated by what the editor considers good taste as well as by contemporary community standards. Although it is true that standards tend to grow more liberal, most editors make a serious ef-fort not to offend the sensibilities of their readers. Obscene language used during a trial, the gruesome details of a brutal murder, the "inside" story behind a politi-cian's downfall, or the "real dope" about the divorce of a prominent citizen may be censored from the story. The reader may not be given all the information about reported events or reports on all events. The newspaper to this extent fails to re-port the news fully.

Just how far this censorship on behalf of "decency" should go is debatable. Often, it may not be the public's taste as much as the editor's that generates the censorship. An Ohio editor was dismissed for allowing an infamous four-letter word to remain in a quote by a man known for the use of that type of language, despite the fact that only a handful of readers complained. The publisher, how-ever, felt the use of the word was bad for the image of the paper and dismissed the editor. In practicing self-censorship, a newspaper must take care that it does not use this power on behalf of a special interest or a special cause. If it does, its pol-icy reporting will be indefensible.

The Moral Purpose

Another excuse for faulty reporting and for allowing policy to influence the news may be the intention to do good. A story may purposely be warped to emphasize a moral—to teach a lesson. Many feature stories become nearly fiction in the process of passing from the scene of action through the reporter's mind, aglow with an honest (or possibly dishonest) emotion, to reach the printed page. Liter-ary license is taken with the facts in many stories to stir readers. Sometimes it may be as "innocent" as the ever-recurring faithful dog story in which a dog allegedly saves its young master from drowning. In actual fact, the dog may have plunged in only when its master staggered into shallow water. Yet many reporters cannot resist the temptation to make a hero of the dog. Photographers rush to the home for the traditional boy-dog picture. Is no harm done? Does it make a good story? Maybe. But is it true? After all, the function of the newspaper is to present the news fully, accurately and truthfully, and this type of story is neither accurate nor truthful.

There is another hazard in stretching fact for so-called moral purpose. Sometimes the well-meaning story can backfire. In one case out of the books on libel, a newspaper was found guilty of libeling a family it had tried to help. The father was out of work and the family without much food when the youngest child died. In an effort to help the family, the newspaper printed a sad and touching story of the family's misfortunes, including a statement that the child would have to be buried in a pauper's grave alongside the remains of drunks and derelicts. In the rush of emotion and a desire to move the readers to help the family, the reporter overstated the family's plight. The family sued, charging that it had been held up to ridicule through no fault of its own. The jury agreed and found the paper guilty of libel.

Dilemma in Weighing Stories

Another excuse for playing up a story on behalf of a policy may be found in an occasional dilemma. When two stories are of approximately equal value, it is almost too much to expect a city editor to bury the policy story. For example, if the newspaper is campaigning for a bond issue, the whole editorial staff might value the policy stories more highly than competing stories. Every item bearing on the need for the bond issue may appear to be important. In weighing stories that have a bearing on newspaper policies, the newspaper cannot excuse itself like a judge whose son is to be tried for murder. Must it not either favor its own child or commit the equal error of "leaning over backward"? The reporter and the staff need almost superhuman objectivity to present the news fully, accurately and truthfully.

A problem sometimes arises when an editor, seeking to please the owner or publisher, gives special treatment to certain stories he or she thinks will please the publisher. Such a story may not have any real news value that given day, yet it may be prominently displayed, perhaps even on page 1. Often organizations deliberately name publishers to their boards in an attempt to gain favorable treatment in the newspaper. And they are quite successful, because many editors would not risk playing down a story they believe might be a "sacred cow" of the publisher.

In pursuing a policy, the newspaper and the reporter have an opportunity to serve the community by placing emphasis on fullness, accuracy and honesty in reporting. A policy to promote worthy causes may indeed be noble. But a newspaper that vigorously promotes the local community chest fund drive year after year but never carefully checks how much of that money goes for campaign overhead compared to how much is used to really help the people of the community is not reporting fully, accurately and honestly.

The issues reported in the press are too commonly the plain and unvarnished facts. They lack the intelligible background that an enterprising reporter would gather from library investigations, from studies of experiences of other communities and from other sources of information. Reporters should never forget that not all newsworthy material is collected on the regular beats. The encyclopedia, librarian, schoolteacher and scientific laboratories are rich in background material outside the established boundaries of news beats. The reporter can offer a service to the community of a rare order of usefulness if he or she will utilize the cultural tools the community offers. In many cases the average citizen lacks the time and ability to use those tools, but in the hands of an enterprising reporter they can help report not only accurately and truthfully but also with the fullness needed by people trying to manage their own processes of government.

Certainly, the coverage of the White House scandal in the 1990s was not the finest hour for either print or electronic journalists. But the situation is not as diabolical as press critics would have the public believe. No newspaper would survive if it did not present a fair, accurate and balanced account of the day's events most of the time.

It is equally true that there is genuine concern among leaders in the news profession about the credibility of the press. That issue has dominated programs at meetings of newspaper editors, publishers and reporters for nearly a decade. It is that concern that led the American Society of Newspaper Editors to undertake its Journalism Credibility Project cited in Chapter 1, and the Pew Charitable Trusts to underwrite the Project on the State of the American Newspapers to scrutinize what big media companies are actually doing for, and to, America's newspapers.

Still, there are large numbers of individuals who believe that newspapers are unduly influenced by the whims—political, economic, ethical, social—of their owners, especially large corporate owners.

EXERCISES

1. Study the editorial page of your local daily newspaper for a week. List the editorials that appear by local, state, national and international topics. Write a brief report on your findings.

2. Invite the publisher or editor of your local newspaper to class to discuss the editorials you studied. Also ask her or him to outline for the class the newspaper's policies on such local issues as local property and sales taxes as opposed to an income tax, bond issues for public building projects, city–county government consolidation and other significant public issues. Write a story on that class discussion.

3. Often newspapers disagree with public officials and express that disagreement in editorials. Examine your local newspaper carefully for a month to find any stories or editorials critical of public officials.

4. Using those stories or editorials, contact the public official or officials and interview them on their response to the newspaper's editorial stand.

5. Some newspapers print rumors, others do not. Collect a sampling of rumors floating around your community that have not appeared in print, then interview the editor of your local newspaper to ask why some were printed and some were not.
   Write a news story on that interview.

6. Invite two or three persons who have been the subjects of articles in the local or
   campus newspaper to class to discuss their views on how fair and accurate the stories about them were.

7. Using your class as a focus group, ask them to read the local daily newspaper (use
   the campus daily if one is published) critically for a week. At the last class of the
   week, examine the paper, page by page, story by story, to elicit their comments,
   praise, criticisms and suggestions. Write a report detailing their likes and dislikes
   and suggestions for improving the paper.

PART FOUR

Writing the General Story

"Newspapers should do a better job of what they do best: Being the primary source of vital information about their communities," Charles W. Dunagin, editor and publisher of the *Enterprise Journal*, McComb, Miss., wrote in *The American Editor*.

Today, more and more newspapers are doing just that. They are emphasizing local stories about religion, sports, business and education as well as crime and politics.

A number of newspapers have increased their local coverage by 10 percent but still continue to report important state, national and international news because readers haven't lost their appetite for it.

Although there is a basic tendency to label all stories by subjects, many stories overlap. A sports story might also be a business story. An education story could also be a political story. And a political story certainly could be a crime story as well.

Labels are a convenient way to classify stories as well as a quick indicator of the department that will handle a particular story and where it probably will appear in the newspaper. However, those divisions are becoming more and more blurred in many newsrooms.

15 Personals and Briefs

"Local news is the name of the game," Jennie Rae Buckner, editor of the Charlotte (N.C.) *Observer,* said. "And we are not as far ahead as we ought to be."

Her remarks came in conjunction with a national study that found people look to newspapers for local news and shopping information.

She said newspapers should cover their communities better and more intently. And the *Observer* has been doing just that. When the newspaper sought to gain circulation outside its core market, its editors talked to readers in those areas where suburban newspapers were pushing "hometown" news.

They asked what the *Observer* should offer them to compete successfully with community newspapers. Among their suggestions were one-year birthdays, anniversaries, Little League, obituaries and wedding announcements. In short, more personal news.

Few items in any newspaper are more local than personals and briefs, which is why newspapers, especially community newspapers, carry so many of these short stories, often no more than a sentence or two long. Some collect them in "People" columns. Others use them as individual stories with their own headlines.

As a general rule, metropolitan newspapers carry briefs or personal items about only the most prominent persons. Frequently those items are collected in a column. However, community newspapers usually carry briefs and personals about practically everyone in town.

Many community newspaper editors say that personals are the best-read stories in their newspapers. Personals may be grouped into a column with a single headline in the family living or lifestyle section, or they may be scattered through the regular news sections. Occasionally an editor or one of the staff may write a personal column and use brief items about citizens in the community. The use and placement of briefs or personals is unlimited.

Briefs and personals serve several important purposes: They provide information on activities of various citizens as well as social, civic and religious groups in the community, and they can be used to facilitate makeup by filling in small spaces left after longer stories are placed on pages. Even when serving this last purpose, they should be written with the same care and effort that go into the main story each day. A mistake in a name, an address or a fact in a personal item is just as serious as a similar mistake in any page-1 story.

Personals and briefs are arbitrarily classified here as a separate story type. Actually, they are a type only in the sense that they emphasize personalities and are short. Otherwise they are relatively unimportant in news value in relation to the news value of the page-1 stories. In subject matter, personals and briefs range the entire spectrum of human activity. All of the subject-matter story types discussed more fully in later chapters are represented among them. At some newspapers they are considered to be merely elementary stories that the beginning reporter is often assigned to write. However, every seasoned reporter knows their value and regularly collects them.

Personals

Names make news. This is a newspaper clichè, but it is also true. And they do not always have to be prominent names. Newspapers have always recognized the news value of names of quite ordinary persons. The names of visitors, guests, committee members, and those sponsoring or attending dinners, banquets, conventions and so on are usually listed by newspapers as fully as space permits. Lack of space, not failure to recognize the essential news value of names, excludes many of these smaller items from newspapers in larger cities. However, a number of metropolitan newspapers use such items as fillers in place of buying filler material from the news syndicates.

Announcements of trips, visitors, parties, newcomers and a large assortment of relatively minor events that take place in any community are considered to be personals. The lifestyle pages or family pages (discussed in Chapter 27) often use many such items, but other personals are used throughout the paper as one, two and three-paragraph stories with headlines.

News Value

It is often difficult to classify personal items by the standard tests for news value—disaster, progress, conflict and so forth—although a careful study of them will show that in a minor way they may fall into those categories. Mrs. Nancy Parker goes to the hospital, and that might border on disaster for her family. David Thomas is made a first-class petty officer in the Navy, and that suggests progress. If these items were of greater consequence, they would be expanded into longer stories to be classified as illness, death or business. They are very seldom novelties. They contain little human interest of an emotional or dramatic nature. They might represent borderline eminence—that is, if they were about a reasonably well-known local person.

Why run them? Personals, as a class of story, would seem to be a composite of all the news values. Individually, they may be of little consequence except to the persons immediately involved; yet collectively they record life in any community on a very fundamental level. They contain virtually all human interests—gossip, birth, death, illness, conflict and the rest. They give the readers of any newspaper a daily look at the activities of their fellow citizens, not just the prominent ones. And they are extremely well read.

The most common characteristic of most personals is that they are quite local in nature. If a member of a local social club is planning an event—plant sale, card party or fashion show—it is local news of a personal type. A similar event in a community 50 miles away would mean nothing. The personal is a standard item in the columns of newspapers in smaller communities. It is usually unnecessary to belong to an organization or take part in a major news event to be mentioned in the news columns of a small-town newspaper—daily or weekly. A shopping trip to a nearby city or the purchase of a new tractor may be sufficient for one to get his or her name in the local newspaper in many small communities. In the large city dailies the personal is somewhat confined to the more or less prominent persons, the activities of prominent local groups and clubs, and the personalities of so-called high society. Rural or urban newspapers, however, consider the personal items as an important reader-interest and circulation builder.

Sources of Personals

Most personals are telephoned, mailed, faxed, e-mailed or brought to the newspaper office by interested persons. Hostesses report their party plans, themes and guest lists. Mothers announce schools or vacation plans for their children. Families report on out-of-town visitors. Dinners, parties and other social events are similarly brought to the family editor of the paper. The mail brings a steady stream of press releases from vacation hotels, convention centers and other tourist attractions reporting the local persons who visited there recently. Every regular beat yields personals and briefs to the alert reporter. Public officials and employees go on business trips and vacations. They have children going off to school, babies at home. Behind the public front of every person on every beat are many personal items of interest. Hobbies, along with other recreation and sports activities, are fertile fields for personals. On a rare occasion a personal item can lead to an even bigger story. The social activities and travels of a midwestern state official some years ago piqued the interest of a beat reporter who eventually discovered that the official had stolen $14 million from the state.

One community editor reports that she takes a notepad with her everywhere, even to church, and records items about individuals that later appear in the "Personals" column in her paper. Her reporters are required to bring personals in from their beats, and many readers phone or mail in items for the column. "It's one of our most popular features," she said.

Writing Personals

The personal should be written as a straight news story. It should have a well-written lead and contain all the necessary information to make the story complete.

The lead requires:

1. The five W's. These are essential in all stories, of course, though some of them may be implied in the lead.

2. Identification of the person or persons mentioned. If a long list of persons is given (for example, the names of new club members), do not try to use them all in the lead. Write a more general lead and include the names in the second paragraph along with their identification. But if the item reports the activities of only one or two individuals, each should be identified. Wherever possible, a descriptive identity should be included to intensify reader interest. The descriptive identity, lacking in the first of the following personals, is *italicized* in the second item.

> Mrs. Gaylord Hampton, 1202 Briarcliff Ave., is making a month-long auto trip through the Southwest.
> Mrs. Gaylord Hampton, 1202 Briarcliff Ave., *whose Southern cookbook was published in June*, is making a month-long motor trip through the Southwest. *She will collect recipes for a Chicano cookbook.*
> Evelyn Biggs, 2412 Bradford Ln., is touring southern Louisiana for two weeks with her granddaughter, Shannon.
> Evelyn Biggs, 2412 Bradford Ln., *whose photographs of life in the Smoky Mountains have been reproduced in national newspapers and magazines*, is touring southern Louisiana for two weeks with her granddaughter, Shannon. *She plans to photograph a day in the life of a Cajun family that will be used in a book on ethnic Americans to be published next fall.*

Here is how to handle a personal with a long list of names:

> Eight members of the Clay County Garden Club will exhibit floral arrangements in the Piedmont Flower show in Raleigh next month.
> They are: (List the club members and their addresses. If descriptions of the floral arrangements are available, include them. But do not include any if you cannot include all of them.)
> Ten members of the Recreation Department's Ceramics Club will enter their work in a juried crafts show sponsored by the Southern Guild of Folk Artists in Asheville next month.
> They are: (List the club members and their addresses. If descriptions of their ceramic pieces are available, include them. Do not include descriptions of some pieces and not others.)

Stressing an Interesting Feature

Reporters should always look for interesting features when writing personals and not be satisfied to use only the basic five W's. To say that "The Rev. Thomas O'Neal will leave for Rome Friday" is interesting to friends and members of his church. But what is he planning to do in Rome? Is he just on vacation? Is he attending a church meeting? Will he be going to school there? The minister probably would be willing to answer a few questions, and the reporter may find an interesting feature somewhere.

The following is an example of how a personal item might be improved by adding a few details:

Bobby Mason, daughter of Mr. and Mrs. Jackson Mason, 117 Maplewood St., has been named to the dean's list at the University of the Pacific, Stockton, Calif.

Bobby Mason, 117 Maplewood, a senior accounting major at the University of the Pacific, Stockton, Calif., has been named to the dean's list for the seventh quarter in a row. She is the daughter of Mr. and Mrs. Jackson Mason.

In writing a personal, every effort should be made to avoid referring to persons by such terms as "widely known," "popular" and "beloved." (In newspaper offices, such words are called "puffs.") This is not only poor writing, but also editorializing and should not be permitted in personals or briefs, just as it should not be permitted in any straight news story.

Briefs

It is often difficult to distinguish between a personal and a brief. Perhaps the best distinction between them is that briefs generally do not pertain to persons. The change in city library hours, the post office's holiday schedule, dates for obtaining new auto licenses, announcements of minor fund-raising events and dozens of other short but newsworthy items would be classified as briefs.

Briefs are usually one- or two-paragraph stories dealing with incidents or occasions having broad appeal. Naturally, the wider the appeal—perhaps the closing of public buildings for a holiday—the more prominently they will be displayed in a newspaper. Briefs may be rewrites from other papers or new stories picked up by beat reporters or phoned in by interested persons. They are used because they are news, and they may be grouped together in a "News Briefs" column or used as fillers throughout the paper.

It is difficult to establish a dividing line between a brief and a longer, more important story. An event worthy of no more than two paragraphs in some newspapers may be "blown up," with the inclusion of more details, to five or six paragraphs in other newspapers. The size of the community and its newspaper, the availability of local news and the interest of the readers are factors to be considered by the reporter. A story's relative significance—the proportion of readers it will interest—is the major space-measuring device for the reporter.

Here is an example of a brief from a community newspaper:

The Twentieth Century Club will hold a rummage sale Oct. 4, 5 and 6 at its clubhouse, 1722 Washington Ave.

Sale hours Oct. 4 and 5 will be from 9 a.m. to 5 p.m. Oct. 6 the hours will be from 9 to 11:30 a.m.

Like a personal, a brief is obviously a single-feature story—and hardly more than a lead at that. The five W's, with the proper play given to the most important W, usually compose the whole story. Further explanation of one or more of the W's may call for a second paragraph.

Careless reporting, notably the lack of an inquiring attitude, sometimes makes potentially long stories into briefs. If the beginning reporter becomes too "brief" conscious, feeling that every story should be told in two paragraphs, he or she may fail to ask the kinds of questions that could develop a possible page-1 story. On the other hand, insignificant news events should not purposely be blown up or overplayed.

Fillers

The standardization of advertising format in recent years and the trend toward six-column makeup throughout newspapers has reduced some of the need for fillers. However, many editors still are faced with awkward and often tiny spaces to be filled, especially above advertisements.

Some newspapers use briefs and personals to fill those spaces. Others keep on hand a supply of very short items to "plug" those holes. Such fillers are usually inserted without headlines. They usually contain information, perhaps trivia, rather than news in its classic sense.

Fillers come from a variety of sources, but the most common source is a news feature service (syndicate). A number of organizations, such as the National Geographic Society or the American Cancer Society, distribute fillers free to newspapers. Other special-interest groups include them in their press kits or publicity releases.

A number of newspapers develop their own fillers from almanacs, government reports, census data, history books and encyclopedias. They are selected with some care to present unusual facts, "fascinating" information or descriptive items highlighting the local community. Many newspapers coordinate fillers with the general subject of the page or section of the newspaper in which they are used. Fillers about food are placed on the food pages, and so on. Humor and quotes from famous people also are used as fillers.

Here are some examples:

Be a reading tutor:
Call 623-1336

"A little learning is not a dangerous thing to one who does not mistake it for a great deal."—William Allen White

Marion County has 117 churches representing every major religious denomination.

Life has its disappointments but there is no reason to be one of them.

State Park Information: 8 a.m. to 5 p.m., Mon.-Fri., 753-2027.

To prevent food from sticking to a new fry pan, boil a little vinegar in it before using it the first time.

CONTRIBUTE TO THE COMMUNITY CHEST

BUY U.S. SAVINGS BONDS

Other newspapers use the space at the end of columns and above advertisements to promote the paper and some of its services. Here are several examples:

What's Sunday without The Daily News?

The New York Times Magazine

Illuminates the news.

The Plain Talk's Classifieds

Work for you—619-3354

EXERCISES

1. Interview five of your fellow students about their social, academic or sports activities and write a one- or two-paragraph personal item for the hometown paper of each one.

2. Copy or clip from several weekly newspapers available to you, five examples of personal items or briefs. (Often they are found in the Living section). Compare them to five examples of personals or briefs you find in several larger daily newspapers. (They usually are found collected in columns). Write a brief report on how they are similar and how they differ.

3. Country or rural correspondents write from many community dailies and weekly newspapers. Using several weeklies or small dailies, clip two or three examples of such columns. Circle each example of overwriting in them, such as phrases like "ever popular," and "beloved" and others discussed in this chapter.

4. Read each of the following personals or briefs and underline the basic flaws in each. Then rewrite them in an acceptable news style:
   a. The annual Lowery–Housley family reunion was held on Saturday at the Cove Lake State Park picnic shelter. Descendants of Jim and Martha Housley-Lowery attended and a good time was had by all the 200 who attended, ranging from great-grandparents to babies in arms.
   b. Donald O. Berendt and his wife, Mary Edith, will celebrate 48 years of wedded bliss on Saturday evening at 8 p.m., in the Fellowship Hall of the United Baptist Church of Jonestown. All six of their sons and their wives and children—26 in all—will be on hand to honor the happy couple. Cake and punch will be served.
   c. Members of the Industrial Board of Clay County would like to show their appreciation for local businesses and industries so they are having a cookout on October 12 at 2 p.m. in Krutch Park, just for fun and fellowship. Everybody is invited.
   d. There will be a parent meeting at the Hillside K through 8 Elementary School, November 13, starting at 3 p.m., to offer parents the opportunity to learn about Lauderdale County's Federal Education programs. Please come and register for a door prize drawing.

e. Andrew Wilkenson is happy about finishing with a perfect score of 24 in the State Children's Bible Drills held at Concord Wesley Methodist Church and receiving a State Winner Superior Seal. He's the 9-year-old son of Jake and Rhonda Wilkenson of Jacksboro.

5. Write personals or briefs from the following notes:
   a. Ruth Ann Poovey
      First Grade Teacher
      East Townsend Elementary School
      Taught there 24 years
      Honored this week as
      Blount County American Federation
      Of Teachers "Teacher of the Year"
      Received $100 gift certificate

      (Source: Nikki Mundy, AFT president)

   b. 4-H Poultry Show and Sale
      Thursday at 5 p.m.
      Union Planters Bank parking lot
      Cocke County 4-H Club selling
      Rhode Island Reds, Barred Rocks,
      New Hampshire Reds and Black Australorps
      All proceeds go to support
      4-H poultry projects

      (Source: Tim Barr, 4-H leader)

   c. Bethlehem Christian Fellowship
      Will hold Vacation Bible School
      In Fellowship's Family Center
      June 15–19 from 7–9 p.m.
      "Hooked on Jesus" is the theme
      Classes for all ages
      Persons attending are asked
      To bring covered dish
      For potluck supper
      Classes open to the public

      (Source: Pastor Sonny Boy Vaughn)

   d. O'Connor Senior Center
      Offering classes in
      Old-fashioned clog dancing
      For senior citizens
      Every Wednesday in June at 2 p.m.
      You must be 65 or older
      To sign up for the free classes
      Advanced registration required
      Call Vera Mae Chapman 619-8703

      (Source: Laura Mae Gouge, center director)

6. Using material available to you in the college or city library, the local chamber of commerce or the city's web page, if it has one, write at least six fillers containing information about your city.

16 Speeches, Publications, Interviews

"If you haven't struck oil in your first three minutes, stop boring!" the late George Jessel, actor, author and professional speaker, advised all other speakers.

The same should be said about speech stories—or any other story for the matter. If you haven't created reader interest in the first three paragraphs, you've probably lost the reader.

Studies show that readers skip over hundreds of stories generated by speeches, press conferences, interviews and articles in professional journals or magazines because they are boring.

Although these stories may be vastly different in subject matter, basically they come from a single source and are a collection of direct and indirect quotes from that single source. A potential for dullness often is built in.

Too many times, reporters settle for the obvious: "Mayor Willie Brown said today . . ." or " Actor Michael J. Fox revealed today . . ." or " A National Cancer Institute study released today shows . . ." when a feature approach might have been more lively and interesting.

These stories require skillful handling to keep them from being dull, especially if the speaker is not very articulate or the subject isn't very interesting.

Speeches

While speech stories are a staple in American newspapers, they often are neglected as "just another routine story" unless they are speeches given by major public figures. Many of these stories are poorly written because the reporter lacks interest in the assignment.

Covering a speech and writing a story about it can be exacting. It takes considerable skill to report a 7,500-word speech in 300 words and still give the reader an accurate report of what was said. It takes time, thought, hard work and writing talent.

For example, a reporter assigned to cover a meeting in Washington, where the speaker was to review the book *The Spanish Armada*, took the assignment on with dread. But it was a "must" assignment. The meeting, sponsored by a Washington women's group made up of the wives of prominent federal officials, congressional leaders and military commanders, drew a stellar crowd of senators, representatives, cabinet officials and admirals and generals to a church hall across the street from the White House. The speaker didn't like the book and said so pointedly. The reporter, casting around for a way to handle what was basically a rather dull event, decided to use a feature lead. Here it is:

> The Spanish Armada was sunk again today—across the street from the White House.
> While two generals of the army, several four-star admirals, a marine commandant and what appeared to be a platoon of highly decorated Air Force brass looked on, Spain's glorious fleet was sent to the bottom in 35 minutes, with time for questions and answers.

The remainder of the relatively short story focused on direct quotes from the reviewer as he told why the book was, for him at least, dreadful. The final paragraph gave some details of the club and its membership to help the reader understand why there were so many prominent individuals in the audience at a program sponsored by a social club. A basically dull assignment was turned into a lively short feature because the reporter used his imagination.

Some reporters dislike being assigned to cover speeches because speakers often are not very good and what they have to say is not very interesting. Yet every speech, no matter who is giving it or what is said, offers a chance for a reporter to show his or her resourcefulness and talent as a writer.

All speeches, whether formal addresses on special occasions or impromptu remarks during an unstructured gathering, are handled very much alike. The reporter must consider the following three elements:

1. The speaker
2. The audience
3. The speech

A fourth consideration is the possible interpretation that any of the three elements may need. The proportion of the story to be devoted to each element varies with the comparative importance of each, but no speech story is complete without all three. Generally, in speech stories the emphasis should be put on what is said.

The speaker should be properly identified in the lead. Sometimes this can be done with a title or a short sentence. If more identification is needed, it can be in the body of the story. This is an amplification of the basic principle of identifying persons named in the news. The reader needs to know who the speaker is and why his or her statements are worth quoting. Even a description of the speaker's distinctive characteristics and manner of emphasizing certain points is sometimes woven into the story to give it more color. But this type of material should not be used in an attempt to hold the speaker up to ridicule.

The audience also should be described. How many people were there? Who were they? Why did they meet? The reporter looks over the crowd, talks with the leaders and reads any available program carefully to help answer those questions. The names of persons in the audience need not be given unless it would be of interest to the reader to know the names of a few of the more prominent ones, but the reporter should tell whether they are bankers, teachers, taxpayers or miners. These facts are implied, of course, at regular meetings of civic clubs and similar organizations, when nothing more than the name of the organization is required. Audience reaction is frequently worth noting.

The speech—what the speaker had to say—is the most important of the three elements. "What is the most important thing the speaker said?" is the first question that a reporter should ask when starting to write the story. Two reporters covering the same speech may not agree on what the most important thing is.

Here are leads on two stories covering the same speech by Federal Reserve Chairman Alan Greenspan:

> WASHINGTON—Alan Greenspan, the Federal Reserve chairman, said today there is little evidence that the economy is slowing down. But he warned for the first time since the stock market's most recent run-up that equity prices might be getting excessive.
>
> WASHINGTON—Federal Reserve Chairman Alan Greenspan suggested Wednesday that the high-flying stock market has risen too far. But he made clear that the central bank would not raise interest rates just to bring it back down.

Some interpretation of one or more of the three necessary elements may be needed. Perhaps the audience is not as representative as it appears to be for the occasion. Applause may be staged by partisan supporters of the speaker. Perhaps the speaker has affiliations or a record that should be presented to clarify his or her significance. Perhaps the speech content should be related to larger national movements, editorial campaigns or other programs. Frequently the speech will have significance in local issues. For example, if the speech concerns establishing new national parks and if the community is campaigning for a national park, a story ignoring this relationship would be inadequate and noninterpretative. Interpretation, however, must avoid editorializing. The interpretative reporter is not authorized to express an opinion. Interpretation must be merely the presentation of pertinent facts to give the reader a clearer picture.

Getting the Speaker's Words

Ideally, a reporter should obtain an advance copy of a speech. However, many speakers do not provide advance copies, so the reporter has to attend the speech and make extensive notes. Most reporters do not take stenographic notes of everything the speaker says. Usually they make notes only on the important statements and arguments or points made by the speaker.

A careful reporter will make every effort to place only the speaker's exact words within quotation marks, particularly in matters that may be controversial. Many reporters like to tape a speech while taking notes to make certain the quotes are exact. Because direct quotations tend to add emphasis, the reporter should avoid quoting routine, obvious or minor points from speeches. Accurate paraphrasing is usually sufficient to convey the less important elements of a speech.

However, a reporter should not paraphrase too much. Direct quotes should be used liberally throughout a speech story. Under no circumstances should a reporter turn in a speech story with few or no direct quotes.

A speech may have one or several features just as any other type of story. In organizing the material, the reporter should look for the central theme, the logical division and unusual or provocative quotes. A good speech will have all of those elements. However, the reporter does not have to play up the central theme if some other aspect of the speech may have more reader appeal.

The Speech Story Lead

On most speech stories, the lead should feature the most important point the speaker made. That is the whole point—to focus on the most newsworthy element of the speech. It can be done by using direct quotations, indirect quotations or interpretations. Summarizing the entire speech in the lead is acceptable; however, it can result in a long and dull lead. Summary leads should be used sparingly on speech stories. Here are several examples of speech leads:

> NASHVILLE—"A few dozen hecklers" will not deter the United States from its mission in Iraq—containing Saddam Hussein and reducing his ability to use biological and chemical weapons, Secretary of State Madeleine Albright said here today.
>
> "Our goal . . . may not seem really decisive. But we're trying to contain Saddam Hussein. Whenever he puts his head up, we push him back . . ."

> Assembly Speaker Peter Cutraro, one of the state's most-high profile political leaders, told his fellow Democrats today, "I won't run for governor."
>
> "I gave it serious consideration," he told a partisan audience at the state Democratic Party's annual legislative conference here. "But I've decided I can be more effective serving as speaker of the General Assembly."

> Bilingual education "will set this country back a century," Joshua Bilek, a Fairfield lawyer who is leading the opposition to adopting the controversial educational program, told the Downtown Rotary Club today.
>
> "If we fail to teach children English soon enough, if at all," Bilek said, "we will do the nation and them irreparable harm . . ."

There are some exceptions to the rule of leading with the most important point the speaker made. The occasion itself may be important enough to be featured in the lead. Here are two examples of how reporters at different papers handled the story of the Pope's visit to Mexico City. The first as a straight news speech story, the second focusing on the event:

> MEXICO CITY—Speaking before a multi-ethnic crowd estimated at more than 1 million souls, Pope John Paul II sternly warned Catholics Sunday to rebuff the temptations of other faiths, including Protestantism.
>
> On the third day of his triumphant return to Mexico, he assailed "fallacious and novel ideologies" in a veiled reference to the growing number of Protestant evangelical groups in this predominantly Catholic nation.

> MEXICO CITY—Pope John Paul II flew down from the skies in a white helicopter into a racetrack today to say an outdoor Mass for more than a million Mexicans, who chanted his Polish childhood nickname, "Lolek," in greeting.
>
> The Pope, who has been here three times before, chose Mexico for his first papal trip after his election 20 years ago, and many Mexicans feel that they have a special, personal bond with him.

The writer didn't directly quote the Pope until the fourth paragraph. Here's that paragraph:

> "Faith in Christ is an integral part of the Mexican nation," the Pope said in a homily that included special mention of the indigenous peoples of Mexico, the poor and others in difficulty. "Do not let this light of faith be extinguished! Mexico still needs it in order to build a more just and fraternal society."

The Body of the Speech Story

The body of the speech story should be direct quotations, indirect quotations and interpretative summaries of the speech. They should be fairly well balanced, but the writer should remember that direct quotes often carry more impact than indirect quotes or summaries. Readers respond more favorably to direct quotes because they give a story more authority.

Quote-Summary-Quote Story

Newspaper reporters have over the years developed a popular form for stories containing a large number of direct quotes. Commonly referred to as a "quote-summary-quote" story, it can best be explained in this example and accompanying diagram:

The Diagram	*The Written Story*
Lead summarizes all or emphasizes a major feature of the speech as this example does.	Changes in society are creating strains on family relations that could eventually threaten the existence of the family unit, one of the nation's leading psychiatrists said here today.

Quote on Feature
or Features in
Lead

"I think there have been a lot of subtle changes such as the effect of affluence on young people," Dr. Walter Menninger said.

"Those who don't have to work to help support the family have more free time, become bored more easily and may be more likely to use drugs or look for other artificial highs."

Dr. Menninger spoke at a workshop on "Parenting in a Changing Society" at Lakeshore Mental Health Institute. He is a senior faculty member at the Menninger School of Psychiatry and director of the division of law and psychiatry at the Menninger Foundation in Topeka, Kan.

Summary of
Other Features or
Details

Other important changes in society include the changing role of women and the rapid advances in technology, he told the 250 persons at the workshop, which was sponsored by Child and Family Services, Inc.

Quote: Details

"One of the biggest problems facing families today is the loss of a clear definition of roles," he said. "Instead of staying home to raise the family as their mothers did, many women today have to work full-time. And the number of single mothers who have to work has increased dramatically over the last decade."

Summary: Details

These changes have had a major impact on the family as a unit, he said.

Quote: Details

"In fact, sometimes it means not having a family at all," he explained. "When a couple meets in college and they each have an agenda that often precludes having a family, their relationship tends to be viewed with less of a commitment to permanence."

Most people have conflicting ideas and feelings about such issues as commitment to work and family, he said. "And it is important for them to sort out these ambivalent feelings so they can more easily resolve conflicts with others," he added.

Summary: Details
(or new feature)

Menninger said he was concerned about the impact of our rapidly changing technology on the family as well.

(Remainder of story deals with Menninger's views on how technology has changed the way we live and as a result has changed the family.)

Take note of how the writer attributed all statements to the speaker. Attribution (the source or authority) is always a problem for news writers. Some tend to overuse it, others don't use it often enough. In this example, the writer was careful to use attribution throughout the story to remind the reader that the speaker, not the reporter, made the statements. Obviously, attribution is not needed in every sentence if the story is carefully organized so there can be no doubt who is being quoted. Attribution can be omitted with a quoted statement if the source of the quote is clear. Generally speaking, however, every paragraph containing indirect quotations should include some attribution.

Complete Reporting

The example of the quote-summary-quote story is straight news reporting. Some speech stories, however, require additional information to give the reader the full background. Here is an example of information added by a reporter to give the reader a more complete picture of the issue discussed in the speech:

> Gov. Frank G. Munger told members of the state Press Association today he would ask the State Legislature again for a one-cent increase in the sales tax to fund his Better Schools program.
>
> "We cannot compete for new high-technology industries in the future if we cannot provide a highly trained and educated work force," he said.
>
> "The time is now. It is critical. We must start improving the education of our young people or they won't stand a chance in the high-technology future facing them."
>
> The governor introduced his Better Schools program last year. It includes increased math and science requirements as well as computer training for all students. The program was bitterly opposed by the state Education Association and the State Legislature refused to raise the sales tax to fund it.
>
> "I think we have worked out our differences with the state Education Association over this program and I am confident the Legislature will not let the people of this state down this year," Governor Munger said.

The rest of the story follows the quote-summary-quote approach.

The importance of such interpretative reporting—if the occasion requires it—is apparent. Without editorializing, the fourth paragraph assembles additional pertinent facts to help the reader evaluate the speaker's comments, giving the whole story an altered significance and enabling the reader to understand the possible motivation involved.

Story Contents

A speech story should include:

Facts

1. Speaker
   a. Present position
   b. Experience
   c. Description (if apropos)
   d. Unusual speaking characteristics

Sources

1. Speaker, various Who's Who publication, members of group before whom speaker speaks, observations of reporter

2. Audience
   a. Name and type of organization
   b. Number present
   c. Purpose of meeting
   d. Reaction to speech
   e. Description
   f. Important persons present

2. Officials of organization, observations of reporter

3. Speech
   a. Theme
   b. Divisions
   c. Title
   d. Quotations

3. Speech

Publications

The *New England Journal of Medicine* may be the most quoted publication in the nation. Each issue produces at least one if not more news stories about important advancements in medicine, medical research and human behavior. Those stories often make the front pages of the daily newspapers.

Dozens of other national magazines also are a source for news stories. Celebrity interviews in *People, Vanity Fair* and other magazines often result in news stories carried by the national wire services. News and opinion magazines such as *Time, Newsweek* and *The National Review* publish articles that frequently are the source of important news stories. Even newspapers with national circulation such as *USA TODAY,* the *New York Times* and the *Wall Street Journal* are sources of stories picked up by the wire services and used by other newspapers. Many newspapers try to localize those stories if there is a logical tie-in.

In addition, thousands of issues of specialized publications, trade journals, academic journals and regional and local magazines are checked regularly by reporters searching for news and feature story ideas. In some cases, a story may have only local news value. However, in many cases the story may have state, regional or even national significance.

Here are several examples of newspaper stories based on articles that appeared in other publications:

> Most U.S. transplant centers meet or exceeded their expected survival rates, based on how sick their patients are, says a report put out today.
> And survival rates for transplants of all organs except the heart are improving over time—surprising since both recipients and donors are getting older, according to the study published in the *Journal of the American Medical Association.*
>
> *USA TODAY*

> Draconian cuts in dietary fat may be no better for lowering cholesterol levels than moderate fat restrictions, and may even be harmful, a study says.
>
> The finding in today's *Journal of the American Medical Association* supports the National Cholesterol Education Program's calls to limit total fat to less than 30% of overall caloric intake.

> *USA TODAY*

Here is an example of a story based on an interview that ties in with a major national holiday:

> Nashville's skyrocketing violence could be avoided if the young offenders had been raised with Dr. Martin Luther King Jr.'s vision of peace, but they haven't.
>
> "Our children have not really been told about the struggle and some of them can't conceive of what was going on during the '40s and '50s," says Russell Merriweather of Nashville.
>
> "He told us that there was no need to fight back and if he could see us today, he would be shocked that we are not making progress toward alleviating the violence and crime," Merriweather says.

> *Nashville Banner*

Reporting articles such as these should not be confused with a book review or with a critical analysis. The news story based on an article is not an evaluation of the ideas in the article. It is simply a news story based on what the article says, nothing more. The reporter should follow the same general principles and form that are used in reporting a speech.

There is very little difference between a story on a speech and a story on a published article. As in a speech story, the content of the article and not the fact that the article has been written is usually the substance of the lead. The remainder of the story can be handled effectively as a quote-summary-quote story. And, of course, a description of the publication in which the article appeared (name, type of publication, frequency of publication) may be necessary, just as a description of the occasion (audience, time of presentation) is necessary in reporting a speech.

Personal Interviews

Virtually all stories in a newspaper are the result of interviews, which is why a reporter has to know what to ask, whom to ask and how to ask to be effective. Even reporters who witness events must ask questions of persons involved and others to obtain additional facts and quotations for a story. Police, hospital officials, witnesses and others are questioned for facts about an automobile accident or a fire, for example. A club president is interviewed about a program featuring a prominent speaker or unusual events. A public official is asked to reply to charges made by a political opponent.

Reporters should never stop asking questions—interviewing. Without asking the right questions, a reporter simply cannot write a complete story.

Interviews directly related to a news event or a public issue are done to collect facts rather than to draw out the personalities of the persons involved.

Here's the start of a personality profile based on an interview that appeared in *USA TODAY:*

> WASHINGTON—Senators fretting about decorum could decide this week whether witnesses will be called in the impeachment trial of President Clinton.
>
> "They needn't worry," political humorist Mark Russell deadpans. "I'm sure Monica will wear her most formal black thong."
>
> Russell, 66, has been making mirth for a living since the Eisenhower administration. His Watergate gags 25 years ago earned him a small measure of fame. Now, he gets to tell impeachment jokes again.
>
> "I knew if I waited long enough," he says. "Or as Dan Quayle might have put it: 'Andrew Johnson got impeached—but he and Lady Bird got over it.'"

In the personal interview story the reporter is trying to make the subject come alive on paper. In addition to basic biographical information, the reporter tries to capture for the reader the subject's mannerisms and personality as well as to elicit answers to questions that will give the reader additional insight into that person. To do that successfully, the reporter has to be able to ask good, often provocative, questions and to observe the subject carefully. Additional information often is collected from the subject's family, friends, coworkers, admirers and even detractors, if there are any.

Throughout the history of American journalism, a number of writers have made names for themselves as excellent interviewers. They range from Horace Greeley and his interview with Brigham Young to some of the brightest "stars" of the 1960s. Rex Reed became almost as prominent as some of the famous Hollywood stars he interviewed. Tom Wolfe and Gay Talese developed the basic interview story into an art form, helping to create the so-called New Journalism of the 1960s. Although it is true that Wolfe and Talese frequently wrote about the famous or infamous, they did not start out interviewing only that type of person. Each did his share of interviews with persons who were, at best, notable only on a local scale. Yet their interviews—even the ones written early in their careers—show that they went into their assignments prepared.

Advance preparation is essential to any successful interview. Without it, a reporter will be hopelessly over his or her head. One of the famous stories of interviewing illustrates that point beautifully. Mary Martin, a major star of the American musical theater, was making one of her rare American tours in the 1960s. At a press conference on one of the first stops on the tour an unprepared young reporter asked: "Who are you?" The fact that a reporter did not know the first lady of the American musical theater made a nationwide story and caused the reporter's publication—and surely the reporter—considerable embarrassment.

Every reporter must know at least some important bits of information about the person he or she is going to interview if the story is to be a major personality interview. Various Who's Who publications may provide a brief biography. The newspaper's library or morgue may contain photographs and biographical data in news clippings or press bureau material. Countless other reference books covering major personalities in practically every field are available at most libraries. Often only one or two reference books may be of help. A *World Almanac and Book of Facts* and a handy one-volume desk encyclopedia should be a part of every reporter's personal reference library. If no standard reference material includes information on the person the reporter has to interview, a telephone call to the city library's reference desk may supply the needed background. With even a slim amount of information, the reporter can begin to formulate a few questions that can be asked in an interview.

Planning Questions

In general, questions should pertain to the work, life or personal interest of the person interviewed, but the questions should be planned to bring answers that will interest the general newspaper reader. Questions should be timely and, to whatever extent possible, local. Comments of a prominent person on a current national event in the person's field are timely. If there is a local angle to the national event, then questions about the local situation should also be asked. Of course, if the subject has absolutely no knowledge of what is happening locally, his or her time should not be wasted by asking questions about such subjects. Obviously, visitors to the city would not feel competent to comment on a strictly local issue.

Questions should be tailor-made for the subject's profession or background. If a television star is not particularly known as a political activist, do not spend a great deal of time asking him or her political questions. Most readers are not interested in how their favorite star votes. They usually want to know what the stars are really like. Are they as nice as they appear on television? Are they as tough? Are they like the characters they play?

In preparing questions, the reporter should keep in mind that one question should lead to another. The interview should move along in a conversational, informal manner while the reporter jots down on paper, tape-records or commits to memory the answers and attitudes revealed. Constantly taking notes is inadvisable except for dates, figures and the like, although in some cases it may be permissible to keep a pencil busy throughout the interview. If a reporter wants to use a tape recorder during a private interview, he or she should ask the subject for permission (some persons do object).

However, in the case of a mass interview with the electronic media represent, no special permission is needed because radio and television reporters will be recording the interview on tape. The reporter should always be aware of whether note-taking or recording makes the interviewed person self-conscious and "quote timid"; if so, the use of pencil or tape recorder should be limited. As soon as possible after the interview, however, the reporter should type up the interview notes because the exact responses of the interviewee are then still fresh in the reporter's mind.

The reporter should watch as well as listen. The interviewee's mannerisms, dress, distinctive features and other personal characteristics make copy for the personal interview story. No matter how important the interviewee's statements, there is always room for a few phrases describing the subject. In this lead, Henry Mitchell of the *Washington Post* captures the language of his subject as well as the speech patterns of the region she lives in and writes about:

> JACKSON, Miss.—Some say Eudora Welty writes best of all, in all Hinds County, but she has never taken on prideful airs. Others say she's the best in all central Mississippi or all America.
>
> "Shoot!" she says, or "Foot!" when the paid-for, or you might say, store-bought critics start up their steady song of praise.
>
> "Now, Eudora," a friend once said to her, "how come you read those reviews? Lots of writers don't read reviews at all."
>
> "I know a lot of writers that don't," she said, "but I do. I've got too much curiosity not to."
>
> Which is, as the Lord knows, true. Miss Welty has more curiosity than a tiger cat. Besides, though she won't exactly say so, it's fairly nice to pick up a paper or magazine and see them having consistent and urgent fits about both your last two books. She writes them for hours off and on in her bedroom right here in Jackson and they are, as some would say, a wonder to behold.
>
> One fellow in the *Washington Post* (writer Reynolds Price) just flung up his arms in print and said there's no point comparing *"Losing Battles"* to other American novels. He suggested, for starters, you might compare it with *"The Tempest"* by the late W. Shakespeare, and then just took it on from there.
>
> "Yes, I know he did," said Miss Welty when I had the pleasure of her company and her cooking for two days recently, "and I am really going to speak to him about it. Shakespeare is a bit much."

The rest of the story was written in much the same tone, giving the reader the "flavor" of this unusual writer and the way people in Jackson respond to her.

Some reporters bring themselves into the personal interview far more than Henry Mitchell did in his story on Eudora Welty. However, the circumstances of the story rarely justify extensive personal references about the reporter. The reader wants to know about the subject of the interview, not the reporter.

Because of the increasing role of science and technology in our lives, reporters may find themselves having to interview persons in highly technical fields. Faced with such an assignment, a reporter has to make advance preparation. A reporter has an obligation to the interview subject to do some homework. The library usually is the best place to start. A speech the subject gave may have been reprinted in *Vital Speeches*. Articles the subject has written may be listed in the library catalog. General or special magazines may have carried earlier interviews with the subject. Reporters frequently are criticized by interview subjects for not being prepared or for pretending to know about a topic or issue when they do not.

John Jamison, director of corporate communications for the North Carolina National Bank, developed this "Interview Bill of Rights" as a guide for the reporter and the subject:

Rights of the Interviewee

— The right to an objective listening to the facts presented.
— The right to an accurate representation of his or her position.
— The right to a fair and balanced context for all statements.
— The right to know in advance the general area of questioning and to have reasonable time for preparation.
— The right to reasonable flexibility as to when to have the interview. (Just as there are times when a reporter cannot be interrupted near a deadline, there are times when others cannot be interrupted.)
— The right to expect the interviewer to have done some homework.
— The right to withhold comment when there is good reason without having this translated as evading or "stonewalling," for example, information governed by the Securities and Exchange Commission regulations, competitive secrets, matters in litigation or negotiation, information that could damage innocent persons.
— The right to an assumption of innocence until guilt is proven.
— The right to offer feedback to the reporter, especially to call attention to instances in which the story, in the honest opinion of the interviewee, missed the point or was in error—and to have this feedback received in good faith.
— The right to appropriate correction of substantial errors without further damage to the credibility or reputation of the interviewee's organization.

Rights of the Interviewer

— The right to access an authoritative source of information on a timely basis.
— The right to candor, within the limits of propriety.
— The right to access information and assistance on adverse stories as well as favorable ones.
— The right to preparation on a story the reporter has developed exclusively, until it has been published or until another reporter asks independently for the same information.
— The right not to be used by businesses for "free advertising" on a purely commercial story.
— The right not to be reminded that advertising pays the reporter's salary.
— The right not to be held accountable for ill treatment by another reporter or another medium at another time.
— The right to publish a story without showing it to the interviewee in advance.
— The right not to be asked to suppress legitimate news purely on the grounds that it would be embarrassing or damaging.

— The right not to be summoned to a news conference when a simple phone call, written statement, news release or interview would do just as well.

Jamison's "Bill of Rights" was originally published in the May 28, 1977, issue of *Editor & Publisher* and is just as valid today as it was then.

Conducting the Interview

Most reporters begin personal interviews with a brief period of small talk to establish rapport with the subject of the interview. This often is the most critical part of the interview. It gives the subject a chance to size up the reporter. Those first few minutes often determine the tone of the interview.

A good reporter will move quickly into the questions prepared for the interview. The questions should be arranged in order of their importance. The general questions should come first. The tough, intimidating or offensive questions should be asked near the end of the interview. If the tough questions are asked at the outset of the interview, the subject may refuse to answer and terminate the interview immediately.

A reporter should listen carefully to everything the subject says and be prepared at any point in the interview to ask the subject to clarify an answer. When in doubt, ask for the correct spelling of all names mentioned in the interview and for verification of important times, dates, places, addresses and statistics. A subject's memory may be hazy, and the reporter must not be too timid to ask for verification of the facts presented.

Interview Problems

Special problems can arise during interviews. The most common are off-the-record comments by the subject, sources who do not want to be identified in print, and requests by the interviewee to read the story before it is printed. Before agreeing to any of these requests, a reporter should know the newspaper's policy on each. It also would be helpful to the reporter to know the state's law on the protection of confidential sources. Some states give reporters total freedom to protect confidential sources. However, the U.S. Supreme Court has ruled that the First Amendment does not provide for protecting confidential sources in federal criminal cases.

In addition, there often is a credibility problem when unnamed sources are used in stories. Several readership studies show that readers often do not believe stories in which the source of information is not identified. Some readers have told researchers they suspect the reporter may have made up the information when a source is not identified.

The problem created when sources demand to read a story before it is printed seem to grow annually. Most newspapers refuse to allow sources to read stories in advance. However, it is common practice among reporters to check quotes, especially those dealing with highly technical or scientific subjects, with the source. A reporter should never agree to let a source read the story in advance without checking with the editor first.

Telephone Interviews

Many interviews are conducted by telephone. It saves time for the subject of the interview and the reporter. However, many reporters consider the telephone to be ineffective for conducting personality interviews because they are unable to observe the subject's reactions to the questions. Reporters also say they are unable to observe the subject's mannerisms, dress, distinctive features and other personal characteristics that add a special dimension to personality profiles.

A reporter should prepare for a telephone interview the same way he or she prepares for an in-person interview. When conducting a telephone interview, the reporter should observe all the simple courtesies used during in-person interviews. The reporter should give his or her name and make certain the subject knows the information being collected will be used in print. The reporter also should (1) speak clearly and calmly and avoid long, rambling questions; (2) avoid irrelevant or obvious questions; (3) save the tough or embarrassing questions for the last; and (4) try not to obtain so much information in the telephone interview that the subject of the interview grows impatient.

Interview Story Forms

In the personal interview, the reporter finds that a variety of approaches will apply, depending on the person interviewed and what is said. But all interview stories have one thing in common: many direct quotes. A reporter can make use of the quote-summary-quote form in the body of the story, and in that regard the interview story is somewhat similar to the speech story. The lead can be a summary, an outstanding feature, a quote or an anecdote, or, to set the scene, it can be descriptive. The lead, of course, can contain the substance of the interview, but often a striking word picture of the speaker is more desirable if his or her personal characteristics are particularly impressive. By all means, somewhere early in the story, the importance of the interview must be established, although it does not have to be in the lead or first paragraph.

Another story form that has gained considerable popularity in interviews, especially in some magazines, is the "question-and-answer" structure. Newspapers, however, use this form sparingly because it generally requires large amounts of space. In this form, the reporter simply writes a short introduction similar to an editor's note, giving a brief biographical sketch of the interviewee, and then reproduces the questions and the interviewee's answers. Often these interviews are done on tape recorders and are simply transcribed and perhaps edited for style and length. Some of the best examples of question-and-answer interviews can be found on the opinion page of *USA TODAY.* The newspaper has effectively adapted the question-and-answer form to limited space.

EXERCISES

1. Study your local daily newspaper or a national newspaper such as the *New York Times* for a week, count the number of stories that are based on speeches, stories

that originated in other publications and interview stories. Write a brief report on what you find.

2. Select one of each type story and write a brief analysis of it. Pay particular attention to the lead, story organization and the use of full and partial quotes.

3. Using an issue of *Vital Speeches* in your college or community library, make a copy of one of the speeches. Write a news story based on the speech. Turn in the speech with your story.

4. Attend an event on your campus or in the community featuring a prominent speaker. Take notes and write a news story on that speech. Many local political and service clubs have speakers at their weekly lunches or dinners. Do not use a copy of the speech even if one is available. Hand in your notes with the story.

5. Check radio and television listings in your city for coverage of a speech by a major public figure. Listen to the speech on radio or watch it on television. Take careful notes and then write a news story based on them. Do not copy the version that appears in the local newspaper. Hand in your notes with the story.

6. Write a speech story on the following excerpts from a speech by Dr. Marleen Chin, director of student conduct for the state Department of Public Education. She spoke at an annual conference of the Parent Teacher Organization in the state capital:

    Misbehavior is on the rise in public schools in the state and nationally.

    It is the violent acts—the killings and gang activity—that gets the headlines. But mouthing off to teachers, breaking rules, smoking in the boys' and girls' bathrooms and destruction of school property are rampant.

    Such disruptions damage learning.

    The problems caused by disruptive students are widespread. Nationally, one in five principals is battling with students who verbally abuse their teachers up from 13 percent in 1990. Two-thirds of the principals report that tardiness is a problem. In fact, it has grown by 50 percent in the last seven years.

    The state's figures match those of the national ones. And it erodes the learning environment for all students.

    A study of the state's eighth-graders shows that one in 10 feels unsafe at school. Six percent of them say drug use is a problem in their school, virtually the same as the national average.

    The state's junior high school students say more racial and cultural conflicts exist than their peers nationwide. Sixteen percent of the state's eighth-graders say such tensions are moderate to serious. Nationally, the figure is only 4 percent.

    Studies show there is a connection between misbehavior and lower test scores in all subjects. Those who reported taking drugs or being suspended from schools had lower scores in all subjects. So did students who admitted to minor offenses such as cutting class or talking back to the teacher.

    The key point is this: The consequence of student disorder is not merely more disorder; disorder also erodes the learning environment for all students.

    Schools that strictly enforce rules such as required hall passes at all times and prohibiting students from leaving during the day reported fewer problems. Tough suspension policies work.

Another way to cut down on misbehavior is less obvious—making classes more interesting. Good teaching will capture students' attention and their respect.

Schools should work to reduce tensions between different groups and teach students how to build better relationships.

If you have to attend to survival issues, you aren't able to attend to learning as much.

7. Write a news story based on these excerpts from an article that appeared in *Neurology*, the scientific journal of the American Academy of Neurology. It is based on a study of 241 stroke patients at Hermann Hospital in Houston by Dr. Lewis Morgenstern, an assistant professor of neurology at the University of Texas Medical School.

Women stroke sufferers aren't brought to the hospital as fast and are evaluated more slowly than male stroke victims. Their death rate is higher than men.

Delay in getting women to hospital means that fewer of them are candidates for treatment with a clot-busting drugs, a tissue plasminogen activator that recedes the injury that strokes can cause.

His study showed that it took women 46 percent longer to get to the hospital after stroke symptoms were recognized than it did men stroke victims. And once they were there, it took 49 percent longer to be seen by a doctor.

Delay in getting women to the hospital could result from the fact that women live longer than men and therefore are often alone in their older years. They may not be able to call 911 quickly.

The delay in treating may come from the fact that doctors generally believe that vascular disease is a disease of men, not immediately associated with women. Yet in his study, 61 percent of the people who die from stroke in his state were women.

He recommended persons showing signs of a stroke call 911 and be taken to the hospital in an ambulance. His study showed that patients who arrive at a hospital by ambulance are seen more quickly than those who arrive in a private vehicle.

A stroke is deadly and is the No. 1 cause of disability in the United States.

8. Review a number of professional journals and research publication for teachers, doctors, lawyers, political scientists in your college library. Select a by-lined article dealing with an interesting study or event and write a news story based on it. Turn in the original article with your story.

9. Interview the most interesting person you know and write a story on her or him. Do not use a star athlete, head coach or campus political leader for this assignment.

10. Write an interview story from the following notes.

Dr. Michael Simpson, a veterinarian, operates an obesity clinic for overweight pets whose weight problem is serious enough to be life-threatening. He sees corpulent cats, chubby dogs, plump parrots, and even the occasional horse with a pot belly, but most of his patients are housepets. Food is love, and people love their pets, Dr. Simpson said. That leads to the same problem people have when they eat too much and don't exercise.

The percentage of obesity in the human population matches that in the animal population. The fact is, a lot of people who come in with overweight pets are overweight themselves.

It's a delicate matter talking to people about dieting dogs when they need to be on a diet themselves.

The first thing I do is put the animal on a diet. I banish treats. Did you know one Milk-Bone treat can contain as much as 20 percent of a dog's caloric intake?

For pet birds, the problem is seeds. They are the junk food of the bird world. Mostly fat, not a single nutritional bit in them. And for cats and dogs who eat commercial animal food, well, they are getting heavy doses of fat.

Once we begin to get them on a diet, we put them in a swimming pool or on a treadmill to get them exercising. And we clip a heart-rate monitor to their arms to check their heart rate and blood pressure.

It isn't always easy to get an animal on a treadmill. Dogs are a bit more adaptable than cats. So I've devised a harness to keep cats on the treadmill. They still don't like it though.

I became interested in animal obesity when I discovered my own dog, Lola, a small beagle, started putting on weight. I put her on the scales and discovered she was six pounds overweight.

I put her on a diet and started feeding her carrots, broccoli and frozen grapes as snacks. At first she didn't like them. But now she will eat them raw.

I got her walking on the treadmill and now she likes it because she gets a carrot treat at the end of her exercise period. She lost the six pounds and three others besides.

Several studies show that an overweight pet has seven times the number of joint and muscle diseases, three times the number of skin disorders and are twice as likely to die between the ages of six and 12.

I've had animals in here that were 10 or more pounds overweight. One dachshund weighed 26 pounds when it should only weigh 16. The extra weight was so overwhelming, it broke the dog's back. It had to be put to sleep.

Simpson is a tall lean man who exercises on the treadmill and treats himself with raw carrots, broccoli and frozen grapes, just like he does his beagle.

CHAPTER

17 Meetings and Special Events

"Create in the reader the impression that you were there. You saw, you heard," the late Red Smith, perhaps the best sports writer of the century, advised other writers.

Unfortunately, in writing meeting stories many writers don't give the reader the slightest clue of what the meeting was really like. Yet newspapers cover dozens of meetings every day. And, unless it is one with a high-profile speaker, most meeting stories are flat and dull. They offer the reader little more than what the speaker said. No color. No description added.

It's true that a lot of meetings that newspapers cover are fairly colorless. But an observant reporter will almost always find a splash of color to put a little life into the story.

Newspapers simply cannot cover every meeting, so editors have to decide which ones are the most important and interesting. In doing so, they consider such questions as:

— Do we write an extensive advance story about what is expected to happen, and then a brief follow-up after the meeting?
— Will a brief advance story do, with a detailed report on what actually happened?
— Do we rely on a press release for our advance, and in some cases, the follow-up?
— Do we assign a reporter and perhaps a photographer?

There are almost as many answers to those questions as there are editors and meetings. But, as a general rule, editors consider meetings of non-governmental organizations particularly newsworthy if:

1. There is a prominent speaker or significant program that would interest readers.
2. There will be a large number in attendance.

Meetings about real issues often make important news. But significant stories can and do come from what may appear to be just another routine meeting. For example: A routine talk at a service club luncheon by the new director of a medium-sized southern city's art museum became the lead story in the "Local" section of the morning newspaper when the speaker used a very gamey reference to the male anatomy to explain how a person could determine if a photograph was obscene. It generated follow-up stories because the head of the museum's board of trustees hastily issued an apology to the service club while praising the director for his excellent work on behalf of the artistic community and art-loving public.

Obviously, not all speeches at service clubs generate that kind of coverage. But it is important for reporters to keep in mind that when reporting on a meeting, the most important aspect is to tell the reader what took place and why she or he should care.

Once an event has occurred, there is no news value in the simple fact that it happened. Even at meetings where little or nothing goes on, the reporter should look for a news peg or interesting fact for the lead. Far too many stories begin "The Downtown Business Circle met for lunch yesterday in Morrison's Cafeteria and heard an interesting talk by Superintendent Margaret Lopez." Tell what she said. That's the news. Even when writing an advance story about a meeting, the reporter should look for something interesting to put in the lead. Never settle for "A meeting will be held . . ."

Types of Meeting Stories

The Advance

Most groups rely on newspapers to publicize their meeting through a story or stories printed in advance. Some groups mail or phone in announcements of upcoming meetings. Often the information they provide is incomplete, and the reporter has to call a representative of the group to obtain additional details to write a full and accurate story that will interest many readers—not just members of the organization.

Information needed for a meeting story includes the correct, formal name of the organization (and local chapter name if it is part of a national group); the exact time, date and place; and details on the program such as speakers, entertainment, election or installation of officers. The more the reporter knows about the organization, the easier it will be to write an interesting and informative story. Compare these two meeting leads:

Weak:
Parents Without Partners will meet in the auditorium of Westwood Elementary School at 7 p.m. Wednesday to hear a talk by narcotics officer Patsy Hammontree on drug abuse by pre-teens.

Better:

Patsy Hammontree, a 10-year veteran of the police narcotics squad, will speak on drug abuse by pre-teens at a meeting of Parents Without Partners Wednesday. The meeting, at 7 p.m. in the Westwood Elementary School auditorium, is open to the public.

Avoid starting meeting stories in the following ways:

There will be a meeting of the Cocke County Senior Citizens Club at noon . . .

At 7:30 p.m. Wednesday, members of the Del Rio Rescue Squad will . . .

An evening of fun awaits members of the Cosby Kiwanis Club when country comic Buster Curry . . .

The first example is not written in news style; the second one focuses on the time element, which rarely is the most important fact in the story; and the third one is editorial in nature. How can the writer be sure everyone will have fun? Maybe Buster will be a bust in the opinion of some members of the Cosby Kiwanis Club.

In the body of the story, the reporter should avoid editorial comment on the caliber of the program, such as "an excellent talk was given by" and a "thrilling presentation of operatic excerpts." Such expressions as "All members are urged to attend" and "The public is cordially invited" should be omitted. If the meeting features a speaker and the club or organization would like others to attend, include that the "meeting is open to the public."

The Follow-Up

Most meetings worthy of more than a bare announcement will have produced something of substance on which the reporter can build the story, including:

1. A definite action—passage of a law, adoption of resolutions, announcement of plans, endorsement of candidates or issues
2. One or more speeches
3. Discussion and debate—conflict, difference of opinion, voicing of views, criticism
4. Personnel—election of officers, nominations, new members, resignations, membership drivers, visitors, prominent members or guests, interesting personalities
5. Miscellaneous features—music or other entertainment, unexpected interruptions.

The lead on the follow-up story can vary greatly from a summary of the entire meeting to a single outgoing feature followed by a summary of other features.

In many cases, reporters attempt to develop a general theme for the entire story if there seems to be a central theme to the meeting:

> An urgent appeal for $2 billion in emergency federal aid to fight recession in the nation's big cities was made at the U.S. Conference of Mayors in Boston yesterday.

The remainder of the story would be built around the central theme of the recession and its effect on the cities and their need for more federal help.

A reporter should not try to develop a theme, however, if one does not logically exist. Often some feature that is far from the main purpose of a meeting will be the most logical lead because it has stronger reader appeal. The reporter's responsibility is to the reader, not the sponsors of the meeting. The story should be written with that in mind. At the same time, the story should not present a distorted view of the meeting.

It is important that the story be told in a logical order, with the most important thing that happened at the meeting being told first. The story should not be written in chronological fashion, and it should never sound like the minutes taken by the club secretary.

The lead on the follow-up story can vary greatly from a summary of the entire meeting to a single major feature that would be followed by other activities at the meeting. Here is an example of a follow-up story about a city council meeting in Barnwell, S.C., from the *People's Sentinel:*

> Barnwell City Council approved a $2.5 million dollar budget with no tax increase at Monday's meeting.
>
> City council had time for a public hearing on the budget at Monday's meeting, but no one showed up.
>
> "We passed another budget without a tax increase. This is very important for the community," city attorney Tony Boulware said.
>
> The council also passed an ordinance to raise the mayor's salary by 17 percent and council members salaries by 15 percent.

The story went on to give the new salaries which it pointed out was done behind closed doors at an earlier meeting. It also listed five other actions the council took.

Conventions

Conventions have always provided newspapers with a wide variety of stories and, increasingly, they are becoming the focal point for major news breaks. Planners often schedule a particularly newsworthy speaker to attract the attention of newspeople as well as delegates. Speakers frequently use the convention platform to announce new scientific discoveries, plans for world peace or formation of a new political party or pressure group.

Handling the stories generated by a large convention can be a major undertaking for any reporter. A big-scale convention is in reality a series of meetings that offer the reporter a wide variety of features and frequently requires the writing of multiple news stories. It is not uncommon for several staff members to be assigned to a large convention. If the convention is a major event—a political party convention or the national meeting of an organization that might attract several thousand delegates—a special convention staff of a dozen or more reporters and photographers under the direction of a special editor may be assigned.

Many newspapers make special efforts to "cover all angles" of a large local convention, frequently devoting more space to it than that warranted by its appeal to local readers. This type of treatment can be justified on several counts: Each of the many delegates is interested in the coverage and is a potential buyer of the newspaper and, furthermore, newspapers generally give broad coverage to such meetings as a matter of civic spirit. Conventions are important to the economy of any city, and the newspaper joins other organizations of the city in welcoming the visitors and promoting the city as a convention center.

Of course, a large convention also has many angles of local interest. Although it may attract little attention in the largest cities, several hundred visitors in the average city will create news in itself. Even the smallest of conventions might attract prominent visitors, newsworthy speeches and discussions, resolutions on important issues, unusual persons or incidents and participation of local persons. Any of these should generate considerable local reader interest and make the convention worthy of coverage.

This story from the *Miami Herald* not only reported on a special event, it served as an advance for an upcoming meeting:

> The chairman of the Miami Herald Publishing Co., David Lawrence Jr., will appear before the Miami–Dade Commission next month to ask it to pass a countrywide gay-rights ordinance.
>
> Lawrence received an award Saturday night at the Dade Human Foundation annual dinner in Miami for his work on behalf of the gay community.
>
> During his acceptance speech, he told an audience of about 500 that he would address the commission on behalf of the controversial ordinance . . .

Preliminaries

If the editors of a newspaper decide to give maximum attention to a convention, a reporter may have weeks—perhaps even months—to begin preparing for the event. Long before the opening of the convention, the reporter may write stories almost daily to feature all phases of the upcoming event.

Most organizations planning a convention will have a publicity committee or manager to work with reporters, providing them much of the information needed to write stories. Often complete press kits are given to reporters to help them cover the event. A kit usually includes the complete program, pictures and biographical sketches of the speakers and officials of the organization, a history of the group, an explanation of important subjects on the program and a variety of other material that could be used for stories.

Some publicity managers also provide copies of speeches in advance. But they insist that a story on the speech not be printed until after it has been given. A copy of the speech can be extremely helpful because it gives the reporter time to read and digest the speech completely before writing the story.

Even with a copy of the speech in advance, a reporter should attend the meeting to make certain the speech actually was given and to record any material the speaker might add. On some occasions, often with permission of the speaker, a newspaper will publish an advance speech story in its editions on the day the speech is to be delivered. In those cases the lead usually contains the phrase "in a speech prepared for delivery at the (name) convention today."

All this help from publicity representatives does not relieve the reporter of the responsibility for gathering material for stories on the convention. If a publicity manager is not available to help, it is the reporter's job to get as much material as possible about the convention in advance by writing or phoning officials of the organization and the speakers. Reporters should also work with the local convention bureau or the hotel or office serving as convention headquarters to gather information about the convention.

Sometimes the number of speakers and the variety of sectional meetings of a convention are so large that the newspaper must omit details of the less important ones. As in every other story, it is important for the reporter to develop a keen sense of what really is news when gathering and writing convention stories.

Presenting Convention Features

In preparing a number of advance reports on a convention, the reporter must plan stories to avoid repetition of the same features. Each story should have something new in its lead, but the time, date and place of the convention should be repeated somewhere (not necessarily in the lead) every time.

The first story lead generally announces that the convention will be held in the city. Often it emphasizes the approximate number of persons who will attend along with the time, date and place of the convention. Story leads of follow-up stories will highlight different phases of the program (speakers, officers, entertainment). A summary of other features (minus details) will be included in the body of the story. If a summary of all other features runs the story length beyond the space allotted for it, some of the less important features usually are omitted. It is also acceptable to play up—in the lead—features that have been summarized in the body of the preceding stories even though they are not new developments.

From the day before a convention opens—especially if it is a major one—until the day after it closes, there is a real rush. Often photographers and other reporters team with the reporter in charge to gather speeches, conduct interviews and search out other significant information that was unavailable in advance. In addition to reports on business and the speeches of the convention, many newspapers seek out human-interest stories on interesting delegates, unusual events in connection with the meeting, comments from delegates on the convention and the city, or other material.

All aspects of a convention may be put together in one long story, or they may be divided into a number of stories. The larger the convention, the more stories, generally speaking. If the stories are divided, one main story will be devoted to the major—most newsworthy—event of the convention and include such essential information as number of delegates and other general information. Other stories will present reports from sectional meetings within the convention, interviews and other sidelights. The exact manner in which the convention is covered depends on its size, overall newsworthiness in relation to all other news that day and the amount of space available in the newspaper.

This lead on a major conference focuses not only on the expected attendance, but also the reason for the conference:

> At least 18,000 women are expected to attend a conference in Washington this weekend where a female team of Christian speakers and singers have pledged to celebrate the strength of their gender.
> The Women of Faith gathering is part of a growing trend for men, blacks and now women who seek to reaffirm their beliefs outside the traditional ecclesiastic settings.
> "When you're delineating with worship in the church, it's not really geared to women's needs and issues," says Linda Reter, 45, a federal employee who lives in Baltimore. "We're hungry for a woman's experience of faith. . . ."

Special Events

Fairs, festivals, dedications, exhibitions and other large events that attract a great number of persons offer much the same sort of problems as do convention stories. Each presents the possibility of some significant straight-news reports as well as dozens of features. Advance preparation is necessary to obtain details. Several stories, each playing up a different feature, are required before the event takes place, and adequate coverage of all features is necessary while the event is in progress. If the program of the special event is simply substituted for the convention program, the whole assignment involves the same procedure.

Some events are given coverage by the press because of their unusual nature. The ongoing debate over abortion rights has been covered extensively by the press. So an event such as the one described in this lead was certain to draw the attention of the press:

> Celebrity items always draw big money at auctions, even at the Banquet of the White Rose. Last year's White Rose auction featured a black jacket worn by an arsonist when he was caught torching a Falls Church, Va., abortion clinic. It went for about $125.

FIGURE 17.1 It was a special event when Mark McGwire of the St. Louis Cardinals broke all homerun records by hitting 70 in the season, and it rated a special commemorative edition of the *St. Louis Post–Dispatch* with this colorful and artistic cover page.

(Reprinted with permission of the *St. Louis Post–Dispatch*.)

At tonight's banquet in College Park, Md., auction items include a hand-knit cap and camouflage booties made by Rachelle Shannon, an Oregon woman serving a 31-year prison sentence for trying to murder a Kansas abortion doctor, George Killer. She shot him in both arms.

The militant foes of abortion who will gather for the fourth annual White Rose banquet will honor the murderers, arsonists and others in prison for "defending the unborn . . . "

USA TODAY

EXERCISES

1. For one week, count the number of stories in your local or area daily newspaper that pertain to meetings. Include both advance and follow-up stories. Pay particular attention to the number of stories that stand alone compared to those that are listed in a calendar of events. List any stories in the calendar of events that you think may rate a larger, more complete story and tell why.

2. Using those same stories, list the various kinds of meetings they are about, such as church, civic, social and service groups as well as business and professional organizations.

3. Using your campus daily or the calendar of events at your campus student center, select the event you think is the most interesting. Then call the sponsors of that meeting and obtain information for an advance story. Write the story and turn in your notes as well as the name and phone number of your source.

4. Most newspapers print a calendar of upcoming meetings of civic, professional, and political groups. Attend one of those meetings and write a story about it. Hand in the notes taken at the meeting along with your story.

5. Every campus has special events such as holiday festivals, international student celebrations and other campuswide activity. Contact the sponsors of one of those events and obtain enough information to write an advance story. When the event takes place, attend it and write a news story.

6. Craft shows, art exhibits, fairs, flower shows, river festivals and other special events are common in most communities. Pick one in your community to attend and then write a human-interest story about it. Emphasize the color and excitement and unusualness of the event in your story. Turn in your notes.

7. Second Harvest, an organization that provides food for the poor, is sponsoring a fund-raising event featuring 10 top chefs from restaurants in the area preparing their favorite entrees. It will be in the Civic Center from Noon Wednesday through Noon Thursday. A number of food suppliers and brokers will have booths at the event displaying the products they supply. A 3-night luxury package at Charleston Plane, an Orient-Express Hotel, in Charleston, S.C., will be offered as a door prize. Tickets are $35 each. Write a story using that information along with the schedule of events:

11 a.m. Wednesday	Doors open. Tickets available at the door.
Noon	Lite Lunch, featuring Tandori Chicken, with Cucumber Raita, Green Peas and Basmati Rice. Prepared by Cesare Casella, chef–owner, Casella's, Greeneville.

2:30 p.m.	Spring Partners featuring Cumin-Crusted Sea Bass with Celery Root Puree and Spinach. Prepared by Waverly Root, executive chef, The Spa in Ware's Valley.
4:30 p.m.	Talking Turkey, featuring Peppered Turkey with Cranberry–Grape Relish served with Broccoli and Wild Rice. Prepared by Attica Marston, chef–co-owner of Zelma's in Sunbright.
7:30 p.m.	Rustic but Romantic, featuring Beef Medallions with Cognac Sauce served with Mashed Potatoes laced with Pancetta and Leeks. Prepared by Gilberto Palato, executive chef at the Covey in Carmel Valley.

Vintners from leading wineries in the state will provide a list of wines to serve with each entrée.

9:30 a.m., Thursday	Brunch for a Bunch, featuring Baked Apple Pancakes served with Buttery Cinnamon Sugar and Applesauce, with Bacon piled on the side. Prepared by Sheridan Whitesides, executive chef at Anasazi's in Soddy-Daisy.
11 a.m.	Forgettable Food Fads, an illustrated talk by Andre Huguet, humor columnist and food commentator for National Public Radio.
12:30 p.m.	Flashy Finishes, a demonstration of four classic chocolate desserts. Prepared by Geraldine Watterson, executive pastry chef at Windows on Wallen Pond, Scottsdale.

The door-prize drawing will be held immediately after the dessert demonstration. You must be present to win.

8. Call the local Chamber of Commerce and ask for a schedule of upcoming conventions or conferences in your city. Select one that is featuring a prominent speaker, attend that speech and write a story about the speech.

PART FIVE

Writing the Simple Story

The prime goal of the writer . . . has to be clarity: the statement of his case in the simplest, most precise and most direct words . . . ," Lewis Lapham, former *Harper's* editor, said in his column, "The Easy Chair."

That is sage advice, especially for beginning reporters, who generally start out writing the simpler stories that require little interpretative writing and little background. But they are important stories and should be written with the same care and precision as major stories.

The classification of stories as simple or complex is a convenient and arbitrary decision that most editors use when making assignments, even though there is no real technical significance in this classification. To most editors, single-incident stories—automobile accidents, deaths, illnesses, funerals, minor crimes—would fall into the "simple" classification. Those stories requiring little interpretative writing and little background might be added to the editor's list—an award or public appointment, for example.

However, it should be noted that any single story may turn out to be either simple or complex, depending on the facts and their news values. For purposes of proceeding from the less difficult to the more difficult stories, the "simple" or "complex" classification has proved useful.

18 Illnesses, Deaths, Funerals

"Obituaries are the last writes," Dr. Peter Lawrence wrote, with tongue in cheek no doubt, in his amusing book, *Peter's Quotations: Ideas for Our Times.*

For many young reporters they may be the first "writes," so to speak, because some editors still assign the newest staff members to write obituaries. It's the editor's way of testing the new reporter. Sloppy and careless work marks a reporter as someone not to be trusted with important stories. Careful, thoughtful and dignified work brings more rewarding assignments.

Fortunately, that is no longer the practice at many newspapers. Most editors now know that the obituary is one of the most important stories in the newspaper. It is read and reread, clipped, bound in plastic and often pasted in the back of the family Bible. It has the potential of making more enemies and more friends for the newspaper than almost any other kind of story.

Sadly, in recent years there has been a trend at some larger newspapers to standardize all obituaries. They all sound exactly alike, except for the name of the deceased and the time of services. Often they begin:

> John Smith, 91, of Blythville, a retired warehouse manager, died Friday at his home after a stroke.

Or:

> Services for Lula Mae Pullen, 86, a retired teacher, will be held at . . .

Often standardizing obituaries so they all sound alike distresses the family of the deceased. But it also may cause the newspaper to miss a good story by not collecting additional details about the person's career or background. Why not talk to people who know the deceased, use their quotes, give some depth to the person you are writing about?

Writing obituaries requires a particular sensitivity. Family members will remember the newspaper for the careful, accurate way it reported even the smallest details during their time of sorrow.

News Values

Why are obituaries and stories about illnesses and funerals so important? Evaluating their news value shows they all fall on the disaster side of human experience. They are disruptions of the status quo, and they are of consequence in the community. The removal of almost any human being from the local scene requires social and economic readjustments among relatives and friends. His or her place must be taken; his or her job must be filled by another. The home may be offered for sale; the widow or widower may move to another city; the daughter or son may withdraw from college. All such changes touch the lives of others.

Factors of Magnitude

The importance of the news story is determined by several factors. Illness is measured by its gravity, approaching death as its climax. And both illness and death are measured by the number of persons affected in the community. Thus the prominence of the person and the nature of the illness may determine story importance. A rare disease or accident, even one involving someone who is comparatively unknown, is interesting because it is unusual.

Even more important may be stories about the threat of epidemics of quite common diseases. Since prominence usually means being well known, in addition to holding a position of importance, the community is more generally affected by matters involving prominent persons. Multiple deaths or cases of illness extend importance of the news. Although the story of illness or death (and of the funeral) may frequently stand stripped of its disaster appeal, its news importance may sometimes be heightened by prominence, novelty, consequence, human interest and even conflict.

Illnesses

Illness—grave illness—is reported less frequently than its news importance justifies. Patient, family, physician and hospital are often unwilling to have the illness known. Physicians and hospitals usually tend to avoid publicity even in the case of very prominent persons. Family and patient may wish to avoid unnecessary alarm to friends, employer or employees and sometimes the family wants to hide information from the patient. Often if the person is very prominent—a public official or a major entertainment figure, for example—the illness may not be disclosed in order to assure the person's privacy.

Illness can affect business matters, contracts, perhaps even diplomatic negotiations, as well as various other obligations. Always in the background is the thought that tomorrow or the next day the patient may be well and the less uproar about the matter the better. If the patient's family, physician and hospital all refuse to give a statement on the illness, the reporter should use whatever information is available with extreme caution.

Illness is not easy to report properly. Highly technical or tenuous conditions may characterize the illness itself. The physician might not know the exact nature of the illness. The nature of the illness itself might be so technical that it is extremely difficult to translate into language the average reader can understand. Some medical schools, however, now have special courses to teach medical students how to write and speak in non-technical language.

The reporter should always keep in mind the emotions and the sensitivities of the patient as well as the family. Once the brief bulletin on the patient's condition is announced, little substance is left for the reporter to take hold of and expand, as a general rule. However, if the person is prominent—a major entertainer or perhaps the governor of the state—the attending physicians sometimes will hold a press conference and explain the nature of the illness and the patient's condition.

In the prolonged illness of such a prominent person, regular medical bulletins will be issued and the comings and goings of delegations, friends, relatives and others as well as their public statements may provide copy. The illness stories of lesser persons will usually be brief, however, unless they suffer from a rare or unusual ailment.

Although a list of patients admitted to and dismissed from hospitals often is published each day in newspapers in many smaller communities, the reporter gives individual attention to only a few. In addition, "tips" sometimes will lead the reporter to interesting stories about illnesses.

Story Content

Many accounts of illness contain only one, two or three paragraphs and are usually handled similarly to a personal. The following information is usually given:

1. Name and identification of the person who is ill
2. Cause of illness
3. Condition (fair, serious, critical—an accurate quotation from the doctor or hospital)
4. Name of hospital (sometimes "at a local hospital" if person is in a private institution such as a mental hospital)
5. Duration of illness
6. Members of family at bedside
7. Effect of illness on person's public position (especially in the case of an elected official) or business.

The "Who" is the most important "W" in most illness stories and should be in the lead. For variety, or if the disease or operation is unusual, the cause of the illness or the condition of the patient may be featured. However, if the story is a follow-up, the condition of the patient is usually the feature. Note these examples:

Who

Dr. James Witherspoon, president of State Technology University, was taken to Widner Memorial Hospital today for observation after suffering several dizzy spells while working in his office at home.

Cause

A severe ear infection caused Dr. James Witherspoon, president of State Technology University, to suffer several dizzy spells while working in his office at home, doctors at Widner Memorial Hospital said today. He will remain in the hospital for several days.

Condition (a follow-up)

Dr. James Witherspoon, president of State Technology University, is in good condition at Widner Memorial Hospital, recovering from a severe ear infection. He was taken to the hospital Wednesday after he suffered several dizzy spells while working in his office at home.

Hospital Notes

Some newspapers regularly carry a hospital column. It may be merely a list of "Admitted" and "Discharged" with no details given. Some hospitals refuse to make such lists available; others have a more liberal policy on publicity. It is common practice at many hospitals to ask a patient or the family if there is any objection to being listed as a patient in the daily report to the press. But with or without the cooperation of the hospitals, many personals deal with hospitalization. The following are some common examples:

Gilbert Rader, Parrottsville, underwent hip surgery Wednesday at Tokamoa Hospital, Greenville. He expects to be released in six days.

Alicia Alfredo, former Hendry County School superintendent, has returned home from New Orleans, where she underwent heart bypass surgery seven days ago at Oschner Clinic.

Jim McMillan, 6, son of Mr. and Mrs. Tom McMillan, 1831 Newberry St., suffered a broken left arm today when he fell off a swing in the playground of West Hills Elementary School. He was admitted to Methodist Hospital where he is reported in "good" condition.

Deaths

Death is an important item of news. It may contain all the news values discussed previously. Regardless of news values, death is reported as a public record. No person ever becomes so unimportant that he or she is not valuable as a vital statistic. The public health records chart all deaths, and state laws fix standard forms of physicians' reports. Even the nameless drifter found frozen to death under a superhighway overpass is not overlooked. The drifter fits somewhere in a chain of persons and events. Although practice will vary from paper to paper in the treatment of death stories, all newspapers report deaths.

One of the best descriptions of an obituary was given by Arthur Gelb, deputy managing editor of the *New York Times*. He said:

> An obit is the summing up of a person's life, the last statement about him for the record. It has to have fairness, balance, accuracy, substantiation of fact. We see obits as short biographies, an analysis of the man and his time. What did his life mean? What was his impact on civilization? What was his paper? . . . We try to put him in the context of history and of his field and what he meant to the people in that field.

Obituaries

Just as the practice of reporting deaths varies, so the terms used to describe this type of news story will also vary. At some newspapers, the word "obituary" means a news story written about the death of a person that is published with an individual headline. At others the obituary is the black, agate-type alphabetical listing of everyone who has died and has not yet been buried. This list is also called "Death Notices" at some newspapers. All newspapers publish stories of deaths free if they use them as separate stories. Many newspapers, however, make a per-word charge for death-column notices just as they do for classified advertisements, and such charges become part of the funeral costs. Whether the obituary is a paid item or not, the form used by the newspaper is standardized to get all essential information. Many newspapers and funeral homes use a standard form such as the one illustrated on page 276.

From a report of this kind a rather standard notice is printed in the alphabetical listing in the newspaper. Funeral arrangements usually are included when they are available. Here are two examples of death notices written by family members or funeral home officials:

> LELAH H. DIETZ—Age 93. Born June 17, 1897, in Page, N.D., died Friday. She moved to Spokane in 1920 and taught high school science for several years at Central Valley High School and other schools in Idaho and Washington. She was a member of the Catholic Daughters of America. She is survived by a niece, Betty D. Westin of Seattle, and a nephew, Edward J. Dietz of Arlington, Va., and grand-nieces and nephews. Mass of Christian Burial will be celebrated Wednesday at 9:30 a.m. at St. Joseph's Church, Spokane. Burial will be at Holy Cross Cemetery, Spokane. Evergreen Funeral Home is in charge of services.

> RUSSELL, MARY EDITH (JONES)—Age 80, was funeralized Oct. 22, in Indianapolis, Ind., at Bethel Faith Tabernacle. The Rev. Merritt Taliaferro officiated. She was a graduate of Anderson College and taught public school for 45 years. Attending the obsequies were: nieces, Mrs. Mattie S. Smith; Mrs. Joyce Williams; and Miss Theodosia Perrin.

The amount of information in a death notice will vary. Because it is paid for by the family, it can include such information as the names of the pallbear-

```
                              OBITUARY

    Name_____Age_____

    Address_____

    Place of death_____Date_____Time_____

    Cause of death_____

    Date of birth_____Place of birth_____

    Parents_____

    Education_____

    Occupation_____

    Husband or wife (maiden name)_____

    Date of marriage_____Place_____

    Residence here since_____

    Previous residences_____

    Name of present employer_____

    Previous employers_____

    Military record_____

    Church affiliation_____

    Clubs, fraternal organizations, other affiliations_____

    _____

    Special interests or hobbies_____

    Survivors with relationships and addresses_____

    _____

    _____

    Body at_____

    Funeral arrangements_____
```

ers, the name of the officiating minister and other material. At some newspapers, these notices are handled by a clerk or a secretary using information provided by the funeral homes. Others have reporters write the notices from the funeral home reports.

FIGURE 18.1 It was not your traditional obituary. But then singer Frank Sinatra was not a traditional individual. His death rated three-fourths of the front page of the *San Jose Mercury News* with three more pages devoted to the singer on the inside. It is an excellent example of how a major daily covers the death of a larger-than-life public personality.

(Reprinted with permission of the *San Jose Mercury News*.)

Death Stories

Reporters are called on to write death stories (or obituaries) that are handled in regular news style. Some newspapers publish these on the same page as the paid notices. Others have separate pages for them. The *Indianapolis News,* for example, has for years done an excellent job of reporting deaths in that city and its surrounding area. Each death is handled as a separate news item, and the stories vary in length depending on the person and the amount of available information. Other newspapers limit these stories to persons who are newsworthy enough to justify extra attention. In most large cities, the death of a person who has gained no prominence and who died of natural causes would be reported only in the paid notices column.

Although the information in the paid notice or the funeral home's report provides the basic facts for the news story, the reporter often must seek additional information by telephoning or visiting relatives or others mentioned in the notice. If the person is prominent, the reporter frequently checks the newspaper's morgue or library for additional information and calls friends, business associates and others for material on the deceased. If the person is exceptionally prominent, a reporter should refer to several standard reference books, such as *Who's Who in America,* for additional material.

The wire services and most large newspapers maintain rather complete files of hold-for-release obituaries on most big names—national and international leaders, for example. Many smaller newspapers maintain similar stories, ready for print, on the most prominent citizens in their communities. These usually are brought up to date at regular intervals.

Story Content

If a newspaper does carry individual stories on deaths, any reporter assigned to write them should keep in mind that the story must provide the following information:

1. Name and identification (address, occupation, and affiliations) of the deceased
2. Age
3. Day and time of death
4. Place of death
5. Cause of death
6. Duration of illness
7. Names of members of the immediate family (survivors)
8. Effects of death on the person's public position (if applicable).

Although this information is routine, there should be nothing routine about the writing of the story. The reporter should use every journalistic device to show what manner of person the deceased was. This, of course, depends on details. The reporter should look for colorful incidents, anecdotes, personal traits and personal remembrances of friends and family to convey exactly why this particular death is news.

The first paragraph should sum up the circumstances of the death with name, age, identification by position or profession and time and place of death. The remainder of the story should be a carefully constructed biographical sketch of the person in an effort to picture for the reader what he or she really was like. It should not be a mere routine summation of the facts of his or her life and career. Although it should contain colorful highlights of the deceased's life history, it should not be light or frivolous.

For example, when musician Carl Perkins, a rock 'n 'roll pioneer, died, the *Nashville Banner* played the story across the top of the front page with the largest headline of the day. The story with its eight-column headline and a picture of Perkins filled nearly 15 inches of space on the front page and continued for another 20 inches inside. The story began:

> JACKSON—Carl Perkins, a rock 'n 'roll pioneer whose song, "Blue Suede Shoes" and lightning-quick guitar playing influenced Elvis Presley, the Beatles and a slew of other performers, died this morning. He was 65.
>
> Perkins died at 10:30 a.m. at Jackson–Madison County Hospital from complications related to three strokes he suffered in November and December, family spokesman Albert Hall said. Funeral arrangements are incomplete.

The story continued for 10 more paragraphs on the front page before being moved inside, where it ran for another 20 inches.

When veteran comedian Henny Youngman died, the Associated Press (AP) sent this story over its wires. It was prominently displayed in hundreds of newspapers:

> NEW YORK (AP)—"Dear God—take Henny—please," the rabbi said Friday at a funeral for Henny Youngman that was rich with rimshot humor.
>
> With Alan King, Jerry Stiller, Anne Meara, Larry Storch and Soupy Sales among the mourners, Rabbi Noach Valley followed solemn prayers with vintage gags from the King of One-Liners.
>
> An overflow crowd of more than 200 mourners could pick up a pamphlet of Youngman's insults at the door along with condolence books.
>
> The comedian whose signature line was, "Take my wife, please," died Tuesday at 91 of complications of the flu.
>
> The rabbi recalled that Youngman told him from a hospital bed with a broken hip two years ago: "The doctors are a bunch of crooks—they all wore masks."
>
> "One doctor was OK. If you can't afford the operation he touches up the X-ray."

The rest of the story recounted Youngman's remarkably long career and was sprinkled with a number of his best one-liners recounted by a host of friends from show business.

Similar treatment is given by other papers to prominent citizens in the community. That is especially true in many weekly newspapers. When long-time civic leader Leo Lobertini died in LaFollette, Tn, the *LaFollette Press* started his obituary on the front page under a three-column headline accompanied by a photograph and continued it to an inside page. The story reviewed his long public career and included quotes from current and former public officials who had served with him. Newspapers will often publish an editorial in which they pay tribute to a prominent person who has died. Here's the start of an editorial from the *Nashville Banner* when Henry R. Cannon, husband of country star "Cousin Minnie Pearl," died:

> Fans of "Cousin Minnie" were familiar with her comedy routines about her "men problems." But those familiar with the late Sarah Cannon knew she had no such trouble.
>
> Her husband, Henry Rolffs Cannon, was a gentleman of the first order, a man completely devoted to his famous wife. It is with deep sadness we note his death Friday at the age of 80.

The rest of the short editorial praised him for his unstinting support of his wife's career and for his good works in the community.

Obviously not every newspaper has the staff or the space to treat the death of a prominent citizen in the community in the same manner as the major dailies. However, a number of them often seek ways to present an additional tribute to someone who touched the lives of many. Here is an example of that type of story. It was written by Sam Venable, columnist for the *Knoxville News–Sentinel* in Tennessee:

> You don't have to read Miss Manners' column to know letters must be written in black or blue-black ink.
>
> Not if you were a student of Miss Geneva Anderson of Maryville, who died Friday at age 79 and will be buried today at Grandview Cemetery.
>
> Nor did you split your infinitives nor dangle your participles, splice complete sentences with commas nor (sin of sins) chew gum in class.
>
> "Now cherubs," she would say, "someone in this room is chewing gum. We will stop our lesson until this matter is resolved."
>
> That's when silence would fall upon her class—like an anvil. And tiny slivers of contraband Juicy Fruit in your mouth would balloon into a pumpkin.
>
> But if you were lucky enough to be assigned to Geneva Anderson for a year of senior English, you came away with more than the basics of letter-writing and etiquette. Just ask the thousands of pupils who studied under her at Robertville, Everett, Walland, Porter, Hixon and Young schools. Many students kept in contact with her until late this summer, when she suffered a debilitating stroke.
>
> In nearly two decades of formal education, I came in contact with countless dozens of teachers. Most were good, a few excellent . . . and, alas, a handful so poor they give "tenure" a bad reputation. Geneva Anderson was the bluest chip of them all.
>
> We met in the fall of 1964, the start of my final year at Young. English had never been a particularly difficult subject for me; but for three years, I had heard upperclassmen warn about nine months of enslavement if your name was included on her roster.
>
> Mine, gulp, was . . . and with fear and trembling, I entered her room.

What I happily discovered was not a female Simon Legree but an utterly charming, humorous, knowledgeable and challenging tutor.

Whenever Miss Anderson was particularly pleased with your work, she would write "sheer delight" at the top. I am here to tell you she was sheer delight from that first class in September until graduation in June.

Geneva Anderson could read "Macbeth" aloud and you could smell the cauldron bubbling. She could transform a vocabulary lesson into an exciting quest for new words. She could show you how to decode Harbrace and use it as a road map into the world of communications. And she made a certain four-eyed lad believe people would pay him to write, and then he wouldn't have to work for a living.

Firm? Indeed. But not strong-arm firm. On rare occasions of civil disorder, all Miss Anderson had to do was cut her eyes and stare for a moment—and calm was instantly restored.

I do hope St. Peter has everything in order. If that poor boy is chewing gum when Miss Anderson arrives, or tries to sign her up with green ink, he's gonna wish he had applied for a transfer.

The reporter must write death stories objectively and with dignity. Every effort should be made to resist the temptation to make the reader weep. The language of the story should be simple and precise, avoiding saccharine words and phrases such as "he will be missed by all." A person "dies" instead of "passes away"; he or she is "buried" instead of "interred," no matter what the family and the funeral director say. However, the reporter should learn the practices of the various religions and refer to them properly in the story.

Occasionally, a reporter is faced with a problem in writing a death story about a person whose past was marred by a scandal—a prison term, disbarment or a messy divorce that had made the front pages. If the person was entirely private, many newspapers would elect to leave out such facts, especially if the person had lived down the incident. However, if the person who was once a convict later became a prominent public official, the story must mention the prison term. Because the deceased was a public person and the criminal case was a well-known fact, the newspaper cannot leave it out. Facts of that nature, no matter how unpleasant, are essential to an adequate story.

When a death is announced in the afternoon newspaper, the next day's morning newspaper in the same city generally does not repeat the same lead. It usually features a different angle—the announcement of the funeral services, for example. Even if the funeral arrangements were carried in the original obit, they are the feature of the lead for the second-day story.

Funerals

The funeral announcement is the follow-up of a death story, except in the case of more prominent persons whose funerals might attract large numbers of mourners. As in any follow-up, a brief summary of the preceding story must be included, but the lead features the funeral.

Story Content

1. Time
2. Place
3. Whether public or private (open to the public unless otherwise stated)
4. Who will officiate
5. Place of burial
6. Active pallbearers
7. Honorary pallbearers.

Here is a typical funeral story:

> Funeral services for Col. E.B. (Buck) Ewing, 71, who had served as mayor of Hernando for two terms after he retired from the U.S. Army, were held at 11 a.m., Monday, at Calvary Baptist Church. Burial was in Hernando Memorial Cemetery.
>
> The Rev. Charles Louis Griffen, pastor of the church, praised Mr. Ewing for his "dedicated service to the nation and his untiring efforts to make Hernando a better place for all of us to live."
>
> Mr. Ewing, who died Saturday after suffering a heart attack at home, served as mayor from 1973 to 1981. During that time, he brought several industries to the community and established the 911 emergency telephone system.
>
> He did not run for re-election after his second term and later became chairman of the Hernando Park Commission. He helped develop a public park downtown on land donated to the city.

The remainder of the story would include the highlights of his military career, his education, his civic and fraternal memberships and a list of survivors.

The funeral story of a prominent person would be greatly expanded and reported in the same manner as any other news story of similar importance. It would include excerpts from the minister's eulogy, description of the service and an account of relatives and prominent friends and members of associations who attended in addition to any other information required to report the funeral adequately to readers.

The *New York Times,* for example, reported the funeral of Archbishop Fulton J. Sheen, the famous television priest, under the headline "Sheen Rites at St. Patrick's." The story was accompanied by two photographs of the funeral services. The story began this way:

> Behind the high altar of St. Patrick's Cathedral, the ornate bronze doors of the crypt stood open yesterday as Terence Cardinal Cooke said the funeral mass for Archbishop Fulton J. Sheen, who died Sunday at the age of 84.
>
> More than 50 ushers dressed in dark suits helped seat the hundreds who attended and then cordoned off the pews as they became full.
>
> Archbishop Edward T. O'Meara delivered the homily, praising Archbishop Sheen for his work during 63 years in the priesthood, during which time he wrote more than 50 books and gained lasting fame and the affection of millions through his radio and television ministry.

Most newspapers prefer to list the cause of death. However, some families either refuse to give that information or request it be withheld. This is particularly true in the case of certain diseases such as cancer and acquired immunodeficiency syndrome (AIDS). Newspapers generally defer to the family's wishes. But increasing numbers of families have consented to have AIDS listed as the cause of death.

A similar situation exists with listing the survivors. Some individuals who have died of AIDS have had long-term relationships with a companion. An increasing number of death stories list that person among the survivors, if that information is provided.

Here is how the Associated Press (AP) reported the memorial services for Canadian AIDS activist David Lewis:

> VANCOUVER, B.C.—AIDS activist David Lewis was surrounded by friends and family when he changed his intravenous drip solution from a harmless saline solution to a "sleeping potion," says a man who was with Lewis when he died Aug. 24.
>
> "David died supremely happy, at first frightened, then peaceful," Roedy Green told 40 people who attended a memorial service Tuesday evening for Lewis.
>
> Lewis attracted international attention in July when he revealed that he helped eight people with AIDS kill themselves during the past nine years.
>
> He said he placed overdoses of their drugs within the AIDS sufferers' reach.
>
> "I think it's immoral and unethical to not help someone die if that's what they want," Lewis, who was 38, said at the time.
>
> His own health then deteriorated from a number of illnesses related to acquired immune deficiency syndrome (AIDS) and he announced last month he would commit suicide rather than endure a painful and undignified death.
>
> "David did not want to die," said Green. "He enjoyed his life immensely, even to the very last second."

EXERCISES

1. Interview the city editors of a daily and a weekly newspaper in your area about their policy on obituaries. Write a short report on your interviews.

2. Study the illness and death stories in both those newspapers and write a brief report on how they are similar and how they are different. Pay particular attention to the style in which they are written, their length and where they are displayed in the newspaper.

3. Many newspapers and the AP wire service prepare obituaries on prominent women and men in advance and have them ready to print in the event of that person's death. Select a prominent person in your community or state whose death would be a significant news story. Make a list of the facts about her or him that you would need to write a story. Using all sources available to you (but do not call the person or any immediate relatives), collect all the facts for a story. Organize those facts similarly to the form described in this chapter and turn it in to your instructor along with the list of sources.

4. Check your college or university library to determine which major newspapers it receives or keeps on microfilm. Then select a prominent person who has died in the past year and look how the major newspaper handled the story. If microfilm of your local daily newspaper is available, compare how it handled the same story. Write a brief report on your findings.

5. Write illness or death stories from these notes:
   a. Johnny Mack Brewer
      Speaker of state's
      House of Representatives
      Tripped and fell on
      State Capitol steps
      Broke his right hip
      His right wrist
      Suffered five-inch gash
      On his forehead
      Rushed to Memorial Hospital
      Underwent six hours of surgery
      Condition listed as fair
      Will be hospitalized
      At least several weeks
      But expects to be on hand
      For opening of session
      Of State Legislature
      Two months from now
      Aide Thomas Ballard said
      Brewer apparently slipped
      Patch of ice on steps

      (Source: Ballard, Hospital spokeswoman Jane Pope)

   b. The Rev. Dr. Albert Sidney Harrigan
      Senior Minister at
      New Covenant Evangelical Fellowship
      Largest charismatic church in city
      More than 6,000 members
      Has not conducted services
      In more than a month
      Staff refuses to comment
      The Rev. Marianne Flintridge
      Has been conducting services
      Phone disconnected at
      Harrigan home which
      Appears closed up
      Many rumors among congregation
      From absconding with church money
      To absconding with church organist
      But no one speaks on the record
      Police say they have no
      Missing persons report on him
      Harrigan founded church

Ten years ago after
Breaking away from Church of God
Said it was "too stuffy"
His church featured
Multiple choirs, orchestra
Stage productions with
Themes from the Bible

(Sources: Church members, earlier stories in newspaper clip file)

6. Using the information in the death report (below) write a story about his death for a newspaper. Refer to that type story shown earlier in this chapter.

7. Using the information in the death report plus this additional information write an expanded story about Mr. McCord that includes the funeral services from the funeral report shown here.

8. Obtain from your college or university public relations office a copy of the vita or any type feature story they may have prepared on the president of your school. Double check it against reference works like *Who's Who*. Write an "advance" story, similar to those prepared by the wire services and major newspapers on prominent individuals. Do not list a cause of death or funeral details. At the end of the story list the prominent and not so prominent people you would get statements from about the "death" of the president.

9. Write an advance death story about yourself, using only the facts of your life as they now exist. Do not add any imaginary details but you could include comments from persons who know you well—fellow students, your minister and the like.

Death Report

Date _March 17_

Name _Joe Thomas (Red) McCord_   Age _78_

Address _716 Pine Ridge Road_

Place of death _Memorial Medical Center_   Date _March 17 (2:30 a.m.)_

Cause of death _Heart attack_

Date of birth _October 25_   Place of birth _Cleveland, Tennessee_

Parents _Mr. and Mrs. John A. McCord (deceased)_

Education _Cleveland Public Schools, Vanderbilt University AB Music_

Occupation _Professional musician, band leader_

Husband or wife (maiden name) _Sally Marie McCord (deceased)_

Date of marriage _June 16, 1937_   Place _Cleveland, Tennessee_

Residence here since _1946_

Previous residences _Cleveland, Tennessee; Knoxville, Tennessee_

Name of present employer _Retired after leading own band many years_

Previous employer _WSM Radio, Ted Weems Orchestra_

Military record _Captain, U.S. Air Force, 1941—45, military band leader_

Church affiliation _First Baptist Church_

Clubs, fraternal organizations, other affiliations _American Federation of Musicians Bluff City Lions Club_

Special interest or hobbies _Collecting early sheet music_

Survivors with relationship and address on each _Mrs. Joan Counts, 1421 Spencer St.; two grandsons, Joe Thomas Counts and Donny Counts_

Body at _Woodlawn Funeral Home_

Funeral arrangements _Incomplete_

FUNERAL REPORT: Joe Thomas (Red) McCord

Time 2 p.m., March 19

Place First Baptist Church

Officiating The Rev. William Robert Scrubbs

Burial place Lakeview Cemetery

Active pallbearers Representatives of the American Federation of Musicians

Honorary pallbearers none

Remarks Music for funeral services will be provided by members of Musicians Union who played in various bands with Mr. McCord. In lieu of flowers, family requests donations be made to American Heart Association.

19 Fires, Accidents and Disasters

"Tell the story in terms of people." Editors have been telling reporters that for decades and supporting their advice by referring their writers to *The Elements of Style*, a classic on clear writing by William Strunk, Jr. that was rescued from obscurity and revised by E.B. White.

Most stories can be told in terms of people if the reporter works at it. That is especially true of stories about fires, accidents and disasters. They are filled with drama.

Here's a lead on a fire story from the *New York Times* told in the terms of people:

> Generous to the last, Kitty Meyer struggled up the burning staircase of her multimillion-dollar, art-filled town house on the Upper East Side before dawn yesterday trying to save a house guest.
>
> But the flames were too fierce, seeming to almost explode from the windows of the neo-classical building, witnesses said, and Mrs. Meyer and Zohra Lahrizi Zondler, a Moroccan-born actress and socialite, were forced out onto the fifth-floor balcony.
>
> Then, even as a firetruck wailed down East 67th Street, throwing out its hoses, the women plunged to their deaths.

The remainder of the story gave details of the fire, details of Kitty Meyer's life and quotes from friends.

By contrast, here is a lead from the *San Francisco Chronicle* with the emphasis on the blaze:

> A fast-moving, four-alarm fire swept through the top of a Polk Gulch residential hotel last night, forcing 80 to 100 people into the bone-chilling cold and sending a beacon of flames into the sky.
>
> Although causing only one injury—to a San Francisco firefighter who received a minor head wound—the blaze ruined the holiday season for most of the tenants of the Leland Hotel, who were displaced.

Except for the truly dramatic fires and accidents, much of the information for this type story comes from records of the police and fire departments. But to avoid writing a dull and routine story, an alert reporter will attempt to get additional information by telephone or in person from witnesses—policemen, firemen, spectators and the persons involved if possible. Without that additional information the story may sound like a hundred other fire and accident stories. A lead that says:

> CAVE CITY, Ky.—Fire destroyed part of Guntown Mountain Amusement park early yesterday.

doesn't exactly reach out and grab the reader. Neither does an accident story that begins:

> A two-car accident at Central and Vine at the height of rush hour yesterday tied up downtown traffic for more than an hour.

In some major cities, newspapers are connected with the fire department's alarm system, and the fire bells ring in the city room as well as at fire headquarters. Most newspapers monitor the police radio so they can dispatch reporters and photographers to accident and fire scenes.

No matter how the information is gathered, certain facts are always required for a complete story. The newspaper reader is eager to know who was killed or injured; the extent and amount of property damage; and the disruption the event caused, such as blocked streets and traffic delays. If, in addition, the drama of major events can be effectively presented, so much the better. But the drama should be implicit in the facts. The reporter shouldn't overwrite for effect.

Here's an accident story from the Associated Press (AP) with an unusual twist:

> CLEVELAND—A woman chasing a $20 bill across a highway was killed early yesterday when she stepped into the path of a pickup truck.
>
> Karen Byers, 24, of Dalton, Ga., was driving on U.S. 64 with her boyfriend around 4:15 a.m. when she accidentally threw the bill, along with a cigarette butt, out the car window.
>
> She had just crossed the median in an effort to retrieve it when she was struck. She was pronounced dead at Bradley Memorial Hospital.
>
> The truck driver could not see her in the dark and did not have time to swerve, Tennessee Highway Patrolman Jake Butcher said. No charges were filed.

Facts and Sources

Story and Contents

The following formula indicates the facts and sources usually available in a major fire or accident story. Minor stories use fewer details:

Facts	*Sources*
1. Casualties	1. Police, firemen, hospitals, funeral homes, friends and relatives of dead and injured, witnesses, neighbors
a. Name and identification of every person killed and injured	
b. Manner in which persons were killed or injured	
c. Nature of injuries	
d. Disposition of head and injured	
2. Damages	2. Police, firemen and property owners
a. Damages to property	
b. Description of property	
c. Owner of property	
d. Insurance	
e. Other property threatened	
3. Description	3. Police, firemen, persons involved, witnesses
a. Cause	
b. Time and duration	
c. Chronological account of incidents	
d. Relief work of firemen, police or others	
e. Spectators	
4. Escapes	4. Police, firemen, persons involved, witnesses
a. Rescues	
b. Experiences of those escaping	
5. Legal action	5. Police, firemen, fire marshal, property owners, lawyers
a. Investigations	
b. Arrests	
c. Suits	
6. Sidelights (human interest, as part of main story or as separate story)	

In a major fire and accident story the number of persons dead or injured is usually featured. The amount of property damage is commonly featured if there are no injuries or deaths. But involvement of a prominent person, an unusual cause, a dramatic rescue or any one of the five W's may sometimes be featured in the lead.

Story Forms

Fire and accident stories can range in form and size from a brief to a lengthy several-feature story. The multiple-casualty story form is often used when such treatment is justified.

These are examples of accident and fire story leads:

A Brinks armored truck on a routine daily trip to the Keys—and carrying an unspecified amount of money—flipped over during the morning rush hour Wednesday in Florida City, backing up traffic on U.S. 1.

The driver, Juan J. Prado, and two passengers suffered minor injuries. Only Jesus Naranjo, who was riding in the front seat, was taken to Homestead Hospital. He was released after being treated for muscle strains, hospital spokeswoman Marcey Stevens said.

Brinks General Manager Angel Guinea said that though the truck's back door broke open, only a couple of rolls of pennies escaped. "We lost maybe $5," he said.

At least two people died and two were injured when a tanker truck collided with a car at the intersection of U.S. 441 and Interstate 595, sloshing 9,000 gallons of fuel over the major roadways at the tail end of the rush hour and igniting a blaze visible for miles.

The tanker was exiting 595 onto 441 when it apparently took the ramp's curve too fast, hit the car and tipped over at about 6:48 p.m. Minutes later, the truck's fuel burst into flames in three explosions.

The remainder of the story described how other drivers tried to rescue passengers in the car and quoted other witnesses and police. In addition, two sidebar stories accompanied the story. One was an interview of the man who pulled a woman to safety. The other was a story about the 2,400 gasoline trucks that use the highways near the accident scene.

Frequently, an accident or fire story's aftermath can result in a dramatic story. Here's the lead on one that followed an accident in which three popular coaches were killed:

CATHEDRAL CITY (AP)—On the end of the big high school football game, round one of the playoffs, excitement ran high in this working-class desert town of stucco mini-malls between the much richer Palm Springs and Rancho Mirage.

Then came shocking news: Three popular football coaches for Cathedral City High School were killed when their Jeep Wrangler went off a remote road in Thursday's early morning darkness.

The accident left the city and the school's 2,000 students numb. Crisis counselors were called in. Students walked the halls in a daze. Some called in sick. The Friday night playoff game was rescheduled for Saturday afternoon.

For the 44 young players, many from middle-class families, many Latino, many for whom football means everything, the accident stripped then of friends and confidants and left them struggling to prepare for the most important game of their lives.

"Everybody was getting all pumped up for the game, and it was like, I couldn't believe it," 17-year-old senior Tim Bohan, a line-backer on the varsity squad, said Friday. "How could this happen? I didn't know what to think. We were real close, like we're all good friends."

The remainder of the story recounted how the team was told about the accident and their immediate response, gave details of the accident and background on the coaches and how the town reacted to the tragedy.

Not all fires burn building. In fact, in many states forest fires are a major story. Here are several leads from stories involving forest fires:

CRAWFORDVILLE—The latest and largest of a string of forest fires was still burning out of control Tuesday over a 1,500-acre swath of wilderness area deep within the Appalachicola National Forest.

Despite the efforts of 105 firefighters and three helicopters to extinguish it, the fire burned out of control.

Abnormally dry weather and temperatures in the high 90s each day have turned the great woodland into a virtual tinderbox. No homes or structures are threatened by the blaze, about seven miles west of Crawfordville . . .

FILLMORE—Firefighters patrolled for embers and hot spots yesterday after controlling a fire that burned more than 12,000 acres of hilly brushland in Ventura County.

Ghostly wisps of smoke rose from the hills near this farming town of 13,000, but fire crews were demobilizing and preparing to leave after controlling the week-old blaze on Saturday evening . . .

DAYTONA BEACH—Weary firefighters continued to lose ground Monday as flames swept across parched woodlands in several Florida counties.

Record high temperatures, low humidity and desert-like dry conditions have made for the state's worst wildfires in half a century.

So far this month, fire has ripped through more than 85,000 acres in 65 counties, injuring 17 people, destroying 72 houses, damaging 42 others and causing more than $100 million in damages to forests and crops.

Disasters

A spectacular chain-reaction auto crash involving 75 cars resulting in multiple deaths and injuries is generally treated as a disaster by most newspapers. So, too, is a fire that may threaten a whole city block of stores and office buildings. And certainly, an epidemic of a disease that may pose a threat to the lives and property of hundreds, maybe even thousands, is considered a disaster by editors.

When one occurs, editors, reporters and photographers usually work as a team to provide in-depth coverage of the initial event and continuing coverage for days, weeks and maybe even months because disasters often disrupt communities and the systems that make them work.

And in many disasters, the newspaper may be the chief link between victims and other residents of the community and authority. The newspaper often provides vital information not easily obtainable from other sources.

In addition, newspapers not only report the basic event, but the underlying causes and what public officials are doing to help in recovery as well as starting programs to correct potentially dangerous situations—flooding, for example:

Because each disaster is different, the checklist will be adjusted for the specific incident. However, most newspapers devote enormous effort and time to provide blanket coverage, not only of the initial disaster but the aftermath as well.

Perhaps the most shocking man-made disaster of the 20th century was the bombing of the Murrah Federal Building in Oklahoma City. At the *Tulsa World*,

Executive Editor Joe Worley created a special team of reporters, editors and photographers to cover the story and its aftermath.

The front page of the *World* the morning after the bombing was devoted to three stories about the bombing and two spectacular color photographs. Fifteen other stories, seven photographs, a map and a diagram were spread across four inside pages, none of which carried advertisements. They included eyewitness accounts, interviews with survivors, statements from government officials and stories of police protection for property to prevent looting.

Here's the lead on the *World's* main story written by Brian Ford:

> OKLAHOMA CITY—In the deadliest U.S. bombing in 75 years, a massive car bomb ripped apart a nine-story federal building downtown Wednesday, killing at least 31, injuring hundreds and leaving at least 200 missing.
>
> At least 12 of those confirmed dead Wednesday evening were children, Assistant Fire Chief John Hansen said.
>
> The American Red Cross said more than 1,000 people received first aid downtown, and about 60 people were transported to local hospitals in critical condition in ambulances. More than 300 people were admitted to area hospitals. The blast was felt as far away as Stillwater . . .

In the following days, the *World's* coverage remained intensive, concentrating on the protracted search of the building's ruins for bodies of the victims and the impact of the bombing on the survivors as well as the city and the efforts of law enforcement agencies to arrest a suspect in the bombing (see Figs. 3.1 and 3.2).

Vocabulary and Fact Reporting

In reporting accidents—notably automobile accidents, because of their frequency—the reporter must use words carefully, with an eye to precise meaning. Only moving objects collide, strictly speaking. Therefore, "*struck* a parked car" is better than "*collided with* a parked car." "The accident occurred *when the car in which they were riding*" is awkward, yet "their car" is usually inaccurate. A number of newspapers, however, have come to accept the latter.

Libel actions grow out of inaccurate phrasing, and shortcuts of language should be used with care. Except in reports of storms, earthquakes and other "acts of God," colorful language should always yield to fact reporting. The phrase *completely demolished* (or *destroyed*) is redundant. To *demolish* or *destroy* means completely, so the word *completely* is unnecessary. A statement that a person is *not expected to live* should be reported as *critically injured* unless a direct quote is available from a physician using those exact words.

Factual reporting and careful language will also help the reporter write without expressing an opinion on the person responsible for a fire or accident. The reporter does not attempt to fix that responsibility. Who the guilty person is may seem apparent from the facts, the arrests and the statements of officials as reported in the case; but the reporter makes no effort to point out the guilty party, for that is the job of the courts.

If the facts of a story tend to point the finger of guilt at a person, the ethics of fair play require that the reporter make an effort to get that person's side of the story and report it at the same time. If the reporter is unable to reach the person, then the story should indicate that fact.

Complete Reporting

Most disasters are treated adequately when presented as straight news, with little interpretation. However, if such events accumulate into a daily threat to the security of life and property, the newspaper may feel compelled to develop a story or series of stories dealing with the problem.

Most communities face the serious continuing problem of automobile accidents. Occasionally there may be a series of fires, and there are epidemics of disease and crime. What causes those disasters? How do they occur? How could they be avoided? Before the community can protect itself or take the proper remedial steps, it must know the facts. That is where the reporter and the newspaper come in. In such cases it is the reporter's job to report not merely the surface events but the underlying causes as well. Often it is the reporter and the newspaper who force reluctant or foot-dragging public officials to undertake programs to correct potentially dangerous situations.

Almost every newspaper, at some time during the year, will print a story or series of stories touched off by a single news event such as an accident or fire. Three school bus accidents in less than a month caused a midwestern newspaper to do a series on how carefully the buses were checked for mechanical failure. The stories forced the school board to institute rigid new inspection policies. Fires in three apartment complexes in a southeastern city sent reporters checking county building codes that turned out to be virtually nonexistent. County and state officials quickly promised a new enforcement program.

Some newspapers have used news events to bring about improved traffic enforcement and better sanitary conditions at public housing and sewage treatment plants, for example. In each case, the reporter and the newspaper saw a need to reach the heart of a community problem. Rather than stopping with the initial report, the newspaper assigned the reporter to go beneath the surface of the initial event and through investigation and interpretative analysis present the problem to the public and public officials. Public service awards are won each year by many newspapers that investigate and report on communitywide problems.

EXERCISES

1. Fires and accidents are costly, not only for victims and survivors, but for the city as well. Select a significant fire or accident story from the local daily or one from a nearby city. Then interview the police or fire chief to find out how much it cost in manpower, time and equipment to handle the fire or accident. Talk to an insurance

executive to find out what impact fires and accidents have on local insurance rates. If there were injuries, check with hospital officials to find out what the medical treatment cost. If a major building burned, interview the owner to find out what impact it had on the businesses and professional persons who occupied the building. Ask local officials what the loss of the building means to tax collections. Write a news story on your findings.

2. Make a week-long inventory of the accident stories that appear in your local newspaper. Do the same with fire stories. Write a report on how the newspaper handled the stories. Include the size of the headline, the length of the story and where it was placed in the newspaper.

3. Interview officials of social service organizations such as the Salvation Army and the American Red Cross to find out what services they provide victims of fires and accidents. Write a news story on your findings.

4. Write stories based on these notes:
   a. Patricia Hope Lyons, 26
      Driving 1995 Geo
      Southbound on 1-75
      Between Lake City
      And Clinton exits
      Near Clinch River Bridge
      About 4:40 pm. Sunday
      Lost control of her car
      It crossed the median
      Stopped in northbound lane
      Struck by a 1990 Ford van
      Driven by T.J. Sparks, 64
      Of Speedwell in Blount County
      He and his wife, Jimmie, 58
      Were treated for minor bruises
      Patricia Lyons and daughter
      Brittany Nicole, two,
      Killed in collision
      Another daughter, Tiffany, six
      In critical condition
      At University Medical Center

      (Sources: State Trooper Paul Pullen, hospital spokesperson)

   b. 70-car train carrying
      7,000 tons of rocks
      To FEC's Hialeah yard
      Just two miles from destination
      Train crew heard loud explosion
      Second engine, first four cars
      derailed about 6:30 a.m. Friday
      Three employees jumped before
      Cars turned over causing
      Estimated $200,000 in damage

To the train and tracks
Derailment shut down railroad
Operations here for the day
Railway workers had to
Lay new tracks, upright cars
Clean up spilled rocks
Cause of accident undetermined

(Source: Jim Keely, chief of police for railroad)

c. David and Cindy Crawford
Children Dillon and Cameron
Sleeping in their home
At 118 Stone Ridge Parkway
About 6:15 a.m. a propane gas tank
Exploded and burst into flames
Crawford was jolted out of bed
He got his children out
Went back helped wife to safety
Crawford suffered burns
To most of his body
Wife Cindy broke her right ankle
Children suffered minor burns
Family taken to Vanderbilt Hospital
By Rutherford Rescue Squad
All were treated and released
Propane tank blew off
Back of the house
Crawford's truck and car
Both were destroyed in fire
La Vergne Fire Department
Fought the blaze two hours
House was a total loss
Noise from explosion
Woke neighbors as far away
As Woodlawn subdivision
About a mile away
Firemen sprayed neighboring
Houses to keep them from
Catching on fire
Trust fund established
In family's names at
First National Bank
To receive and manage
Donations to help the family

(Sources: La Vergne Fire Chief Bill Coleman, neighbors)

d. Sean Hickman, 56,
Flying single-engine
Piper Cub plane
Crash-landed on
Northwest Dade Lake

About 12:45 p.m. yesterday
Two miles west of
Island Home Airport
He radioed he was
Having engine trouble
He was unhurt but
Plane began to sink
He stood on top of it
Until the tail went down
Then he started swimming
Manuel Pedrosa, 19, on
Water jet rescued Hickman
About 150 yards off shore
National Transportation
Safety Board and Federal
Aviation Administration
Are investigating crash

(Sources: Pedrosa, Jorge Prellezo, safety board regional director)

6. Interview a member of a local Rescue Squad or Ambulance Service about their work and write a story about it. Turn in your notes with your story.

CHAPTER

20 Seasons, Weather, Natural Disasters

"**O**bviously, you don't prepare to cover a plane crash, but I think you prepare by what you do every day," said *Newsday* reporter Adam Horvath, who accepted the Pulitzer Prize for his newspaper for its reporting on the crash of TWA Flight 800 off Nova Scotia.

Tornadoes, hurricanes, earthquakes, floods, ice storms, blizzards, terrorist's explosions and plane crashes that result in hundreds of deaths all challenge the ingenuity of reporters, editors and photographers. And most often, they respond with determination to tell the story in detail as quickly and as thoroughly as they can.

When a tornado devastated downtown Clarksville, Tn., including the office of its daily newspaper, the *Leaf–Chronicle*, the staff still produced a 24-page edition within 24 hours. They worked out of a hotel, the home of the publisher and the office of the *Kentucky New Era* newspaper in Hopkinsville, Ky., a half-hour away. And the *New Era* printed the paper because the *Leaf–Chronicle's* presses were standing in water and there was no electrical power.

In its coverage of the Clarksville tornado, the *Tennessean* in nearby Nashville, a sister-paper to the *Leaf–Chronicle* (both are owned by Gannett), devoted most of its front page to the Clarksville tornado. It ran two major stories and two pictures, one seven columns wide by six-and-a-half inches deep. And it devoted four inside pages to 10 stories, five pictures and a large map showing the tornado's path through downtown Clarksville. It also carried a column telling tornado victims how to get help and a story on how others could help the tornado victims.

That type coverage is standard for newspapers when a disaster strikes. Everyone on the staff contributes, and disaster coverage often brings out the best in reporters, editors and photographers.

The impressive results of their individual and team efforts can and do result in national recognition. The *San Jose Mercury News,* for example, won the 1990 Pulitzer Prize for its coverage of the earthquake centered in the Santa Cruz Mountains.

But there is an equal challenge in having to write about the weather on a daily basis, especially when the forecast changes little from day to day. Until recently the daily weather story in many newspapers was dumped on the newest or weakest reporter in the newsroom. But not any longer. The continuing popularity of television weather forecasts and the excitement generated when *USA TODAY* introduced its four-color weather map and detailed regional summaries changed all of that.

Newspapers pay attention to the weather story every day now, not just when there is a blizzard or thunderstorms that send creeks and rivers over their banks. And many newspapers send their reporters to seminars and short courses in meteorology and climatology to help them improve their ability to write about the weather accurately and authoritatively.

Weather Stories

Mark Twain was half right when he said everybody talks about the weather but nobody does anything about it. Everybody does talk about the weather. Newspaper editors know that the weather story is consistently one of the best-read items in the paper every day. Many newspapers carry a regular front-page news story about the forecast. Almost all newspapers carry a detailed weather map, frequently in color, and complete local, regional and national forecasts that are provided by independent weather forecasting services or the National Weather Service. A listing of high and low temperatures in major cities across the nation generally is included.

A reporter assigned to write the weather story is often faced with making the same or nearly the same forecast sound fresh and interesting day after day during extended hot or cold, wet or dry, spells. It's not easy. During a heat wave in Memphis, Tn., a local restaurant owner gave the writer of the weather story a different angle. Here's the lead on that story:

> Attempting to meet a hot demand, a Memphis restaurant showered its customers with water Friday.
> The Cottage Restaurant at Summer and Holmes perched oscillating lawn sprinklers atop its entrance. So despite a hazy blue sky and temperatures in the 90s, water drops marked the lunch crowd's clothes as they took their seats.
> The Cottage may not have to resort to such tactics this weekend, however. "The outlook for rain this weekend is the best it's been since July," said meteorologist Brad Grant of the National Weather Service.

The remainder of the story gave the complete weather forecast for the area and recapped the daily temperatures for the week. It also included information about school closings.

To avoid a routine story based on the day's forecast only, many editors insist that the reporter look for a human-interest approach. But reporters should avoid trying to be overly cute or clever. Adding imaginary elements or stretching the facts could change or misrepresent the forecast and lead to angry readers. It could also bring a rebuke from federal officials. It is a violation of federal law to falsify a weather forecast.

Hyped up, overly dramatic efforts to give a lead a dramatic impact (such as this example from the *Atlanta Constitution*) not only fail but can be an embarrassment to the newspaper. This story was compiled from the wire services, but perhaps it should have been credited to the Armageddon Press International:

> Pigs screamed in the heat Wednesday and died on broiling Illinois farms. Chickens keeled over in North Carolina. The sturdy old brick homes of St. Louis turned into deadly ovens for the elderly and sick.
> The heat wave that has oppressed the nation's eastern half for more than a week groaned on and got worse. Temperatures soared from the 90s toward the 100s in much of the torrid zone.
> Across the nation the blistering weather was blamed for at least 29 deaths. Ten died in the St. Louis area alone, where a heat emergency was in force and 50 civic cooling centers were open.

If humans were dying, shouldn't they have been mentioned before the pigs and chickens? And is St. Louis really in the nation's eastern half or more toward the middle?

Frequently, the weather figures into other stories. When heavy winter rains brought flooding and mudslides to Northern California creating havoc for motorists as well as homeowners, it was front page news in the *San Jose Mercury News*. Here's the lead on just one of its front page stories:

> Bay Area motorists kept a nervous watch on traffic reports Sunday, fearing that more rain could bring additional havoc to their commutes today.
> Despite the apparent easing of the rain, highway officials and commuters remained concerned about travel conditions today and in the days ahead. Highways and vital roadways around the Bay Area still were plagued by pooling water, potholes and other damage, collapsed lanes, mudslides and potential flooding.
> At the top of the worry list was Montague Expressway, where Sunday night only one lane remained open in the westbound direction.
> "There are probably 75,000 employees in the North San Jose area," San Jose spokeswoman Kathy Thornberry said.
> "Any impact on traffic in this area is critical. . . ."

The story continued to the inside, where it, along with three large pictures of water-covered highways, people sandbagging their homes and a large map showing closed roads, power outages, sinkholes and mudslides, airport delays and areas where flood watches were posted, filled an entire page. Two other inside pages were filled with weather-related stories including a list of where to get free sandbags.

When a rare tornado ripped its way through downtown Miami, the *Miami Herald* photographers captured it in a dramatic color photo that covered about a third of the front page and the lead on the main story said:

> A towering tornado ripped its way through the middle of Miami, Biscayne Bay and Miami Beach right after lunch Monday, smashing cars and windows, tossing trees skyward and scaring the dickens out of thousands of people who were transfixed by the uncanny sight.

No one was seriously injured. Damage, although spread across a wide swath, was mostly minor, with some glaring exceptions . . .

The *New York Times* reported the continuing effects of a powerful winter storm that gripped eastern Canada this way:

MONTREAL, Jan. 12—First it was ice, then a paralyzing darkness when power lines fell and lights blinked out. Now weary residents of Eastern Canada, already reeling from the most damaging winter storm in memory, are shivering under a dangerous cold spell.

At least 15 people have died since the storm began to lash the area on Jan. 5. The police are now going door to door in some places, warning residents, particularly the elderly, that they should move to community shelters as temperatures dip within a few degrees of zero . . .

Special Weather Stories

Often the weather may become the lead story or one of the major stories of the day. A special story is demanded if:

1. The weather results in disasters—floods, hurricanes, tornadoes, droughts, dust storms, blizzards, lightning and other weather quirks that cause deaths or serious damages
2. There are sudden changes—cold waves, early snows, heavy rains or other out-of-the ordinary conditions
3. Records are approached or broken—highs and lows in monthly and annual temperatures or rainfall
4. A special event is affected by the weather—football and baseball games or other major sports events, parades, other outdoor events and even some indoor events.

Readers are interested not merely in data but also in the social and economic effects of unusual weather. The effects of weather on crops in farming areas can be of major local interest and perhaps even have national and international implications. A poor Russian wheat harvest resulting from bad weather eventually affected the price of bread in the American supermarkets, for example.

Such news is obtained from a variety of sources: the hospitals for deaths, injuries, and illnesses; the police for accidents and traffic problems; the fire department for fires and rescues; the charity agencies for suffering of the poor; government offices for relief work; transportation and utility companies for interruptions in service. There is also a variety of reports that come into the newspaper office from eyewitnesses. All are usually bound together in one weather story.

The multiple-casualty story (discussed in Chapter 9) is a popular form to use for weather stories concerning a number of deaths and injuries. Even if there are no casualties, this same form may be used as a convenient method of presenting

FIGURE 20.1 When a savage winter snowstorm almost stopped the state of Kentucky in its tracks, closing schools, highways and business and government offices, the *Lexington Herald–Leader* published a special "Portrait of a Storm" section, depicting the storm and its impact in both words and pictures.

(Reprinted with permission of the *Lexington Herald–Leader*.)

reports on a wide variety of property damages and other effects, the list of damages in this instance taking the place of the list of dead or injured.

Story Contents

The facts and sources of various weather stories include:

Facts	*Sources*
1. Statistics	**1.** Weather Service
a. Temperature (high and low)	
b. Precipitation	
c. Visibility	
d. Humidity	
e. Wind velocity	
f. Flood stage (if any)	
2. Forecast warnings	**2.** Weather Service, police, fire
a. Crop warnings	department, relief workers,
b. Sea or lake warnings	agriculture extension agents
3. Casualties	**3.** Police, fire department,
a. Names and identification of	hospitals, friends and relatives,
dead and injured	witnesses
b. Cause of deaths and	
injuries	
c. Nature of injuries	
d. Disposition of dead and	
injured	
4. Damages	**4.** Police, fire department, rescue
a. Damages to property	workers, owners, witnesses
b. Description of property	
c. Cause of damage	
d. Property threatened	
5. Relief	**5.** Police, fire department,
a. Relief done	charitable agencies, city
b. Relief needed	officials, relief workers
6. Escapes	**6.** Police, fire department, relief
a. Experiences of those who	workers, witnesses
escaped	
b. Rescues	
7. Legal action	**7.** Police
a. Arrests	
b. Investigations	
8. Tie-in or tie-back	**8.** Newspaper file, reference books

Natural Disasters

Some natural disasters are so monumental that they dominate the news for weeks and occasionally much longer because of their devastating impacts. The October

17, 1989, earthquake that caused more than $10 billion in damages from Watsonville and Santa Cruz to Oakland and San Francisco in northern California is a classic example.

A year later, it was still making news because many private homes, particularly near the epicenter in the mountains near Santa Cruz, had not been rebuilt. The business district of Santa Cruz remained in shambles and behind a wire fence. For miles, the collapsed double-decker freeway running through Oakland was being torn down. Across the bay, miles of its counterpart leading into San Francisco remained closed, causing horrendous traffic jams and a threat to the livelihood of merchants in Chinatown, while city, county and state officials were still debating who would pay for repairs.

Some newspapers are prepared to continue their operation whenever a natural disaster strikes. They have disaster plans that encompass all aspects of their operation, from gathering the news to printing and delivering it. Others unfortunately, do not.

It was just such a plan that permitted the *San Jose Mercury News* to publish a complete 104-page newspaper with a 12-page ad-free earthquake wraparound the next morning and to distribute 175,000 extra copies of it. Although the earthquake knocked out power throughout the area, including San Jose, the *Mercury News'* backup generators provided the power for the editorial and production staff to work through the night. The *Mercury News* was on the streets by 6:30 a.m.

On succeeding days the paper contained a 16-page earthquake section on October 18; a 12-page section on October 19; and a 16-page commemorative section, "We will never forget," on October 21. For its distinguished coverage of one of the worst natural disasters to hit the United States that year, the *Mercury News* won a Pulitzer Prize.

A basic checklist for stories on a disaster includes what the disaster was, who and how many were killed, who and how many survived, when it happened, the weather, extent of damage, emergency and law enforcement agencies involved, evacuation, shelters provided, medical aid at the scene, hospital emergency rooms and disaster information sources.

The lead of a disaster story should describe the extent of the disaster, focusing on the human element—casualties in particular. Here is the lead on the *Mercury News'* main earthquake story, written by David Schrieberg:

> The biggest earthquake since 1906—7 on the Richter scale and possibly higher—hit the Bay Area at 5:04 p.m., Tuesday, killing at least 76 people, injuring more than 460, setting off fires in San Francisco and sending buildings, highways and bridges crashing down on people and cars across the region.
>
> The quake, centered in the Santa Cruz Mountains, lasted from 20 to 40 seconds and frightened millions from Ukiah to San Diego. It was as strong as the quake that ravaged much of Soviet Armenia in December.
>
> Damage throughout the Bay Area was staggering, as death and injury reports poured in to disaster centers and rose by the hour. Lt. Gov. Leo McCarthy said the damage could reach $1 billion.
>
> In Oakland, officials feared that up to 200 people may have died when an elevated section of Interstate 880 toppled onto another part of the road. And the Alameda County coroner said the toll was expected to grow.

MURDER TRIAL
Defense attempts to deflect blame
PAGE 3A

DEFENSE SECRETARY
Former Republican Cohen sworn in for cabinet role
PAGE 7A

COUNTY BATTLE
La Vergne sweeps Smyrna foes
PAGE B1

The Daily News Journal

149th Year-No. 325   SATURDAY, JAN. 25, 1997   MURFREESBORO, TENN.   35¢

Twisters rampage

Tornadoes destroy homes and utilities, injure many people

BY SANDEE SUITT
SUZANNE GHIANNI
ANGELA CANNON

More than 100 homes, businesses, schools and utilities were damaged or destroyed in wake of Friday area freak storm sent tornadoes ripping across Rutherford County.

A constant wail of sirens piercing the darkness created an almost surreal atmosphere throughout the county after twisters left millions of dollars of damage in Smyrna, Barfield and southeast Murfreesboro.

The twisters damaged as many as 100 homes in the Barfield community alone, spread destruction across several other locations and injured many people. Some houses were nothing but a pile of rubble while others had little left but a concrete slab.

Shelters were opened, emergency services mustered as many personnel as they could and the National Guard was asked to assist in what Tennessee Emergency Management Agency reportedly called the hardest hit area in the state.

A Tennessee Highway Patrol helicopter was expected before 9 last night to fly over the area hit by the Southridge subdivision just southeast of Murfreesboro, to assist in the search for possible storm victims who were unaccounted for late Friday, said

(See Tornadoes, page 2A)

Injured listed

Twelve people were treated at Middle Tennessee Medical Center as the result of injuries suffered when tornadoes ripped through the area Friday night, according to Rebecca Chisam, vice president of public affairs at MTMC.

The injured appeared in apt Park 1 to be:
- Clover identified those injured, all from Murfreesboro, as:
- • Virginia Johnson, 36, treated and released for abrasions and contusions.
- • Linda Barrom, 66, treated and released, lacerations and abrasions.
- • Colter Grayson, 39, treated and released for rib fracture and laceration.
- • Jonathon Grayson, 3, treated and released.
- • William Grayson Sr., 4, treated and released.
- • André Grayson, 17, treated and released.
- • Mary Jo Bell, 45, treated and released for abrasions, contusions.
- • Estey R. Tuuku, 79, treated and released, abrasions, lacerations.
- • Kimberly Kelch, 35, released (no condition available at print time).
- • Katina Kelch, 11, treated and released for lacerations.
- • Sherri Bell, 46, treated and released for abrasions, contusions.
- • Mary Barney, 38, treated and released for abrasions and contusions.

Rutherford County Sheriff Truman Jones.

"They're going to light up that area and give us a better assessment if there's any people over there or not," Jones said.

"A lot of the houses are nothing but rubble. So far, we haven't found any casualties or any major

(See Tornadoes, page 2A)

TORNADO TOUCHDOWN
INJURIES CONFIRMED
MAJOR DAMAGE

TORNADO TOUCHDOWN

Havoc wreaked throughout county

DNJ Photo by Jim Davis

Estimates of the damage and destruction left in wake of Friday's tornado have yet to be tallied, but well over 100 buildings were damaged or destroyed. Top left, Marsha Chunkey and Ray Bohrer of the Southeast Rutherford Fire Department survey what's left of the truck building at South Church Street Neill-Sandler Toyota, which was moved over a hundred feet before being deposited by the storm. Above, emergency workers survey the remains of a home on Southridge Drive, which received the brunt of the storm's fury.

Storm tears homes in Barfield asunder

BY BYRON HENSLEY
MIKE WEST
AND KELLY LOCKHART
Staff writers

At least 30 houses were destroyed as a tornado jumped Stones River and touched down in Southridge subdivision off Barfield-Crescent Road just south of Murfreesboro shortly before 5 p.m. Friday.

At the worst point of devastation, five houses were taken down to the dirt with little foundation remaining.

"Oh, my God. Oh, my God," screamed one Southridge resident as she saw just the foundation of her home. Deputies first comforted her and then escorted her inside the yellow police tape.

"I want to look," she cried. "I want to

see."

A second deputy stopped her precious son with a fatherly bear hug as he ran screaming "No! No! No! No!" over and over again.

Despite that damage, sheriff's deputies who were searching the wreckage for survivors discovered a gold-colored corgi dog buried under debris. The dog was shaken but not injured.

On nearby Kerry Lane, five houses were destroyed when the tornado initially crossed the river.

"I saw it bounce over the river then touch down. It was a big black cloud. It looked almost like a big fire, but then I saw all the roofing tiles twirling around

(See Storm, page 2A)

Smyrna feels ravages of Friday funnel clouds

BY DAN WHITTLE
Staff writer

SMYRNA — A tornado, high winds, golf-ball size hail and driving rain left a trail of destruction and high anxiety for Smyrna residents late Friday.

The Hickory Groves area, Chalet Apartments, Food Lion, Smyrna Middle School and Gileville were among the places hit by the tornado.

Smyrna resident Richard Swader, who has relatives living in the Hickory Groves area, appeared highly agitated at not being able to get into the rural area on Old Jefferson Pike that was hit at about 5 p.m.

A Smyrna police dispatcher could not confirm any injuries Friday night. However, residents said they knew of some people who had been hurt.

"I know that friends Karen Hardy and Kershanda Shepherd have received injuries and there were

> "It was a distinct funnel cloud. It sounded like a herd of big trucks going through the community."
>
> Claude Cooper
> Jefferson Pike
> Smyrna

three ambulances dispatched to the area, but we are blocked from Smyrna in trying to get the region where numerous houses have been wiped out," noted Swader, who lives on Jefferson Pike on the eastern edge of Smyrna. "It appears the tornado hit on the border between Murfreesboro and Smyrna."

Swader appeared to be near a state of tears as he voiced concern for his relatives and neighbors.

Claude Cooper of Jefferson Pike

in Smyrna was an eyewitness to the tornado.

"It was a distinct funnel cloud," noted Cooper. "It sounded like a herd of big trucks going through the community. We looked out our front window and saw debris and items flying through the air overhead and headed toward the Hickory Groves community."

Smyrna Mayor Paul Johns confirmed there were personal injuries in the apartment complex that was hit.

Some power lines were knocked down at Smyrna Middle School and the Thurman Francis Elementary in the downtown area of Smyrna. Various businesses throughout the city reported sign damage from the tornado, high winds and driving rain and large pieces of hail that rained from the sky.

Smyrna resident Brian Clayton, a sacker at the Smyrna Food Lion Store, described the swirling winds

(See Smyrna, page 2A)

INSIDE...

Ramsey parents never hit their children: former nanny

A former nanny for JonBenet Ramsey's parents said "they never hit their children" when investigators inquired about the possibility of abuse.

SEE STORY PAGE 3C

INDEX
Classified C3-7
Comics 2C
Opinion 4A
Sports B1-4
TV 8A
Weather 6A
Public Record 8A
NASCAR 10C
Auto Saturday 9C

DNJ photo by Jim Davis

Without a home
Kenny Curtis, left, and Scott Gibson of Southridge subdivision south of Murfreesboro prepare to be transported to MTSU's Murphy Center Friday night after their homes were destroyed by a tornado.

SERVING MIDDLE TENNESSEE SINCE 1849   www.dnj.com

FIGURE 20.2 The *Daily News Journal,* a small daily in Murfreesboro (Tn), devoted its entire front page to tornadoes that swept through its area, injuring at least a dozen people and destroying more than 100 homes and businesses. This front page is an outstanding example of how a newspaper can concentrate all its efforts covering a major disaster.

(Reprinted with permission of the *Daily News Journal,* Murfreesboro, Tn.)

Writing the first story of a major disaster such as an earthquake or tornado presents a particular challenge because of conflicting reports of the casualties and damages. Officials often are unsure and can only guess, as those in Oakland did, about the total number of people who might have died when the interstate collapsed, and as the Lieutenant Governor did when he underestimated the total damage by about $9 billion. But they are the most reliable sources at the time, and it is important to give the readers those figures. The readers know that they will be adjusted in subsequent stories.

The *Mercury News* editors just like their counterparts at other papers know that the real story of a natural disaster is in the human element—the people who are killed, those who are rescued, those who rescue them, the homeless, the displaced. That is why one of the prime elements of disaster coverage is the feature or human-interest story focusing on the individuals whose lives were dramatically impacted by the disaster.

Here is the lead on the *Mercury News'* story of one of the most dramatic of all the rescues of the quake victims. It was written by Laura Kurtzman, Dan Stober, and Philip J. Trounstine.

> OAKLAND—They were dirty, drained and demoralized after a fruitless search for life in the rubble that once was the Cypress Street Viaduct.
>
> Then, unbelievably, a Caltrans engineer in a cherry picker saw a movement—a faint promise—in a 3-½-foot-high concrete tomb.
>
> And from the flattest and most hopeless section of I-880, rescue workers on Saturday pulled 220-pound dockworker Buck Helm from his squashed silver Chevrolet Sprint—89 hours after he was buried.
>
> "Thank God, I'm alive," said the 57-year-old Weaverville man, according to one of the rescue workers who cheered and wept as Helm waved weakly from his gurney.

The feature treatment was also given to a follow-up story on the tornadoes in Illinois that killed 26 that appeared in the *Los Angeles Times*. It was written by Tracy Shryer and Bob Sector.

> CREST HILL, Ill.—Dazed and heartsick, Joann Eads stared absently into space Wednesday as she sat on the curb outside what only the day before had been her trim two-story townhouse on Cedar Drive.
>
> Next to her lay a bottle of blue antacid. Behind her, total devastation.
>
> "You wanna buy a house cheap?" she asked facetiously.
>
> Eads was just one of thousands of people struggling with tears, black humor and hope to piece together their scattered lives and possessions after a series of monster tornadoes unleashed their fury across parts of the south-western Chicago suburbs Thursday afternoon.
>
> The storms killed at least 26 people, injured 350 more and caused destruction to homes, businesses, schools and churches on a scale not seen in these parts in more than two decades.
>
> "It was like the devil came to visit," said Mike Brewer, who safely rode out the twister in the bathroom of his now-mangled pizza parlor in nearby Plainfield.

Seasons

Seasonal stories are a staple in most newspapers. They also can become a problem for a reporter. How can he or she make this year's St. Patrick's Day story different from last year's? Is there a new angle to St. Valentine's Day, Mother's Day, and the dozens of the other holidays and anniversaries newspapers dutifully write about each year? Fortunately, most newspapers handle seasonal stories as features. If a reporter has an active imagination and a flair for words, what might have been a routine story can be turned into a clever, original and highly readable feature.

The handling of some seasonal stories became complicated when Congress passed a law making Monday the day of observance for five federal holidays, no matter which day the holiday actually came on, in order to create three-day weekends. They are Washington's Birthday, Memorial Day, Labor Day Columbus Day and Veterans Day. Starting in January 1986, the birthday of the late civil rights leader Dr. Martin Luther King Jr. has been observed on the third Monday in January. The matter can get even more confused because on some of those holidays, in some states, only federal offices are closed. State and local officials may elect to keep their offices open. For example, most Southern states do not observe Memorial Day as an official holiday.

Weaving the Story

The key to writing all seasonal or holiday stories is to combine the present and the past—to tell not only how the holiday will be observed but also why it is being observed—and to make the story sound fresh. Something is lacking if a feature on Columbus Day fails to recall highlights of the discovery of America. In addition, the story is really incomplete if it mentions nothing of local residents' plans to observe the holiday.

The sources for seasonal stories is evident. In developing a feature, the reporter has to go to reference books or other sources to obtain facts of the past. But reporters also have to interview informed persons for facts of the present. This information has to be woven into a coherent and interesting story. To give the story timeliness, the reporter often puts emphasis on the present in the lead.

Research is the key. A reporter should not settle for the quickest, easiest reference work—an encyclopedia. Much historical, and sometimes scientific, research is done annually in many areas that might give a reporter a new approach to a holiday. Reports of such research often are listed in the standard periodical indexes available in most libraries. For example, a check of such indexes turned up a scientist who had made a study of Ireland and produced a theory that it was the Ice Age and not St. Patrick that drove the snakes out of Ireland. This gave a fresh touch to a St. Patrick's Day story and brought dozens of responses by mail and phone from staunch supporters of the good saint.

Sometimes the cause of the celebration does not date back to a historical event—the vernal equinox, for example—and the reporter must develop a scientific rather than a historical background. The reporter may assume that many persons will approach a certain day with interest, and it is permissible to predict what will be done as an unplanned observance of that day. Depending on the tenor of the story, the reporter sometimes may make his predictions imaginative as well as factual. However, this approach requires imagination similar to that of an Associated Press (AP) reporter who wrote a personality sketch on a turkey as a Thanksgiving feature. Often an offbeat feature can be developed on one of the lesser known "days," such as Bachelor's Day on February 28.

Seeking information on local celebrations, the reporter naturally will question leaders of clubs and organizations. The American Legion and Veterans of Foreign Wars might be the principal sources for a Veterans Day story if there is no government-sponsored observance planned. The labor unions should provide information for a Labor Day story. Schools observe most anniversaries by class programs. Most other organizations will announce such special programs in advance.

Here are several seasonal story leads, including an offbeat one by Nancy Klingener of the *Miami Herald:*

> When the August moon approaches full, the thoughts of coral turn to love.
> Or at least reproduction.
> Coral spawning, the annual event that has intrigued scientists and divers, will occur next week. Several Keys dive shops offer night dives to showcase the spectacular display.
> Normally a fairly passive animal, coral polyps show their stuff once a year when they send out bundles of eggs and clouds of sperm into the Ocean.

> Fall leaf lovers can expect a normal fall with good color in the Great Smoky Mountains National Park.
> The best time to see colorful leaves will be the last two weeks of October, Nancy Gray, park ranger, said.
> "Conditions over the summer and the first part of fall have been good as far as determining how colorful the leaves will be," Gray said. "Rainy summers, warm days and fair nights make for the best colors."
>
> (The *Knoxville News-Sentinel)*

> As the Fourth of July approaches, those uninhibited public relations people in Philadelphia are at it again, shamelessly bragging for the third straight year about having "the world's largest birthday cake."
> If only it were true; but, alas, the claim seems half-baked.
> Once again, the concoction, sponsored by convenience store operator Wawa Inc., will be 80 feet long, 10 feet wide and weigh about 1,800 pounds. On the nation's birthday, an estimated 25,000 people milling around the Liberty Bell will be offered a little taste of freedom, including a portion iced to look like the American flag.

The story, written by Alex John London for the *Wall Street Journal*, detailed how the Philadelphia claim was disputed by Martin Day, editor for the *Guiness Book of World Records* in London, who said the world's largest cake—90,000 pounds, 84 feet by 114 feet—was served up in 1986 in Austin, Texas, to celebrate the 150th anniversary of the founding of the Republic of Texas.

Story Contents

The formula for a seasonal story is:

Facts	*Sources*

1. Explanation of seasonal event
   a. History
   b. Past observances
	1. Reference books or reliable local historians

2. Observances
   a. Formally by organizations
   b. Informally by whole city
	2. Officials of organizations, reasonable predictions of reporter

Chase's *Calendar of Annual Events* and Appleton's *Book of Holidays* are two good guides to seasonal and other special events. The accompanying chart points out some of the events and dates that may receive attention by newspapers. Not all of them are reported by any one newspaper, although all are potential stories. Local interest and available space in the newspaper may be the deciding factors.

To this list may be added many seasonal events of local interest only: anniversaries of Revolutionary or Civil war battles, admission of the state into the Union, anniversary of the founding of the city, and various "weeks" (Book Week, National Newspaper Week, and so on) are proclaimed during the year. When it occurs, an astronomical phenomenon such as an eclipse, sun spots or the arrival of a comet is also covered extensively in the newspaper.

January

  1—New Year's Day
  8—Jackson's Birthday
17—Franklin's Birthday
18—Martin Luther King's Birthday
19—Lee's Birthday

February

  2—Groundhog Day
12—Lincoln's Birthday
14—St. Valentine's Day
15—Women's Suffrage Day
22—Washington's Birthday
29—Leap Year Day (every four years)

March

17—St. Patrick's Day
21—Vernal Equinox

Last of month—evidence of Spring, first robin, spring fever, outside activities

Between March 22 and April 25—Easter, first Sunday after full moon following equinox; Good Friday, Friday before Easter; Passover

April

1—All Fool's Day
13—Jefferson's Birthday
26—Arbor Day (varies in different
     states)

May

1—May Day
     Second Sunday—Mother's Day
30—Decoration or Memorial Day

June

6—D-Day
14—Flag Day
Third Sunday—Father's Day
22—Summer Solstice
During month—vacations, trips,
     picnics

July

4—Independence Day

August

During month—height of "dog
     days"

September

First Monday—Labor Day
17—Constitution Day

23—Autumnal Equinox
During month—Rosh Hashana, Yom
     Kippur, school openings, harvest
     time, fairs

October

12—Columbus Day
Fourth Monday—Veterans Day
31—Halloween

November

First Tuesday after first
     Monday—Election Day (not every
     year)
Fourth Thursday—Thanksgiving
During month—beginning of winter
     sports, migration of birds

December

First of month—Christmas shopping
22—Winter Solstice
25—Christmas
28—Wilson's Birthday
Last of the Month—Ramadan,
     Kwanzaa, Hanukkah.

EXERCISES

1. On most college campuses there is at least one faculty member who is a climatologist or meteorologist and some even offer a major in meteorology. Contact the weather expert on your campus. Interview him or her about local weather patterns and trends and write a story using the information you obtain in the interview.

2. Then, using the local library as a reference point track down the local weather "prophet," who may predict the weather by the number of fogs in fall, the travels of woolly bear caterpillars across the highway, the length of a billy goat's beard and so forth. Interview that person. Compare his or her weather predictions to those of the campus weather expert you interviewed. Write a story based on your interview.

3. Contact the local chamber of commerce or the local chapter of the state historical society to see if they have records of any unusual celebrations that were held or are

held in your area, such as the Collard Greens festival or the Repeal of Prohibition (the Volstead Act). Write a feature story about the event.

4. Using the Internet, click on to the National Weather Service's web page and search for the long-range forecast for your area. Write a news story based on the forecast.

5. Write news stories using the following notes:
   a. Today's weather forecast
      High: 50, gradual clearing
      West winds 5–10 mph
      Tonight: Low: 34
      Fair skies, calm winds
      Tomorrow: High: 58
      Partly cloudy, warmer temperatures
      Light and variable winds
      Tuesday–Thursday
      Sunny Tuesday and Wednesday
      Partly cloudy skies
      Thursday highs: 59–62; lows: 35–38
      National Weather Service
      Forecaster Grady Blount says
      "We are in for some nice days
      "As temperatures warm up."

      (Source: Local Office National Weather Service)

   b. Classes to resume Thursday
      At Alberta State University
      Had been called off
      For five days because
      Tornado badly damaged
      Six classroom buildings
      In heart of campus
      ASU President Sidney Luft
      Spoke to faculty today in
      University's gymnasium
      First time since tornadoes
      Faculty returned to campus
      He told them "I'm happy to
      Go on with classes"
      He gave them each a
      T-shirt with a drawing
      Of a tornado on it in red
      He announced classes
      Would resume Thursday
      Students returning to
      All dorms but Hess Hall
      Which lost its roof
      Students from that dorm
      Will be housed in local motels
      President also praised

Campus employees for
Their action during the
Tornado and in the
Cleanup afterwards
The tornado struck
Campus about 6:30 a.m. Friday

(Source: State University spokesman John Clark)

c. Heat wave continues
16th consecutive day
Of 100-degree weather
On Tuesday tied record
For most 100-degree days
In a single year
Set in 1953, tied in 1985
Says National Weather Service
Meteorologist Douglas Cain
But a cold wave is coming
Down from Canada
Cooler temperatures expected
By the weekend
But temperatures will still
Be in mid to upper 90s
With high humidity
"It's still going to be
Pretty miserable," Cain said
Social agencies say
Demand for help
Up about 100 percent
Ask for donation of
Electric fans of all sizes
No reported heat deaths here
But 124 across the nation
Local utility board says
Demand for power has
Jumped nearly 100 percent
Doesn't anticipate blackouts
City hospitals report
Fifty percent jump in
Heat related illnesses
Treated in emergency rooms
Summer school classes
Have been canceled
For rest of the week
School buildings not air conditioned

(Sources: Cain, spokespersons for social agencies, school board, utility company)

6. Extreme weather conditions have a serious effect on homeless people. Contact several social agencies such as the Salvation Army and the local Rescue Mission to find out how they prepare for the extra demand on their resources in times of extreme weather. Contact the Office of Emergency Planning in your city to find out what the city does for homeless people in case of extreme weather. Write a story based on the information you gather. Using the Internet, click on to one of the many web sites devoted to global warming. Using information gathered from several of those web sites, write story analyzing the global warming debate. Check with a professor who teaches meteorology on your campus for her or his views on global warning. Include them in your story.

8. Write a news story based on the following information about the aftermath of a major snow storm that hit your entire state:
More than 20,600 homes
Across state still without power
Storm dumped 17 inches of snow
In the city over two days
Starting last Wednesday
And 22 inches across the state
Five days later crews hustling
Only one reported death
Retired teacher Ruth Montgomery, 80,
Died Thursday in McCreary County
After loss of electricity
At her home rendered
Her oxygen tank useless.
Governor called it "a miracle
That there has only been one death"
But emergency crews are still
Searching remote areas across the state
For possible victims of the storm
Schools across the state
Will remain closed until
All roads have been cleared
So schoolbusses can travel safely
State Education Department said
National Weather Services said
Temperatures will gradually
Reach about 40 by tomorrow
Which should improve conditions
And allow work crews to reach
More remote areas in efforts
To restore power.

(Sources: State Police, State Highway Department, State Education Department, Power Utility, National Weather Service, McCreary County Sheriff's Office)

9. Make a list of newsworthy pictures about the aftermath of the storm you would have taken based on notes in Exercise 8. Write appropriate cutlines for them.

10. Write a 90-second newscast based on Exercise 8.

CHAPTER

21 Crime

"Sensational crime stories in newspapers make a pure mind almost impossible," Anthony Comstock, the self-appointed guardian of the nation's morals in the last half of the 1800s, wrote.

"They open the way for the grossest evils. Foul thoughts are the precursor of foul action," railed the founder and secretary of the New York Society for the Suppression of Vice, as he sought to rid the nation of what he called a "deadly stream" of crime stories pouring into "thousands of homes . . . breeding scoffers and breaking down restraints and counteracting the sweet influences of religion."

More than a century later, those same views are being expressed by both professional and amateur critics of the press. But the crime story still remains a staple in American newspapers.

Although many cities are reporting dramatic decreases in murders and other capital crimes, skeptics question the accuracy of their statistics. Many police departments has been accused of "doctoring" their figures.

Whether crime is actually up or down, newspapers continue to report murders, robberies, the illegal drug trade, police scandals involving bribery and brutality along with rapes, robberies, holdups and other traditional crime stories. But increasingly, they are giving extensive coverage to stories about child abuse, incest, child pornography, battered wives and husbands, white-collar crime such as bank fraud, embezzlements, stock fraud, theft by computer, tax fraud and crime on the Internet, especially child pornography.

Newspapers are devoting more space to crime victims and the human cost of crime. And they are putting more emphasis on patterns and trends as well as the causes.

Although too many crime stories still begin:

> A 27-year-old Ferndale man was shot to death yesterday in a drug deal that "went bad," police said . . .

More and more coverage of crime has spread to other beats, including religion, occasionally. Stories about college football players stealing thousands of hours of cellular phone air time, elementary and high school students killing fellow students in school, computer technicians stealing valuable information from employers and selling it to the competition and ministers who defraud their flocks are not uncommon.

As a result, crime stories are no longer exclusively the work of the police or investigative reporters. They turn up on almost every beat, including sports, business and religion. For example, the *New York Post* led its business section with this story about reputed crime families manipulating stock in a health-club company:

> Mobsters booted from the Fulton Fish market set their sights on the stock market—and joined forces with brokers and execs to make a killing in a massive "pump and dump" scheme, prosecutors charge.
>
> Nineteen people were indicted yesterday in the scam, in which the penny stock for a health-club company called Health-Tech International was artificially inflated and sold at a huge profit.

The Salt Lake City Olympic bribery scandal got as much play on the sports page as it did on the front pages. And charges of embezzlement and fraud against the head of one of the largest religious organizations in the nation dominated some religion pages.

Occasionally, a "police" story may even touch on fashion, in a manner of speaking, as this story from Portland, Ore., did:

> PORTLAND, Ore. (AP)—Earrings probably won't become de rigueur among the ranks of Portland's finest, but policemen wishing to adorn their ears with dainty pieces of precious metal may now do so.
>
> The city attorney's office has advised the department to allow male officers to wear earrings after a policeman filed a labor grievance recently.
>
> Police officials say they'll follow the city attorney's advice, but they don't have to like it.
>
> "I don't think the public is prepared to see a male police officer wear an earring," said Capt. Wayne Inman.
>
> The grievance challenged rules that specified female officers' earrings must be small and non-dangling, but didn't address the question for male officers.

The city police, the county or parish sheriff's office, state police and other state agencies and numerous federal agencies are involved in various aspects of law enforcement. Sometimes they enforce identical laws, but each has its separate law-enforcement machinery. For the most part they work closely together and share information.

In most cities, the chief source of crime news is the city police station, but in a major city there may be as many as a dozen agencies, all with law-enforcement powers. A wide variety of important news is reported to the police—murders, robberies and other criminal acts, accidents, fires, missing persons. City police generally enforce state laws on murder, larceny and other crimes in addition to ordinances covering crimes and regulations that apply within the city limits.

The county jail, where the sheriff and other county law-enforcement officers are headquartered, is also an important source of crime news. County officers function chiefly outside the city limits to enforce state and county laws, but they also have authority within the city.

Federal officers make few arrests compared to city and county officers, but even this number is increasing as the incidence of crime in general is soaring. Often stories resulting from federal arrests can be of a more spectacular nature than the crime story growing out of an arrest by a city or county officer. Federal officers enforce laws dealing with kidnapping, counterfeiting, narcotics (smuggling and sale), federal tax evasion, mail fraud, manufacture and sale of illegal beverages, and hijacking of airplanes as well as trucks involved in interstate shipment of goods, interference with civil rights and similar matters.

The states generally maintain state police for highway patrol duty, a state bureau of criminal investigation, fire marshals, tax collectors and investigators, game wardens, forest rangers and other units of law enforcement that will produce crime and other news stories.

Often the first beat assigned to a new reporter is the police beat, which includes some if not all of the law-enforcement agencies. The police beat is an excellent training ground for beginning reporters because it offers good practice in the fundamentals of reporting, in cultivating news sources, in gathering all the facts needed to write an accurate story (often requiring the checking of several sources) and in writing under the pressure of approaching deadlines. It also presents some serious hazards for the lazy reporter who does not check the facts or the reporter who gets too close to police sources and begins to serve as a police spokesman rather than a fair and accurate reporter.

Reporting crime news can be demanding. At times, if properly done, it is a public service that can be a deterrent to certain types of crime. But, badly handled, it can show how to commit crime successfully. It can give a false impression of the amount of crime, or build sympathy for or glorify criminals. Crime news also can help criminals by informing them of police strategy or hamper justice by "trying the case out of court"—making it difficult to get a fair trial. And, of course, it can turn the spotlight on the law-abiding family of the criminal, adding to their humiliation. Fortunately, over the years, leaders in the news media have come to recognize these problems, and most newspapers today practice considerable restraint in handling crime news. At the same time the news media continue to fight for its First Amendment rights to report freely and fairly all crime news, despite repeated efforts over the years to force controls on them.

Crimes

Before examining the content of the typical crime story, the reporter should know what is meant by "crime." A breach of law is a crime and may be either a felony or a misdemeanor. A felony is one of the more serious crimes, usually carrying a penalty of long imprisonment and sometimes death. (Although the Supreme Court held in the 1970s that the death penalty was "cruel and unusual punishment," it later reversed that stand and a number of executions have been carried out.) A misdemeanor is a minor breach of law, usually resulting in a fine and no imprisonment, although some misdemeanors provide confinement and penalties. A study of most state laws will show that the following crimes are usually regarded as felonies:

Homicide (killing a person)
1. Manslaughter
   a. Voluntary (intentional, in a fit of passion)
   b. Involuntary (unintentional, through negligence)
2. Murder
   a. First degree (with evident premeditation)
   b. Second degree (no premeditation but intent to kill)

Assault
1. Assault with intent to kill or maim
2. Felonious assault
3. Mayhem (maiming)
4. Kidnapping

Violating Property Rights
1. Larceny (illegally taking property)
2. Burglary (entering dwelling to take property, housebreaking)
3. Robbery (larceny with assault, threatened or committed against a person)
4. Embezzlement (larceny through trust)
5. Forgery
6. Arson
7. Receiving stolen property

Obstructing Justice
1. Interfering with an officer
2. Perjury
3. Bribery
4. Contempt of court

Conspiracy in Crime
1. Accessory before fact
2. Accessory after fact

Others
1. Illegal gambling
2. Manufacture, possession or sale of illegal beverages and drugs
3. Disturbing peace (fight, riot)
4. Sexual crimes
5. Criminal libel

FIGURE 21.1 Reporter/photographer Fred Petke was on the scene when two jail escapees were recaptured by police in Corbin, Ky. His story and photographs were spread across two-thirds of the front page of the *Times–Tribune*. It is an example of outstanding news coverage of an important local event in that southeastern Kentucky community.

(Reprinted with permission of the *Times–Tribune*, Corbin, Ky.)

Misdemeanors include such violations as public drunkenness, speeding, illegal parking, simple assault and a variety of lesser infractions ranging from littering to public nudity.

In crime stories the reporter must be sure to write only privileged facts gathered from public records, and they must be accurate. Of course, accuracy is important in every news story, but it is vital in crime stories because a libel suit lurks behind every one of them. If a person is arrested and charged with a certain crime, the reporter can say just that. It is a matter of public record. But a detective's chance remark that a certain person committed a crime is not a matter of public record and therefore is not privileged. Its publication may result in a libel suit. Even in cases in which police obtain confessions, the reporter must exercise care. In one case on the records, a man arrested for a crime confessed. During the trial he repudiated his confession and was found not guilty. He then sued the newspaper that had reported his confession and won the libel suit.

A person who is arrested is not necessarily guilty of a crime. No matter how damaging the evidence may appear, the reporter's story should not imply guilt. The story should include the evidence the police have against the person, but it should be fair and accurate and should not draw conclusions.

Reporters should always remember that a person is arrested on "charges" of a certain crime, not for the crime. And reporters should be cautious when reporting the evidence police or prosecutors say they have against a prisoner. The reporter should ask to see the evidence to make certain it exists. At one infamous murder-rape trial in Illinois, a prosecutor claimed he had a pair of the prisoner's blood-stained undershorts, which he even showed in court. During the appeal process in the case, it was proved that the undershorts did not belong to the prisoner and that the "blood" on them was red dye.

If doubt exists that the prisoner gave a correct name, newspapers often write that the person "was booked at the city jail as John Smith" or the prisoner "gave his name as John Smith." If a prisoner refuses to give an address, the reporter should say so or write "address not given." Some newspapers no longer publish the addresses alleged criminals give to police because quite often they are fictitious and create problems for the legitimate residents at those addresses. Instead, the newspaper may print "John Smith, who said he lives in the 1200 block of South Park Street, has been charged." But before resorting to that, reporters should use telephone books, city directories and other available sources to check on the correct name and address of anyone arrested for a crime. In fact, it is good practice to check all names and addresses automatically, no matter what the arrest record may show. Police have been known to make mistakes.

Stories involving juveniles are particularly sensitive. Some states have laws prohibiting the publication of a juvenile's name in connection with a crime report. Juvenile cases are generally not tried in open courts, and juvenile judges establish the standards for releasing names and information. Most newspapers do not use the name of a juvenile unless it is a major offense—perhaps a son's killing a father—or unless the prosecutor elects to try the juvenile as an adult.

Here's how the *Los Angeles Times* handled one story involving a juvenile burglary ring:

> A gang of tiny toughs, ages 9 to 14, used a cutting torch to crack safes in seven businesses in Salinas and may have committed up to 50 burglaries during a downtown crime spree, police said Friday.
>
> Thousands of dollars in cash and goods were taken during the series of break-ins over an eight-month period and the little burglars often vandalized the stores they broke into, investigators said.
>
> The case was broken late Thursday when two boys, one 11 and the other 12, were arrested after they allegedly robbed an elderly person in front of a fast-food restaurant, police Lt. Rick Anderson said.
>
> When police questioned the two youngsters they confessed to the burglaries and named four accomplices. Anderson said police had a half-dozen boys—one age 9, one 11, one 12, two 13 and one 14—in custody and were sifting through a mound of burglary reports.

More often stories involving juveniles get this treatment:

> A 10-year-old boy from Orange, N.J., was charged yesterday with murder and aggravated sexual assault in the beating death of a 4-month-old girl who had been left in his care late Saturday night while the baby's mother went out to a local fast-food restaurant, Essex County prosecutors said.

The name of the 14-year-old Kentucky boy who shot several of his schoolmates, killing three and wounding five others, was released almost immediately. So, too, were the names of the two elementary school boys who shot and killed their schoolmates in Jonesboro, Ark., and the two who shot and killed classmates at Columbine High School in Littleton, Col.

Police Records

Two types of records commonly yield local crime news in most localities: (1) city and county jail "blotters" and (2) complaint sheets or bulletins. The first is an entry or log book of arrested persons maintained at city and county jails; the second is a record of complaints made to police and of investigations by police. The accompanying illustration of this type of record has been condensed to conserve space.

These records give the reporter only a few bare facts about a case. Many cases are so trivial that they either will be a one-line entry in a crime log published in many newspapers or will be ignored. Additional facts about the more interesting cases have to be collected through interviews with the officers and the persons involved in the case.

Here is an example of a major crime story that required the reporters to gather facts from a variety of sources other than the police record alone:

> A prominent San Francisco attorney was shot and killed yesterday in his Market Street office by an assailant who was gunned down just minutes later in an exchange of shots that left two police officers wounded.

The slaying took place shortly before 1 p.m., when the suspect, described as a man with a wooden left leg, shot Garfield Walton Steward, 75, who had offices on the sixth floor of the historic Flood Building at 870 Market Street.

After police responded to an emergency call reporting the shooting, they cornered the armed assailant on the third floor and ordered him to drop his gun, police said. When he refused, he was fatally wounded in an exchange of gunfire.

(San Francisco Chronicle)

In addition to the details of the shooting provided by the police, the reporters interviewed the police chief and several other occupants of the building who either saw the gunman or heard the shooting. They also talked to numerous persons who knew the lawyer as well as members of his family.

The *San Jose Mercury News* handled the story this way:

SAN FRANCISCO—Police killed a gunman who walked into a busy downtown office building Tuesday, shot a lawyer to death and then wounded two police officers.

The lunchtime gunbattle was fought in the marble hallways on two floors of the James Flood Building at the crowded corner of Powell and Market streets.

The slain lawyer was Garfield Steward, 75, according to the coroner's office.

The story also included interviews with police officers who had been at the scene during the gunbattle and three other persons who worked in the building and were present during the shooting.

Access to police records and other public records varies from state to state. By the early 1980s, nearly all states had open records laws requiring police and almost all other records to be open for inspection by the public as well as the press. Every reporter should learn what his or her state's law on open records is. Many state press associations have published their state's laws in convenient booklets for reporters to use.

As a general rule, law-enforcement officials cooperate with the press. This is not always the case, however. As a result, a number of newspapers resort to court action to force police and other public officials to open public records.

The computerization of public records has presented some problems for the press, but in a number of states with open records laws, the information stored in computers is considered public and must be made available to the public and the press.

A reporter must use extreme care when copying information from a police blotter and especially in the use of complaint sheets. Both of these records frequently contain misspellings of names and incorrect addresses. In addition, complaint sheets often contain misinformation, exaggerations and, from time to time, outright lies. They usually are a form of interoffice correspondence between the complaint desk and the investigating officers. Reporters should verify everything in the complaint sheet with the investigating officers before making use of complaint-sheet information. The reporter also is expected to use good judgment in handling information from police sources if publication would aid a suspect in escaping, prevent a fair trial or cause other difficulties.

Although the form on page 324 pertains to city police, similar forms are kept by other types of law-enforcement officers—county, state and federal. Every reporter should know that federal law-enforcement agencies, as a general rule, tend to be far less open than city and state officials in revealing information to the press. Although there is a federal freedom of information law designed to open federal records to the public, the release of certain criminal information is exempt from the law.

The coroner is another public official whose records are often important in crime news, although coroners usually are not considered law-enforcement officials. The coroner, in many states a medical doctor, conducts an inquiry (inquest) into deaths from "unnatural causes"—those in which foul play, violence, suicide or unusual circumstances may be involved.

If the coroner's report shows that the cause of a death points to evidence of crime, arrests by law-enforcement officers may result. However, the coroner's functions are limited to determining the cause of death only. The coroner does not "try" a case against persons who may be accused of causing the death. Any legal action arising from the coroner's report must go through the regular legal system in the usual manner.

Story Contents

The usual information and sources for a crime story might be outlined as follows:

Facts	*Sources*
1. Casualties	1. Police, hospitals, friends and
a. Name and identification of persons	relatives of dead and injured, witnesses
b. How persons were killed or injured	
c. Nature of injuries	
d. Disposition of dead and injured	
2. Damages	2. Police, property owners
a. Value, property stolen or destroyed	
b. Description of property	
c. Owner	
d. Insurance	
e. Other threatened property	
3. Description	3. Police, involved persons,
a. Chronological account	witnesses
b. Description of involved persons	

KNOXVILLE, TN. POLICE DEPARTMENT   EVENT REPORT

FORM PD 370 6/80   PAGE _____ OF _____ PAGES

VICTIM

2. VICTIM/FIRM	SEX	RACE	D.O.B.	3. COMPLAINANT'S NAME	SEX	RACE	D.O.B.	4. COMPLAINT NO.

5. HOME ADDRESS	6. COMPLAINANT'S ADDRESS	9. WHEN REPORTED

8. BUSINESS ADDRESS/SCHOOL	6. T / BUS. RES.	7. BUSINESS ADDRESS	10. T / BUS. RES.

EVENT

11. CLASSIFICATION	12. OFFENSE/EVENT	13. LOCATION OF EVENT	14. NEAREST CROSS STREET	15. ☐ PUBLIC ☐ PRIVATE	16. BEAT	17. RELATION TO VICTIM

16. TIME OF OCCURRENCE _ _ _ _ - _ _ _ _ - _ _ _ _	17. TOOLS/WEAPON USED	20 METHOD USED

M.O. INFORMATION

Type of Structure		Point of Entry	Security Used	Impersonated	Suspect Actions

21 Non-Residential
- 1 ☐ Convenience
- 2 ☐ Drug
- 3 ☐ Medical
- 4 ☐ Financial
- 5 ☐ Mfg./Const.
- 6 ☐ Other Retail
- 7 ☐ Public Bldg.
- 8 ☐ Restaurant/Bar
- 9 ☐ Transportation
- 10 ☐ Wholesale
- 11 ☐ Fast Food
- 12 ☐ Other

22 Residential
- 1 ☐ Apt./Condo.
- 2 ☐ Duplex
- 3 ☐ Hotel/Motel
- 4 ☐ House
- 5 ☐ Mobile/Camper
- 6 ☐ Townhouse

23 Type Lock Defeated
- 1 ☐ Chain/Bolt
- 2 ☐ Deadbolt
- 3 ☐ Padlock
- 4 ☐ Springlatch
- 5 ☐ Other

24 Target(s)
- 1 ☐ Cash Register
- 2 ☐ Display Items
- 3 ☐ Person
- 4 ☐ Safe Box
- 5 ☐ Sales Area
- 6 ☐ Vending Machine
- 7 ☐ Attic
- 8 ☐ Basement
- 9 ☐ Bathroom
- 10 ☐ Bedroom
- 11 ☐ Den
- 12 ☐ Family Room
- 13 ☐ Garage/Carport
- 14 ☐ Kitchen
- 15 ☐ Living Room
- 16 ☐ Storage
- 17 ☐ Other

25 Weather Conditions
- 1 ☐ Clear
- 2 ☐ Cloudy
- 3 ☐ Fog
- 4 ☐ Rain
- 5 ☐ Snow
- 6 ☐ Other

26 Point of Entry
- 1 ☐ Unknown
- 2 ☐ Front
- 3 ☐ Garage
- 4 ☐ Rear
- 5 ☐ Side
- 6 ☐ Door
- 7 ☐ Duct/Vent
- 8 ☐ Roof/Floor
- 9 ☐ Trunk/Hood
- 10 ☐ Wall
- 11 ☐ Window
- 12 ☐ Other

27 EXIT:

28 Victim/Offender Relationship
- 1 ☐ Family
- 2 ☐ Acquaintance
- 3 ☐ Friend
- 4 ☐ Co-Offender
- 5 ☐ Other
- 6 ☐ None

29 Security Used
- 1 ☐ Alarm
- 2 ☐ Bar/Grate
- 3 ☐ Dog
- 4 ☐ Ext. Light
- 5 ☐ Guard
- 6 ☐ Int. Light
- 7 ☐ Locked Doors
- 8 ☐ Locked Windows
- 9 ☐ Neighborhood Watch
- 10 ☐ Photo/Camera
- 11 ☐ Fence
- 12 ☐ Other

30 Point of Entry Visible From
- 1 ☐ Adjacent Structure
- 2 ☐ Alley
- 3 ☐ Street
- 4 ☐ Not Visible

31 Lighting Conditions
- 1 ☐ Dawn
- 2 ☐ Daylight
- 3 ☐ Dusk
- 4 ☐ Dark (street lights off)
- 5 ☐ Dark (no street lights)
- 6 ☐ Dark (street lights on)

32 Impersonated
- 1 ☐ Survey
- 2 ☐ Customer
- 3 ☐ Delivery Person
- 4 ☐ Disabled Motorist
- 5 ☐ Drunk
- 6 ☐ Employee/Employer
- 7 ☐ Friend
- 8 ☐ Ill/Injured
- 9 ☐ Use Phone
- 10 ☐ Police/Law
- 11 ☐ Renter
- 12 ☐ Repairman
- 13 ☐ Salesman
- 14 ☐ Seeking Assistance
- 15 ☐ Directions
- 16 ☐ Relative
- 17 ☐ Seeking
- 18 ☐ Selling
- 19 ☐ Soliciting
- 20 ☐ Other

33 Suspect Actions
- 1 ☐ Unknown
- 2 ☐ Bound Victim
- 3 ☐ Blindfolded Victim
- 4 ☐ Child Molest
- 5 ☐ Demand Cash
- 6 ☐ Demand Jewelry
- 7 ☐ Disabled Phone
- 8 ☐ Ate/Drank
- 9 ☐ Hideout
- 10 ☐ Injured Victim
- 11 ☐ Sex Acts
- 12 ☐ Ransacked
- 13 ☐ Raped
- 14 ☐ Smoked
- 15 ☐ Took Money
- 16 ☐ Took Tools
- 17 ☐ Took TV
- 18 ☐ Took Stereo
- 19 ☐ Took Vehicle
- 20 ☐ Threats
- 21 ☐ Had Lookout
- 22 ☐ Demand Note
- 23 ☐ Forced Entry
- 24 ☐ Used Matches
- 25 ☐ Stolen Vehicle
- 26 ☐ Used Tools
- 27 ☐ Vandalized
- 28 ☐ Vehicle Needed To Remove Property
- 29 ☐ Was Neat
- 30 ☐ Snatched Purse
- 31 ☐ Other

34 Place of Attack
- 1 ☐ Structure
- 2 ☐ Vehicle
- 3 ☐ Street/Alley
- 4 ☐ Lot/Park/Yard
- 5 ☐ Other

35 Description of Surrounding Area
- 1 ☐ Residential
- 2 ☐ Business
- 3 ☐ Indust./Mfg
- 4 ☐ Recreational
- 5 ☐ Institutional
- 6 ☐ Open Space
- 7 ☐ Other

36. IS THERE A SIGNIFICANT M.O. PRESENT? IF YES, DESCRIBE IN NARRATIVE IF NO PLACE AN X IN BOX A →	A.

PROPERTY/UCR

37. IS STOLEN PROPERTY TRACEABLE?	IF NO PLACE AN X IN BOX B →	B.

38 PROPERTY CODE	(D) DAMAGED	(V) VEHICLE FROM WHICH THEFT OCCURED	(S) STOLEN	(A) VEHICLE USED BY SUSPECT	39. CONFISCATION NO.
		(R) RECOVERED (L) LOST (E) EVIDENCE (F) FOUND (O) OTHER			

40	SER. NO./OP. I.D. NO./DRIVER'S LIC. NO.	COMP VALUE

YEAR	MAKE	MODEL	COLOR	BODY	TAG/STATE/YEAR	VIN. NO.	TOTAL VALUE

40. IGNITION LOCKED ☐ YES ☐ NO	41. VEHICLE/PROPERTY INSURED BY	42. IDENTIFYING CHARACTERISTICS
KEYS IN IGNITION ☐ YES ☐ NO		
DOORS LOCKED ☐ YES ☐ NO		

43. CAN SUSPECT VEHICLE BE IDENTIFIED?	IF NO PLACE AN X IN BOX C →	C.

44. TIME SUSPECT VEHICLE INFORMATION BROADCAST.	PLACE TIME IN BOX 44 →	

45. IS THERE SIGNIFICANT PHYSICAL EVIDENCE PRESENT? IF YES, DESCRIBE IN NARRATIVE. IF NO PLACE AN X IN BOX D →	D.
46 HAS EVIDENCE TECH WORK BEEN PERFORMED? (9 -) REQUESTED? IF NO PLACE AN X IN BOX E	E.
TECH WORK PERFORMED/REQUESTED: ☐ PHOTO ☐ FINGERPRINT ☐ COMPOSITE ☐ OTHER	

OFF.

47. INVESTIGATOR NOTIFIED	I.D. NO.	48. SUPERVISOR NOTIFIED	I.D. NO.	49. CRIME LAB TECHNICIAN ASSIGNED	I.D. NO.

50. REPORTING OFFICER	I.D. NO.	51. SECOND OFFICER	I.D. NO.	52. SUPERVISOR	I.D. NO.

4. Escapes	4. Police, involved persons
a. Rescues	
b. Experiences of those escaping	
5. Legal action	5. Police
a. Investigation, clues, evidence	
b. Arrests	
6. Tie-backs	6. Library–morgue

The length of a crime story is usually determined by the seriousness of the crime. Other factors that add paragraphs and increase the size of the headlines are the prominence of the persons involved, the place of the crime, unusual circumstances and incidents of human interest. Often one of those factors leads a reporter to write a feature lead, or an entire feature story, about the incident instead of a straight-news story. In selecting facts to go into the story and in the treatment of those facts, the reporter must be careful to observe the ethics of the newspaper. How much gory description should be included in the story of a particularly gruesome murder, for example? (A review of newspaper ethics would be appropriate in this connection; see Chapter 5.)

Here are some examples of leads on crime and crime-related stories:

Vella Schmid, 73, who robbed a 91-year-old "friend" at gunpoint in February, is out of jail after being sentenced earlier this month to two years of house arrest and eight years' probation.

(The *Miami Herald*)

Rather than surrender after he was caught shoplifting a $40 shirt, Thomas A. Majors drew his gun, fired at police and then died in a barrage of returned shots.

(*Nashville Banner*)

A former teller at a Princeton bank that was robbed of about $140,000 on Thursday has been arrested and accused of planning the robbery. He even drove the getaway car, the Federal Bureau of Investigation said yesterday.

(The *New York Times*)

WASHINGTON—More than 1 million women are stalked each year, according to a Justice Department study released Thursday.

(*USA TODAY*)

DAYTONA BEACH—(AP)—A man who exchanged gunfire with police on a crowded street during Black College Reunion weekend early Sunday injured six people before he was shot and killed.

They've been bound and gagged, shot and stabbed, dumped in a river and set on fire.

They've been beaten, clubbed and drugged, run over with cars and hammered.

They are Nashville's murder victims.

Statistics released last week by the FBI show Nashville, the 24th largest city in the country, had the 18th most homicides last year with 112.

(The *Tennessean*)

An Oakland man killed in a botched Financial District bank holdup was a convicted bank robber wanted for questioning in four other Bay Area bank heists, including one in San Francisco, police said.

(*San Francisco Examiner*)

A 17-year-old Gilroy youth was arrested Friday in connection with what police believe was the rape of a 13-year-old Gilroy girl in San Martin, Santa Clara County Sheriff's officials said.

(*San Jose Mercury News*)

CLINCHPORT—A Scott County man has been charged with first-degree murder after he allegedly shot his brother in the face with a 12-gauge shotgun Saturday afternoon, authorities report.

And there is always a dumb criminal to report on, as in this story from the *LaFollette Press*, LaFollette, Tn:

After revealing his first name and the phone number of his best friend during an armed robbery, a Caryville resident is in the county jail facing criminal charges . . .

Rapes

Traditionally, newspapers do not print the names of rape victims, even during the course of a trial. However, the issue became a topic of considerable discussion among journalists, lawyers and women's rights advocates in the early 1990s after one victim permitted her name to be used by the *Des Moines Register* in a five-part series that detailed the emotional pain she experienced after the rape.

This, of course, was not the first time a rape victim's name had been printed. It did not lead to a flood of similar stories, although several did appear in major newspapers such as the *San Jose Mercury News*. Yet critics of the policy expressed their concern that the Des Moines series and the support it received from a number of journalists as well as women's rights advocates could lead to a wholesale printing of the names of rape victims without the victim's consent. That has not happened. Most newspapers still do not print rape victims' names.

However, in 1991 when a woman charged that she had been raped by William Kennedy Smith (a nephew of Sen. Edward M. Kennedy) on the grounds of the Kennedy family estate in Palm Beach, the National Broadcasting System and the *New York Times* used her name about a week after the initial news story. Both news organizations were criticized.

The *Times* drew particular fire from critics because in addition to its basic news stories, it printed a story that detailed the young woman's troubled personal history. That story included information about her mother's divorce and subsequent marriage to a wealthy businessman; it also quoted acquaintances of the women who discussed her alleged "high living" lifestyle in Palm Beach.

Accompanying the story about the woman, the *Times* printed an explanation of why it elected to use her name. The statement said, in part:

"Like many other news organizations, the *New York Times* ordinarily shields the identities of complainants in sex crimes, while awaiting the courts' judgment about the truth of their accusation."

The *Times* pointed out that it used her name finally because "NBC's nationwide broadcast took the matter of her privacy out of the hands" of its editors.

"The practice of withholding names became almost unanimous in the 1970s when women argued that it would make rape victims more likely to come forward," the *Times* story said.

Many editors said that using names would increase the pain of a traumatic experience. But some editors now believe that failing to identify rape victims perpetuates the idea that rape is a crime that permanently damages a woman's reputation.

Generally speaking, rape stories are relatively brief. They may include:

Facts	*Sources*
Statement of alleged victim	Police
Hospital treatment	Hospital officials, police
Arrest of suspect	Police
Possible statement of suspect	Suspect, suspect's attorney
Possible court action	Police, district attorney

It should be noted, however, that in many rape cases the victim is unable to identify her attacker or the attacker is never caught.

The *Miami Herald* reported a kidnapping and rape this way:

Hialeah Police charged a man Tuesday with repeatedly raping a woman after kidnapping her and her son and keeping them hostage for eight days in a West Okeechobee Road motel.

The man allegedly beat the woman's face with his fist and hit her 5-year-old son, police spokesman Jose Caragol said.

Luis Median was charged with armed kidnapping with aggravated assault, assault with a deadly weapon and three counts of armed sexual battery.

Here is the lead on an Associated Press (AP) story about court action in a rape case:

> JOHNSON CITY—A civil court judge has awarded $4 million to a woman who claimed she was sedated and raped by her doctor nearly two years ago.
>
> She may have a tough time collecting, however. The bondsman who posted $100,000 bail for Dr. Mohamed F. Ali and an attorney for the state Board of Medical Examiners says he's left the country.
>
> Washington County Judge Thomas Seeley awarded the woman $1.5 million in compensatory damages and $2.5 million in punitive damages on Wednesday. She had filed a $10 million suit against Ali, an Egyptian native.
>
> Ali, 36, is believed to have fled the country last year before criminal charges of rape and attempted bribery were tried.

Suicides

In covering a suicide, the reporter must be extremely careful. The official police report, not the reporter's judgment, determines whether a death is a suicide. In many states police can determine if the case is a suicide; in others a final ruling has to await action by a coroner. Even if a man plunges from a 14-story window in front of a large crowd, it may not be a suicide. Even if a woman is found dead on a lonely road with a pistol in her hand and a bullet in her head, there may be no definite evidence that she fired the bullet. Until police or the coroner complete the investigation, the reporter should say only that the person was "found dead," or "plunged," or "fell." If police report they found a suicide note or say that the wound was self-inflicted, the reporter should quote them. But the reporter should not say the case was a suicide without quoting an authority.

It may be possible to discover a motive, after suicide has been clearly established, but the reporter must be careful. Reporters should not piece together certain facts about the person's ill health, financial difficulties or love affairs and then conclude that they were the motives. If there is a definite, authentic statement of motive from a suicide note or a close relative, it is generally safe to use that information in the story. However, if no motive is found, the reporter should say so in the story by quoting an authoritative source.

Even more caution is necessary in reporting attempted suicides. Unless the suicide attempt is evident and backed up by statements of authorities, or unless the person admits the suicide attempt, the reporter must give only the facts. It is wise to be cautious even in cases in which the person admits the attempted suicide. It could be a grandstand play for attention or a fabrication for some other reason.

The method of suicide is usually described only in general terms. Newspapers never give details of methods because that might show others how to commit suicide. For example, the name of a poison or drug is not used in suicide stories. The means of suicide is simply called "a poison" or "a drug." Gory details are nearly always omitted in suicide stories.

Story Contents

The following is a formula for the usual suicide story:

Facts	*Sources*
1. Name and identification a. Disposition of body	1. Police, coroner or coroner's report, hospital, relatives, friends

2. Method
  a. Cause of death
  b. Circumstances surrounding death (when and how found)
	2. Police, witnesses

3. Motive
  a. Suicide note
  b. Statement from relatives, physician, friends, business associates
	3. Police, relatives, friends, physician

Any of the three principal facts named above may be the feature of the suicide story. An unusual method or motive is usually the feature, unless the person's prominence overshadows that feature. Under no circumstances should the reporter attempt to treat a suicide story in a lighthearted or humorous manner.

Here is an example of a suicide story from the *New York Times*. The story was given considerably more attention than most suicide stories because of the prominence of the family.

> A retired Wisconsin newspaper editor and publisher who had been suffering from cancer shot and critically wounded his wife yesterday and then killed himself in their home on a Rockefeller estate in the Adirondacks, state police said.
>
> Miles J. McMillan, 69 years old, who retired four years ago from *The Capital Times* of Madison, Wis., and his wife, Elsie Rockefeller, 58, were found by her daughter and their son. Both were shot in the head.

The story quoted state police as its authority for McMillan's cancer, saying he had undergone radiation and chemotherapy treatment at the Mayo Clinic in Rochester, Minn. It also said the couple was found on a bed, and a .22 calibre automatic pistol was nearby. But it gave no other details of the shooting.

EXERCISES

1. Increasing numbers of police departments have web pages. Check with the police and sheriff's departments in your area to find out if they have such a page. If so, talk to the department official or the person who is in charge of it about its purpose and usefulness. Write a story based on what you learn.

2. The issue of publishing the names of convicted sex offenders has created controversy in states where it is allowed by law. Interview the police chief, the prosecut-

ing attorney and the head of the American Civil Liberties Union in your area to obtain their views on the issue. Write a story on your findings.

3. Interview the chief of your campus police about crime on your campus. Ask for crime statistics for the past three years. Write a story based on the interview and the statistics detailing how safe your campus is.

4. The following are reports on several crimes reported to police. On a separate sheet of paper explain how you would handle the story on each. For example, explain if you would simply write a straight news story based on the available information or if you would expand the story to include quotes from police or behavioral psychologists commenting of this particular type crime.

   a. David Harry Rogers, 42, 6380 S. Manor Circle, Pinehurst, was arrested for exposing himself to 10-year-old girl riding a school bus. He was charged with four counts of lewd and lascivious acts in the presence of a child. Lt. Armando Guzman said Rogers was seen following buses in his car several times in the Kinloch area. Before school Oct. 6, Guzman said, Rogers exposed himself to girls who were on a bus stopped near Northwest 43rd Avenue and 11th Street. He was arrested before lunch Thursday at the law firm where he works, Brown and Potemkin, 5201 Blue Lagoon Dr., Guzman said.

   b. A city police SWAT team was celebrating the end of a tough three-week training course at a Foley Beach Bar. Twenty members of the team, Police Chief Roberto Sosa, and Assistant Chief Jimmy Kaplan were there. Witnesses said a brawl erupted. Someone hit Officer Marco Zappata over the head with a beer bottle. He landed in the hospital where doctors put eight staples in his head to close the wound. Four men, not police, were arrested. Assistant Chief Kaplan said it wasn't a brawl. He called it a "minor disorder by a large crowd." Said he was clueless as to what started it. However, the chief called it a mini-riot. Witnesses said it started when someone grabbed Zappata's girlfriend. It all happened Thursday about 6:30, during happy hour at the bar.

   c. Republican leader of the state House of Representatives arrested for drunk driving. State Trooper Bill Bible stopped Rep. Barney Kockman about 10:30 p.m., about 10 miles west of Crossville on Interstate 40. He said Kockman's car had been weaving all over the road. He said Kockman at first claimed immunity from arrest because he was a legislator. He refused to take a breath test. Kockman released after posting $10,000 bond and surrendering his driver's license. He issued a statement saying his arrest Friday proves "that people are not perfect. They make mistakes." He said he would not resign his leadership post. "They'll have to force me out," he said. Two years ago Kockman was acquitted of drunken driving in a neighboring state after convincing a judge that cold medicine affected his breath test for alcohol.

5. Write news stories using the following notes:
   a. Andrea Singleton, 21, of Pinewood Drive
      Don Callahan, 21, of Virginia Drive
      Arrested for murder and robbery
      Police Chief Floyd Geiger says
      They beat Hollis Alpert, 81
      To death with a lug wrench
      Saturday night for $1

Callahan lived next door to Hollis
The couple was arrested
Shortly after the murder
They were walking home
Just before midnight
Stopped to talk to
Patrolman John Williams
At corner of Stevens and Scott streets
He noticed blood on them
Asked for identification
Callahan pulled out a wallet
It turned out to be Alpert's
He arrested them, took them to jail
Chief Geiger said "It was a terrible
Crime for any amount of money."
They face a preliminary hearing
Friday in General Sessions Court

b. Police searching for
Two armed men
They smashed through glass door
Of a Dixie Lee Junction gas station
About 3:20 a.m. Friday
Forced store clerk into cooler
Took $19,300 in cash and store items
Stole two safes containing $6,800
In cash, $10,000 in prepaid phone cards
And 2,500 lottery scratch-off game cards
From Best Buy Gas Station and Market
At 2230 W. 68th St.
Police have not arrested anyone
But have a surveillance video
Of the crime clearly showing
The two men who robbed the store
The owner of the store is offering
A $1,000 reward for information
That leads to arrest.
Police ask anyone with information
To call Crime Stoppers
At (316) 619-TIPS (8477).

c. Downtown Federal Courthouse
Evacuated about 10:30 a.m. today
Police bomb squad called
To check a package found
By a court employee
In shrubs on south side
Of the building at 301. N. Saratoga Ave.
Police blocked off area
Around the courthouse
Put the package in special

Container and exploded it
It was not a bomb
Just a cluster of flares,
Wires and timing devices.
"The maker went to great lengths
To make it look like a real bomb,"
Police spokesman Delbert Campbell said
Courthouse workers allowed
To return to building
About an hour later
Police are investigating

d. A convenience store owner,
Oscar Gazien, shot a shoplifter
Who tried to sneak out
With a $2 can of Spam
He had hidden in his pants pocket
Halley Lightfoot, 30, of Claiborne Street
Was wounded in the upper right cheek
Taken to Memorial Hospital
Treated and released
Police arrested Gazien
On a charge of attempted murder
They say shooting wasn't warranted
The two men had running feud
Over Lightfoot's free-style
Shopping methods, police said
Gazien claimed Lightfoot stole
Merchandise many times
He had barred him from the store

e. Jimmy Dean Wilson, 41,
Shot and killed
By another motorist
At a tollbooth exact change lane
On Merrit Island Parkway
In remote area of
South Knox County
Witnesses told police
Wilson reached exact-coins lane
At Boggy Creek exit
Had no change
Motorist behind Wilson
In black Chevy Blazer
Honked at Wilson
Who got out of his truck
And was shot by the motorist
Who drove off without
Witnesses getting license number
Wilson airlifted to

McArthur Regional Medical Center
Shortly after the 8:30 p.m. shooting
Pronounced dead an hour later
Police are searching
For a black Chevy Blazer

f. 4,000 pounds of cocaine
Worth about $34 million
Seized Monday by
U.S. Drug and Customs agents
From luxury yacht that
Sailed into port here
Tied up at Pier 66
Where drug-sniffing dog
Named Lola alerted them
To the stash
Agents escorted the yacht
To a government dock
Ripped it apart
And found drugs
In storage lockers
Below cabin deck
Five people aboard
The rented $1.5 million yacht
One woman, four men
Arrested on charges
Of drug smuggling,
Possession of drugs
With intent to distribute
Drug agents said they
Had followed the yacht
Throughout the Caribbean

g. Nikki Batista, 27, of Venice Ave.
Arrested for child neglect
Police say she left
Her 2-year-old son, Buster,
Locked in her car
In Wal-Mart Parking lot
at 17250 N.W. 57th St.
While she went shopping
About 2:30 p.m., Wednesday
When the temperature
Was in the low 90s
A passerby noticed
The unattended child
Inside the car
Which was locked
And windows rolled up
He called police

They used a slim jim
To open the car door
Child in physical distress
From extreme heat in car
Police said child's
Temperature was 101 degrees
He was treated at
Palmetto General Hospital
Suffered heat exhaustion
Police said he will
Be released to Department of
Youth and Family Services
Mother faces felony charge

7. Write a one-minute newscast from Exercises 4b, 4c, 5a, 5c, 5d, and 5e.

PART SIX

Writing the Complex Story

"It is no longer adequate to cover the fires, murders and political intrigue," Madelyn Ross of the *Pittsburgh Press* told a Scripps Howard seminar on Public Affairs Reporting.

"We're now asking reporters to find out why events occur, to provide connections between seemingly unrelated events, to explore complex social problems, so that readers come away from a story with understanding rather than just information."

That approach to journalism is a reflection of the fact that society continues to change, so newspapers must continue to change the way they report on it.

Few newspapers today simply tell the reader what happened and stop. Life is now far too complex for that kind of treatment of the news. Editors are aware that many stories require explanation and interpretation if the reader is to grasp their true significance.

Here are some of the problems reporters may encounter in covering complex fields:

1. Stories often involve a web of conditions and events stretching into the past, the future and even into related fields.
2. The reader must be told not merely the facts but also the significance of those facts.
3. Because much interpretation is necessary, the reporter needs to develop a knowledge of the field he or she is covering.
4. The reporter might need a technical vocabulary in order to communicate with the specialists he or she is writing about and has to have the ability to translate that technical vocabulary into words the reader can understand.

Many newspapers seek reporters who have professional training in various specialized fields. However, a good reporter can, through study, practice and experience, develop the skills needed to handle complex stories successfully.

22 Courts, Trials, Lawsuits

"Justice is truth in action," Benjamin Disraeli, prime minister of Great Britain in the late 1800s, said.

But that was long before DNA and the discovery that a lot of what has passed for justice in American courts wasn't justice at all. And while forensic techniques such as DNA testing has created more public interest in the justice system, much of what is being written about the courts still is as dull and boring as a legal brief. In fact, many court stories are so loaded with legal jargon they sound as if they were written by a last-semester law student.

Part of the problem stems from the fact that reporters who cover civil and criminal courts often get bogged down in the workings of the court system and ignore the human element, except in the most spectacular trials.

Court stories often are as tedious as the case itself because reporters are overwhelmed by the complexity of the legal process or they simply lack the imagination or writing ability to make court stories lively and interesting. They tend to forget that the public wants to know about who those people are in the courtroom and why they are there. It is the people, not the process, that fascinates the public.

Lawsuits and court cases are boringly alike, which creates a problem for a reporter who spends much of his or her time sifting through blizzards of legal paperwork in the offices of various court clerks before getting into a trial. In fact, newspaper court reporters spend very little time in courtrooms covering trials. Most of their day is spent going from one clerk's office to another and talking to lawyers about cases pending in court. Not every trial rates on-the-spot coverage, and not every case goes to trial. But that does not mean they aren't worth writing about.

There is an added danger not only from the reporter's point of view but also from that of the principals involved in the case because of the continuing debate about pretrial publicity and its possible influence on the outcome of the case.

Strong arguments have been made on both sides. But there still is no conclusive evidence to prove that in most instances pretrial publicity prevents a fair trial. Usually the issue arises only in the most spectacular or sensational cases.

For the most part, stories about criminal court cases, in particular, are concerned with events that have appeared previously in the news. So, in a sense, the court story is a follow-up. The crime, already reported at the time of commission and arrest, will reappear in the news as a trial for murder, larceny, arson or embezzlement. Fires and accidents, already reported, may reappear as lawsuits developing from them. Many business conflicts may result in litigation. And, of course, litigation can and does develop from such areas as medical and legal malpractice, violation of civil rights, unfair labor practices and many other alleged violations of both criminal and civil law.

After evaluating the importance and newsworthiness of a trial or lawsuit, the reporter may ignore it or write a story summarizing it. Often a reporter may never attend such a trial, obtaining information about it from court officers and documents or from the attorneys involved. Usually trials given lengthy coverage have to do with the more controversial or sensational cases.

In previous chapters, the newspaper's right to public judicial proceedings as privileged materials was pointed out. In this chapter, it is important to explain that judges have the power to limit a newspaper's rights and freedoms to some degree where cases in their own courts are concerned. Judges can back up their power by having reporters (as well as attorneys and court personnel) jailed on contempt-of-court charges for refusing to abide by court orders pertaining to the conduct of a case. This is not to say that all judges use this power wantonly, although in some cases judges have gone beyond the bounds of both reason and law.

Reporters have the right to appeal any restrictions placed on news coverage by a judge, and a number of reporters have appealed such restrictions. For the most part, the higher courts have upheld the rights of reporters to cover trials in open court.

The problem from a news point of view is that if a newspaper elects to obey a judge's unconstitutional gag order and then appeal, the coverage of the trial obviously will be inadequate. Disobeying the gag order, on the other hand, could mean time in jail. Reporters involved in contempt-of-court disputes with judges generally do not spend long periods in jail; however, several have been locked up for as much as 50 days before a conflict was resolved.

The conflict grows out of two provisions of the United States Constitution, one guaranteeing freedom of the press and the other guaranteeing an individual a fair and impartial trial. No ethical journalist would want to deny anyone a fair trial, but reporters are aware that judges, lawyers and law-enforcement officers are not necessarily ethical, nor are all trials fair. In such cases, reporters frequently believe that the only way the defendant will receive a fair trial is with the presence of the media. Some reporters feel so strongly about their First Amendment rights that they are willing to risk jail by defying judicial orders.

Judges and lawyers generally feel otherwise. If a judge thinks the presence of newspaper reporters, photographers or television cameramen in the court will affect court proceedings to the extent that the rights of the individual in receiving a fair trial may be impaired and justice obstructed, the judge has the power to limit the number of communications representatives in the courtroom. In some cases, judges have even barred reporters and photographers from the courthouse itself. Others have issued extensive rules of coverage for the media along with stern lists of instructions to all the lawyers and participants as well as court officers in regard to discussing the case with the media.

Judges in the lower federal courts began in the early 1990s to reconsider allowing photographers for newspapers and television stations into their courtrooms. But not the justices of the U.S. Supreme Court. The experiment was short-lived. Photographers are not allowed in federal courts. However, all but five states and the District of Columbia permitted photographic coverage of both criminal and civil cases by the start of the final decade of the century.

The practice varies from state to state and, in truth, from court to court in those states. For example, in more celebrated cases some judges will bar photographers but permit artists to sketch courtroom scenes for newspapers and television. Some lawyers, however, have even objected to allowing artists in the courtroom during a trial.

Restrictions on a trial's coverage naturally will depend on the individual judge. In most cases such restraints are really unnecessary because newspapers today generally exercise caution in their coverage. They are interested, of course, in seeing that a fair trial is conducted. But they also want to avoid the embarrassment and loss of credibility with their readers that they might suffer if a conviction were reversed upon appeal due to unfair or sensational publicity. Reporters also would prefer not to be cited for contempt of court by a judge, for that could mean a fine as well as a jail term.

The press does have the right of "fair comment and criticism" on the action of a judge or the court. As a general rule, newspapers will not editorialize while a case is still in court. However, they have that right. To be successful in holding a newspaper in contempt, a judge has to show that its editorial and/or trial coverage presented a "clear and present danger" to the successful completion of the trial.

The judge does have absolute power in the courtroom (subject to review by a higher court), and, to lessen the animosities between judges, lawyers and reporters, a number of state press and bar associations have worked out sets of guidelines for trial coverage acceptable to both groups. In other states, members of press associations have voted against such guidelines, seeing them as an infringement of their First Amendment rights.

Before covering a trial a reporter should:

— Do the homework. Make sure to read the court file. Know as much about the case and the charges as possible.

— Talk to the attorneys involved in the case. Usually, attorneys are willing to explain terms and give background information.
— Find out who the key witnesses in the trial will be.
— Know who the members of the jury are and how to contact them after the trial. It is not uncommon for judges to instruct jurors not to talk to reporters after a trial.
— Summarize each day's events with key quotes from witnesses and attorneys made during the courtroom action.
— Observe the reaction of the people who attend the trial, particularly those who are related to or associated with the principals in the case.

Story Forms

No definite forms can be prescribed for reporting trials and lawsuits. But the general principles of good news writing should always apply. The lead of a typical trial story should either summarize the events of the day in the courtroom or emphasize an outstanding feature such as a particular bit of testimony or legal maneuver by the lawyers.

Here are the leads of two court stories that are inherently interesting because of their unusual circumstances:

> BATON ROUGE, La.—A 41-year-old Louisiana man faces up to 50 years in prison after being convicted of shooting his girlfriend's brother for eating a slice of his lemon meringue pie.
>
> *(Reuters)*

> CLEARWATER, Fla.—A man is suing a topless club, claiming a dancer gave him whiplash during his bachelor party when she bumped him with her prodigious breasts.
> "I saw stars," said Paul Shimkonis, a 38-year-old physical therapist.
>
> (The Associated Press)

The body of the story should amplify the lead, as in other types of stories. However, it is essential in the case of a trial that continues over several days to include a tie-back (summary of the case so far) high in the story. Some reporters work the tie-back into the second or third paragraph, as in this example from The *Knoxville News-Sentinel*.

> A Knoxville doctor testified in U.S. District Court Tuesday that he gave $30,000 to his girlfriend to halt a drug investigation. But he said he did not know he was being set up in a bribery scheme.
> Dr. Richard Winn Henderson, who operated the East Tennessee Medical Clinic on Washington Pike, is on trial in U.S. District Court, charged with attempting to halt a federal probe of his operation by paying off an assistant U.S. Attorney.

Henderson is accused of making payments totaling $30,000 earlier this year to an undercover FBI agent, who posed as the brother-in-law of Assistant U.S. Attorney Mike Mitchell.

Mitchell was directing the investigation of the clinic, which began after Henderson's girlfriend, Alex Wright, went to authorities following a fight with the doctor last January.

In organizing the story, the reporter should use both direct and indirect quotations with interpretative summaries interspersed. Because trials can be difficult to follow, reporters often will present what happened in court in chronological order.

Much of what happens in trials is window dressing and legal posturing. A reporter must learn to evaluate what is important and what is not. The use of character witnesses at trials is a classic example of window dressing. Many lawyers, especially if they have a weak defense, seek to influence the jury with a parade of witnesses who are willing to testify to the accused's good name and character. Most of the time this testimony would rate not more than a sentence or two in a story.

Unless the information elicited from a witness is startling in nature, most trial stories do not include extensive direct testimony. Quotations from testimony are usually presented either in chronological order or in short question-and-answer form in the body of the story.

A reporter may choose one of two forms in handling questions and answers. Here is a narrative style that is common for brief excerpts of testimony:

Assistant District Attorney Ronald Miller questioned Booth's contention that he was only firing to protect himself.

"You fired 10 times and you didn't mean to hurt them?" Miller asked.

"It was so frightening. I didn't know how many times I fired," Booth said.

The second form is used for extended questions and answers and is used especially when reporting key testimony:

Q—How many times did you fire?

A—I don't know. I was just trying to protect myself.

Q—Isn't it true you fired 10 times?

A—I don't know. I just stuck the gun out the window and started firing. I didn't mean to hurt them.

Q—You fired 10 times and you didn't mean to hurt them?

A—It was so frightening. I don't know how many times I fired.

Quotation marks are not necessary in the Q-and-A form. Before testimony is given in this form, it must be preceded by an explanation such as "Booth's testimony follows."

In addition to noting feature highlights in court proceedings, the reporter should take notes on the background of court actions—descriptions of the crowd, witnesses, jury. Sometimes a lead feature comes from an event not included in regular court procedure. For example, outside the courtroom the attorney's actions could have a direct bearing on the case and provide a far more significant lead than anything that happened in the courtroom that day. Reporters should be particularly observant during trials, for the courtroom is an excellent source of human-interest stories.

Although most court stories are reported as straight news, a considerable amount of interpretation might be necessary to enrich and clarify the significance of facts and procedures.

Background and Interpretation

In addition to having an understanding of the organization of the courts in the state, the reporter assigned to cover any trial must acquire a background of facts and relationships of the particular case. Is the embezzlement of bank funds related to a previous bank failure, to business conditions or to personal problems of the person charged in the case? Is the case a striking parallel of other cases? When, where, how and by whom was a suit filed? The same questions should be answered about the crime itself. Have there been any previous consequences? Are other suits or indictments pending? What consequences will develop from the case? Is there a particularly interesting problem of law, court jurisdiction or other novel feature involved in the case? Only with such a background can the reporter do full justice to the case and write a clear account for the newspaper's readers.

A reporter must have a thorough knowledge of legal terms and procedures to write effectively about a case. In law there is a difference, for example, between "evidence" and "testimony." A reporter must use those and other legal terms properly. In addition, a reporter must be able to translate legal terms clearly for the reader. Court stories should not sound like legal briefs. Many legal terms mean nothing to the average reader.

The reporter should explain legal terms as well as the consequence of legal action. "The grand jury returned a no-true bill against Sidney Westchester . . ." might be understood by a few readers but not the majority; but "The grand jury freed Sidney Westchester of charges . . ." would be clear.

If the case involves the constitutionality or validity of a certain law being tested in the courts, the reporter must explain the consequence of the court ruling. For example, "The State Supreme Court today upheld the constitutionality of the new open-meetings law in the Palm County School Board case" isn't as meaningful as "The Palm County School Board was told by the State Supreme Court today that it could not meet behind closed doors anymore." Readers are not expected to be interpreters of court decisions. The newspaper must tell them, in language of the layperson, exactly how a decision affects their life routines.

This is an example of a lead emphasizing the prosecution's opening statement in a trial:

> LARGO—(AP)—A respected Baptist preacher was a con man who looked people in the eye and smoothly swindled millions in church funds to finance a lavish lifestyle, a prosecutor said Monday.

The Rev. Henry Lyons "led two totally different lives. He led one public life . . . but there was a second side, a hidden side to Henry J. Lyons, a side that caused him to be brought here to this seat," Assistant State Attorney Robert Lewis said in opening statements at Long's racketeering and grand theft trial.

Here is an example of a lead on the sentencing of a convicted person:

A psychologist convicted of defrauding Medicare of more than $480,000 was sentenced Friday to 5 years and 10 months in prison in U.S. District Court in Chicago.

Carol Hoogenboom, 36, formerly of Glenview and now of Worth, was convicted in June after a bench trial by U.S. District Senior Judge Milton Shadur on 14 counts of mail fraud, false claims, money laundering and obstruction of justice.

(Chicago Tribune)

ORLANDO—(AP)—A former exotic dancer-turned-infomercial guru and his wife were sentenced Monday to 24 years each for swindling customers with a get-rich-quick real estate scheme promising no debt, lower taxes and early retirement.

William J. McCorkel appeared stoic and his wife, Chantal, cried silently in response to U.S. District Judge Patricia Fawsett's sentence for their widespread scheme. They netted more than $72 million from sales of videotapes, books and seminars promising a business partnership that would never exist.

In nearly five hours of testimony Friday, Fedell Caffey repeatedly denied he killed Debra Evans and two of her children, insisting, "I could never do nothing like that."

Caffey, 24, spoke out for the first time since his arrest in the grisly slayings Nov. 16 and 17, in which Debra Evans' full term fetus was cut from her womb.

He spoke in a soft monotone vice, rarely making eye contact with jurors.

(Chicago Tribune)

In a trial that sounded like a case thought up for a law school class, a drunken driver was convicted of manslaughter and not murder Friday in the case of a Jehovah's Witness who died after refusing blood transfusions.

The jury deliberated 3½ days before reaching the verdict against Keith Cook, a 32-year-old auto mechanic.

Cook had acknowledged drinking on March 7, the day he plowed his truck into a car, pushing the vehicle into Jadine Russell, who was standing by the side of the road.

Russell, 55, suffered broken bones and severe bleeding. But she told emergency workers and doctors "No blood" at least 10 times, and even tried to pull out an intravenous line, relatives said.

(San Jose Mercury News)

Sometimes government agencies sue each other and one city sues another, as these leads show:

The St. Louis County Boundary Commission has asked the courts to restore a $67,750 cut from the agency's annual budget request of $235,400 by county administration and the County Council.

> The suit, filed in St. Louis County Circuit Court on Thursday, said state law set up the commission as an independent agency. The county action, the suit said, "was an arbitrary and capricious abuse of discretion."
>
> *(St. Louis Post–Dispatch)*

> The town of Surfside filed suit against its neighbor, Indian Creek, in Miami-Dade Circuit Court on Thursday, trying to stop construction of Indian Creek's new government building.
>
> (The *Miami Herald*)

Some cases are settled before a verdict is reached in court:

> A $5.7 million out-of-court settlement was announced Monday for two lawsuits filed by West Indian sugar cane cutters who alleged they were underpaid by Florida's largest sugar companies.

> A county high school course designed to teach the Bible as history will be renamed, and students will be required to take world history or comparative religion along with the Bible course, according to an out-of-court settlement between Lee County school officials, parents and civil liberties groups.

And some litigants aren't satisfied, so they appeal, as in this case:

> WASHINGTON—Paula Jones announced yesterday that she will appeal a federal judge's decision to dismiss her sexual-harassment case against President Clinton, declaring in a voice soaked with tears, "What Mr. Clinton did to me was wrong."

The Law and the Courts

Two general types of law are recognized: "civil," comprising suits for damages involving two or more persons; and "criminal" under which charges of offenses against society may be brought by a governmental officer or a citizen against one or more persons. The authority for enforcing the two types of law comes from the Constitution ("constitutional law"), the acts of legislative bodies ("statutory law"), and customs and judicial precedents ("common law"). There is another type of law on the federal and state levels, called "administrative law," generated from the powers granted governmental regulatory bodies such as the Federal Trade Commission or (state) Public Utilities Commission to enforce certain rules over particular industries and businesses. The two fundamental types of law are further classified as follows:

1. Civil cases
   a. *Cases in law,* which abide closely by the law
      1. *Contracts*—cases in which the plaintiff (the person bringing the suit) claims the defendant (the person against whom the suit is brought) did not follow the terms of an oral or written contract.

2. *Torts*—cases that treat private injuries not arising from a breach of contract. For example, it is usually a tort for a person to damage someone or his or her property purposely or negligently.

   b. *Cases in equity,* which are distinguished from cases in law rendering "equitable" judgment by not following definite laws. Persons go to an equity court when they can get no relief from the definite writs existing in the regular law courts. This relief often is obtained by compulsory or preventive decrees (mandates and injunctions) issued by the judge. Controversies over property ownership are usually brought to an equity court.

2. Criminal cases

   a. *Misdemeanors*—minor criminal cases usually resulting in fines, sometimes in imprisonment

   b. *Felonies*—major criminal cases usually resulting in imprisonment and sometimes death by execution (see Chapter 21, Crime)

State courts—which also include county and city courts serving by authority of the state—and federal courts deal with these types of law. Local affairs and cases concerning state laws are tried by state courts. Cases concerning federal laws and interstate cases are tried by federal courts. The dual system of courts is outlined in the accompanying chart.

To obtain a better understanding of the chart, and at the same time to learn a few of the most common legal terms, it is necessary to trace the route of a criminal case and a civil case in a state court. (Be sure to learn the meaning of each italicized term.)

Route of a Criminal Case

1. In a court of limited jurisdiction (county or city magistrate court):

   a. A warrant is sworn out charging a person with a crime and enabling officers to bring the person before a magistrate (judge).

      (1) If the person has been arrested on a warrant from another state, an extradition order is obtained; this will enable officers from that state to take the prisoner back to that state to stand trial.

      (2) Attorneys who feel their clients are being held illegally may obtain a writ of habeas corpus from a superior court and get an immediate hearing. The arresting officers must prove that the prisoner is being held for a just cause.

   b. The magistrate hears the case.

      (1) If the crime is a *misdemeanor,* the accused may be fined (within prescription of state law).

         (a) Fines may be appealed from this court to a court of general jurisdiction, where such cases are tried anew.

      (2) If the crime is a *felony,* the magistrate may *bind the prisoner over* to the grand jury.

         (a) The prisoner may *waive* the preliminary hearing and be bound over to the grand jury.

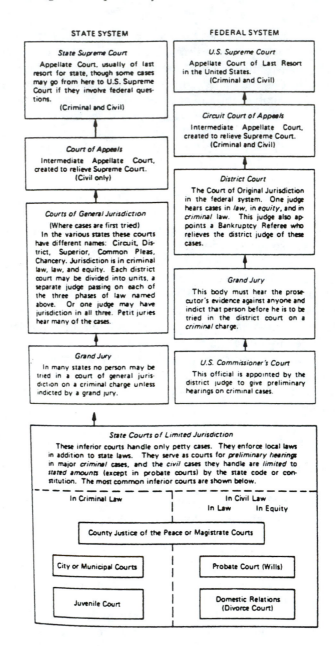

STATE SYSTEM

FEDERAL SYSTEM

State Supreme Court

Appellate Court, usually of last resort for state, though some cases may go from here to U.S. Supreme Court if they involve federal questions.
(Criminal and Civil)

U.S. Supreme Court

Appellate Court of Last Resort in the United States.
(Criminal and Civil)

Court of Appeals

Intermediate Appellate Court, created to relieve Supreme Court.
(Civil only)

Circuit Court of Appeals

Intermediate Appellate Court, created to relieve Supreme Court.
(Criminal and Civil)

Courts of General Jurisdiction

(Where cases are first tried)
In the various states these courts have different names: Circuit, District, Superior, Common Pleas, Chancery. Jurisdiction is in criminal law, law, and equity. Each district court may be divided into units, a separate judge passing on each of the three phases of law named above. Or one judge may have jurisdiction in all three. Petit juries hear many of the cases.

District Court

The Court of Original Jurisdiction in the federal system. One judge hears cases in *law,* in *equity,* and in *criminal* law. This judge also appoints a Bankruptcy Referee who relieves the district judge of these cases.

Grand Jury

This body must hear the prosecutor's evidence against anyone and indict that person before he is to be tried in the district court on a *criminal* charge.

Grand Jury

In many states no person may be tried in a court of general jurisdiction on a criminal charge unless indicted by a grand jury.

U.S. Commissioner's Court

This official is appointed by the district judge to give preliminary hearings on criminal cases.

State Courts of Limited Jurisdiction

These inferior courts handle only petty cases. They enforce local laws in addition to state laws. They serve as courts for *preliminary hearings* in major *criminal* cases, and the *civil* cases they handle are *limited* to *stated amounts* (except in probate courts) by the state code or constitution. The most common inferior courts are shown below.

In Criminal Law	In Civil Law
	In Law In Equity

County Justice of the Peace or Magistrate Courts

| City or Municipal Courts | Probate Court (Wills) |
| Juvenile Court | Domestic Relations (Divorce Court) |

(3) In binding the prisoner over, the magistrate *sets the bail bond,* which the prisoner may post in order to be released until trial.

(a) In some very serious cases, the magistrate may not allow the prisoner freedom from jail but will bind him or her over *without bond.*

2. In the grand jury:

a. Evidence is given to members of the grand jury *ex parte,* or without the presence of the defendant.

(1) Only the evidence against the defendant is heard. This is not a trial body. Cases are not heard in public.

    b. If the grand jury feels the evidence against the defendant warrants a trial, it may return an *indictment,* or *true bill,* against the defendant, arraigning him or her for trial in a court of general jurisdiction.

    c. If the grand jury feels the evidence is not sufficient or in order, a *no-true bill* is returned, and the defendant is released.

3. In a court of general jurisdiction (officers of this court usually include the judge, clerk, attorney, jury and bailiff).

    a. The trial opens with charges made against the defendant.

    b. Pleas and motions are made by attorneys. Some of the pleas and motions that could be made are

        (1) "Guilty" or "not guilty."

        (2) Motion for continuance.

        (3) *Demurrer*—challenge the sufficiency of the indictment.

        (4) *Plea in abatement*—contention, among others, that the indictment is illegal.

        (5) *Motion to quash indictment*—contention that indictment is unfair or defective.

        (6) *Nolo contendere*—defendant does not admit guilt but decides not to fight case.

        (7) *Nolle prosequi*—prosecuting attorney decides not to prosecute the case because new evidence indicates the person's innocence or because the prosecutor believes the case against the defendant is weak.

        (8) Plea of insanity—claiming defendant is mentally ill and not responsible.

        (9) *Motion for change of venue*—defense attorney claims it is impossible to get a fair trial in that district and asks to have the case transferred to another legal district.

    c. The judge acts on pleas or motions.

    d. *Petit* (or *trial*) *jurors* are selected if the case continues.

        (1) The jurors are selected from a *panel of veniremen,* or a list of persons who have been *summoned* for jury service.

        (2) Attorneys on both sides may *challenge* certain prospective jurors and prevent their serving on the jury.

        (3) The judge also excuses from jury service those who show evidence that they might be prejudiced in the case or are disqualified for other reasons.

    e. Opening statements of the prosecutor (in most states) are made to the jury in which the prosecutor outlines the state's case against the defendant.

    f. Opening statements of the defense attorney are made to the jury.

    g. Testimony is given by witnesses who have been subpoenaed to testify for the prosecution.

        (1) Prosecuting attorney questions witnesses—the direct examination.

        (2) Defense attorney questions same witnesses—the cross-examination.

(3) Depositions, usually written sworn statements, from witnesses who may be forced to be absent or are not present for other reasons are entered into the trial record.

h. Testimony of witnesses for the defense is heard (same procedure as for prosecution).

   (1) The trial is concluded with arguments of attorneys to jury.
      (a) The prosecutor speaks first, reviewing what has been "proved."
      (b) The defense attorney speaks next, attempting to show jury prosecution did not prove its case against the defendant.
      (c) The prosecutor speaks again.

i. The judge instructs jury on the law in the case.
   (1) Explains what verdicts it can return.
   (2) Explains certain points of law in the case.

j. The jury deliberates in secret.
   (1) If jurors cannot agree unanimously, a mistrial is declared.
   (2) If jurors can agree, they report their verdict to the judge.

k. Motions may be made by the attorney for the defendant who is found guilty.
   (1) Judge may be asked for a new trial based on the claim that errors were made in the trial proceedings or that new evidence has shown up.
   (2) Judge may be asked for an arrest of judgment.

l. The judge can reject all motions and pass sentence if the defendant is found guilty.
   (1) The judge may send defendant to prison immediately, issuing a *mittimus*, a court order of commitment to prison.
   (2) Judge may declare a suspended sentence (in some states), holding up imprisonment. Judge can reserve the right to put the sentence into effect later or keep it suspended indefinitely, as long as the defendant gets into no more trouble.
   (3) Judge may (in some states) place the defendant on probation, which might be called a suspended sentence on good behavior for a certain period of time.
   (4) Judge may fine the defendant (within the limits of the law).

4. In an *appellate court* (appeal made on errors, with a *transcript* or *record* of trial sent to appellate court):
   a. The decision may be *reversed*.
   b. The decision may be *affirmed*.
   c. The case may be *remanded* (and reversed or affirmed) or returned to the court in which it originated and a new trial ordered.

5. After a case has been tried and possibly appealed:
   a. The governor may *commute* (or decrease) the sentence.
   b. The governor may issue a *reprieve*, staying for a time the execution of the sentence.
   c. The governor may *pardon* the prisoner outright.
   d. The prisoner may be put on *parole* and allowed his or her freedom after serving part of the sentence. But the prisoner has to report to parole officer periodically.

Route of a Civil Case

Because a civil case is in some respects like a criminal case, explanations of similar steps and terms are not repeated.

1. In the court of limited jurisdiction (the case may be heard here if the amount involved is lower than the maximum fixed by law for such courts):
   a. The plaintiff submits a *declaration* or *complaint* that he or she is due relief or compensation.
      (1) If the case involves recovery of property, the magistrate may issue a *replevin*, which is a court order enabling officers to take the property.
      (2) The magistrate may also issue a *writ of attachment*, usually when convinced that the defendant may dispose of certain property involved in the suit. By that writ, the court takes charge of the property until the case is settled.
   b. The defendant is summoned to answer the complaint.
   c. The magistrate hears the case and passes judgment. Either party may appeal the case to higher court, where it is tried anew (*de novo*).
   d. The magistrate may attach the funds of the defendant (if the case is lost) to carry out the judgment. This order may be served on a third party, who may owe or will owe money to the losing party. In other words, the magistrate may *garnish* the losing party's income if the court's judgment is not paid.
2. In the court of general jurisdiction (cases may originate here, or they may come up from courts of limited jurisdiction; in either case, they are handled similarly):
   a. The plaintiff submits a declaration, which is recorded with the clerk (the declaration sometimes is not necessary in appeals from courts of limited jurisdiction).
   b. The defendant is summoned.
   c. The defendant may submit motions and demurrers attacking the complaint.
   d. The defendant submits an *answer* or *plea*, which is recorded with the clerk.
   e. The plaintiff submits motions and demurrers attacking the answer.
   f. The case is set for trial, which may be held by a judge without a jury.
   g. If the trial is by jury, the jury is selected.
   h. The attorney for plaintiff makes an opening statement (in some states), explaining the case and outlining arguments.
   i. The attorney for defendant makes an opening statement.
   j. The plaintiff presents evidence.
   k. The defendant presents evidence.
   l. The plaintiff may present more evidence in rebuttal.
   m. The defendant may also present more evidence in rebuttal.
   n. The plaintiff's attorney makes a closing argument.
   o. The defendant's attorney makes a closing argument.
   p. The plaintiff's attorney makes a rebuttal.

q. The judge renders a decision in the case (if tried without a jury) or instructs the jury.

r. The jury deliberates and returns a verdict if agreed on unanimously.

s. Motions may be made by the attorney on either side, such as asking for a new trial or arrest of judgment.

t. The judge renders judgment on any motions.

u. The judge acts on the verdict.

3. In the appellate court:

a. The decision may be reversed.

b. The decision may be affirmed.

c. The decision may be remanded (and reversed or affirmed) to the lower court and a new trial ordered.

Cases in equity are usually not tried before a jury. The judge (sometimes called a *chancellor* when there is a separate court of equity) hears cases and renders verdicts and judgments.

The *probate court*, named in the accompanying chart, has a limited jurisdiction in the disposition of a deceased person's property. If the person dies *testate* (having written a will), the probate judge has the *executor* named in the will to carry out its provisions. If the person dies *intestate* (without a will), the judge appoints an *administrator* for the property.

Only a small portion of cases will be followed through the full routine outlined in the preceding pages. Still, nearly every step may result in a separate news story if the case is important enough. The outline should be checked against local variations because each state determines its own court procedure.

Here are the leads on several civil cases:

> Six current and former female employees at Lawrence Livermore National Laboratory filed a class-action lawsuit yesterday on behalf of 3,000 women workers they say have been systematically denied pay equal to that of male employees.
>
> The suit, filed in Alameda County Superior Court in Oakland, charges the University of California regents, who operate the lab under contract with the U.S. Department of Energy, with gender discrimination. Also named in the suit is C. Bruce Tarter, the lab's director . . .
>
> *(San Francisco Examiner)*

> LOS ANGELES—(AP)—An actress–singer claims a Taco Bell burrito she ate caused a sharp pain in her throat and has ruined her voice.
>
> Noreen C. Kelly, whose stage name is Kelly Ryan, has filed a lawsuit against the fast-food giant in Superior Court. She is seeking unspecified damages . . .

EXERCISES

1. Study the court coverage in your local daily newspaper for a week, paying attention to the location and space given to criminal cases compared to the treatment given civil cases. Write a report on your findings.

2. Interview the presiding judge in both the civil and criminal court systems in your city about their courts with emphasis on the number of cases tried each year, the number of cases that are postponed, the size of the case backlog, and other pertinent information about the courts. Write a story on your findings.

3. Visit the office of the clerk of both the civil and criminal court divisions in your county and interview the senior court clerk (Note: this is not the same person as the court reporter). Write a story about the clerk's offices.

4. Visit the court that handles traffic violations and minor offenses in your city, and observe a number of cases being tried. Write a feature story on your "day in court."

5. Most college and universities have a "judicial" system to handle cases of misconduct by students. Interview the dean of students about that judicial system and write a feature story about it.

6. Attend a major case underway in a criminal court in your city and write a news story on the events that occurred while you were there.

7. Write brief news stories from the following notes:

a. Ramond Dominguez, 56
   Owner of Athena Health Care Systems
   Pleaded guilty to defrauding
   Medicare of $12 million
   By false billings
   For unperformed treatment
   Sentenced to six years
   In federal prison today
   By U.S. District Judge
   William Dimitrouleas
   Domingues told judge
   He was "repentant."
   He was ordered to
   Repay government $12.9 million
   His partner in Athena,
   Rene Corvo, goes on trial
   In early March

b. Criminal Court Judge Michael Simpson
   Refused to admit
   Lie-detector evidence
   In case of Brian Kennedy, 28
   Charged with murder of
   Girlfriend Jennifer Brooks'
   9-month-old son, Bobby Joe
   Kennedy charged with
   Shaking baby to death
   When it wouldn't stop crying
   When he was baby-sitting
   The couple shared house in
   Suburban Beech Grove
   Kennedy's lawyer Harold Hill
   Sought to introduce
   Results of tests of Kennedy
   He said they would prove
   Ms. Brooks, not Kennedy,

      Shook the baby to death
      Kennedy's trial is in
      Its second week
      If found guilty
      He could be sentenced
      To life in prison

c. Edward Wright 54, Chatham
      Charged with murder
      Of his daughter
      Francesca Regina Wright, 28
      On Nov. 24 when he was angered
      Because she charged
      Thousands of dollars
      Worth of calls to
      The psychic hot lines
      He hacked her to death
      With a hatchet, cut up body with chain saw
      Jury selection for his trial
      In Sullivan County Criminal Court
      Gets underway today
      More than 200 prospective
      Jurors have been called
      Judge Robert J. Wiandt
      Said he aims to have
      Jury picked in a week
      Police Chief Billy Freeman
      Called the crime the worst
      He's dealt with in 30 years

d. Commonwealth Attorney Steve Barnette
      Said he will offer deal
      To Barbara Jean Neal, 19
      To testify against
      Bennie Gamble, 21, Frankfort
      Charged with first-degree murder
      In choking, beating death
      Of William (Spuds) Bradley, 21
      His trial is to begin Nov. 25
      Neal pleaded guilty to murder
      In the Bradley case Thursday
      Barnette said he would offer
      Neal a 25-year sentence
      On the murder charge
      In exchange of her
      Testimony against Gamble
      Criminal Court Judge Jeff Bradley
      Said he would wait until
      After Gamble's trial to
      Decide on Barnette's offer
      If Neal testifies

8. Interview a leading criminal defense attorney in your city about her or his career and write a feature story based on that interview.

23 Government and Politics

"**M**ost of the journalists think they have satisfied their role when they come talk to you, get a quote, go back to the office, describe the numbers and then go to some chronic naysayer and get a counter quote."

That harsh criticism came from Wayne Curry, supervisor of Prince George's County, Md., who said that there is a lack of firsthand knowledge of how government works among journalists.

It may be something of a sweeping overstatement. But Jack Cox, head of the Foundation for Advanced Communications, agrees. He told a session on "Redefining Government" at a national convention of the American Society of Newspaper Editors that "Reporters need better education in economics, political science, business and other areas . . ."

Dramatic changes in government at all levels are changing the way many newspapers cover government and politics. Of course, some newspapers cling to the old formula government story, based on covering meetings and turning out dull, boring and confusing stories.

Most government stories tend to focus on legislative bodies, bureaucracies, and the terminally dull reports and surveys all branches of government turn out. What reporters often fail to do is tell the reader what all of that has to do with her or him and the quality of their lives.

Here's an example of one of those peopleless government stories from the Associated Press (AP):

> The nation's employment rate sank to a near 24-year low of 4.9 percent in April as Americans reaped the benefits of a robust, low-inflation economy.
>
> The stunning drop reported by the Labor Department today, from a seasonally adjusted 5.2 percent a month earlier, came despite a second month of modest growth in employer's payrolls. They increased by 142,000 jobs in April after a downwardly revised gain of 139,000 in March.
>
> The rate, propelled by decreased joblessness for both whites and blacks, was the lowest since December 1973 when Richard Nixon was president and years before workers now in their 20s and 30s obtained their first full-time jobs.

The story continued for three more paragraphs in which it reported the reaction of the stock market to the unemployment figures and noted that another government report on key economic indicators rose 0.1 percent, a modest but continued indication of economic growth.

Who needs sleeping pills when they can read stories like that? It didn't really tell the reader what it meant to him or her. It didn't say what those "benefits of a robust, low-inflation economy" actually were. It did not quote anyone who was "reaping" those benefits. Why it didn't even bother to give the name of the government bureaucrat who wrote the report.

Increasingly government stories are attributed to buildings and departments in this way: "The White House said today," "The Governor's Office said today," "The Treasury Department said today." Houses and bureaucracies can't talk. Someone has to talk for them. Readers know that. So why not name the ventriloquist who's giving the White House a voice?

Admittedly, writing about government is challenging because governments are complex, multi-billion-dollar enterprises changing often as a result of new laws, court decisions interpreting those laws and new department regulations established as a result of both.

To add to the difficulty of covering government, many of its activities are so repetitive a reporter is faced with a serious challenge of how to cover them in ways that are both informative and meaningful for readers. In addition, many elected and appointed officials, as well as bureaucrats, have a penchant for operating in secret.

But the people must be informed if democracy is to work. Without the press to report regularly on what is happening in city hall, the state house, Congress and state legislatures, most citizens would have no source of government news, other than the government itself. They would have no broad base with which to evaluate the performance of government.

The press is an important source of information for the government as well. Every day the president gets a new summary culled from dozens of newspapers, television news programs and news and opinion magazines. The president's office is equipped with television monitors turned to all the major networks. In every congressional office staff aides clip newspapers from the home district to keep the representatives and senators they work for informed of current events "back home." Government agencies at both the federal and the staff levels frequently subscribe to the wire services in an effort to keep informed. They also monitor the television network news programs. The mass media provide the foundation on which many public officials base their knowledge of current events. Naturally, they supplement this knowledge with information from many other sources.

Government News

What do people want to know and need to know about government? What is meant by "government news" and "political reporting"? Much news that comes from government offices is one or more of the various types discussed in other chapters. Some of the stories include:

Type of Story	*Sources*
Crimes and accidents, suicides	Police, sheriff, state police
Illness, deaths, accidents	Public hospitals
Fires and accidents	Fire departments
Trials and lawsuits	Courts
Weather	National Weather Service
Meetings, new laws	Legislative bodies and boards

In other words, government is a source of virtually all types of news. In reporting such matters the reporter is giving an account to the public of government activities. Over and beyond these reports of daily activities are other important materials that need reporting as government news by a political reporter. They do not constitute a story type; nevertheless, they can be illustrated and studied, and they must be written if the public is to have a complete report on its government.

Here are some leads on stories involving local and state governments:

WEST PALM BEACH—(AP)—Thousands of people in Florida received food stamps even though they couldn't possibly need the help: They were dead.

Florida and three other states gave the benefits to 25,881 dead people during 1995 and 1996, for a loss to the federal government of $8.5 million, a report from the General Accounting Office says.

ATLANTA—Lobbyists spent $350,000 making Georgia legislators feel comfortable during the three-month legislative session that ended in March.

Most of the money went for mass dinners and receptions, but some went for food and drinks after hours.

(The *Valdosta Daily Times*)

Gov. Roy Barnes' plan to create a new transportation superagency to deal with pollution and traffic gets its first legislative hearing today as it moves along a fast track that could put it up for a vote in the full Senate before week's end.

(The *Atlanta Journal–Constitution*)

Starting in July, LaFollette will implement a new pay plan for city workers while maintaining the same tax rate for property owners despite a plea from one council member to raise taxes.

During the regular City Council meeting Monday, members approved a $4.7 million budget and a $1.07 per $1000 of assessed valuation property tax rate for the fiscal year.

(*LaFollette Press*)

The Political Reporter

A political reporter does not cover a political campaign or a political personality only, although much time may be spent following a candidate, listening to the same speech over and over again. Most of a political reporter's time is spent looking at the purely political aspects of government and the men and women who run the government.

Although it is true that on a national level news organizations assign reporters specifically to cover the president, most other political reporters have to cover far more territory. A political reporter covering state government, for example, does not report on the activities of the governor only. There are the members of the cabinet as well as the leaders of the state legislature to write about. In addition, a vast array of department heads and supervisors in state government are potential news sources.

Although the political reporter may not visit state hospitals, inspect highway construction projects or spend a day in a food stamp office as part of the daily routine, he or she must be in regular contact with the commissioners who run those departments as well as other cabinet officers. Along the way the good reporter also will collect and pass along to the city editor tips for other stories as well as personal items and briefs about the men and women in government.

The good political reporter goes beneath the surface of routine government news and comes up with stories on issues and policies and the broad aspects of government. Routine government news generally is provided in press releases by government press agents. The chief role of the political reporter, therefore, should be to interpret government actions and policies for the reader.

There are specific matters—and others not so specific—that the political reporter should look for and report. The specific items include:

Legislative actions (whether of the state legislature, the city council, the governing body of the county or Congress)

Executive branch actions (whether of the governor or mayor, or department heads)

Judicial decisions (of the Supreme Court usually—not trials and lawsuits, but precedent-making decisions)

Financial and budgeting matters (including bond issues, debt reductions, taxes and tax delinquencies).

Less specific items would include the following matters pertaining to any governmental office whenever they are of sufficient importance to affect policies and trends:

1. Daily records
2. Periodic reports
3. Changes in personnel
4. New projects and programs
5. Speeches
6. Discussions
7. New laws
8. Enforcement of laws
9. Taxes imposed and paid
10. Publications

11. Changes in policies
12. Interviews and features.

The substance of these items can be determined only by the reporter in contact with, and thoroughly informed about, a specific official over a period of time. The political reporter should be so well informed about the activities of a governmental office and its officials that he or she can detect any significant changes that should be reported to the public. The reporter should not have to wait for the changes to be announced by the officials. Often the unannounced changes involve political developments that should be exposed.

A reporter's duties as both a government news and political news reporter require a thorough knowledge of government itself. The following brief analysis of governmental forms and their news potential should prove helpful.

Forms of Government

In general, there are four levels of government: city, county, state and federal. Each provides the citizen certain services, paid for ultimately by taxes. Each has a legislative, an executive and a judicial branch. The legislative branch, composed of representatives elected by the voters, enacts the laws that make possible the government's services and imposes the taxes that bring in revenue to support those services. The executive branch, composed of elected and appointed persons, carries out the laws of the legislative branch, performs the services and collects the taxes to pay the bill. The judicial branch, composed of persons either elected or appointed, administers justice, interpreting the laws enacted by the legislative branch as well as common laws and constitutional laws. In addition to the four levels of government, there may be others such as special districts created by legislative act to perform and charge for special services (such as water and sanitation). On a state and federal level there are regulatory agencies empowered to enforce administrative law governing numerous state and federal agencies such as public utilities commissions and the Federal Trade Commission.

City Government

The accompanying charts show sample forms of city government. The specific form of any particular city can be found in its charter, which is granted (enacted like any other law) by the state legislature. The charter will define the duties and powers of city officials and otherwise outline the corporate structure of the city. A city can change its form of government, but such a change usually requires a popular election and in some cases approval of the new charter by the state legislature.

No reporter should attempt to cover city hall or report on any aspect of city government or political affairs in a city without a complete understanding of that city's charter. The reporter will find that no one else (probably including the

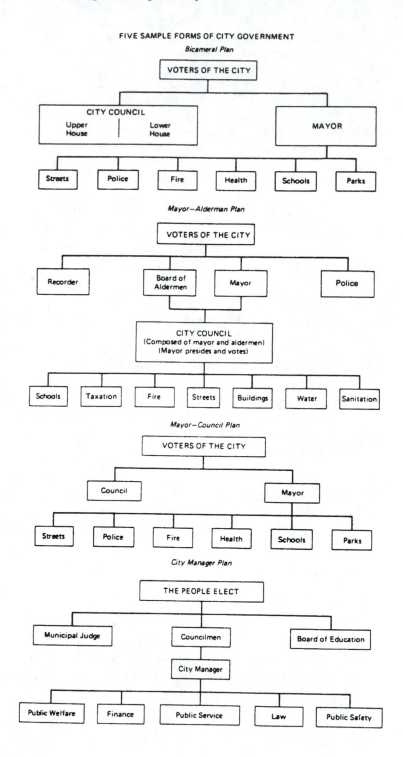

FIVE SAMPLE FORMS OF CITY GOVERNMENT

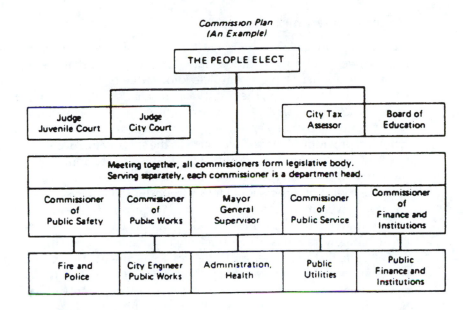

*Commission Plan
(An Example)*

mayor and the city law director) is thoroughly acquainted with it. Reporters who know the charter have an advantage because such knowledge will lend strength and authority to their stories.

The city charter (and a chart the reporter should draw from for personal use) will suggest the many important areas of city government that should be reported. Major issues should be checked with the proper city officials from day to day. The reporter should resist the tendency to rely only on the mayor's office for all information. It is important that the city hall reporter know every department head and most of the subordinates in a department as well as the office staff, visiting them regularly. Every official pronouncement from the mayor's office about any department in the city should be checked with additional sources in that department and outside sources that may have knowledge of it or a vested interest in it.

It is important to keep in close contact with department sources inasmuch as problems change from time to time. One month may find the major public issue to be teachers' salaries. The next month it may be the traffic plan, zoning irregularities or garbage collection. In most cities today, problems tend to fluctuate in importance, so none should be overlooked or ignored.

Knowledge, background and personal acquaintance with city officials and employees are paramount for success in reporting city affairs. But reporters should not become the captives of their sources. They must have independent sources of information to ensure that government sources do not use them as press agents.

County Government

Forms of county government (page 361) vary from state to state and in some cases even between counties within a state. It is important that the reporter covering county government have a complete knowledge of the local county government structure. Unlike the city, the county has no charter. It derives its forms and powers from acts of the state legislature and from the state constitution, and perhaps from precedent. In many areas, the county government acts as an arm of state government, providing state services such as the sale of auto licenses. The way county governments are formed often makes the task of learning about their structure difficult and may force the reporter to spend time reading old legislative acts in the state code. But it is essential for the reporter to know very specifically how the county's government evolved in order to understand its power and authority.

Without a complete understanding of how county government is structured and what powers it has, a reporter may be unable to recognize the special political interests that may attempt to control government. The reporter may thus become an unwitting press agent for those interests. To get a firm grasp on county government, many reporters draw up a chart listing county officials and their duties and note the specific enabling act under which that department operates. It is essential to keep abreast of new enabling acts, passed by each successive state legislature, that might affect county government.

State Government

A sample of state government structure is shown in the accompanying chart (page 362). But state governments differ, and reporters therefore must acquaint themselves with the structure of the state government they are reporting about. Knowledge of the state constitution is an important tool for any reporter. But there will be many reorganizational statutes that alter the basic pattern established by the state's constitution, setting up the current organization of government. Every state regularly publishes a "Blue Book," a reference volume of the state's government. Included are the state's constitution as well as descriptive information on all branches of government and biographical data on governmental officials. Every reporter on state government should have a personal copy of this reference book. In addition, many states publish (often through a major state university) a statistical abstract, a reference volume giving statistical data on each county. Such a volume can be an important research tool for a reporter, and an up-to-date copy, if published, should be available in the newspaper office.

Many states have created special agencies to help the smaller cities as well as the counties to operate. These agencies provide legal and technical advice for elected officials who serve only part time in office. They can be an important source of information for the reporter.

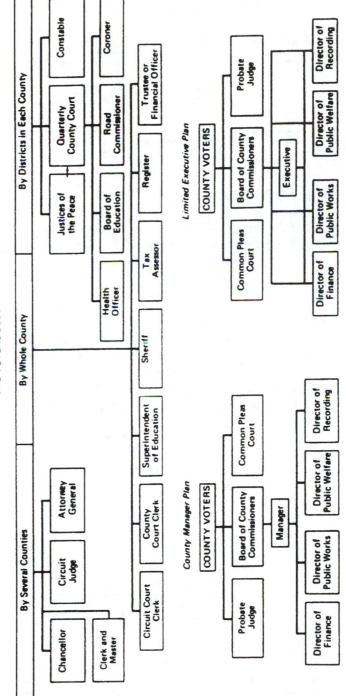

THREE FORMS OF COUNTY GOVERNMENT
"Long Ballot" Plan Used by Some Counties

THE VOTERS ELECT

ORGANIZATION OF A SAMPLE STATE GOVERNMENT

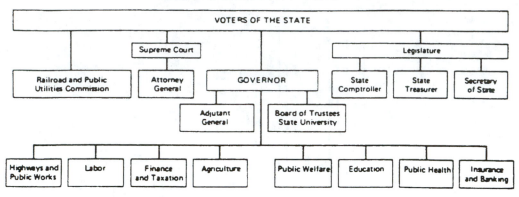

Specific News Materials

All of the story forms previously discussed and diagramed are employed in reporting government and politics. They are used to present the following types of specific story materials.

Legislative

No aspect of the state legislature, city council or governing body of the county should be ignored. Frequently, what happens behind the scenes at committee meetings, occasional secret sessions of public officials and lobbyists and seemingly routine staff conferences can be more important and significant than what happens at the public sessions of legislative bodies. It is at these private sessions that much of the groundwork of government is done, decisions made and deals struck.

A reporter covering government has to be alert. New laws are important news, but even more important may be proposed laws, proposed changes in zoning or plans for projects that would commit the taxpayers to enormous public debt. The public record is replete with examples of public officials who, by behind-the-scenes maneuvering, have cost taxpayers billions of dollars through unneeded and occasionally foolhardy projects. The public depends on the reporter for advance information that will help prevent this type of abuse by public officials.

Citizens frequently want the opportunity to be heard. Once alerted, citizens can act to arouse public opinion against unnecessary waste of the tax dollar. The reporter can serve as a watchdog of the public welfare by carefully observing and reporting trends in legislation. It is important not only to cover the action on the floor of legislative bodies but also to follow bills through committee rooms and public hearings. The reporter should poll authoritative opinion and canvass similar legislation in other states and communities to determine whether it has been successful or constructive. Finally, the reporter should tell the reader what the legislation will cost and what specifically the taxpayer will get in return.

A SUMMARY OF GOVERNMENTAL SERVICES
PROVIDING SOURCES OF NEWS

Services and Activities	City	County	State	Federal*
Protection of person and property	Police Fire Courts Building inspectors	Sheriff Magistrates Deputies Constables Courts	State police, courts, fire marshals, rangers, game wardens, National Guard	Army Navy and Marines Air Force Coast Guard FBI inspectors
Promotion of health	Water supply Health Department Garbage and sewage disposal, Hospitals	Health Department	Health Department	Public health service
Regulation and promotion of agriculture	None	Agricultureal agents and departments	Department of Agriculture	Department of Agriculture and other agencies
Regulation and promotion of business of industry	City ordinances enforced by inspectors	Licensing	Department of Commerce (may have another name)	Department of Commerce and other agencies
Regulation of working conditions	Usually none	Usually none	Department of Labor	Department of Labor and other agencies
Construction and maintenance of public roads	Department of Public Works, Streets	Department of Highways	Department of Highways and Public Works	Bureau of Public Roads and other agencies
Education	School boards Superintendents Libraries	School boards Superintendents Libraries	Department of Education and state institutions	Office of Education and other agencies
Conservation of natural resources	Parks Planning agencies	Agricultural agents Planning agencies	Department of Conservation	Department of Interior, Regional agencies
Regulation, control, and operation of public utilities	City water Power Light	Rural electrification corporations	Utilities and Railroad Commissions	Interstate Commerce Commission
Promotion of general welfare Social Security	Department of Welfare, almshouses Hospitals	Almshouses Hospitals	Department of Welfare, mental hospitals Special schools	Social Security and programs of many other agencies
Other major services		Property and other records	Regulations and controls	Post Office, Department of State (foreign relations)
Administration	Taxes Budgets Regulations Routines	Taxes Budgets Regulations Routines	Taxes Budgets Regulations Routines	Taxes Budgets Regulations Routines

* Federal agencies form too vast a network to permit detailed analysis here. Only standard services are suggested.

Executive

An alert reporter covering government will be aware of the relationship between the executive branch and many new laws. Although officials of the executive branch may insist that they are only the executors of the law, they in fact often are the sponsors of legislation for reasons that may not always be the most honorable. A good reporter will know what government official is behind a law and why.

Once a law has been passed, a reporter must be aware of its permanent news potential. If it is a tax law, for example, the reporter should follow its effects, checking with the proper official—perhaps the commissioner of finance or city financial director. What is its yield? Is it easily enforced? And, naturally, the reporter should check with the public to see whether the law is popular and how it directly affects taxpayers.

Aside from its function in the execution and enforcement of new legislative measures, the executive branch of government (governor, mayor, county judge or manager and chief department heads) is a permanent news source. Are the laws being enforced? Too strictly? Not strictly enough? What specific problems arise from day to day? What new policies are in effect? The reporter also must make certain that the executive branch (through the specific departments of government) is providing the proper services to the public as required by law and paid for by tax dollars.

The reporter not only keeps the public informed but also aids the executive branch in educating the public about matters of government. But the reporter must be careful not to become an unquestioning mouthpiece for the executive. The governmental reporter plays a key role. Without the reporter as a news channel, the interaction of government and the people would be difficult.

Judicial

A political reporter must also watch the courts closely. Here the same laws that were enacted and put into operation may come up for adjudication. Trials and lawsuits will usually be covered by other types of reporters, but sessions of the Supreme Court or any court in which decisions fraught with economic and social consequences—in which the constitutionality of laws is involved—will find the political reporter present.

Fiscal

Revenues and expenditures—the budgets of state, county and city—demand careful attention from the political reporter. Bond issues, taxes, delinquent taxes, special assessment and the entire financial structure, fixed and current, need adequate interpretation to the people. The cost of government increases every day, whereas the quality of governmental services sometimes declines. The reporter must tell the public why this is happening and what can be done about it. Government officials may tell why costs are going up, but usually the explanation is wrapped in technical terms and governmental double-talk. The reporter is responsible for translating all of this into plain language the public can understand.

Public Records and Meetings

To cover government effectively, a reporter must have access to public records and the right to attend meetings. Even in states that have open meetings and open records laws, questions arise over what is and what is not a "public record" or a "public meeting." National and state journalistic organizations continue to conduct crusades charging officials with too much secrecy in government and demanding that all public records and meetings be open to the public and the press, for the press must base its claim for access on the public's right of access. The Tennessee Press Association, for example, sponsored such a campaign with a slogan, "What the People Don't Know WILL Hurt Them," and was able to obtain a state law requiring that all public records be open to the public and the press. It followed with campaigns to protect the confidentiality of news sources and to open all public meetings. Although all three laws have been tested in the courts and upheld, public officials still seek ways to circumvent them and conduct public business in secret.

Of course, there generally is no quarrel over certain types of public records and meetings, such as property transfers, delinquent tax notices, arrests, periodic fiscal reports, city council meetings and sessions of the state legislature. The disputes have been over certain types of records that officials claim are not open to public inspection, despite the word "all" in the laws, and certain types of meetings (special sessions of the city school board, for example, when personnel matters are being discussed) that officials do not want the press or public to attend even though public business is being conducted. Newspapers have had varying success in opening records and meetings that have been closed for unjustified reasons.

In any event, if there is no open record or open meeting law in a state, the press still can demand the right to see records and to attend meetings that are accessible to anyone other than specific government officials and employees. In addition, the press can insist that final action on a legislative or governing matter (such as action taken by a school board) be taken in open session. In states where open meeting laws exist, the press has successfully sued public bodies, forcing them to rescind action taken in secret meetings. In states where such laws do not exist, the press should bring the pressure of public opinion, legislative action and the courts to force governmental bodies to conduct the public's business in the open.

Elections

Despite the efforts of the press to inform the public on the issues and the candidates, public apathy is not uncommon in most elections. At all levels of government, increasing numbers of citizens are not voting. A reporter assigned to election coverage has a special responsibility to write accurately and fairly so voters can be fully informed. The complexity of the nation's various election laws complicates the reporter's job. The nation's system of political parties and election practices has grown up by trial and error. Although various state laws have stabilized them somewhat, both primary and general election practices require a broad knowledge and considerable political acumen if they are to be properly interpreted for the public.

PARTY ORGANIZATION AND METHODS OF
CALLING CONVENTIONS
(Democratic and Republican Parties)

National Executive Committee

Composed of representatives from each state and territory chosen by the national convention. In general, manages the national party affairs and issues the call for the national convention.

State Executive Committee

Composed of representatives from each congressional district chosen at biennial primary elections. In general, manages state party affairs and, in response to call of National Executive Committee, issues call to County Executive Committees for the election of delegates to the State Convention.

Congressional District Executive Committee

Composed of the chairman of, or other delegates from, the County Executive Committees of the particular district. Frequently inactive.

County Executive Committee

Created usually by party usage. Its organization is different in each of the political parties and is not uniform in the counties, even in the same party. The committee issues call for county convention or primary election to nominate party's candidates.

The accompanying charts are simplified pictures of party organization. The national party system is made up basically of two parties, with third-party efforts sometimes emerging in response to the intensity of the issues before the public at a given time. Third-party campaigns are most often launched during a presidential campaign.

Although the organization of the two major parties and their practices are somewhat uniform on the national level, states show considerable variation in their party organizations and practices. The political reporter has to have the same understanding of the state's election laws as of state and local government operations in order to report political campaigns adequately.

The political reporter also is expected to evaluate candidates for readers, and it is therefore essential that not only the election machinery but also the issues and personalities be understood. Without editorializing—unless writing a signed column—the reporter must present a fair and factual evaluation of all candidates. Obviously this takes careful study or long experience and close contact with the politics of the community, state or nation.

During a political campaign, a reporter will interview candidates, write biographical sketches and evaluate the candidate's position on major issues while reporting daily on the candidate's activities. In major political races, often the same

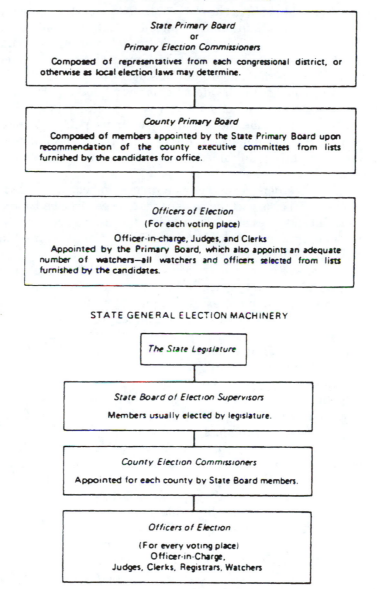

STATE PRIMARY ELECTION MACHINERY
(Democratic and Republican Parties)

State Primary Board
or
Primary Election Commissioners

Composed of representatives from each congressional district, or otherwise as local election laws may determine.

County Primary Board

Composed of members appointed by the State Primary Board upon recommendation of the county executive committees from lists furnished by the candidates for office.

Officers of Election
(For each voting place)

Officer-in-charge, Judges, and Clerks
Appointed by the Primary Board, which also appoints an adequate number of watchers—all watchers and officers selected from lists furnished by the candidates.

STATE GENERAL ELECTION MACHINERY

The State Legislature

State Board of Election Supervisors

Members usually elected by legislature.

County Election Commissioners

Appointed for each county by State Board members.

Officers of Election

(For every voting place)
Officer-in-Charge,
Judges, Clerks, Registrars, Watchers

reporter will follow a candidate, report on his or her speeches and the audience reaction to them, and be on hand at campaign headquarters on election night to report on the victory or concession speech.

Interpretation of Politics

Covering politics offers endless pitfalls for a reporter. Some reporters become too close to a candidate and find it difficult to write a critical article if the need arises. Some candidates deliberately try to "use" a reporter to plant favorable stories. Even the most routine handout from a candidate must be carefully interpreted to prevent the reporter's innocently advancing one candidate over another.

To cover a political campaign fairly, a good reporter must "know the politics" of the men and women involved. It is important for the reporter to understand the facts behind the so-called news in the political handout, the motives for certain governmental action during a campaign and the behind-the-scenes maneuvering of the political leaders that could have an effect on the outcome of an election.

Many readers depend on newspapers to help guide them in making a political choice. They expect the newspaper to expose the bad and commend the good deeds of candidates as well as public officials. A good reporter will look for motives in everything a candidate for office says or does, and those motives should be explained to the readers.

To represent the newspaper's readers faithfully, the reporter of governmental news must know the men and women to hold public office and all the political, social and economic pressures that influence their actions. Who are their associates in and out of office? Who contributed to their campaigns? Which lobbying groups have access to them? What political debts do they owe? How do they rank with their fellow party members? How do they rank with the opposition party? What is their voting record?

In short, a reporter should know as much as anyone else, if not more, about the people who are currently holding office as well as those seeking office and should know about the political party organizations of both incumbents and candidates. However, reporters should not bargain their rights as reporters to obtain a close working relationship with sources. Reporters should not make deals with sources. Developing a broad knowledge of politics and establishing important sources takes time. That is why the political reporter often is one of the older and better reporters on the staff—a person who has the ability and personality to be an important figure in the political life of the city.

James A. Hogan, a partner in Coopers & Lybrand, then one of the top four accounting firms in the world and one doing more municipal auditing than any other firm, made a list of questions that should be asked any politician responsible for making financial decisions. They were presented by Sylvia Porter in her syndicated financial column, "Your Money's Worth." They are:

1. What are you doing to retain and gain private-sector businesses and jobs for the area you represent?

2. Have you maintained autonomy by not increasing the city's dependency on the federal government for resources with strings attached?

3. What steps are you taking to assure provisions of only those services which citizens demand and are willing and able to pay for?

4. Are you insisting that proven management methods (zero-based budgeting, for instance) be used to set new priorities for the types and levels of public services to be provided to keep taxes and spending down?

5. Are you making sure that goals and objectives are written into new laws so their effectiveness can be measured and reported to the public?

6. What efforts are you making to find new ways to deliver essential public services more efficiently?

7. What plans are you making to increase the percentage of our government's income that is used to pay for current services instead of general administration—and to pay off old debts and retirement benefits earned in the past?

8. Will you help in publishing a simple annual city report that anyone who usually reads business news can understand?

9. Will you seek improved credibility of financial reports by calling for mandatory adults by a qualified independent firm?

10. Have your bond ratings improved in relation to other governmental units?

Of course, it is important that the government reporter check regularly to make certain the official is doing what was promised in answer to each of those questions.

Reporting politics and government is a year-round job, but at election time most newspapers devote special attention to the campaign and the candidates. The public turns to newspapers for information about the candidates for office, the issues at stake, the political alignments and maneuvers. The reporter must wade through the propaganda being dished out by the candidates and their staffs to tell the voters what they need to know about the issues as well as the men and women seeking office. When the final votes are counted, the reporter must analyze election statistics so that they mean something to the reader.

Frequently newspaper policy (see Chapter 14) is involved in reporting politics and government. This will arise if the newspaper has partisan views on those holding or running for office or if it has a policy relating to governmental affairs. Such policies may range all the way from efforts to consolidate the city and county school systems to a campaign to change the entire form of city government. More than all other communications media, newspapers have taken the lead in crusading for governmental reforms. The public has come to expect the newspaper to be not only a guardian of governmental conduct, but also an adviser on progressive steps needed in governmental organizations. Newspapers rejecting their responsibilities and conducting unreasonable partisan coverage of election campaigns (and some still do) are doing a disservice to the public and their communities. Obviously, candidates seeking endorsement of newspapers may be swayed by the opinions of the press when they set their platforms. It is essential that a reporter recognize this. With such great responsibilities, the reporter who covers governmental and politics must be one of the most competent members on the staff.

Here are several political story leads:

> PENSACOLA—(AP)—It was biscuits and grits, a bus and the Oak Ridge Boys singing "Elvira" in the Florida Panhandle for Republican gubernatorial candidate Jeb Bush on Thursday.

> The state Board of Elections will meet Monday to consider ballot challenges and a proposal to computerize campaign finance reporting.
> The meeting starts at 10 a.m. in Room 9-040 of the James R. Thompson Center, 100 W. Randolph St.
> Board members will take up challenges to the validity of signatures on nominating petitions filed by the U. S. Taxpayers Party and Libertarian Party candidates in the November elections.

> *(Chicago Tribune)*

> Two candidates for statewide posts made stops in Valdosta and Flagler counties Thursday, trying to drum up a few more votes before Tuesday's general election.

> *(Valdosta News–Journal)*

And the writer of this political story took a feature approach:

> PHILADELPHIA—Appearing here recently as the Wizard in a stage show "The Wizard of Oz," Mickey Rooney stopped in at City Hall to present Mayor Edward G. Rendell with a special souvenir.
> As he accepted a ceremonial key to Oz, Mr. Rendell took a moment to congratulate the 78-year-old actor for a lifetime of charitable work. Mr. Rooney was taken aback by the Mayor's remarks. "I'm not through yet," he insisted, promoting Mr. Rendell to cut him off.
> "I keep telling people here I'm not through yet, either," Mr. Rendell said.
> Embarking upon the last of his eight years as Philadelphia's Mayor and foremost cheerleader . . .

> (The *New York Times*)

This story is a follow-up to a local election:

> Until newly elected county officials are sworn into office on August 31, Campbell County is apparently without a full-time Sessions Court judge.
> Defeated Judge Rocky Young will be paid more than $4,500 in August for holding office, even though he hasn't been back since the election.
> Following his defeat in the August 6 election, Young announced to Circuit Court Clerk Brenda Boshears early the following week that he wouldn't be back, despite the fact that, since he did not tender his resignation, he will be fully paid for his services through August 28.

> *(LaFollette Press)*

Political Polls

The increased use of polling to measure the public's attitude toward nearly every aspect of our lives has presented an added problem for the political reporter. Every candidate sponsors polls. So do political parties, citizen's groups and the news media. So much attention has been focused on poll results that the public can easily be misled if the reporter is not careful.

It is the responsibility of the reporter to understand polling techniques and not to misinterpret the results of a poll. Before writing about the results of a poll, it is important for the reporter to know who sponsored the poll; who conducted it (was it a reliable polling organization such as Harris or Gallup, or was it the candidate's own staff?); the wording of the questions (to make certain they weren't biased in favor of one point of view over another); how many persons were questioned; where they were questioned; when they were questioned (was the survey done in a day or over a long period of time?) under what circumstances (at home, by telephone or on the street in person); the characteristics of the persons in the sample (were they all young, old, registered voters, unemployed, etc.?); and the response rate, including the number who said they did not know or did not have an opinion.

When reporting the results of any poll, responsible newspapers will always explain to the reader exactly how the poll was conducted. Some newspapers include the information as a part of the story. However, others carry a separate story giving the reader all the information about the mechanics of conducting the poll.

In an article for the *Washington Journalism Review*, Evans Witt, a reporter on politics and polls for AP, offered these rules for journalists covering polls.

1. Do not overinterpret poll results.

2. Include the results of other polls, even if they cast doubt upon the latest results.

3. Always include and be aware of sampling error.

4. Never forget the base.

5. Look at the exact wording of questions carefully.

6. Do not use non-scientific readings of public opinion for anything except entertainment value.

7. Be very, very careful when writing about polls conducted for candidates, special interest groups or political parties.

8. Never forget that polls give little hint about the depth of people's emotions or commitment.

9. Do not disguise your own interpretations as poll results.

10. Use common sense and do not fall under the spell of numbers.

And the National Council on Public Polling offers these guidelines for public pollsters:

1. State who sponsored the survey.
2. Give the dates of interviewing.
3. Define the method of interviewing.
4. Describe the population interviewed.
5. Reveal the size of the sample.
6. Describe and give the size of any subsamples used in the analysis.
7. Release the wording of all questions.
8. Release the full results of the questions on which the conclusions were based.
9. Do not remain silent if a client publicly releases and misrepresents a poll's results.

Reporters should be leery of any pollster who does not follow those guidelines.

Political polls often rate top play on the front page of newspapers. Here are two examples:

> Most Americans now condemn the Senate for its handling of the impeachment trial as much as they did the House, and Republicans are taking most of the blame. The party's fortunes have so sagged that half of even conservative Republicans say their party's prospect for the 2000 elections have been damaged, the latest *New York Times*/CBS News Poll shows.
>
> (The *New York Times*)

> WASHINGTON—President Clinton, backed by a public that overwhelmingly supports his presidency and record-high approval ratings for his handling of the economy, delivers his State of the Union address tonight before lawmakers who are debating whether to remove him from office.
>
> A *USA TODAY*/CNN/Gallup Poll shows Clinton with a 69% overall approval rating.
>
> Although a record-low 24% view Clinton as honest and trustworthy, more than eight in ten say his presidency is a success. Other findings . . .
>
> (*USA TODAY*)

But we poll about everything, as this story from *USA TODAY* shows:

> More than a third of elderly parents say their grown children have failed to help them in a time of need in the past five years, according to research to be released today. But when asked the same question, only 15% of adult children agree.
>
> Findings from two major polls conducted by AARP, an organization that focuses on issues of people over 50, show a generation gap when it comes to children dealing with elderly parents.

Meetings

Every governmental body and local group have meetings that reporters spend a great deal of time covering. The problem with meeting coverage is that it can be repetitive and dull if the reporter does not strive to make every story interesting and informative. Polls of readers have found that many simply do not read local government stories because they are dull and boring.

Fred Palmer, writing in the "Editorially Speaking" section of the *Gannetteer*, a magazine for Gannett Group people, recommended two initial steps to his fellow editors that he said would make a meeting story readable and, maybe, excellent:

— Convince beat reporters that the newspaper office is a place where they can pick up their mail and see who is trying to get in touch with them. The office is not a place where they work.
— Convince beat reporters that the city hall, the county courthouse or the police station are only starting points on their beats. Warn them that those places are almost as deadly as the newsroom.

Palmer said nothing much really happens at city hall.

People draw maps, apply for grants, gripe about the declining sales-tax revenues and talk to reporters.

All of that is very boring.

It is difficult to take something that is basically very boring and turn it into a story that anyone would want to read.

But if we get away from city hall, we can find people who think their street needs to be fixed, who don't like it when rainwater backs up into their toilets and who worry a lot about an iron deficiency in their oak trees.

These people also will talk to reporters and very often what they have to say has something to do with a meeting.

In that same issue, Kathleen O'Dell, a veteran Gannett reporter, columnist, city editor and editorial writer, said she would tell reporters covering meetings to:

— Do your homework. Meeting coverage seems to be 60 percent background work and 40 percent actual meeting. Find out what is expected to happen, and background yourself on those points. Attend the study sessions that often are scheduled days before the regular meetings of school boards and city councils.
— Break the news before the meeting. The days before a meeting offer a good chance to run stories exploring issues that are expected to be raised at the session.
— Background yourself on the names, personalities and special interests of the board members or meeting principals.

— Be sure your quotes are correct. If you miss part of a quote during a meeting, pull the speaker aside later and get it.

— Don't rely on your memory to get answers to quotes or correct name spellings after the meeting. Jot down questions as they occur.

— Immediately alert your city editor by phone or messenger if something unusual happens at the meeting. That will allow time to plan for space needed or to send a photographer.

— If possible arrive at the meeting early. This will allow you to keep an eye on board members and time to interview people about meeting issues.

— Read agendas and meeting handouts carefully, and as much before the meeting as possible.

— Get details, such as the number of people attending, any protest signs that were displayed, applause, heckling and any gestures or mannerisms the speakers made that you can include in your story to add life to it.

— Always keep in mind this question: "How will it affect the readers?" It will prompt you to ask the most important questions for the story and help you write the lead as well as the rest of the story.

— Watch for trends that develop over weeks or months of meetings of the city council, county commission and other governing bodies. Some stories don't happen at meetings but do stem from information that you can pick up there.

— If you decide not to attend a meeting, cover yourself. Arrange for a trustworthy person at the meeting to alert you during it if something important happens and always talk to the person after the meeting to check on what happened.

This example shows that the reporter used imagination in covering a meeting and came up with a bright lead that might not be considered politically correct by some:

> The No. 2 man in Lebanon is now a woman.
> Fourth Ward Councilwoman Jeannie Smith, who in 1985 became the first woman elected to the council, scored another first last night when she was elected mayor pro tem—or vice mayor—by the Lebanon City Council.
> Smith, a 39-year-old homemaker, sees her position as something all women in Lebanon could take pride in.
> The city's No. 1 man, newly elected Mayor Bobby Jewell, said Smith's election was a positive step for equality.

The following lead on a story in the *Knoxville News–Sentinel* played off on the way announcers wind up each episode of a soap opera with a series of questions:

> Will Stella Brookshire be reinstalled? Will the absent members of the County Housing Authority attend the next meeting? Does Executive Director William G. (Bill) Pierce have the power to hire and fire? Will tenants' support of Stella have weight in the authority's decisions?

All those questions and more were left unanswered yesterday when Authority Chairman Cas Walker was the only board member to attend a meeting he had called, presumably to hold a hearing on Mrs. Brookshire's firing by Pierce Jan. 28.

Here is a meeting lead that never should have been written:

City Council members were told last night that because of nearby potential hazards to children, it might be "inadvisable, perhaps even negligent" to site 45 units of public housing designed for low income families on the so-called "Federal Office Building Tract" because of potential dangers from heavy equipment, plating solutions and radioactive materials in that area.

Budgets

The budget story often is the most important story a reporter covering government will write in any year. The budget always gives the public a fairly clear understanding of where the administration places its priorities. On a national level in recent years, the major priority obviously has been defense. In many states, the top priority has been public education (more than half the annual budget in some states is allocated to the public schools). In some cities and counties, law enforcement agencies get the biggest slice of the budget.

Ideally, every reporter covering government should have more than one course in city, county, and state government finance and perhaps a course or two in accounting. In addition, a reporter must know how to read a budget. If a reporter does not know how to read a budget, it is important to seek help. Perhaps the newspaper's own accountant can conduct a quick course in budgets.

Government budgets usually come with a quick and easy summary at the beginning. Often the summary is prepared to make the official submitting the budget look good. The reporter should not become a captive of the official summary. The real story of the budget is buried deep inside the tables, graphs and charts it contains. A good reporter should be able to dig out the financial picture.

The original budget story often is somewhat routine. It should include the total amount of the new budget for the coming fiscal year; whether that amount represents an increase or a decrease over the preceding year; if an increase, where the money will come from; if a decrease, what services are being cut; what new taxes, if any, the budget calls for; if there is an increase in property taxes, in particular, what this will mean for a typical home owner; any pay increases (or decreases) for public employees; and a review of the departmental allocations, including the largest and the smallest, and any departments that may be marked for dramatic changes.

Here is an example of a good budget story lead from the *New York Times:*

ALBANY—Jan. 27—After a two-year detour into government largess, Gov. George E. Pataki today returned to the conservative path of his early years, proposing a $72.66 billion state budget with substantial cuts in health care and education. He proposed eliminating programs aimed at expanding pre-kindergarten classes and lowering class sizes.

Though the state is flush with money, with a surplus expected to top $2 billion, Mr. Pataki called for a spending increase of just 1.8 percent in the fiscal year that begins April 1.

WASHINGTON—(AP)—With a promise of huge federal surpluses, President Clinton on Monday unveiled a $1.77 trillion budget for fiscal 2000 that would buttress Social Security and provide billions for everything from troops to teachers.

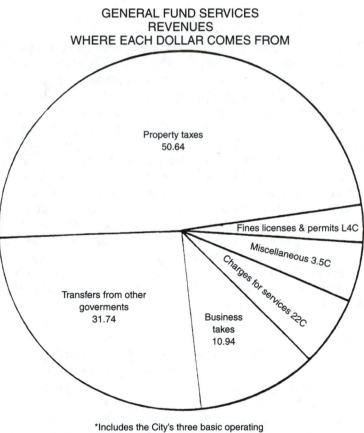

GENERAL FUND SERVICES REVENUES
WHERE EACH DOLLAR COMES FROM

Property taxes
50.64

Fines licenses & permits L4C

Miscellaneous 3.5C

Charges for services 22C

Transfers from other goverments
31.74

Business takes
10.94

*Includes the City's three basic operating funds-General Fund, Revenue Sharing, and State Street Aid. Total Amount $71,810,299

FIGURE 23.1 Budget documents usually contain pie charts that help the reporter—and the public—understand the overall budget. This one shows the source of revenue for a city.

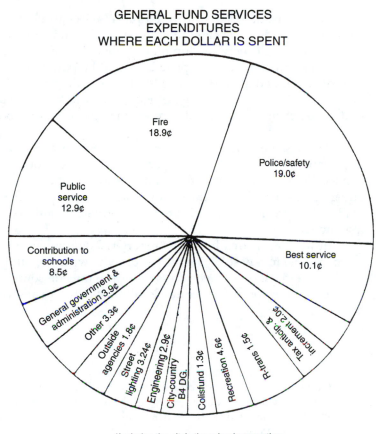

GENERAL FUND SERVICES
EXPENDITURES
WHERE EACH DOLLAR IS SPENT

*Includes the city's three basic operating
funds-general fund, revenue sharing, and
state street aid. Total amount $71,810,299

FIGURE 23.2   This pie chart shows where each dollar of the budget is spent.

This example of a budget story focuses on what a mayor emphasized in his budget proposal:

> The city tax rate of $4.80 per $100 assessed valuation should not be changed. City employees should receive an average 7% raise. And the city's automobile registration fee should be abolished.
> Those were among recommendations Mayor Joe Jones forwarded to the City Council yesterday with his $43.6 million budget for the coming fiscal year.

Budget-making is a year-round process. Departments usually submit their requests for funds six to eight months before the budget is completed. A series of conferences is held between top officials, budget officers and department heads before the final budget is completed. A careful reporter keeps track of the budget as it develops and should be able to predict with some certainty what the final document will be like, although officials prefer to keep most of the work on the budget secret until it is officially presented to the legislative body that must act on it.

At the same time, the reporter must keep track of all revenue sources. It is important to know if taxes on property, businesses and other specialized areas are being collected on time. It is important to know if funds from the state and federal governments have been reduced. In short, is the income meeting the projections made in the previous budget? If not, what impact might that have on the upcoming budget?

In working with a budget, a reporter should never guess at anything. It is important not to rely solely on the people who write the budget for an interpretation. A reporter should have access to several outside sources—an accountant or perhaps a professor of finance at a local university—to answer questions about a budget.

EXERCISES

1. Obtain from the mayor's office or the city public relations office a chart of city government structure. Make certain you have the names of each of the major department heads as well as the names of all city council members. You will need them for later exercises.

2. Do a one-week inventory of all the government stories in your local daily newspaper. Analyze them carefully, paying particular attention to their content. Categorize them by city, state and national government and then by topic—council meetings, budgets, public issues and public events involving government leaders.

3. Arrange to accompany the city government reporter for your local daily on her or his rounds one day. Write a feature story on that experience.

4. Attend a city council or county commission meeting and write a story about it. Turn in your rough notes with the story the following morning. Do not copy the story printed in the morning newspaper about the meeting. But you should compare your story to the one in the local paper later.

5. Interview the mayor or the chief county executive. Question her or him about current problems facing local government. Also ask about recent accomplishments or achievements of government that benefited the citizens. Write a story using the information gathered in the interview.

6. Arrange a focus group of six individuals (not all students) and have them discuss the quality of local government and government services. Write a story about what they said.

7. Arrange a similar focus group on campus using students, faculty members and staff workers. Ask them to discuss the quality of the university administration and the services it provides students, faculty and staff. Write a story on what they said.

8. Interview the city finance director about the fiscal state of the city. Write a story based on the interview.

9. Interview a state representative or senator from your district about the major issues confronting state government in general and any issues that may apply specifically to his or her district. Write a story based on the interview. Turn in your notes with the story.

10. If your city or state has its own web page, click on it and see what it contains. Write a story about what citizens can learn about their city from reading the web page.

11. Write a news story from each of the following sets of notes:

    a. City Manager Dale Burton
       Said he plans to ask
       City Council Members
       To revise work week
       For city employees
       He wants employees
       To work longer days
       And get every other
       Friday off
       He wants employees to work
       Eight nine-hour days,
       One eight-hour day
       Every two weeks
       Then have one day off
       It works out to
       A 40-hour work week
       Burton says the change
       Will serve the public
       Since it will keep
       City offices open
       Until 5:30 p.m. daily
       He has put the item
       On the council's agenda
       For its meeting Thursday.
    b. Fire tax issue
       Up for discussion
       At tonight's meeting
       Of City Council
       Controversial plan
       Adopted last year
       Estimated to raise
       Between $24–27 million
       To help pay off
       Some city long-term debt

Practically every building
Including churches and schools
Taxed under the plan
Mayor Dennis Lopez
Said today he plans
To ask City Council
To exempt churches
Synagogues and other
Places of worship
From the controversial tax
Mayor said he had met
With church leaders
Who convinced him
To seek these exemptions
No other group has
Asked for exemptions
However, School Board Chairman
Bunny Moss said she would
Urge full board to ask
For a full exemption
She estimates tax costs
School board $600,000 annually

c. State Representative Lois Willey
Plans to introduce bill
Requiring health plans
To pay for birth control pills
If they plan to pay
For Viagra pills for men
Lobbyist for insurers
And employers who offer
Health care plans
Claim her plan
Would drive up
Cost of health insurance
Force businesses to drop
Coverage for workers
Rep. Willey said
"They cry wolf all the time
"If they are going to
"Pay for men to be able
"To produce children
"They ought to be made
"Pay to help women
"From getting pregnant
"Fair is fair"
She admits chances slim
For bill's passage
"Because men outnumber
"Women 10 to 1
"In state legislature"

CHAPTER

24 Business, Industry, Agriculture, Labor

"Business will be better or worse," President Calvin Coolidge once proclaimed. He was right—it's been both.

Fortunately, the writing about business in American newspapers has gotten better and better over the years as business news broke out of the confines of business news sections and started regularly making the front page of most newspapers.

Reporters assigned to cover business frequently saw their stories on the front page as the economy set new records in the late 1990s, the stock market reached new heights, major corporations from automobile to communications giants merged into even larger giants, and the collapse of the Japanese and Brazilian economies presented serious threats to American investors.

Here are the leads on several business stories that made the nation's front pages:

A year of pleasant economic surprises ended with the biggest one of all: a last-minute burst of growth that surpassed even the most bullish predictions.

America's gross domestic product—the total of goods and services produced—surged at a 5.6 percent annual rate in the final quarter . . .

Ford Motor plans to buy the car unit of Sweden's Volvo for about $6 billion, say those close to the deal, which is to be announced today in Sweden.

The deal is likely to be cash: Ford has $24 billion on hand.

And when Alan Greenspan, the Federal Reserve Board chairman, spoke about interest rates or the use of federal budget surpluses to shore up Social Security, it made the front pages.

Editors recognized that there is an economic angle to literally every story. A football game that brings 95,000 persons to a city on a Saturday afternoon, for example, has an economic impact on local businesses. A prolonged and harsh winter, normally thought of as just a weather story, will send the cost of heating homes, schools, businesses and industrial plants skyrocketing. It could also lead to plant closings, delay spring planting and cost local governments large sums of money for repairs to damaged streets, highways and bridges.

The greatest change caused by increased attention to the economy has been in the business pages. Once many editors were content to reprint publicity releases (perhaps rewritten) from local industries or their parent companies, together with the wire service stock quotations and call it a business page. Being a business-page reporter then was not a particularly demanding job. Today's business- or financial-page reporter, however, must have more than just a passing knowledge of economics and finance. The reporter must be able to understand what is going on and explain it to readers in a language they will understand.

Several trends have brought this about. Probably the most significant is the changing nature of ownership of American businesses and industries. Millions of small investors now own stock in major corporations, either directly or through pension and retirement plans, and have an interest in their success. In addition, the nation's unprecedented economic expansion during the first three decades after World War II was followed by a dramatic slowdown in the 1980s that sent shockwaves through the public. To report and interpret those developments, the business- or financial-page reporter has had to become something of a specialist in economics and finance.

National and international economic events and trends often have direct influences on local business, industry, agriculture and labor just as national and international political events have. A depression, major unemployment, inflation, a poor wheat crop in Russia, frost damage to the coffee trees in Brazil—all can have a direct effect on the economic life of a community.

It should also be pointed out that the economic health of a community will have an effect on the newspaper. Being a business itself, the newspaper derives its financial support as an advertising medium for the establishments that compose the economic structure of the community. As a general rule, newspapers do not open their new columns to free advertising space just to please advertisers. At the same time, most editors realize that there are many legitimate news items developing within the business community that have strong reader interest.

Even the routine business stories usually have local consequence, affecting the pocketbooks, jobs, household budgets and general plans of local citizens. The stereotyped real estate transfers reported in a "column" will be read by many adult readers. The price paid for the corner building lot may reflect the value of every piece of property in the block. Will a service station be located there? Or perhaps an all-night market or a laundromat? If so, it may be the first sign of decay of a substantial residential neighborhood. Progress or disaster thus might exist below the surface of a routine as well as a major business story. The announcement of the consolidation of two major steel firms in the other cities might have a direct bearing on a local steel plant that is a subsidiary of one of the merged firms. Will they phase out the local operation or perhaps expand it, bringing new money into the community and creating new jobs?

Although it is true that handouts, publicity releases and promotional stories may save the business reporter a lot of leg work, a reporter must always question their news value. Is a fashion show, a Santa Claus parade or a Washington's Birthday sale legitimate news or free advertising? The news policy of the individual newspaper will determine how much and in what manner such material will be accepted. Many newspapers join with local merchants in promoting some events. Some national "weeks" and "days" with a commercial tinge may be publicized. Mother's Day, Father's Day, Harvest Moon Sale Days (with special entertainment features provided by the stores) and other worthy though special-interest occasions may find the reporter writing not news but promotion and publicity. In all such cases the safeguard of honest reporting is the ability to distinguish the wolf in sheep's clothing. A Washington's Birthday sale, for example, can be a legitimate news story if traditionally thousands of people start lining up outside stores at midnight to get first crack at the bargains when the doors open in the morning.

Types of Establishments

Establishments and organizations that come within a community's economic complex include:

Retail stores

Wholesale distributors

Real estate agencies

Insurance agencies

Transportation firms—passenger and freight—both surface and air

Industries

Communications—telephone, telegraph

Business and industrial organizations—chamber of commerce, Better Business Bureau, various trade associations, automobile club

Farms

Agricultural markets

Agricultural organizations and agencies—state, county and federal

Labor—organized and unorganized

Various types of service establishments, some indigenous to the locality

But newspapers have broadened their coverage way beyond those areas. Stories as diverse as the microbrewery revolution in beer making, Super Bowl advertising rates, the banana war between the United States and Europe, the proliferation of telemarketing and overcharging by supermarket scanners regularly are the lead stories on business pages.

Even stories about the personal life of prominent figures in business have made the front page of business sections. When the wife of the chief executive officer of a major corporation sued for divorce and demanded half his assets, the *New York Times* carried the story on its business front page. And when the publisher of two major national magazines decided to dramatically change his lifestyle, leaving his wife for another man, it made the front page of the *Wall Street Journal.*

The extent to which a newspaper will cover each of these activities may depend on local characteristics. If a sizable number of the newspaper's subscribers are engaged in one of these activities, special sections of the newspaper may periodically be devoted to news and timely information published for the benefit of those subscribers and other interested readers. Such sections range from the fairly common farm page used in regions that have substantial agricultural interests to a special section on a new airport, for example.

Many newspapers put out annual business and industry editions or so-called progress editions devoted to the economic growth of the community over the previous year. Whether or not any special sections or pages are printed on a regular basis, stories from all of the listed economic activities are published as the news becomes available. Frequently the story, if of major significance, may appear on the front page. A prolonged drought in an agricultural region is sure to make page 1, just as a strike that idles a large number of the city's work force may be the main story of the day.

Types of Stories

The great variety of stories from business, industry, agriculture and labor will not conform to any simple general type. Some will be reported as meetings, speeches, interviews and publications. Some will appear as trials and lawsuits. Even crimes, accidents, fires, illnesses, deaths and funerals may affect the economic life of the community and require an interpretation of their influence.

The following are some general varieties (rather than special types) of news on economic developments that appear from day to day in the newspapers:

1. *Markets.* Stocks and bonds, livestock, and commodities—mostly tabulations and stereotyped reports, national and local, but accompanied by interpretative stories.

2. *Real estate.* Routine transfers, new additions, large sales, improvements and expansions of buildings, construction permits issued.

3. *Merchandising.* Retail and wholesale stories—expansions and improvements, new corporations and partnerships, mergers, bankruptcies, prices, cost of living.

4. *Financing and banking.* Stockholders' and board meetings, dividends, bond issues, discounts and interest rates, the money market in general, refunding, trends.

5. *Industry.* New industries, new products, improved processes or methods, expansions, removals, bond issues, mergers.

6. *Transportation.* Changes in schedules, rights of way, board meetings, stocks and bonds, refunding rates.

7. *Labor.* Wages and hours, unemployment, strikes, lockouts, relief, policies.

8. *Business and government.* Taxes, legislative acts and court decisions affecting business, regulations and enforcement.

9. *Agriculture.* Crops, sales, droughts, new methods of farming, regulation by government, new varieties.

For all of these varieties, stories on personnel changes (including human-interest stories on retirements and the like) along with a countless supply of features are available to the imaginative reporter.

Story Forms

Stories about business, industry, agriculture and labor are not limited to a single form. Although the straight-news style is still fundamental, many reporters write human-interest, feature and interpretative stories to help readers understand the often complex issues involved. The *Wall Street Journal* consistently uses the feature approach to tell business and economic news.

Here is the lead on a *Journal* article about a small Ohio community, once the home of eight underwear manufacturers, that bills itself as "The Underwear Capital of the World." It was written by Clare Ansberry:

> PIQUA, Ohio—Madonna would have felt at home here a week ago. People were walking around town in their underwear.
>
> There was Mary Miller, a bartender at the Best Western, heading down Main Street in red long johns. Visiting New Zealander Peter O'Toole strolled about in a red lace bra (36-C) while singers belted out these words to the tune of the World War I ditty "Over There":
>
> "Underwear. Underwear. Wear it here, wear it there. Everywhere.
>
> "It's a stylish fashion, for work or passion, a far-out treat for those who dare."
>
> "Underwear. Underwear."
>
> The normally inhibited become uninhibited at the two-day event called the Great Outdoor Underwear Festival, which promotes Piqua's newly self-proclaimed position as the underwear capital of the world. Until 1988, the town's big claim to fame was "Home of the Mills Brothers." A granite monument in the town square honors the singers as musical ambassadors who "made the world a better place" with songs like "Glow Worm."
>
> But the rainless summer three years ago caused a drought delay in the town's annual Heritage Festival and sent festival yearing Piquads (yes, Piquads, pronounced PICK-wads) scrambling for a proxy. Bereft of a major crop such as tomatoes or strawberries to anchor the festival, Piqua (population 21,000) picked underwear.

This sampling of other leads will give some indication of the breadth of coverage found on business-news page.

When Lycos, a mainstream East Coast Web search engine company, purchased Wired Digital, once the on-line arm of *Wired* magazine, the *San Francisco Examiner* led its business section with this story about the impact of the deal:

> It's an unglamorous end of the digital revolution.
>
> In the stark, white San Francisco offices of Wired Digital, sullen, black-clad employees manipulate computer spreadsheets.
>
> Instead of being on the cutting edge of the on-line world, many of them are trying to figure out how they're going to make their quirky Web sites—with titles like Web Monkey and HotBot—meet the bottom-line demands of their new corporate owners at Lycos, a mainstream East Coast Web search engine company.

> The decades-old war between environmentalists and business is heading for a new battlefield. The next fight is not over a smoke-belching vehicle or smokestack, but the outboard engines that power small boats and the ubiquitous water scooters.
>
> California, often considered a bell-weather of environmental standards, has proposed air-emissions standards for carbureted two-stroke outboards that have marine manufacturers and boating groups rallying in protest.

The rest of the *Chicago Tribune* story presented both sides of the debate and cited how manufacturers of outboard motors in a nearby city have been working for years on new technologies that would sharply reduce emissions and noise.

> The check's in the mail.
>
> A little more than a year from the deadline, the people on Music Row who generate royalty payments already are reassuring songwriters that year 2000 computer glitches won't cripple the complicated systems that collect data and cut checks.

The story in the *Tennessean* in Nashville, where music publishing and playing is big business, went into detail what ASCAP, SESAC and BMI, the industry's Big Three music licensing agencies, were doing to assure songwriters would get paid should the "Millennium Bug" strike.

In Atlanta, where Coca-Cola is king, the *Journal–Constitution* carried this story about a drop in earnings at Coke's biggest rival, Pepsi Cola:

> Pepsico's earnings fell 27 percent in the fourth quarter, as the No. 2 U. S. soft drink company boosted advertising spending for its new Pepsi One diet cola.
>
> The maker of Pepsi-Cola and Lay's chips said profit before a gain and charges fell to $25 million, or 22 cents a share, from profit from continuing operations of $446 million, or 29 cents, a year earlier.

The rest of the story detailed efforts by Pepsico to update its image, move into the juice drink business and test new drinks to better take on rival Coca-Cola.

Even sex of a sort makes the business pages as this story from the front page of the business section of *USA TODAY* shows. It combines two sure-fire topics of interest to readers—sexy clothing and the Internet:

> Sex sells, but Victoria's Secret sells more. The lingerie company strutted its models on Wall Street and onto the Internet Wednesday to show investors what the future of on-line retailing could look like.
>
> Victoria's Secret broadcast its exclusive New York fashion show live on the Internet to as many as an anticipated 500,000 viewers Wednesday night. Company officials said they would not have estimates of viewership and sales until today.
>
> But no matter how they turn out, the Webcast was a high-stakes attempt to untie the Gordian knot that has thwarted all on-line marketers: how to draw masses of people to a commercial Web site.

Interpreting the News

Interpretation is the key to most stories on business, industry, agriculture and labor—even most of the routine stories. The reader wants to know what happened, why it happened and what it means. The reporter has to be able to tell all this in a language the reader understands. The worlds of business, industry, agriculture, and labor have languages—jargon—all their own, and the reporter must not fall into the trap of using this jargon without explaining to the reader what it means.

Statistics seem to be a language common to business and industry, for example, so a reporter should learn to simplify figures for the reader without distorting them. The average reader probably would not take the trouble to analyze "A total of 60,613 of the 147,604 persons in Thomasville own automobiles, according to . . ." The figures probably will slip right past the reader. But "Two out of every five Thomasville residents own an automobile. . . ." might be more of an attention-grabber.

The significance of statistics should be made clear. Usually a comparison is needed. How do the figures compare with other figures? Are they high or low? How do they compare with figures of past years and other sections of the nation? Most figures are meaningless unless comparisons are made. When the reporter writes that local automobile sales increased 50 percent last month, the reader needs to know how many automobiles were sold last month and the month before if the percentage figure is to have any meaning.

The following list of technical terms used by business, industry, agriculture and labor will emphasize the need for interpretation:

partnership	strikes and lockouts	contracts
corporation	clearinghouse	overhead
articles of incorporation	assets and liabilities	trustees directors

charter	discounts	interlocking boards
bonds	interest	pyramiding
refunding bonds	dividends	holding companies
serial bonds	premiums	public utilities
sinking-fund bonds	exchange	municipality
common stock	liquidation	debt and deficit
preferred stock	credit	"blue sky" laws
bankruptcy	trusts	audits
referee in bankruptcy	monopolies receiver	balance sheet tariff
"bull" and "bear" markets	Federal Reserve surplus	state capitalism parity
collateral	socialism	balance of payments
call loans	communism	gold reserve

In using such terms the reporter should either translate them or use them within a context that enables the reader to understand their meaning.

Some economic terms may require only simple definitions, but others require analyses that are possible only if the reporter knows the language of business and industry. Such documents as an auditor's report, a profit and loss statement or a market report require special knowledge in economics to be read and translated accurately.

The Reporter's Background

A reporter needs an academic foundation in economics, sociology, economic history, economic geography and political economy in order to cover business, industry, agriculture and labor with any degree of success. These subjects generally are studied by journalism students at college, but never make the assumption that those few required economics courses provide a sufficient background for depth reporting on the economic structure of the community. They help, but the college graduate stands at the entrance, not at the exit, of all economic education.

College courses will give a reporter the general theories, principles and history of economics, but a successful business- or financial-page reporter needs more than that. The reporter must learn the specifics of economic activities in the locality where he or she works and be able to tell readers how national and international events and trends affect the local economic community. The reporter should have ready answers to basic questions on the area—population, wealth, chief sources of income, chief occupations, tax rates, school enrollment, bank deposits, labor force, value of properties and other vital facts about the community and the people whose economic life he or she will attempt to interpret. Most of this information is available in standard reference works such as atlases and state statistical surveys. However, the local chamber of commerce will probably be able to provide more up-to-date information on the community.

Even with all of this, the reporter is just starting. To be established as a competent journalist on economic affairs, a reporter needs to acquire additional expertise in each of the four areas of economic coverage.

Business

A thorough knowledge of the business houses and a more than passing acquaintance with the business executives of the city are major requirements for a business-page reporter. Retail and wholesale stores, finance houses, transportation agencies and other firms, particularly the principal officers of those firms, are news sources for the business reporter. The reporter must know about these businesses to get the real news and must be able to separate free advertising and publicity from legitimate news in order to present an accurate picture of the city's economic progress or decline. The reporter should develop a relationship with the major business executives in the city. If the reporter is respected, business executives will be willing to answer penetrating and sometimes distasteful questions, and a number of them will volunteer tips that can lead to important stories. Since business firms are private enterprises and a reporter has no legal right to see their records (in most cases), it is essential to cultivate contacts. An alert reporter with good contacts should be able to anticipate most stories that will develop on the business beat.

Business stories often come from other beats. Here's one that originated at a hearing of a government agency:

> The Public Service Commission got an earful from angry consumers who turned out in droves Wednesday to accuse Atlanta Gas Light Co. of everything from mangling the English language to price gouging.
>
> Extra security was added when about 200 people—more than for any public hearing in recent years—showed up to vent their frustrations following last week's rate settlement between the PSC and gas company.

Industry

Most industries have their sales sights on a regional or national rather than a local market. Nevertheless, the people employed by a local industry are local citizens, and their activities as well as the industry's well-being are of interest to all the people of the community. They are vital to the local economy, especially if the number of industries in the community is limited. The reporter covering industries should know them well—the products they manufacture, the number of persons they employ, the distribution of their products, the sources of their raw materials and the people who manage and operate them. As in the case of covering local businesses, the reporter must cultivate and keep alive all news sources in industry.

Court decisions involving industry often generate stories for the business page. Here's an example from the *New York Times*:

> Companies do not have to share surpluses in their pension plans with their workers, even if the workers contributed to the plans through money withheld from their paychecks, the Supreme Court ruled unanimously yesterday.
>
> Pension experts on the employer side hailed the decision as either a great victory for management or a confirmation of established law. Those who represent workers said the decision showed how a 1974 federal law intended to protect workers benefits had been twisted into a tool to restrict those benefits while enriching corporations.

Agriculture

One does not have to be a farmer to be interested in agricultural news. In fact, what happens on the farms of the nation can and does have a day-to-day effect on the lives of everyone. A prolonged drought that wipes out the corn crop is reflected in the prices on the supermarket shelves. Freezing weather that damages the truck crops can send prices of fresh vegetables skyrocketing. And an extended farm laborer strike might cut the supply of some products completely.

In dozens of ways each day, the news emanating from the nation's farms influences our lives. Well-written, informative farm news should hold the interest of most readers. The local agricultural community can be an important source of news. The county agricultural and home demonstration agents, farm bureaus and other offices of agricultural agencies and associations have long-standing affiliations with hundreds or thousands of individual farm operators, and those offices generally are the primary sources of agricultural news. The reporter must know the officials and the scope of services of those organizations to be effective.

Knowledge of agriculture is also required if the reporter is to explain accurately the how and why of farming to the reader. It is all too easy for a "dude" reporter to make a screamingly funny mistake in writing about planting peas or milking cows. A few such errors will cost a reporter the confidence of both news sources and readers. A reporter from a non-farm background can learn to avoid mistakes through reading and regular visits to farms. A reporter who does not know about farming should not be afraid to ask questions or to look up information. Even reporters with farm experience should refer to books and other publications regularly to keep abreast of the latest developments in the field.

In many areas farm production is seasonal, and the harvesting of a major crop ranks as a major news event.

In Kentucky, where tobacco is a major cash crop, the *Lexington Herald–Leader* took a look at who holds the right to grow tobacco under federal quotas and produced this interesting story at a time when the fight against tobacco by the American Medical Association and others was reaching fever pitch:

> Kentucky doctors own enough tobacco to produce 63 million packs of cigarettes a year.
>
> But they say they don't want you to smoke them.

At a time when volumes of research blame smoking for a growing number of deadly illnesses, more than 300 of Kentucky's 7,000 doctors own the right to grow and sell tobacco, according to a federal database of tobacco quota holders.

The list includes obstetricians, family doctors, rural and urban physicians and even heart and lung specialists.

The rest of the story quotes the doctors who hold tobacco quotas who generally defend their quotas while admitting they were torn about what to do with their tobacco. It also pointed out that the state medical association had argued for non-smoking sections in public areas and pushed the tobacco industry to eliminate advertising that attracts children to smoking, but it did not take a stand on whether owning and selling tobacco creates an ethical conflict for doctors.

Here's a story with a strong agriculture tie even though it isn't about crops or livestock. It's from the Scripps-McClatchy News Service:

STOCKTON—John W. Abel expressed his eternal gratitude after the federal government stepped in to help save his family's Colusa County farm during the Great Depression of the 1930s.

Now that he is gone, he has left Uncle Sam a great big thank-you gift.

In what government officials said is one of the largest single bequests in memory to the United States, Abel has willed the government $2.3 million.

Labor

The labor beat can be one of the most significant of a newspaper's beats, especially in a highly industrialized and unionized area. A community's labor force, which constitutes much of the total population, cuts across the areas of business, industry and agriculture. This makes the job of the labor reporter particularly sensitive, especially in times of labor disputes. A strike against a major advertiser, for example, might present serious financial problems for the newspaper if the advertiser did not like the tone of the stories reporting the strike. The struck firm might seek to influence coverage of the strike by threatening to withdraw its advertising from the newspaper. That does happen, but it is the exception rather than the rule.

The labor force can be organized by crafts or industries or not at all. As a result, covering the labor beat involves developing many sources of news. The general run of labor news offers no more than briefs on elections, routine meetings, social events and the like. But when strikes are threatened or in progress, or contracts are up for renewal, such developments may become front-page news. A labor reporter should make every effort to report the labor-management affairs that are settled without strife just as vigorously as those that threaten or result in conflict. News sources cultivated by the handling of routine stories often become quite valuable during periods of labor strife. Moreover, to develop latent reader interest in labor news, the reporter needs to search for stories and features that are not centered on conflict.

A labor reporter should not be a crusader for labor or a spy for management. A careful reporter does not choose sides. It is important to know the pros and cons of both sides of an issue. For example, a good reporter will be well versed in the role of organized labor in the local community, the structure of labor organizations, the extra benefits resulting from labor union membership (such as pension funds), the salary scales of union as well as non-union laborers and other information important to local workers.

It also is important to have a working knowledge of the major labor laws that affect all workers, as well as those laws that have a direct bearing on local industries. The reporter should know and understand the position of business and industry in any labor dispute. This knowledge is essential if a reporter is to give labor stories depth and interpret labor news accurately for readers of the newspaper.

Labor stories demand careful balance. When writing of strikes and lockouts, for example, a reporter must be objective, giving the facts but not stacking the deck for one side or the other. Even in violent strikes, the reporter should resist the temptation to write them as if they were military warfare. Strike stories should be factual but not inflammatory.

Retraining of workers dislocated by mergers and by companies moving their plants to foreign countries became a major concern of the federal government and labor unions in the late 1990s. Here's a *Wall Street Journal* article about a plan to retrain workers for the trucking industry:

> The Labor Department has pledged $1.2 million to train dislocated workers to drive long-haul trucks.
>
> In part because of the booming economy, the government estimates that an additional 40,000 truckers will be needed over the next two years. "This investment makes sense," Vice President Gore said in announcing the grant.
>
> Classes will be conducted at driver-training centers in Pennsylvania and Tennessee affiliated with the American Trucking Association, an industry group based in Alexandria, Va. Susan Coughlin, director of the ATA's research arm, says driver shortages are trucking firms' biggest problem. Many new drivers quit prematurely because the job takes them away from their families.

Complete Reporting

The most important form of interpretation in reporting the economic life of a community is that which reaches below the surface of events and brings forth significance and trend. Stock market figures, commodity prices, car loadings and other financial data are usually not significant in themselves. Compared with what they were a year ago or last month, however, they may have a meaning and be a prophecy of the future. This does not mean that the reporter should become a forecaster; on the contrary, he or she must be cautious about making forecasts on business conditions because serious consequences could result—stock shifts, sales slumps and the like. Nevertheless, the reporter can point up the trends of the past. Although analyses of business conditions may be the prerogative of "business analysts" or special columnists, the reporter cannot afford to restrict questions to the obvious facts.

Is a factory to be established in the community? What, then, will be its effect on the labor situation, unemployment, housing, taxes and the demands on city utilities and services? No columnist or analyst writing for a wire service can interpret this sort of local story for the citizens. Only the local reporter can provide this service. Complete reporting is expected of the reporter as a public service. Concerning a new city auditorium, a new freeway through the city, a strike at a major industry or the status of retail sales during a recession, the question is not just "What is happening?" but also "What does it mean in the lives of local people?"

Personal finance stories became increasing popular on business pages. Many use syndicated columnists but others have their own columnists. Here's an example of a personal finance column written by Candy McCampbell, personal finance editor of the *Tennessean*, Nashville:

Who's going to save the kids? The ones who are bombarded every hour of every day by ads urging them to spend, whether they need to or not?

Parents, the advice-givers say, should start training their children early, letting them know about shopping lists and budgets, limiting their choice to one item at the store.

Before they start kindergarten children can learn about money, learn to count their money and learn the relative values of money.

The remainder of the column discussed strategies parents could use to teach their children about money and how to use it wisely. The column quoted both local and national sources.

EXERCISES

1. Interview the director of the local office of the Department of Employment Security about the rate of unemployment in the state and in your area. Also contact the human resources office on your campus and ask its director to provide you figures about employment on campus. Write a story based on your findings. Make certain you compare local figures to national figures.

2. Call the finance director of the city in which your college or university is located for an interview. Ask her or him to give you a briefing on the state of the city finances. Write a story on that interview.

3. Most states have a statewide statistical abstract of business and industry. Check with your library, or a Business Research Bureau if one exists on your campus, for a copy. Study it closely and then write a news or feature story on a single industry that is profiled in the statistical abstract.

4. Call the Economics Department in the College of Business at your college or university for the name of a faculty member who is an expert in the state's economy. Ask her or him for an interview and write a story based on that interview.

5. If you live in an agricultural area, contact the local county extension agent for an interview about the general state of farmers in your county and section of the state.

If possible, interview several farmers. Then, write a story based on the information you collect.

6. Write stories using the following notes:
   a. City Councilwoman Mary Johnson
      Asked City Law Department
      To seek a court order
      Forcing The Funeral Store
      A local crematorium
      To remove large billboard
      Near its business
      At 2554 Calle Oche
      That says in giant letters
      "Don't Be A Dirt Sandwich
      Cremate—Only $395.00"
      Johnson says sign is offensive
      "It implies we just dump
      People in the ground"
      Law director says it
      "Probably a matter of free speech"
      But he said he would look into it
      Outdoor sign company
      Owner Tom Barry refused
      To discuss the matter
      William Lohman, owner of
      The Funeral Store
      Did not return phone calls
   b. Efforts to promote
      International trade
      For state's agricultural
      And manufactured products
      A top priority for
      Gov. Ray Price
      He proposes in his budget
      For next fiscal year
      $3.5 million for
      Promoting international trade
      That's up $1 million
      From last year
      Increase will allow
      State Department of
      Industry and Trade
      To hike number of
      Trade representatives
      From 10 to 15
      They will travel
      To dozens of other countries
      Promoting the state's product
      Governor made the announcement

In a speech to State
Chamber of Commerce
c. County Agent Kirk D. Wallace
Reports county's
Strawberry fields are "loaded"
Despite bad weather it's
"Best crop in years"
Fields are so "flush"
Farmers are urging people
To come pick their own
At $2 to $2.50 a pound
Quality is good, size is good
And prices are good
Says grower Buddy McKay
Who operates five U-Pic fields
They will be at peak
This weekend, he said
Weekend also marks opening
Of the annual Strawberry Festival
In nearby Plant City
Berries will be good
For next 10 days, Wallace says
Heavy rains that damage crops
In other parts of the state
Did not hurt crop here

7. Using the following information, write a news story:
   Dr. R. Carlyle Kennard
   Economic Adviser to
   Governor Ray Price
   Spoke at annual meeting of
   Small Business Association
   350 in attendance
   At Civic Center
   Made following comments:

It can't get any better than this.

The nation's economy—and ours in this state—is the best most of us have ever seen. And both state and national surveys show that the public agrees. Nationwide, some 60 percent say the economy is the best they've ever seen. On a state level that number goes to 68 percent.

When we ask people across the state about their economic condition, most tell us things like, "Financially, I'm much better off than at any time in my life."

People have good reason to feel that way. You have to go back to 1965 to get this kind of economic high water mark. That's due to the great performance of the stock market, low unemployment and minimal inflation.

It's true that the people who feel strongest about the economy are more apt to earn more, own more stocks and tend to be older. For example, the greater the household income, the more optimistic respondents in the surveys are about the economy.

Among those with annual income of at least $75,000, 81 percent were bullish on the economy compared to 56 percent earning $20,000 to $30,000.

The older the respondents, the better they rated the economy. Of those 50 and older, more than 73 percent said it was good or excellent compared to 61 percent of 18- to 29-year olds.

Of course, not everyone agrees about the strength of the economy. There are people struggling because of mergers in industries and businesses and some farmers, especially hog farmers, are having a bad time right now. But I anticipate that will turn around soon. But basically, people are looking in their pocketbooks and say they feel pretty good right now.

8. Using these items taken from press releases sent to the business desk by local firms, write a "Business Briefs" column. Keep each item to one or two short paragraphs:
   a. Robert Kollar & Associates
      Public Relations firm
      Specializing in
      Visual Communications
      To buy Filmette
      A local video studio
      For undisclosed price
      Kollar said the acquisition
      "Will allow us to better
      Serve our current customers
      And attract new ones"
      A large video and editing
      Studio will be added to
      The Kollar building at
      1127 Sunset Drive
   b. Big Noise Entertainment
      Management Company announces
      Carlotta Craig, a former
      Member of the singing group
      The Sound Machine
      Has been named director
      Of Artist Development
      She'll work with new artists
   c. Wayne Matusiak
      Owner of Mighty Good bakery
      To move from his tiny
      Home kitchen to a
      Full-service bakery
      In the Green Hills Mall
      He gained fame for his
      Giant cinnamon rolls
      Now he will add cookies
      And European pastries
      And breads in his now
      Take-out-only store
      Which will be open

        6:30 a.m. to 6:30 p.m.
        Monday through Saturday
  d. Free Internet Workshop
        Offered every Saturday
        In May and June
        By John Bailey
        Professor of Technology
        Palmdale Community College
        Workshops are from 10 a.m. to Noon
        To register call
        (656) 822-5043
  e. Judith Dockery
        Promoted to manager
        State Teachers Credit Union
        She's a 29-year-veteran
        Of financial services industry
        Anna Lutz named
        Assistant manager
        She was previously
        A loan officer at
        The credit union

25

Education, Research, Science, Technology

"America is the best half-education country in the world."

Nicholas Murray Butler, the late educator, president of Columbia University and Nobel Peace Prize winner, expressed that opinion decades ago. But if you listen to the resounding chorus of complaints about the poor quality of America's public education today, you might think he had said it just last night on the Larry King television show.

Rarely does a month go by without a new report on poor scholastic test scores, crowded classrooms, crumbling school buildings, unreasonable teacher–student ratios, lack of qualified teachers, serious disciplinary problems, drug use and a shopping list of other problems.

Parents, community leaders, business people and politicians repeatedly call for higher standards and improved quality of instruction in public schools. Improving education became a battle cry in almost every political campaign at local and national levels. Here's the lead on a report on the popularity of education as a campaign issue from *Congressional Quarterly*:

> WASHINGTON—Listen to some of the ideas put forth in the state of the state addresses delivered by the nation's governors this year: It sounds like the agenda at a local PTA meeting.
>
> Across the country, education has climbed to the top of state legislative agendas. And in a year when 36 governorships will be on the ballot, it has become the top political issue as well.
>
> That is as good a gauge as any for assessing the atmosphere. When the top agenda item is schools, it is a good bet that unemployment, crime, inflation and interest rates are all under control.
>
> President Clinton repeatedly called for more classroom teachers and national standard achievement tests for public school students. And the issue of school vouchers kept surfacing regularly.

Increasingly, newspapers put more emphasis on the education beat. Their efforts paid off with important stories about local schools, not just routine coverage of school board meetings. More and more editors and education writers came to realize that the education beat had a strong built-in interest for readers because it involves two things that most people value highly—their children and their money. The cost of education often is the largest item in any local government's budget. In fact, the cost is of special concern because everyone in a community helps pay for public education, whether he or she attends school or has children who attend, through sales or property taxes.

In addition to their educational role, schools are important news sources because they frequently play a major role in the social life of a community. Moreover, the press has a particular interest in schools because they are producing tomorrow's consumers of newspapers.

The criticism of the public schools has made many newspapers rethink their coverage of education. Enrollment figures, bond issues, faculty changes and the fortunes or misfortunes of the athletic teams still form the backbone of school-news coverage. But increased emphasis is being placed on stories that try to help the taxpayer understand what is happening not only in local schools but also across the nation.

Problems in school financing, trends in classroom teaching, changes in graduation requirements, increased standards, labor negotiations with teachers and dozens of other significant problems are being reported with renewed vigor. Newspapers are also showing increased interest in church-related and private schools as well as the trade schools that have developed in many areas.

After California passed a $1 billion measure designed to reduce the number of students in classes, the *San Francisco Examiner* took a look at its impact so its taxpayer–readers would know how successful the effort was. This is the lead on its story written by Julian Guthrie:

> The most costly and popular education reform measure in California history is stirring tension between new groups of haves and have-nots: teachers with small classes and those without.
> As a majority of kindergarten through third-grade teachers in California delight in having classes of 20 or fewer students, their next door neighbors—fourth- and fifth-grade teachers with 30 or more students—are beginning to ask, "What about us?"

The remainder of the story included interviews with teachers, administrators and political leaders about the success as well as the shortcomings of the state's effort to improve schools.

Research and education go together. Persons in the field of education, especially those on the upper levels, seek not only to teach but also, through research, to add new knowledge. Research, of course, is by no means confined to educational institutions. Government agencies, industries, hospitals and clinics and private laboratories sponsor many research programs. A large percentage of those programs, however, are linked to educational institutions, either through special contracts or through the services of educators as consultants. In any event, educational institutions train most if not all of the personnel qualified to operate research programs.

Research is conducted in both scientific and non-scientific fields. Studies by researchers in the basic sciences, medical sciences and engineering often result in scientific breakthroughs that become significant news stories. But equally important is the research being conducted in other fields of knowledge. Studies in the humanities and social sciences, for example, also lead to important news stories. Many newspapers now have writers who cover medicine as well as the latest developments in pure science, the humanities and social science.

Here's the lead on a story about research at the University of Massachusetts that attracted worldwide attention:

> Researchers at the University of Massachusetts said Tuesday they have cloned three genetically engineered calves, harbingers of a bovine baby boom to be used for the mass production of drugs in milk.
>
> The calves, George, Charlie and an unnamed brother, were created through a combination of cloning and genetic engineering—manipulation of the animal's genes so that they can produce foreign proteins.
>
> And there are six more calves waiting to be born.

(USA TODAY)

The education beat cuts across virtually every other subject a newspaper covers: politics, religion, business, courts, sports, race relations, social issues, even lifestyles and fashions. An imaginative reporter can find enterprise stories in all of those areas and more. The list of potential stories beyond routine coverage is endless.

A reporter does not have to be a former schoolteacher or have taken education courses in college to cover education effectively. But he or she must have an understanding of the education system and must keep informed about what is happening in education generally and on the local scene specifically. The education beat cannot be covered from the city room or the school superintendent's office. The education reporter has to be involved daily.

To cover the education beat, the reporter must know the organizational structure of the public and private school systems in the community and the state. Whether it is a single school or a large school system encompassing many schools, the organizational pattern of each will be much the same. At the top is some type of board, elected or appointed, on which membership is generally considered to be a public service. Board members generally serve without pay. The board meets regularly and is responsible for the total operation of the school or the system.

Voters elect or empower the board to employ an individual, usually a professional educator, who serves as the chief administrator (superintendent, president, chancellor, headmaster) of the school or system. Some communities still elect the school superintendent along with school board members, although there is some research that indicates appointed superintendents are more effective than elected ones. From this point on, the functions of the board and the administrator usually are clearly defined.

The board, after consultation with the administrator, normally sets the basic policies for the operation of the school or the system. The board decides on capital-outlay measures and formalizes regulations concerning appointments, retirements, leaves of absence and terminations of faculty and staff. The administrator usually is in complete charge of operating the school or system within the policies set forth by the board and makes recommendations on the appointments, terminations and other matters requiring formal school board action.

Board members are not expected to move into the professionalized area of administration, nor should the administrator extend his or her authority beyond the policies fixed by the board. In actual practice, it does not work that way. Board members often get involved in such matters as teacher assignment, new curricula, student disciplinary matters and other areas on a day-to-day or individual basis.

Many superintendents have been known to "dictate" to boards on a variety of policy issues. The latter is especially true in cities and counties where the superintendent is an elected official. The operation of school systems in such major cities as Baltimore, Boston, Chicago, Minneapolis, Philadelphia, St. Louis, Washington, D.C., and San Francisco and of those in dozens of smaller cities has been jeopardized because of disputes between board members and superintendents that have grown out of the wide range of difficulties facing the schools—squeezed budgets, rising teacher militancy, increased crime in the schools and, in some areas, race problems.

The top organizational officials, as well as the subordinate ones (supervisors, principals, directors, department heads), are vitally important to the operation of a school or an educational system, but more important is the teacher–student relationship. Everything should be done for the purpose of getting the teacher and the student together, giving them adequate facilities for the learning process, with the hope that the student will absorb the desire for learning as well as the knowledge that the teacher can transmit. Presumably, if the organization is efficient and effective at the top levels, it will achieve those goals at the teacher–student level. It does not always work that way, however, and it is essential that the education reporter be aware of that fact.

However, cooperation between superintendents and boards are the rule not the exception as this story from the *Chattanooga Times* shows:

> Hamilton County Board of Education members took a detailed look at this year's school budget during a work session Thursday.
> Superintendent Jess Register and his financial staff walked board members through the 120-page, line-item budget they use to manage the district day-to-day.

Scope of Coverage

The education reporter usually is expected to cover activities at all levels of the school system from the policy-making boards to the teachers in the classrooms.

Large or small, the education beat offers the opportunity for many routine stories as well as major news breaks, features and interpretative pieces. Routine stories may be written about subjects such as:

1. Scheduled dates—opening and closing, holidays
2. Enrollments—statistics, comparisons, trends
3. Honors—citations of students and faculty
4. Changes in curricula—courses added and dropped
5. Commencements—speakers, graduating students
6. Personnel changes—appointments, resignations, retirements
7. Board meetings—policies, budgets, capital-outlay plans
8. Activities of affiliated organizations—education associations, parent–teacher chapters, "booster" groups, alumni.

Major stories develop in such areas as teacher strikes, academic freedom of teachers, racial strife, crime in the schools, rejection of bond issues by taxpayers and a long list of other troubles that often beset school systems. Although these are important stories and generally rate the front page, there are numerous other major interpretative and feature articles that can come out of the schools. The alert reporter will be looking for them constantly.

Here are some examples of school stories covering a wide range of subjects:

TALLAHASSEE—High school students would be required to study algebra, chemistry and biology and take fewer electives under a bill that moved Monday through the Senate Education committee.

"We've got to demand more from our students in an attempt to get them to do better," said the bill's sponsor, Sen. Bill Turner, D–Miami Shores. "The more you demand from students, the better they do."

(The *Miami Herald*)

Most days, Naomi Franklin and Lidia Jimenes and Jiao Liang are standing in front of the classroom teaching, as they have for years. But nights or weekends, they are the ones sitting at the desks, taking remedial classes to prepare for the state exam for a teaching license, which they have failed again and again and again.

Now, their jobs are on the line.

(The *New York Times*)

Tennessee's state colleges and universities will need more than $1 billion next year for operating and capital expenses, officials say.

The Tennessee Higher Education Commission considered higher education funding for the next fiscal year at its quarterly meeting here today. The budget included $1.46 billion in operating expenses; $1.54 billion for capital outlay projects; and $16.6 million of capital maintenance at the state's higher education institutions.

(*Nashville Banner*)

Schools often are involved in lawsuits, as these story leads show:

> COVINGTON, Ky.—Two 17-year-old high school students who say they were denied membership in the National Honor Society because they were pregnant are planning to sue their schoolboard in Federal court here on grounds of sexual discrimination.
>
> (The *New York Times*)

> High school students in Lee County can still learn about the Bible, but it will no longer be taught as history.
> The School Board voted to settle a lawsuit by dropping a controversial class, History of the Old Testament, and replace it with a secular version called Introduction to the Bible. The new class, like the old one, is an elective .
> Parents opposing the Bible classes sued in December. In January, U.S. District Judge Elizabeth Kovachevich issued an injunction against the New Testament class, and ordered the schools to videotape the Old Testament classes.
>
> (Associated Press)

> WEST PALM BEACH—(AP)—A high school freshman forced to endure hours in the "Slacker's Box"—a 3-foot by 4-foot space under a classroom sink—has filed a federal lawsuit against the teacher who put him there.

A problem facing all education reporters involves the cooperation of board members and the school officials with the press. School board members and officials are extremely sensitive to criticism from the media or the community. They are equally sensitive when the press reports (as it should) on major problems such as student unrest. Boards frequently meet in private to conduct "public" business, and school officials sometimes decline to provide information needed for a reporter to write a balanced story.

However, as noted earlier, in almost all states there are open-meetings laws and open-records laws on which reporters can rely to obtain their information if officials are uncooperative and if the newspaper elects to follow that course. Ideally, school officials and the press should cooperate in an effort to inform the public and improve the cause of education.

Story Forms

Education stories range from the one-feature brief to the multi-feature report on a significant board meeting. In between can be found all story forms, including human-interest stories on students and teachers and feature articles on school activities.

Covering Research and Science

Newspeople are having difficulty keeping up with the new knowledge pouring out of the millions of research projects and studies being conducted by scientists and other scholars. These developments push the boundaries of man's knowledge to new heights almost daily. The public is not always aware of these advancements because the changes are frequently so specialized that it is difficult if not completely impossible for a layperson to understand them. As long as science and scholarship remain enshrined in technical language, society cannot understand them fully. They must be interpreted to the people, reduced to terms laypeople and legislators can comprehend.

Newspapers have become increasingly aware of their responsibility not only to keep the public informed about scientific developments but also to interpret their implications for the public. That is why a number of newspapers have employed reporters specially trained in science and medicine who can communicate with scientists almost as equals and can then translate new developments accurately and clearly for the reader.

The science editor or the reporter covering research has problems and responsibilities that must be understood and mastered. Reporting a research project—giving the public an understandable explanation of research findings—is quite often an assignment unlike any other given a journalist. The reporter often faces three significant challenges: first, the researcher (or researchers); second, the research project; third, writing an accurate and interesting interpretation of the project for the public. Any one of these can become a difficult experience for a reporter.

The Researcher

In interviewing a researcher, the reporter must keep in mind that the subject of the interview may not be eager for, or even mildly interested in, newspaper publicity. Often a researcher prefers to present his or her finding in a scientific publication or at a scientific gathering. Because scientific news has been poorly handled in the past, a researcher may be afraid of both inaccuracies and sensationalism in the newspaper account. Having spent days or months on a carefully worded paragraph, the researcher may be averse to having an article slashed to bits in a three-minute effort by a reporter to emphasize an "interesting" feature.

Dullness, often attached to preciseness, is a researcher's prerogative. Frequently, a researcher does not see and may be indifferent to the utility or human-interest aspects of a project. Consequently, the researcher may have no sympathy whatsoever for the reporter's problem in writing the story for the general public.

A researcher may even be antagonistic toward publicity. A newspaper article on a particular project will mean little if anything to the researcher's professional career. In fact, it might have negative effects. The researcher might be branded as a publicity hound, especially by a fellow scientist who might be nearing a breakthrough in the same area. He or she might be hounded by well-meaning people as well as kooks who phone, write or even come in person seeking help. For that reason medical researchers generally are extremely careful about announcing breakthroughs in the mass media. Usually, they make their reports in a major medical journal. Fortunately, as newspapers have made a serious effort to improve science writing, many leading scientists have become more willing to share their findings with the public. They realize that they have an obligation to do so just as a newspaper has a responsibility to report scientific discoveries carefully and accurately.

Obviously, then, the reporter's first task is to establish a good relationship with the researcher, winning enough confidence for at least a chance to show a sincere desire for accurate interpretation. When handling a scientific story, a reporter should never guess. At the risk of delaying a story, the reporter has the responsibility to make certain that the story is accurate. When in doubt about any aspect of a story, the reporter must check back with the original source and any additional sources available in the scientific community.

Most major institutions and organizations have men and women on their public relations staffs to assist reporters in their efforts to work with scientists and researchers. Public relations people can be a valuable asset, but the reporter should not rely on them alone for information. The major source always has to be the man or woman who conducted the original research.

Here's the start of a story in which the professionals cooperated fully with the reporter. It was written by Stephen Smith for the *Miami Herald*:

> On a good day, Tori Cameron's skin blisters in a half dozen spots. Then there are the bad days, when 30, 40, even 50 welts rise from head to toe on the 8-week-old infant, her body turning on itself, raw wounds cast in shades of red and black.
>
> So her Miami doctors decided to try something that once was possible only in the minds of science-fiction writers. They're giving the Broward baby a new suit of artificial skin, piecing it together with three-inch swatches of bio-engineered material that look for all the world like skinny slices of mozzarella.
>
> It is the first time anywhere that doctors have used the bioengineered substance to replace the diseased skin of a child born with the condition threatening Tori's life.

The remainder of the story included interviews with her doctors and other scientists who have studied the disease called epidermolysis bullosa and detailed the child's first difficult eight weeks of life.

The Research Project

A reporter should recognize the two broad types of research: (1) basic or fundamental research and (2) practical or utilitarian research. Further, it is important to understand that a basic research project may be the predecessor of valuable practical research, even though this might not be immediately apparent to the reporter.

Many projects that may have appeared on the surface to be pointless, even frivolous, have proved to have enormous consequence. Sir Alexander Fleming's early experiments with molds eventually led to the wonder drug penicillin. A research project to study aggression in apes provided important data on aggression in humans and helped the National Aeronautics and Space Administration in the selection of astronauts for the space program. If a reporter or the public does not understand the value of a basic research project, that does not make the project any less justified. In most instances, neither the average reporter nor the general public is competent to judge its value.

Many thousands of research projects, basic and practical, are being conducted at considerable cost to the people of the nation through the National Science Foundation and other federal and state agencies. Some will turn out as failures, but others will pay spectacular practical dividends that make the total cost of research look small indeed.

It is fairly easy to report a project dealing with an improvement in the rate of emission of pollutants from automobiles by the use of a new catalytic converter. But what can be done, for example, with a project "concerned with the synthesis and biochemical evaluation of drugs which influence psychological processes through their effects upon the central nervous system"? The answer calls for interpretative skill.

Interpretation of the Research Project

Although dullness is the researcher's prerogative, it is the reporter's enemy. Given the task of writing an interesting story, the reporter must seek to humanize the research project, spelling out for the reader what it means in clear, careful and accurate words. The reporter must find out what the discovery or theory means or may mean eventually to the average person and then provide the details necessary to give the layperson a clear picture of the research.

Early on, a reporter who starts writing research and scientific stories must develop a dictionary of the scientific or professional words used by the researchers in the field being covered. It is also necessary to work with researchers to develop accurate definitions or synonyms for scientific words that an average reader will understand. Far too many reporters—not only those covering science but also those covering other professional fields—fall into the trap of writing in professional jargon and not in the language of the general reader.

The keys to research projects that are designed to fill specific practical needs are ready-made, but the secrets of many basic projects are not easily unlocked. For basic research the reporter must interpret the nature and findings of the project without stretching facts in an attempt to indicate practical value. The interpretation can perhaps explain that a project reveals knowledge that may contribute to the solution of practical problems, but this must be done with extreme caution. There is a world of difference, for example, in what is being said in the following two paragraphs:

> The reaction of cells to certain acids manufactured by the human body is being studied by Dr. A. B. Count, Southeastern University zoology professor, who hopes his findings will contribute basic knowledge to science's fight against cancer.

> A cure for cancer is being sought by Dr. A. B. Count, Southeastern University zoology professor, in studying the reaction of cells to certain acids manufactured by the human body.

If the first paragraph is accurate, no one can blame Dr. Count for becoming furious with the reporter who takes the liberty of "interpreting" the basic research project as is done in the second paragraph. As a researcher who demands facts and accuracy, he cannot shrug off such "sensationalized" reporting. He considers such extravagant claims as damaging to his professional career, and he remembers this the next time a reporter approaches him for a story.

Every effort should be made—with the researcher's help—to inform readers of any practical use of a research project. However, the reporter must recognize that there are times when no practical angle is available. This may be true in the case of pure basic research being performed solely for the purpose of finding new knowledge. Sometimes that new knowledge or the search for it is itself interesting enough to give the reporter the key to a story. Other times, the subject of the research may be so complicated and so far from public interest that the reporter must abandon the story.

In gathering information to interpret a research story, the reporter must not be afraid to ask questions. The best rule of thumb is: "If you don't know, ask." To write an accurate story, the reporter must have a clear understanding of what he or she is attempting to explain. It is imperative that a reporter check with the researcher before writing the story to make certain that his or her interpretation of the facts is accurate.

One of the major criticisms researchers and scientists have of the press is the tendency of some reporters to want a quick, five-minute explanation of a project that has taken five years to develop. Reporters writing a story on a scientific development or a research project must allow time to conduct a thorough and careful interview so that there can be no misunderstanding of the information collected. Careful, thoughtful, accurate research stories cannot be written in a few minutes. They often require hours, even days, of multiple interviews.

Story Forms

Increasing numbers of newspapers are following the lead of the *New York Times*, the *Boston Globe* and other metropolitan dailies and establishing special sections each week devoted to science, research, medicine and technology. In addition, the wire services regularly distribute news stories dealing with major scientific topics, and syndicates distribute to the daily press articles from a number of specialized magazines such as *Prevention* and *Longevity*.

A review of these stories will show that all the story forms discussed earlier are used in writing about research. As a general rule, if the research has significant practical value or is the first report of a major breakthrough, the straight-news form is used. As practical value diminishes, reporters tend to use the feature-story form to tell the story.

These leads illustrate the scope of research, science and medical stories that appear in newspapers regularly:

ORLANDO, Fla.—What does it cost to save a life? About $2 per life per year, says a study out today.

Thanks to a wonder drug called aspirin.

Rohit Arora of Columbia University and his colleagues reported Tuesday that aspirin now rescues 6,665 heart attack sufferers a year. They say the drug could benefit 318,750 others for just $2 each annually.

(USA TODAY)

Scientists may have found a simple way to take the sting out of vaccinations.

Research on mice suggests that vaccines spread on the skin can be effective against diseases as well as reduce the risk of spreading disease through contaminated needles in developing countries.

"It's conceivable one could just wear a Band-Aid or a patch overnight," said Dr. Gregory Glenn, scientific director of the Iomal Corporation of Washington and an author of the report in today's issue of the journal *Nature*.

(Associated Press)

ANAHEIM, Calif.—Scientists say they're ready to create life from scratch in a laboratory.

A project to create a bacterial cell from inanimate chemicals for the first time will go ahead as soon as it is passed by an ethics committee.

Craig Venter, a pioneer of gene discovery, said molecular biology and genetics had advanced enough to take what would be a momentous step.

(Financial Times)

A 7,000-square-mile dead zone in the Gulf of Mexico caused by the runoff of fertilizer is getting worse and the only solution may be to change farming practices throughout the Corn Belt, experts say.

Every spring and summer, nitrogen from agricultural fertilizer washes down the Mississippi River and into the northern Gulf of Mexico. The nutrient-rich waters trigger a bloom of algae which strips the water of oxygen.

Researchers attending the national meeting of American Association for Advancement of Science conference over the weekend said . . .

(Associated Press)

For a century, chemists doubted that such a substance could exist, but scientists at an Air Force laboratory have created a freakish form of nitrogen believed to be one of the most violently explosive substances ever made.

A team of chemists headed by Dr. Karl O. Christe and Dr. William W. Wilson at the Air Force Research Laboratory at Edwards Air Force Base, Calif., reported their achievement at a recent meeting of the American Chemical Society.

(The *New York Times*)

Medicine

Most newspapers have dramatically increased their coverage of medical news. Many have weekly medical and science sections such as the *New York Science*

Times on Tuesday, which covers both medical and scientific news. The acquired immunodeficiency syndrome (AIDS) epidemic originally created medical, ethical and legal challenges for newspapers.

However, over the years when AIDS was no longer labeled the "gay" disease and had spread to other groups, in particular intravenous drug users, newspapers reported the story aggressively. They still do.

But they also pursue other medical stories with the same diligence. Stories such as tobacco-related illnesses; the debate over a national health care plan; dramatic advances in transplant techniques; the ongoing battle to conquer cancer; the development of new drugs for everything from strokes to sexual dysfunction; and dozens of other exciting medical advances.

Here are several medical story leads:

WASHINGTON, March 12—For the first time since the 1930s, the number of new cancer cases in the United States is declining, Federal officials said today in announcing a sharp reversal in the incidence of diseases that kill more than 1,500 Americans each day.

Deaths from cancer are also dropping, continuing a trend that was first reported in November 1996.

(The *New York Times*)

Doctors for the first time have grown new blood vessels to shunt blood past heart patients' blocked coronary arteries without surgery, says a report out today.

Researchers at Fulda Medical Center in Germany report in the journal *Cardiology* that they triggered the growth of the new blood vessels using a genetically engineered human growth factor called GFG-1.

(*USA TODAY*)

The "window of opportunity" for stopping a stroke has just gotten bigger, researchers report.

To be effective, conventional clot-busting drugs must be given within three hours after the onset of stroke symptoms. Few patients get to the hospital in time for them to work.

Now a new drug, tested at more than 50 centers, including Nashville's Centennial Medical Center, can prevent the devastating consequences of stroke in many patients when given up to six hours after symptoms begin.

Findings were presented yesterday during an international stroke conference at Opryland Hotel attended by 1,700 doctors and scientists.

(The *Tennessean,* Nashville)

CHICAGO, Jan. 31—The riddle of the origin of the AIDS virus has apparently been solved, according to an international team of scientists who reported today that they had traced its roots to a related virus in a subspecies of chimpanzee in Africa.

(The *New York Times*)

FIGURE 25.1 The *San Jose Mercury News* devotes an entire section each week to Science and Technology. This section featured the marine research laboratories at Monterey Bay.

(Reprinted with permission of the *San Jose Mercury News*.)

Technology

The rapid advances of technology, especially computer technology, began a major news story in the last half of the 1990s. While the *San Jose Mercury News* has long covered the computer industry, which developed in Silicone Valley, with stories on its front page, in its business section and in a special computer section each week, most major papers didn't begin to devote space to the advances in technology until more recently. The development of the Internet and its impact on business, industry, education and life in general became a major news story. Many newspapers created a separate beat to cover technology and developed special sections devoted to it.

Papers from the size of the *New York Times*, with its special "Circuits" section Thursdays, and *USA TODAY*, with special sections such as its "The Digital Frontier," to smaller papers like the *San Luis Obispo Tribune's* "Personal Tech" section have recognized the importance of computer technology and are reporting on it vigorously.

Here are two technology story leads:

A new search engine is tailored to help students from kindergarten through high school do their homework. The site, www.searchopolis.com, includes databases on sites in various school-related categories, like history, math, science and social studies.

The site, created by two Internet content developers, Look Smart of San Francisco, and N2H2, of Seattle, also includes a reward for homework well done: television listings.

(The *New York Times*)

Shoppers increasingly are turning to the Web for a painless shopping experience. They're drawn by the chance to browse among millions of options—and maybe pick up a bargain or two in the process.

And sellers, eager to test their entrepreneurial instincts or to find customers they might not ordinarily reach with traditional businesses, are venturing on-line and setting up their own Web sites or storefronts in cybermalls.

(*USA TODAY*)

The Internet has become a major research tool for journalists. Unfortunately, a reporter can waste a lot of time searching the Internet for information. Alan Schlein, a Washington-based researcher for several newspapers and networks, recommended in an issue of *Quill* that before reporters start a computer search, they ask these five W questions: WHO is the research about. Subjects? Sources? WHAT type of information do I need? Text? Public record? WHEN? The Internet is a great short-term reference, but useless for historical searches. WHERE are you going? Where have you already looked? WHY are you searching? For a single fact, or for general background? And, HOW much information do you need?

He and ABC PrimeTime Live producer Olive Talley cited the Clinton–Lewinsky coverage as an example of combining electronic and shoe-leather searches. The Internet revealed that former White House intern Monica Lewin-

FIGURE 25.2 USA TODAY is one of the leading newspapers in the nation in coverage of technology and its impact on society. This front page from a special section of the Digital Frontier is one example of their excellent regular coverage of the subject.

sky's parents had been divorced in Los Angeles. Courthouse reporters used this to unearth details about the family's lifestyle.

Schlein's web site—www.deadline.on-line.comm—provides many tips for reporters, including how to find phone numbers, set up a personal information "tracker," and use news groups to locate sources.

A number of other Internet discussion lists offer reporters an opportunity to talk to each other and seek support and information on-line. The two most popular are SPJ-L, which is affiliated loosely with the Society of Professional Journalists; and IRE-L, a service of the Investigative Reporters and Editors, Inc. In response to a question from a list member on how to find sources on a specific topic, for example, fellow members generously respond with suggestions.

Some other more specialized journalism discussion lists (complied by the *Columbia Journalism Review*) include: CARR-L (Computer-Assisted Reporting and Research) Copyediting-L; NICAR-L, similar to CARR-L; Online-News/Online Writing; CCR-L, deals with crime and court reporting; FOI 1-L, devoted to Freedom of Information questions; JOURNET-L, aimed at journalism professors; and YNGRPTR, for journalists just starting their careers.

EXERCISES

1. If there is a College of Education on your campus, interview the dean about her or his views on the state of public education. What's good about it? What's bad? Are the critics right or simply ill-informed? Write a story on that interview.

2. Interview the director of finance for your local public school system about the annual budget. Find out the ratio of how much money is spent on actual classroom teaching compared to administration and how much support comes from the state among other issues. Write a story on that interview.

3. Arrange through the school superintendent's office to spend a day in a school where student scores on standard achievement tests are the highest in the system and a school where student scores are low on those tests. Write a story comparing the two schools.

4. Contact the president of the Parent–Teacher Organization at several schools in your area and interview them about the contribution their organizations make to the schools in money and in volunteer work. Write a story based on the facts you collect.

5. Write news stories for the next day's newspaper using the following notes:
   a. Jordan Ragsdale, senior at
      William Blount High School
      In Jefferson City
      Took American College Test
      A standard college entrance exam
      Scores a perfect 36
      Only one of 23 students
      Nationwide with perfect score
      Only student in state

To make a perfect score
Perfect score means
Only two questions missed
Math Teacher Janine Jennings
Called him "brilliant"
"A good, good soul"
He also took the other
College entrance exam
Scholastic Assessment Test
And scored 1,580 out of 1,600
His only comment
"I'm pleased"

b. 200 students at
George Washington High School
Required emergency treatment
For nausea, diarrhea and stomach cramps
After eating lunch in
School cafeteria yesterday
Some students blamed the hot dogs
Others said it was a
"mystery meat" patty
"I should know better than
To eat anything hidden
Under thick gravy"
Senior Don Campbell said
Dr. Eleni Sadaka, medical director
County Health Department
Said her lab is analyzing
Food and water samples
Said the outbreak was
Food poisoning of light variety
Of short duration
Hits one day, gone the next
Schools officials have ordered
Cafeteria closed for
Complete sanitation
Students will be permitted
To go off-campus for
Lunch the rest of the week

c. Attorney L. John Tonti
Said he plans to sue
The state in his ongoing
Battle for equal pay for
All teachers across the state
Claims in poor counties
Teachers are paid up to
$17,000 less than those
Teaching in urban schools
He told House Education Committee

The problem is in how sales taxes
Are distributed to counties
He wants legislature
To order sales taxes
Distributed to counties
By student population
Instead of letting
Counties keep all
Sales taxes they collect
Since rural counties have
Fewer tax-generating businesses
His proposal would mean
Loss of revenue for six
Largest counties in state
He pointed out that under
Current tax distribution
Marion County teachers
Paid an average of $11,000
More than those in
Rural Jackson County and
$9,500 more than those in
Hancock County
Education committee members
Said they'd study his proposal

6. Attend a meeting of your local city or county school board. Write a story about the meeting and turn it in the next morning with your notes.

7. Interview the county health director about the kind of medical services the county provides for the poor and indigent. Write a story on that interview.

8. Most colleges and universities publish a report on the research done annually by faculty members. Check with the public relations office on your campus to see if such a report exists. If so, select one research project listed, interview the faculty member who conducted the research, and write a story about it. Make certain to include an overall view of the kinds of research being done on campus and the amount of research dollars being generated.

9. A new post called "director of technological services" has been added at many colleges and universities. Find out if someone on your campus holds that or a similar post. If so, interview her or him to find out the kinds of technological services available on campus.

10. If your college or university has a web site, click on it and analyze what's there and then write a short feature story on what students will find if they go to that web site.

11. Often a college or university has a research hospital or medical center. If there is one in your area, contact the doctor who serves as its director and do an interview with him about the kinds of research being done by staff members. Write a story based on the information you collect.

12. If your local daily has a reporter assigned full-time as a science or medical writer, invite her or him to class to discuss techniques used in covering science, medicine and research.

13. Write a 90-second newscast based on the notes in Exercise 5.

CHAPTER

26 Religion and Philanthropy

"If you look at recent news coverage, you could come to the same conclusion that one religion editor did when she said, 'God is hot right now,'" religion writer Steve Rabey told a writer's symposium sponsored by the San Diego Professional Chapter of the Society of Professional Journalists.

Stories about people's faiths and beliefs are of increasing interest in newspapers, even though there are fewer than 100 fulltime religion writers in U.S. newspapers, according to Rabey. He is former religion editor of the *Gazette Telegraph* in Colorado Springs, Col., a city that is headquarters to about 90 national and international religious groups.

Although many newspapers do collect news of religion on a single page either Friday or Saturday, a careful review of many others shows that religion has nearly equal news status with education, business, health and occasionally sports. And why not? After all, more people are in church on any given Sunday than attend all sports events put together during a whole month.

Some newspapers such as the *Tennessean* in Nashville carry a local religion story almost every day and place stories about religion throughout the paper as the individual story merits. Often such stories merit being on the front page as leaders of religious denominations and their followers engage in spirited and occasionally violent debate over nuclear arms and chemical warfare, abortion and euthanasia, genetic tinkering and even American foreign policy in Latin America and the Middle East.

More and more, newspapers are analyzing trends and movements ranging from the rise in popularity of Eastern religions in the West and the continuing battle over women's becoming priests to debate over ordination of homosexuals in several denominations. Those stories might compete successfully for front-page space because they often involve conflict. That conflict is the news peg, but, more than that, it sharpens the issues and makes visible the important underlying questions and issues.

This example, by Andy Newman of the *New York Times,* is one type of story about religion that is certain to rate front page across the nation:

SOMERVILLE, N.J., Nov. 9—Eleanor Boyer missed 7:30 mass this morning. Some of her old friends at the Church of the Immaculate Conception were worried about her.

"She wasn't here yesterday, either," said Nino Cavallero, 77. "She's all caught up in that lottery stuff. For her to miss Mass yesterday and today, you know darn well she's upset."

But just before 9 o'clock Mass started, Ms. Boyer, an indomitable 72-year-old woman in a mustard velour cap with a gray raincoat, strode into the Roman Catholic church, stole a quick hug from her pastor, Msgr. J. Nevin Kennedy, and turned to face the wall of flashbulbs and television cameras to explain her absence.

"My car's in the shop," said the woman who—for the time being is a millionaire eight times over. "I had to get a ride with somebody. Now that's enough, all right? I want to pray a little bit."

The story went on to explain how Ms. Boyer had won a lump sum of $11.8 million, before taxes, in the New Jersey lottery and gave half of it to her church and the rest to the town rescue squad, the volunteer fire department and some other groups that serve the town she grew up in.

A visit to the United States by the Pope rates front page coverage in many newspapers. For example, when Pope John Paul II visited Mexico and then St. Louis, Missouri, his trip was covered by several hundred reporters and religion writers. The day he arrived in St. Louis, the *Post–Dispatch* published a 14-page special section devoted to him. It included everything from a current biography of him to a story on his tailor. But there were also stories on Catholicism's history in St. Louis.

Other religion related stories often make the front page also. Occasionally, they are about an unusual religious group such as one about a Taiwanese group whose members moved to Texas and whose leader predicted that "At 10 a.m. on March 31, 1998, God shall make His appearance in the Holy Land of the Kingdom of God: 3512 Ridgedale Dr., Garland, TX 75041, U.S.A." God did not show up that day, and the group left Garland.

Prominent clergy who fall from grace so to speak often find their missteps on the front pages. Here's an example from the *Miami Herald*:

> The Rev. Henry J. Lyons, embattled leader of one of the nation's largest religious groups, was charged Wednesday with transgressions generally associated with mobsters rather than clergymen: racketeering and grand theft.
>
> State prosecutors charged Lyons, 55, with engaging in a "systematic" scheme to steal at least $300,000 from several corporations and organizations—including the Anti-Defamation League, a Jewish group.
>
> Lyons is president of the National Baptist Convention, USA, which claims 8.5 million members and calls itself the largest black religious group in the nation . . .

The rest of the story detailed the charges against the minister and detailed his lavish and somewhat unorthodox lifestyle.

Of course, a general circulation newspaper should advocate no religion but should be a channel of communications for all religions. Freedom of religion, like freedom of the press, is protected by the Bill of Rights of the United States Constitution, and the press must recognize both the place of religion and the right of religious choice in its columns.

Although the proportion will vary from community to community, a conservative estimate is that substantially more than half the people served by a newspaper are members of a church, mosque or synagogue. News of religion, then, should have many potential readers. Even though religious institutions have a large total membership, the news interest of an individual member is, first, in his or her own church; second, in the denomination; then, to a milder degree, in other churches. Sometimes churches are competitive to the point that publicity given to one may stir up envy in the members of others—even of the same denomination. Religion news must therefore be broad enough in denominations, diverse enough in the same denominations and selective enough in the newsworthiness of materials that readers will recognize the stories on religious activities as solid news rather than puffery or press agentry in favor of a particular minister, church or denomination.

As noted earlier, many newspapers publish a weekly page or special section devoted largely to news of religion in the community, appearing generally on Friday or Saturday. A member of the staff may hold the title of religion editor or church editor (often in addition to other duties), and it is his or her job to gather and write the material for this page or section. Much of the material comes by the way of press releases or telephone calls from ministers or persons acting in a public relations capacity for a church or religious organization. As a general rule, the news stories appearing on this page or in this section would not be classified as major news stories dealing with religion.

A hotly contested pastor-vs.-a-faction-of-the-congregation controversy, however, may be reported on the front page. A split in a major congregation, especially if it lands in the courts; the filing for divorce by a popular minister; or the leaving of the church by a local priest or nun to get married are stories that almost surely will get front-page play. News sources cultivated by the religion editor in handling routine stories often prove valuable in gathering information when such special stories develop.

The religion reporter must learn the organizational patterns of the churches covered, for the sources of news on religion include church-governing officials as well as local churches. But the reporter must have outside sources as well. Church leaders frequently are unwilling to discuss controversial issues with the press. Church organization varies widely among the different denominations. Some are completely independent, selecting their own ministers and setting up their own programs. At the other extreme, some local churches are under the strong control of a central governing body that assigns ministers to the various churches and also has a strong influence on the local program of each church.

The program of a church encompasses many activities in addition to worship services and Sunday schools. It may also include the sponsorship of such projects as foreign or domestic missionary work, local relief projects, kindergartens, grade and high schools and colleges and universities. It is not uncommon for religious leaders and their congregations to be involved in very controversial moral, social and political issues in a planned and organized way. Such activities always make news, whether they are in the "Religion" section, in the "Education" section, or on the front page or other sections for special news stories.

The Religion Section or Church Page

Newspapers that carry a regular page or section on religion should use a systematic plan of compiling news for that section. Church officials should be informed that they must submit materials for the section by a specific deadline; this puts the burden of getting publicity on the churches and at the same time protects the religion editor from the criticism of members whose churches are not mentioned in the news. Some highly newsworthy stories can often be developed from materials submitted by the churches, but for the most part these handouts must be condensed into one- or two-paragraph stories, if used at all. On the other hand, the reporter might have to get additional information to develop the potentially better stories than are submitted.

A religion editor or reporter takes pride in the assignment and considers the news on religion to be as important as much of the other news in a given edition. If the Religion section reflects accurately the community's religious or moral tone, it can be a strong influence on the life of the community. To do an effective job, the religion reporter must make the page or section more than just a bulletin board compiled from church press releases.

Like many other sections of a newspaper, the religion pages have to be planned in advance. The seasonal stories are obvious—Christmas, Easter and the like—but a good reporter will develop significant news and feature stories on the most important trends in the religious life of the community as well as on the most newsworthy national and international developments and how they affect local churches. That is why it is important for the religion reporter, like the reporter in any other specialized field, to be constantly aware of what is happening in the field of religion. Current trends or controversies frequently can be localized into significant stories.

The following are some subjects and types of stories that the reporter may develop from materials submitted by the churches and from other sources:

1. Regular worship services (some newspapers publish a weekly listing of church services)

2. Sermons—if unusual

3. New buildings or other facilities

4. Changes in church personnel

5. Special events and campaigns—evangelistic efforts, fund-raising drives for worthy causes, attendance promotions

6. New policies of local church or denominational groups.

7. Meetings of denominational groups, ministerial associations and lay groups

8. Human-interest feature stories—on unusual church members, historical anniversaries, retiring pastors, interesting projects of Sunday school classes, work of missionaries.

The following examples are typical of stories often found on religion pages in newspapers:

> After 7½ years of leading Bethel Temple Assembly of God to new heights both spiritually and physically, the Rev. Steve Allen has resigned as pastor of the church to shepherd a flock near Nashville.

> Highland Park Baptist Church will celebrate its 100th anniversary on Sunday with State Rep. David Copeland and Judge Steve Bevil as special guests.
> Dr. J.R. Faulkner, pastor, will speak on "Where Do We Go From Here?" during the 10:50 a.m. service.

> Each United Methodist Church in the nation has been asked to read a pastoral letter from the Council of Bishops Sunday. The letter seeks to have each church member join the bishops in fasting, in prayer and in helping the denomination become more vital.
> In part, the letter seeks to end the denomination's self-termed "spiritual malaise" and reverse a 22-year decline in membership.

> Each Sunday at 11 a.m., prime time for U.S. Christian church services, a handful of Vietnamese Buddhists begin their weekly chanting in a house near Grant Park.
> In Vietnam, services are held three times a month on a lunar calendar, said Phong V. Le, a temple secretary. "That's hard to do here."
> By scheduling the traditional Buddhist worship at the Chua Quang-Minh Temple according to American custom, its leaders are preserving the culture of the old country while adapting to life in the new.

Here's how Francis Meeker, then religion editor at the *Nashville Banner*, reported a convention in which conservatives were pitted against liberals for control of the Tennessee Baptist Convention:

> JACKSON—Leadership, not conquering power, will be the mark of his presidency, says the new conservative-backed head of the Tennessee Baptist Convention.
> The Rev. Doug Sager of Knoxville defeated moderate-supported Rev. Earl Wilson, also a Knoxville pastor, Tuesday night in a vote of 968–850 for the presidency of the convention that represents about one million Tennessee Baptists.

The story went on to detail that there had been a decade-long battle between conservatives and moderates within the denomination over theological issues and support of Baptist colleges.

Here are the leads on several stories that deal with broader topics involving religion that do not fit the routine church-story category and were used in the regular news sections of papers:

> On a warm Saturday evening, 17 gays and lesbians sit in a small chapel in Westwood and sing a Catholic hymn called "Be Not Afraid." The lyrics tell of "crossing a barren desert" and "wicked men who insult and hate you."
>
> There is a deliberate poignancy here, as the song and voices echo off the rafters.
>
> In the eyes of the Roman Catholic church, these men and women are infidels—spurned because their active gay lifestyle is regarded as a sin. Although they have not been excommunicated, they pray alone, without a priest to lead them. Except for the grace of another religion's pastor, they would not even have a place to worship.
>
> In 1989, Archbishop Roger M. Mahony ordered priests in the vast Los Angeles Archdiocese to stop saying Mass for members of Dignity/Westside and two other local chapters of the 21-year-old national organization for gay Catholics.
>
> Mahony's decision was a major defeat for the beleaguered Dignity, with 84 chapters and 4,200 members nationwide, for the decision signaled agreement with most other U.S. bishops.

The remainder of the story, which was written by Hank Stuever for the *Los Angeles Times*, described the service and the struggle gay Catholics have with recognition and acceptance from their church.

> NEW YORK—(AP)—Moslems, long isolated from America's religious mainstream have started edging into it.
>
> An initial step into working collaboration with Christians and Jews came last week as national Islamic representatives joined a major interfaith operation, Religion in American Life.
>
> Dawud Assad, president of the Council of Mosques of the United States, said that in taking the step, "we look forward to some good cooperation in the future" with "our brothers and sisters."

Unexplained phenomena of a religious nature often are used in the regular news section of a paper because of the attention they have generated. Here is an example from the Associated Press (AP) that was printed in hundreds of papers:

> NEW YORK—Thousands of people are flocking to a Greek Orthodox church to see an icon that they believe began shedding tears last month after a special prayer session for peace in the Middle East.
>
> The icon of St. Irene, patron saint of peace, has drawn Christians of many denominations and smaller numbers of Moslems, Jews and the curious to the St. Irene Chrysovalantou Cathedral, church officials say.
>
> Visitors have come from as far away as France, Japan and India, according to Maria Galiatsatos, assistant secretary at the church in a largely Greek neighborhood in Astoria in Queens.

She says she receives up to 500 calls a day.

"We have had more than 100,000 people visit here since she began crying," Galiatsatos said. "One Sunday we didn't close the church until 4 a.m. and we re-opened at 6 o'clock in the morning."

The church's Bishop Vikentios of Avlon says he believes the icon of St. Irene—whose name means "peace" in Greek—is weeping for the Persian Gulf.

Church "trials" are not commonplace, but when they happen, they get wide-spread coverage, as in this example:

KEARNEY, Neb.—(AP)—A pastor who performed a lesbian unity ceremony is not guilty of disobeying church rules, a Methodist church panel ruled today.

Had he been found guilty by the jury of fellow ministers, the Rev. Jimmy Creech could have lost his position as senior pastor of Omaha's largest United Methodist Church and been stripped of his ministerial credentials.

The case was the first challenge to United Methodist policy on homosexual marriages, and the jury's decision could shape how the 9.5 million member de-nomination interprets rules governing its treatment of gays.

The story went on to detail the ceremony Mr. Creech conducted and pre-sented the arguments offered by the church and the minister's defense. It also re-ported on what other denominations did about conducting same-sex ceremonies.

And when a group of monks turned to cyberspace to spread the gospel, *USA TODAY* told their story:

SANTA FE—Some missionaries do God's work in China, others in Africa or India. Until now, though, none set their sights on cyberspace.

Yet that's where souls will be won or lost in the 21st century, says Brother M. Aquinas Woodworth.

The soft-spoken monk, 32, already is known on-line and in religious circles for turning a group of financially strapped Benedictines into Web page designers and for consulting on the Vatican's recently renovated site.

But his new project is the most ambitious yet: founding a religious commu-nity whose mission will be in a virtual country inhabited by a new generation— one that doesn't seek God because it's too busy surfing the Net and playing video games.

The remainder of the story told how Brother Aquinas had founded a group called the Scribes of St. Peter to produce spiritually oriented web sites compelling enough to compete with the likes of Microsoft and Disney.

Interpreting Religious Terminology

It is essential that any reporter writing about religion make a serious effort to learn the technical words and phrases commonly used by the various denominations. Not every minister, for example, is called "reverend" or "pastor." "Father," "rabbi," "elder" and "brother" are just a few of the formal and informal titles used for ministers by various denominations. The reporter should know which is applicable within the denomination being covered.

Reporters should also learn and correctly use the terms associated directly with the various worship services of denominations. Many groups have prepared a glossary of the terms and phrases that are used in their churches. They usually are available through the headquarters of the denomination. If one doesn't exist, a reporter should prepare one for his or her use. In the interest of accuracy, most ministers would be willing to help prepare a glossary.

In covering religion, a reporter should be thorough and objective, applying the same standards of accuracy that are required elsewhere in the paper. A reporter doesn't have to be religious to cover religion effectively, but he or she needs to be knowledgeable. Knowing which terms and titles are used in each denomination is just as vital as understanding the issues and trends.

Philanthropy

The basic meaning of "philanthropy" is "love of mankind." However, a secondary and more general meaning has developed that involves the expression of such love and concern for others in terms of hard cash. By the start of the 1990s, Americans were contributing more than $100 billion in hard cash annually to philanthropic causes. In addition, they contribute billions of hours of volunteer time to thousands of organizations devoted to the health, welfare and betterment of individuals as well as the community as a whole.

Philanthropy includes a wide diversity of activities. Among them are projects designed to promote and support religious and educational institutions and programs, the cultural arts (music, drama, art), character-building youth groups, welfare agencies, senior citizens' organizations, Christmas charities, disaster relief, hospitals, community civic projects, historical observances, recreational facilities, the treatment of and research for the cure of diseases and disabilities and other promotions requiring the raising of funds.

Not all philanthropic movements ask for money, however. Some solicit a person's time; a pint of blood; housing accommodations for visitors or the needy in an emergency; old clothes and newspapers; or a pledge to drive safely or to eliminate fire hazards. Whether for money, time or blood, all these movements are in the public interest—the service of humankind—and, as such, are associated with philanthropy. All of them can generate not only promotional stories but also special stories of major significance to the community.

Often individuals take on philanthropic projects of their own. Here is an AP story about one individual committed to feeding the poor:

> BOSTON—A dilapidated truck and its near-bankrupt owner parked outside a church in one of the city's poorest neighborhoods yesterday and out stepped Nancy Jamison, on her daily rounds to feed the less fortunate.

"Millions of pounds of food, darlin', are dumped every day while people are starving," she said. "Mayonnaise sandwiches are a reality, my dear."

Jamison, 40, a former fashion designer, is a one-woman food program, delivering vegetables and bread to the city's neediest people. Her truck, running perpetually in second gear because the transmission is shot, is always met at the Pilgrim Congregational Church in the city's Dorchester section by hungry people.

Sponsors of philanthropic movements are many times more numerous than the types of movements. Included are the Community Chest or United Fund organizations; Red Cross; Salvation Army; the YMCA and YWCA, along with their youth counterparts in other religions such as the YMHA; Boy Scouts and Girl Scouts; all types of civic and service clubs and fraternal groups; drama, music and art societies; recreation organizations; health associations, such as those serving in the areas of tuberculosis and heart disease; societies to assist the blind, deaf and physically handicapped; and churches, schools, colleges, hospitals and similar institutions. Newspapers also sponsor their own philanthropic promotions. Some of the various philanthropic movements are short-term drives; others are long-term continuing efforts, generally on an annual basis.

The newspaper, a public service institution itself, is by its very nature interested in philanthropic programs and promotions. Much space, as well as the time of reporters and editors, will be contributed to the success of worthy causes. In these cases the newspaper often will make an exception to its regular demands for stories based strictly on newsworthiness, and it will accept material that is more promotional than informative.

One of the paradoxes of the newspaper profession is that its critics frequently cite the "negative" or allegedly "sensational" content of newspapers while rarely mentioning the thousands of column-inches of free space given to community promotion and philanthropic drives. A study might reveal that there is indeed a much better balance between "good" news and "bad" news than critics would have the public believe.

Many individuals fulfill their need to be philanthropic by creating scholarships as this press release from the University of Tennessee shows:

An Atlanta couple with ties to Alcoa and Maryville high schools has established a $50,000 scholarship fund at the University of Tennessee.

The scholarship, which gives preference to Blount County students, is a memorial to Alan K. Thompson, son of Herman and Peggy Thompson.

And when a truly major act of philanthropy takes place, it rates front page news. Here's how the *San Jose Mercury News* reported the work of the David and Lucile Packard Foundation starting on page 1. The story was written by Paul Rogers and was accompanied by two color pictures, a chart and a graph:

Glance into your rearview mirror, Henry Ford.

On the highway of American philanthropy, David Packard is cruising into the passing lane.

Early next year, all the stock that Packard owned in Hewlett-Packard Co. at the time of his death in March 1996—shares worth roughly $5.5 billion today—will be transformed from a family trust to the charitable foundation that bears his and his late wife's name.

The event marks both a coming of age for Silicon Valley and a landmark shift in U.S. charitable giving. At that moment, the David and Lucile Packard Foundation probably will emerge as the largest charitable foundation in the United States, wealthier than the family charities established by the Rockefellers, Fords and Carnegies generations ago.

The story continued on the back page of the front news section and covered all but about 10 inches at the bottom of the page. It was accompanied by a pie-chart showing where the Packard Foundation's donations had gone between 1982 and 1996 and a color map of the United States indicating the growth of foundation giving in western states compared to the decrease in most other regions. There also was a chart listing the 20 largest foundations and their total assets.

Problems in Publicizing Philanthropy

Handling news of philanthropy poses some special problems for a newspaper. Often an editor must take the responsibility for deciding whether the publicity being sought is intended to promote the self-interest of an individual or organization rather than a charitable or other social goal. If a newspaper uses all of the publicity that certain groups wish, it risks loss of reader interest and consequently of circulation. On the other hand, if it restricts such publicity sharply, the newspaper risks loss of the good will of the groups involved.

The number of different philanthropies has increased to the point that the public has insisted on the consolidation of some of the fund-raising campaigns under a Community Chest or United Fund plan. Even though such plans have combined many campaigns—in some cities 50 or more charitable or welfare-type agencies receive funds from such plans—some social service and charitable groups still elect to carry on their own local and national campaigns with special weeks or months set aside for fund drives. Newspapers generally bear a heavy portion of the promotional work for such plans as United Fund and Community Chest. Occasionally an editor may decline to support a campaign that he or she believes should be part of a united drive. However, most editors find it difficult not to give space to any legitimate cause. As a result, most newspapers spend considerable time and money in writing about these various public-service activities.

Promoting Philanthropic Movements

Newspapers serve as the principal channel of communication for most of the promotional efforts of philanthropic and civic projects. However, various media are used in the campaigns and drives—letters, brochures, meetings, radio, television, billboards.

Despite all the publicity in newspapers and other news media, the most effective method of soliciting funds is the person-to-person approach—the volunteer workers who visit prospective donors. Many employers arrange a plan for monthly deductions from donors' paychecks, which contributes greatly to the success of such fund drives. Solicitation by mail and other means is used when the number of prospective donors is so great that direct contact is impractical. Numerous professional fund-raising organizations have come into existence to conduct local as well as nationwide campaigns for a fee. Like the amateur fund-raiser, they rely on the newspaper for publicity.

How does the newspaper fit into these approaches? Publicity given a project in the press will "set the stage" and help develop a climate of generosity among prospective donors. And, of course, the recognition afforded by publicity stories is important in obtaining and encouraging volunteer workers. However, the sponsors of the project will be greatly disappointed in expecting such publicity to do the whole job. While many people may be inclined to give to a worthy cause publicized in the press, very few remember to respond to their inclinations unless a solicitor visits them or a letter reminds them. There are things that the reporter and the campaign sponsor should keep in mind, or they may expect too much from newspaper publicity.

A newspaper can publish many promotional stories for philanthropic movements and projects. The following is a listing of some of the developments that could be reported:

1. Initial announcement of campaign or project

2. Appointment of persons in charge of project

3. Appointment of personnel or committees who will assist

4. Various meetings of campaign workers—goals, campaign plans, time schedules

5. Series of straight-news stories, features and human-interest stories reporting recent benefits of the project

6. Special stories on large donations

7. Progress reports on campaign

8. Stories on conclusion of campaign and its achievements.

Here are several examples of leads on stories reporting philanthropic activities:

> The United Way of Greater Knoxville, has broken its $5.8 million goal, its campaign chairman announced Friday.
> "We made $5,802,452, which is 6.6 percent over last year," Sam Furrow said at a press conference. "It is about $360,000 more than we raised last year . . . It

shows what a caring and loving community we are, and that we take care of our own."

The United Way funds 48 non-profit agencies and community organizations.

(The *Knoxville News–Sentinel*)

When Nashville's inner-city Boy Scout troops collected cans for the Second Harvest Food Bank, Scout leaders said they were also gathering food for thought.

Boys in Troop 2000 were among the 15,000 Middle Tennessee Scouts who went door to door collecting food for the needy Saturday. They hoped to bring in 360,000 cans this year to top last year's 350,000 total.

Troop 2000, which is for inner-city youth, played a special role in the collection because many come from homes that are not financially well off, said Chuck Simmons, spokesman for the Middle Tennessee Council—Boy Scouts of America.

"What makes it so important to these Scouts is that most of them have very little, yet they're going out asking the community to feed those who have even less than they have," Simmons said.

"There's a great lesson for them and for us," he said. "You can always help others, regardless of your situation in life.

(*Nashville Banner*)

Philanthropy is not always for the obviously needy, as this *Washington Post* story indicated:

WASHINGTON—Friends of Dan and Marilyn Quayle raised $340,000 in tax-deductible funds from nearly 200 contributors around the country to add children's bedrooms on the third floor of the vice president's residence, his office says.

Of that amount, about $140,000 was spent on improvements, supplementing $200,000 in money appropriated by Congress last year in response to an indirect appeal by Marilyn Quayle.

EXERCISES

1. In the research department of your college or university library, look up the Foundation Directory and write a feature story on the range of philanthropic foundations and organizations in the United States. In addition to the famous ones like the Ford and Packard foundations, cite some of the more obscure ones and tell what type organizations they support.

2. Most libraries subscribe to publications such as the *Chronicle of Philanthropy and Giving*. Check your library to see if it subscribes to any. If so, read several issues and write a story about what they contain. (Note: If copies of the publications listed in the two previous assignments are not available in your library, click on the web site of the American Institute of Philanthropy and gather information for your stories from there.)

3. Interview the local executive director of an umbrella religious organization such as the National Conference of Christians and Jews or the local council of churches.

Discuss with her or him the state of religious tolerance or racial harmony in your city. Write a story based on your interview.

4. Churches are known for their charitable works. Interview several ministers in your city to discuss the charitable work sponsored by the churches year round, not just at the Christmas holidays.

5. In many cities, doctors, dentists and nurses take part in the medical missions to Latin American and other countries. Call a number of churches in your city to find out if medical professionals from their congregation participate. If so, interview them and write a story about their work.

6. Women ministers are still in the minority, but most cities have at least one or two. Call the local council of churches office and ask for the name of a woman minister. Then, interview her and write a story based on that interview.

7. Write stories for a religion page using the following notes:
   a. The Metropolitan Mass
      A Capella Chorus
      Made up of 70 singers
      From Churches of Christ
      Throughout the city
      Recently released CD
      "Speaking in A Capella Psalms"
      Containing African-American
      Spirituals, hymns and traditional
      And contemporary songs
      Chorus will present
      A concert based on the album
      6:30 p.m. next Friday
      In the Civic Coliseum
      Love offering will be taken up
   b. Captain Ric Branson
      Head of local Salvation Army
      Reported at last night's
      Annual civic dinner
      Called "Angels Among Us"
      That the nonprofit organization
      Served 32,000 meals
      Provided 20,000 nights lodging
      Hosted 16,000 worship services
      Conduct 14,000 home visits
      Worked with 11,000 in youth programs
      He also reported that
      During the year, the Army
      Had $846,454 in revenue
      $482,619 came from public donations
      $229,876 from thrift store
      $10,000 from Federal Emergency
      Management Agency
      $121,766 from United Way

       $2,307 balance from last year
       Expenses totaled $835,129
       Included $208,057 staff compensation
       $579,573 for programs and services
       $47,499 to Salvation Army headquarters
       "God sends a host of angels
       Who work through all seasons
       And all through the night," Branson said.

c. Eighth grade class
       At St. Mary's Elementary School
       Begin drive this Saturday
       To collect small suitcases
       To be donated to foster children
       So they won't have to carry
       Their belongings around
       In plastic garbage bags
       Will accept slightly
       Used suitcases or
       Donations to buy
       New suitcases
       Mary Claire O'Neal
       Originated the idea
       After reading a story
       That said children
       In foster care move
       Between families an
       Average of eight times
       Donations can be brought
       To St. Mary's School
       At 1421 Northshore Drive
       During school hours
       For information call
       730-555-8192

8. Using a search engine, locate the web site address of a major religious organization and write a story on the type information that is posted there.

9. Contact the head of a local organization such as the Shriners or Rotary Club and interview him or her about the charitable work of the organization. Write a story about the group's work.

10. Most newspapers sponsor various charitable activities of their own as well as supporting others in the city. Interview the public service director and/or editor of your daily newspaper about its charitable contributions to the city and write a story about it.

PART SEVEN

Writing the Special Story

Straight-news stories make up only part of the content of a newspaper. Readers want more. That's why a good newspaper is a careful mix of hard news and special stories.

Special stories appear in the sports pages; the section devoted to family, foods, fashion and social events; and the reviews or criticisms of television, movies, music, books and the fine arts. In addition, many newspapers have regular sections on developments in science, medicine and technology. These special areas usually are operated as separate departments with their own editors and staffs, who are responsible to the managing editor.

Even though the departments are specialized, the principles used in gathering and writing straight-news stories apply to special stories as well. News is always paramount. However, special stories often employ writing devices not commonly used in straight-news stories. It is essential that every reporter learn the techniques needed to handle special stories because most reporters are required to write them from time to time.

CHAPTER

27

'Lifestyle' Section

"If you live long enough, you'll see everything."

That folk saying from Leo Rosten's *Treasury of Jewish Quotations* certainly applies to today's newspaper "Lifestyle" sections.

Take a look at several dozen "Lifestyle" sections and you'll find stories dealing with significant social, political, moral and ethical issues: "The Extramarital Affair," "Lust or Trust," "How to Protect Your Child from a Molester," "Incest: A Family Affair," "How to Tell If You Are Becoming an Alcoholic," "The Great Abortion Debate," "Date Rape," and dozens of other topics that 20 years ago might not have made the newspapers. Editors of the long-ago women's or society pages probably are turning over in their graves.

Certainly, most "Lifestyle" sections still carry the traditional engagement, wedding, fashion and social notes in some form. But those subjects often are secondary to stories about every phase of living known to woman and man. Stories about the environment, the economy, personal finances, family nurturing and loving, personal values, leisure activity, personal relationships and parenting are featured regularly.

While the sections often deal with such issues as the woman alcoholic, the woman shoplifter, the unwed mother, the problems of a single mother and the runaway mother, they also tackle such topics as the househusband, the single father, the male rape victim, the impact of AIDS and other provocative stories. These dramatic changes have caused some critics to complain that the once proud, but prissy "Women's Page" has been neutered. Others see the broad sweep of most "Lifestyle" sections as a reflection of the diversity of interests of men as well as women.

Most "Lifestyle" sections do what Kent W. Cockson, then executive editor of the *Pensacola News–Journal* in Florida, said they should do: Everything. And anything. He said if he had to write the "lifestyle law," it would say that the typical section would be: entertaining, helpful, informative, lively, personal, reflective, septic (as opposed to antiseptic), topical, trendy, useful, versatile, well planned and it should convey a sense of community, with no less impact than a ton of feathers.

Today's better "Lifestyle" sections are a pleasing blend of substance and fun. For the most part they are a showcase for quality reporting, quality writing, quality editing, quality packaging and quality graphics, as Ruth D'Arcy, who directed the J.C. Penny–University of Missouri Awards Program for many years, said in an article in the *Bulletin* of the American Society of Newspaper Editors.

Many newspapers follow a regular pattern in their "Lifestyles" sections, perhaps using general features on Monday and Tuesday, food stories on Wednesday, fashions on Thursday, entertainment on Friday, family-oriented features on Saturday and a cover story on a major social or moral issue on Sunday. The pattern varies from paper to paper. This arrangement allows for a vast range of stories generated by staff writers or provided by the wire services or feature syndicates. In many cases, a lifestyles writer will seek to localize a wire or syndicate story or will write a separate local story as a sidebar to the major story.

Generally, the traditional lifestyles news is given secondary play. However, some newspapers do reserve special days for printing engagements and weddings, columns covering local social events, syndicated features, club announcements and service features such as special sections for senior citizens.

In addition, many newspapers have developed specialists in consumer news who write stories designed to help the reader cope with the problems often associated with making major or even minor purchases of every possible product or service. A story might be about something as simple as how to tell if your butcher is cheating you or how to cope with a doctor who will not give you adequate time to discuss your medical problems. Often these stories have enough reader interest to be used as the cover story in the section.

The following are some leads from stories that have become commonplace in the "Lifestyles" sections of many newspapers:

A vacationing couple fears the popcorn they bought at a gas station is contaminated.

A woman panics when an employee sneezes while scooping her ice cream.

A man wonders if he could be infected by shaking hands.

Some worry about using public restrooms or hot tubs or being bitten by mosquitoes.

More than 3,000 times every day people with concerns like these call the toll-free National AIDS Hotline. The world's largest health-information telephone service, the hotline has fielded nearly 5 million calls since 1987.

Hotline staff members say that many of the callers are panicked and seek reassurance and information about whether the disease that has killed more than 100,000 Americans since 1981 can be casually transmitted.

(*Washington Post*)

Susan holds up the hand mirror and studies her eyelashes. Jane shakes her head to test the bangs of her newly-cut wig. Gayle's quick smile is evidence enough that she likes her change in lipstick color.

Pretty not only is as pretty does. For these cancer patients, pretty is as pretty feels.

"Look Good . . . Feel Better: Caring for Yourself Inside and Out" is a new program developed by the Cosmetic, Toiletry and Fragrance Association Foundation, the National Cosmetology Association and the American Cancer Society specifically for cancer patients undergoing chemotherapy or radiation treatments.

The program has given Gayle Lauer a new lease on life.

(The *Knoxville News–Sentinel*)

They live by the numbers: two careers with a combined six-figure income, at least one child in a top-ranked private school, one nanny, a house in a socially accepted ZIP code.

They pace their frantic lives by the clock: leave home early, come home late, carve out "quality time" for their children.

The payoff for these "fast-track" parents is achievement—commonly measured in earnings that provide for the house, the cars, the nanny, the school tuition and the endless array of lessons and things that keep the household up to speed.

But what does this mean for their children?

That's what experts are asking.

(*Los Angeles Times*)

Most people have a legal will that outlines how their valuables should be disbursed after death.

Others also may have a living will, which lays down the conditions of death, detailing what extraordinary measures, if any, people want medical professionals to take on their behalf when they're at death's door.

But most people have done nothing to protect and distribute the most valuable things they possess: the values, ethics and blessings family members deserve to know about.

A movement has developed that encourages people to write their ethical and spiritual convictions and publish them in a document for posterity.

The rest of the story from the Knight–Ridder Service includes quotes from a physician who has written his own ethical "will" and developed a kit that helps the average person sort out what's important to her or him.

The "Lifestyles" section of most newspapers is under the supervision of a special editor. On larger newspapers, the editor may have one or more assistants. Writers assigned to this section generally operate independently of the city editor. They are responsible for gathering and writing news and feature stories for the "Lifestyles" section only. However, it is not uncommon for their stories to appear in the news section, depending on the news value they possess. The copy editing, rewriting, headline writing and makeup may be handled within the section but coordinated with the copy desk and graphics department.

One of the major changes in "Lifestyles" sections over the years has been the change in staff. The sections are no longer exclusively a "woman's world." Many have men as writers, columnists, copy editors and graphic designers. At a number of larger newspapers the "Lifestyles" editor is a man.

Traditional Social News

Most "Lifestyles" sections still carry traditional social news—engagements, weddings, personal items, club notes and the like. The personal items might be collected in a column, or they might be used as individual stories with headlines of their own. Their reader appeal may be measured by the various news values (Chapter 15), but their largest single value is prominence.

The prominence of persons involved in the stories determines the importance and therefore the length of social news stories. Prominence in this sense must be understood as local and relative rather than national. The smallest and most unsophisticated community will have its socially prominent persons, usually based on wealth or professional position. In fact, the first "Society" pages were originated by New York City newspapers in the last half of the nineteenth century to report the purely social activities of the wealthy and socially prominent.

Initially only the social activities of the so-called elite were reported. However, this began to change gradually, and in the period immediately after World War II most newspapers broadened their concept of "society" and began to cover the social activities of a broader range of individuals in the community. Although the banker's daughter generally got the biggest picture and story when she announced her engagement, no longer was the engagement of the baker's daughter ignored. In more recent years, many newspapers have sought to standardize the coverage of engagements and weddings by using the same size of picture and story for everyone, regardless of social standing in the community.

Nevertheless, prominence is still a major news value. Most newspapers still base their general policy on the principle that names, especially the widely known names in the community, make news. But they recognize that all names make news if they are involved in certain types of activities suitable for the "Lifestyles" section.

In addition to engagements and weddings, which are not given the same prominence in many newspapers as they once were, basic social-news stories that appear in the "Lifestyles" section include:

— Personals and briefs not carried elsewhere in the newspaper
— Births, if not published elsewhere
— Receptions, teas, parties, dances, luncheons, showers, dinners
— Women's clubs and organizations: routing meetings, programs, speeches and special activities such as benefits, bazaars, recitals and charity events
— Social columns or social notes that sometimes are gossipy and include editorialized comments by the writer about the local social scene
— Stories and columns on fashions, food, child care, interior decorating, family relationships, home and beauty tips
— Stories and columns on local women and men in the business and professional world, if they are not carried elsewhere in the newspaper

News Sources

The editors and writers who handle social news generally become personally acquainted with the individuals in the community who are principal news sources. This is particularly true in smaller communities. Clubs and organizations usually have someone in charge of publicity who seeks out coverage for their events. Often tips on significant events can come from florists, caterers and others whose services have been engaged by the family or organization sponsoring the event. Far from having to seek social news, the editor is generally under pressure for more space to use everything that comes in by mail or phone or is delivered in person. Although a great amount of news is unsolicited, to have a well-rounded section, the "Lifestyles" staff has to seek other sources of timely stories and features.

Writers for "Lifestyles" sections often become specialists in such fields as foods and nutrition, family relations, child development, textiles and clothing, interior decorating, fashion and other subjects and write by-lined columns in addition to news and feature stories about their specialized areas. But it is important for any writer to be versatile and be able to write about engagements, weddings, clubs and other social events with care and accuracy.

Problems of Social-News Sections

One of the most serious problems facing the reporter handling social news is the lack of story substance. Social-news stories do not have the impact of hard news, although they are an important ingredient in a well-balanced newspaper. Social events not only are categorized but also tend to be stereotyped. Yet the reporter must strive for freshness and variety. The monotonous, stereotyped story forms must be avoided.

A second and very definite responsibility of the social-news reporter is to spell all names correctly. To misspell a name or use the wrong initial of a person is to strike at the heart of social (or, for that matter, any kind of) news. There can be no acceptable excuse for carelessness. Also, great care must be exercised by the reporter and editor in checking sources of announcements of engagements and weddings to ensure validity. Many a practical joker has sent a phony engagement announcement to the newspaper "to get a laugh on a friend," and some of those announcements have unfortunately been printed.

Lead Features

One of the most critical problems for the reporter in avoiding stereotyped forms and writing more effectively is the selection of the proper feature or features for the story lead. Any social function or occasion will produce the following subject matter, in which the feature may be sought:

1. The occasion itself may be defined. Perhaps it is an anniversary or the hundredth anniversary of an event. Perhaps it is devoted to a "cause," or it might have other special features or a theme.

2. The place itself might be significant—an ancestral home, a national shrine or the site of a local historical event.

3. In general, the persons present at the function offer the most obvious feature. Hosts and guests, honorees, distinguished visitors, those in the receiving line, those who "poured," committee members, famous names—all are available features.

4. Decorations and color schemes might be features—or costumes, gowns or jewelry.

5. Refreshments and music or other forms of entertainment may also be featured.

Here are several examples of leads on social-event stories. Most come from community newspapers. However, larger newspapers often include personal items of this nature in a personal or social column that appears once or twice a week.

> Three pink and blue showers honored Mrs. Terry Dale Mantooth, the former Crystal Gregg. The events on three consecutive Fridays this month were held in the Gold Medallion Room at the Newport Beach Hotel.

> The turkey was off the hook for the Thanksgiving hunt at Thomas and Kelsey Nelson's farm in Strawberry Plains. It was the fox that led the chase.
> The farm was the site of the second annual Green Valley Hunt Club fox hunt that officially opened the social season.

> It was a happy 90th birthday that Asa Bundy celebrated Sunday with a party given by his daughter, Bonnie Sue Jochaim, and her husband, Joe. Autumn flowers, balloons and a collage of memorable photographs were used in the decorations.

> A beans and wieners dinner, lots of children's activities and prizes will proceed the Del Or Woman's Club annual charity auction Saturday in the Community Center.

Frequently items like this one will appear in a column of social notes in larger newspapers:

> The City Symphony League's annual gala holiday ball on Saturday evening at the Cherokee Country Club promises to be a fashionable event. Lucky Schwartz, League President, is wearing a black, burgundy and gold gown . . . Freddie Tubbs is going with black and gold, too—black velvet skirt with black and gold silk top . . . Muffin McVey is wearing ivory silk charmeuse encrusted with pearls and sequins.

Often these columns focus on charitable fund-raising events, as in this example:

> The $100,000 netted from the eighth annual awards dinner of the Arts & Education Council made a great kickoff for the council's $2.1 million fund-raising campaign, according to Steve Sawyers, chairman of the Fund Drive.
>
> Marie Branson, CEO and president of the A & E Council, had the happy task of announcing that a combination of extra events last year resulted in raising an additional $90,000 for use of the 160 organizations enriching the cultural life in the metro area.

The rest of the column named the recipients of various art awards, names of the cochairwomen of the awards dinner and a long list of persons who attended.

Writing Style

Writers of social news should strive to overcome the stereotyped story without straining for effect. Even in standardized columns, announcements may become monotonous if every story begins "Mr. and Mrs. James VanSycle Howard Brewer announced the engagement of their daughter Lotty. . . ." In describing social events, the writer has the freedom to use a few more adjectives than are used in news stories. However, the story should be accurate and avoid puffy or gushy language. Not all luncheons are "delicious," nor are all brides automatically "pretty" or "lovely." And certainly not all parties or dances are the "biggest social event of the season." Such expressions as "everyone is cordially invited" and "a good time was had by all" should not be used. Restraint should be the guide when writing social news.

Engagements and Weddings

Although many newspapers have standardized their engagement and wedding stories, in many smaller newspapers they are given considerably more space with larger photographs. Newspapers rely on families to provide the basic information for both engagement and wedding stories and pictures. To ensure accurate information, newspapers have detailed questionnaires for prospective brides to complete. They call for the names and addresses of those participating; descriptions of gowns, flowers, ribbons, etc.; themes; and all other essential information about the event and the couple and their families. In most cases, the story is written directly from the form, although a reporter might call the prospective bride or her mother for additional details if needed. In every case, engagement and wedding announcements brought to the newspaper or mailed in should be verified to avoid a hoax.

Here are several examples of engagement announcements and wedding story leads:

An Engagement Announcement Lead

A summer supper Saturday at the home of Roberta and Walter McIntire celebrated the announcement of the engagement of their daughter, Mildred, to Beau Lolly. An August 31 wedding is planned at the Church of the Immaculate Conception.

Newspapers that have standardized their engagement announcements generally use this type of lead:

Mr. and Mrs. Walter McIntire, Blackberry Farms, announce the engagement of their daughter, Mildred, to Beau Lolly, son of Mr. and Mrs. Buford Lolly.

A Wedding Story Lead

The chapel of First United Methodist Church was the candle-light setting for the nuptials of Patricia Dagmar Motte and Anderson Kurt Huffman.

In a standardized announcement, the lead generally is more direct:

Patricia Dagmar Motte and Anderson Kurt Huffman were married June 2 at First United Methodist Church.

Both styles of engagement and wedding announcements have merit. The danger of the first type of story is that the writer may get a bit too flowery. The problem with the standardized version is that it is colorless and boring, especially when 16 to 20 wedding stories, reading exactly alike except for the names, are displayed on a single page.

Most metropolitan dailies no longer carry long and detailed wedding stories, unless it's royalty or the rich and famous. However, that type of wedding story still is standard in community newspapers. Here is an excerpt from one:

Kymberly Kay Napier and Robert Bradley Byrge exchanged wedding vows in a candlelight ceremony on Saturday, April 11, at Central Baptist Church in Caryville. The Reverend James Wilcox performed the traditional Christian ceremony.

Kym is the daughter of Ms. Ernestine Napier of Jacksboro and the granddaughter of Ernest and Gladys Napier of Caryville. Brad is the son of Ms. Sherry Byrge of Caryville and Robert Byrge of Elk Valley. He is the grandson of Faye and the late Odel Harness of Caryville and the late Tom and Minnie Byrge, also of Caryville.

The church was beautifully decorated by the bride and her maid of honor. Cream-colored magnolias surrounded by candlelight adorned windows and pews.

The mothers and grandmothers were seated to "Mama, Food For My Soul" by Boys II Men. The wedding party entered the church to "Can't Help Falling In Love" by Elvis Presley. Vocalist Rebecca Walden, cousin of the bride, sang "The Lord's Prayer." Rusty Massengill was pianist. Mrs. Cindy Chadwell was wedding coordinator. Greg Byrge and Judy Massengill were music coordinators. Other musical selections included "Going to the Chapel" by the Dixie Cups, "On the Side of Angels" and "You Light Up My Life" by LeAnne Rimes and "Can't Help Falling In Love" by the UB40's.

The remainder of the story detailed the bride's wedding gown, listed the attendants and described their gowns, named the two best men and the groomsmen, described the gowns worn by the mothers of the bride and groom and described the wedding reception including the wedding cake and the groom's cake.

Miscellaneous Stories

In smaller newspapers the largest group of strictly social stories are provided by receptions, teas, parties, dances, luncheons and dinners. The prominence of the persons involved and the magnitude of the occasion often determine the amount of space allotted to the stories. In some cities, even large ones, there still is a formal social season and debutantes are introduced at a banquet and dance. Newspapers cover them in depth, sometimes devoting the front page of the "Lifestyles" section to a single event. But for the most part, individual events might be confined to no more than three or four paragraphs.

Another large group of stories appearing in "Lifestyles" sections includes the reports of churches and club activities, which might be largely social yet also have significant substance such as a charity auction or a scholarship fund-raising banquet. The following examples demonstrate the variety of miscellaneous stories that appear in "Lifestyles" sections:

Parties

The American Cancer Society will have a "plaid shirt affair for the black tie crowd" Tuesday evening at the home of Goldie and Nelson Barnes.

The barbecue will honor Billy Baldwin, Dr. Walter Frickel and Bootsy Bartlett, veteran Cancer Society volunteers. Entertainment will be by the Sundowners Trio.

Clubs

The Middle Tennessee Reading Association will meet at 6 p.m. Tuesday at John Trotwood Moore Middle School, 4425 Granny White Pike. This year's theme is "Literacy Links the World."

Ruth Ann Leach, *Nashville Banner* columnist, will speak on motivation. Admission is free and open to the public. Call 262-6685 or 333-5170 for more information.

Baked goods, plants, crafts and antiques will be available to the highest bidders at the annual auction of the Neartsease Garden Club at 7 p.m. Monday in the Cosby Civic Center.

The club uses funds raised at the auction for its city-wide beautification programs. Last year the club planted more than 1,000 flower plants in city parks.

Trips

The "Lifestyles" sections of community newspapers often carry announcements of trips local people make to visit friends or relatives or for vacations. Similar items are used in larger newspapers if they have a column of social news. Usually the names used in the larger papers are of the city's more prominent citizens. The following are common examples:

> Mrs. Edwin Maples has returned from Savannah, Ga., where she visited her son and family, Stephen, Susan and Scott Maples. She also visited her brother, Sam Craig, and helped him celebrate his 92nd birthday.

> Mary Ruth Emrick and her husband-to-be Floyd Ginger drove to Hooker's Point Saturday evening where they were honored at a dinner party given by Mr. and Mrs. Elbert Hooker at the Okeechobee Country Club. Mrs. Hooker is Mary Ruth's sister.

> Kitty Sue Crumpton has just returned from a 15-day tour of the Southwest by Greyhound. She visited Texas, Oklahoma, New Mexico and Arizona.

Guests

Hosts and hostesses with out-of-town guests frequently ask newspapers to report the fact not only to honor the visitor but also to inform other friends who might wish to entertain them. Here are several examples:

> Misty and Roland Greenberg of Dallas are spending two weeks with her mother, Mrs. Irene Jacobe, 4718 Greenbriar Lane, so their first son, Jason, who is just three months old, will get to know his grandmother.

> Ingrid and Ryan Dauphin of What Cheer, Iowa, have joined her parents, Bobbie Joe and Elmer Scott, at their condo in the Smoky Mountains for two weeks. Ryan was manager of the Free Service Tire Store here for five years before being transferred to Iowa.

Births

Some newspapers, especially in smaller communities, regularly carry birth announcements. They may be used as individual stories, grouped in a column or simply printed under hospital notes. The stories usually give the names and addresses of the parents; time and place of birth; weight and sex of the infant; name, if one has been chosen; and the names of grandparents. Here are two examples:

> Robin and Mitch Coakley are the parents of a daughter born Nov. 1 at Cocke County Baptist Hospital.
> Mara Paige weighed seven pounds, five ounces. She is the couple's first child.
> Her grandparents are Evelyn Webb and Wayne Fine and Holland and Beverly Coakley.

> Barron Mark Suggs, born yesterday at Greeneville Memorial Hospital, has been named in honor of his uncle who is president of the First National Bank, Wartburg. He is the first son of Mr. and Mrs. Randy Suggs of London, Ky., formerly of Wartburg.

Consumer News

A number of newspapers continue to devote special pages to consumer news, which gained considerable attention in daily newspapers in the 1960s and 1970s. However, many other newspapers use consumer news as a part of their offerings in their "Lifestyles" sections, arguing that it should not be singled out for special treatment. Some editors oppose reporters' playing the role of advocate, as do newspaper advertising managers.

Although the so-called action-line columns to help the average reader who might be having difficulty with the local store or a government agency are not as popular as they once were, some newspapers still have them and display them prominently. Some editors say their action-line column is one of the most popular features in their newspaper.

The more aggressive consumer reporters launched a wide range of investigations that produced front-page news stories and often brought about reform or spurred legislation to protect the consumer. Dozens of reporters investigated such things as the shabby workmanship and exorbitant prices of local television and auto repair shops or the unsavory practices of used car dealers. Others tested the often exaggerated claims of advertisements. Banks, funeral homes and other institutions that had been considered untouchable were being investigated in the name of consumer advocacy. Several newspapers established buyer panels of citizens who tested products and reported their findings to readers. The comparison-shopping story, in which a reporter compared the price of the same brand-name product at a number of retail outlets and reported the findings, became commonplace.

Although there has been considerable business backlash, most papers that established consumer reporting continue to engage in some form of it. They cover newsworthy consumer events, write about product safety, cover changes in laws affecting consumers, provide shopping guides for products and services, and make critical assessments of everything from food to colleges.

Those newspapers without consumer reporters of their own often run consumer-oriented stories from the wire services or a syndicated consumer column. Consumers Union syndicates material from its magazine *Consumer Reports,* for example. And many newspaper chains have a consumer reporter whose work appears in all of the papers in the chain.

After an initial flurry of consumer-news reporters and even some consumer newspapers, a number of dailies began incorporating consumer news in their "Family Living" and "Lifestyle" sections. The rationale behind this decision was that consumer news is not unlike the reports on foods, fashions, home furnishings, and other family and home-oriented articles that have become the staple of this type of section. The *New York Times,* for example, reports on weddings and engagements separately in its Sunday edition. The *St. Louis Post–Dispatch* combines fashions, decor, wine and food in its "Lifestyle" section on Sunday. The *Washing-*

ton Post mixes fashions, food, culture, entertainment and even books and health in its "Style" section.

Many smaller dailies and weeklies also have developed family and living sections that include social news as well as consumer-oriented stories, food, fashions and entertainment. The *Montgomery Journal,* an award-winning newspaper from Chevy Chase, Md., calls its section "Tempo." The *Jackson Sun* in western Tennessee includes a broad range of consumer stories in its "Living" section and tends to downplay the traditional engagement, wedding and social-event type of stories.

No matter where the consumer story appears, it requires particular care. It is a form of business reporting, but the emphasis is placed on the role of the buyer or user rather than the producer. As such, it is frequently critical of the producer or seller. This type of story can damage a person or a business and can bring a libel suit.

In most newspapers, consumer news is broadly defined. While it could be a story on a sales fraud or misleading solicitations for charity, it also could be a story to help readers cope with a particular problem. The following examples will demonstrate the range of consumer stories. The first, from a special section called "fortysomething—Creative Planning for the Years Ahead" in the *San Francisco Chronicle,* is a story on how to ensure that your parents are provided for:

> Many of the dilemmas of caring for an elderly or infirm parent can be minimized by planning ahead, yet adult children often don't have all the information they need to help.
>
> Many seniors think that as long as they've drafted wills that's all that they need to do. Others are afraid that their children will take advantage of them. Still others may find it a relief to talk to children about their concerns.
>
> Here's how experts suggest meeting your parents' needs without threatening their independence and dignity, and preserving the financial and emotional resources of both generations.
>
> Skidding across the ice into the guardrail was bad enough. The $3,000 repair bill was worse. But perhaps the biggest shock of all came when his insurance company declared his 1978 car a "total loss" because the cost of repairs exceeded its value. This gave Bob Garfield's budget a terrific beating.
>
> Rather than pay for $3,000 worth of repairs, the insurance company paid him $2,500 for the "totalled" car—its current market or book value. This was less than he still owed on his auto loan. Then came the real sting—Garfield had to pay $8,200 for the 1982 model of the same car.
>
> (*Palm Beach Post*)

The story went on to detail a new type of auto protection called "replacement cost auto insurance" being offered by major insurance companies.

Increasingly, newspapers are using their "Lifestyle" front pages to show case stories that deal with health and wellness issues, such as how to live with hypertension and the sometimes fatal immune system disorder Lupus, which afflicts

2 million Americans. Here's an example of a lead story from the Life section of the *San Jose Mercury News:*

> Alex Wright looks cool in his first set of wheels, laughing as he drives the vehicle in tight little circles.
>
> He runs into chairs, bystanders and a Palo Alto building. But his mother, Patricia, isn't concerned. In fact, she's cheering him on.
>
> "All right, Alex-gator!"
>
> Alex is three; his wheels are battery-operated; and no one has ever been injured by his reckless joy rides. If anything, his adventures in this miniature cart are considered beneficial to his health and development, and are encouraged by his doctors and therapists.
>
> Alex has cerebral palsy, a nervous system disorder that causes muscular disability and mobility problems. While many kids his age have mastered the skill of running, Alex still has difficulties crawling and walking.

The *Los Angeles Times* explored the longtime complex ties between the city's Latino and Jewish population in this lead story in its Life & Style section:

> It was a coalition that started to change the face of L.A. politics, uniting two ethnic communities and electing a groundbreaking minority to citywide office.
>
> The year was 1949, a quarter century before Tom Bradley rose to power on the strength of a cross-town alliance between Jews and Blacks. The politician then was Ed Royal, who broke the Anglo stranglehold on the City Council with the help of a progressive labor coalition, most of whose members were Eastside Jews and Latinos.
>
> Royal's historic ascendancy is but one chapter in the mostly ignored relationship between L.A.'s Jewish and Latino communities. These ties will be explored in two programs being presented as part of the Yiddishkayt in L.A., a weeklong citywide festival continuing through Sunday.

The rest of the long story went on to track the history of the relationship between the two groups, focusing not only on their cooperation with each other, but also on how in recent years the two groups have gone their separate ways.

EXERCISES

1. Contact one of the social service agencies in your city that provides support for homeless women and arrange an interview with its director and several of the women the agency has helped. Write a feature story on the information you gather.

2. Using any daily and weekly newspapers available to you, compare the "Lifestyle" sections. Catalog the type of stories that appear in both and then write a report on the results.

3. Make an informal and unscientific survey of businesses and industries in your area to determine what their policy is about allowing a male employee to leave when his

wife has a baby. If possible, locate a man who has taken a leave to help care for a newborn child and interview him. Write a feature story on the information you collect.

4. Interview the director of the local office of the state's Child and Family Service Agency about the issue of child abuse in your area. Ask for a copy of any reports that give statistics on the number of cases handled by the office. Write a story on your findings.

5. Using the local Employment Security Office as a starting point, locate one or more women who may be holding nontraditional jobs and interview them for a story on how they got the job and the problems they have had to overcome with coworkers and supervisors.

6. Do an informal survey with several marriage and family counselors who are listed in the yellow pages of the phone book about the "state" of marriage in your city. Ask them what is the main cause of family problems. Find out their individual track record for repairing broken marriages. Include statistics on the number of marriages compared to the number of divorces in your city or county. Write a story on your findings.

7. Contact the local chamber of commerce and ask if it maintains a list of all the self-help organizations and groups in your city. Usually there is an umbrella group for them that may be listed in the phone book. Write a story on all the ways a person can get help for a variety of problems—health, social concerns, parenting, substance abuse, eating disorders, and the like.

8. Visit a senior citizens center in your city, interview its director and some of the people who come there for its various services and write a feature story about it.

9. Using the yellow pages of the phone book, look up several consumer credit counselors. Interview them for a story on how to get out of debt and stay out.

10. Interview at least six of your fellow students about the problems they have had dealing with the bureaucracy at your college or university—delayed financial aid, class scheduling mixups, housing problems, lousy food in the dorm cafeteria and inadequate parking, for example. Then contact the official responsible for each of those areas and ask her or him why the problem exists and how students can avoid a hassle in the future. Write an action-line-type column based on the questions and answers.

11. Write short stories based on the following notes.

   a. Child & Family Services
      3105 E. Shelly Place
      To offer ongoing
      Supportive workshop called
      "Divorce Through
      A Child's Eyes"
      For children in
      Grades kindergarten
      Through eight
      It will run every

Monday 4:30–5:30 p.m.
Cost is $10
For more information
Call 861-9377

b. Graduates of five
Local high schools
To have reunions
In June
Charles Page High School
Class of 1989
June 11–12
Meadows Country Club
Contact (324) 555-2000
East Central High School
Class of 1969
Contact Cathy Jones
At (324) 555-0087
Memorial High School
Class of 1989
Call (324) 555-1371
For more information
Union High School
Class of 1989
June 25–26
Doubletree Hotel
Contact Billy Rae Brewer
(324) 555-5377
Will Rogers High School
Class of 1989
Call (324) 555-3331

c. Habitat for Humanity
Completed new house
At Woodlawn and Claiborne drives
House to be dedicated
3 p.m., Sunday
Ceremony open to public
Program will include
Dedication of house
Introduction of family
Who will live in house
Appreciation to contributors
National, state, county leaders
Invited to participate
For more information
Call 555-6667

12. Arrange to attend a wedding and write a story about it.

13. Most university centers are the site of numerous social and cultural events. Ask the director of the one on your campus for a list of all the events scheduled for the next

week. Call the contact person for several that sound interesting to obtain more information and then write a column about the upcoming events.

14. Write a photo caption from the following information.
    Jan Hitt, volunteer at
    City Animal Shelter
    Surrounded by eight dogs
    Holding large black cat
    All these animals and more
    Are available for adoption
    When Animal Shelter
    Holds its annual
    "Take Home a Pet"
    Adoption Sunday
    From noon til 4 p.m.
    Sunday, June 16
    Shelter is located at
    3722 Holston Hills Rd.
    No over-the-phone reservations
    For adoptable pet

CHAPTER

28 Sports

"Everyone who writes reflects the age in which he lives, and this is no less true of the sports reporter than of the dramatist, essayist or historian. Games and people who play them have a place in our culture . . ."

The late Red Smith, the most literate sports writer of the 20th century, wrote that in the introduction to a collection of his columns, "Strawberries in the Wintertime," in the late 1960s.

Today, many critics complain that games and the people who play them have come to dominate our culture. To shore up their argument, they point to the way newspapers and other media cover sports at the expense, they claim, of far more important and significant events and issues.

The frenzied "end of the world" type headlines when Mark McGwire raced Sammy Sosa for the single-season home run record proved their point, critics said. Each new home run seemed to rate a bigger headline. And when McGwire hit his 70th home run at the end of the season, newspapers went wild with headlines and stories but none could match the *Post–Dispatch* in St. Louis, where McGwire played for the St. Louis Cardinals.

In addition to stories on the front page and the sports section, the newspaper published a special 24-page commemorative edition devoted to McGwire's accomplishment. It contained more than a dozen separate stories, more than 100 color and black and white photographs, and assorted charts, graphs and listings of his accomplishments.

Overkill? Not hardly, when you consider the *Post–Dispatch* tripled its press run to 900,000 the day after McGwire hit his 62nd home run and sold a half million extra copies. So many fans lined up outside the paper's lobby that managers installed a pair of portable toilets. And when McGwire finished off the season with 70 home runs, the *Post–Dispatch* sold another 900,000 copies, reportedly almost running out of ink in the process.

Sports is no longer the toy department of life. It's serious business, and big business too. That is reflected in the dramatic changes that have been made in the content of sports pages since the late 1970s.

Although game coverage remains the lifeblood of most sports pages, readers want more. They want to know who played, what they did or did not do on the field or court, who won and who lost and why in national sports and especially in local sports. They know national sports writers will automatically analyze why Atlanta did so poorly in the Super Bowl, and they expect a similar analysis when their favorite Central High Bobcats are eliminated in the first round of the basketball playoffs.

Equally as important to readers of sports pages are those stories about complex contract negotiations and the migration of multimillion-dollar sports franchises with their effects on a community's economics, and the drug, mental health, alcohol and gambling problems of players and coaches. Often those stories move from the sports pages to the front page of a newspaper.

Some of the best-written and most interesting stories in any newspaper, on any given day, appear on the sports pages. But some of the worst-written stories in any newspaper, on any given day, appear in the sports sections also. To a talented writer, the sports page offers an unlimited challenge because sports reporting allows far greater freedom of expression than straight news.

A number of writers—Grantland Rice, Damon Runyon, Paul Gallico, Red Smith, Jim Murray and others—made sports writing an art form. All, of course, had several things in common: discipline; a thorough knowledge of sports; imagination; and, most important, a command of the language. This lead on a famous Notre Dame football team by Grantland Rice remains a sports writing classic:

> Against the gray October sky, the Four Horsemen rode again in legendary lore. Their names are Death, Pestilence, Hunger and Fire. These are only aliases. Their real names are Stuhldreyer, Crowley, Miller and Layden.

Unfortunately, too many sports writers, lacking imagination or a flare for the language, produce leads like this statistic-laden one from a large daily:

> BIRMINGHAM, Ala.—A freshman, Bo Jackson, ended a 67-yard drive with a 1-yard plunge with 2:26 left to give the Tangerine Bowl-bound Alabama a 23-22 triumph today over Georgia.

But many sports writers repeatedly grab readers with their storytelling. Here's an example by Ben Walker of the Associated Press (AP):

> NEW YORK—Those Yankees boasted of Babe Ruth, Lou Gehrig and Murders' Row. These Yankees do not have anyone among the top 50-home run hitters in the majors.
>
> Those Yankees had six players eventually elected to the Hall of Fame. These Yankees did not have a single player elected to start the All-Star game.
>
> Those Yankees are considered the greatest team ever. And yet, these Yankees are the ones winning at a historic rate.
>
> That said, is it baseball heresy to compare this club to—yikes!—the 1927 New York Yankees?

The remainder of the story continued its comparison of the two teams and ended with the comment that there really wasn't a way to tell which was the better team. But it sure made interesting reading.

The sports reporter's field is broad and interesting enough to test the finest talent. Each sport has rules and records. Each has its gallery of personalities and hall of fame. Perhaps in no other field of reporting is the opportunity greater for a writer to hone his or her talents.

World of Sports

Although it shouldn't be, at most newspapers the sports section is a world unto itself. Generally, on larger newspapers, it is operated as an independent department, often isolated from the news department, and has little contact with other writers and editors. The sports editor and staff are responsible for all phases of gathering, writing and editing. This freedom often results in sports pages that feature flamboyant graphic design with large headlines, large photographs and imaginative graphic illustration.

Some readers may see a curious misconception of news values at a newspaper that prints a three-paragraph story with a one-column headline about a $1 million cancer-research grant in its general news section and a 20-paragraph story with an eight-column headline and three photographs on the sports page about a high school or college football game on the same day.

Most newspapers respond to criticism of too much sports coverage by pointing out the high readership of the sports section. They also note that the countless hours devoted to coverage of sports by television have simply whetted the reader's appetite for more sports coverage. Several studies indicate the many sports fans who watch a game on television automatically read the newspaper's story about the game. That has forced sports writers to use greater care and accuracy in reporting. No longer can sports writers take too much license with what happened on the field, as their counterparts in radio used to do in those days when former President Ronald Reagan was a radio sportscaster.

News Values of Sports

The whole scale of news values characterizes sports news. Clustered around conflict as the pivotal appeal are prominence, progress, disaster, human interest and —in the sports sense—consequence. Moreover, the reader is a "fan," highly conditioned for ready response, at once appreciative and critical. The sports reporter— usually a by-lined writer—acquires a "public" that may become a valuable career asset. Thus there is something over and beyond news values—something of camaraderie and clan esprit—that enhances reader interest in the sports page. Men particularly, but also women and children, look at the sports section for news on their favorite teams and frequently to see what their favorite writer had to say about a game or a team.

The rise of women's collegiate sports, especially women's basketball with powerhouse teams from the University of Tennessee and the University of Connecticut, created legions of new fans among women. In the late 1990s, both those teams drew larger crowds to their games than many men's college teams. And they often rated coverage on the front pages of sports sections across the nation.

Often stories of women's college basketball games sound much like the game story for a men's team, as in this example:

> Top-ranked Tennessee held visiting Mississippi to 25% shooting from the field to route the Rebels 96-58 Thursday.
>
> (USA TODAY)

The story in the hometown newspaper, the *Knoxville News–Sentinel,* had more of a feature approach:

> The start of the Tennessee's women basketball game against Ole Miss on Thursday night was delayed briefly by fire.
> Lady Vols game management staffer Todd Dooley was the man for the moment, climbing a basket support and deftly wielding a Gatorade cup in dousing a lingering ember from the pregame fireworks.
> Ole Miss (13, 4–6) should have taken a cue from those heroics. But the Lady Rebels would have required a tireless bucket brigade to combat the Lady Vols' raging inferno.
> The defending national champions bolted to an 18-point lead at the outset and proceeded to a 96–58 SEC victory before 12,547 fans at Thompson–Boling Arena.

Qualifications of a Sports Writer

The sports reporter has certain responsibilities that are perhaps not different from, but merely more obvious than, those in less specialized reporting. Two of them have been mentioned—background and judgment gained from either experience or extensive reading.

Background can be acquired. One does not have to be a former football player to write about football, but a detailed knowledge of the fine points of the game is certainly essential. Many sports reporters are "addicted" to one or more sports and have been since childhood. Although this can be a help, it also can be a hindrance, especially if their "addiction" clouds their judgment.

Some sports may have to be mastered vicariously. Story backgrounds should be historical as well as technical. A fire, an accident or an occasion may be reported adequately from within the event. Too frequently, also, sports reporting confines itself in the same manner. But the richness of reporting from a full background outside the event should be evident in the story.

The Kentucky Derby winner has to be compared with Derby winners of all time and of all tracks. The reader should be told if the "sire" and "dam" are of distinguished ancestry. Many—perhaps even most—readers will have partial knowledge of this background. They want not only to be told what they already know (and it had better be correct), but also to have their knowledge expanded. They want the whole significance of the event, and they look to the sports reporter as interpreter and final authority. They demand that the reporter have an adequate background. If the background of the reader is deeper than that of the writer, the writer is faced with a serious credibility gap.

To some extent, also, the sports reporter can acquire good judgment if aided by adequate knowledge. Familiarity and experience with various sports will ac-

FIGURE 28.1 When your team loses, why not have a little fun? That's what the *Athens Daily News/Athens Banner–Herald* did when the University of Georgia football team lost to arch rival, the University of Tennessee. This clever headline and front-page display is an outstanding example of creativity by a newspaper staff.

(Reprinted with permission of the *Athens Daily News/Athens Banner–Herald*.)

quaint the reporter with the standards used to measure the merits and demerits of plays and players. Ultimately, though, the reporter will succeed or fail because of the accuracy or inaccuracy of his or her independent judgment.

A reporter's ability to see beyond the surface and the statistics is a tremendous asset. It is insight, too, and not background, that must detect the cause of weakness or the source of strength of a team or of an individual player. (Some call it a "gut" feeling.) Nor can a sports reporter take comfort in the thought that, if he or she fails to detect and report an error or an achievement, no one will be the wiser. Unlike other reporters, the sports reporter writes for a public, some or many of whom have observed the same event in person or on television with a highly critical eye. A positive requirement for success is sound judgment.

A third desirable qualification of the sports reporter is perspective, or detachment, which should be the result of sufficient knowledge plus good judgment. Being a fan of a particular game or a team does not always make one the best of sports reporters. Thumping the drums for the local team with brass and bias is not detached reporting. The reporter's responsibility is to the public and not to the local team. Although the fans are quick to resent any lack of unrestrained support for local heroes, they will, in the long run, respect the sports reporter's honesty, accuracy and detachment.

The sports reporter is a judge as well as a reporter. But the good one avoids the arrogance of trying to usurp the coach's authority and run the team through the newspaper's columns. There is a difference between good critical judgment and second-guessing, and every sports reporter should learn this early.

Scope of Sports Writing

Sports writing ranges from straight-news reporting through all degrees of interpretative and feature writing and the editorialized column. A sports event may be treated in any one of those degrees or in all of them combined. The general practice is to treat the important event as straight news, utilizing any of the lead and story forms already discussed, with sufficient interpretation to enrich the report with background. Separate stories, features and columns devoted to the sidelights supplement the straight-news account. Many newspapers permit sports writers to use a highly informal style, often with few restrictions on editorializing, even in a story handled as straight news. Careful reporters keep their editorial comments to a minimum in their straight-news account of a sports event.

For important sports events, "buildup," or advance, stories and articles sometimes are used for days, even weeks, before the event. The event is thoroughly covered when it occurs, and "post-mortem" stories may be used for days afterward in commenting on what took place.

Here are several examples of free-wheeling leads on sports stories:

NEW YORK—Sassy and flashy and psyched to the max, Andre Agassi put on a show of blast-away tennis to set up a fiery Saturday match against Boris Becker in the U.S. Open semifinals.

(The Associated Press)

It's that time of the year again, the time when normally sane people start wearing deflated basketballs on their heads and their hearts on their T-shirts.

(Chicago Tribune)

News Sources

Local and regional schools and colleges, recreation departments, professional teams of all types, sponsors of all kinds of sports leagues (such as Little League teams, bowling leagues and country clubs) and other local organizations that promote or conduct sports events all are covered by the sports staff. The editor has, on the one hand, to avoid overlooking some activities deserving space, and on the other, to avoid giving too much space to some teams and groups having very active publicity directors or chairpersons.

A sports staff could not begin to cover all events deserving space, but with the proper encouragement and instructions a sports writer can get valuable assistance in gathering news from many of the people engaged in the various sports. Many newspapers arrange with high school and even junior high students to phone in results of games the newspapers are unable to staff. Little League coaches or their spouses, interested parents, bowling lane owners and tennis and golf club professionals generally are willing to call in the results of an event.

A word of caution is needed on sports news sources. Gambling on sporting events seems to be a national pastime, but the sports staff should be cautious about quoting gambling odds on sports events, although the practice has become more commonplace today in reporting on upcoming professional sporting events. (Gambling is illegal in most states.)

Style in Sports Writing

Good sports writing should be vigorous, virile and audacious. It should not be hackneyed or so exaggerated that it strains the boundaries of believability. It should not be dull. Each reporter must develop a style of writing that is bright and readable but that does not violate the principles of standard English rhetoric. The basic rules of English grammar apply to sports writing as well as to all other newspaper writing.

A sports reporter's objective is to bring the event to the reader with all of the impact that event had on the spectators. Twisting, straining and mangling the language should not be used to accomplish this. The informality of writing on most sports pages may tempt a weak writer to fall back on cliches and hackneyed expressions.

The most effective and vivid sports writing is achieved through the use of active rather than passive verbs and the judicious use of precise adjectives. There is a great difference between carefully selected, precise verbs and adjectives and worn-out cliches such as "banged the apple" and "smacked the pill."

It is important for the sports reporter to remember that the story should be written for the reader-spectator and not the athlete and the coach. The language must not be so technical that the general public will not understand it. At the same time, however, the reporter must be aware that the coach and the players will be reading the story. If the writing reveals an ignorance of techniques and misuses the language of the sport, those involved in playing the sport are not likely to respect the writer and may not be willing to cooperate on future stories.

Sports Story Leads

The sports page contains stories on a wide variety of events. Most space is devoted to such major sports as football, baseball, basketball, golf and tennis, but other sports that may be written about include swimming, hunting, fishing, automobile and horse racing, track, volleyball, trapshooting, bowling, boxing, wrestling and gymnastics. Depending on the season, and perhaps the section of the country, skiing, hockey, soccer, polo, rowing, rodeos, hiking and a variety of other sports might get even more space than some of the major spectator sports. In an effort to be complete, most sports pages try carry stories on all major events in all sports. In many cases these include horse shows, dog shows and other events that might not be classified as true sports.

Sports stories are usually reported in a news fashion. Although allowed more freedom in the use of language, the sports reporter usually follows the regular news principles in building the story. The five W's are generally in the lead of the straight news account of the event, and the features usually are summarized at the beginning and elaborated in the body of the story. The general principles of the single-feature and the several-feature lead also apply to straight-sports writing. However, many sports stories, particularly the second-day story or a sidebar story, take a strong feature approach.

No matter what type of sports event is being covered, the reporter may look for one or more of the following elements to provide features for the story:

1. The score of the game or the outcome of the event (The final score may be subordinate to other features, but it should be in the lead or no later than the opening sentence of the second paragraph.)

2. Spectacular plays

3. Scoring plays or sequence of plays

4. Individual stars

5. The significance of the game—championship or effect on record

6. General comparison of teams or opponents

7. Background of game—weather, crowd, special occasion.

These leads illustrate the use of various features of an event:

The Score or Outcome

Quincy Lewis scored the last six of his 36 points at the foul line to give No. 21 Minnesota a 90–83 overtime victory Tuesday against No. 15 Indiana at Minneapolis.

FIGURE 28.2 High school sports are important in every community. The staff of the *Valdosta Daily Times* recognizes that by devoting an entire front page of its sports section to prep sports. Chances are it was the best read page in the paper that Sunday.

(Reprinted with permission of the *Valdosta Daily Times*.)

Campbell County's boys dropped their fourth game in a row Tuesday night with a 99–73 loss to visiting District 3-AAA foe Clinton.

Individual Performance

Chris Weinke threw a career-high four touchdown passes and Florida State's defense yielded only 129 yards and five first downs in a 48–0 blowout of Clemson.

COLUMBIA, S.C.—This sun-soaked afternoon belonged to the golden right arm of Tee Martin, who set three NCAA passing records.

The Vols surged to a 21-0 halftime lead as Martin completed his first 23 passes against the Gamecocks. He broke the NCAA season record with 24 straight completions, which included his final pass of the Alabama game. He also broke the single-game record by hitting 23 in a row.

Significance of the Game

A prince and a pauper met in the middle of a 100-yard field Saturday afternoon. When they had finished pounding on each other, the long-time underling had emerged from beneath the boot heel of NFL royalty to remain the only one standing.

And a crowd of 70,262 in the Georgia Dome went nuts.

The Atlanta Falcons, long one of the NFL's doormats, defeated the old nemesis San Francisco 49ers 20–18 to advance to next Sunday's NFL Championship Game for the first time in the franchise's 33-year history.

(The *Atlanta Journal–Constitution*)

Recruiting is always an important sports story. Here are two examples, one with an unusual twist:

It has been nearly three decades since the University of Texas finished No. 1 in college football. Now, at least in the national recruiting race, the Longhorns can claim a national title.

Thanks to a change of mind by quarterback Chris Simms, Texas signed a recruiting class Wednesday that most experts rated the nation's best.

(*Fort Worth Star Telegram*)

Three-inch heels, a black mini-skirt, earrings and a white satin blouse aren't typical attire for an athlete signing a college football scholarship. Then again, Riverdale High's Tonya Butler isn't your typical signee.

The female placekicker was one of six Riverdale players to sign a national letter of intent Wednesday morning. Butler, headed to Middle Georgia Junior College, is the first female to earn a football scholarship in a state college.

(The *Atlanta Journal–Constitution*)

Feature Leads

The use of feature leads on sports stories is more popular than ever since they were introduced by writers on afternoon newspapers as a way of gaining a fresh look on a game that was already 24 hours old. This type of lead may be based on a quote, an after-the-game visit to the locker room or perhaps an analysis of a player's or team's style. Some writers also use descriptive leads effectively.

Sometimes a good quote tells the story of a sports event better than the score alone. One of the better quote leads of all times didn't get into print because the sports editor thought it would offend the readers. Here it is:

> Reporter: "What happened, coach?"
> Coach: "They beat the hell out of us!"
> That's how Rebel coach Buster Jones explained his team's humiliating 56–0 defeat by the Western Raiders last night.

Reporters who elect to use feature leads often collect most of their material after the game, talking to the coach and players in the locker room, interviewing happy or disappointed fans, observing crowd reaction as the game draws to a close. That is the material television often misses.

Here's an example of a feature lead on a game story:

> FOXBORO, Mass.—It seems as if Bill Parcells' walkout made all the difference for the New York Jets.
> Parcells, not happy with the way things were going during the week following the Jet's lackluster effort in a loss to the St. Louis Rams on Oct. 10, took his assistant coaches and walked out on the players at last Friday's practice. That got his players thinking—and put them in the right frame of mind for Monday night's 24–14 victory over the New England Patriots.
>
> (Associated Press)

The feature approach often works well in other sports stories. Here's *USA TODAY's* story on the question whether Notre Dame should remain independent or join the Big Ten Conference:

> SOUTH BEND, Ind.—Maybe a few puffs of white smoke would be appropriate. Notre Dame's board of trustees will emerge Friday from a meeting in London and render a decision a bit more corporal—but perhaps only a little less anticipated—than the traditional election of a new pope.
> Should the Fighting Irish football program, the most famous in the land and representing the most famous of all Catholic universities, remain independent? Or should it abandon more than a century of tradition and seek a home in the Big Ten Conference?

Chris Broussard of the *New York Times* used this approach in his story on the New York Nets basketball team:

> They start a point guard who prefers shooting to passing, a small forward who is more comfortable in the backcourt and a center who is a shade shorter than his listed height of 6 feet 10 inches. Their top shooting guard, though graceful and athletic, is reed-thin and their rising star at power forward has been labeled by many basketball analysts as a tweener.
>
> But the Nets, one of the most peculiar and unorthodox units in the National Basketball Association, makes that collection of talent work.

Here's Kirsten Haukebo's tribute to Mr. Prospector, the oldest and most valuable living stallion, that appeared in the *Louisville Courier-Journal*:

> It's a quiet fall morning at historic Claiborne Farm, the 3,000-acre spread near Paris, Ky., where great racehorses have become great stallions for generations.
>
> Secretariat stood at stud here and is buried behind the farm's main office, alongside thoroughbred legends Bold Ruler, Nijinsky II and Nasrullah. Fresh flowers rest against Secretariat's headstone, the champ died 9 years ago, but fans still send bouquets every few days.
>
> Only one plot remains in the small cemetery. It's being saved for Mr. Prospector, the oldest and most valuable living stallion and one of the most important of all time. He has earned $160 million during his stud career.
>
> Mr. Prospector has had more starters in Breeders' Cup races than any other sire, 37 in the event's 14 years.

And Mike Diovanna's disappointment shows through in this report on the poor showing of the San Diego Padres in Game 2 of the World Series. It's from the *Los Angeles Times*:

> NEW YORK—This wasn't a baseball game—it was an ambush, a classic New York Yankee-style mugging in which the San Diego Padres were so thoroughly plundered they should have stopped by a Bronx precinct afterward and filed a police report.
>
> Putting together their first complete game of the playoffs—and we don't mean a pitcher going the distance here—the Yankees throttled the Padres, 9–3, in Game 2 of the World Series on Saturday night to take a commanding 2–0 lead in the best-of-seven series.

Most newspapers have one or more sports columnists. Some of them are not very good. Others are tremendously talented. One of the best is Jim Murray of the *Los Angeles Times*. He is often witty and not afraid to poke a little fun at sports and sports figures. The following is an example of one of his column leads:

> Wait just a darn minute here! Hold it! Time out!
> What's going on in the United States of America?
> Let me ask you something: didn't we used to win international athletic events with monotonous regularity? Didn't the rest of the world have trouble keeping up with us? Didn't we used to win Wimbledon, U.S. Opens, golf and ten-

FIGURE 28.3 Eye-catching graphics have become a hallmark of many sports pages as demonstrated by this example from the *Boston Sunday Globe* featuring a story about Robert Edwards, a rookie running back for the New England Patriots. (Reprinted courtesy of the *Boston Globe*.)

nis, British Opens, French Opens, auto races, foot races, Olympic games? Like clockwork?

The rest of the world got sick of hearing "The Star Spangled Banner," right? Well, take a look around you. What's happening here?

A guy whose name you can't pronounce without a mouthful of marbles, Jose Maria Olazabal, has just won the World Series of Golf, our World Series of Golf, by—hear this!—12 shots.

That wouldn't be so bad—but a Briton won our Masters tournament this year. An Aussie won our PGA.

A Swede won Wimbledon and will probably win the U.S. Tennis Open. Unless, of course, a Czech or German does.

The rest of the column catalogued other events American athletes once won but haven't won lately, including the Little League World Series.

The Body of the Story

The body of the sports story must, of course, complete the development of the lead. If the lead is a summary, the body may proceed in the logical development of the various features as presented in the summary lead. If the lead is an outstanding feature, it must be followed by a summary of the features and by the subsequent development of each feature. These are the general principles of lead and body development that have been observed from the beginning of our text as applying to all types of stories.

In many sports stories, however, two types of body development must be utilized: (1) the general interpretation and (2) the running story. The general interpretation is essential. It is merely the development of the lead or lead block. The reporter must narrate and explain (interpret) the highlights (features) of the event. This is the logical body development that is used in other types of stories. The running (chronological) story (play-by-play, inning-by-inning, round-by-round) sometimes appears after the general interpretation or is printed separately under its own headline. Play-by-play or blow-by-blow accounts of sports events are used only infrequently by some newspapers and not at all by others, particularly when radio or television covers the major event.

EXERCISES

1. Select a major sports event (the Super Bowl, the Indianapolis 500, the NCAA basketball tournament final game, for example) and compare the coverage in a major daily—the *New York Times, Chicago Tribune* or *Los Angeles Times*—with the coverage by AP and a national sports publication such as *Sports Illustrated.* Write a report on how they are similar and how they differ.

2. Read the sports stories in your daily newspaper for one week. Make a list of all the clichés you find. In each case, select a better word or words that could have been used in place of the cliché.

3. Football and basketball tend to dominate colleges and universities and get the most attention from the press. Select one of the so-called minor sports on campus and write a story about the coach and team.

4. Attend both a major sports event and a minor one on your campus and write a feature story comparing the fans at both.

5. Invite the sports editor or the leading sports columnist from your local newspaper to class to discuss sports coverage in his or her newspaper. Write a story on that interview.

6. Interview the head of food services for the dormitories on your campus and the person who supervises the food served athletes at the training table. Write a story comparing the food served at both.

7. Interview the quarterback for your college football team, the captain of the basketball team, the top swimmer, the leading tennis player and the outstanding track runner. Write a story based on their views on how difficult it is to be involved in a college sports team and a full-time student at the same time.

8. If your college has one or more female intercollegiate athletic teams, interview the leading player on each and write a story about them similar to the story in Exercise 7.

9. Contact the official who is in charge of maintaining the football stadium or basketball arena at your college or university. Interview him or her and write a feature story about the strange items found after a sporting event.

10. Interview the person in charge of concessions at football and basketball games and write a story about how much food and drink—and what kind—is consumed during a single sporting event and for the entire season.

11. Write short stories using the following notes:
    a. Cherokee Country Club
       On short list for
       Major PGA tournament
       Golf pro Mark Pizarek
       Said it's too early
       To even speculate
       Acknowledged that PGA
       Officials had talked
       To him and club officials
       "If it happens it won't
       Be before next year"
       It would be first
       PGA championship
       Tournament in the state
    b. Sunshine Wellness Exercise
       And Therapy Center
       811 Holiday Blvd.
       Seeking entrants for
       First annual Touch-and-Go
       Bench Press competition

To be held last Saturday
In the month
Competition categories
Overall lifting, all weights
Among other competitions
Divisions for men, women
Masters (over 40)
For information call
794-0065

c. State Wildlife Federation
Announced plans for a
Fisharama, Duckarama and
Bass Madness trade shows
David Houston, spokesman says
Shows will make city
"A mecca for outdoor enthusiasts"
Fisharama and Duckarama
Will be held June 16–18
At the City Expo Center
Expect 40,000 to attend
Bass Madness show
Will be held
In Jacobs Building
State Fairgrounds
July 10–12
Seminars hourly on
Fishing techniques
Fishing competition
On nearby Douglas Lake
Admission to events free
Call Wildlife Federation
For more information
(661) 555-9000

d. Richard Albright, 40,
Route 1, Bulls Gap
Hospitalized Saturday
After duck-hunting accident
Wildlife Resources Warden
Tommy McNamara said
Albright and four others
Setting up a duck blind
On end of Norris Lake
He was loading his shotgun
It accidentally discharged
Into some rocks
Ten pellets ricocheted
Off the rocks
Struck Albright
In face and neck

Other hunters not hit
Albright taken to
Morristown Hamblin Hospital
Later transferred to
University Medical Center
Listed in serious
But stable condition
Wildlife Officer Jim Robins
Is investigating the incident

12. Using information you collected in Exercise 4, write a 1 minute-radio sports news report.

29 The Arts, Entertainment, Criticism

"Criticism is the stage on which journalists do their fanciest strutting," William Zinsser said in his book, *On Writing Well*.

Not everyone agrees, especially those who have been criticized. Writer Kenneth Tynan once described a critic as "a man who knows the way but can't drive the car." Actor Robert Morley warned that "if the critics were always right, we should be in trouble."

Composer Igor Stravinsky said he dreamed of critics who were "small and rodent-like with padlocked ears, as if they had stepped out of a painting by Goya." And actor/director Elia Kazan put it more bluntly. Criticism, he said, is "a big bite out of someone's back."

Despite the criticism of the critics, there is no shortage of individuals who want to write criticism of arts, music, literature, films and popular entertainment for newspapers and other publications.

Nearly every young journalist seems to harbor a desire to be a critic or a reviewer, even though he or she may be tone deaf, admire paintings done on black velvet and rank Barbara Cartland's romance novels as great literature.

It's obvious from the comments just quoted that artists and performers do not like critics and reviewers. There have been some notorious feuds between writers and performers, due in part to the fact that there are no absolute standards in the arts. The late Pauline Kael, long-time movie critic for the *New Yorker* wrote: "There is no final authority. There is only fallible judgment."

Unfortunately, some critics and reviewers write as if their judgment was indeed infallible. When they move on, there are countless others waiting in line who also believe their judgment is truly the final authority.

The late television critic, syndicated columnist and author John Crosby, once lamented that the job of the critic is to be "literate about the illiterate, witty about the witless and coherent about the incoherent." That's not a very encouraging job description. Nevertheless, the job of the critic or reviewer often is the most coveted one at a newspaper.

Being a reviewer or critic is much more than simply saying, "I know what I like, so I can write about it." It is not an easy path to glory. It requires a strong background and understanding about drama, literature, film, music and fine arts to be able to write about them literally and with authority.

In writing about cultural subjects, the reporter has far more latitude than that offered in almost any other area. Unlike the straight-news story, much of what is written about entertainment or fine arts is appraisal and evaluation for the reader. Obviously, hard-news stories do come out of these fields, and they often have a news peg—a new book or play, a concert, an art show or a performance by a musical group or drama company that leads to the coverage by the newspaper. But for the most part, the prime purpose of a review or critique is to help readers enjoy, understand and appreciate the performance or work of art.

Reviewing vs. Criticism

The difference between reviewing and criticism might be mainly one of definition. In practice, at most of today's newspapers and magazines, the terms are almost synonymous. Yet there is a distinction.

A reviewer, who is not competent by way of background and knowledge, should not criticize the performance or work of another. A review should present facts without editorializing. For example, a reviewer assigned to cover a popular music performance should tell the reader who performed, mention where and when the concert took place, give a summary of the performance and describe the reaction of the audience. A reviewer should tell the reader what the performance was like without attempting a critical evaluation of the performer's musicianship. Of course, in a number of newspapers, reviewers are allowed to engage in various degrees of criticism in their reviews.

Pure criticism, on the other hand, requires expert judgment. Usually a newspaper will not engage in criticism unless it has a qualified staff member to handle the assignment. Many smaller newspapers buy columns from syndicates and feature services written in such areas as theater and music. At times, however, a newspaper may assign its most qualified reporter or employ an outside specialist (musician, artist, author) to write criticisms of public performances.

The good critic uses his or her knowledge and understanding of a particular field to evaluate the performance or work of art. Critics should know the respective standards of each art form and be able to measure fairly the success or failure of the work or performance in attaining those standards. The work or performance should be compared with others in its class, and the ability of the artists, performers or musicians to present it successfully should be carefully evaluated.

A critic must make certain that his or her judgment is not clouded by a particular bias against a composer, a style of art or music or an individual performer. Criticism can be clever, sarcastic, even cutting, but it should also be insightful. For example, this clever line by drama critic John Mason Brown remains a classic today: "Tallulah Bankhead barged down the Nile last night as Cleopatra and sank." But criticism should never be mean-spirited.

FIGURE 29.1 The *San Francisco Chronicle* packages its daily entertainment and arts section in its Datebook.

(© *San Francisco Chronicle*. Reprinted with permission.)

Entertainment, literature and the fine arts that are the subjects of review or criticism in newspapers include:

1. Books and articles
2. Dramatic performances
3. Concerts and other musical performances (classical and popular)
4. Recordings
5. Films
6. Radio and television programs
7. Lectures
8. Art—painting, sculpture
9. Architecture
10. Professional dancing
11. Photography
12. Nightclub performances.

Principles of Criticism

The person assigned to write a review or a critical piece should remember that the standards of good writing always apply. Far too many critics write more in the jargon of the particular field they are covering than in the language the typical reader of a mass publication can understand. This is particularly true in such a field as abstract art.

The following are important points anyone writing a review or critical article should consider.

1. It is important to give readers a view of the woods before pointing out individual trees. The reader is interested in knowing what to expect in the book, play or performance. What is the nature of the work? Is it sensational, intellectual, calm or boisterous? Is it worthwhile and in what way?

2. The work should be criticized in the light of its intentions and within its genre. A detective story or mystery play should not be compared to a classic drama. Amateurs have a right to compete with other amateurs without being judged by professional standards. However, amateurs should not be praised lavishly if they do not deserve it. It is generally wise to report the amateur performances fairly, emphasizing audience reaction.

3. The contents of books or plays should be outlined only to the extent needed for readers to determine whether they are interested and not so fully as to give away the plot. One purpose of the critic is to promote popular interest, not to discourage it.

4. The criticism should be interesting in itself. Readers will not read dull criticism any more readily than they will read dull news. Good criticism may rise to the heights of literature itself.

5. The critic is addressing lay readers who do not possess technical vocabularies. Some of them cannot be expected to know the difference between crisis and climax or protagonist and antagonist, for example, and they may not be familiar with Aristotle's theory of catharsis. So the critic should write a language the reader will understand and not attempt to "show off" his or her literary prowess.

6. The significance of the work should be suggested. Is it extraordinary, distinguished, superior, mediocre, below standard? Does it have social or economic implications?

7. If the critic likes or dislikes what is being evaluated, he or she should explain why. It is not enough merely to praise or to condemn a literary or artistic production. Critical comment should be supported with examples.

8. The critic may stay within ethical and legal bounds (see Chapter 5). In using copyrighted material, he or she may quote a reasonable amount with no fear of violating the law. A reasonable amount might be interpreted as "a taste but not a full swallow" of the quality of the material. In other words, the critic cannot present the full impact of a reviewed work's quality under the guise of a critical review.

9. Above all, the critic must keep in mind that his or her major responsibility is to the reader, not to the authors, performers or painters. It is important to tell readers whether the production is worth seeing or hearing and why. A critic must be honest with the reader and fair to the artist. A critic should never become a public agent for a performer or production.

A reader would get a pretty good idea from this review by Tom Shales in the *Washington Post* that this television show might not be worth viewing:

> Simplistic and ridiculous, NBC's "The 60s" exploits, trivializes and occasionally trashes a decade of horror and glory in American life. The four-hour miniseries is a dizzy, busy mishmash of newsreel footage from an era and hokey dramatic sequences about two fictitious families living through it.

Writing Style of Criticism

Some newspapers use a set form to give essential data at the beginning of a critical review. It generally is set off in a box and often is in bold type. Here is an example of the style used by the *New York Times* for films, television, opera and musical performances:

The Last Days
Directed and edited by James Moll; director of photography, Harris Done; music by Hans Zimmer; produced by June Beailor and Ken Lipper; presented by Steven Spielberg and Survivors of the Shoah Visual History Foundation; released by October Films. This film is not rated. WITH: Representative Tom Lantos, Alice Lok Cahana, Renee Firestone, Bill Basch and Irene Zisblatt.

The review by Stephen Holden began this way:

> James Moll's documentary film "The Last Days," a concise, devastating his-
> tory of the Nazis' decimation of Hungary's Jewish population during the final
> days of World War II, offers a ghastly inverse kind of reassurance. It reminds us
> that yes there are still images and stories of the human cruelty and degradation
> that we can never get used to, that we shouldn't get used, no matter how intensely
> the mass media have flooded us with pictures of human nature at its vilest.

Other papers do not have an established pattern for presenting these details. The
reviewer or critic will work most of them into the article, which often takes the
form of an essay. First-person is permitted because the critic or reviewer is expressing a personal opinion, and the story will carry a by-line.

Most small newspapers do not offer many opportunities for beginning reporters to develop their critical faculties. Even many medium-size newspapers
purchase their critical reviews of the arts and entertainment from syndicates or
use those distributed by the wire services.

A reporter interested in developing as a reviewer or critic should read the writ-
ings of other critics, especially the good ones, and analyze all the devices and techniques they use. But the beginning critic should not copy the writing style of other
critics. It is important for anyone writing criticism to develop a personal writing style.

Subjects of Criticism

Books and Articles

Most metropolitan dailies have book-review columns or pages. They often are a
part of the Sunday or weekend edition. Many newspapers use reviews written by
members of the staff as well as reviews from the wire services and syndicates.

The public frequently looks to the reviewer or critic for guidance in selecting
books, and often the critic can help mold public taste. The better critics do not
limit themselves to writing about new books. Often they write about literary
trends as well as the business and economics of the publishing industry.

In judging a book, the critic must not lean too heavily on the publisher's
publicity release announcing the book. Nor should a critic write a review from the
notes on the dust jacket, a practice many authors insist is commonplace. Publicity
releases and dust-jacket notes can be used as aids, and some critics may find that
they agree with their assessment of the work, but publicity material should not influence the critic's own appraisal.

These examples will illustrate the range of writing style in book reviews:

ANOTHER KIND OF AUTUMN
By Loren Eisley (Scribner's $8.95)

Harriet Van Horne said it best: A friend I never knew died last weekend. Let me
paraphrase it: A friend I met only once died a few weeks ago. There is a large hole where

he vanished. One can only hope that as with those problematic black holes in space, there is a compensating white hole in some far part of the universe where his energies are a source of never-ending wonder.

Loren Eisley is the name of the friend met only once, a shy man, seemingly unaware of his genius. His new and last book of poetry is properly titled "Another Kind of Autumn." Autumn was always in his work, as was poetry. His earliest essays, 30 years ago in *Harper's*, struck an awe into me that never stopped, but went on from article to article, prose-poem to prose-poem and finally to his poetry itself, the poems with brightness in them, but with autumn narrowing the light.

(Ray Bradbury, *Los Angeles Times*)

EVENING NEWS
A Novel by Marly Swick
Published by Little & Brown
368 pages, $23

Marly Swick has written a novel that might be lifted right out of the headlines—a story of a family shattered by loss when a 9-year-old accidentally shoots his half-sister.

The all-too-familiar opening scenario has Teddy's best friend Eric showing off his dad's handgun. When Eric hears his mother coming, he gives Teddy the gun, which goes off and kills 2-year-old Trina.

In the aftermath of the shooting, the pieced-together stepfamily begins to unravel . . . "Evening News" is a book that lingers in the mind and heart.

(Colleen Kelly Warren, *St. Louis Post–Dispatch*)

MEDICINE MEN
By Alice Adams
Knopf, 239 Pages, $23

Alice Adams' new novel is both a delight and a disappointment, just what we have come to expect from this venerable American writer. "Medicine Men" opens with intrigue and promise: Molly Bonner, 40ish, is a recently widowed San Francisco resident made rich by insurance money following the helicopter accident of her daredevil filmmaker husband, who had decided to leave her . . . Adams' splendid prose and dialogue are punctuated by wonderful details about her character's behavior . . .

(Patty Shillington, The *Tampa Tribune–Times*)

Movies

For the young writer, movies present one of the best opportunities to develop as a critic or reviewer. Students interested in this type of writing would benefit greatly from some of the film courses now being offered at many colleges and universities. They should also study the works of a wide range of critics writing for major newspapers and magazines as well as the many collections of movie reviews in book form. The collected reviews of James Agee, for example, are excellent for style, form and critical judgment. And the works of Pauline Kael, film critic for the *New Yorker*, should not be overlooked.

A movie reviewer or critic should prepare for the job by studying the works of the great critics while making every effort to keep current on the economic as well as artistic trends in the film industry. Too often newspaper writers who report on films content themselves with simple reviewing when they have an opportunity for conscientious criticism in the manner of Agee and Kael. The critic has an opportunity to do more than create audiences for films. The critic can exert much influence on the medium and can help bring about a higher type of entertainment. In the final analysis, the moviegoer is the one who really determines the fare offered. However, an effective critic can do much to refine the moviegoer's taste.

Although the temptation might be great, a reviewer or critic should resist seeking personal attention through snide and devastating comments. A review or critique should be an honest and fair evaluation of the work. Criticism is not synonymous with slurs. A fair critic—one who gains the respect and even the admiration of readers—is not constantly negative; neither does he or she forever praise every film. Few works are entirely good or entirely bad. A reader who has been misled by a reviewer or critic generally ceases to be a reader.

The following are leads from several movie reviews:

"I Still Know What You Did Last Summer"
*

— Rating: R (violence, language)
— Cast: Jennifer Love Hewitt, Brandy, Freddie Prinz, Jr., Mekhi Phifer
— Director: Danny Cannon
— Writer: Trey Callaway
— Running Time: 1 hour, 36 minutes

"I Still Know What You Did Last Summer" still stars teen queen Jennifer Love Hewitt, who's still being menaced by that creep in the raincoat, who's carrying around a fish hook the size of Rhode Island.

Still, that's no excuse for how tired a sequel it is.

(Julie Hinds, *San Jose Mercury News*)

"Still Crazy"
*** (out of four)
Stars: Stephen Rhea, Billy Connolly,
        Jimmy Nail
Director: Brian Gibson
Distributor: Columbia
Rating: R for profanity, sexuality and drug content
In limited release today

Middle age, in and of itself? Not that funny.
Middle-age men trying to rekindle their flaming youth? Sort of funny.
Middle-age musicians revisiting their '70's glory days with a reunion tour? Sex, drugs and a belly roll—now you're rockin'.

Still Crazy is less crazy than This Is Spinal Tap, the most sterling example of heavy-metal mirth on film and less fulfilling than The Full Monty, whose male strippers have a certain pub-gritty kinship with these British past-their-primers . . .

(Susan Wloszczyna, *USA TODAY*)

Some larger newspapers use capsule reviews on movies opening in a given week while others run condensed versions of original reviews to up-date what's playing at the movies. Here's a capsule review from the *San Francisco Chronicle*:

"JOHN CARPENTER'S VAMPIRES". James Wood stars as a ruthless vampire slayer who must hunt down Valek (Thomas Ian Griffith), the vicious, 600-year-old leader of the undead, in the deserts of New Mexico. Co-starring Sherly Lee, Daniel Baldwin and Maximillan Schell. Opening Friday at Bay Area theaters. Rated R. 107 minutes.

In its movie guide on Fridays, the *New York Times* may recap earlier reviews of a dozen or more films. Here's one example:

"AT FIRST SIGHT," starring Val Kilmer and Mira Sorvino. Directed by Irwin Winkler (PG-13, 128 minutes). In this overlong and often desperately banal version of a case study reported by Dr. Oliver Sacks, Mr. Kilmer plays a man whose nearly lifelong blindness was suddenly alleviated by surgery. Ms. Sorvino plays the bright-eyed New York career woman who falls in love with him, then urges him to change his once-peaceful life. But the film brings more than case-study data to communicating how this man's restored sight affected him, or what made it a mixed blessing. Sample dialogue: "Have you ever listened to the rain? I mean, really listened?" (Maslin)

Television, Radio, Recordings

The television industry produces major news stories almost daily. The decrease in audience shares of the major networks, the shabby treatment of a beloved morning news/entertainment program hostess, the networks' fight with the rating services, the astronomical cost of advertising during the Superbowl, the multi-million-dollar contracts of new anchors and dozens of other news stories often make the news sections of most newspapers because television plays a major role in the daily lives of millions of persons.

Major daily newspapers have staff writers and columnists who cover television both as a business and as an entertainment medium. Often they write about radio as well. In addition, the wire services and most feature syndicates distribute news stories, special columns and features on television and radio.

The same basic standards that apply to all news and critical writing apply to writing about television and radio. The news stories should be complete, fair, accurate and balanced. The critical reviews should be informed, fair and just. Flippant reviews can be amusing, but they serve no useful purpose in most cases. Television, in particular, has far too great a social, cultural and economic impact to be treated lightly. It should be written about as the serious social phenomenon it is.

Here are several examples of news stories about the industry and a review of a major television drama:

> You may be experiencing fewer *deja vú* moments on television these days.
>
> In a small but encouraging sign, the Big Four networks are airing fewer repeats. The 22-episode season—an industry standard for more than 15 years—is being stretched to 24 or 26 new episodes, particularly for hit shows.
>
> The reason is obvious: Viewership drops off sharply when a show is in reruns. The networks, which are battling severe rating erosions as cable's numbers climb, can no longer afford those losses . . .

Cable television, the favorite whipping post of pundits, politicians and just plain folks who subscribe, takes a media beating when it fouls up. Here's a story from the *Atlanta Journal–Constitution* when the cable system went out during the Super Bowl:

> Perhaps the only thing worse than watching the Atlanta Falcons lose the Super Bowl was not watching them lose. Tens of thousands of metro Atlantans were outraged by cable and electricity outages during Sunday night's big game . . .
>
> MediaOne spokesman Reg Griffin estimated about 20,000 cable customers were without service for part of the game . . .

The possible change in programming at a local radio or television station often rates a major story as this example from the *Miami Herald* demonstrates:

> At WTMI's Coconut Grove Studios, Howard P. "Woody" Tanger, owner of South Florida's only classical music radio station, sits twirling an unlit cigar and contemplating the future. The suspenders he sports, over a natty blue-striped shirt, are decorated with miniature portraits of Beethoven, one of his cultural heroes.
>
> "I'm wearing my Beethoven suspenders purposely because I'm making a statement," he said last week. "WTMI will remain a classical music station, come hell or high water, until Dec. 31, 1998."
>
> After that, it's anyone's guess what will happen. Though Tanger intends to develop another revenue source for WTMI over the next year, there are no guarantees. But at least the year of reprieve is better news than the station's 250,000 weekly fans heard last month when Tanger, expressing disappointment in the station's relatively weak revenues, hinted he might sell it or change its programming to a more profitable format, such as rock.

Here is how the *New York Times* reported the return of Walter Cronkite to television, even though it was only a brief encore:

> John Glenn's return to space has the ring of nostalgia for a generation of Americans, and CNN will add to that flavor by bringing Walter Cronkite back as a co-anchor for its coverage of the event.
>
> The cable network announced yesterday that Mr. Cronkite, who was closely associated with the American space program in his role as the CBS News anchor in

the 1960s, would join John Holliman in presenting CNN's coverage of the launching of the space shuttle Discovery on Oct. 29 and the planned landing on Nov. 7 . . .

The *San Francisco Chronicle* led its Datebook entertainment section with the Glenn–Cronkite story.

New television shows generally are previewed by the major newspapers. Here's what Matt Roush of *USA TODAY* told his readers about ABC's "The Practice" the day it was scheduled to be telecast for the first time:

> Before you shrug it off with "Just what we need, more TV lawyers," it's worth checking out the scrappy employees of The Practice.
>
> Don't expect the new or revolutionary. There's nothing the least bit special about this ensemble drama, set at a barely-scraping-by Boston law firm, except that it's all so well done.
>
> The assets are nothing to sneeze at: sharp writing by David E. Kelly, a coast and a world away from his tony L.A. Law days, returning to realism after all those Picket Fences allegories; a commanding and sympathetic leading man in the strikingly handsome Dylan McDermott as Bobby Donnell for the defense; and (in the three episodes previewed) spectacular guest casting.

Radio

Radio's local programming formats and its declining influence as a national entertainment medium, except in music and sports, has caused many newspapers to limit their coverage to an occasional important news story and a limited listing of programs. However, some newspapers continue to carry a locally written radio column and report on such activities as changes in format by local stations, ownership changes and the arrival or departure of radio personalities. When a popular morning radio personality is pulled off the air during sticky contract negotiations with the station, it's an important local news story. Many newspapers also supplement their coverage of radio with wire service stories and syndicated columns.

Pirate broadcasting stations have been in and out of the news for years. When the Federal Communications Commission started a crackdown, here is how Brad Kava reported it in the *San Jose Mercury News:*

> The knocks on the door came last Sunday, like something out of a Franz Kafka novel. Two government agents stood there, grilling people and leaving some with threatening letters.
>
> This was part of a crackdown by the Federal Communications Commission against what they call pirate broadcasters.
>
> The broadcasters call themselves fighters for speech or micro-broadcasters. They operate low-wattage, homemade radio transmitters, sometimes out of their bedrooms, playing music and talking about local issues on shows heard at most 10 miles away.
>
> Five of them in San Jose and Los Gatos were called on by agents from the Haywood FCC office. They said the agents also spoke with landlords and parents, hinting at darker actions if the stations weren't shut down. Several of the broadcasters are under 21.

Recordings and Music Videos

The recording industry in the late 1980s and early 1990s was the source for two major news stories—one as a result of technology and the other of duplicity. The introduction of compact discs that offered clearer sound literally revolutionized the record industry and brought an end to the era of long-playing vinyl record albums. In addition, the candid admission that an immensely popular and award-winning singing duo had not sung a single note on their best-selling album shocked the public and the music business much the same way as the 1950s payola, drugs and sex scandals had damaged the credibility of the industry.

Although these hard-news stories capture the public's attention briefly, it is the columns, reviews, critiques and feature stories about recording artists written by the music writers and critics that readers rely on for information and a fair evaluation of recorded performances. Most larger newspapers have assigned staff writers with some musical training to cover the recording industry. But many smaller papers purchase columns and features about music and musicians from feature syndicates. At some newspapers, the critic or reviewer who covers live musical performances also writes about recordings.

The stars of the musical field—especially the popular music performers—are national and international heroes to their fans, and a reporter who attempts to write about them and their work must be knowledgeable or risk the wrath of legions of irate followers. A performer's work should not be dismissed or degraded simply because it does not please the taste of the reviewer.

In addition to evaluating performances, the reporter writing about recordings also has a responsibility to keep the public informed, not only about new releases, but about the many fads, trends and other changes in the field, especially the technological changes that continue to reshape the industry.

One of the most significant changes came about with the advent of the music video, which revived the sagging rock music industry through MTV, a cable network devoted entirely to music videos. It became the hottest basic operation in the history of cable. Its popularity spilled over from rock music into other popular music as well as country music. Music videos became a staple in all fields except classical. And newspapers across the country began reviewing them just as they do records.

These leads from record and music-video reviews illustrate the style commonly used by writers. Often the reviews are limited to three or four paragraphs, and many newspapers group them in a column under a single headline.

> Ani DiFranco
> "Up Up Up Up Up Up"
> Righteous Babe, $15.98
>
> Ani DiFranco is a changeling. In the past two years, she has transmuted from punk-folk singer with a small but dedicated fan base into a punk-folk star whose lovely mug appears from magazine racks as frequently as it does from CD bins . . .
> Her 13th album, "Up Up Up Up Up Up"—that's exactly five more "ups" than R.E.M. boasted on its 1998 album title—finds DiFranco turning outward from

the first-person focus of "Castle" and its predecessor, "Dilate." . . . "Up" incorporates intimate relationships into the larger world.

(San Francisco Chronicle)

Ask many of today's neo-swing bands about Rudy Vallee and you get the impression these Gen-Xers in zoot suits would likely reply that he must be a character in the Scooby Doo cartoon.

Listen to Terry Kinakin and his new CD, *Neither Here Nor There*, and you believe the Canadian-bred Nashville resident damn well knows about Vallee, the 1930s singer and other vintage swing-era performers. That is to say, Kinakin isn't jumping on the swing band bandwagon. This singer and banjo, mandolin and guitar player displays a genuine love for the music of the '30s and '40s . . .

(The *Tennessean* Nashville)

Home Videos

The video cassette recorder became a technological sensation in the late 1980s and changed the way millions of Americans watched television and movies. Renting or buying videotapes of major motion pictures became a multi-billion-dollar business and cut into the audience share of network television. Video rental stores popped up like convenience markets. Some cities passed ordinances to control the types of videos that were being sold or rented when it became apparent that so-called X-rated films on tape were in great demand.

Newspapers quickly introduced columns announcing the latest releases and providing readers with brief reviews. Larger newspapers assigned the task to staff writers, while smaller publications used reviews provided by the wire services and feature syndicates.

John Beifuss of Scripps–Howard News Service started his review of *Cat Women of the Moon*, which was released on video about the same time that astronaut John Glenn made his return to space after 30 years, this way:

> If John Glenn ever saw *Cat Women of the Moon*, he never gave it any credit for fueling his interest in space, despite the fact that the film reveals that Earth's craterpocket satellite is inhabited by a race of showgirls in black body stockings who occasionally perform ritualistic jazz dance routines.
>
> Even by the standards of 1954, *Cat Women of the Moon*, starring Sunny Tufts, was a ridiculously unbelievable movie. Heck, it's ridiculous by the standards of 1854.

In its weekend entertainment guide, the *San Jose Mercury News* provides quickie summaries of new video releases. Here's an example:

Artemisia
French filmmaker Agnes Merlet allows nudity and sex to overwhelm her bio-drama about Artemisia Gentileschi, widely regarded as Western civilization's first major female painter. (R—graphic sexuality, nudity: Buena Vista).

For Richer or Poorer
        Tim Allen and Kirsti Alley play wealthy, warring New York marrieds who go on the lam in Amish country to avoid the IRS. (PG—13—Universal).

Life Performances—Music, Drama, Dance

Newspapers cover a wide range of live performances—popular singers and musical groups, plays, classical music concerts by individual artists as well as orchestras, nightclub performers, outdoor dramas, dance companies, jazz singers and instrumentalists, among others. Good critics/reviewers are careful observers as well as listeners. They do not simply label a performance "good" or "bad," "adequate" or "inadequate," because that does not tell the reader much. Rather, they use verbal images that help the reader visualize what they saw on the stage or platform.

Although writing reviews and critiques of live performances certainly is not as restrictive as writing hard-news stories, the same principles of fairness and accuracy certainly are called for. Although it is true that the review or criticism is the personal opinion of the writer, the principles of criticism (pages 469–470) should still apply.

The critic of a live performance should always describe and evaluate a performance for the reader. But he or she may have to make certain allowances for unexpected or unpleasant conditions (which should be pointed out in the review) that might affect the performance. The critic should not pounce or dwell on a minor defect if the performance as a whole is excellent. But if the orchestra was so loud that the audience had difficulty hearing the singers, it should be pointed out. If the costumes were shabby, the reader should be told. If the sets were poorly executed and the lighting ineffective, the reviewer should say so because sets, lights and costumes are all part of the performance.

When reviewing the performance of a star who appears both in concert or in plays and in the movies, the critic should avoid scathing comparisons. Most performers who appear in films are helped immeasurably by a film editor who can save most performances with careful editing. Live performance can be a minefield for even the most seasoned performers. On the other hand, a performer is expected to act like a professional, and the critic has an obligation to give an honest appraisal of a live appearance. If the performance is shoddy and unprofessional, the critic should say so. Readers who may be planning to attend should be told what to expect.

In the case of a stage play, especially a new one, the critics should evaluate how well the author succeeded in the writing as well as how successful the actors were in presenting it. The same applies to performances of new musical compositions or a newly created dance. If a widely known work is being performed, comparisons can be made with interpretations by other performers.

Performances by amateurs should not be judged by rigid professional standards. They should neither be lavishly praised out of a sense of loyalty nor be viciously attacked. A critic can and should be as encouraging as critical to amateurs.

Many critics or reviewers try to develop a personalized style in their writing. Since first-person is acceptable in reviewing, critics often write highly personal reactions to performances. But not all criticism should be written in that style.

The first two examples are reviews of the same theatrical production from two different papers:

> NEW YORK—From the very first minutes of "The Lion King," you feel yourself on new ground—no, in a whole new world. Disney's newest stage musical doesn't just leave its blockbuster animated-film roots behind. It's a different kind of Broadway creature. (***½ out of four)
>
> Animals—a savannah's worth, played by actors with stilts, masks and tails—saunter down the aisles of the New Amsterdam Theater, swaying to the sounds of "The Circle of Life." It's a theatrical flourish as intoxicating as any you've ever experienced . . .
>
> When "The Lion King" is good, it's enthralling. It may run as long as the tamer "Cats."
>
> (*USA TODAY*)

> Suddenly, you're four years old again, and you've been taken to the circus for the first time. You can only marvel at the exotic procession of animals before you: the giraffes and the elephants and the hippopotamuses and all those birds in balletic flight.
>
> Where are you, really, anyway? The location is supposed to be a theater on 42nd Street, a thoroughfare that has never been thought of as a gateway to Eden. Yet somehow you have fallen into what appears to be a primal paradise . . .
>
> Such is the transporting magic, wrought by the opening 10 minutes of "The Lion King," the director Julie Taymor's staged version of the Midas-touch cartoon movie that has generated millions for the Walt Disney Company.
>
> (The *New York Times*)

> The current revival of "Follies," the much-revered 1971 musical with book and lyrics by Stephen Sondheim and book by James Goldman, at the Paper Mill Playhouse in Milburn, N.J. is quite a theatrical event. This is the first major revival of the work since its debut, except for a 1985 concert version at Lincoln Center and a 1987 version in London. For this musical about memory and regret, the new production, under Robert Johnson's canny direction, has assembled a remarkably colorful cast skilled in putting over the work's palette of emotions.
>
> (*Wall Street Journal*)

> Nobody can embrace and light up an audience quite like Joe Williams, the grand master of the suave jazz blues. With his soulful singing and loose, glowing presence, he creates an intimacy that makes a big hall feel almost like a club.
>
> That's what he did Wednesday at Masonic Auditorium, opening the 15th annual San Francisco Jazz Festival with the venerable vocalist Nancy Wilson. The charismatic Williams, a great artist and a great entertainer, put on a terrific performance that mixed serious music-making with earthy humor, the carnal with the spiritual.
>
> (*San Francisco Chronicle*)

Old is old and on the surface there doesn't seem to be much to say for it. But give old a second thought and it really isn't all that bad. Some things actually do get better with age, like loafers and jeans, some wines, the best of friends—James Taylor.

In these days of yapping rappers and bombastic heavy-metal types, Taylor, 44, is an oasis of understatement. His music comes with spry and simple melodies and words that unfold less like lyrics than short stories. On stage, he doesn't rant and pose; he teases with wry anecdotes and warm and witty asides.

(San Jose Mercury News)

Three young, women singers take their place at the center of the stage, to the left of the band. The programmed beat kicks in, with a staccato bass line and snapping electronic drums overlaid by a wispy synthesizer.

They harmonize a familiar melody: "Candy," an '80s rhythm and blues hit by the group Cameo. Before long, everyone in the place—3,500 strong—is standing and clapping and singing along.

While the song is familiar, the words have been rewritten. Instead of Cameo's mildly salacious "it's like candy," the girls are repeating. "We're so happy/This is the day the Lord has made . . . !"

The performance is not in a concert hall, but a church—the huge Brookhollow Baptist Church off of West Little York, near Highway 6.

And the minister of the church, Pastor Ralph Douglas, a fine singer himself who has just finished a powerful sermon, is on stage with the women, dancing behind them, waving his hands over their heads.

Welcome to gospel music in the twilight of the 20th century, where the beats are as funky as anything in the secular world, but the message is straight-up sanctified.

(The Houston Chronicle*)*

Art—Paintings, Sculptures, Photographs

The "I know what I like and this isn't it" school of criticism is of little value to any reader and often reveals the shallowness of the critic. This is especially true in reviewing art, where it is essential for the critic to have a broad knowledge of the different art forms and various interpretations of them.

Like all other critics, the arts writer must not let personal prejudice for or against a particular art form or style influence the critical assessment of the work. To be effective, a critic must have some understanding of what the artists sought to do before being able to evaluate the work fairly.

A writer hoping for a career as an art critic should at least study art history and read the works of major art critics. Colleges and universities offer numerous art courses that will give a writer a solid foundation for art criticism.

Here are several leads of art stories and reviews:

The ones with snaky gum trees, billabongs and kangaroos have to be Australian.

Those with Hudson River colors, buffalo, Mohicans and Winchester '73s are, of course American, which ought to make it easy to divide "New Worlds From

Old: 19th Century Australian & American Landscapes," at the Corcoran Gallery of Art.

But this very smart exhibition is not a show about the obvious. Its seams are subtle. So companionably mixed are the vistas that it opens that you don't always know which continent you are looking at . . .

(The *Washington Post*)

BROCKTON—You first see Chris Gustin's bulging pastel forms from above, looking down from the Fuller Museum's balcony into the big gallery below. Gustin's stoneware "Vessels" look like strange, mutant beings that can't decide which way to grow so they thrust into space in all directions. They also look pillowy and even squishy; it's easy to imagine yourself sinking into them.

Gustin's are the opening pieces in "ReFORM," a show of mostly recent work by 11 accomplished ceramists . . .

Photography has finally been recognized as an art form by the nation's leading art museums. And newspapers regularly review major exhibits. Here's the lead from a photography review in the *New York Times*:

You know that magazine ad that says "We get closer"? If only they had known Weegee.

Weegee (1899–1968) got close to crooks, corpses and kids. He climbed into paddy wagons to photograph the passengers, and crouched on the sidewalk where blood had been spilled. He popped a flash in the stunned faces of accident survivors. He photographed lovers and sleepers on the sly. He crowded the mike when the fat lady sang.

"Weegee's World: Life, Death and the Human Drama," an enormous show of 329 photographs open today at the International Center of Photography Midtown. . . . The largest show ever devoted to this photographer, it includes many images never seen before or unseen for half a century, as well as some films by and about Weegee.

EXERCISES

1. Contact the director of a play that is being prepared by the drama department on your campus. Ask her or him to let you spend a day or two with the cast while the play is in rehearsal. Write a feature story based on what you see and hear.

2. When the play opens, attend a performance and write a review of the performance.

3. A number of artists, writers, musicians and filmmakers receive grants from state arts groups or the National Endowment for the Arts. Locate one of them and interview her or him about the impact of that sponsorship on her or his creativity. Check with the head of the art and music departments for possible names of grant winners. Write a story based on the interview.

4. Compare the review of a Broadway production in the *New York Times* to the review of the same production in one of the major news magazines—*Time* or *Newsweek*. Write a report on how they are similar and how they differ.

5. Check your campus or community library to see if a copy of the book *Agee on Film* is available. If so, read several of the movie reviews he wrote when he was a critic for *Time* magazine and the *Nation* at the same time. Write an essay on how they differ in form and in style.

6. Most campuses and communities have an art gallery or museum. Contact the director of the one nearest to you for an interview. Among other things, ask her or him about support for the arts on campus or in the community. Write a story based on that interview.

7. Make an informal survey of about 25 students on your campus and ask what books they are reading for pleasure (not their textbooks) and then interview the manager of several local bookstores that cater to students and ask what books students are buying. Write a story based on your survey and those interviews.

8. Television specials are a staple on most networks and cable. View one and write a review of it. Compare your review to one appearing in a major daily newspaper or a news magazine such as *Time* or *Newsweek.*

9. Attend one or more of the following (as assigned by the instructor) and write a review: a motion picture, an art show, a live pop or classical musical performance, a live dramatic performance or a photographic exhibit.

10. Attend an athletic event on campus and write a review of it, just as you would for a stage or musical performance. Do not write a sports story, although somewhere along the line do include the score.

11. If you have access to the Internet, go on-line and try to determine how many entertainment and cultural sites include reviews. Write a story about what you find.

12. Write a review of the classroom "performance" of one of your instructors this semester, but not necessarily the instructor in this course, unless you are a risk taker.

30 Editorials and Columns

"I love writing editorials. But, God, how I hate reading most of them," Maura Casey, editorial page editor of the *New London Day* in Connecticut, wrote in the *American Editor.*

"Too many are ponderous incantations to the status quo. They're as bland as a bowl of warm custard."

Daniel Henniger, deputy editor of the *Wall Street Journal's* editorial page, agreed. Writing in the same July–August 1998 issue of *The American Editor,* he said, in part: "The hard-hitting, high muzzle-velocity editorial has given way to essays felt to be more measured, more analytical, even 'balanced.' But is this 'thoughtful,' if not particularly opinionated, editorializing, going to attract and hold readers' eyes in the brutal daily competition of their time? I don't think so."

Their call for editorial writers to stop writing boring editorials and start writing ones that provoke thought again certainly isn't new. Editorial pages have long been criticized for their blandness by people both inside and outside of newspapers.

However, many newspapers are making a concerted effort to strengthen their editorial pages with thought-provoking editorials and commentary. And they have sought to broaden them as well by soliciting and presenting diverse opinions on the editorial page or its companion "OpEd" page, which usually features local and syndicated columnists.

Still, few editorial pages today are like those in earlier times during the so-called days of personal journalism. That's when strong-willed editors interpreted current events as they saw them (there were few female editors or editorial writers then) and when readers were about as familiar with the name of the editor as they were with the name of the newspaper. In that era, the policies and opinions of the editor for or against a public issue or candidate were known by the readers and often influenced the editor's presentation of the news. At a few papers, it still happens today.

In the coverage of the presidential campaign that followed the Civil War, for example, there could be no doubt where the editor of the *Chicago Times* stood on General Ulysses Grant's candidacy. Here is part of his scathing editorial after Grant received the Republican nomination:

> Hiram Ulysses Grant, did you resign your commission in the army in 1853, for fear that you would be court-martialed for conduct unbecoming an officer and a gen-

tleman? Did you scandalously foul a soup tureen? Was it your habit frequently to get into a state of beastly intoxication when you were living on a farm of your father-in-law, General Dent, near St. Louis? In Galena, were you supported by charity of your father and brother, although you were then in good health? Were you intoxicated on the day of the battle of Belmont? Were you intoxicated on the day of the battle of Shiloh? . . . Is it true as charged by . . . prominent members of the Republican party that you "cannot stand before a bottle of whisky without falling down?" . . . Did you get into a controversy with President Johnson in which was mixed a question of veracity and did you come out of that controversy branded a liar and as a man who was guilty of an act of inexpressible meanness and dishonor?

Perhaps it is because most editorial writers—except at the *Wall Street Journal*—refrain from such direct, slashing attacks that they are branded as timid by media critics. As modern journalism evolved from those early personalized newspapers, the news was presented in a more objective (and, presumably, more accurate) manner by reporters. The editor, however, retained the right to express opinions and state policies on the editorial page. The by-lined opinion column developed early in the 20th century as an adjunct to the editorial page.

A major criticism through the years has been that the editorial page is a closed shop, that only the editor's opinion is expressed and that editors print only columnists who reflect their own points of view. That may have been a valid criticism once, but no longer. Most newspapers now present a diverse set of opinions to the public through the use of conservative, middle-of-the-road and liberal columnists. In addition, most newspapers have expanded their use of "Letters to the Editor" in which the newspaper and the editor may be criticized for a particular stand on an issue.

One of the most successful ways editorial pages have been opened up is through the "Op-Ed" or commentary page pioneered by the *New York Times*. Editors of these pages regularly seek the views of persons who differ with the newspaper's stand on public issues. Political, social, religious and academic leaders are asked to write for the page. Some newspapers present, side by side, the views of two persons who differ on an issue. In its editorials, on the opposite page, the newspaper's editorial writers may present still another point of view.

On its editorial page, *USA TODAY* always follows its editorial with an opposing view. They label the two as "Today's Debate." For example, in one issue it published an editorial questioning the effectiveness of a federal lawsuit against the tobacco industry to recover damages caused by smoking. It suggested higher taxes and more regulation would be more effective. The editorial was followed by a commentary critical of the lawsuit and arguing that smokers were already paying more than their share of taxes. It was written by Sam Kazman, general counsel for the Competitive Enterprise Institute, a nonprofit free-market group in Washington, D.C. Unfortunately, the newspaper did not tell its readers where that group got its funding.

The commentary page is also an outgrowth of the concept that on the modern editorial page readers have a right to express their opinions and that they may

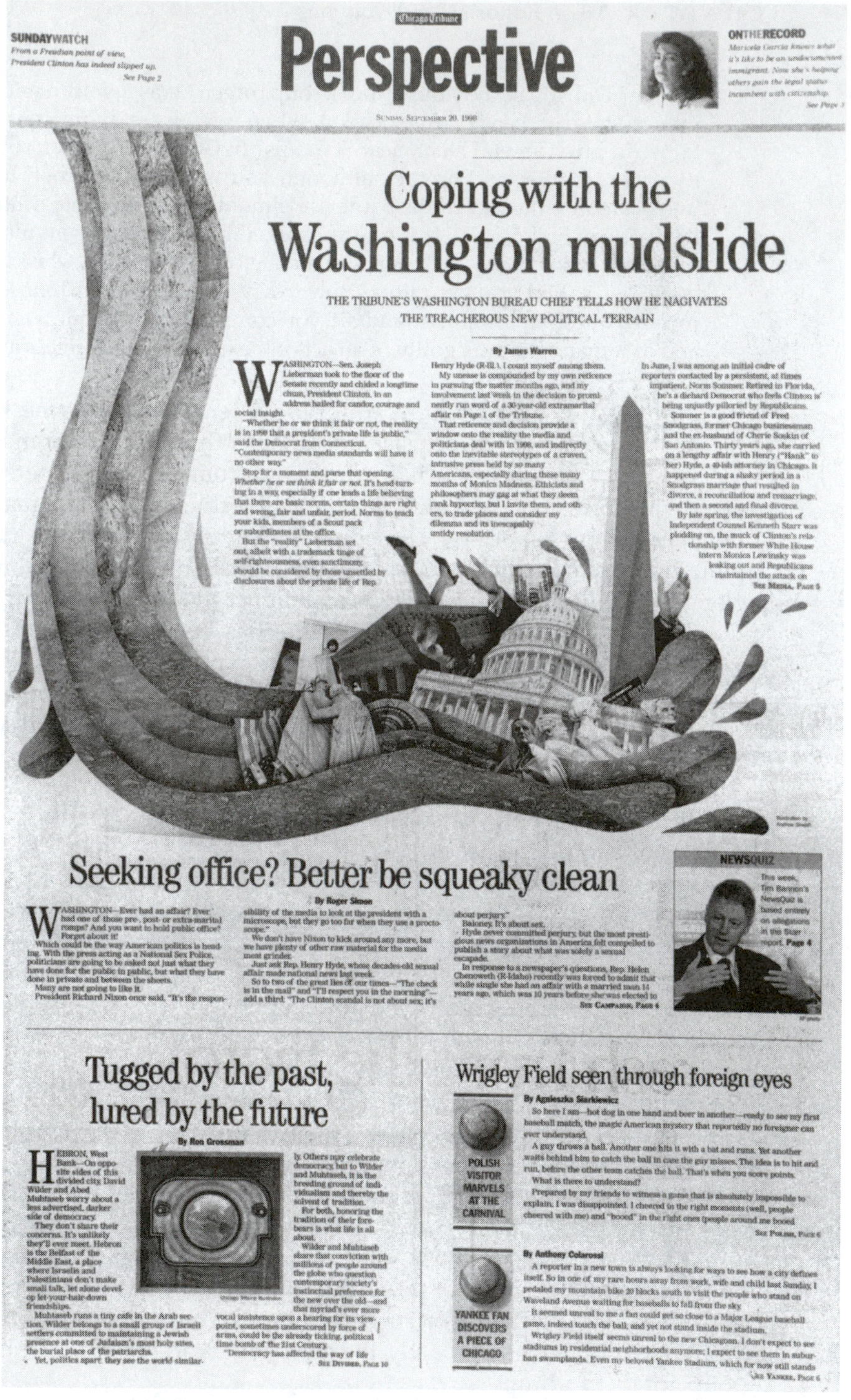

Chicago Tribune

Perspective

Sunday, September 20, 1998

SUNDAYWATCH
From a Freudian point of view, President Clinton has indeed slipped up.
See Page 2

ONTHERECORD
Maricela Garcia knows what it's like to be an undocumented immigrant. Now she's helping others gain the legal status incumbent with citizenship.
See Page 3

Coping with the Washington mudslide

THE TRIBUNE'S WASHINGTON BUREAU CHIEF TELLS HOW HE NAGIVATES THE TREACHEROUS NEW POLITICAL TERRAIN

By James Warren

WASHINGTON—Sen. Joseph Lieberman took to the floor of the Senate recently and chided a longtime chum, President Clinton, in an address hailed for candor, courage and social insight.

"Whether he or we think it fair or not, the reality is in 1998 that a president's private life is public," said the Democrat from Connecticut. "Contemporary news media standards will have it no other way."

Stop for a moment and parse that opening. *Whether he or we think it fair or not.* It's head-turning in a way, especially if one leads a life believing that there are basic norms, certain things are right and wrong, fair and unfair, period. Norms to teach your kids, members of a Scout pack or subordinates at the office.

But the "reality" Lieberman set out, albeit with a trademark tinge of self-righteousness, even sanctimony, should be considered by those unsettled by disclosures about the private life of Rep. Henry Hyde (R-Ill.). I count myself among them.

My unease is compounded by my own reticence in pursuing the matter months ago, and my involvement last week in the decision to prominently run word of a 30-year-old extramarital affair on Page 1 of the Tribune.

That reticence and decision provide a window onto the reality the media and politicians deal with in 1998, and indirectly onto the inevitable stereotypes of a craven, intrusive press held by so many Americans, especially during these many months of Monica Madness. Ethicists and philosophers may gag at what they deem rank hypocrisy, but I invite them, and others, to trade places and consider my dilemma and its inescapably untidy resolution.

In June, I was among an initial cadre of reporters contacted by a persistent, at times impatient, Norm Sommer. Retired in Florida, he's a diehard Democrat who feels Clinton is being unjustly pilloried by Republicans.

Sommer is a good friend of Fred Snodgrass, former Chicago businessman and the ex-husband of Cherie Soskin of San Antonio. Thirty years ago, she carried on a lengthy affair with Henry ("Hank" to her) Hyde, a 40-ish attorney in Chicago. It happened during a slushy period in a Snodgrass marriage that resulted in divorce, a reconciliation and remarriage, and then a second and final divorce.

By late spring, the investigation of Independent Counsel Kenneth Starr was plodding on, the muck of Clinton's relationship with former White House intern Monica Lewinsky was leaking out and Republicans maintained the attack on

See Media, Page 5

Seeking office? Better be squeaky clean

By Roger Simon

WASHINGTON—Ever had an affair? Ever had one of those pre-, post- or extra-marital romps? And you want to hold public office? Forget about it!

Which could be the way American politics is heading. With the press acting as a National Sex Police, politicians are going to be asked not just what they have done for the public in public, but what they have done in private and between the sheets.

Many are not going to like it.

President Richard Nixon once said, "It's the responsibility of the media to look at the president with a microscope, but they go too far when they use a proctoscope."

We don't have Nixon to kick around any more, but we have plenty of other raw material for the media meat grinder.

Just ask Rep. Henry Hyde, whose decades-old sexual affair made national news last week.

So to two of the great lies of our times—"The check is in the mail" and "I'll respect you in the morning"—add a third: "The Clinton scandal is not about sex; it's about perjury."

Baloney. It's about sex.

Hyde never committed perjury, but the most prestigious news organizations in America felt compelled to publish a story about what was solely a sexual escapade.

In response to a newspaper's questions, Rep. Helen Chenoweth (R-Idaho) recently was forced to admit that while single she had an affair with a married man 14 years ago, which was 10 years before she was elected to

See Campaign, Page 4

NEWSQUIZ

This week, Tim Bannon's NewsQuiz is based entirely on allegations in the Starr report. **Page 4**

Tugged by the past, lured by the future

By Ron Grossman

HEBRON, West Bank—On opposite sides of this divided city, David Wilder and Abed Muhtaseb worry about a less advertised, darker side of democracy.

They don't share their concerns. It's unlikely they'll ever meet. Hebron is the Belfast of the Middle East, a place where Israelis and Palestinians don't make small talk, let alone develop let-your-hair-down friendships.

Muhtaseb runs a tiny cafe in the Arab section. Wilder belongs to a small group of Israeli settlers committed to maintaining a Jewish presence at one of Judaism's most holy sites, the burial place of the patriarchs.

Yet, politics apart, they see the world similarly. Others may celebrate democracy, but to Wilder and Muhtaseb, it is the breeding ground of individualism and thereby the solvent of tradition.

For both, honoring the tradition of their forebears is what life is all about.

Wilder and Muhtaseb share that conviction with millions of people around the globe who question contemporary society's instinctual preference for the new over the old—and that myriad's ever more vocal insistence upon a hearing for its viewpoint, sometimes underscored by force of arms, could be the already ticking, political time bomb of the 21st Century.

"Democracy has affected the way of life

See Divided, Page 10

Wrigley Field seen through foreign eyes

POLISH VISITOR MARVELS AT THE CARNIVAL

By Agnieszka Siarkiewicz

So here I am—hot dog in one hand and beer in another—ready to see my first baseball match, the magic American mystery that reportedly no foreigner can ever understand.

A guy throws a ball. Another one hits it with a bat and runs. Yet another waits behind him to catch the ball in case the guy misses. The idea is to hit and run, before the other team catches the ball. That's when you score points.

What is there to understand?

Prepared by my friends to witness a game that is absolutely impossible to explain, I was disappointed. I cheered in the right moments (well, people cheered with me) and "booed" in the right ones (people around me booed

See Polish, Page 6

YANKEE FAN DISCOVERS A PIECE OF CHICAGO

By Anthony Colarossi

A reporter in a new town is always looking for ways to see how a city defines itself. So in one of my rare hours away from work, wife and child last Sunday, I pedaled my mountain bike 20 blocks south to visit the people who stand on Waveland Avenue waiting for baseballs to fall from the sky.

It seemed unreal to me a fan could get so close to a Major League baseball game, indeed touch the ball, and yet not stand inside the stadium.

Wrigley Field itself seems unreal to the new Chicagoan. I don't expect to see stadiums in residential neighborhoods anymore; I expect to see them in suburban swamplands. Even my beloved Yankee Stadium, which for now still stands

See Yankee, Page 6

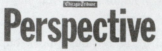

FIGURE 30.1 The *Chicago Tribune* devoted this front page of this Sunday "Perspective" section to a combination of local, national and international issues.
(Reprinted with permission of the *Chicago Tribune*.)

"talk back" to editors and columnists. They do this in "Letters to the Editor," which are used in increasing numbers by both daily and weekly newspapers. Some newspapers, *USA TODAY* among them, often solicit the opinions of readers on a particular topic with survey forms printed in the paper or special telephone numbers for readers to call. Often these form the basis for a front-page news story. On several occasions newspapers have used letters and survey responses to cover a front page: these letters and responses then were continued on several inside pages.

Only bona fide, signed letters are generally used, and the editors reserve the right to reject a letter or to reduce its length to meet space limitations or to conform to ethical codes or the laws of libel. In a sense, each of these letters is an editorial, but it is an expression of the opinion of a reader instead of an editor.

With by-lined columns, however, the situation is different. Although these often appear on the editorial page or the "Op-Ed" page, the editor does not necessarily agree with the views expressed by the writer. It is not uncommon for a newspaper's own editorial opinion to differ with that of the by-lined columnist. Some editors have on occasion either edited offending material from a column or withheld the column completely, for which they have usually faced a storm of accusations about stifling free speech.

But for the most part, publishers and editors today believe that a newspaper has a social responsibility to seek out and publish the opinions of writers who effectively represent all points of view. Both the editorial and the by-lined column represent personal journalism and have some things in common; chiefly, they are an expression of personal opinion. But in writing style and form they often are radically different.

Editorials

It is essential for the writer to recognize that there is no formula for writing editorials. They will vary widely, depending on the writing style of the editor. But a good editorial is always a carefully constructed analytical essay in which the writer explains, interprets and appraises an event or public issue. It shouldn't be simply a restatement of an issue with a few lines of criticism or comment tacked on at the end. The following are some generalized statements about the attributes, purposes, value and content of editorials that can serve as guidelines for editorial writers.

Attributes of Editorials

To comment on current events, editorials should be timely. Readers are more interested in news than in history, unless there is a historical tie-in to the day's news. What happened today affects readers today, and they are open to suggestions and opinions on such matters. This factor dovetails with the second essential attribute—consequences. Minor news stories rarely make interesting editorials. The

"USA TODAY hopes to serve as a forum for better understanding and unity to help make the USA truly one nation."
—Allen H. Neuharth
Founder, Sept. 15, 1982

USA TODAY
EDITORIALS

David Mazzarella
Editor

Karen Jurgensen
Editor of the Editorial Page

Thomas Curley
President and Publisher

Yes, impeachment polls matter, but how much?

When the House votes on impeachment later this week, it will have one eye on public opinion and the other on the Constitution. The question is, how much should each count?

At the White House, the view is that polls are definitive. On Monday, Vice President Gore cited polls as reason Congress should reject impeachment and censure President Clinton instead.

Among Congress' most staunch impeachment advocates, meanwhile, the view is just the opposite. Polls shouldn't count, the issue is simply one of principle.

Neither is right.

The core of Gore's argument is that the polls for months have shown steady public opposition to impeachment. Typical is the latest USA TODAY/CNN/Gallup poll. The number of people opposing impeachment dropped seven points in a week, but 59% still oppose such action, and Clinton's overall approval ratings are riding as high as the economy.

But the larger picture is more complex.

For one thing, Gore's alternative, along with all others, also misses the public mood. While most people prefer censure, they also demand that Clinton admit lying. He hasn't done so, and Congress can't compel him to do so.

In addition, as pollsters constantly remind us, no matter how constant poll numbers seem, they are subject to change. In Watergate, President Nixon achieved high approval ratings, with most people seeing the issue as "just politics" until late in 1973. A majority, for impeachment didn't emerge until 1974.

The change was attributed to unforeseeable events: Discovery of the White House tapes and a downturn in the economy.

Further, national polls aren't what House members care most about. They care about opinions among voters who elect them, particularly the most energized — a factor that pushes politicians toward extremes and certainly is not sound basis for such a weighty judgment.

At the same time, to ignore polls is to deny that national consensus is important in deciding to negate the public's electoral choice. It's not the

sole criterion, but it is a significant one.

Indeed, the proper way for House members weighing impeachment to regard polls is as one important set of criteria in a complex judgment. What will be the impact of impeachment, or the absence of it, on the presidency? On the nation? Since their vote will not remove Clinton but send him to trial, should they pass the issue to the Senate and hope for national consensus later? What does the Constitution demand? What does justice demand?

The complexity of the decision is the reason for representative government.

As a young congressman once wrote about lawmakers he admired, "A man does what he must — in spite of personal consequences, in spite of obstacles and dangers and pressures — and that is the basis of all human morality."

That man was Clinton's political inspiration, John F. Kennedy, writing in his Pulitzer Prize-winning book *Profiles in Courage.* The writers of the Constitution, had they anticipated polling, could not have put it better.

The public's view

A majority of the public so far consistently has expressed opposition to the impeachment of President Clinton for the abuses alleged in the Monica Lewinsky scandal.

···· Impeach — Don't impeach

(chart showing Oct. 9-12: Impeach 34%, Don't impeach 62%; Dec. 12-13: Impeach 38%, Don't impeach 59%)

Today's debate: Pro team palaces

Stop stadium blackmail

OUR VIEW Hartford deal is latest to subsidize local dreams with federal taxes.

"You really overwhelmed me," New England Patriot owner Robert Kraft told a rally in Hartford, Conn., last month after announcing his plans to move his NFL team there.

You'll be overwhelmed, too, if you got what Connecticut Gov. John Rowland promised Kraft — a record-setting gift of public largesse that will be voted on in slightly modified form today by the state legislature.

What a deal: a $375 million facility for your team, including guaranteed payments by the state if attendance is off. You get a shot at an extra $30 million in income a year simply by moving your team, with all the risk of losses borne by taxpayers.

Unfortunately, you aren't Kraft. You're just a federal taxpayer. So, rather than receive, you'll give, helping pick up that tab through a variety of tax breaks and openly federal grants that grease the great sports bidding war.

More than $8 billion has been dumped into building new stadiums and arenas around the nation, with most of the money put up by communities and now, increasingly, by states.

Here's the way these owner payoffs work: Owners tell communities they've simply got to have a new pleasure palace if they are to remain competitive. If a community, or now a state, balks at putting public money into owners' hands, the owners threaten to move.

Denver and San Diego recently succumbed

to such threats. Pittsburgh and Philadelphia want to, but state legislators are balking at putting up $150 million. Massachusetts, on the other hand, saw Connecticut's offer, the biggest stadium bid so far, and folded.

Rowland argues this is smart investment, a chance to invigorate the sagging economy of Hartford, the state capital. That's a dubious notion judging by economic studies that rate a pro sports team no more valuable than a mall, but it's the state's risk, or take. What's absurd is that taxpayers elsewhere, including in Massachusetts, put their money behind such bids.

In Connecticut's case, at least $200 million of the $374 million in bonds sold for the project would have a preferred rate because of federal tax exemption. In addition, half the cost of the club seats sold to businesses would be deductible from federal taxes — a $23 million a year write-off if all are sold.

The state also hopes to use some of the funding for the Patriots' stadium to obtain matching federal grants. (It gets $2.4 billion of them a year already.) And Hartford is applying for federal empowerment-zone money to meet its neighborhood needs, which frees up state funds for the stadium plan.

Why should this be?

Congress could end stadium blackmail simply by withholding federal support to cities that feel rich enough to subsidize wealthy owners. In fact, only Congress can do it. And until it does, the deals will become increasingly overwhelming, to the glee of owners and dismay of taxpayers everywhere.

Stadium will revive city

OPPOSING VIEW The price is worth it to return hope to Hartford.

By William A. McEachern

Connecticut legislators decide today whether to build a new stadium in Hartford for the New England Patriots. Hartford has been losing population, jobs and hope. A mere 17 square miles cover-sixth the average area of U.S. cities over 100,000, the city has had little flexibility in addressing its urban problems.

The stadium will catalyze existing plans to make the city a more vibrant and more exciting place to work, to shop, and to live. It should also provide a greater sense of community, enhance civic pride, and help develop a clearer presence on the national stage. Indeed, the Patriots and an upgraded UConn football team that will call the new stadium home should help attract and retain young people, a group now in critically short supply statewide.

If tax support remains strong, taxes on tickets, concessions, and players' salaries should pay for the stadium. But if ticket sales go badly, the state

might have to come up with as much as $20 million a year — no question a substantial amount, yet a sum that would run state government less than a day. In this worst-case scenario, the cost per state resident would average about $6 a year.

Although polls show majority support for the new stadium, NBC Nightly News last Thursday branded the deal "The Fleecing of America," devoting to the safety and fairness of a drive-by shooting. Now USA TODAY weighs in to question the use of tax-exempt bonds for the stadium. Connecticut pays more than its share of federal taxes.

According to the Tax Foundation, Connecticut last year received only 67 cents in federal spending for each dollar of federal taxes paid.

This was the lowest return in the nation and a multibillion-dollar drain on the economy of the state. We don't expect thanks from the rest of the country, but don't tell us we're ripping you off as we try to bring a city back to life.

William A. McEachern, a University of Connecticut economics professor, is editor in chief of The Connecticut Economy: A University of Connecticut Quarterly Review.

(cartoon caption) IMPEACHMENT'S THE ONLY WAY TO GO AS FAR AS WE CAN SEE!

LETTERS

Creating human embryos for 'adoption' is immoral

Embryo adoption may present no ethical problem.

For example, an infertile couple has a frozen embryo conceived by another couple implanted in the wife's womb, in effect adopting the embryo and saving a human life from being destroyed ("100,000 frozen embryos: Is adoption the answer?" Cover Story, Dec. 8).

There may be no problem as long as the adopting couple had nothing to do with the artificial reproduction of the new human being and its being frozen.

However, the USA TODAY article clearly states that some fertility clinics are intentionally conceiving new human beings in vitro for the express intention of having them "adopted" by infertile couples.

This certainly is immoral.

The language itself betrays the denigration of human life conceived in artificial reproduction. The article spoke of the frozen embryos as the "unused," the "surplus," and the "leftovers."

Who would ever conceive new human lives and refer to them this way? Is any human being unused, surplus or leftover?

USA TODAY asks: "How did an estimated 100,000 or more embryos end up in tanks of liquid nitrogen?"

The answer is clear and simple: Because artificial reproduction reduces newly conceived human lives to the level of a mere commodity. In violation of their human dignity, these new human beings have been pathetically and immorally reduced to the level of things.

Monica Migliorino Miller, Ph.D
Milwaukee, Wis.

The writer teaches theology at Marquette University.

Public wants censure not impeachment

It's interesting that USA TODAY rebukes President Clinton for not resigning, which would, in the words of Monday's Our View, "require the president to put the nation's interests ahead of his own" ("Clinton can still act honorably — he can resign," Impeachment Opinion, Dec. 9).

Yes, the editorial doesn't mention the fact that congressional Republicans are putting their political interests ahead of those of the American people.

TV personality Cokie Roberts outlined a striking example of this by citing a Republican member of Congress who complained that his hands are tied; if he doesn't vote for impeachment he will forever remain in middle management and activists in his state will prevent him from successfully running for governor or the U.S. Senate. Somehow, this doesn't strike me as putting the nation's interests ahead of his own.

Despite the fact they were elected to carry out the will of the American people, most Republicans in Congress are ignoring that, choosing instead to tell us we are too stupid to know what is good for us and too shortsighted to remember their actions in the 2000 elections.

They are wrong on all counts.

While Clinton's actions were reprehensible, they do not warrant impeachment. A president should not be impeached because a special-interest group such as the Christian Coalition insists its beliefs and stated hatred for this man should overturn two national elections. This lowers the bar for impeachment to frightening levels that will affect every future president.

Americans are tired of this fiasco and have made it clear they want Clinton censured, and the Congress and the country to move on. It is high time for the Republicans to recognize this.

As an educated woman and voter, I assure them I will remember this episode. It will inspire me to use my time, energy and money to ensure their defeat in 2000.

Elizabeth Paciotti Weiner, M.D.
Churchville, Pa.

Nixon had decency to resign

Monday's Our View calling for President Clinton to resign was one of the most refreshing pieces I have read in a newspaper for a long time.

As the editorial says, Clinton will fight to the end to preserve his place in history regardless of what it does to the country or his Democratic Party.

Regardless of one's opinion of Richard Nixon, at least he had the decency to resign prior to a House vote. Maybe some Democratic leaders should pay Clinton a late-night visit, in the same way Barry Goldwater and others visited Nixon the night before he decided to resign.

As to former Texas governor Ann Richards' response, "Resignation demand outrageous," I think the kindest thing to say is that maybe she should stick to doing TV ads (Opposing View).

Contrary to what Richards says:
► Clinton has yet to come up with any idea of his own concerning Social Security, building more schools and hiring more teachers will not guarantee that the children who use them are going to be any more literate when they graduate than they are now.
► This administration's policies concerning Bosnia, Northern Ireland and the Middle East are being literally shot to pieces every day.
► The budget is not balanced. The economic expansion started way before Clinton came to power and has far more to do with the Federal Reserve Board than with the White House.
► Hundreds of business executives, university faculty members and senior armed forces personnel have had their careers ruined merely on accusation of sexual misconduct.

Paul Lundy
Omaha, Neb.

GOP destroying presidency

Bill Clinton merely ruined a good dress. This Republican vendetta, on the other hand, has ruined several people's lives, tied upon basic legal tenets such an

attorney-client privilege, wasted millions of dollars on a case of entrapment, and made the rest of the world question the sanity and stability of our political system.

Who is the real culprit who should be impeached?

I know the Republicans are shortsighted. One needs only to look at their stances on education and the environment to realize that.

But if they succeed in overthrowing the election and seizing the office of the presidency, they will have established such dangerous precedents that the presidency won't mean anything anymore.

They will have destroyed what they're trying to save.

James Fletcher
Los Angeles, Calif.

Do the right thing

For the first time in my life, I am starting to question my pride in being an American. The actions of the present occupant of the White House and his supporters bring shame to all our country stands for. Throwing mud at everyone else does not cleanse the president.

I personally don't know anyone who supports the president. If polls are accurate and do not just represent people dependent upon the government for their livelihood and ultraliberals, we are near the edge of the cliff apart from the righteous, the cliff stands upon which our country has founded. I fear for our country.

It is time for our elected officials to stand up and do the right thing and forget about political expediency. I loved Ronald Reagan's first in arms: "Bull" Fisher, when a young flyer told him he didn't want to lend men back into battle because it was time for great men and he was too raw. Halsey's — Cagney's — response was something like, there are no great men, only ordinary men who, through the chance of circumstance are called on to do great things.

Now is one of those times for our elected leaders to do the right thing.

Delbert R. Mathers
Lithonia, Ga.

FAA policy reckless

After reading the article last month about the Federal Aviation Administration (FAA) employing intersecting runway procedures, I was not surprised to see "Pilots protest procedure after air scare" (News, Wednesday). I think this is the most outrageous, reckless and stupid idea ever conceived to wring out a bit more capacity from our overworked air traffic system.

I should think that, at a minimum, the FAA would not clear another airliner for takeoff until it was assured that the landing jet could, in fact, stop clear of the intersection. Its operation otherwise is tantamount to playing "Russian roulette" with those of us traveling on U.S. airlines.

I'm a 3 million miler on Delta Air Lines and log about 200,000 base miles on Delta per year. I encourage my Delta pilots to decline such landing conditions when asked to "sign up" for them. I only hope they get the same opportunity when asked for an

accident caused by a drunken driver. The blame is simply misplaced.

Millions of retreaded tires are safely used by school buses, emergency vehicles, commercial airliners, package delivery services and trucking companies.

They are economical and environmentally friendly.

We are an industry association and would be happy to send a free booklet and video about tire defects to any readers and contact us.

Our toll free number is 1-888-473-8732. For readers who wish to learn more about retreaded tires, we invite them to visit our web site: www.retread.org.

Harvey Brodsky, managing director
Tire Retread Information Bureau
Pacific Grove, Calif.

Any tire poses hazard if misused, mismatched

Although we sympathize with the writer of the letter to the editor, "Truck retreads road hazard," and share his concerns about tire debris on highways, he has no way of knowing if the piece of tire tread he struck even came from a retread (Friday).

Much of the tire debris on our highways comes from tires that have never been retreaded.

More importantly, nearly all of the tire debris comes from tires that have been improperly maintained.

When tires are abused — run underinflated, overloaded, mismatched on dual-wheel positions, etc. — they will fail, and it doesn't matter if they are new tires or retreads.

To blame retreads for rubber on the road is like blaming an automobile for an

To comment ...

We welcome your comments on editorials, columns, other topics in USA TODAY or its subjects important to you. Only letters that include name, address and day and evening phone numbers, and that are verified by USA TODAY can be considered for publication. Letters to the editor of 250 or fewer words have the best chance of being published. Letters are edited for length, accuracy and clarity. Send letters by e-mail to editor@usatoday.com, fax to 703-247-3108, or mail to USA TODAY, 1000 Wilson Blvd., Arlington, VA 22229. Letters to the editor and guest columns submitted to USA TODAY cannot be acknowledged or returned. By publication, letters to the editor of 250 or fewer words have the best chance of being published. Letters are edited or distributed in print, electronic or other forms.

FIGURE 30.2 *USA TODAY* offers its editorial page readers a debate on a major issue each day. In this edition, it spoke out against subsidizing stadiums with federal tax dollars and let a supporter of public support for stadiums to house privately owned sports teams offer a counterargument.

(Copyright 1998, *USA TODAY*. Reprinted with permission.)

editorial writer usually may choose from a large selection of important events—events that attract and affect a large number of readers. The current issues and problems arising from events, rather than the events themselves, often form the subject matter for editorials.

Value of Editorials

The editorial is valuable to both the newspaper and the reader. It gives the newspaper a chance to present its policies and beliefs without coloring the regular news stories with biased statements. If the newspaper believes taxes are high, it can carry on a campaign to get them lowered, using every timely opportunity that arises to present its arguments. The newspaper's appraisal of local, state, national and international events can be offered effectively in this manner.

On the other hand, readers benefit from the expert interpretations and opinions on current events offered by the well-informed editorial writer. The key word here is "expert." To be believed and respected, the editorial writer must be a trained thinker, a keen student of society and a skilled interpreter.

Editorial writing requires knowledge in many fields as well as patience and aptitude for careful research. The average reader who spends somewhere between 30 and 45 minutes a day reading a newspaper has neither the time nor the ability to unravel the complexities of major political and social events. The typical reader does not have the general background or knowledge to know if the city really will benefit from a proposed new eight-lane highway through the heart of a residential district. The editorial writer has a responsibility to research the proposal and tell the reader if it is worthwhile and why.

Types of Editorials

The ultimate purpose of most editorials is to convince, whether or not the writer hopes to stir the readers to immediate action. An analogy can be made between an editorial writer and an attorney speaking to a jury. "Here is the evidence," the attorney declares. "With these facts before you, the verdict should be as I have indicated."

Just how far the writer goes in trying to influence the reader varies from editorial to editorial. It depends on what the writer wants to accomplish. In one editorial the writer may merely interpret an event and offer no specific recommendations of reader action. This type of editorial should add dimension to the reader's knowledge and understanding of an issue. In another type of editorial, the writer may suggest, outright or subtly, one or more courses of action. And in a third, the writer may demand action on the part of public officials or exhort readers to take immediate action because of the gravity of the issue. Of course, a writer who shouts "Wolf!" too often without sufficient cause or evidence to support the cry will quickly go unheeded.

Still another type of editorial is the short, humorous kind intended to lighten the seriousness of the editorial section and to inject an element of amusement or lightheartedness into the day's events, although it also can be a humorous jab at a serious subject. No matter what type of editorial it is, the writer should keep it reasonably short. Some experts recommend 1,000 words as the outer limit of length.

Contents of Editorials

Editorials usually have a news peg, an introductory statement explaining the subject, followed by the writer's interpretation and appraisal of the topic. The two parts should be tied together in a unified essay. The facts and the arguments for or against should be organized in a logical pattern to bring the reader around to the writer's point of view. (Courses in argumentation and debate or participation in college debating can give a writer an excellent background for preparing editorials.)

The reader must understand the question being written about before he or she can understand comments on it. The editorial writer often has to assume that the reader knows little or nothing about the event under consideration. The writer must prepare the reader by briefly reporting the news that has prompted the editorial. That part of the editorial is similar to the tie-back in a follow-up story. After setting the scene, the editorial writer then presents an interpretation of the event and recommends a course of action.

No standard form or style, except that of effective newspaper English, is used in writing editorials. The writer is free to use any dramatic device—open letters, mock reviews of documents (as of the city budget), question-and-answer, and even verse—that will effectively enhance the arguments presented. In style, however, the editorial should be as polished as anything in the newspaper. Editorial effectiveness is a blend of sound thinking and good writing, and the two are often indistinguishable. A catchy headline and opening will be helpful for any editorial, no matter what subject is discussed. The concluding paragraph also deserves special care in the writing, for it is the last chance the writer has to impress the reader on the points being made in the editorial.

Jenkin Lloyd Jones, editor and publisher of the *Tulsa Tribune* until it ceased publication, said the editorial writer's trick is "to be both right and positive . . . We must catch their eye, intrigue them and entertain them. We must leave them with the impression that we know whereof we speak and that our suggestions are associated with their own self-interest . . . A good editorial is not a battle-ax. It is a rapier. It doesn't smash. It thrusts, parries and drives its point home."

Maura Casey wrote that when it wasn't possible to write editorials that expose corruption and storm conventional wisdom, "I am for writing editorials that elicit emotion; they make readers feel sad, glad and mad—and most important— make readers think.

"Passion is good. So is writing short editorials, they tend to be better written and are more considerate of readers' time."

Here are several examples of editorials dealing with national and local issues. The first was written by Randy Schultz, editor of the editorial page of the *Palm Beach Post*.

'HUMANE EXECUTIONS?'
There is no such thing

One thing about Florida. We may not be interested in finding money to give every child a good school, but we'll do everything to make sure the electric chair works.

Seven years ago, with a cop killer named Jesse Tafero in Old Sparky, flames shot up six inches from his head when the executioner threw the switch. The incident prompted calls for a more "humane" method by which the state could kill someone. Federal courts began ruling that a supposedly inhumane electric chair violated the constitutional ban on cruel and unusual punishment.

So Gov. Bob Martinez ordered up a bizarre test in which a kitchen colander (head), a vat of saline solution (body) and pipe (legs) substituted for an inmate. With signs of relief, the state pronounced the death chair to be mechanically sound, and executions resumed.

Now rulings by the Florida Supreme Court and a Duval County judge have blocked all executions until April 24 because a similar problem developed during the March 25 killing of Pedro Medina. A malfunction sparked foot-high flames that burned the mask over Medina's face and filled the execution chamber with smoke. So Gov. Chiles called in "experts." They issued a death penalty version of Hints from Heloise. Use a natural sponge on the head. Test the chair regularly.

So far, however, the courts aren't convinced. Meanwhile, the ludicrous debate continued over whether the malfunction caused Medina to feel pain. The governor keeps saying no. Defense attorneys keep saying yes.

Of course, Medina felt pain. The electric chair kills people. You can argue that anyone who gets the death penalty deserves the same anguish his victim felt, but it's silly to argue that any instrument of capital punishment is humane. The question is whether state-sanctioned inhumanity can be administered fairly, and it cannot.

Take Medina's case. He was convicted of killing an Orlando teacher in 1982, but in the days before his execution, the victim's family urged the state not to go through with it. Medina insisted he was innocent, and the family agreed. Pope John Paul II appealed for leniency. Medina died anyway.

Then last month, after pleas from family and friends, the same jury that convicted Kim Cain of killing Palm Beach resident Geraldine Pucillo decided he should get life in prison. Cain's crime was just as terrible; he murdered the former owner of Petite Marmite after trying to steal jewelry. Judge James Alderman, however, probably will agree with the recommendation when he rules on April 28.

Florida employs 13 lawyers in the attorney general's office who do nothing but handle death penalty appeals for the state. Florida taxpayers spend $5 million per year to operate the Office of the Capital Collateral Representative, which handles death penalty appeals for inmates. The office won't win any popularity contests, but until someone changes the Constitution, it's the price Florida pays for capital punishment.

Nearly 400 men sit on Florida's Death Row. Since the Legislature created the OCCR in 1985—to speed up executions, so the state won't have to scramble to find lawyers—the average time between crime and punishment has been about 13 1/2 years. Before OCCR, it was 9 1/2 years.

The death penalty is costly and mostly frustrating. Florida's list of conditions that justify and mitigate against capital punishment may satisfy the Supreme Court's conditions, but they result neither in fairness for the guilty nor complete satisfaction for the victims. Otherwise sensible people sound foolish when trying to explain the unexplainable and defend the indefensible.

There is nothing soft about a maximum sentence of life without parole. Aside from saving money and closing a case when it should be closed, abolishing the death penalty might let us do more to keep these horrible crimes from happening in the first place.

Here's how the *Houston Chronicle* began its editorial criticizing the National Football League on the awarding of the league's 32nd franchise, which Houston hoped to land:

> GAME PLAYING
> Houston, McNair deserve better from NFL
> Now that the Super Bowl is over, the National Football League's big game is determining when it will award the league's 32nd franchise. The NFL and Commissioner Paul Tagliabue didn't put it into a halftime advertisement at the Super Bowl, but it's pretty clear that Los Angeles will be the winner this spring, despite the fact that Houston businessman Bob McNair has in hand a better proposal to bring a team here than either the two competing groups in Los Angeles.
> The game in other words is a sham. And that's a shame.

The *Tennessean* in Nashville began its editorial in support of lowering the blood-alcohol limit for drunken driving this way:

> ### Lower blood-alcohol limit
> If the Davidson County delegation to the General Assembly needed any more common-sense input about Tennessee's DUI law, it got some last week from the Metro Council.
> The council passed a resolution asking the county's legislative delegation to vote to reduce the blood-alcohol content level for drunken driving from .10% to .08%. While Tennessee has dallied over the measure, 33 states have made .08% the threshold. Tennessee should toe the line too.

Newspapers with Sunday editions generally devote an entire section to editorials and commentary. They are called "Perspective" and "Outlook" and "News Analysis" and dozens of other names. But most follow the same pattern. The front page of the section is devoted to a major local or national issue. It could be how your tax dollars are spent or can Social Security be saved or, in the case of the *St. Louis Post–Dispatch* during Mark McGwire's record-setting home run streak, the use of performance-enhancing dietary supplements.

Inside the section is the newspaper's own editorial page with a cartoon, letters to the editors and local columnists, the OpEd page with both local and nationally syndicated columns. They usually range from 8 to 12 pages.

Columns

An opinion column is closely related to an editorial. But the two differ in a number of ways. While a columnist often makes editorial comments on a public issue or subject, the column represents the views or opinions of the writer alone. An editorial, on the other hand, speaks for the newspapers. The writing styles of the two are quite different. Some columnists choose to write in first-person because the column carries a by-line. Editorials are rarely signed and even more rarely written in first-person.

Columns usually reflect the personality of the writer who seeks to develop such a rapport with readers that they will turn to the page on which the column regularly appears to see what the writer has to say. Many columnists, both local and syndicated, have large followings who turn to them before reading anything else in the paper. Columnists who do not maintain significant numbers of readers usually are dropped by newspapers.

Essential Qualities of Columns

How does the column writer cultivate box-office appeal? First and foremost, by having something to say. And then by having the knowledge and resources to qualify as a commentator on a given subject. Trying to write a political column, for example, without a broad knowledge of politics and politicians and the resources needed to obtain information would be pointless.

Next, the columnist must be interesting. The most erudite individual may fail as a columnist if he or she is unable to write in a readable, interesting style. Having something to say and saying it with style and grace are absolute requirements for a successful columnist.

Some columnists fail to attract broad readership because they are too heavy-handed, too pedantic. On the other hand, many influential columnists writing on the national political scene frequently depart from a more serious tone to present a subject in a witty and entertaining manner.

The acid test of a columnist is durability. Successful columnists maintain high quality day after day and week after week. The one who runs out of something to say or falls into the trap of saying everything exactly the same way loses box-office appeal and risks being cancelled.

Types of Columns

There are several broad types of by-lined opinion columns. The largest group, one that includes a wide variety of offshoots, is the public affairs or straight-editorial type, in which the writer comments on current issues and events. This type dominates the editorial pages of most newspapers. David Broder, George Will, Anthony Lewis, Cal Thomas, William Safire, Mary McGrory and Debra Saunders are a few of the dozens of writers whose columns are syndicated in American newspapers. A number of other columnists, however, are known for their light-hearted approach to some of the more serious topics of the day. The *New York Times'* Russell Baker was a master of the art, but he has retired. Molly Ivans, an irreverent Texan, is now among the best of columnists with a sharp pen and a slashing wit. Arthur Hoppe of the *San Francisco Chronicle* is another.

Here is a lead from a classic Baker column:

> The idea behind the MX missile system is sound enough. Place bomb-bearing missiles on wheels and keep them moving constantly through thousands of

miles of desert so enemy bombers will not have a fixed target. To confuse things further, move decoy missiles over the same routes so the enemy cannot distinguish between false missiles and the real thing.

As my strategic thinkers immediately pointed out, however, the MX missile system makes very little sense unless matched by an MX Pentagon system. What is the point, they asked, of installing a highly mobile missile system if this command center, the Pentagon, remains anchored like a moose with four broken legs on the bank of the Potomac River?

This is why we propose building 250 moveable structures so precisely like the Pentagon that no one can tell our fake Pentagons from the real thing and to keep all of them, plus the real Pentagon, in constant motion through the country.

Among the other types of columns prominent in most newspapers are sports, humor, advice and social. There are columns covering almost every topic imaginable from pets to stamp collecting. Most newspapers use their own staff members to write sports and social columns that deal with local personalities and buy columns from syndicates dealing with national sports, entertainment and other public personalities.

Most of the columns dealing with the national scene are used in the section or on the page of the paper most closely related to their subject. However, they can be used anywhere in the newspaper.

EXERCISES

1. Make a week-long inventory of the editorials in the daily newspaper that circulates in your area and a corresponding one of the editorials in a national newspaper such as the *New York Times, USA TODAY* or the *Wall Street Journal.* Write a report on the number of the subjects the editorials in each covered, paying particular attention to the number that deal with local, state, national or international issues.

2. Using any newspaper available to you, select three news stories on local issues that you believe worthy of editorial comment. Write an editorial on each. Make one editorial interpretative, another an editorial recommending a course of action to solve a particular problem, and the third a humorous comment on a particular event or situation.

3. The National Conference of Editorial Writers publishes a quarterly called *Masthead.* If your university or the local library subscribes, review the back issues for several years and write a report on the various issues discussed in the publication.

4. If copies of the *Masthead* are not available, use your computer to go to the editorial writers' web site, www.ncew.org. and review it. Write a report on what you find there, especially the various problems of the editorial writing trade discussed on it.

5. Interview the editor and the chief editorial writer of your local newspaper. Discuss with them the newspaper's editorial stand on an important local issue. Write a story on that interview.

6. During that same interview, ask the editor and editorial writer their policy on endorsing candidates for public office. Then, interview two elected officials and a candidate seeking public office for their opinion of editorial endorsements.

7. Interview the news director of a local or area television station about that station's policies on airing editorial comments. Write a story on that interview.

8. Write a "Letter to the Editor" expressing your views on a particular local or national issue. Submit the letter to a local newspaper for possible publication after you have turned in a copy of it to your instructor.

9. If your local newspaper has an in-house editorial cartoonist, interview her or him about their work. Write a story based on that interview.

10. Write a 650-word column on any topic of your choosing. It can be an editorial column or one dealing with any other subject—music, drama, sports—and it can be serious or humorous. Turn in a copy to your instructor and submit a copy to the campus newspaper for possible publication.

PART EIGHT

Editing the News

"They ran my story through the dull machine again," reporters often complain when they see their story in print after it has been edited.

"I call it the Dullatron," says another, who, like most writers, doesn't like anyone to edit his stories.

The truth is, writers need editors, although they don't want to admit it. That's why newspaper stories pass through an editing process before they appear in print. It is essential that a reporter know, understand and appreciate that process. This section deals with what happens to a story after it has been written.

Once a story has been completed and before it appears in print, it is handled by several other individuals. Generally, a story will pass through all or most of the following stages:

1. It may need to be rewritten
2. It must be copy edited
3. It must have a headline written on it
4. It must be set in type
5. It must be proofread
6. It must be assigned a place in the newspaper by the makeup editor
7. It must be printed
8. The newspaper must be delivered to homes or newsstands or mailed

Only the first, second, third and sixth steps are the responsibility of the editorial department. They will be discussed in detail in this section.

It is essential that a reporter learn these steps. On smaller newspapers, reporters frequently edit their own stories and write headlines on them. Understanding the copy editing process will help a reporter prepare clean, clear copy that requires minimum corrections. Many reporters serve as copy editors from time to time. Copy editing, even for a limited time, invariably strengthens a reporter's grasp of his or her work as a writer.

31 Rewriting Faulty Stories

"Hello, sweetheart, give me rewrite," a handsome reporter, wearing a snap-brimmed fedora with a press card stuck in the brim, says into the phone on a colorful and nostalgic poster that appeared in newsrooms in the days before political correctness became politically correct.

The poster is long gone from newsrooms, but not the word "rewrite." Rewriting is still a crucial part of the editorial process. The word actually has three or more meanings in most newsrooms, depending on the particular circumstances.

In Chapter 11, "Rewrites and Follow-ups," two of those meanings were discussed: rewrites of stories appearing in competitive newspapers and stories written in the office from facts phoned in by a beat reporter or a reporter at the scene of an event in an effort to meet a deadline.

The third use of the word is in connection with stories that have to be rewritten by the reporter, if time allows, or by someone assigned "rewrite" duties by the city desk because the original has serious flaws in construction, organization or perhaps tone. Occasionally, copy editors may be called on to rewrite a story. However, most newspapers prefer to have the reporter who wrote the original story do the rewrite after consulting with his or her editor.

Serious Errors

Few reporters turn out completely errorless copy. That's why newspapers have backup systems—the city or section desk and the copy desk. Many errors in news stories—such as those involving grammar, style, spelling and punctuation—can be corrected by a copy editor if they slip past the city or section editor. However, some errors are so serious they require that the story be rewritten. When the original writer of the story is not available and the story is being pushed because of an upcoming deadline, the story is turned over to another writer who is assigned rewrite duties. Often larger newspapers have a group of women and men assigned full-time to rewrite. They handle all three kinds of rewrites. Frequently they are among the newspaper's most experienced staff members and write with skill, grace and speed.

What are those "serious" errors that would require a story to be completely rewritten?

The Main Feature Might Not Be Stressed in the Lead

The choice of the news hook of any story generally is a matter of opinion. Generally, the most important point of the story is obvious. The reporter's sense of news values is usually an excellent guide in selecting the facts to feature in the lead when there are several to choose from. However, reporters sometimes overlook what is undoubtedly the outstanding feature and may bury it deep in the story. For example, suppose a reporter wrote a lead about a fire in a nursing home, using two or three paragraphs to describe the scene and mentioning for the first time in the fourth or fifth paragraph that 11 persons died in the fire. The story, or at least the lead, probably would be rewritten at most newspapers to emphasize the 11 deaths in the opening paragraph, if not the opening sentence.

Some reporters like to "set the scene" for the reader. But often they fail to get to the point quickly enough. Here are several examples:

> DAYTON, Ohio—One student likes to throw scissors across the classroom.
> Another lies on the classroom floor every morning and screams. Some repeatedly call teachers names or curse.
> Although most children come to class ready to learn, Lebanon teacher Sara Oeder has heard dozens of horror stories about unmanageable students.
> Oeder and a group of Warren County educators and business leaders think it is time teachers reclaim control in their classrooms. They've proposed a change in Ohio law that would grant teachers more power to punish unruly students without fear of legal action.
> State Rep. George Terwilleger, R-Maineville, and nine other legislators have introduced a bill based on Warren's proposal in the Ohio House.

The remainder of the story describes the type of discipline teachers would be permitted to use under the new law. It also quotes school administrators and others who reacted to the proposal.

The problem with this story, as interesting as the scene setting may be, is the reader has to go through four paragraphs before finding out that a new law has been proposed to give teachers more authority to discipline unruly students. The writer kept the reader in the dark too long.

In this example, readers have to get through four paragraphs of scene setting before getting to the heart of the story—the mayor is asking the railroad commission for some kind of local authority over rail traffic:

> STAFFORD—From the start, Mayor Leonard Scarcella and the 12,000 residents of his Fort Bend County city have had a love/hate relationship with the railroad.
> Without the railroad, there would be no Stafford.

History—not to mention the city logo—credits Stafford as home of the first railroad in Texas.

But while the bonds are lifelong, the trains that roll through the city daily have chafed the nerves of motorists and agitated the mayor so much that he once had a policeman chase a train outside the city limits to issue a speeding ticket.

The most recent train incident spurred Scarcella last week to take his concerns to Austin, where he pressed upon Texas Railroad Commission officials the need for some kind of local authority over rail traffic.

The Story Might Be Poorly Organized

In some stories the main feature may be handled properly in the lead, but the body of the story may be jumbled and confusing. Or the reporter might not support the lead with information until five or six paragraphs into the story. In other stories, it may be that the reporter jumps too quickly into a chronological account of the event, forgetting to summarize all features before relating details. Sometimes only a few paragraphs need to be changed, and this might be done by an editor or the copy desk by simply rearranging the paragraphs on the computer screen. But other times a completely new and rewritten version of the story might be needed.

The Story Might Be the Wrong Type

Deciding just how to handle a story properly can present a problem for some reporters. Obviously, some stories should be handled as a feature, but the reporter—especially one not accustomed to writing features—will ignore that approach and produce a lackluster hard-news story.

At other times, the reporter may try to write a feature about an event that should be handled as straight news. The results often appear strained, and that may be obvious to the reader. The switch from straight news to feature or feature to straight news usually requires a complete rewriting of the story. Generally, a major rewrite can be avoided if the reporter discusses the story with the editor before starting to write it.

Rewriting should not be done capriciously, and the rewritten version of the story should always be better than the original. If the reporter cannot handle the rewrite, the person assigned to do it should first read the story carefully to get a clear picture of what the story is about and how it is organized. During the rewriting process, the reporter should be consulted to make certain the new version is an accurate representation of what took place. Special care must be taken during the rewriting process not to make errors of fact. The person doing the rewriting should never assume anything and never guess. When in doubt, questions should be asked and facts checked. If a fact cannot be verified, it should not be used.

Persons assigned to rewrite and copy editors often have to combine several stories into a single one. Although some try to blend the stories by moving paragraphs around, the most effective way to handle this type of assignment is simply to rewrite the facts from the stories into a single new one. Trying to blend two or more stories into one can lead to awkward transitions, missing facts or incomplete names.

EXERCISES

1. Using any newspaper available to you, clip at least four examples of stories that you think need rewriting. Analyze each story and write a report on what you find wrong with the story and how you would rewrite it to improve it.

2. Using any newspapers available to you, clip at least four examples of short straight-news stories that you think could be made more interesting if given a feature treatment. Rewrite those stories as features, and hand in both the clipping and your version of each story.

3. Read the following short story carefully. Make a list of any flaws you may find in how the story is written. If you believe the story is acceptable, explain why.

> Nabisco Inc., was blocked from throwing goldfish into the snack food market by a federal judge in New York who ruled Wednesday that the company's new fish-shaped cracker would unfairly ride on the success of Pepperidge Farm's established product.
>
> Nabisco plans to ask the judge to stay the effect of her ruling while it seeks an emergency appeal because the product that was ready to be shipped this week is perishable, said Hank Sandback, a company spokesman.
>
> U. S. District Judge Shira A. Scheindlin found that Pepperidge Farm had spent considerable amounts of money boosting the image of its Goldfish cracker and making it a signature product of the Pepperidge Farm label.

4. Using the information in the story in Exercise 3, rewrite it with a feature lead.

5. Rewrite the following stories to make them more interesting, using only the information in them. Do not embellish the facts:
   a. William Bowen and his fellow jurors sat through two weeks of testimony in a civil case in Los Angeles, then never got to pass judgment because the judge dismissed the case.

   > Bowen is so sure that Joanne Bragg got a raw deal in the case that he has offered her a gift of $5,000 to help finance an appeal. He said he took an informal poll of his fellow jurors and they all agreed that Bragg deserved a judgment of at least $250,000.
   >
   > Bragg, whose lawsuit claimed a bank helped her ex-husband steal money from her, has never met Bowen but said she is thrilled by his gesture.

   b. A Protestant minister is resigning from the Bakersfield Interfaith Ministerial Association because a practitioner of witchcraft was allowed to become a member.

   > The association approved membership for Terry Cheeseman, a Wicca prince, in an attempt to broaden itself beyond Christian religious groups.
   >
   > That caused the Rev. Marc Mullins, pastor of Bakersfield's First Christian Church, to quit the ministerial association Thursday.

Mullins said he thinks recognizing witchcraft is carrying religious tolerance too far.

c. Give me your money or I'll slather you!

Franklin police are looking for a man about 30 who approached an elderly woman Tuesday as she got into her car at Cool Springs and sprayed her with ketchup.

Then, as he attempted to help her clean the condiment from her clothing, two females approached under the pretense of lending assistance.

But, police said, one of them tried to pilfer the "red" faced victim's purse. Foiled by the woman, all fled.

Police are looking for two well-dressed females and a man about 6 feet tall with a dark complexion.

32 Copy Editing

"Our collective ability to deliver information far outstrips our ability to create it and package it, to make it understandable and useful and entertaining . . . to do, in other words, what copy editors do," Bill Connoly, senior editor at the *New York Times* told members of the American Copy Editors Society.

The society was formed in 1997 to give copy editors a greater voice in their publications, to sharpen professional skills and to raise up a new generation of copy editors, who are a crucial link in the process of producing a truly outstanding newspaper.

To be useful and understandable, information needs to be digested, explained and presented to the reader in a clear, coherent and interesting fashion. That's the role of the copy editor since comparatively few stories, when they have been completed by the reporter are perfect. They need careful checking and expert editing.

John McIntyre, chief of the copy desk at the *Baltimore Sun,* told a workshop of the Mid-American Press Institute: "American newspapers are largely written in a journalese that is increasingly removed from the way people speak, and write, impenetrable bureaucratic jargon, relentless clichés, with structurally unsound development and shocking lapses in English grammar and usage . . ."

His comments reflect those of James J. Kilpatrick, syndicated columnist and author of *The Writer's Art,* who said in the late 1980s that he had a gut feeling that the indispensable function of a venerable copy editor has been dispensed with at many newspapers.

Not quite. But as newsrooms become more electronically controlled, some copy editors fear, as Kilpatrick said, "the path from the computer terminal" in the newsroom "runs straight to the waiting press."

The copy editor's main function is to read the story carefully, eliminate mistakes, improve the language and write the headline. As the last person to check the story before it is set in type, the copy editor must be the watchdog for the newspaper and something of a guardian for the reporter, although reporters often do not see it that way. Often reporters accuse copy editors of butchering stories and destroying creativity, while copy editors believe reporters need to be reminded that they do not have a license to kill the English language. Despite their differences, reporters and copy editors have one thing in common: the readers of their newspaper.

Copy editing is one of the most important and painstaking jobs on a newspaper because the number of possible errors in a news story is great. Many of the most common ones that need to be corrected are a result of carelessness on the part of the reporter. Other errors are far more complicated. That is why a copy editor must have a commitment to accuracy; a knowledge of and respect for the English language; the ability to grasp not only what a story says, but also what it fails to say; and enough sense to know the difference between good, tight, creative editing and butchering.

The copy editor:

1. *Checks the story for accuracy.* A careful and well-informed reader of the newspaper, the copy editor should know the background of most news events or where background information can be found. Doubtful statements should be checked automatically. In addition to familiarity with the city—its streets, buildings, leading citizens and officials—such standard references as the city directory, dictionary, atlas, encyclopedia, clippings and other information should be readily available. Personal knowledge and reference to material help the copy editor catch most errors unless the error has to do with a fact that can be verified only on the scene or at the source of the story.

2. *Makes corrections of grammar.* Haste and carelessness on the part of the writer often result in grammatical errors. The copy editor makes certain that standards of good English are observed in all newspaper stories.

3. *Eliminates verbosity in newspaper copy.* Newspaper writing style should be lean and crisp. The copy editor, by killing one word or even a complete paragraph, can often make a dull, wooden story come alive.

4. *Eliminates libelous statements.* Potentially libelous statements should be toned down or eliminated. "When in doubt, leave it out" is an excellent guideline if a statement in a story could be interpreted as libelous. Of course, no copy editor can catch libelous statements resulting from erroneous reporting.

5. *Simplifies the story.* All confusing or ambiguous statements and all words that will not be understood by the layperson are eliminated. Technical terms or professional jargon is replaced or defined.

6. *Eliminates editorialized matter in news stories.* Editorial opinion should not be included in news stories. If a story is by-lined, however, a certain amount of editorial expression is sometimes permitted when the writer is relating a first-hand account.

7. *Checks all stories for adequacy.* If the reporter evidently has omitted certain essential facts, the copy editor often returns the story to the city desk. The story might be given back to the reporter or to a person on the rewrite desk for completion.

8. *Sometimes trims or shortens a story.* If the story is longer than the news editor desires, the copy editor might be instructed to cut it down to a certain length by eliminating the least essential paragraphs.

9. *Makes the story conform to the newspaper's style.* Each newspaper has certain rules covering optional forms of punctuation, abbreviation, capitalization and spelling and the copy editor sees that every story observes those rules.

10. *Attempts to polish and improve the story.* Generally, copy editors should not completely rewrite a reporter's story unless it is hopeless. However, they should try to transform every story into a smooth and lively account by inserting or deleting certain words and phrases or by rearranging paragraphs and sentences.

11. *Writes identifying labels and instructional notes.* For each story, certain codes, labels and instructions must be provided to expedite processing through the computer in the mechanical department. They include identifying labels for each story, codes for typesetting and instructions for type face and size of the headlines to be used on the story. Some newspapers include the section and page number where the story will appear. Each paper, however, has its own set of codes and instructions. While they might be similar in a number of ways, each has its own particular way of handling stories sent from the copy editor to the composing room.

At most newspapers, the copy editors work at computer terminals grouped in one section of the newsroom, still referred to as the "copy desk." Copy editors generally handle all stories for the paper. However, at larger newspapers some special sections such as "Sports" and "Lifestyles" may have their own copy desks. Some newspapers have been experimenting with assigning copy editors to other sections of the paper as well. In those cases, the copy editor would work at a computer next to the section editor. When the editing and headline process has been completed, the copy editor sends the story from that section directly to the composing room, where it is set in type.

Electronic Editing

Computers dominate the newsrooms of American newspapers. Reporters write their stories on computers and store them in the computer's memory bank. City editors and section editors use computers to call the story up from storage for review and preliminary editing. Copy editors use them for the final editing and headline writing.

The so-called front-end system will vary from newspaper to newspaper, depending on the particular equipment purchased. However, most computers are quite similar and once a reporter or copy editor has learned one system, using a different one requires very little adjustment.

The computer is considered a blessing by some copy editors. Others still are not sure. There is no question that a computer is more flexible than a typewriter. A copy editor can perform the following functions on a computer:

1. Delete characters, words, lines and paragraphs as well as move entire blocks of copy within a single story
2. Delete the entire story
3. Add new text at any location in the story being displayed on the computer screen
4. Instruct the computerized typesetting machine how wide to set the copy and what type size and typeface to use for a particular story
5. Write the headline for the story

A wide range of electronic editing systems are available, and they are being refined and made more sophisticated every year. The functions that can be performed depend entirely on how sophisticated the equipment is. Some, for example, have split-screen capabilities that allow two stories to be shown at the same time should a copy editor want to compare or possibly combine the stories.

It is important to remember that the computer is the central device for the system. The codes a reporter and copy editor must learn will vary from newspaper to newspaper, and the keyboard on the computer may vary slightly. However, all systems are essentially the same.

The early 1990s also saw the introduction of the personal computer (PC) in the newsroom. Graphic artists at many papers used them for a number of years before they began being used as a supplement to the front-end system. In fact, in some places they have supplanted the front-end system. For example, the *Miami Herald* added PCs to an existing front-end system. The *Houston Chronicle,* the *Chicago Tribune* and many smaller papers installed complete systems based on PC technology.

USA TODAY is a leader in the industry in the use of personal computers. They are used in the editorial art department, the photo department, the library and the sports department to produce some of the agate sports results listings. Reporters use them to tap into outside databases and for developing their own databases.

A number of newspapers have named "systems editors" whose responsibility is to know everything there is to know about the particular computer equipment used in the newsroom and other editorial departments. The systems editor serves as a troubleshooter for the editorial staff when glitches develop in the computer system.

Wire News

Most copy coming into newspaper offices from the Associated Press (AP) is fed directly into the newspaper's computer, eliminating the need for clattering teletype machines and reams of paper copy. Copy editors retrieve the wire stories from the computer on their computer and complete the editing and headline writing process before sending the story to the composing room to be set in type.

Generally speaking, newspapers follow the style set in the AP Stylebook, so wire stories may not require extensive editing to make them conform to the style in such matters as spelling, grammar, punctuation, use of titles and the like. How-

```
(DBO:) DESK1: HOSTAGE STORIES;6   11-DEC-90   09:05:10          PAGE: 1
11    <7297 CHARS, 3089 POINTS, 561.6 AGATE, 42.9 INCHES, 282 LINES>
12
13    *b48*[p47.4v49.4][c41]/]
14    Ex-hostages relate/1
15    frightful ordeals/]
16    /1
17    /1
18    *m24*[c11.7]Man, dog hid/1
19    in air duct/1
10    for 23 days/1
11    /1
12    /1
13    *9*[c11.7]/1
14    *bi*ByPatLeisener@Associated Press@/mTAMPA, Fla. . . A Florida
15    man trapped in Kuwait by Iraqi
16    invaders hid for 23 days with his
17    dog in a tiny crawl space, eating
18    only uncooked spaghetti.</P>
19    A New Mexico man defended
20    his hide-out with a machete, kii]<L-
21    >ing an intruder. </P>
22    A freed Baltimore man told of
23    watching a Kuwaiti man gunned
24    down by a platoon of Iraqi sol<D-
25    >diers. </P>
26    The family of a Missouri man
27    who endured four months in hid<L-
28    >ing plans to burn his passport so
29    he can't leave the United States
30    again.<\P>
31    Tales of captivity ranged from
32    those who cringed inside dark<L-
33    ended apartments in terror to a
34    hostage held in Kuwaiti royal
35    palace who ate off fine china and
36    drank from gold-rimmed crystal
37    goblets.<\P>
38    Tom Kreuzman of Holiday,
39    Fla., hid with his Yorkshire ter<L-
40    >rier, Chu Chu, in an apartment
41    air-conditioning duct about 8 feet . . .
```

FIGURE 32.1   An Associated Press (AP) story after it was edited and a headline was written for it by a copy editor at the *Nashville Banner*. All the codes, symbols and typesetting instructions were entered on the computer by the copy editor.

ever, a number of newspapers have their own style, which may differ from AP style. In such cases, the copy editor follows the newspaper's style.

Copy editors often shorten wire copy, rewrite stories to emphasize a local angle, or combine several wire stories into one. Here is an example of an original version of a wire story:

> WASHINGTON—The Senate clerk whose reading of the roll has become familiar to viewers of President Clinton's impeachment trial was struck and killed by a motorist in Arlington, Va., Friday night.
>
> Yesterday's Senate trial session began with prayers and a moment of silence for Raymond Scott Bates, 50, a legislative clerk who worked at the Senate for almost 30 years. His wife, Ricki Ellison Bates, also was struck in the accident and was injured critically.

This is how a copy editor might have changed it to emphasize the tribute to the Senate clerk, which was a newer angle to the story:

> WASHINGTON—The Senate clerk whose sonorous voice had become familiar to Americans during roll call votes at President Clinton's impeachment trial was eulogized on the Senate floor yesterday as a good friend and an admirable colleague.
>
> Scott Bates, the Senate's legislative clerk, was struck and killed Friday night while crossing the street with his wife, Ricki Ellison Bates, near their Arlington, Va., home. His wife was critically injured.

A few newspapers and some special publications, newsletters and journals are still edited by pencil rather than on a computer screen. For the convenience of persons who edit by pencil, a set of standard computer copy editing symbols appears in the Appendix.

Newspapers simply cannot function without copy editors. It has been tried in the past and the product was a monumental failure.

EXERCISES

1. Ask for permission to spend a shift observing the copy editors at your local newspaper. Spend time with several of them. Note their editing and headline writing techniques. Then, write a story about what you observed.

2. Using a copy of *The Associated Press Style Book and Libel Manual* as your authority, read at least one locally written story from every section of your local newspaper. Compare the style of punctuation, abbreviation and capitalization used in the local stories to the instructions on those topics in the *AP Stylebook*. Write a report on what you find.

3. Team up with a classmate. Each of you write a story and make a printout. Exchange stories and then edit each other's work, using the *AP Stylebook* as your guide.

4. Retype the following sentences as they appear here and then edit them to conform to AP style:
   a. Bait shop Owner Wayne Pullen, 42-year-old, of Blairsville, walked away wednesday with the larges check written todate by the state Lottery.
   b. The national Symphony Orchestra from Wasginton, D.C., makes its Debut tonight at 7:30 pm, in Powell shyphony hall, conducted to Music Director Michael Tilson Thomas.
   c. He slipped across the US boarder with Mexico fifteen years ago and has lived in the United State ever since.
   d. The United States Senate will here final statements starting at noon today with three hours alloted to each side.
   e. Senator Richard Branson, Democrat from Michigan, said he would vote for an across the board seventenn percent tax cut.
   f. Ticekts to the Lady Vols NCAA title match at seven o'clock Friday night against Purdue will go on sale at 1 p.m. at the campus ticket office. They cost $25,000 each and are not reserved.
   g. 19 Webb High School students were being questioned today after a brawl in the parking lot of the civic coliseum about 11 last night following a performance of the City's Living Natavity Pageant.
   h. She attended the state university of Illinois at Northern, Illinois, from 1996 to the year 2,000.
   i. The award winning movie, "The Thin Red Lion," opens Wed., May 5, at the OLympia theatre.
   j. State Police Trooper Stan (Bubba) McKay said he clocked by Mayor Benjamin Franklin Thomas with his Radar gun going 80 in a 50 mph zone.

5. Using several newspapers available to you at your college or university, compare how they edited and displayed the same major wire story that day. Select a weather, political, election or natural disaster story that you are certain would be used by every major daily. Write a report on how the editing and the display of that story differed in each newspaper.

33 Proofreading

"Murphy's Law assures us that no amount of proofreading will uncover all the errors of a work about to be published," Arthur Plotnik reminds us in his book, *The Elements of Editing: A Modern Guide for Editors and Journalists.*

He's right. Despite the concentrated efforts of writers, editors and proof-readers, errors still appear in every issue of every newspaper. Often they can be embarrassing. Occasionally, they can lead to a libel suit.

When a sports reporter at a Tennessee newspaper slipped a salacious paragraph about a high school soccer player into a story, the copy editor and proof-reader failed to catch it. And despite public apologies on the part of the publisher and editor, the player sued and won a large monetary settlement.

That type of careless editing and proofreading reinforces critics, both inside and outside the newspaper profession, who charge that newspapers have given up on proofreading. Many of them insist that the computerization of the writing and editing processes at newspapers has resulted in the elimination of "backshop" proofreaders who generally make the final check on a story after it has been set in type. They also claim that it is more difficult to edit and proofread on a computer screen than it is working with story proofs.

There is some evidence that the critics may be right. At a large daily in the South, for example, section editors do the final checking for errors, not a proof-reader working in the composing room. Most smaller dailies and weeklies have always had reporters proofread their own stories as well as those written by others.

The object of proofreading is to eliminate any errors made during the editing and typesetting process. Although proofreading and copy editing are similar in that their chief purpose is to catch errors, the responsibility of the proofreader is to see that the proof follows the original copy—that no words, sentences or paragraphs are jumbled or omitted—and that there are no typographical errors. However, proofreaders generally correct misspelled words, incorrect English and other blunders that might have slipped past reporters and copy editors.

Using Proofreading Symbols

Many proofreading symbols are similar to copy editing symbols, but there is an important difference in their use. The copy editor uses symbols within the body of the story, making changes at the point in the text at which the error occurs. The proofreader places all of the proofreading symbols in the margin of the proofs, indicating at which point changes are needed in the story. This speeds the process of correcting errors after the story is in type. The person correcting the mistakes need only scan the margins, not read the entire story word for word.

Two methods are used by proofreaders to indicate that corrections are needed:

1. The correction is noted in the margin directly to the right or left of the line in which the error appears, with an additional symbol within the line pointing out the error. The correction should appear in the margin closest to the error.

```
A 33-year-old Brooklyn woman was accused of killing her          #
husband . . .
```

If the line contains several errors, the correction symbols are placed in sequence and are separated by slanting lines.

```
A 33-year-old Brooklyn Woman was accused of killing her          lc/tr
husband . . .
```

2. The correction is noted in the margin with the correct symbol marking the point of error.

```
A 33-year-old Brooklyn woman was accused of killing her          tr
husband . . .
```

Corrections requiring words and short phrases usually can be handled in the margin by either of the two methods just illustrated. However, if a complete line of copy has been omitted or jumbled, the proofreader may mark "See copy" in the margin and return the original copy with the corrected proof. The proofreader must indicate exactly where the words and phrases are to be changed or added. For example:

```
A 33-year-old Brooklyn woman was accused of her          killing
husband . . . killing
```

If the error is only a single letter, the correction can be made this way:

```
A 33-year-old Brooklyn woman was accused of killing er          h
husband . . .
```

As an additional duty, the proofreader must check the method of dividing words between lines and correct the words that are not divided between syllables

Symbol	Definition	Example of Use
X	A defective letter	Civil liberty is freedom from restraint by any law, save that which conduces in a greater or less degree to the general welfare.
ℐ	Delete material	To do what I will is
℈	Letter is inverted	natural liberty. To do what I will, consistently with equal rights of others, is civil liberty,
#	Insert space	the only liberty possible in a state of civilized society.
w.f.	Wrong font	
stet……	Do not make change. Let copy stand as it is.	If I wish to act, in every instance, in accordance with my own unrestrained will, I am made to reflect that all
;	Insert semicolon	others may do the same. In which case I shall meet with so many checks and obstructions to my
(	Close up space	own will, that liberty and happiness will be far less than if I, with the
tr.	Transpose	rest of the community, were subject to the restraints of reasonable
^	Insert comma	laws applying to all.
⊙	Insert period	So it is, that proper and adequate laws are essential to the well-being and good order of
¶	New paragraph	civil society. But legal restraint, for no other
cap ≡	Capital letter	reason than mere restraint, is certainly unphilosophical, and inherently wrong, be-
l.c. /	Lowercase letter	

Symbol	Definition	Example of Use
Rom ++++	Use Roman type	cause it amounts to a deprivation of natural liberty without any compensating benefits to the public at large.
Ital —	Use italics	James C. Carter, in his "Origin and Function of Law," says,
⊙ (colon)	Insert colon	"It is the function of government to define the limits or sphere
] or [	Move to right or left, as indicated	in which the individual may act, as a member of the social state, without
(move up/down)	Move down or up, as indicated	at the same time encroaching upon the freedom of others.
# ⌣	Equalize spacing	It follows, therefore, that to live under
ᵛ	Insert quotation marks	civil government is to surrender a portion of our natural
spell out ◯	Spell out circled word	liberty for the public good, in order that that which remains to us may be
ᵛ	Insert apostrophe	the better safeguarded by the strong arm of the law. But liberty may be
)	Push down slug that prints	destroyed by law. The Romans furnish a concrete example. The prevailing ethos or national spirit of the Romans
! /	Insert exclamation mark	was law. Did not law regulate everything. A citizen could not fix a
b.f.	Use boldface type	price upon his own goods. It was the oppression of law which cheap-
? /	Insert question mark	
= /	Insert hyphen	ened the desire for life.

FIGURE 33.1

according to accepted usage. A dictionary is usually the best guide for this purpose. Split-word corrections are made as follows:

```
suit filed in State Sup-
preme Court in Manhattan.
```

The more common proofreader's symbols are shown in the accompanying chart (Fig. 33.1).

EXERCISES

1. Using any newspaper available to you, make a collection of errors you find in stories, headlines and photo captions that slipped past the proofreader. Clip and paste them on sheets of paper and, using standard proofreading symbols, make the necessary corrections.

2. Here are several newspaper stories as written by reporters, and below each is a galley proof of that story. Proofread each galley proof. To avoid defacing the text, make a copy of the galley proof and use it to complete the exercise.

   a. Women are twice as likely as men to suffer depression, says a study sponsored by the American Psychological Association.

   Depression hits 1 of every 4 women vs. 1 in 8 men. Other findings: biological factors (other than infertility) are not significant cause of depression in women. Abuse early in life, unhappy marriages and poverty are important factors.

   Depression goes untreated in most women or is misdiagnosed 30% to 50% of the time, the study says.

   > Women are twice as likely as men to suffer depression, says a study sponsored by the american Psychological Association.
   >
   > Depression hits one of every 4 women vs. 1 in 8 men. Other findings: biological factors (ohter than infertility) are not significant cause of depresion in women. Abuse early in life, unhappy marriages and poverty are important factors.
   >
   > Depression goes untreated in most women or is misdiagnosed 30 percent to 50 percent of the stime, the study says.

   b. The State Supreme Court today upheld a 1951 law making it a misdemeanor for groups such as the Ku Klux Klan to wear masks in public.

   The 6-1 decision overturns a lower court judge's ruling to drop charges against Klan member Shade Miller Jr. The high court ruled that the law prevents violence and intimidation by mask-wearers, and does not violate free speech.

   > The State Suprmem Court today upheld a 1951 law making it a misdemeanor

for groups such as the Ku Klux Klan to wear masks in public.

The 6-1 decision overturns a lower cour judge's ruling to drop charges against kaln member Shade Miller, Jr. The high court ruled that the law prevents violence and intimidation by mask-wearers, and does not violat free speech.

c. A commuter plane carrying eight passengers landed safely yesterday after it apparently was hit by lightning on a flight from Springfield to Municipal Airport here, airport officials said.

No one aboard the Midwest Express turboprop plane was injured. However, the plane sustained slight damage to one of its propellers, Dennis Rosenbrough, a spokesman for Municipal Airport, said.

The pilot and co-pilot landed the craft without incident about 9:30 a.m., and taxied it to the gate without assistance.

Midwest operates three daily fights between Springfield and Municipal Airport, Rosenbrough said.

Allan Miller, a public relations executive coming here for a professional meeting, said "the whole thing was a bit frightening."

A commuter plane carrying 8 passen-gers landed safetly yesterday after it apparently was hit by lightning on a light from Springfield to Municipal Airport here, airport officials said.

No one aboard the Midwest Express turboprop plane was injured. However, the plane sustained slight damage to one of its propellers, Dennis Rosenbrough, a spokesman for Municipal airport, said.

The pilot and co-pilot landed the craft without incident about 9:30 a.m., and taxied it to the gate without assistance.

Midwest operates three daily flights between Springfield and Municipal Airport, Rosenbrough said.

Allen Miller, a public relations executive coming her for a professional meeting, said "the whole thing was a bit frightning."

d. A motorist was killed and two others suffered minor injuries when a tractor-trailer truck and a car collided on the Golden State Freeway in Sun Valley Friday night, the Highway Patrol reported.

The truck landed on top of the car in the northbound lane near Hollywood Way shortly after 8 p.m., Trooper Dean Malsono said.

A Corvette "lost control and spun out in front of the semi-tractor-trailer carrying a load of bricks," Malsono said.

The Corvette hit the center divider and caught fire, then the truck hit the divider and ran up over the car. The driver of the Corvette was killed, but his passenger and the driver of the truck suffered only minor injuries.

The name of the Corvette driver has not been released, pending notification of next of kin. The passenger, Ron Wright, 23, of Newport, and the truck driver, Jose Martines, 51, were treated at Sun Valley Memorial Hospital and released.

A motorists was killed and two others suffered minor injuries when a tractor- trailer truck and a car collided on the Golden State Freeway in Sun Valley Friday night, the Highway Patrol reported.

The truck landed on top of the car in the northbound lane hear hollywood way shortly after 8 p.m., Trooper Dean malsono said.

A Corvette "lost control and spun out in fron of the semitractor trailer carrying a load of bricks, Malsano said.

The Corvette hit the center divider and caught fire, then the truck hit the divider and ran up over the car. The driver of the corvette was killed, but his passenger and the driver of the truck suffered only minor injuries.

The name of the Corvette driver has not been released, pending notification of the next of kin. The passenger, Ron Wright, 23, of Newport, and the truck driver, Jose Matines, 51, were treated at Sun Valley Memorial Hospital and released.

CHAPTER

34 Headlines

"Good leads and headlines are the quick summaries that get a reader to pause and read the story," Brian Cooper, executive editor of the *Telegraph Herald*, Dubuque, Iowa, wrote in the column "The Write Stuff" in *The American Editor*. He cited this combination as an example of an enticing lead and headline:

MAD ABOUT BREW
Success and love of beer keeps
Meister Brock Wagner hopping

It's a burnt-caramel odor, a cloying, woody smell that gets in your nostrils and stays there. See, in a charred, pungent way. Not very pleasant, to tell the truth. A smell only a genuine brewmeister could love.

The headline was written by Renee Kientz and the lead was written by Melissa Fletcher Stoeltige of the *Houston Chronicle* for a Lifestyle cover story about a microbrewery.

Writing good headlines is almost an art. It is also one of the most difficult and demanding parts of a copy editor's job. What a reporter said in 30 words or less a headline writer might have to say in six words or less. And the headline has to be accurate, fair, clear, precise, punchy, thoughtful, inviting, relevant, urgent, and readable. It can be done, but it requires skill and a command of the language. Most of all, it requires imagination.

Here's an imaginative headline on a Valentine's Day story in the *Nashville Banner*:

Roses are red,
marriage is blue,
love is more
than just 'I do'

Headlines are, in a sense, an advertisement for the story. A good headline will reach out and grab the reader. When it is bright, informative, clear and accurate, the readers are hooked. They read on, and that's the whole object.

In addition to grabbing the reader's attention, a headline should:

— Summarize the story so a hurried reader can get the gist of the story at a glance.
— Help the reader evaluate the news.
— Help make the newspaper attractive and interesting to the reader.

All of this must be done clearly and intelligently in a small amount of space, within the additional restrictions placed on the headline writer by the required type size.

Generally, the headline on most straight-news stories should be drawn from the lead. The headline should be the lead translated into sharp, punchy, dramatic words. Material from the body of the story is used in the secondary head, or deck, if the newspaper's headline style permits decks. If a headline writer has to go into the body of the story for the headline on a straight-news story, chances are the lead needs to be rewritten.

Some headline writers are intimated by the limited space they have to work with. They tend to think first of something to fit the space rather than the idea they want to convey. As a result, their headlines often are dull, little more than vague labels.

Advance on how to write good headlines abounds. Some suggest that you get what you want to say down on paper first without worrying about headline count, then refine and polish those words. One copy editor suggests: Write the headline, then imagine swinging open a barroom door and shouting it. Depending on how many heads turn, either set it or forget it.

A good headline does not require translation. The reader should understand it immediately, unlike the following example (that was actually used):

BN VP at BS

It translates "Boys Nation Vice President at Boys State." Although that is an extreme example, many headlines are almost as difficult to grasp because they are vague, such as:

Trip needs volunteers

What trip? Where? How many volunteers? Actually, it referred to a trade mission to Ireland. But you'd never know from that vague headline. Some copy editors read their headlines aloud to make certain they "read" smoothly. If the copy editor stumbles over his or her own headline, then the reader will almost certainly do the same.

Reading the following headlines aloud could have spared the writer and the newspaper some embarrassment. They are from *Columbia Journalism Review's* "The Lower Case" page:

School board member
suspected of honesty

Bomb caused church bombing

Most newspapers have a list of guidelines for writing headlines. Although they often are quite similar, some vary according to the particular views of the editor and copy desk chief. Here are the rules followed by the *Bellingham Herald,* Bellingham, Wash., which were included in a special section on better headline writing in the *Gannetteer:*

1. Make the headline say something: don't write non-heads.
2. No headline may start with a verb.
3. Conjunctions, prepositions and modifiers in headlines may not be placed at the end of the line.
4. Commas or semicolons may be used at the end of a line in multideck heads. Single-line heads may have commas or semicolons, but they should be used sparingly.
5. Do not pile modifiers one after another.
6. Do not split the parts of verbs from one line to another.
7. Do not use pronouns alone and unidentified.
8. It is NOT always necessary to use a verb in a headline. But when you do not, the omission must help make a better headline.
9. Do not use "hit" or "flay" or "rap" or "score" or "blast" or anything in that category of verbs, unless the word means precisely what it says.
10. Fill out the lines in your head.

The paper then tells its copy editors to "break the rules" if it will help make a better headline. Substance outranks form.

Copy editors have considerably more freedom in writing heads now than they had in the past. Here's a clever headline on a column in the *Miami Herald* about a psychiatrist who died of a heart attack after a lawyer pulled a gun on him:

Case of fatal
distraction
kills doctor

And on a story about states fining wineries for shipping their products into their states in violation of their laws, a copy editor wrote this clever headline:

Drink no wine
before it's fined

Copy editors have always had greater freedom in writing headlines for feature stories than they had for straight-news stories. That doesn't mean they can take an "anything goes" approach. After all, the feature head should reflect the tone of the story, and it should not necessarily summarize the facts as a straight-news head would. Moreover, feature heads should not divulge a story's surprise ending or unusual twist.

The *San Francisco Examiner* used this headline on a front page feature about a former woman surgeon who became a street person:

From Easy Street to mean streets

And a copy editor used a play on words to come up with this clever head on a story about the flu season coming early:

Fall may begin early
exerting its influenza

Trends in Headlines

In modern typography the trend is toward simplicity. This means shorter main heads and fewer, if any, secondary headlines. Some newspapers have eliminated decks completely. Others still use them. And some mix them up. Many others have introduced a variety of headline techniques, often similar to those used in magazine makeup and even advertising.

The flush-left headline is still the most common in modern newspaper typography because it is based on the instinctive pattern in which the reading eye moves in Western cultures—from left to right. The following are several examples of flush-left headlines:

Disney	**Lesson in gun**
Ship not	**safety ends**
in shape	**with shooting**

Many newspapers, however, use a variation on the flush-left theme. Here are some of them:

1. *Inverted pyramid*—two or three inches, each one indented one character more than the previous one.

Secret payments made
by coal firm
suit says

2. *Drop or stepped lines*—two or three lines, each approximately the same length. The top one is flush left, the second line is indented one space, and the third line is indented two spaces.

A Museum Merger:
The Modern Meets
The Ultramodern

3. *Hanging indentation*—two, three, or four lines, the first line longer than other lines and flush left. Other lines are equal and are indented an identical number of spaces at the left.

Weak regulations, greed
blamed as investors,
home owners lose out

4. *Crossline or barline*—a single line, centered.

Waitress Bags Suspect

The variety of headlines used by newspapers is endless. Four- and even five-line heads are showing up frequently. Decks and banks are making a comeback. Headlines in all capital letters are used more often now than they were in the early 1970s, even though they are considered more difficult to read than those written in capital and lowercase letters.

Kickers and reverse kickers are popular at some newspapers. The kicker usually is about one-third the width of the main headline and should be approximately one-half the type size of the main head. A 60-point headline should have a 30-point kicker. Kickers most often are used on multicolumn headlines, although they can be used on one-column heads if they are kept short. With a kicker, the main head should have no more than two lines, as a general rule, and a deck should not be used. The main head under a kicker should be indented several spaces but the kicker is set flush left or centered over the main head. The combination of the kicker and the indention of the main head creates white space around the mass of type in the head, and white space tends to attract the reader's eye.

The use of the kicker led to the introduction of a reverse kicker, also called a hammer. In this style, the headline writer simply reverses the size of the main head and the kicker. The reverse kicker usually is twice the size of the main headline and it is set flush left. It should be no wider than half of the headline space, which means it should not be attempted too often in two columns of space and never in one. The main head under a reverse kicker also is intended to help balance the area of white space at the right created by the kicker.

Here are examples of a kicker and reverse-kicker headlines:

The Compromise
A Suggestion
Of Conviction
Minus Ousting

MT. MO
Brave Bobbie before birth of Miracle Seven

Kickers and reverse kickers allow the headline writer to expand the ideas to be conveyed in the headlines. However, they are difficult to write and unless done with care can be pointless. Even when excellent kickers are written, the reader should be able to get an accurate message from the main headline alone. If a kicker, using a qualifying word or phrase for the main head, is accidentally left off, the main head might end up to be more of an editorial comment than a straight headline.

One of the more popular headline styles is called "down" style. Only the first letter of the first word in the headline and any proper names are capitalized.

Here are just a few examples of headline styles selected at random from daily newspapers across the nation:

Enough Turkey
Leftovers for All
On Networks

Bus gives granny the boot

Brothers' feuds
Shooting leaves man dead

Illinois frees first 18 inmates
after sentencing law is voided

Almost 2,600 prisoners
are affected by ruling

Padres Run Out of Town
    Game 2: Yankees use 16-hit barrage,
    good baserunning and Hernandez's pitching
    to win, 9–3, and take 2–0 lead in Series

Counting Heads

Headlines can be either all caps or caps and lowercase. The choice will make a difference in the number of units of space in the headline, depending on the size of the type—the smaller the type, the more letters and spaces. The headline writer must compose a headline that will fit into that limited space allotted for the headline. However, it is possible on most computer terminals to "squeeze" in extra letters by very slightly reducing the headline's point size. Some newspapers do not allow squeezing headlines in that fashion. At others, substance outranks form.

Although the headline count will vary from newspaper to newspaper depending on the type family used, the following is a typical schedule. For heads set in capital and small letters, use this unit count:

One-half Unit
Small i and l, capital I, numeral 1
Punctuation marks (except dash and question mark)
Spaces between words

One Unit
All small letters except i, l, m and w
All figures except 1
Dash and question mark

One and One-half Units
Small m and w
All capitals except M and W (and I, which is ½)

Two Units
Capital M and W
For all-capital heads the following applies:

One-half Unit
I, numeral 1
Punctuation marks (except dash and question mark)

One Unit
All letters except I, M and W
All figures except 1

Spaces between words
Dash and question mark

One and One-half Units
M and W

If, for example, a headline writer is told to write a three-column, one-line, 30-point head, caps and lower case, he would count it this way:

$1\frac{1}{2}$ $\frac{1}{2}$ 1 $1\frac{1}{2}$ $1\frac{1}{2}$ $\frac{1}{2}$ 1 $1\frac{1}{2}$ $1\frac{1}{2}$ 1 1 1 1 $\frac{1}{2}$ 2 $1\frac{1}{2}$ 1 $\frac{1}{2}$ 1 1 1 1 $\frac{1}{2}$ $1\frac{1}{2}$ 1 1 1 1 $\frac{1}{2}$ 1 1 1 1 1
F i r e H i t s L a u r e l H e i g h t s A p a r t m e n t s

This is the accepted method of counting in headlines, but headline writers on some staffs do not follow the system carefully. Writing heads on a computer, they count each letter and space as one unit, depending upon the compositor or paste-up person to space the lines correctly. In most cases such headlines will fit the space, but sometimes they must be rewritten because they are too long. Most computers are now programmed to "count" headlines and signal the writer if they are too long.

Writing good headlines requires a mastery of the language, an affinity for words, a lively imagination and a bag full of tricks. The good headline writer always remembers that she or he has only a few milliseconds to grab the reader's attention. A headline that may be perfectly clear to the writer because he or she has read the lead, the first three paragraphs or the whole story may be confusing, even meaningless, to the reader who knows nothing about the story.

Selecting the Headline

The practice will vary from newspaper to newspaper, but the responsibility for evaluating news stories and deciding what size headline should be written for each is the job of the news editor, often in conjunction with the makeup or graphics editor. They may be the same person at a smaller newspaper.

How does an editor determine what headline should go on a story? In general, the importance of the story or the local interest in it dictates the size of the headline on the story. The position the story will occupy on the page also influences the headline size. Longer stories frequently get larger headlines, partly out of reader interest, but also because a large head on a long story generally makes the page more attractive. Stories compete with each other, not only for length and headline size but also for position in the paper. A short news story may be the most significant that given day and may end up with a large headline, prominently displayed on the page. So length does not automatically ensure a large headline.

News is inconsistent. A fairly interesting story may get a rather large headline on a day when outstanding stories are scarce. On other days, several leading stories might be of equal importance, but the editor cannot use the same type and size of headline for all of them. In such a case, the editor attempts to make all of them approximately equal but uses a variety of typefaces and headline combinations to signify to the reader their relative importance.

The importance of the story should always dictate the approximate size of the headline. Although planning is necessary, stories should not be greatly overplayed or underplayed to meet space requirements or a predetermined page design.

Here are a few suggestions for selecting heads:

— Nearly every page will need a few large heads with one more dominant than the others.
— Double-column and other multicolumn heads improve the appearance of the newspaper's pages.
— Both Roman and italic typefaces are available and should be used. Italic type is generally used to break the monotony of the darker Roman type often used for headlines on hard-news stories.

Principles of Headline Writing

Good headline writing is an art practiced under the pressure of deadlines. Every headline writer will develop individual techniques, but a study of headlines, good and bad, will show that there are some general principles usually practiced at all newspapers.

1. The headline should tell the story's essentials and tell them accurately. It should be based on the lead in the case of news stories and should give as many of the five W's as necessary, playing up the proper W. Each head should be a complete sentence with unnecessary words omitted:

Poor

**Man Sustains
A Fatal Injury**

Better

**Guard Killed
In Gun Fight**

2. The symmetry of line length required by the style of a particular headline should be achieved. The lines must not appear to be too crowded with type or too empty. They should not appear grossly unbalanced:

Poor

**McDonald to
Head FBI Office**

Better

**McDonald Named
FBI Agent Here**

Poor

**Mayor
Urges
Crackdown**

Better

**Mayor Urges
Crackdown**

3. If a headline is made up of several different forms, each part should be a full statement and should stand alone:

Poor

**Huge Oil Slick
100 Miles Long**
**Reported by
Coast Guard**

Better

**Huge Oil Slick
Threat to Coast**
**Covers 100 Miles
Reports Guard**

4. A thought should not be repeated. Each deck or bank should advance the story with additional information:

Poor

**Heavy Truck
Bill Postponed**
**Truck Weight
Increase Sought**

Better

**Heavy Truck
Bill Postponed**
**Public Hearings
Planned for Fall**

5. Involved, confusing or ambiguous heads should be avoided:

Poor

**Aged Fight Pension
Plans for Future**

Better

**Aged Group Fights
New Pension Plans**

6. Feature stories should have feature headlines:

Poor

Dog Is Favorite White House Pet

Better

'Dogging' It at the White House

Poor

**Patrons Borrow Free
Umbrellas Permanently**

Better
Free Umbrella Idea
Picked up Quickly

7. Each headline should contain a verb in order not to appear as a mere label. The verb should be in the first line if possible, but the headline should not start with a verb.

Poor	*Better*
College Mall	**College Mall Opens**
—	—
Urge Milk Fund	**Milk Fund Urged**
For City's Needy	**For City's Needy**

8. Headlines generally should be written in the active voice, not the passive, for impact:

Poor	*Better*
Strikers Warned	**Mayor Warns**
by Mayor	**Rail Strikers**

9. Headlines should be written in the historical present tense (or future). However, some newspapers permit past tense in headlines:

Poor	*Better*
Penal Farm Inmate	**Penal Farm Inmate**
Escaped Into Woods	**Escapes Into Woods**

10. The headline should use vivid, fresh language; avoid dull and trite words:

Poor	*Better*
Congress Studies	**Congress Takes Aim**
Gun Control Again	**At Gun Control Again**

11. Words should not be repeated in the headline:

Poor	*Better*
Strike Conference Ends	**Mediation Session Ends**
Steelworkers Strike	**Steelworkers Strike**

12. Headlines should be specific. Try to find the exact word to convey a thought:

Poor

**Youth Injured
In Knife Battle**

Better

**Youth Slashed
In Knife Fight**

13. Provincial slang expressions should be avoided:

Poor

**Stockers Sales
Cut in Half**

Better

**Local Cattle Sales
Drop 50 Per Cent**

14. The headline writer cannot use simplified spelling (such as "tho") unless it is the style of the newspaper:

Poor

**Rain to Continue
Thru Another Day**

Better

**Rain to Continue
Through Tomorrow**

15. Single quotation marks should be used in headlines.

Poor

**Kidnaped Boy
"Buried Alive"**

Better

**Kidnaped Boy
'Buried Alive'**

16. Abbreviations should not be used unless standard, conventional and generally understood, such as U.S., FBI:

Poor

**500 of ASE
At Meeting Here**

Better

**500 Engineers
Convene Here**

17. Words, phrases consisting of nouns and adjective modifiers, prepositional phrases and verb phrases should not be split between lines:

Poor

**Council Passes Sales
Tax Despite Protest**

Better

**Sales Tax Passes
Despite Protest**

18. Opinion headlines should be attributed or qualified:

Poor
Taxes Too High
On Businesses

Better
Taxes Too High
Say Businessmen

19. Articles and other unnecessary words should not be used, except with names of books and other proper titles:

Poor
Fireman Saves
A Little Puppy

Better
Fireman Saves
Dog from Blaze

20. "Half truths" must be avoided. Sometimes such heads can be libelous or misleading.

Poor
Pastor Sought
In Larceny Case

Better
Pastor Sought
As Eyewitness

Subheads

Subheads are boldface lines of type used to break up the body type in long news stories. They are a typographical device to relieve the grayness of long columns of type. As a general rule, they start after the first three paragraphs of a story and are placed evenly three or four paragraphs apart throughout the story. The last one generally is placed three paragraphs before the story ends. Some newspapers set their subheads in all caps, boldface type slightly larger than body type. Others use boldface-cap and lowercase subheads. The general principles of headline writing apply to subheads. They should not fill the entire line, nor should they be too short.

A number of newspapers have eliminated subheads in favor of other devices to break up the monotony of large masses of solid body type. One is to boldface whole paragraphs, parts of paragraphs or even parts of sentences—the first four words of a sentence, for example. Others take sentences or paragraphs right out of the story, set them in larger type and insert them into the body of the story with ample white space around them.

Trends in newspaper headlines come and go just as they do in the overall design of newspapers. But the principles of headline writing remain the same. Good headlines say something.

EXERCISES

1. Using the daily newspaper in your city and a paper available to you from a city in another state, study their headline styles to note the similarities and the differences. Write a report on your findings.

2. Interview the copy desk chief at the local daily newspaper about the role of a copy editor at the newspaper. Write a story based on that interview.

3. Select a major story of national interest—the resignation of a major political leader or a major natural disaster—and compare the headline on the story used by the local daily and six other daily newspapers that are available to you in your college library. Note the difference in size, wording and placement of story and headline in each. Write a brief report on your findings.

4. Using any daily newspaper available to you, rewrite all of the headlines on the front page. Try to improve them. Do not change the type size or column width of the original headlines. Turn in the originals with your rewritten version.

5. Select the major story from any newspaper front page and using the headline schedule at the end of Chapter 35, write the following size headlines on that story: No. 1; 2a; 3a; 5b.

6. Read the following stories, then rank them in the importance of news values. Select no more than six of them to use on the front page, then indicate the size headline you would use on each:

   a. Parents blast plan to change how students assigned to schools
   b. University to sell Memorial Hospital to private investors
   c. Democrats seek control of state road projects
   d. Local bait shop owner wins $22 million in state lottery
   e. Bill in state house would aid poor counties with more school tax support
   f. New computer chip raises privacy fears among civil liberties groups
   g. Columbian cities leveled by earthquake killing thousands
   h. Sheriff's deputies bust up fifth methamphetamine lab in county this year
   i. A divorced 37-year-old father killed his four young children, turned self in
   j. City council hikes property tax rate, despite pleas for increase by teachers
   k. City council members approve pay raise for themselves

7. Write a one-column, two-line, flush-left headline on each of the following story leads. Use capitals and lower case with 15 to 16 units in each line:

   a. A Franklin woman died at the scene of a head-on collision Wednesday night in Brentwood, pushing the number of traffic fatalities in the city to 26 this year.
   b. A prison inmate who embezzled $90,000 by promising fellow convicts he and his lawyer could secure them a presidential pardon was convicted on fraud charges today.
   c. Minors caught with guns would have to be locked up for five days on a first offense and up to 30 days for a second offense under a bill introduced today in the state House of Representatives.

d. A highly publicized pill for baldness, called Propecia, will be considered for approval Thursday by a Food and Drug Administration advisory panel.

e. Doctors are trying to save the left leg of 1-year-old Jonathan Smith, the youngest of three children hit Tuesday by a county school bus in North Dade County.

35 Newspaper Design

"What is hip today will probably look hopelessly out-of-date in a decade or two. Tastes change; newsroom philosophies change, too. The same goes for theories in page design," Tim Harrower of the Portland *Oregonian* says in his book, *The Newspaper Designer's Handbook.*

Like hemlines, newspaper design trends change, but not quite as often or as dramatically.

Perhaps the greatest impact on newspaper design has been the computer. They make it easier to create a page that's logical, legible and fun to read. Using a computer, graphic designers can manipulate type, squeeze heads and move and resize photographs with relative ease. One of the real advantages of pagination programs on computers is that the graphic artist can show the reporters and editors each page just as readers will see it.

Most editors say pagination allows them to find the most effective way to sell stories and clarify information. It gives everyone the opportunity to see how effective the design can be before the newspaper is printed.

Although some newspapers have not yet computerized their design departments, most have. And they have found pagination indispensable because it allows for greater creativity in design, especially when creating front pages for special sections such as lifestyle, sports, business, and entertainment.

There have been other influences on newspaper appearance as well. A major one has been the visual competition offered by television. But for the most part, the appearance of a newspaper still is a reflection of its owner and the women and men who run it.

One of the key players in most newsrooms today is the graphics editor. Working with other key editors, he or she helps to decide what each day's edition is going to look like. Graphics editors take part in daily editorial conferences in which the city, state, wire, sports, business, lifestyles and other departmental editors meet with the managing editor to plan the paper. Each presents a list of major stories, and as a group they discuss which stories will go on page 1, the section fronts and the inside pages. After the stories have been selected and ranked according to their importance, the graphics editor and staff do their layouts either by personal computers such as the Macintosh or by hand.

On smaller newspapers, the news or managing editor might serve as the designer. And at many newspapers, sections such as "sports" and "lifestyles" do their own design.

Changes in Design

One of the more popular phrases heard around newspapers in the early part of the 1990s was "reader friendly." All newspapers were seeking a way to hold on to readers and win new ones as daily newspaper circulation decreased. Newspapers have made a lot of changes, but most continue to display their stories horizontally rather than vertically. There are a few exceptions to that rule, like the *Wall Street Journal's* front page. In most of the new designs, headlines are multicolumn rather than one-column. Pictures are often large and more horizontal than vertical. Charts, graphs, maps and information graphics, frequently in color, are used with stories and sometimes even stand alone. News-summary columns are commonplace now.

Many newspapers continue to place the main story in the top right corner of the front page, as was the practice when the eight-column banner (a page-wide headline in very large type) was the standard headline on the most important story of the day. However, now the headline on that story might be only two or three columns wide. Some newspapers place their main story in the upper left-hand corner, where it catches the reader's eye. Then, they display a story or photograph of almost equal importance in the upper right of the page. A variety of other combinations are used, depending on the length of the stories, their importance, and the photos or illustrations available for the page.

One of the early proponents of modern newspaper topography, Edmund Arnold, cited the following principles of makeup. They are just as sound today as they were when he introduced them:

1. Good typography should be the packaging of content, and content should determine what the package looks like. You must first know what you are packaging. A good layout of any kind must be organic, must grow from what it has to work with—the content, the day's news.

2. The newspaper design should present a lot of different news in a minimum of space.

3. A good newspaper page must be functional. Every element—every line of type—must communicate with the reader, must transmit information.

4. Good typographic layout of any kind must be invisible. It should not overpower the message.

Some design traditionalists argue that the design of *USA TODAY* tends to overpower the message. However, its circulation figures indicate that a lot of readers don't agree. *USA TODAY* has one of the largest circulations of any newspaper in the nation.

Design Procedure

In designing a standard-size page—the front page or an inside page—the first step most designers take is to place a strong attention-getter in the upper left-hand corner of the page. That's where the reader's eyes normally "enter" the page. If there is nothing in that spot, the reader's eyes are likely to go on to something else, perhaps less important in basic news value. One of the functions of design is to help the reader "grade" or "evaluate" the news by its placement on the page and the size of its headline.

The attention-getter should be a strong headline, a large picture or an unusual story placed in a box or a graphic. Whatever is used, it should rivet the reader's attention to the top part of the page, where the most important story of the day is traditionally placed. The attention-getter should be counterbalanced by an equally important item, often the major news story that day. The object is to keep the reader's eyes moving across the page from left to right.

After placing stories and other elements at the top of the page, the designer should plan the center, by using a strong display element. Finally, the lower part of the page is designed, also with strong headlines or other display elements so it does not fade away.

The way the entire top third of the page looks is influenced by where the newspaper's flag (nameplate) is placed. Many papers display their flag at the top of the page and never move it. Some use a strip of promotion boxes above the flag. Other newspapers use three- or four-column flags. Still other newspapers float the flag and place stories above or beside it. (See examples at the end of this chapter).

Another factor that influences the display of stories on the front page is summary or other columns in a permanent position on the front page. For example, the *Nashville Banner* places its promotion boxes in the first column on the left side of the page. *USA TODAY* places a two-column news summary down the left side of its front page.

It is important for the designer to achieve a sense of balance on the front page. The top should not totally dominate the bottom of the page. There should be some strong display elements in the center as well as on the bottom third of the page. Some designers anchor the bottom corners with stories in boxes or the index. Display elements can be a photograph, a graphic or a strong multicolumn headline. The display elements used in the center and lower third of the page should not be larger than those used on the top third of the page.

One of the marks of an attractive front page is the lack of crowding. (The same goes for inside pages.) The use of white space is a significant design tool in attaining a balanced look. It can be used around the flag or art, above headlines, between lines of heads, between the head and the by-line, between the by-line and the credit line, between the credit line and the lead, modestly between paragraphs, between the photo and the caption, and between the ads and the editorial matter.

Many designers attempt to place the headlines so they are not tombstoned (placed side by side) or armpitted (a narrow head placed immediately under a wider one with no body type between them). The separation of heads by lighter body type makes the page more attractive and much easier to read, and it creates contrast. Some newspapers, however, ignore that concept. *USA TODAY* and the *Wall Street Journal* are two examples.

Contrast also is important in the selection of headlines. A range of headline sizes should be used on a page. A variety of sizes provides contrast and also helps the reader grade the value of the stories. The large headline is a signal to the reader that the story has greater news value than the one with a smaller headline.

Although the practice varies widely, it is a generally accepted design principle that the front page should be organized into horizontal blocks, not unlike the page of a book. Research shows that type in horizontal blocks tends to appear to have a smaller mass. Besides, readers are more willing to dive into a shorter story. In some tests, a 15-inch story displayed horizontally attracted more attention and was said to be easier to read than a 15-inch story displayed vertically. This is a signal to reporters, editors and designers that some readers, perhaps even large numbers of readers, may not complete a long story.

The practice of jumping long stories from the front page to an inside page varies from newspaper to newspaper. Research repeatedly has shown that half the readers never turn to the part of the story jumped to the inside page unless it is an unusually compelling one.

Here are some generally accepted guidelines about jumping stories, ignored from time to time by any number of newspapers:

1. Avoid jumping too many stories from page 1. Some newspapers limit the jumps to three. Others allow none. Still others, like the *New York Times*, jump almost every story.

2. Do not jump short news stories. Make room on the page by careful editing. Short jumps are not only unattractive but also difficult for the reader to find.

3. Avoid jumping a story within the first two or three paragraphs. A sufficient number of paragraphs should be placed beneath the headline to balance the size of the headline and prevent it from appearing to overpower the small amount of body type.

4. Do not jump stories from one inside page to another, if possible. Unless there is enough space on an inside page to accommodate the entire story, it should not be placed on that page.

Related Stories

Sometimes a graphics editor will have several stories related to a single event or incident. Generally, these stories should be grouped. A common method is to put one large headline on the most important story and smaller, separate headlines on the secondary stories that are placed adjacent to the larger story. Often the most important story is placed on the front page with a box indicating that related stories are on an inside page. If the front-page story jumps, it is usually jumped to the same page with the related stories.

Front-Page Design

Most newspapers strive for an attractive, readable, well-balanced front page. Every element on the page performs an essential function. Most newspaper designers strive to make their pages clean and uncluttered. Column rules, cutoff rules and multiple decks have been eliminated from most newspapers.

A full-size page will vary slightly, depending on the size of the newsprint roll. Some pages are approximately 15 by 22 inches. Others are approximately 13½ by 22 inches. The standard format is six columns. However, computerization has enabled newspapers to vary the column width considerably. For example, some newspapers mix column widths, setting some stories in the standard width and others a column and a half or two columns, depending on the desired design effect.

Every year, a number of suggestions are floated about professional meetings and gatherings of graphic designers for changing and "improving" the appearance of newspapers. Some include turning the front page into a "super" news summary or capsulization of the day's news into down-sized pages with larger body type. Until that day arrives, these hints for designing page 1 can be helpful:

1. Do not design a page first and then force the news to fit it. That will destroy or distort the news value of the stories and undermine one of the prime purposes of design—to help grade the news.

2. Put the most important story or display items at the top of the page.

3. Avoid placing large multicolumn heads in adjoining columns at the top of the page. Use a picture or graphic to separate them.

4. Avoid tombstoning headlines. Use display devices such as pictures, boxes, graphics, even white space, to separate heads, especially if the heads are the same size.

5. Place at least one strong multicolumn headline in each quarter of the page and the center, if possible.

6. Use pictures generously. If a picture looks good as a two-column, it will look even better as a three-column most of the time. Crop pictures artfully. Do not waste space.

7. Put big pictures toward the top of the page, but do not be afraid to use a big picture at the bottom as well. Just make certain the one at the top is larger.

8. Use multicolumn headlines at the bottom of the page, even a banner. Be certain the banner's type size is not larger than of the main headline at the top of the page.

9. Don't be afraid to float the flag to give some variety in makeup, but always keep it close to the top of the page.

10. Don't let subjects in photographs based in outside columns look off the page, which destroys unity.

11. Run stories horizontally rather than vertically whenever possible. Attempt to keep major stories 15 to 20 inches on page 1. If they run longer, either jump them or make two stories out of one.

12. Run related stories in the same area on the page.

13. Vary the size of body type and the width in which some stories are set. But don't overdo it.

14. Limit the number of one-column headlines on the page.

15. Use a variety of headline sizes to give the page contrast.

16. Do not let the story run out from under the headline.

17. Vary your page design from page to page.

18. Try a few surprises by ignoring these hints from time to time.

Types of Inside-Page Design

The inside pages, unlike the front page, carry advertising—at least most of them do—and this factor presents some special problems in design. The graphics editor usually receives from the advertising department page dummies with the advertisements drawn in. The task then is to make a page as attractive as possible within the framework of the stories and display elements that will fit on the page with the advertisements. Some newspapers automatically leave certain inside pages exclusively for editorial matter. Others keep advertisements to a minimum for the first several pages. Some put no advertisements at all on the front page of a section.

No matter what the custom of ad placement, the designer planning an inside page should remember that the reader's habits do not change automatically when reading the inside pages of a newspaper. The eyes still move from left to right. The upper left-hand corner of the page is still the first place the eyes touch down.

The same basic principles of display that apply to the front page should apply to the inside pages. But obviously the placement of the advertisements on the page will limit the designer's freedom. Advertisements can be pyramided from the right or from the left. They also can be placed up each side of the page, forming a well in the center. They can all be grouped across the lower part of the page, leaving the upper part open. Ideally, pyramiding to the right is most effective because it opens the upper left-hand corner for a display of editorial matter and permits the designer to take advantage of the reader's normal eye movements. The best ad pyramid is one that leaves at least four or five inches of space at the top of the page. This creates a more usable space in the upper-left corner.

Here are some handy guidelines to consider in making up an inside page:

1. Put a strong (multicolumn) headline or a reasonably large picture in the upper left-hand corner of the page at the point of initial eye contact.

2. Use a careful combination of multicolumn and single-column headlines on the page.

3. Restrict the use of banner heads on inside pages. If a banner head is used, do not use another on the adjacent page.

4. Do not tombstone heads. Also avoid butting headlines, especially heads that are exactly the same size.

5. Include a picture (or pictures), cartoon, chart, map or some other graphic device on each page, if possible, except on pages containing advertisements with large photographs.

6. Keep pictures toward the top of the page. Avoid putting a picture right on top of an advertisement or adjacent to an advertisement.

7. Whenever possible, make the headline wide enough to cover all the body type.

8. Do not run the headline for a story across the top of an advertisement. Make certain there are at least one to two inches of body type separating the headline from the advertisement.

9. Use a variety of headline type sizes and widths to give the page some contrast.

10. Avoid the cluttered look. Do not use too many stories, and leave generous white space.

Tabloid Makeup

At one time in our modern history, tabloid-size newspapers were almost the exclusive property of metropolitan areas. Several of the nation's largest newspapers—the New York *Daily News*, *Newsday* on Long Island, and the *Chicago Sun–Times*—are tabloids. Many weekly newspapers and alternative papers use this smaller format. A tabloid page is approximately one-half a full page turned horizontally. The page is usually 10½ by 14 inches, but the dimensions can vary by as much as two inches.

There are two basic kinds of makeup for the tabloid front page. The typical kind used in most metropolitan tabloids is called "poster." It will consist of a large photo (or several photos) and several large headlines. There generally are no stories, just headlines and photos on metro tabloid front pages. The headlines are keyed to stories on an inside page. As a general rule, the lead story appears on page three along with the story for the other front-page heads.

The poster technique, to be effective, requires excellent photos and stories with major impact. For that reason and others, another format for tabloid-size pages has developed. It is referred to as "compact." Although the term has not been widely accepted, the style of makeup has. The compact makeup uses the same techniques used for a full-size page, only with fewer stories, slightly smaller photos and smaller headlines.

Most of the general rules of good page makeup for a full-size page apply to the tabloid page. However, special effort should be made to avoid overcrowding pages with large masses of body type and large headlines. Pages should be designed horizontally with a minimum number of vertical items (stories with one-column heads and vertical photos).

Many tabloids leave four or more pages at the front of the issue free of advertisements to give the news department ample space to create attractively displayed news pages. Frequently several pages at the start of each special section such as the sports section also are left free of advertisements to allow for a more dramatic display of news.

In making up a tabloid page containing advertisements, the general principles used in making up full-size pages should be followed.

FIGURE 35.1 On Sundays, the *Dallas Morning News* uses this nontraditional and innovative front page design to attract readers to its early edition.

(Reprinted with permission of the *Dallas Morning News*.)

NEWS/ 11A
Results from July term of criminal court

JUDGED
BEST LARGE
WEEKLY NEWSPAPER
BY THE S.C. PRESS
ASSOCIATION

Special Sections
A hunting we will go and Best of the Best

TODAY'S WEATHER
HIGH: 91°
LOW: 72°
Partly cloudy; maybe showers
More weather on page 1B

Serving Barnwell, Blackville, Williston, Elko, Hilda, Kline and Snelling

The People-Sentinel

VOLUME 123, NO. 28   WEDNESDAY, AUGUST 5, 1998   6 SECTIONS/84 PAGES/50 CENTS

Area leaders fly to D.C. to lobby for new missions at SRS

STEPHEN GUILFOYLE
News Editor

Area officials flew to Washington D.C. last week to ask two members of the state's congressional delegation to support new missions for the Savannah River Site.

A release from the Tri-County Alliance says state Rep. Wilbur Cave and state Sen. Brad Hutto arranged the flight to Washington.

Tri-County Alliance President Danny Black said the area officials met primarily with U.S. Rep. Floyd Spence and members of U.S. Sen. Strom Thurmond's staff.

Black said the two are members of key congressional committees that control defense spending, and the rest of the projects for Savannah River Site are being controlled through the Department of Defense's budget.

The Department of Energy will handle the two new missions, but they are Defense projects, Black said.

The first mission will be the handling of plutonium from decommissioned nuclear warheads. The plutonium and parts will be removed from the warheads, and the plutonium used to make commercial nuclear fuel.

SRS has already gained the "mixed oxide fuel and vitrification project" which is half of the plutonium mission.

That part of the project will mean up to 500 jobs and $500 million investment. That is the part that deals with the plutonium after it is removed. The local officials want to get the entire project.

The other half of the plutonium mission will involve disassembling the warheads. The disassembly mission will bring up to 500 jobs and $150 million in facilities.

The officials also wanted the other mission, which will mean considerably more jobs and a much larger investment. That mission is the production of tritium to keep up the Defense Department's supply of the radioactive isotope used in nuclear warheads.

The military has more than enough plutonium for the future needs for its nuclear warheads, but tritium is an artificially created nuclear isotope that decays after a much shorter period of time.

"We made it clear to our congressional delegation and to DOE officials that we strongly favor the Savannah River

See Junket, Page 5A

Beating the heat

Zach Williams is a clever 11-year-old. He came up with this idea to cool himself and his brother, Brad, 9, during a hot day last week. They had sprayed water on a trampoline in his grandmother's back yard. But it wasn't cool enough. So when he spotted the can, he came up with this makeshift "pool." His grandmother lives on Main Street in Barnwell. The boys said the water's fine.
Photo/STEPHEN GUILFOYLE

No tax increase for Barnwell City

Council votes to raise pay of Mayor, Councilmen

VICTOR HILL
Staff Writer

Barnwell City Council approved a $2.5 million dollar budget with no tax increase at Monday's meeting.

City Council had time for a public hearing on the budget at Monday's meeting, but no one showed up.

"We passed another budget without a tax increase. This is very important for the community," city attorney Tommy Boulware said.

The Council also passed an ordinance to raise the mayor's salary by 17 percent and City Council's salary by 15 percent. This was the second reading of the proposed increase. The mayor will receive $4,600 per year, up from $4,000, while City Council members' $3,000 salary will increase to $3,500. City

Council discussed the salary increases behind closed doors at last month's meeting.

The City is working with Knowles and Tailer, a Lexington based company, to remove the rotted tree in the Circle. The mayor said three or four trees of comparable size have already been offered to the City. In addition, the company will look at the other trees in the Circle to determine if they need to be replaced.

In other business, the Council:
• went behind closed doors to discuss a police officer, but took no action.
• passed a request to change zoned land on Marlboro Avenue from heavy industrial to general commercial.
• was awarded a $52,000 home grant from the state to repair a house at the corner of Allen and Center Streets;
• said it will apply for a $10,000 federal grant to purchase new equipment for the Police Department; and
• said it finished painting the water tank on Jackson Street and will paint and raise the water tank in Barnwell Heights.

Two Tales of Two Trailers

VICTOR HILL
Staff Writer

A tree destroyed this trailer in Blackville
Photo/VICTOR HILL

was in the bedroom sleeping.

"The wind started picking up like a storm was coming, and then were these sounds and a vibrating sensation," she said. "It started thrusting us around. It was kind of freaky for a while."

That's when the tree, a huge oak situated just outside the trailer, slammed through the roof and into the bedroom. The tree trapped Norman Crawford, Grayson's boyfriend, and knocked him unconscious. Contractors working on a house across the street had to climb through the wreckage to pull him out. Grayson said he may have

BLACKVILLE -- It wasn't an earthquake, but the tree that crashed through Sonya Grayson's mobile home in Blackville did enough damage to make her think it was.

Grayson was doing dishes in the kitchen. Her sister was busy doing laundry, and her boyfriend

KLINE -- The Caroe home is a burned skeleton, its supportive bones blackened by a fire that raged through it a few weeks ago.

Inside, pots, pans, furniture and clothes lie scorched and unusable.

The only sounds are hornets buzzing, making a nest in the corner of the kitchen.

What belongs to William, Peggy, and son, Randy, could salvage are stacked as well as can be expected in the corner of a hotel room.

The Caroes lived in a mobile home in Kline. They had insurance, a policy that covered this kind of disaster, they thought.

It didn't.

After the fire, their insurance company told

them they owed money.

"I never believed something like this would happen to us," William says.

The night of the fire, William and Peggy left to

The ruins of a trailer in Kline gutted by fire
Photo/VICTOR HILL

See Trailer, Page 5A   See Fire, Page 5A

SUBSCRIBE TODAY!
The People-Sentinel
9088 Dunbarton Blvd.
Barnwell, SC 29612
(803) 259-3501

Index

SECTION A
CALENDAR 2
OPINION 4
SPORTS 6

SECTION B
SOCIETY 2
RELIGION 4
OBITUARIES 5

SECTION C
CLASSIFIEDS 4
CROSSWORD 4
TELEVISION
LISTINGS 1, 4
HOROSCOPE 4

"Plus many valuable savings from local advertisers"

© Copyright 1998
CNI Newspapers

County may be looking at 'other' 1 cent sales tax

Specific projects, costs must be stated before referendum

STEPHEN GUILFOYLE
News Editor

Barnwell County Council members have talked about a 1-cent sales tax they could use to help pay for new costs of waste disposal.

During those discussions, they have said more than once that they were discussing the "local option sales tax."

However, the local option

sales tax will raise just about 10 percent of the county's estimates of garbage costs. Most of the money raised by the local option sales tax would be used to roll back property taxes.

The state does allow governments to pass another kind of 1-cent sales tax, different from the local option, which can be used to raise money for specific projects. That tax, however has other specific rules and requirements which the County Coun-

cil has not set out.

That 1-cent sales tax "infrastructure" tax can be used for roads and utilities.

The law relating to that tax says the County Council must spell out the exact projects it wants to use the money for, and exactly how much money it intends to raise with the sales tax.

The 1-cent infrastructure tax can be imposed for either seven years maximum, or until the government raises the amount of money it needs.

Florence County is considering imposing the 1-cent sales tax, and it was passed in York County. Both counties want the money for road projects.

Florence already has the local

option sales tax in place, so if the infrastructure tax is passed, residents will be paying 7 cents on the dollar in total sales tax.

The law also includes specific wording that must be on the ballot, and says the referendum must be approved in a General Election, which comes on the first Tuesday in November each year. It cannot be approved during a special election.

County Council has voted two of the three required times to approve the referendum, but it has been done by a voice motion to just hold the referendum and impose the tax, if the referen-

See Tax, Page 5A

FIGURE 35.2   The *People–Sentinel in* Barnwell, S.C. uses a clean, crisp, modular makeup on its front page that focuses on all local news.

(Reprinted with permission of the *People–Sentinel*, Barnwell, S.C.)

S.F. 26, ST. LOUIS 10

DEFENSE SHINES IN 49ERS' VICTORY

With Packers on tap, secondary's improvement is significant.

▶ *See Page C1*

OAKLAND 27, CINCINNATI 10

BACKUP QB SPARKS RAIDERS

Donald Hollas records his first TD pass in 6 years, then adds another

▶ *See Page C*

San Francisco Chronicle

NORTHERN CALIFORNIA'S LARGEST NEWSPAPER

25¢
SANTA CLARA COUNTY
SPECIAL

★★★★★ MONDAY, OCTOBER 26, 1998 415-777-1111 50 CENT

PENINSULA EDITION

Netanyahu Fighting For Pact, His Future

Israeli leader faces a wall of anger

By Deborah Sontag
New York Times

Jerusalem

Prime Minister Benjamin Netanyahu of Israel, stepping off a plane from Washington into a turbulent political arena, plunged directly into an aggressive campaign yesterday both to stay in office and to secure support for the new peace accord with the Palestinians.

Facing vituperative protests by Jewish settlers and the threat of new elections, Netanyahu kicked off his campaign right at the Ben Gurion Airport yesterday afternoon, mounting a charged defense of what the right wing sees as a betrayal of all it stands for. The furor over of more land to Palestinians control.

In a speech broadcast live on Israeli television, he portrayed himself as a reluctant peacemaker and as a kind of warrior forced to make stomach-turning strategic decisions.

"Standing over even one centimeter or one grain of the soil of the Land of Israel in the Palestinian Authority is difficult and agonizing," Netanyahu said. "We fought with all our might, we fought like lions, to reduce as much as possible, within the framework of Israel's commitments, the land that was handed over."

Appealing directly to his fiercest critics, the settlers in the West Bank, who have promised to topple him, Netanyahu said, "You are us and we are you. We love you."

The sentiment fell on closed ears. The settlers formally broke relations with Netanyahu yesterday.

ISRAEL: *Page A9 Col. 1*

COMMUTER CHRONICLES *Is on Page A11*

■ ELECTION '98 ■

President Clinton greeted supporters after his luncheon speech at the Mark Hopkins Hotel in San Francisco.

Pumped-Up Clinton Cashes In

President raises $2 million on visit to California

By Carla Marinucci
Chronicle Political Writer

Fresh from his triumphant brokering of a Mideast peace accord, President Clinton seized upon his renewed clout and fund-raising muscle to fire up California Democrats one week before Election Day.

From Hollywood to San Francisco, Clinton basked in the glow of praise during a flurry of weekend appearances that raised $2 million for incumbent U.S. Senator Barbara Boxer and state Democrats.

A charged-up Clinton, strolled through San Francisco's Sea Cliff neighborhood to chat with astonished onlookers about the peace process, dined with Hollywood celebrities and spoke to glowingly to Democrats at four separate fund-raisers in an event-packed weekend.

He reveled in telling crowds how he was still feeling the effects of 20 hours without sleep — "I didn't even do that in college" — but repeatedly reminded them that he was in California on a mission.

"We have the message, the candidates and the vision," Clinton told a standing room only crowd in San Francisco yesterday during his 42nd trip to California and the third in last two months. "We are about the business of defining our country."

Clinton warned his audiences they were "not off the hook" with campaign checks, but should work through Election Day to get out the vote. So much was at stake in the California election, he told them, "it's like an election for president."

The president's California weekend, coming one week before crucial November 3 elections that will decide the governor's race, the U.S. Senate race and scores of Congressional seats, marked a dramatic reversal from just four weeks ago, when noisy protesters lined streets with jeering messages like "Jail to the Chief" and "Re-

CLINTON: *Page A9 Col. 1*

Fong Hits Boxer, Defends Donation

Flap over gift to anti-gay group

By John Wildermuth
Chronicle Political Writer

San Diego

With his poll numbers eroding, Republican Senate candidate Matt Fong launched a weekend assault on incumbent Democrat Barbara Boxer, but also found himself defending a $50,000 donation to the anti-gay Traditional Values Coalition.

Fong acknowledged making the "charitable donation" last spring using funds left over from his 1994 campaign for state treasurer. But he said it was intended to help change that group's more extreme position.

"What lets me be a uniter and not a divider is my ability to work with different groups, even with those who would be considered extreme by some people," Fong said.

The Orange County coalition and its founder, the Rev. Lou Sheldon, are opposed to abortion and family planning and have called for quarantining people with AIDS to stop the spread of the disease.

Sheldon also led the successful effort to persuade Republican Senate leaders to torpedo the nomination of James Hormel, a gay San Francisco businessman and philanthropist, as ambassador to Luxembourg.

FONG: *Page A9 Col. 4*

Ballot Test for Gay Marriage in Alaska, Hawaii

By Elaine Herscher
Chronicle Staff Writer

One of the most significant battles over gay rights in a generation is raging not in the urban centers of New York or San Francisco, but in the wilds of Alaska and on the beaches of Hawaii.

Voters in both states will be asked November 3 to change their state constitutions to prevent gays and lesbians from marrying.

The battles have taken on near-biblical dimensions. Proponents of the Hawaii measure say their state faces its "last chance to save traditional marriage." Opponents say if they defeat the measure, gays will "stand within a historical eye blink" of winning marriage rights that they hope will extend across the nation.

Neither state is a gay mecca. Alaska is predominantly Republican and retains a frontier mentality, and Hawaii, while largely Democratic and multiracial, is not known for having a vocal gay community.

But Hawaii has become pivotal to the national debate over gay marriage. The state Supreme Court in 1993 came to close to legalizing lesbian and gay unions that some mainland couples still have their bags packed.

In a preliminary ruling, the court said Hawaii's existing ban on gay marriages should be abandoned as unconstitutional unless the state can prove it had a compelling reason to discriminate against same-sex couples. While the court continued to weigh the state's evidence, attempts to outlaw gay marriage by constitutional amendment failed in the Legislature.

Now the issue is in the hands of the voters.

MARRIAGE: *Page A9 Col. 5*

Victim's Family Finally to See Ng in Court

Trial starts today in serial killings

By Bill Wallace
Chronicle Staff Writer

Santa Ana, Orange County

Paul Cosner had it all: Athletic, good-looking and an excellent health, he was the model of a young, successful entrepreneur. Then, on Nov. 2, 1984, he vanished.

Today, Cosner has reappeared as a number in an Orange County courtroom — Count Four of criminal case 84DF006. People of the State of California vs. Charles Chitat Ng.

Cosner, who was a 39-year-old

auto broker at the time of his disappearance, is among seven men, three women and two children whom Ng allegedly killed in one of the grisliest serial murder cases in Northern California history.

When opening arguments begin in Ng's long-delayed murder

PERSISTENCE: *Page A9 Col. 1*

trial this morning, three people in the courtroom will be listening with particular interest. Virginia and David Neeley, Cosner's mother and stepfather, and Sharon Sellitto, his sister.

This trial may be the only closure they get. Although the family has purchased a plot for him in an Ohio cemetery, the grave remains empty. Cosner's body has never been found.

Seeing Ng on trial is something the family has been awaiting for more than 13 years, Sellitto said in an interview last week.

"There were times when it seemed like we would never get to

FIGURE 35.3 The *San Francisco Chronicle* combines large color photographs with local, national and international stories to create an interesting and attractive front page.

(Reprinted with permission of the *San Francisco Chronicle*.)

******************MIXED ADC 021
PUBLISHER LARRY SMITH
220 1ST ST
LA FOLLETTE TN 37766-2413

►EXAMINING THE TEACHERS TEST — Page 3

BEVERLY CITIZEN

Founded 1851 · Re-established 1995

www.townonline.com/north — Vol. 2, No. 44 — 3 Sections, 116 Pages

COMMUNITY NEWSPAPER COMPANY

WEDNESDAY, JULY 8, 1998 — 50 CENTS

Bonfire of the vandals

Unruly crowd flares at unauthorized Fourth of July bonfire

BY CATHRYN KEEFE O'HARE
CITIZEN STAFF

What started as a little holiday bonfire — illegal, of course — ended up with a melee between revelers and police. One resident was arrested for assault and battery on a policeman and the policeman landed in the hospital where he received 10 stitches for his injury.

Before the night was over, police also confiscated a number of baseball bats, a knife, a pick axe, a night stick, and a black jack.

Police and firemen dodged sticks and stones at about 9:45 p.m. from a crowd of about 100 people gathered around a 10-to-12-foot bonfire in the Gage Street Playground on Saturday, the Fourth of July.

"It's become sort of an annual event," Fire Lieutenant Bob Eastwood said in a later interview.

For the past few years, he said, a number of Gloucester Crossing residents have gathered a lot of trash to make their own, unsanctioned, bonfire.

The blaze was about half-way down the pyre when the fire department arrived, Eastwood said. "It was wholly involved," he said. Firemen doused it with water and broke up the pile, he continued.

BONFIRE, page 23

INSIDE

From the Playgrounds
Page 13

INDEX

RED, WHITE & TRUE

PHOTO BY ROB BRANCH

For showing his true colors, Scott Weber gets a warm greeting from friend Kristin Kelley, in the crowd at the Ryal Side Horribles Parade Saturday. For more faces from the Fourth of July Parades in Ryal Side and Beverly Farms, see page 11.

Gas station slated for Stop and Shop

BY CATHRYN KEEFE O'HARE
CITIZEN STAFF

Excuse me. It's a Fuel Facility, per the Stop and Shop officials who want to build what most of the world calls a gas station in front of the Elliott Street supermarket.

The Zoning Board of Appeals will hear from those officials or their representatives on Tuesday, July 28, at 7 p.m. The construction plans, which are dated June 18, depict a 75 by 20 foot, self-service gas station with three "gas dispensers" — otherwise known as pumps — sitting up front in the current parking lot, close to McPherson Street. The bottom of the sign will be 14 1/2 feet from the ground and will rise another 3 feet, 8 inches to say "Stop and Shop."

According to Building Inspector Tim Brennan, a gas station must obtain a special permit in this commercial zone (CG). In any other zone, gas station advocates need to obtain a variance, which are a little harder to get, he said. The Stop and Shop officials will have to show that a gas station is an appropriate use for the site and that it will have no major impacts on the neighborhood, Brennan continued.

In addition to the pumps, the facili-

GAS STATION, page 7

De-fence-ive tactics

Homeowners fence off the sea wall to stop teens from hanging out

BY MELISSA J. VARNAVAS
CITIZEN STAFF

Taking a stroll along the sea wall from Independence Park to the Washington Street public access point is no longer possible. Despite opposition from Beverly's Coastal Access Group, Lothrop Street home owners Gail and Dennis Meka erected a fence at 59 Lothrop St. overhanging the sea wall behind their property, blocking the historic "Ancient Highway."

Access Group members recently raised awareness of shrinking public access to the coast by issuing a series of maps showing a steady erosion of coastal access since the early 1800s. The maps outline what was known as the Ancient Highway, a public coastal access way which ran from Ryal Side to the Manchester line dating from 1644.

"When you see what was there, and what is there now," Alice Burns, a member of both the Harbor Management Authority and the Coastal Access Group said last week, "you can really see what the issue is."

Meka and her husband, meanwhile, feel caught in the middle between the pressure for public access to the waterfront and the responsibilities of property ownership. "In the days of the ancient way," Meka explained, "people weren't suing each other."

Lothrop Street residents, along

FENCE, page 6

It takes a village to raise the quads

BY CATHRYN KEEFE O'HARE
CITIZEN STAFF

There was an old woman who lived in a shoe. She had so many children she didn't know what to do. (Mother Goose.)

Mary Driscoll loves so many children, and she knows just what to do — call Mom, or Dad, or Auntie, or one of the other 35 people on her list of friends or relatives all lined up to help.

Mary and David Driscoll are the parents of the almost-1-year-old quadruplets born last July 17 within three minutes of each other. And Mary sings in praise not just for these little "miracles," but for all her helpers.

"God help me if they stopped coming," she said in an interview this week.

About 25 hail from the Garden City. After all, even though the Driscolls live in Peabody, Mary was born and raised in Beverly.

Her mother, Ann Englehardt, "feeds us," cooking healthy, hot meals, Mary said. Her father, Bob Englehardt, comes every day to do the laundry. Her uncle, Father Bill Kane, who is Ann's brother, brings Kentucky Fried Chicken when he comes to town. Sister Julie Theresa Kane, another of Ann's siblings who lives now at St. Mary's convent on Chapman Street

QUADS, page 28

The Driscoll quadruplets, 1 year later, are happy and healthy. They are, left to right, Cullen, Emma, Riley and Killian. The quads' parents Mary and David rely on a fan club of friends and family who love to help.

FIGURE 35.4 The *Beverly Citizen* in Beverly, MA., is a tabloid, but it uses traditional broadsheet makeup on its front page to create a clean, easy-to-read newspaper.
(Reprinted with permission of the *Beverly Citizen*, Community Newspaper Co., Beverly, MA.)

FIGURE 35.5 The New York *Daily News* uses traditional metropolitan tabloid style makeup with big headlines and a single picture keyed to main story, which usually starts on page 2 or 3. Other large heads are keyed to secondary stories, also inside.

(New York *Daily News*, L.P., reprinted with permission.)

EXERCISES

1. Analyze the front-page and inside-page design of the four largest newspapers in your state. (They should be available in your college or university library.) Pick days when a major news event took place and compare the way each paper handled the story on its front page. Write a brief report on how they are similar and how they are different. Select the one you believe is the most attractive and easiest to read and explain why.

2. Arrange to spend a day (one shift) with the graphics or design editor of your local newspaper. Write a story about that experience.

3. If your college or university has a graphics department that produces university publications, arrange to spend a day with the designers and observe their use of computers in their work.

4. Using any newspaper available to you, redesign the front page. Use all the same stories, photographs and other display elements—charts, information graphs and maps. It is permissible in this assignment to change the type size and column width of headlines, but do not add additional stories. Use of a different-size masthead also is permissible for the exercise.

5. Using an full-size newspaper available to you, redesign the front page as a tabloid similar to the New York *Daily News* illustrated in this chapter. Then redesign it in the tabloid style of the *Beverly Citizen,* also illustrated in this chapter.

6. Assume the role of a graphics designer who is faced with creating a front page for the special health section of the campus newspaper dealing with the problem of binge drinking. You have one major story plus two sidebar stories that can start on the page and be jumped inside. You can create charts, graphs, lists or other graphic elements as well as any photographs you might want to use. Draw a draft of your front page design indicating headline and picture sizes, amount of each story to be used on the page and any other graphic elements.

7. In your same role as graphics designer, assume your college women's basketball team has just won the NCAA national championship for the sixth time. Design the front page of a commemorative section of the campus paper honoring the team. You can select all the stories and graphic elements and photographs you would use, but you must indicate the headline and picture sizes and you must write headlines for the stories and captions for the pictures.

APPENDIX

Preparing Copy

Most newspaper reporters write their stories on computer screens and follow a set of guidelines for preparing their copy that have been developed for that particular newspaper. In many ways they are quite similar to the instructions for preparing a piece of copy on a typewriter; however, more codes generally are used. (See example in Chapter 32).

For those writers who still use typewriters, here is how your copy should be prepared:

1. Prepare all copy with a typewriter.
2. Begin every story on a new sheet of paper (copy paper is generally 8½ by 11 inches in size).
3. Place your name at the upper left-hand corner of every page.
4. Write the guideline or slug for the story in the same line with your name or in the line below it. This line is a brief identification of the story, such as "fire" for a fire story or "city council" for a report of a city council meeting.
5. Number every page, at the top, following the slug.
6. On the first page, leave ample space between the slug and the first paragraph—from one-fourth to one-third of the page.
7. Leave margins of at least one inch on both sides.
8. Double-space all copy.
9. Type on one side of the paper only.
10. Indent five spaces to begin a paragraph.
11. Do not underline.

Copyreading Symbols

Copy editors use a standard set of symbols that in most instances allows them to indicate changes without using words. Following is a list:

Symbol	Definition	Example
⊗ or ⊙	Period mark	He was there⊗ He was there⊙
⋏	Comma	Therefore⋏ he will . . .
⋎	Apostrophe	Ill let you know . . .
⋎″	Quotation marks	I'll let you know . . .
≡ or ⟶	Make capital letter	later that monday . . .
/	Make lowercase letter	Later in The day . . .
◯	Abbreviate or spell out word or number	(Doctor) Smith said . . . . Dr. (Wm.) Smith said . . . The (2) men were . . . The (twelve) men were . . .
⌐ or ⌐ or ¢	Start new paragraph	⌐The end of the . . . ⌐The end of the . . . ¢ The end of the . . .
no ¢	Do not make this a new paragraph	no ¢ The end of . . .

Correcting Copy

Although stories written on computers are corrected electronically, it is still useful for reporters to learn the standard copy editing symbols. The following are examples of the symbols that are used universally whenever written material is corrected by hand.

Delete letters:

Two men were in the car . . .

Delete word or words:

Two men were were in the car behind us with . . .

Transpose letters or words:

Tow men in were the car with . . .

Spell out or abbreviate (same symbol in both cases):

2 men were in the car with Mister Jones.

Insert word or words:

Two men in the car with Mr. Jones.

Capitalize letter:

two men were in the car with . . .

Make lower lowercase:

Two Men were in the car . . .

Period mark (either of two symbols):

Two men were in the car with Mr. Jones.

Separate letters with space:

Two men werein the car . . .

Bring letters together:

Two men we re in the car . . .

Restore copy that has been marked out:

Two men ~~were in the car~~ with Mr. Jones. _stet_

In deleting copy on more than one line, mark out all the deleted material by drawing a heavy line directly from the beginning to the end of the deleted material:

Located in the center of the little island is a log cabin, ~~built perhaps 100 years ago though no one knows for sure and there is no way of finding out~~ and back of the cabin is the site of the old Indian village.

In correcting misspelled words that have only one or two letters wrong, mark out each misused letter and place the correct letter above it. If a word is badly misspelled, mark out the whole word and write it correctly above:

The b~~a~~y walked ~~nonchalontly~~ _nonchalantly_ into the room.

The reporter should use symbols whenever possible in correcting copy because they are time-saving devices. However, if a phrase (or word) is split between two lines, the simplest procedure is to mark through all or part of the phrase and rewrite it correctly between the lines.

Journalistic Terms

Ad.   Advertisement.

Add.   Copy to be added to a story already written.

Advance.   A preliminary story concerning a future event.

Agate.   Type 5½ points in depth (72 points to the inch).

A.M.   Morning paper.

Angle.   The aspect emphasized in a story.

A.P. or AP.   The Associated Press, press service.

Art.   All newspaper illustrations.

Assignment.   Reporter's task.

Bank.   (1) Part of headline (also called "deck"); (2) table on which type is set.

Banner.   A page-wide headline (also called "streamer").

Barline.   A one-line headline.

Beat.   (1) The reporter's regular run; (2) an exclusive story.

B.F. or bf.   Boldface or black type.

Blind interview.   Interview that does not give name of person interviewed.

Blurb.   A short statement used to promote the sale of a new book or publication.

Body type.   Small type in which most of paper is set.

Boil down.   Reduce in size.

Border.   Metal or paper strips of type used to box stories, ads, etc.

Box.   An enclosure of line rules or borders.

Break.   (1) The point at which a story is continued to another column or page; (2) as a verb, refers to the time a story is available for publication.

Bromide.   A trite expression.

Bulletin.   A brief, last-minute news item on an important event.

By-line.   The author's name at the start of a story—"By John Smith."

C. and L.C. or clc.   Capital and lowercase letters.

Canned copy.   Publicity material.

Caps.   Capital letters.

Caption.   See Cutlines.

City editor. Person in charge of local news; also called "Metropolitan editor" at some papers.

Clip. Newspaper clipping.

Code. Key words or letters on computer to assign functions or routines.

Col. Column.

Condensed type. Type that is narrower than regular width.

Copy. All typewritten material.

Copy desk. Where stories are edited and headlines written.

Copy editor. One who edits and headlines news stories.

Correspondent. Out-of-town reporter.

Cover. To get the facts of a story.

Credit line. Line acknowledging source of a story or picture.

Crusade. Campaign of a newspaper for a certain reform.

Cub. A beginning reporter.

Cut. (1) A newspaper engraving; (2) to reduce the length of a story.

Cutlines. Explanatory lines describing a picture or illustration, usually under the picture; also called "captions."

Dateline. Line at the beginning of a story that includes both date and place of origin of story: "NEW YORK, Jan. 1—."

Deadline. The time all copy must be completed in order to make an edition.

Deck. Part of a multibank headline.

Desk. The copy desk.

Double truck. Two adjoining pages made as one.

Down style. A newspaper headline style calling for a minimum of capitalization.

Dummy. Diagram of a page for use in making up a page.

Dump. Changing stored material from one computer unit to another.

Ear. Small box in the upper corners of the nameplate (flag).

Edition. Issue for one press run, as "mail edition," "home edition," "extra edition."

Editorialize. To include opinion of the writer in copy.

Embargo. A restriction, such as the precise date and time, placed on the release of news.

Filler. Short news or informational items used to fill small spaces in a page.

Flag. Name of paper appearing on first page.

Flash. A short message briefly summarizing a news event.

Fold. Place where paper is folded.

Folio. Page or page number.

Follow or Follow-up. Story giving later developments of an event already written up.

Follow copy. Instructions on copy to set story or word exactly as written, used often to indicate that word is purposely misspelled or that spelling is unorthodox.

Folo. Short for "follow."

Font. Type face of one size and style.

Fotog. Short for photographer.

Future file. File in which stories coming up at later date are kept.

FYI. For your information.

Galley. Metal tray for holding type. In offset, the columns of type to be pasted down also are called galleys.

Galley proof. Proof made of a galley of type.

Graf. Short for "paragraph."

Guideline. A slug line, giving title of the story for convenience of makeup editor and compositors.

Halftone. A cut made from a photograph.

Hammer. See Kicker.

Head. Short for "headline."

Headline schedule. All of the headline combinations used by a newspaper.

Hold for release. Instructions to hold copy until editor orders it printed.

HTK or HTC. Instructions on copy of a "head to come."

Insert. Copy that is to be inserted in a story already sent to the compositor.

Interface. Hardware (the computer's backup machines) "talking to each other."

Itals. Italics.

Jump. To continue a story from one page to another.

Jump head. Headline above a continued story.

Jump lines. Lines such as "Continued on page 6" or "Continued from page 1" to identify a continued story.

Kicker.   A short one-line head, sometimes underlined, either centered above or slightly to the left of main head, usually in type about one-half type size of main head; also called "hammer."

Kill.   To delete or exclude copy.

Layout.   (1) Diagram of page (see Dummy), showing where stories and ads are to be placed; (2) arrangement of pictures on picture page.

L.C. or lc.   Lowercase type.

Lead (lĕd).   (1) As noun, metal pieces placed between lines of type for spacing; (2) as verb, to space out page with these metal pieces in hot-metal typesetting operations.

Lead (lede).   The first paragraph of a news story.

Leg man.   Reporter who gathers news, phoning it in instead of going to newspaper office to write it.

Letterpress printing.   Process of printing that uses metal type or other raised surfaces that make a direct impression on paper.

Library.   Newspaper morgue or files of clippings, photographs, prepared obituaries, biographies, etc.

Localize.   To emphasize the local angle in a story.

Log.   City editor's assignment book.

Make-over.   Rearrangement of stories on page to provide for new copy or to change the position of stories.

Makeup.   Arranging stories, pictures, ads, etc., on a page.

Masthead.   Editorial page heading that gives information about the newspaper.

Matrix or Mat.   A matrix or papier-mâché impression of a cut or of type.

Minion.   Seven-point type.

Modem.   Portable device that allows reporters in field to write stories and feed them by telephone to computer at the newspaper.

More.   Used at end of a page of copy to indicate story is continued on another page.

Morgue.   Files for depositing clippings, pictures, etc. (also called "library").

Mug shot.   Head-and-shoulders photograph of an individual.

Must.   Instructions that story must be used on that day without fail.

Nameplate.   Name of paper on page 1 (also called "flag").

Newsprint.   The grade of paper used in printing newspapers.

Nonpareil.   Six-point type.

Obit.   Obituary.

Offset printing.   Process of printing that uses a rubber roller that takes the impression from a metal plate and transfers it to the printer.

Op-Ed.   Page opposite the editorial page featuring comment, cartoons and other editorial matter.

Overline.   Caption above a cut. Also another word for kicker.

Overset.   Type in addition to that needed to fill a paper.

Pad.   To make longer.

Pasteup.   Method of making up a page for the camera in the offset process—pasting in proofs of headlines, body type, line drawings, etc.

Pica.   Twelve-point type; also unit of measurement, one-sixth of an inch.

Pick up.   Instructions to use material already set in type.

Pix.   Picture.

Plate.   A stereotyped page of type, ready to lock in press.

Play up.   To emphasize.

P.M.   Afternoon paper.

Point.   A depth measurement of type approximately ½ inch.

Policy story.   A story showing directly or indirectly the newspaper's stand on an issue.

Precede.   Material to precede the copy already set in type.

Proof.   An imprint of set type used in correcting errors.

Proofreader.   Person who reads proof to correct errors.

Puff.   Editorialized, complimentary statements in a news story.

Purge.   Eliminate data from the system.

Q and A.   Question-and-answer copy, printed verbatim.

Quad.   A type character or space equal in width and height.

Query.   Question on an event sent by a correspondent to a paper or by a paper to a correspondent.

Queue. Order of priority in scheduling; each schedule is known as a "queue."

Quote. Quotation.

Railroad. To rush copy through to be typeset without careful editing.

Release. Instructions on the time to publish a story, as "Release after 3 p.m. Feb. 6."

Rewrite. (1) To write a story again to improve; (2) to write a story that already has been reported in a competing newspaper; (3) to write a story from facts given by another reporter (sometimes from a leg man over the telephone).

Roll up/down. Commands moving story on a terminal screen.

Rule. Metal strip or paper tape used in separating columns, making borders, etc.

Run. A press run (edition).

Run in. Instructions to make a series of sentences, names, etc., into one paragraph, if each one of the series has been set up as a separate short paragraph or line.

Running story. Story sent to compositor in sections. Also a story reported over several days or weeks.

Runover. Part of a story that is continued on another page.

Sacred cow. News or promotional material that the publisher or editor demands be printed in a special manner.

Scanner. Optical character reader (also known as OCR), which converts typewritten material to electronic impulses and transmits them to a tape punch or computer.

Schedule. List of assignments.

Scoop. An exclusive story.

Second front. The first page of a second section.

Sked. Schedule.

Slant. To emphasize a certain phase of a news event.

Slot. The place occupied by the head of the copy desk (on the inside of horseshoe-shaped desks). Slot man is also called "copy desk chief."

Slug. (1) The guideline at the beginning of the story, to make it easy to identify (see Guideline); (2) a strip of metal, less than type height and used to space between lines; (3) a line of type cast by the typesetting machine.

Sort. Arranging material in a specific sequence.

Squib. A brief story.

Stet. Restore text of copy that has been marked out. (This is a copyreaders' and proofreaders' sign.)

Streamer. Headline stretching completely across a page (also called "banner").

String. Newspaper clippings pasted together.

Subhead. Small, one-line headline used in the body of a story.

System. The computer and computer programs used in a newsroom.

Take. A section of a running story.

Terminal. Common name for computer used by reporters and editors.

Thirty. The end of a story (numeral usually used).

Tie-back or Tie-in. That part of the story which reiterates past events to remind the reader or to give background for the latest developments.

Time copy. Copy that might be held over and used when needed.

Top heads. Headline at top of a column.

Tr. Transpose or change the position of.

Trim. Reduce length of story.

U.C. and L.C. Uppercase and lowercase type.

Wire services. Press associations such as The Associated Press.

Wrong font or W.F. Wrong style or size of type.

THE INTERNET

The Internet is an important research tool for journalists. There are thousands of web sites that provide information quickly. However, because anyone can put anything on the Internet, it is important that Internet sources be checked carefully to avoid spreading incomplete information, unchecked allegations and single points of view. Many newspapers have instituted newsroom policies on checking information collected from the Internet because it is easy to fake Internet return addresses or log on as someone else. However, there are thousands of legitimate federal, state and local government web sites as well as sites maintained by businesses, industries and educational and religious institutions. Search engines such as Yahoo and Hotbot can supply an authoritative list of web sites.

INTERNET TERMS

Chat room.   Where computer users "talk" with others online using a commercial service such as American Online or Compuserve.

Content provider.   Firm or group that generates content.

Flaming.   Aggressive commentary or electronic mail.

Hit.   Web users' request to a server for a file or image.

Home page.   Home or online site for information on thousands of topics.

HTML.   Hypertext Markup Language used to develop World Wide Web documents.

Hyperlink.   The spot on the Internet that links one user to another site.

Hypertext.   Coding system that links electronic documents to each other.

Internet.   Worldwide network of computers that communicate in a common language.

Listserve.   Software that allows computer users to subscribe to mailing lists.

Log on.   The way a computer user identifies him- or herself to gain access to a network.

Mailing list.   A group of subscribers with a common interest.

Search engine.   Means of locating information on the Internet by using keyword(s).

Spam.   Unwanted material. Computer version of junk mail.

Usenet newsgroups.   Bulletin boards, informal forums, or news groups on Internet devoted to wide range of subjects and interests.

The Web.   The World Wide Web; that part of the Internet used to access to information, pictures, and sound.

Web site.   Pages developed by individuals, businesses, and organizations that are accessed through the Internet.

SELECTED READINGS

General References on Journalistic Writing

Berner, R. Thomas. *Language Skills for Journalists.* Boston: Houghton Mifflin, 1984.
Bernstein, Theodore M. *Watch Your Language.* Manhasset, NY: Channel Press, 1976.
Brooks, Brian S., and James L. Pinson. *Working with Words: A Concise Handbook for Media Writers and Editors,* 2nd ed. New York: St. Martin Press, 1993.
Capon, Rene J. *The Word: An Associated Press Guide to Good News Writing.* New York: The Associated Press, 1982.
Goldstein, Norman (ed.). *The Associated Press Stylebook and Libel Manual.* New York: The Associated Press, 1996.
Kilpatrick, James J. *The Writer's Art.* Kansas City: Andrews, McMeel and Parker, Inc., 1993.
Newman, Edwin. *Strictly Speaking: Will American Be the Death of English?* New York: Warner Books, 1974.
Miller, Casey, and Kate Swift. *Handbook of Nonsexist Writing,* 2nd ed. Belmont, Calif.: 1993.
Zinsser, William. *On Writing Well,* 6th ed. Revised and Updated (paperback). New York: Prennial Library, 1998.

Journalism and Society

(Freedom of the press, journalistic ethics, legal aspects of journalism, public opinion.)

Bagdikian, Ben H. *The Media Monopoly,* 2nd ed. Boston: Beacon Press, 1987.
Christians, Clifford G., John P. Ferre, and Mark Fackler. *Media Ethics: Cases and Moral Reasons.* Boston: Allyn & Bacon, 1995.
Goldstein, Thomas. *The News at Any Cost: How Journalists Compromise Their Ethics to Shape the News.* New York: Simon and Schuster, 1985.
Hulteng, John L. *The Messenger's Motives: Ethical Problems of the News Media,* 2nd ed. Englewood Cliffs, NJ: Prentice-Hall, 1985.
Kurtz, Howard. *Media Circus: The Trouble with America's Newspapers.* New York: Time Books, 1993.
Teeter, Dwight L., Don R. LeDuc and Bill Loving. *Law of Mass Communications Freedom and Control of Print and Broadcast Media,* 9th ed. Westbury, NY: Foundation Press, 1998.

References on Special Types of Journalist Writing

Blundell, William E. *The Wall Street Journal: Storytelling Step by Step.* New York: Dow Jones and Company Inc., 1986.
Block, Mervin. *Writing Broadcast News—Shorter, Sharper, Stronger,* 2nd ed. Chicago: Bonus Book, 1997.
Garrett, Annette. *Interviewing: Its Principles and Methods.* New York: Family Association of America, 1982.
Rapoport, Ron. (ed.). *A Kind of Grace: A Treasury of Sportswriting by Women.* Berkley: Zenobia Press, 1996.
Ruehlmann, William. *Stalking the Feature Story.* New York: Vintage Books, 1979.

Collections of Columns

Baker Russell. *So This Is Depravity and Other Observations.* New York: Congdon and Lattes, Inc., 1980.
_____. *The Rescue of Miss Yaskellel and Other Pipe Dreams.* New York: Congdon and Weed, 1983.
Grizzard, Lewis. *Don't Sit Under the Grits Tree With Anyone Else But Me.* Atlanta, GA: Peachtree Publishers Limited, 1983.
Harris, Sydney J. *The Best of Sydney J. Harris.* Boston: Houghton Mifflin Company, 1976.
Quindlen, Anna. *Living Out Loud* (Paperback). New York: Ballantine Books, 1988.
Royko, Mike. *Sez Who? Sez Me.* New York: E.P. Dutton, 1982.
Smith, Red. *To Absent Friends from Red Smith.* New York: Atheneum, 1982.

The Journalistic Profession

(History of journalism, biographies of famous journalists, journalism as a profession)

Berger, Meyer. *The Story of the New York Times*. New York: Simon and Schuster, 1951.

Berges, Marshall. *The Life and Times of the Los Angeles Times: A Newspaper, a Family and a City*. New York: Atheneum, 1984.

Brucker, Herbert. *Communication is Power: Unchanging Ideas in Changing Journalism*. New York: Oxford University Press, 1973.

_____. *Eyewitnesses to History*. New York: Macmillan, 1962.

Buranelli, V., (ed.) *The Trial of Peter Zenger*. New York: New York University Press, 1957.

Canham, E. D. *Commitment to Freedom: The Story of the Christian Science Monitor*. Boston: Houghton Mifflin, 1958.

Carlson, O. *The Man Who Made News: James Gordon Bennett*. New York: Duell, Sloan & Pearce, 1942.

Deakin, James. *Straight Stuff: The Reporters, the White House and the Truth*. New York: William Morrow & Co., Inc., 1984.

Emery, Edwin and Michael Emery. *The Press in America*, 5th ed. Englewood Cliffs, NJ: Prentice-Hall, 1984.

Fowler, Gene. *Timber Line: A Story of Bonfils and Tammen*. Garden City, NY: Halcyon House, 1943.

Gramling, O. *AP: The Story of News*. New York: Farrar, 1940.

Johnson, G. W. *An Honorable Titan: A Biographical Study of Adolph S. Ochs*. New York: Harper, 1946.

Johnson, Michael L. *The New Journalism*. Lawrence, Kan.: University of Kansas Press, 1971.

Kaltenborn, H. V. *Fifty Fabulous Years. 1900–1950*. New York: Putnam, 1950.

Kelly, Tom. *The Imperial Post*. New York: William Morrow & Co., Inc, 1983.

Kluger, Richard. *The Paper: The Life and Death of the New York Herald Tribune*. New York: Alfred A. Knopf, 1986.

Knight, Oliver, ed. *I Protest: Selected Disquisitions of E. W. Scripps*. Madison, Wis.: University of Wisconsin Press, 1969.

McNulty, John B. *Older Than the Nation: The Story of the Hartford Courant*. Stonington, Conn.: Pequot Press, 1964.

Miller, Lee. *The Story of Ernie Pyle*. New York: Viking Press, 1950.

Morris, J. A. *Deadline Every Minute*. Garden City, NY: Doubleday, 1957.

Mott, F. L. *American Journalism: A History of Newspapers in the United States Through 270 Years, 1690–1960*. New York, Macmillan, 1962.

_____. *Jefferson and the Press*. Baton Rouge, LA.: Louisiana State University Press, 1943.

Nixon, R. B. *Henry W. Grady: Spokesman of the New South*. New York: Knopf, 1943.

Pilat, Oliver. *Drew Pearson: An Unauthorized Biography*. New York: Harpers Magazine Press, 1973.

Robertson, Charles L. *The International Herald Tribune: The First 100 Years*. New York: Columbia University Press, 1987.

Ross, I. *Ladies of the Press*. New York: Harper, 1936.

Rucker, Bryce W. *Twentieth Century Reporting at Its Best*. Ames, Iowa: Iowa State University Press, 1965.

Salisbury, Harrison E. *Without Fear or Favor: An Uncompromising Look at The New York Times*. New York: Ballantine Books, 1981.

Seitz, Don Carlos. *Horace Greeley: Founder of the New York Tribune*. New York: AMS Press, 1970.

Starr, L. M. *Bohemian Brigade: Civil War Newsmen in Action*. New York: Knopf, 1954.

Stone, C. *Dana and the Sun*. New York: Dodd, Mead, 1938.

Swanberg, W. A. *Citizen Hearst*. New York: Charles Scribner's Sons, 1961.

_____.. *Pulitzer*. Charles Scribner's Sons, 1967.

Teeter, Dwight L. and Jean Folkerts. *Voices of a Nation: A History of Mass Media in the United States*, 3rd ed. New York: Allyn & Bacon, 1997.

References on New Editing and Design

American Press Institute. *Newspaper Design: 2000 and Beyond*. Restin, VA: American Press Institute, 1989.

Bowles, Dorothy and Diane L. Borden. *Creative Editing for Print Media*, 2nd ed. Belmont, CA., 1997.

Craig, James. *Designing with Type*. New York: Watson-Guptill, 1981.

Design: The Journal of the Society of Newspaper Design, a publication of the Society of Newspaper Design, 11600 Sunrise Valley Drive, Reston, VA. 22091.

Rehe, Rolf. *Topography and Design for Newspapers*. Carmel, IN: Research International 1985.

Solomon, Martin. *The Art of Typography*. New York: Watson-Guptill, 1986.

Index